ERWIN OLAF SPRINGVELD

MISCHA COHEN

ERWIN OLAF

THE BIOGRAPHY

HANNIBAL

WORK HARD, PLAY HARD

CONTENTS

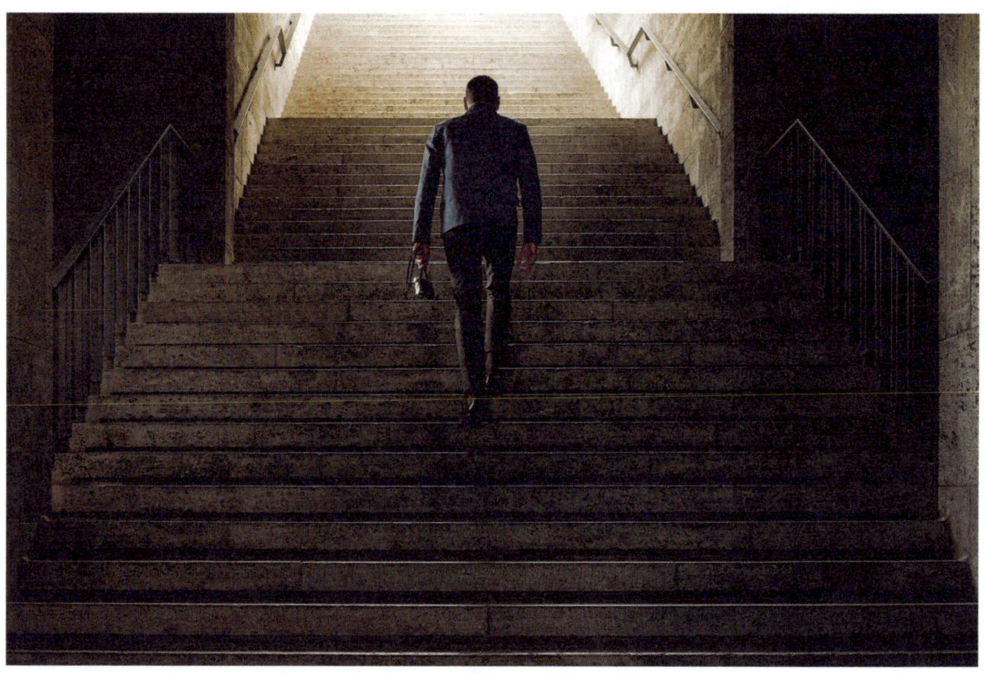

Berlin, Olympia Stadion Westend – Selfportrait 25th of April 2012 from the *Berlin* series.

INTRODUCTION
GOING OUT WITH A BANG

'I don't need to come out looking great... but I do want it to be accurate'

Fifteen black Cadillacs block the streets around Studio Erwin Olaf in Amsterdam's Rivierenbuurt neighbourhood on 27 September 2023. They form the funeral cortège that will convey Erwin Olaf Springveld's body to the Westerkerk. The cars will follow the route that Erwin travelled every day on his electric bike. Today, however, all the junctions are cordoned off by policemen on motorcycles. Starting at the photo studio in IJselstraat, where he worked with his business partner Shirley den Hartog and his assistants on Erwin Olaf's oeuvre, the procession will proceed to the Jordaan, where he lived as Erwin Springveld with his husband Kevin Edwards.

Dozens of friends, colleagues and relatives had paid their final respects the previous weekend at his home on Egelantiersgracht, where he was laid out in an open coffin by the window, with a glass of white wine on a small adjacent table. As a final image, a rainbow flag and a black pennant hung limp and mournful in the autumn rain.

On Monday, thousands of people attended a funeral service at the Westerkerk, which was broadcast live by a local television station. Churchgoers mourned not only the artist but also the activist – the man who had spoken out loudly and indiscriminately against anyone who tried to curtail the freedom of others.

In the meantime he has been brought back to the studio, now in a closed mushroom coffin of his own choosing, grown from fungi that will soon decompose underground, contents and all. Erwin lies in that strangely shaped coffin on a bed of moss. He wears nothing but his wedding ring. The friends in the studio seem startled by the grey contraption, the lid of which doesn't seem to want to close properly and which they will soon have to lift into the hearse. 'It's so ugly!' exclaims Shirley, and everyone laughs with relief. Kevin has lost his husband, but she too is now something of a widow. Shirley first met Erwin almost thirty years ago, and they were soon inseparable. They unanimously agreed on the most important rules of the game: treat everyone alike, whether fan or royalty; always speak the truth; persevere and enjoy life – work hard, party hard.

Many of the mourners have collaborated on this book over the past few years, a project that dovetailed with the major clear-out Erwin had long been working on. He knew he wouldn't live to be very old due to a hereditary degenerative lung disease. It was once predicted that he wouldn't make it to sixty, but he celebrated that very birthday in grand style in 2019, with exhibitions at the Rijksmuseum and the Kunstmuseum Den Haag, where hundreds of thousands of people came to admire his retrospectives.

Although his life expectancy was revised to at least seventy, Erwin wanted to put his affairs in order while he was still reasonably healthy. Transferring part of his archive to the Rijksmuseum was the crowning achievement of those preparations. However, selecting work that was never meant for eternity was also part of the process.

He cleared the studio, reduced the staff, built a vault for the work he still owned, and ensured that Shirley was not just his manager but an equal partner in the company, Studio Erwin Olaf. The idea of a book that would include both Erwins – Olaf and Springveld – aligned with his desire for everything to be neat and tidy in his aftermath, in due course. But having said that, not too soon. He therefore granted access to both his archive and his life: studio shoots, trips to Bruges, Paris, southern England, and Munich, welcoming sessions in the studio canteen, or at his round table at home, which he endured with or without the help of supplementary oxygen and, finally, the last conversations in his isolation room at Leiden University Medical Center.

Inspired by his reminiscences, he re-invited key models from his early photographic career to stand before the camera for this book. The resulting eighteen black-and-white portraits form the series *Muses*: a tribute to the 'actors of the 1/125 second' who had facilitated his meteoric rise in the photography world. It became a series in which he reflected on the passage of time and his own mortality.

Sometimes the attention would get to him, and he'd long for some respite from his role as a semi-famous, outspoken Dutchman. A text message would soon follow: 'I'm totally through with Erwin Olaf.' It was a recent aversion; from a young age, he'd wanted to be recognised, famous even. He also liked publicity, preferably in connection with his photography, but he was also a fierce public advocate, both on television and in the press, participating in debates on LGBTQI+ rights and discrimination.

The antipathy toward his public persona was always fleeting; after a while, he'd cheer up again and start reviewing the rough draft of the manuscript. 'I've started reading again, and it's enjoyable and funny. My goodness, it's a miracle that I didn't turn into a cannabis plant in the 1990s!'

Until the very end, he searched for illustrations and photographs to illuminate his life and work. Coincidentally, he also commented on the text, although, having been formally trained as a journalist, he agreed that he could only correct factual inaccuracies. 'Alright, I hate those controlled, polished biographies of so-called Dutch celebrities. I don't need to come out looking great – and if you look deep into my heart, I don't need anything at all. But I do want it to be accurate.'

Occasionally, there was a debate – his fiery temper and fanatical defence of his personal rights were leitmotifs in his life – and this did not diminish even on his sickbed. 'You cite a piece of research, and it makes me look stupid. But there's another study, you know. And you must include it too.' But he also sometimes had an epiphany. 'Your piece made me look back, and I realised: that is indeed my theme. Jesus Christ – exactly that. The feeling of standing between two worlds. Of never belonging. That you're not at home in either one world or the other.'

That was the basic emotion behind all his photographs, he realised, or at least those of the twenty-first century. It was slightly different in the 1990s, when his photography was more about attack as the best defence. 'Wanting to conquer your place and show that you really can do something.

There were times, in retrospect, when he would have preferred to phrase things differently. Less blunt, perhaps. Less furious, too – although that anger, invariably accompanied by doubt, had also been a driving force. In the quoted letters he is not always subtle, and times have changed. He would not write the same way today. But he certainly wasn't going to get into 'sensitivity reading'. He had been raised with absolute honesty, an open book by nature. He wore his heart on his sleeve, sometimes to his own annoyance.

He wanted his funeral to be grand and theatrical. Over the top? He didn't care; he'd be dead by then anyway. Kitsch, as some had said about his pictures? For him, it was more real than reality itself. As he sometimes said about his photography: 'The essence is that you can cry your eyes out, while knowing that it's all fake.' His reality was simply not that of documentary photography, as he knew. 'Because, you know, if I want to see reality, I'll look out the window.'

'What do you envision when you dream big?' Shirley had asked him when he stayed in Majorca to catch his breath during his final year. Those dreams used to be about conquering the world – getting into the galleries and museums that mattered in major cities. He'd more than succeeded: permanent galleries in London, Paris and New York. Exhibitions in Rome, Sydney, Seoul, Tokyo and Shanghai – to name just a few.

Now they were contemplating his farewell by the pool. It still felt like an abstraction, an unreal thought, though at that point, death was already much closer than they realised. The funeral service should be at the Westerkerk anyway, Erwin thought. He loved the peal of the old Westertoren's bells, often the only external sound that reached his canal house in the quiet part of the Jordaan.

Music: Arvo Pärt. David Bowie, of course. 'Just a Perfect Day' by Lou Reed, the farewell song of a generation. Janet Jackson, who had inspired him with her anti-racist lyrics. The Puur Mokum choir singing 'Aan de Amsterdamse grachten' [On the Amsterdam Canals]. That had so moved everyone at the Black Tea Party in the pop temple Paradiso, one of the many big parties Erwin had organised, as an anthem for all Amsterdammers, irrespective of background. To conclude: 'Ring My Bell' by Anita Ward, a glorious, crowd-pleasing tribute to 1980s disco.

And then, a grave in Sint Barbara's cemetery in Amsterdam-West, and not among the usual suspects on the Amstel. But ideally somewhere by the entrance to the grounds, so you don't spend ages looking for the plot when you visit him. And with a self-designed tombstone, featuring a sunny smiley chiselled into it – the '90s symbol of dance and ecstasy – and the epitaph *Bonum diem habeas*: have a good day. Despite everything, his visitors would leave the cemetery with a smile.

After the burial, Erwin hoped for his last great party, 'Live Dance Kiss', at the Homomonument on Westermarkt. He wanted to go out with a bang, with an event to rival his extravagant parties of old.

They could picture it: the Mayor on stage, in chains and full regalia, with drag performers in outrageous outfits and a DJ alternating between classic house and disco. This was how Erwin's Amsterdam had been, and this was how the city should remain after his departure.

When news broke of Erwin's death, the studio naturally filled with friends who helped address the funeral cards – dress code, 'come as you like yourself best' – and took care of other tasks. Permission was granted for the Westerkerk to be used for the ceremony, and Mayor Halsema promised to speak – both in the church and later, at the Homomonument. It was at this very site that she called Erwin Olaf a 'Rembrandt of our time' and someone who 'lived, as Amsterdam wants to be'. Flowers arrived from King Willem-Alexander and Queen Máxima, whom Erwin had been scheduled to photograph for a new, but never-realised state portrait. After his death, Anton Corbijn took over the job.

When the fifteen Cadillacs depart, the large photo studio is finally empty and soulless. Shirley and the others will attempt to reanimate it, as they promised Erwin. An eponymous foundation will be established to continue his activism and fight for an emancipated society. This Erwin Olaf Foundation will, among other things, organise master classes for students in vocational education and support young people who, for whatever reason, don't fit societal norms and are struggling. Kevin is taken care of, but not too much, as Erwin had urged Shirley: 'Make sure he can live well, but that things remain normal, that he has to keep working.'

But that's all for later. Now, the limousines glide through the city, past the cordoned-off junctions, and arrive at the Westertoren. On this occasion, one of the bells from the carillon has been placed in the vestibule so that the funeral toll can be rung according to Erwin's wishes.

The eight bearers – Erwin's brothers Jos and Ron and six (former) 'first assistants' – place the heavy, flower-laden coffin with some difficulty on the platform in front of the pulpit, next to the self-portrait from the *Berlin* series. The photo captures Erwin from behind, climbing a steep staircase toward the light, a camera dangling loosely in his left hand.

When the picture was taken, more than a decade ago, everyone could have their own interpretation of *Berlin, Olympia Stadion Westend* – one of his most sought-after self-portraits by collectors – in that historically charged location. Here in the Westerkerk, the picture is, by Erwin's own atheistic wish, in exactly the right place. It is the image of the photographer forever transcending earthly concerns and, at once, a tribute to his most important ally: light. Next, Erwin's video installation about mourning and hope, *Life – For Mom*, shines on the big screen next to the coffin. When the sounds of Arvo Pärt's 'Spiegel im Spiegel' fade, it is time for the speakers, standing at the foot of the huge mushroom coffin, to share their grief and tell Erwin Olaf Springveld's story.

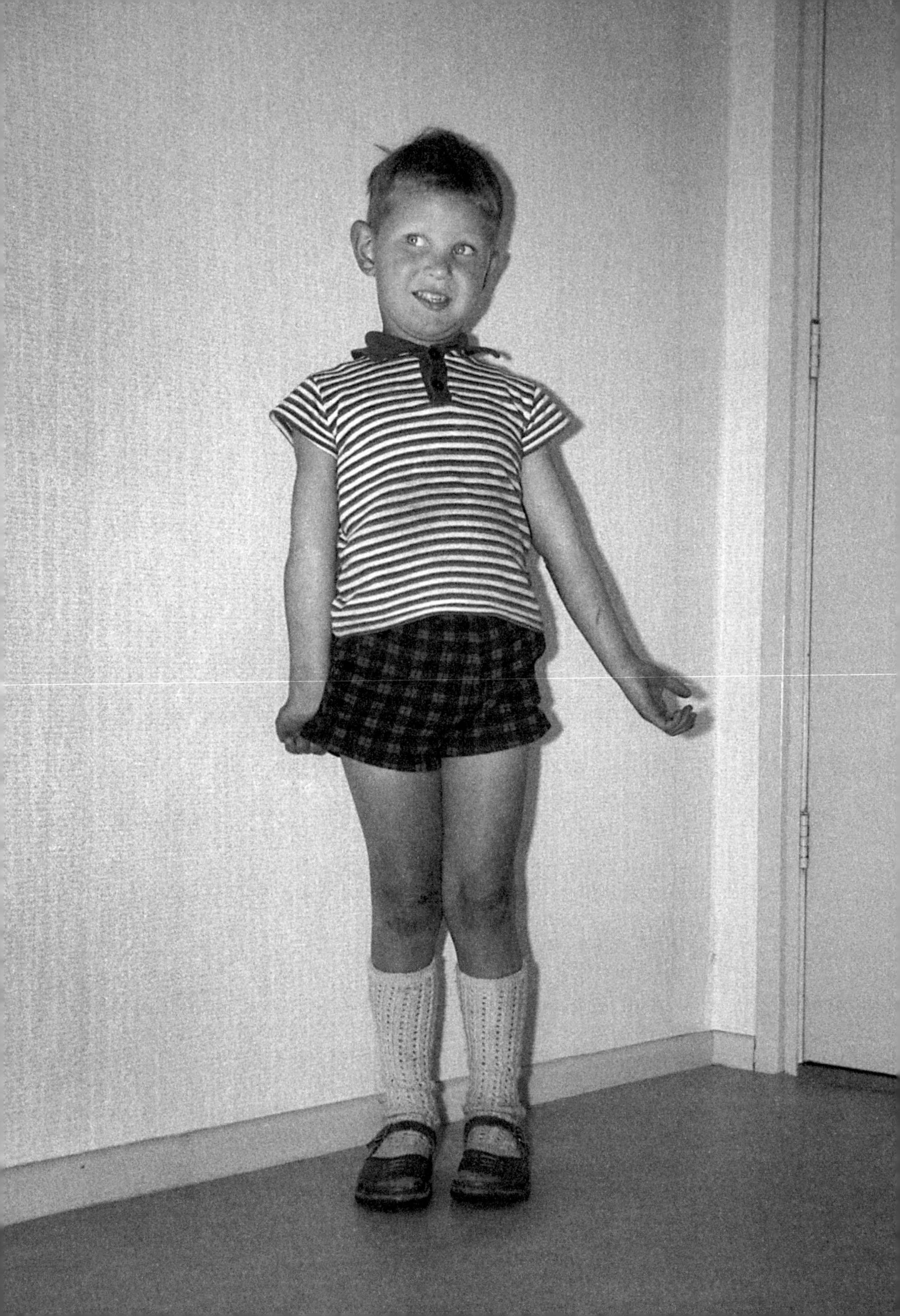

1 BOYHOOD (1959–1977)

'Ideal: general curing of complexes'

THE WHOLE WORLD IN HIS HAND

Visibly moved, Erwin Olaf leafs through diary entries penned by his younger self, occasionally laughing out loud at the thoughts of a somewhat naive twenty-something. The well-thumbed notebook, with its red-and-black marbled cover, lies on a table in the studio. You can quote from it, says Erwin.

He promised me an unvarnished account of his life for this book – and he stayed true to his word. Erwin passes me his red-and-black notebook without pause, asking only for a signed receipt in exchange.

He first opened its covers over forty years ago – at precisely 11 p.m. on 21 August 1980. Just a month earlier, he had celebrated his birthday, newly graduated from the School of Journalism in Utrecht, and had moved to the capital. For the first time, he was living truly independently, renting a flat in a dilapidated social housing block on the Oostelijke Eilanden. Though only a short distance from the vibrant nightlife of central Amsterdam as the crow flies, it felt worlds away in reality.

Standing on the threshold of adulthood, he was filled with plans and desires. But he had no one to share them with and felt adrift in the anonymity of the city. Determined to make something of this low point – because that's exactly how it felt – he began to document his experiences, like a journalist reporting on his own life. He set out to capture everything that moved him, alongside his childhood memories, in an effort to gain some perspective.

He had been living in Amsterdam for six months but still hadn't met anyone with whom he could 'shamelessly share the most inane ideas'. Erwin didn't yet feel aligned with his rebellious contemporaries from the punk and squatters' movements who, earlier that year, had staged fierce protests against the housing crisis during Queen Beatrix's coronation. These countercultural movements had largely passed him by. There wasn't a place in the alternative art scene, or at least not yet, for a young, wet-behind-the-ears journalist.

The red-and-black notebook expanded into a 'repository' for his 'mental excesses', he notes. 'This beautiful little book would be helpful for all my ideas. The thoughts didn't need to be ordered or clearly elaborated.' The process demanded a degree of discipline: 'I must try to have this little book with me at all times.'

I've been having a really bad time lately, he wrote, although, exceptionally, one summer Thursday evening, he says he's feeling pretty great. Nevertheless, he made a resolute decision to enter therapy 'as soon as possible'. His expectations of psychotherapy were not so much far-fetched as realistic and somewhat ironic. He noted:

1. Ideal: general curing of complexes. Losing my inhibitions.
2. Likely impossible, therefore:
3. Get everything in order. The therapist is like a farmer who will teach me to separate the wheat from the chaff and show me the basics of baking bread.

The notebook is a unique, crystallised moment; Erwin produced nothing remotely like it over the ensuing forty-plus years. Nor is it completely filled: he soon found that he didn't need its pages. On closer inspection, Amsterdam was indeed home to a few kind spirits with whom Erwin could share his plans, crazy or not. And above all, his newly discovered medium – photography – soon supplanted the laborious task of writing, an activity that he wasn't truly passionate about anyway.

Although they only span a short period, Erwin's essence already seems to be present in these diary-like texts. They record his desires and fears, but above all the compulsion to make things – although the 'what' is still undefined.

Of importance, for now, is his earliest memory, which Erwin first recorded in the notebook and in which he himself sees the origins of his artistry summarised in a stylised nutshell. It is a scene from early childhood. By way of a title it is headed: 'The history of E.O. Springveld's homosexuality.' His sexual orientation would emerge later; Erwin was only four years old at the time. Seventeen years later, he could still see that scene from his early childhood so vividly in his mind's eye that it seemed superfluous to describe it in detail.

It occurred in Stroeslaan in Hilversum, a street lined with post-war social housing. The flat at no. 99, with a communal walkway, was home to twenty-somethings Simon Jacobus Springveld and Alida Springveld-van 't Hoff, or Siem and Lida to their friends. They had recently moved to the property with their newborn son Jos, their first child, in 1957.

Erwin recalls it being an environment 'of very humble people'. He was born there on 2 July 1959, two years after Jos, followed five years later by Ron, their youngest brother.

There were no artworks on the walls except for embroideries by Lida, who was good with a needle and thread. Nor was there a Bible on the bookshelf in the four-room flat; the Springvelds were strict non-believers.

Siem, the son of a local grocer, was an office supplies representative and a talented salesman. Lida, the youngest daughter of an Amsterdam peppermint maker, was a trained pattern cutter and costumier, and extremely creative. She hailed from a social democratic family. As was typical in the 1950s, she stopped working after marrying Siem in 1955. Lida was devoted to her husband and children and the spider in the web of the young Springveld family. She doted on her middle son Erwin, a shy child with a vivid imagination.

Erwin did not play football like his brothers, and nor was he adventurous; he was more of an anxious dreamer. It complicated the father–son relationship. Siem was slightly awkward around all his children, but he seemed to understand his other sons better than Erwin.

Siem Springveld worked hard and often late into the night. One day, he returned home uncharacteristically early and entered the hallway. Little Erwin, who was sitting there playing, burst into tears. He was inconsolable; his father had stepped on his dog's tail. A genuine flight of fancy because the Springvelds didn't own a dog. Siem was befuddled by what he believed to be complete nonsense on the part of his son. As always, it was Lida who comforted Erwin.

She remembered that whenever Siem Springveld raised his voice, which was often, Erwin would cover his ears with his little hands. 'I love all three of my boys, but right from the outset, there was something exceptional about Erwin. He was much softer than his brothers and deeply attached to me.' A mummy's boy, which also corresponds with Erwin's own recollections. 'My mother was a voluptuous woman, with soft arms that were a delight to squeeze, and cheeks into which your lips would sink with a kiss.' As a consequence, he developed a fascination for strong women.

It was the autumn of 1963. Shortly afterwards, on 22 November, in Dallas, Texas, US President John F. Kennedy was assassinated by Lee Harvey Oswald. One of the most powerful early emotions that Erwin can recall is linked to this event. That day, he sensed an incomprehensible sadness amongst the grown-ups: 'I was well over four years old and I felt that the whole world had come to a standstill, and also in Hilversum. A collective form of mourning, only no one was crying.'

Young Erwin preferred to spend all his time indoors, drawing and inventing games, instead of playing outside with the other children. 'In kindergarten, I was already kind of an outsider.' In his red-and-black notebook, he describes being intimidated by the neighbourhood children. He had a little contact with the girl next door, who was also a loner.

Aged twenty-one, and with scrupulous attention to detail, he described his lonely adventures as a toddler. Erwin was 'wrapped up warm' and gently led outside on an impossible mission: 'to see for himself how much fun it is to play outside'. He remembers standing in front of the block of flats in his autumnal outfit, staring at his peers, who were roller-skating and cycling. There was a small tree in the downstairs neighbours' front garden. As he caressed its leaves between thumb and forefinger, he softly hummed the melody of a hit by the Queen of Gospel – Mahalia Jackson – to whom his mother frequently listened: 'He's got the whole world in his hand.'

This picture of himself as a toddler – gently singing, absorbed in his surroundings but unable to participate – is etched in Erwin's memory. But it would be a while before he could interpret that scene – wherein he is both an outsider and a voyeur – as a source of his artistry. As a 21-year-old struggling with isolation, he described the childhood memory more for therapeutic reasons. 'I think this "childhood snapshot" of an actual event might explain my current fear of loneliness.'

The meaning of this early memory has shifted over time. According to Erwin's first great love, Teun Frieszo, the photographer's aggressive side, and the blind rage into which he would sometimes fly when he encountered bigotry, stemmed from this sense of exclusion. Equally, this anger also fuelled his huge artistic ambitions, a drive to reach an optimal state of invulnerability.

'Erwin has always felt like an outsider, a solitary figure between two worlds,' concurs Frieszo. 'So he decided, early on, to become famous.' He could have achieved that goal by various routes, but photography proved to be the ideal medium. As a studio photographer, he could invite others to step into his self-created world – something that was more problematic in reverse. Only from behind the camera could he construct his own uninhibited and unsullied universe. Looking back, Erwin realises that all his photographs are about 'not belonging'. He says, 'So, I kept dragging the outside world into my inner one.'

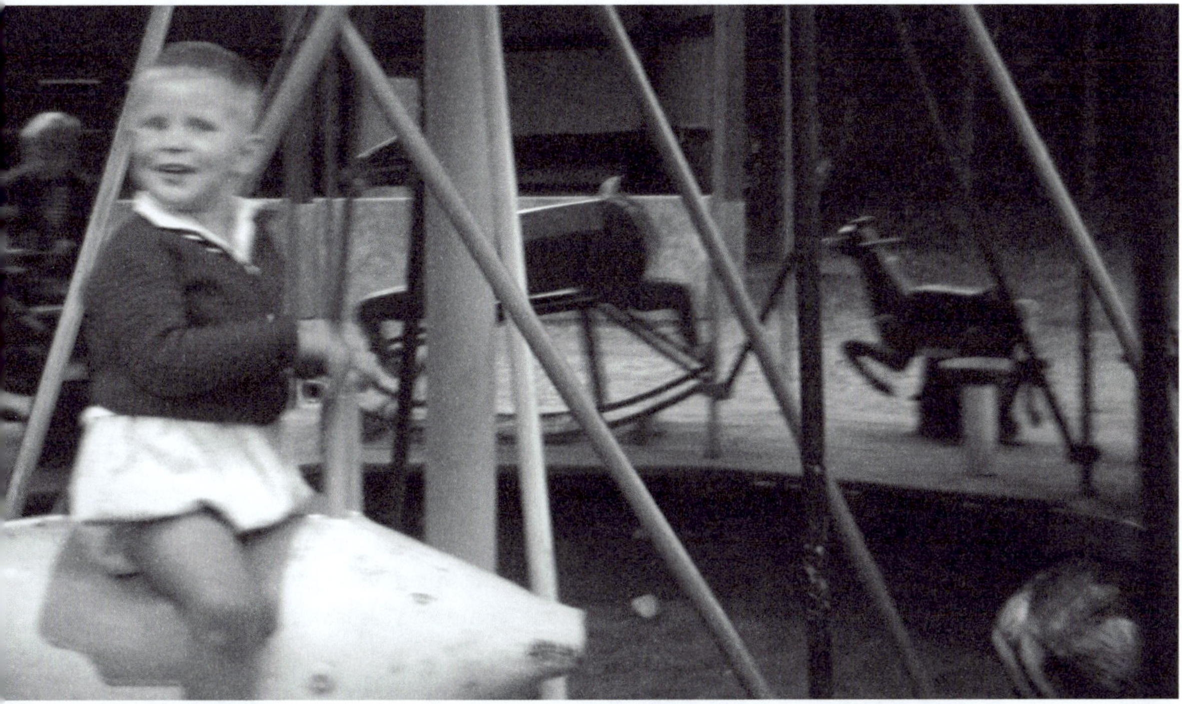

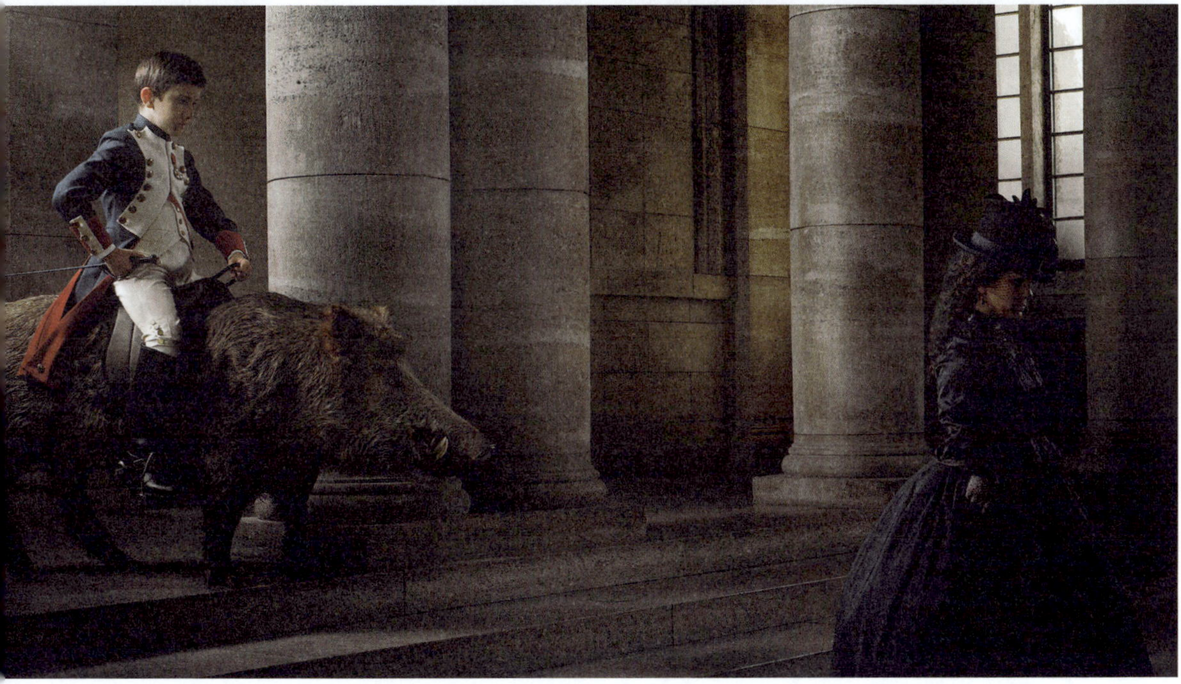

The top photo – Erwin riding a pig on a merry-go-round – inspired the one below, entitled *Altes Stadthaus, Mitte, 8 July 2012*.

Erwin Olaf commenting on the photo on page 12: 'At the age of six you could already tell that I was gay.'

'All the boys in the playground jealously thought, they're fucking!'

REBEL REBEL

'This is the evidence that I'd rather bury my past deep out of sight,' says Erwin as he pulls out one dusty moving box after another from the storeroom of his house in Amsterdam's Jordaan district. The cardboard boxes are full of what you could call, good-heartedly, a personal archive. As a whole, the material paints a picture of a childhood that was far from easy. 'Perfect for your research.' The photos show an ordinary family; Erwin will later refer to it as lower-middle class.

In 1967, the family moved to a newly built house in Hoevelaken, near Amersfoort. This might have been a step up the social ladder for the Springvelds, but it did not bode well for Erwin's social life. 'That environment would be a disaster for any vulnerable child,' he reflects. The bullying, which had started prior to the move, continued. He hardly had any friends in those days, neither boys nor girls. When his father and his two brothers headed off to the football pitch on Saturdays, Erwin stayed at home with his mother. They had the house to themselves and plenty of time to chat.

The cardboard-box archive also contains a folder of school reports. Erwin does not appear to have been a stellar student. He certainly didn't flounder but nor was he particularly diligent or smart. 'The embodiment of a culture hopelessly lost in mediocrity,' as he ruthlessly judges his much younger self. 'When you look back on your life, it's a stark reminder that you're actually very ordinary. It's a constant thought; I can't shake it off. But I do try and make the most of my mediocrity.'

His only advantage in the classroom was never being lost for words, even then. 'Yes, I had the gift of the gab.' Which, to a certain extent, his teachers appreciated.

He was seventeen when he came out, but knew 'it' much earlier. 'At the age of six, you could already tell that I was gay.' As a boy, he loved Robin, the handsome sidekick of TV superhero Batman. 'Batman was a prize jerk, whereas Robin was THRILLING! Only later did I realise that it was a kind of early crush.'

Flipping through his old photo albums, he is as disparaging about his looks as he is about his educational achievements. A 'dull little boy' with 'buck teeth' that inevitably led to braces. Pointing to a photograph of himself, he says, 'Just look, it's pretty obvious why I was bullied.' The Hoevelaken 'hicks', who had initially called him 'girl-crazy', eventually switched to 'poof' or 'pimp'. 'I was wretched. My mother, who was not an intellectual woman but certainly a very wise one, would indignantly retort: "they don't even know what it means".' Despite being ignorant of the definitions himself, Erwin knew instinctively what his classmates meant when they called him names.

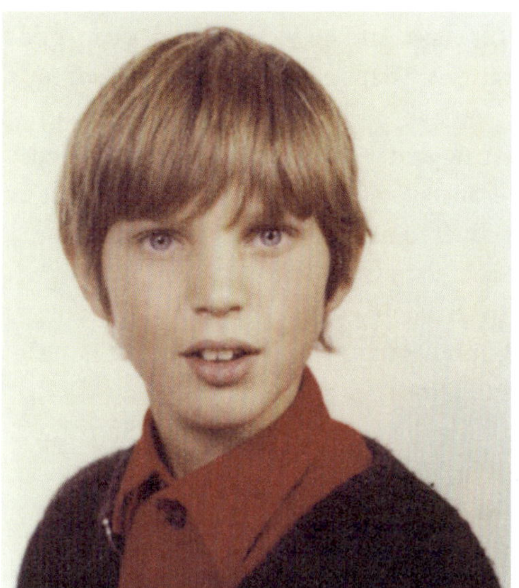

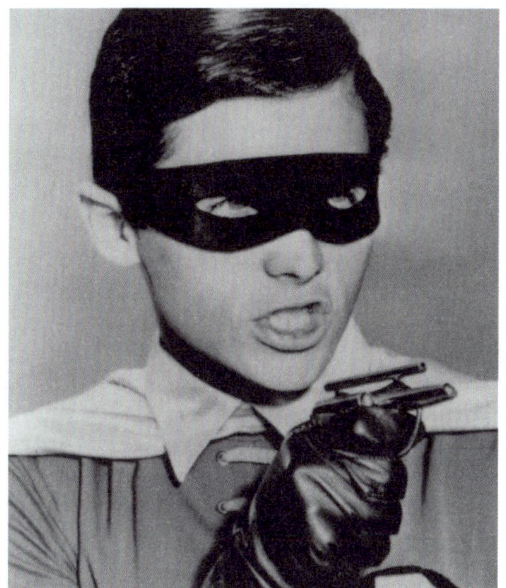

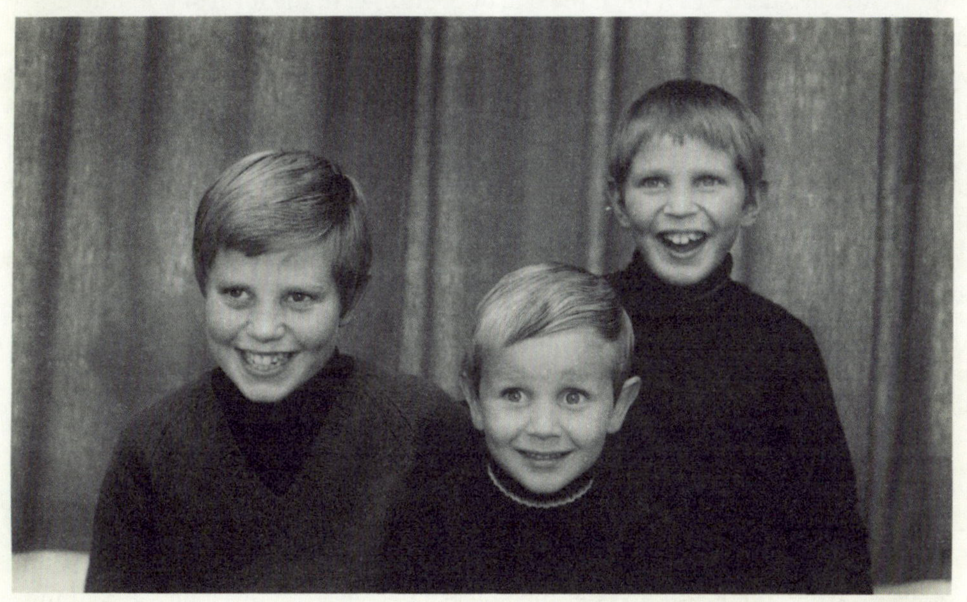

Top left: Erwin at primary school in Amersfoort. 'The bullying continued.'
Top right: 'Batman was a prize jerk, whereas Robin was THRILLING!'
Bottom: The Springveld brothers in 1969. Left to right: Jos, Ron, Erwin.

He was infatuated with some of the boys in his class. And he secretly read 'a very good educational booklet with some horny illustrations. That booklet was right out of my heart. It normalised homosexuality.'

Erwin was raised with clear values and struggled with internal secrets. 'If I lied, my mother would say, I know you're lying because you've got the mark of the cross on your forehead. So, the next time I told a lie, I covered my brow with my hand so she wouldn't see the cross.' His parents told him that they would never be angry if he got into trouble; the most important thing was to tell them.

Telling the truth was fundamental to his upbringing. And if he couldn't be honest, then it was better not to say a word about certain feelings and actions.

Homosexuality was totally absent from daily life, with one exception. Starting when Erwin was twelve, the Springveld family watched a popular TV programme together on Saturday nights. One of the panellists, Albert Mol, had come out on television as gay. But it was difficult, if not impossible, for an insecure adolescent to identify with a pinched, fifty-something who had to resort to innuendo.

Eventually, there was light at the end of the tunnel in the form of a volunteer from a gay rights organisation who was raising awareness about homosexuality. He was an average boy, but it was this very ordinariness that made him seem so exotic to the 15-year-old Erwin. 'The proximity made me giddy. That this guy, barely older than me, could be openly gay. For me, at that age, to have a flesh-and-blood person in front of the class saying, "It's no big deal", was vital. He addressed the entire class but it felt like he was talking directly to me.'

It didn't encourage him to come out there and then: his position at school wasn't secure enough for such a step. But even that was changing, as the worst of the bullying was over. He never forgot the last time he was bullied in high school: an 'obese' boy sat on him pontifically and pinned him to the ground. 'I was beyond distressed but totally helpless. Because, obviously, I couldn't fight back.'

He subsequently wondered if this episode might explain his habit of making vicious and derogatory jokes about big men – a trait that he ultimately regretted. Only much later did he understand that the need to humiliate others often stems from your own degradation. A tragic chain reaction. To put it into perspective: 'It's not necessarily a recipe for disaster if you learn to cope with resistance at a young age, to learn to fight. If you're lucky, it can make you stronger. But the bullying was just as bad.'

Smoking also turned things around: it was considered cool. But what boosted his status more than anything else was spending break times at the rubbish skips in the playground, to the left of the main entrance. It was a coveted hangout spot: anyone who was the least bit hip gathered around the bins.

At the start of his third year at school, a group of fashion-conscious boys of

Moluccan origin suddenly decided to make it their haunt. They were snappy dressers – duck toe shoes, block heels and bell bottoms. After giving Erwin a quick once-over, a tough guy in a green leather bomber jacket with trendy aviator glasses said: you're good-looking but need to buy different clothes. An elegant boy in a Great Gatsby-style suit with belted, pleated trousers backed him up. They saw a kindred spirit in Erwin, who, like them, was resisting mediocrity. 'Those popular guys welcomed me. I liked them; they were cool.'

The 'prettiest and sweetest girls' in the school joined the group as a matter of course. The bullying stopped almost overnight. Cigarettes, gorgeous girls and cool pals were a winning combination – or at least temporarily. 'Suddenly, I was standing next to Henny Dinklage, the school bombshell.' As he would later describe her in a letter, Henny was 'a girl with a gold mackintosh, reddish straight hair and a long, blunt-cut fringe. Smoking like a chimney, yellow fingers, nail-biting. Dashing about, sorting things out. Laughing, occasionally nervous. Crying, sometimes pretending.' She quickly became his best friend. 'All those boys in the playground were jealously thinking, they're fucking! From that point onwards, I was well and truly "in". The leader of the pack.'

Driven by his new-found self-confidence, Erwin started writing for the school newspaper. He described how 'every peasant who can afford intellectual glasses' criticises the school. 'This army of goat-hair-sock-wearing and spotty critics has a new recruit, namely yours truly. That makes you look up, huh? Now, let me tell you this, there is a lot of wrongdoing in this school, which fuels my irritation, like a family of fleas plus all their daughters-in-law.'

It's the 1970s, and even in a provincial high school, anything feels possible. Joints are passed freely by the pond across from the playground. For boys, the look is long hair, a souped-up motorbike with high handlebars – no helmet, of course – and a pouch of shag tucked into the left breast pocket of a denim jacket. Henny Dinklage rode a Tomos with high handlebars and a foot clutch, which was remarkable for a girl at the time. She was as bold as brass, a rebel through and through, and frequently thrown out of class.

Because of her self-professed sense of justice, Henny decided to 'save' Erwin. That friendship helped him, although Erwin still felt out of place. 'At the time, everyone wore a trendy Afghan coat, one of those brown leather jackets that reeked,' she recalls. 'So, Erwin went to Amsterdam to get one of his own. I can still see him rocking up at school in his new acquisition: a black coat with a white fur lining. Beautiful, absolutely beautiful. But then again, it wasn't the right kind of coat. If you wanted to fit in, you had to wear the rough, brown model.'

Siem Springveld became self-employed after losing his job as a sales representative. Erwin's father, who wore his heart on his sleeve, had been openly critical of his employer. He launched a small office-furniture business but suffered a heart attack and stroke in quick succession. Siem, whose was already struggling to stay afloat, was forced to close the business. These were seismic events for the Springveld family. For Erwin, the spectre of commercial failure brought on by ill health became a lasting shadow. It shaped his later drive for financial independence and explains why he consistently accepted commercial commissions alongside his artistic work.

Siem's personality changed after his stroke. He did not become easier to live with but his marriage to Lida survived. 'My parents loved each other and always kissed each other smack on the lips. It's embarrassing as a child, but when you're older, you just think, great!'

As well as Henny, Erwin also hung out a lot with Anne-Marie van Merwijk. 'We were a trinity, Henny, Anne-Marie and me.' Getting to know the Van Merwijk family was an eye-opener for a boy whose family did not hold the arts in high esteem. Erwin enjoyed drawing and writing and noticed that this was appreciated in the Van Merwijks' home. He was determined to make something special of his life, according to Anne-Marie. 'And it was obvious that he'd succeed because he was quite unlike anyone else.'

In addition to films – there was a brief period when he wanted to be an actor and planned to apply to drama school – music and literature opened Erwin's eyes to what was possible in both art and life. It was a time when celebrated Dutch author Gerard Reve waxed lyrical about gay love in novels such as *The Language of Love*, *Dear Boys* and *A Circus Boy*. 'Though I must admit', he reflects, 'Reve's fixation with boys in velvet trousers started to wear thin.' The possibility that some of Reve's texts might also be read as racist hadn't really occurred to him. 'Like many others, I read it as humour, as irony.'

Anne-Marie and Erwin had a trusting relationship and, to the outside world, they even seemed like a couple for a while. That was – 'unfortunately' – a slight exaggeration, according to Anne-Marie. 'It was clear that Erwin didn't want to be like everyone else and that's why I found him so very attractive. Not forgetting those big blue eyes and huge mouth of his.'

It remained an adolescent courtship; an attempt at kissing proved unsuccessful. 'I understood afterwards – whether it's a compliment to me, I don't know – that it was the moment when he realised: no, this isn't working. I really am gay.' Their friendship went the distance, as did their shared fascination with Reve.

Gerard Reve was not Erwin's only hero. There was also David Bowie. Six months after Bowie ended his alter ego Ziggy Stardust and his band The Spiders from Mars, he appeared on Dutch television.

A heavily made-up Bowie with bright red hair, eye patch, gold earrings and a

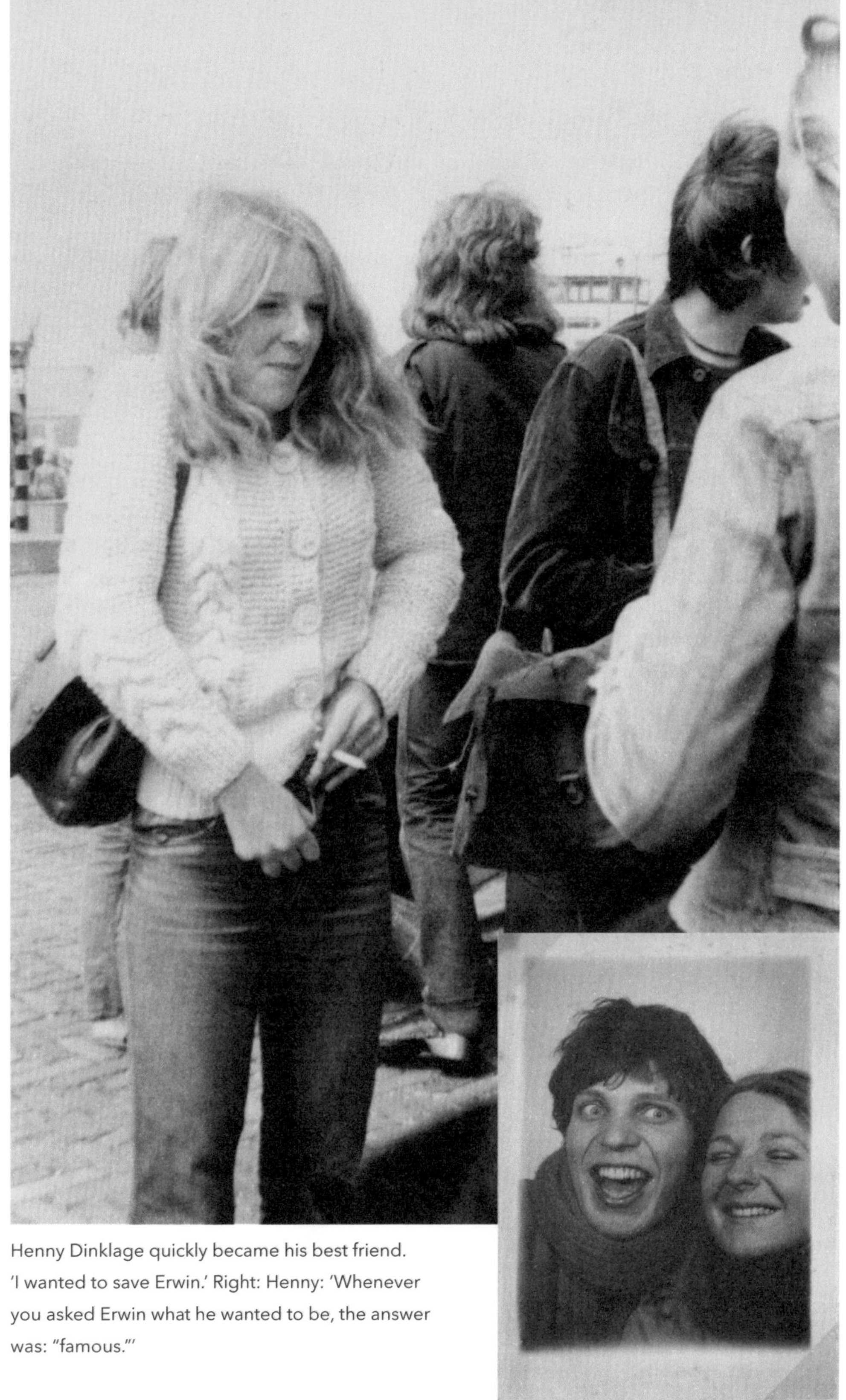

Henny Dinklage quickly became his best friend. 'I wanted to save Erwin.' Right: Henny: 'Whenever you asked Erwin what he wanted to be, the answer was: "famous."'

tight, red jumpsuit, 'lip-synched' to the music and made a half-hearted attempt to pretend he was playing the guitar. Erwin, sitting at home, was stunned by his eccentric appearance.

David Bowie made him realise that being different was not necessarily a bad thing. 'That was out of space.' He heard him sing: 'You've got your mother in a whirl / 'Cause she's not sure if you're a boy or a girl'.

'Rebel Rebel' may have quickly slipped from the charts, but Erwin's love for David Bowie endured. He saw Bowie as a role model: 'That mysterious beauty, the fluidity of sexuality, the constant reinvention, the uber-coolness – it was the whole package. I thought Angie Bowie was great too.'

Erwin and Anne-Marie caught the train to Rotterdam on 14 May 1976 to see their hero perform live for the first time in the indoor arena, Ahoy. Luis Buñuel's short surrealist film classic *Le Chien Andalou* was screened instead of a support act. Erwin watched it with bated breath. 'I understood the balls of it, but the power of the image was overwhelming.' He was mesmerised by Bowie's appearance and his play with transformations.

Anne-Marie's younger brother, Lucas, was a drummer who'd started a band with a few male friends. They were looking for a charismatic frontman. The obvious choice was to ask Erwin to be the lead singer, despite no one knowing if he could actually sing. 'He was a striking figure in the playground, with an androgyny reminiscent of Bowie. And his urge to stand out, to make a mark was palpable.' Erwin didn't hesitate to accept Lucas's invitation. Once in, he wrote songs for the band and immediately came up with the name: Mannekino – derived from mannequin.

Erwin Olaf Springveld was becoming a flamboyant and confident performer instead of a shy boy struggling with his sexual identity. Or so it seemed.

'Terrible. Not least because I wasn't the first to tell my parents'

THE SAINT AND PETE

On the way to Rotterdam's Kunsthal – where his friend, choreographer and fellow photographer Hans van Manen is opening a major exhibition on Robert Mapplethorpe –Erwin reflects on one of his greatest role models. Both he and Van Manen, he explains, drew inspiration from Mapplethorpe. As so often happens, the conversation flows effortlessly from one subject to another: from Mapplethorpe's unapologetic sexuality to the abuse that Erwin suffered in his last year of school. 'If my coming-out story weren't so sordid', he says from behind the wheel of his Audi A3 convertible,

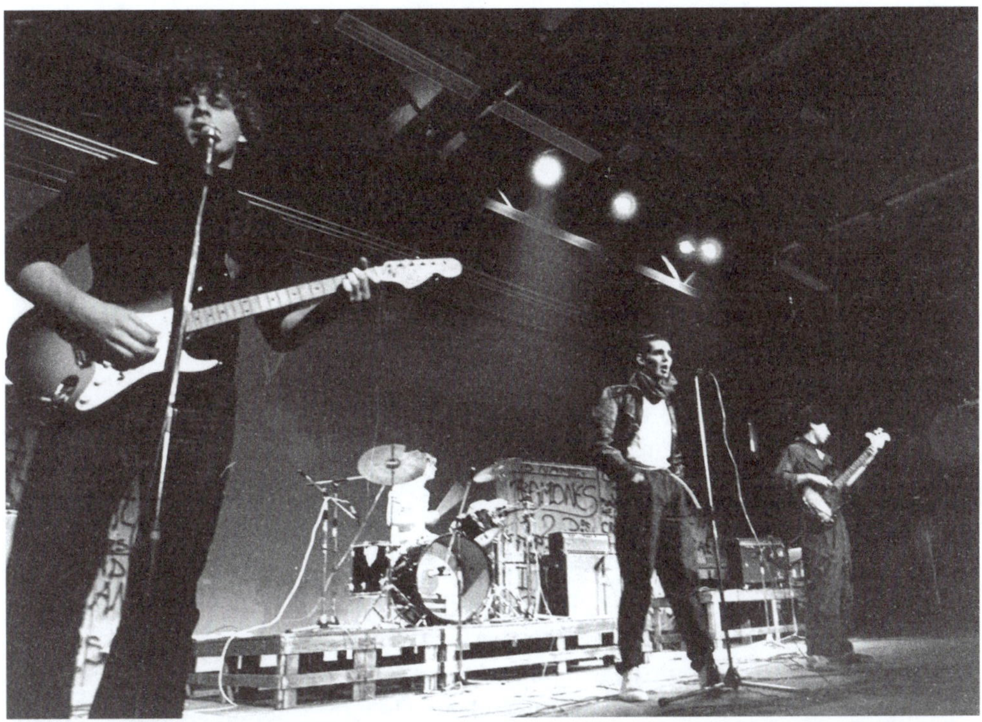

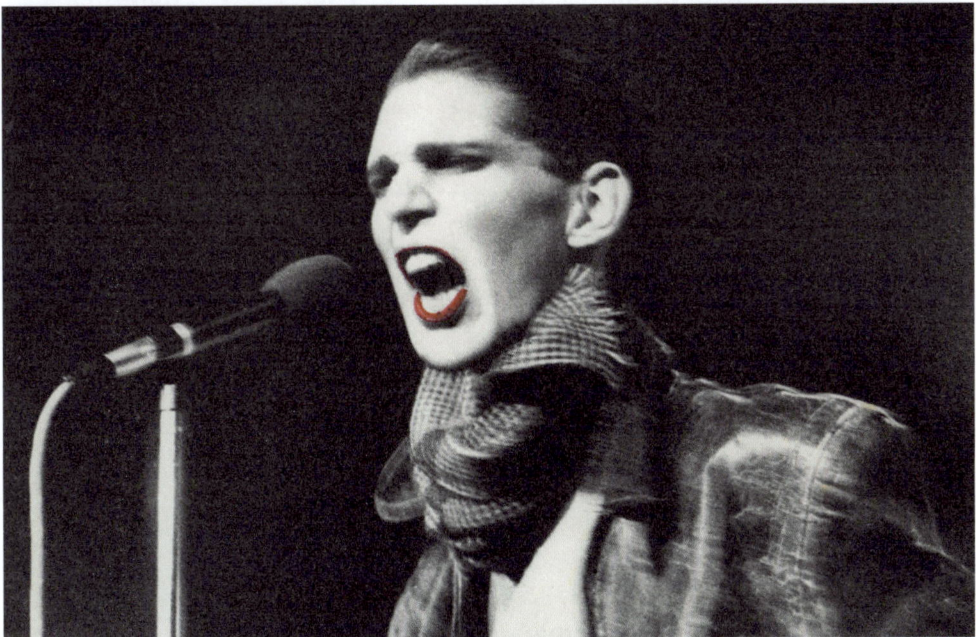

Top: The first performance of the band Mannekino Enterprise, with Erwin in the middle.
Bottom: He made quite an impression as a Bowie-esque lead singer.

'you'd almost think it was slapstick.' St Nicholas plays a role but so does alcohol, a sleazy headmaster and a bold girlfriend.

Singer in a band, popular in the playground, appreciated by not all but some teachers: Erwin felt more confident than ever as he approached his final exams. But the fundamental issue with which he was grappling remained unarticulated. 'I made a pact with myself: when I pass my exams, when I graduate, THEN I will tell my parents.' Things would not go according to plan.

Each year on 5 December, the headmaster would dress as St Nicholas and choose a student to play his helper, Black Pete – as per the centuries-old Dutch tradition that survived until the second decade of the twenty-first century, when it was denounced as racist. In 1976, Erwin Springveld was selected – though the reasons for his 'suitability' would only become apparent in retrospect. He wasn't keen on the role but was too afraid to say no. The headmaster was an authoritarian figure and a 'creepy, scary man'.

The plan was for Erwin to spend the night at the headmaster's home, so they could leave together for school the next morning in full regalia. But the evening took a darker turn in the living room. Looking back, Erwin now recognises it as a premeditated act. At the time, though, he had no such awareness. The headmaster offered the seventeen-year-old – who had never drunk alcohol before – copious amounts of what he claimed was a new kind of 'mixed fruit' soft drink. In reality, it was vodka and juice, served in heavy measure. After an evening marked by unwanted advances from the headmaster, the situation became unmistakably clear. 'I didn't even dare to say the words aloud,' Erwin recalls. 'He more or less coerced me into writing them down. In a private note, he made me confess that I was gay.'

Unaccustomed to alcohol, Erwin soon felt drunk and sick. He fell asleep, only to be awakened by the headmaster attempting to drag him into the bedroom. 'He assaulted me –he touched me. It was extreme, and it was horrifying. I pretended to be asleep, but he kept groping me anyway. In the end, when I was paralysed with fear and not responding the way he wanted, he packed me off to the spare room.'

The next day, teacher and pupil rose early, the latter with a massive hangover. The headmaster yanked himself into his tabard, donned a beard and Erwin transformed into Pete. The duo departed for the St Nicholas celebrations. 'I've never felt as humiliated as I did when we traversed the school corridors, going from classroom to classroom, with St Nicholas prodding his staff into my arse, rubbing it against my black pantaloons.'

The abuse by his headmaster was Erwin's first sexual encounter. A few years later, in the red-and-black notebook, he would describe it as 'rape' or 'extreme physical groping'. 'It was terrible. Not least because I wasn't the first person to tell my parents.'

His mother sensed something was troubling him. A week later, Erwin told her the whole sorry story. 'Which was also an opportune moment to say that I was gay.'

Lida Springveld later recalled that she wasn't wholly surprised by the confession. In her heart of hearts, she'd long realised that her middle son was gay. She'd gradually come to terms with the fact. 'I didn't want to accept it at first. Erwin is such a nice boy, he simply had to have children; that's what I thought.' Only then did it truly dawn on her and she said that, obviously, she loved him regardless: 'So long as you're happy.'

Erwin's father also reacted less negatively than expected, but again, not in a very subtle way. 'It doesn't matter, being gay is no big deal,' he said. Before adding in the same breath, 'provided you don't play the whore.' Erwin understood his father's propensity for rudeness and knew that he meant well. 'My father was a shouter, a real screamer. I'm a bit like him in that respect.'

The abuse warranted a serious response and the family debated the next steps: how to tackle the headmaster? Erwin and Lida Springveld made an appointment with both the headmaster and the relevant alderman. Before Erwin could utter a word, the latter interjected, while the headmaster laughed sheepishly. 'Erwin, we know all about your accusations. But you know, sometimes there are things you want so badly that you dream about them. And then, the next day, you think it's all true. When, in reality, it was nothing more than a fantasy.' Despite his bewilderment, Erwin responded vehemently: 'Do you really think that I would dream of sleeping with an ugly old bloke with a huge scar on his nose and nasal hair? And did I also dream about putting my hand on his cock below his flabby gut?'

He grabbed the cigarettes on the meeting table and flung them at the three men. 'This time, I was assertive, in my own peasant-like way.' He bolted out of the room and, seething with rage, hurled a row of empty coat racks to the ground.

Lida Springveld was just as incensed, forty years later. 'It was totally outrageous to claim that my child was lying about something so terrible. He wasn't raised like that. We're not liars.'
Looking back, she thought they should have still reported it, but she left that decision to her son, who didn't see the point. He was about to take his final exams and was longing for the end of high school.

He did ask his mother, however, if he could at least 'spit in the headmaster's face' after the graduation ceremony. Lida didn't object; however uncouth, it was perfectly justified. It never came to that, however, because the headmaster didn't present the certificates. He never stood on the stage again.

We are approaching Rotterdam and can see posters featuring Robert Mapplethorpe's famous self-portrait – a cigarette dangling from the right-hand corner of his mouth – advertising the Kunsthal's exhibition. After parking his Audi near the gallery, Erwin explains why the abuse ultimately didn't leave any lasting, deep scars.

That he wasn't traumatised by the enforced coming-out and his horrific initiation into gay sex is all thanks to Robert Long, a well-known Dutch singer, writer, composer, cabaret artist and radio and television presenter.

While still in school, Erwin had been conducting a series of interviews with various Dutch public figures for a free local newspaper. Though the project had come to an end, a week after confiding the St Nicholas incident to his parents, the aspiring reporter decided to pick it up again. He arranged to interview Robert Long, the singer and outspoken advocate for gay visibility and openness.

It may not have been David Bowie, but Erwin could still appreciate Long's Dutch cabaret, mainly because his lyrics had a rebellious slant. 'He represented progressiveness and freedom of thought,' Erwin recalls. Unconsciously, he may also have selected him in an effort to overwrite the memory of the predatory headmaster. After all, he admits, he found the 'gold earring-wearing' Robert Long to be 'a rather attractive mophead.'

After answering interviewer Erwin's questions – such as 'Do you too have any fears?' and 'Are you slightly racist?' – the host injected some conviviality to the proceedings: he suggested buying a Christmas tree and decorating it together. He played the piano for his young interviewer, cooked and poured the red wine, 'the first glass of wine – just a half – that I'd ever drunk.' The evening turned amorous, meaning that this time, Erwin only had himself to blame. 'It was the most romantic evening you could ever imagine and Robert Long was incredibly sweet.'

Erwin, still green, had not yet discovered sex as a form of pleasure. He was simply glad to have done it with a man, and a kind and handsome one at that. 'Even though there was a mirror hanging above the bed and I had no idea what he expected of me, it was still my first positive sexual experience. Sweet, tentative sex. For my part, a kind of childlike sex, actually.'

From the assault by a predatory headmaster during the St Nicholas celebrations to Christmas – when a famous singer revealed that sex could be joyful – it had all happened so fast. It numbed the pain of the sexual assault. 'Only now do I realise that it was a form of peasant intelligence on the part of my younger self.' That unforgettable Christmas Eve with Robert Long was a one-off experience: 'He called me just after New Year's Eve. My mother, who was in a total tizz because he was actually quite famous, exclaimed enthusiastically: Robert Long has called! To which I replied (adopts a drawl): "Oh, fun, but I've got my exams and can't hook up."' Robert Long kept calling for months. In vain.

The evening after his graduation ceremony, he met someone from his own age group. Philip, with long black hair, entered the room and said to Henny: 'Budge over.' He sat down in the seat next to Erwin.

Later that evening, they returned to Philip's parents' house. 'It was romantic, new and intense,' Erwin recalls. The next morning, when they came downstairs, Philip's 'rather scrawny' mother and his father – 'wearing a shiny satin dressing gown and oversized glasses' – were seated in the living room. 'They practically jumped out of their skins when they saw me. Philip simply said, "Mum, Dad, this is Erwin. He's my boyfriend, and I'm gay. We're going into town." And he walked out, with me trailing in his wake, slightly embarrassed.'

It was a pivotal moment, the instant when the sexual revolution of the mid-1970s crossed over into Erwin's personal life.

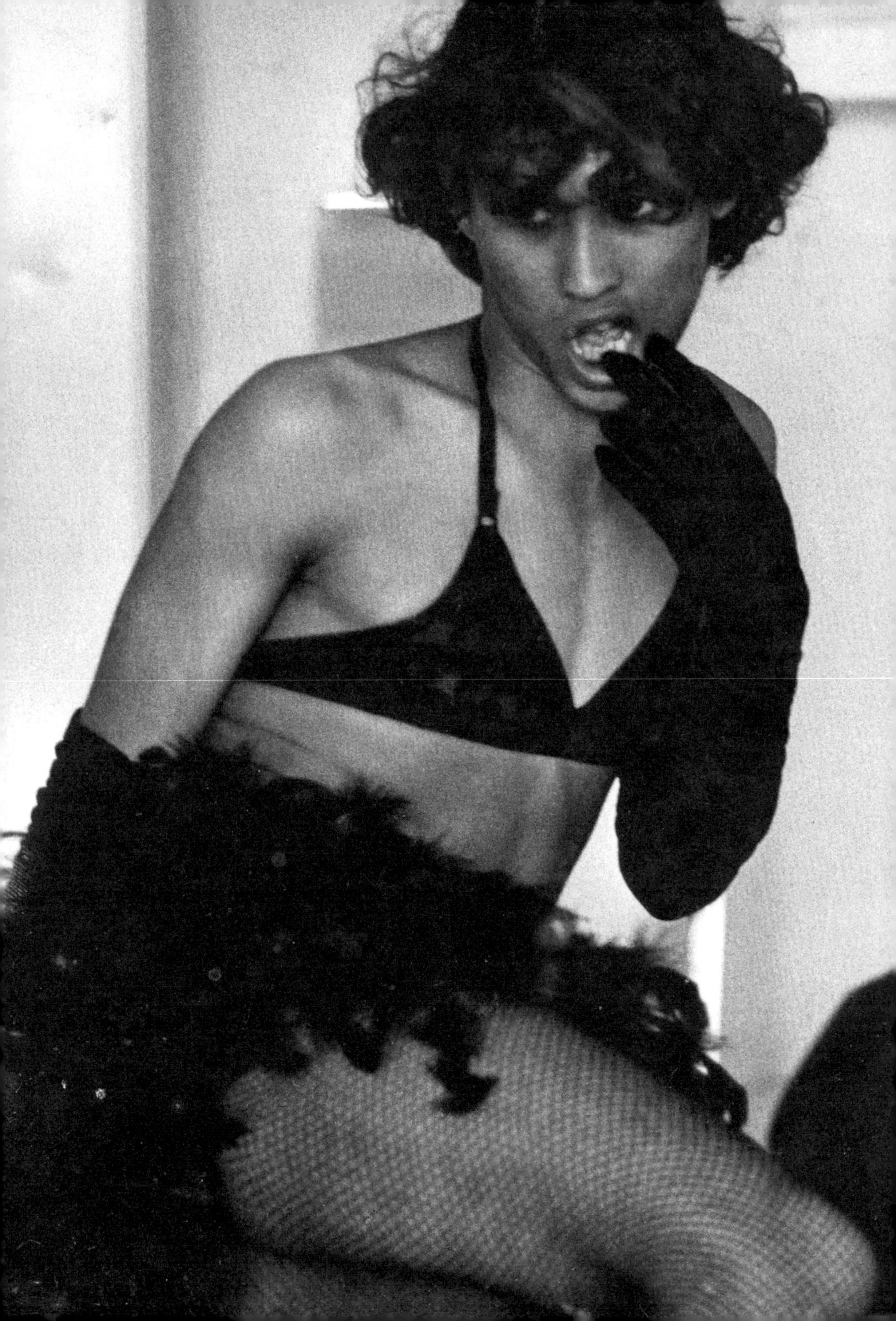

2 LIBERATION (1977–1981)

'I'm not as good as I've long let myself believe'

MANNEKINO ENTERPRISE

On 1 June 2020, a white Motability car crosses Dam Square, navigates the tram lines and pedestrians, and pulls in by the Nieuwe Kerk. Protesters have planned a march against police brutality that led to the violent death of Black American George Floyd. About 5,000 people eventually gather, packed together despite the coronavirus pandemic, shouting anti-racist slogans. Erwin had used their group chat app to encourage his friends to join the demonstration. Erwin, Rudolf Pfalz, Marline Williams and Frans Franciscus (the pseudonym of painter Frans van de Vooren) are four seasoned protesters who have known each other for over four decades.

Erwin has always been engaged with oppressed minorities, especially in the fight for gay rights, a cause that also touched Rudolf and Frans. In the run-up to the Dam demonstration, Erwin saw his friends differently. Marline is the daughter of a black trumpeter from Duke Ellington's orchestra and Rudolf's parents were Indonesian. But Erwin had never considered the two as people of colour. He admitted: 'I'm colour-blind in that respect; it also took me a long time to understand that the N-word was inappropriate. After all, people of colour use it among themselves.' There was now a unified fury, intense emotions, and an awe-inspiring energy surrounding the Black Lives Matter movement.

As the square fills up, Marline worries above all else about her friends. Rudolf's pulmonary emphysema is even more severe than Erwin's. Dam Square is the site of a powerful show of solidarity with the Black Lives Matter movement, as the crowd ignores the risk of coronavirus infection and draws closer. The two chronically ill people, fearful of contracting the virus, eventually decide to leave the protest. They drive their small white car through the crowd as the protesters chant 'I can't breathe', a poignant echo of George Floyd's last words before his death at the hands of the police.

Erwin's decision to study at the Utrecht School of Journalism led, in an indirect way, to his first encounters with Rudolf, Marline and Frans.

Upon discovering in an introductory pamphlet that the programme placed great emphasis on students living in dormitories and fostering an autonomous perspective on the world, Erwin made up his mind. He had been yearning to leave home for quite some time. He wanted to escape 'that stronghold of the far right, the community where the elite gathered at the tennis court, where my brother heard that I was a "queen", and my father expected me to "play by the rules".' He chose the School of Journalism for its reputation as a place of freedom, and once there, the course's anarchist nature suited him perfectly. His friends didn't find his decision peculiar, given his years of writing articles for a local publication. As Henny Dinklage recalls, 'Erwin never harboured a burning desire to write. His true aspiration was to make a mark in public life. ... If you inquired about his career goals, the stock response was "famous".'

Anne-Marie van Merwijk believes that her ex-boyfriend had two sides: one that pursued fame at all costs, and another that was skilled at abruptly severing ties. He was a sweet and gentle boy who could also be extremely ruthless. His incredibly innocent looks opened every conceivable door, yet he could be as cunning as a fox.

They continued to correspond, and Henny 'Dinky Toy' Dinklage occasionally visited Erwin in Utrecht. 'At first, he lived in a tiny room measuring, at most, 12 square metres. It was crammed with friends, on the bed and on the floor. Always Bowie on the turntable. And loads of dope.'

Before sharing Erwin's correspondence from Utrecht with me, Henny consulted her old pen pal. 'I told Erwin, your letters are full of references to weed. Shouldn't I censor those parts?' He agreed, saying, 'Go ahead and black out those sections. Otherwise, people will simply say: it's no wonder that you've got emphysema, you've shot your lungs to pieces. What they don't know is that my lung condition is a hereditary variant.' However, he later changed his mind and said, 'I refuse to dictate what others can and cannot write about me. It's against my principles. And drugs: it was par for the course at the time.' Nor did it stop at dope. 'I was not a prolific drug user, and never injected heroin, although I did snort it on a handful of occasions. But even then, I was totally incompetent: everyone around me would be screaming. No, you're doing it wrong! Watch out, what a crime!'

Utrecht was a big city with a gritty underbelly, which forced Erwin to change his perspective. On his very first night in his new place, he witnessed a young man injecting speed, using a tie as a tourniquet. 'He turned out to be a nice guy. It never changes. I have a bias against someone, only to discover that they are just too unhinged.

And that's what I adore about life.'

The letters reveal that, as a teenager, Erwin Springveld grappled with life, a common experience for many eighteen-year-olds. This isn't the full picture, however, because he was less inclined to express his distress in written form when things were going well. He enjoyed quoting song lyrics, such as a line from David Bowie's 'Time': 'You just scream with boredom.' Underneath, he mused, 'Could that line have been written just for me?'

He dramatically complained that he was not only bored rigid but felt 'desperately unhappy', that he was contemplating 'suicide' and was already considering the method: 'Hanging is cheaper than gas. A gun is prohibitively expensive.' Only to downplay the matter a few paragraphs later, reassuring Henny that she didn't need to panic about the suicidal ideation. 'I have the same kind of depressive episodes at least ten to twelve times a year', wrote Erwin before signing off with a joke, 'don't worry, you know that you'll inherit my scholarship.'

What he was struggling with, clearly, was love – or rather – its absence. He occasionally had sex, but it didn't make him feel good. This included the time, back in Amersfoort, when 'a pockmarked, acned boy' came on to him. They ended up going back to his place. 'Once there, he threw me onto the bed, yanked off my clothes, mumbled, "horny pubes", and gave me a blow job. Whether it was the glaring lights or the two gins I'd imbibed, I became nauseous within minutes and puked.'

While it may have been obvious that he was gay, his sexual orientation in those days was still something fluid. Coming out of the closet did not preclude other routes to love. For example, he wrote a letter to a girl expressing his love for her. 'I wasn't trying to be alluring or confusing, I was being honest.' He wrote about this surprising gesture to Henny Dinklage: 'Infatuation gets me into bed, but beyond that, you know what I mean, right? I could sleep with her, but she'd have to make the first move.'

That the path to love did not run smoothly was one thing, but the freshman also began to feel ever more strongly that he was a huge intellectual failure, and that journalism was ultimately not a good choice for him. 'I've reached the conclusion that I'm not as good as I've long let myself believe. I'm aimless and useless and I loathe myself. I don't fit in here.'

It was hardly unexpected that he struggled to find his niche: someone who liked to be the centre of attention would have been better suited for a different field. Reporting is a service profession – it wasn't about him, but about the stories of others.

What Erwin did find in Utrecht was nightlife. His landlady had an 11 p.m. curfew, but he didn't last that long. Instead, he preferred to smoke dope all day. He had a unique bond with some of his classmates, such as Moos Engels, his friend since their first day at school, and Jan Eilander, who became a writer, screenwriter and director.

In the mid-1970s, the democratic tide from universities swept into colleges, and

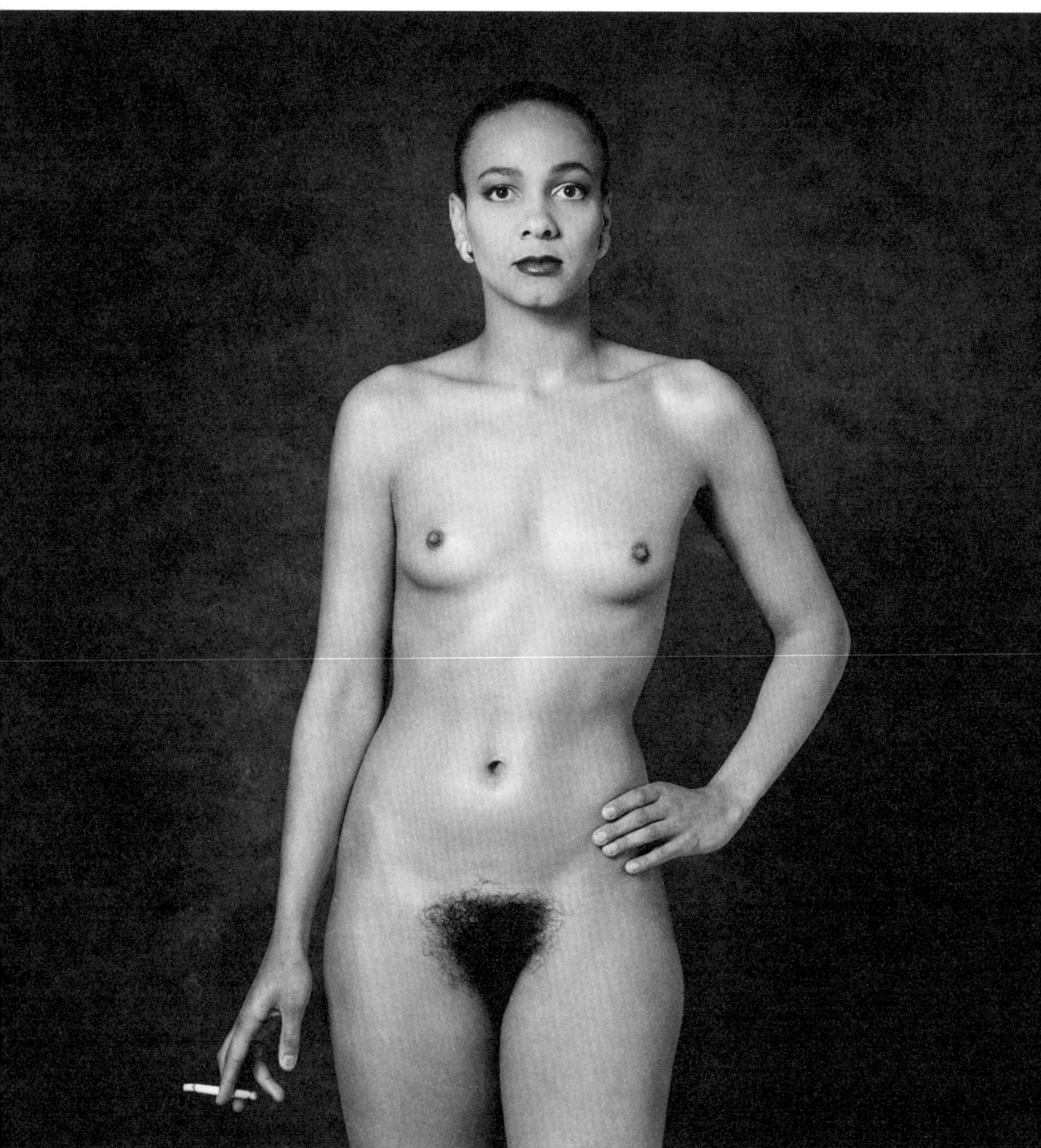

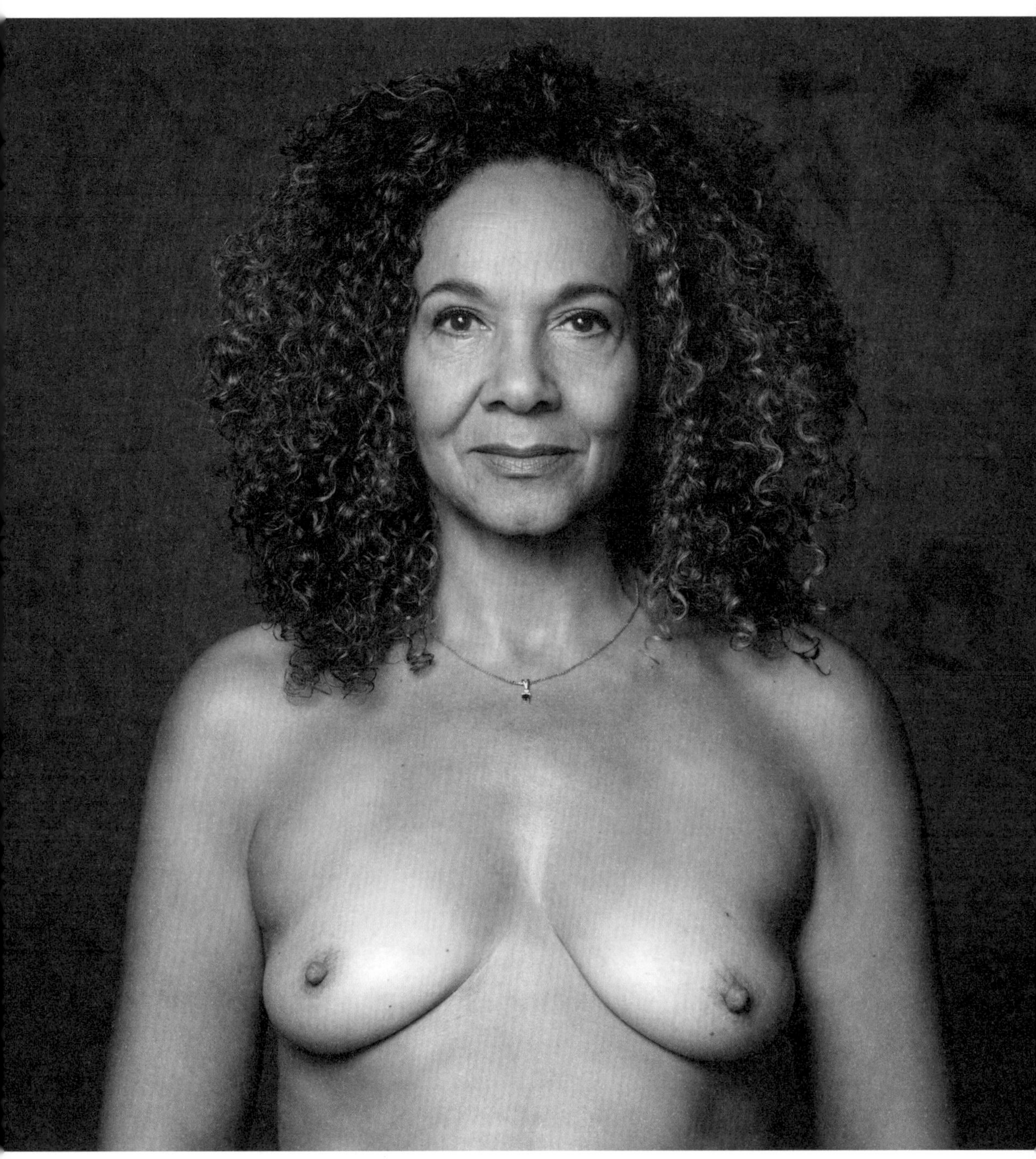

Left: Marline Williams, oldest friend and one of the earliest models. 'For a long time, Erwin was simultaneously my father, my mother, my brother and my sister.' Right: Marline Williams, 2022, from the *Muses* series. Photo on page 30: Rudolf Pfalz, photographed in 1978, was Erwin's first model.

the two were astonished at the power of students to shape the education system. Looking back at his first year, he concluded that it had largely been a waste of time, and he blamed himself above all.

Erwin and Jan Eilander were not interested in the endless discussions on Marx and Engels. Instead, their mutual passion was music, specifically punk, new wave and rock 'n' roll. They spent more and more time together. Eventually, Erwin tentatively asked, 'Jan, do you know that I'm gay?' Jan had no idea: 'I hadn't met a gay man before Erwin.' But it didn't bother him in the slightest and their bond remained strong. In Erwin's room, they listened to vinyl records, including Blondie's latest album, Iggy Pop's *Lust for Life* and, of course, David Bowie.

Student bars and nightclubs existed, as did a gay subculture. In the queer venue, Adonis, he met fifteen-year-old Marline Williams, who had just run away from boarding school. As a lonely teenager, she knew that she wouldn't be hassled by the Adonis's gay clientele. Standing like a wallflower, listening to the disco hits of Foxy, The Tramps and Chic, Erwin approached her with an unexpected opening line: 'So you also love wearing baggy pants?' Williams stated that this was not a typical heterosexual pick-up line. They shared a common interest in fashion and music, and soon became inseparable. 'We lived for nights out and, when we weren't on the town, we smoked joints,' she recalled. Williams wanted to protect herself from predators, so Erwin, who worked part-time in the hospitality industry, gave her a bread knife. From that moment on, Marline kept it hidden in her boot. Better safe than sorry. In turn, she helped Erwin move to a larger room. 'All his possessions fitted into two rubbish bags, so we hopped on the city bus, each with a bag on one shoulder. He sat in the back of a nearly empty bus, wide-eyed, as if it were his own personal limousine. 'Just drive!' he yelled at the driver. I thought, what is this megalomania? As it turned out, Erwin saw it more as the fruits of his imagination. If you can't afford a private driver, why not imagine transforming the city bus into an opulent limousine?

Yet Marline Williams's new friend seemed to possess a greater sense of purpose than she did: 'For me, life was all about survival, making it from one day to the next. I didn't have a plan; I received child welfare payments and nothing more. Erwin, however, harboured lofty ambitions. He was resolute and determined to succeed, aiming to become a force to be reckoned with in the future.'

They lived together for a while, sharing lodgings with a 'very openly gay man'. Kids from the neighbourhood would yell insults at them and throw things at them as they walked down the street. One day, Erwin got fed up, so he invited them to visit his apartment. Look, he said, this is my gay toilet. Here's my gay bedroom, and my gay kitchen with gay sprinkles, gay jam and gay cheese. The street kids understood the joke perfectly. From then on, they were firm friends.

Erwin and Marline eventually moved out, but they lived close by and saw each

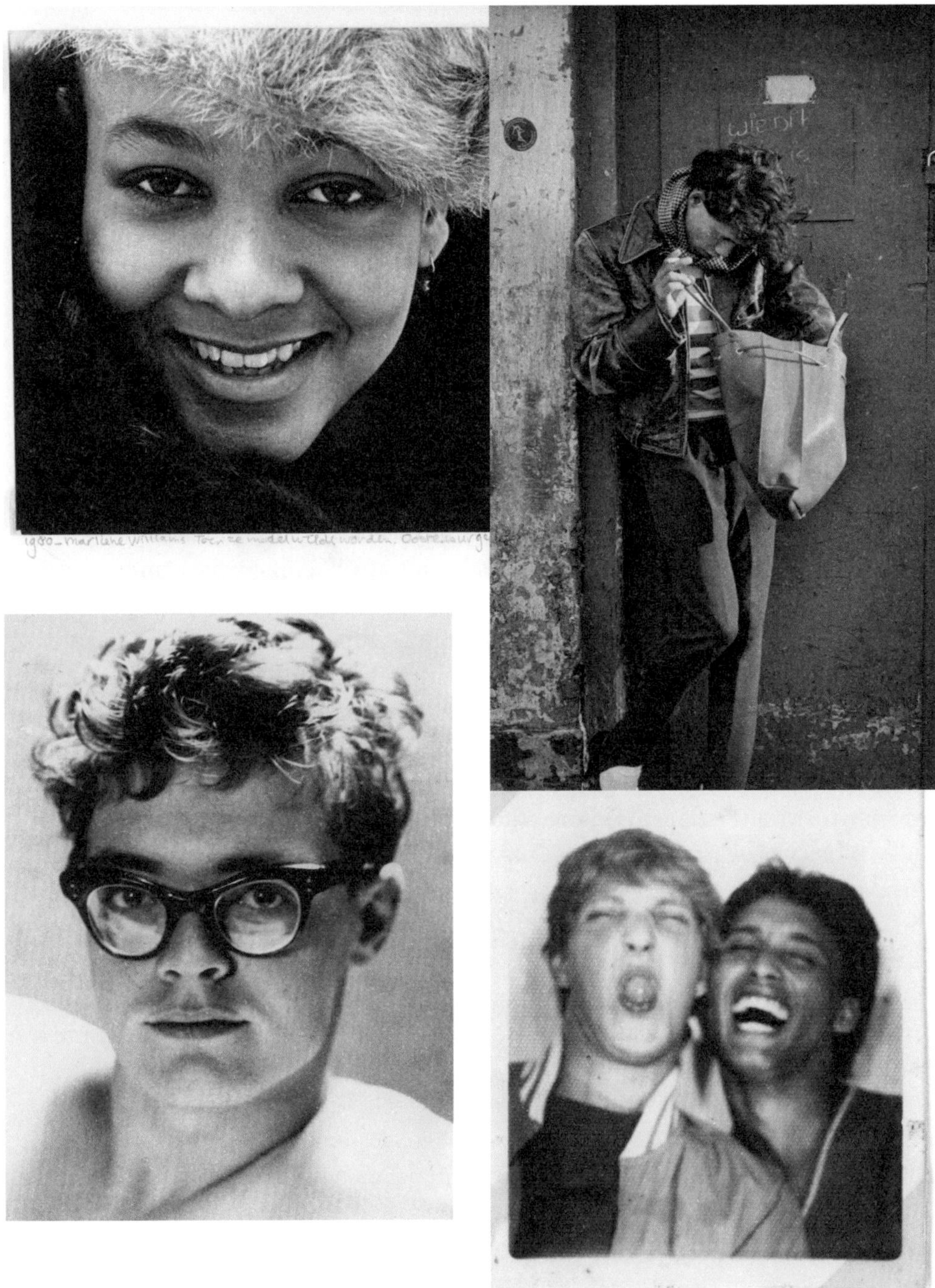

From top left, clockwise: Marline Williams; Rudolf Pfalz in an alley near Lange Smeestraat; Erwin and Rudolf; Frans Franciscus. Next photo spread: the photo wall at home on Egelantiersgracht. In the centre is the picture by Weegee, *Man arrested for cross-dressing*, New York, c. 1939.

other every day. 'Great highs coupled with crushing existential angst, it couldn't be dark enough for us,' Williams says. 'We played *Berlin* by Lou Reed, *Low* and *Heroes* by Bowie. We were spotty, riddled with insecurities and fizzing with brilliant ideas.'

According to Erwin, his emotional state could be characterised as adolescent melancholy. 'I later learnt that it's a normal developmental process for a 20-year-old, but at the time, I was drowning in misery and I felt paralysed, like a sick person without a fever.' Williams says that, as a female teenage runaway, it was nevertheless an 'enormous stroke of luck' that she had bumped into the aspiring young journalist. 'For a long time, Erwin was simultaneously my father, my mother, my brother and my sister.'

Erwin and Marline shared a passion for glossy magazines such as *Avenue*, *Vogue* and Andy Warhol's *Interview*, and they pored over them for all that was cool and fashionable. They admired Helmut Newton's fashion photography, Leni Riefenstahl's films and photos, but also the book *Exposures*, Andy Warhol's Polaroids of the trend-setting New York art scene, which he had published with Bob Colacello in 1979.

Life moved up a gear when Erwin and Marline met budding artist Frans Franciscus, who was also a student of Dutch, and college dropout and *Vogue* enthusiast Rudolf Pfalz. 'I thought Erwin was a hunk,' says Rudolf. Erwin, who was quite shy and 'not at all inclined towards exhibitionism', was captivated by Rudolf's androgynous appearance. He was quite butch but wore feminine accessories, such as heels and feather boas.

Rudolf, Frans, Marline and Erwin formed a tight-knit group, despite the latter's occasional vitriolic letters to Henny. 'Rudolf is captivated by mirrors, obsessed with his own image, and drawn to intriguing individuals. His only problem is acne. Frans is incredibly sweet, although not particularly attractive. You can have long, meaningful conversations with him, but I'm worried he might be in love with me. He is standoffish towards outsiders. Marline is self-obsessed, puts on airs, and thinks she's got it made.' Marline Williams, who became an actress, singer and coach after a brief career in finance, said, 'Erwin is just bloody-minded, to a gross degree. With him, it's like gazing into a crystal-clear mirror.'

The friends often gathered at Frans's loft, which served as a hub for brainstorming and creativity. There, Erwin spontaneously took one of his very first photographs using his first Nikon camera: a nude image of Frans seated in a chair, illuminated by natural light. A portrait of Rudolf in drag, 'the first photo I ever took', he wrote on the back of the print.

Erwin grew more comfortable in Utrecht, making friends his own age who shared his interests. These young people, both men and women, enjoyed partying, drinking, smoking, and passing around joints. For the time being, a lack of funds kept them in check, but Rudolf eventually succumbed to heroin addiction. Despite not yet having reached that stage, Rudolf was permanently excluded from school after a caretaker witnessed him 'rolling a joint'. Even worse, it was alleged that he was selling drugs to his classmates. Erwin alerted the local media, and pieces soon started appearing in the newspaper about how unfairly the school had treated Rudolf, who looks back on the intervention with the utmost respect. 'Erwin's sense of justice is second to none. You wouldn't want to cross him.'

On 10 October 1978, Erwin Springveld, still a student, and Rudolf Pfalz, school dropout, stood on the A27 with their thumbs up. They were hitchhiking to Paris in search of excitement and adventure. For Erwin, the trip held an even greater significance. Although he went to college every day, he was disappointed with how things were going. He planned to make up for his lacklustre performance with two articles: one on David Bowie and the other on Paris.

The Pompidou Centre had only been open for a year when they visited the *Paris–Berlin, 1900–1933* exhibition, where he first encountered the work of Otto Dix, including the famous *Portrait of the Journalist Sylvia von Harden*, as well as *Remember Uncle August, the Unhappy Inventor* by George Grosz, the other great critic of the First World War.

Erwin developed a lifelong fascination with both artists, while the Weimar period – in all its facets – would later inspire his Berlin photo series. He bought a postcard of a Weegee photo in the museum shop entitled *Man arrested for cross-dressing*, New York, c. 1939. It shows a transvestite exiting a prison van. 'There was so much pride and naivete in that photograph. Forty years later, he bought a vintage print of Weegee's photo for $12,000 'because he could'.

Before their Paris trip, he wrote to Henny Dinklage, 'I've fallen in love with a hippie: Teun Frieszo, 28, tall, long brown hair, doesn't smoke pot, plays the church organ, and is smart, handsome and kind. He's super intelligent!' After many flings, this seemed like his first serious relationship, though it came with its own challenges: 'He's been dating someone for five years. Oh God, where do we start?' Before Rudolf and Erwin left for Paris, Teun warned Erwin not to fall in love with him.

Erwin took this as a green light to do whatever he wanted in Paris – and he had the time of his life. As soon as they arrived, Rudolf was eager to ditch their backpacks at the hostel and head straight to the iconic terrace of the Café de Flore. 'Within five minutes, a man approached us and offered to buy us a drink.'

It didn't take long for Rudolf to get a ride in a Mini Cooper, destination unknown, with Erwin following behind on the back of a motorcycle owned by a DJ from the pop station Radio Luxembourg. 'I had my arms wrapped around the waist of a handsome man wearing a leather jacket. We were cruising alongside the Seine towards a stunning apartment with a view of the Opera. His four-poster bed was surrounded by a dozen viewing boxes that lit up at the flick of a switch – but the scenes

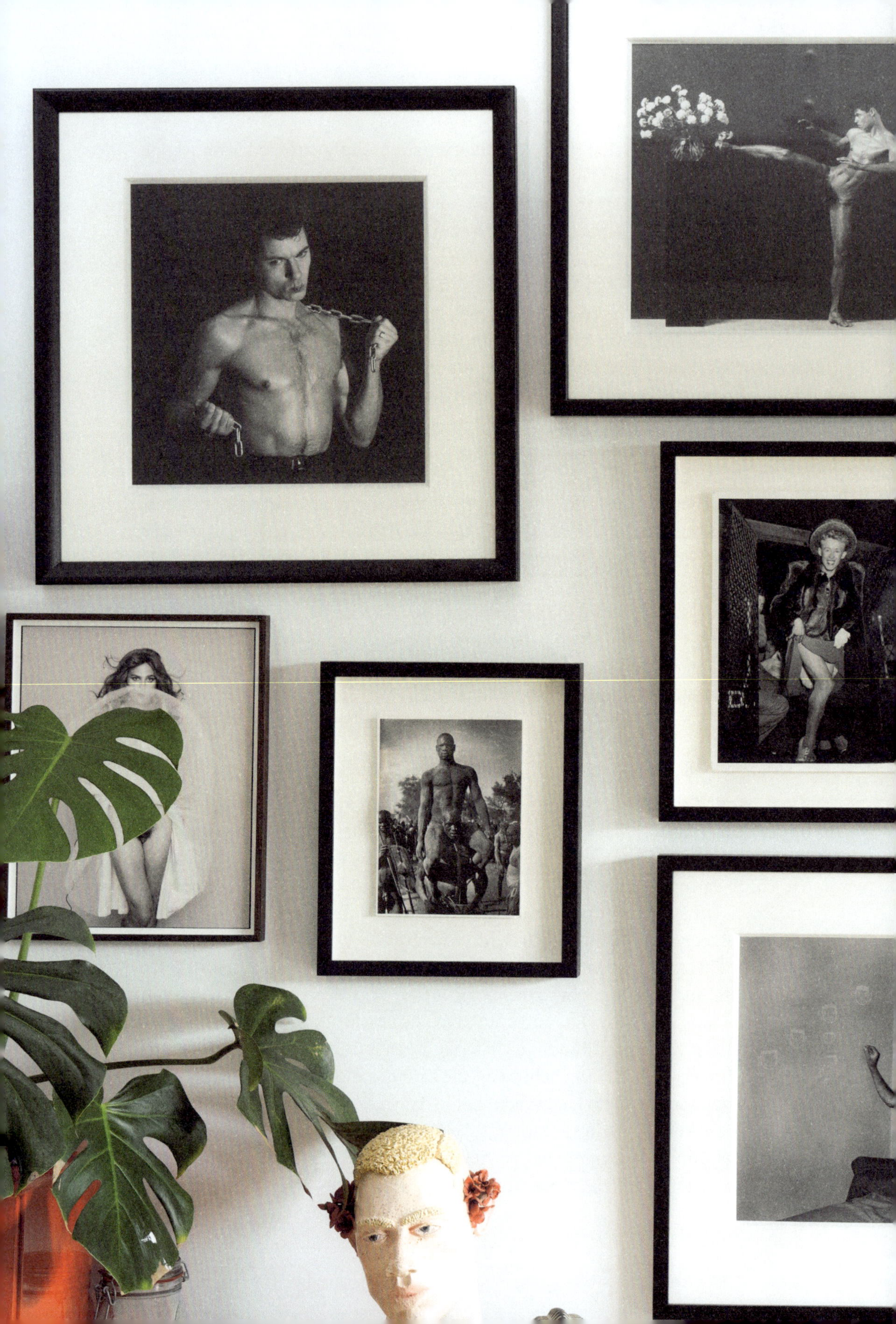

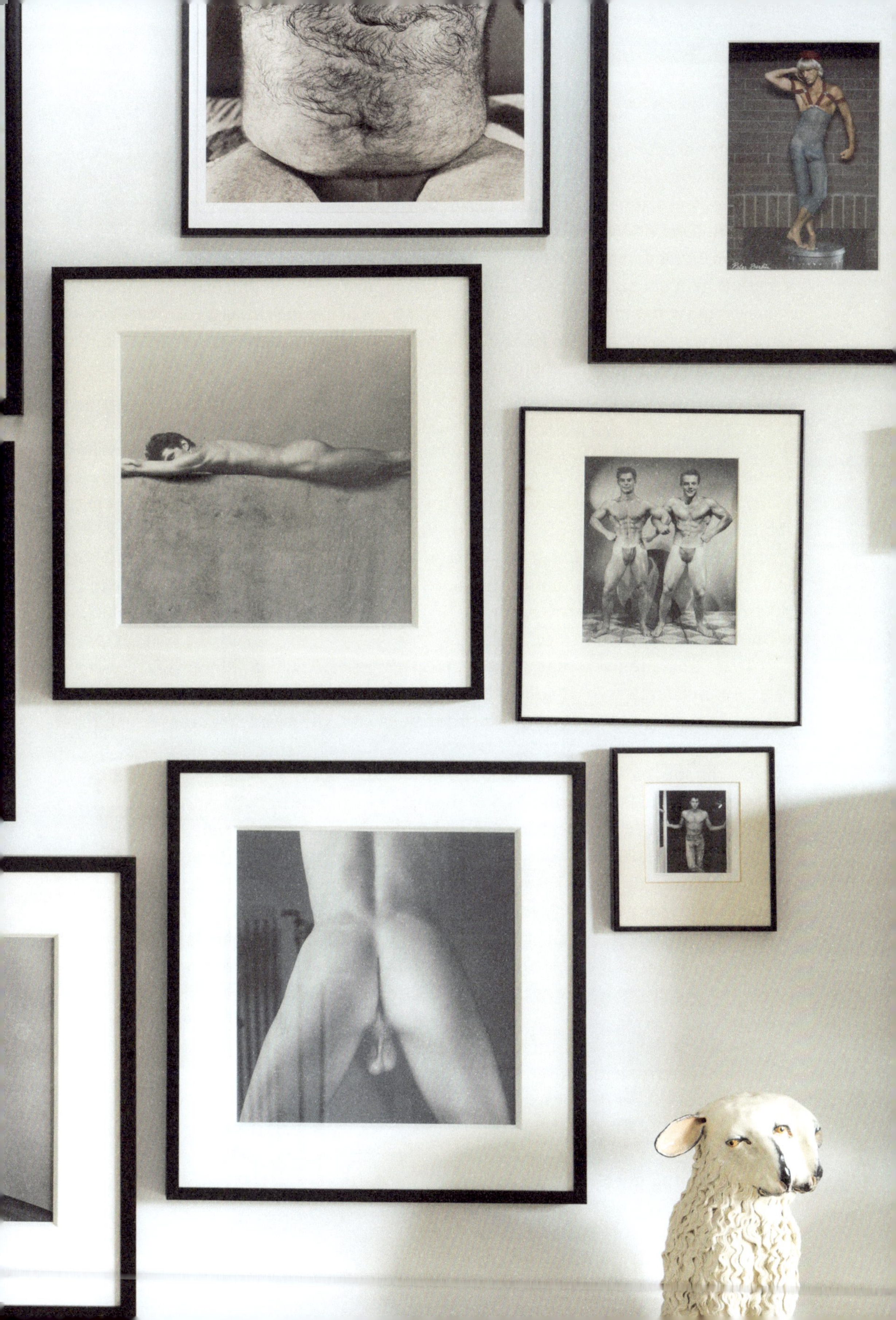

inside the boxes were gory: Barbie and Ken slaughtering each other or mangled in car crashes or skiing accidents. All this on my first ever solo trip to the city!'

They were pampered and taken to late-night dinners. Rudolf: 'Everybody adored us. The men mainly swarmed around Erwin, which really got under my skin. As a result, we initially went out separately in the city.' Later, they met some relatively older, wealthier gentlemen. 'Erwin had a guy who was high up at *Paris Match* magazine, and I was sleeping with a high-ranking official with a huge house in Saint-Germain-des-Prés.' On a joint visit to the *Paris Match* man in his glass-walled penthouse – of whom Erwin, ever the aspiring journalist, thought, 'Well, I never, *Paris Match*' – things became decidedly less agreeable. Their visit took an unexpected turn once they entered. An oversized fruit bowl filled with polaroids of young, partially nude boys caught their attention in the living room. While Rudolf was downstairs spinning records, Erwin found himself alone on the rooftop terrace, conversing with Mr *Paris Match*. 'He toppled me, and my head was halfway down the stairs. The guy was on top of me. Rudolf thought I was joking when I lay there wrestling him, shouting that we had to leave.'

In the hotel room to which they'd decamped, Erwin had another unpleasant encounter, this time with an American boy. 'Suddenly, he lunged at me, pulled down my trousers, and attempted to fuck me. Thankfully, I managed to trip him up and he went flying into the doorframe.'

These were intense events, but Erwin wasn't rattled. 'It was a different era. It was Paris. And you know what? Nothing bad happened. In retrospect, we felt very flattered: someone wanted us. Sex wasn't the priority. I was in the mood for adventure, and the sex was more like an obstacle.'

On the spur of the moment, inspired by the neighbourhood's shady reputation, the boys headed to Place Pigalle. Rudolf approached a prostitute, who pointed out a darkened doorway. Once inside, they found themselves in a sparsely populated bar. They stood on the periphery of the dancefloor, waiting for the venue to fill up. 'Men began to arrive, only to quickly disappear into another room. Rudolf decided to look. I was shaking in my boots. We found them in the dark room, a place we didn't know about back home. It was pitch black, and all you could hear were groans and the sound of creaking leather. Terrifying. Fear paralysed me and I stood there, almost catatonic, unable to move forwards or backwards. As soon as I recovered my senses, I fled.'

Having casual sex with unfamiliar people was not Erwin's idea of love. 'I must click with a sexual partner, although I became less stringent about this in later life.' Furthermore: 'I've set the bar incredibly high in terms of visuals, which is why porn bores me to tears. I find it exhausting to watch a dick repeatedly thrusting in and out of an anus. It's as if I'm watching a video of a diesel engine. My fantasies are infinitely more captivating and visually appealing.'

Paris enthralled Erwin, who returned the following year with Moos Engels to see a major exhibition on Japanese art and the Picasso show at the Grand Palais. The latter made a deep impression on him. He was amazed that so many different styles could be found in one man. This was what it meant to be an artist: constantly evolving and reinventing oneself.

Only later did he discover that things seemed to work differently in the photographic world, which is why he has long avoided art criticism. 'In that milieu, you're only considered a great artist if, like Bernd and Hiller Becher, you begin your career in the late 1950s with face-on shots of factories in slightly cloudy weather. You then continue in this style for several decades. Alternatively, they can take repeated photos of two sisters, consistently using the same backdrops. That's the type of photography preached by contemporary art museums. And it's a circuit that holds sway worldwide.'

Erwin wanted fame at any cost, as Frans Franciscus noticed. 'He seemed unbothered about whys and wherefores.' The conversation takes place in an artists' studio complex on the outskirts of Amsterdam, where over 100 creatives have workshops in a former ammunition depot; Franciscus has a space where he works on his paintings, films and, nowadays, photographs. Back then, he never doubted for a single second that Erwin would succeed in breaking through. 'He could just as easily have been a musician. Don't forget that he was the lead singer in a band despite not being able to sing a note. He simply had the guts to get on stage and steal the show.'

Mannekino created a demo tape and performed their second concert at the Flint venue in Amersfoort. Erwin pulled out all the stops to make it a huge success. Friends and family were pressed into action. The description of what ticket holders could expect foreshadowed the wild photos and parties that he would later host at the Amsterdam venues Paradiso and RoXY. The event by 'Mannekino Enterprise' would be 'compered by a transvestite' and include a 'fashion show to disco music'. He wrote to Henny: 'I'm walking around with a girl weighing more or less 140 kilos. She's a model for swimsuits.' A mime act was booked, and Mannekino, of course, was scheduled to perform. The production team spared no expense, even hiring three backup vocalists. He set his vision down in a drawing: 'I kind of know what I'm going to wear. I'm a saddo, right, to be fixating on the clothes?'

Erwin asked his mother, Lida, to sew him some trousers. He gave her a picture of David Bowie so that she wouldn't get it wrong. His bandmates were stunned by their white-shirted leader. A little further back in the audience, a long-haired, slightly older twenty-something was also listening. Teun was curious to see what his latest conquest would look like on stage and whether he could sing. The music was a bit too bombastic for his taste, but Erwin's immense talent for drama and grandeur was immediately apparent.

While their previous performance was rock 'n' roll, their second one was far more theatrical, with clouds of white balloons, elaborate costumes, televisions showing the game Pong, and a hydraulic stage.

It could have been quite something, although the performance was 'not a great success, but a success nevertheless', as Erwin wrote to his friend Henny. But it wasn't quite enough: Mannekino disbanded at their fledgling peak. Erwin Springveld's music career had ended before it had even begun, with his initial step towards stardom ultimately proving to be a stumbling block.

'I'm not going to lose myself in drink or drugs anymore'

DAVID BOWIE'S DOOR

'I want to start with the bad stuff and get it out of the way. I have never argued with anyone as fiercely as I have with you.' It is a drizzly Saturday in February 2021, and Erwin Olaf is speaking in Utrecht's St Nicholas' Church before the friends and family of his recently deceased former lover and muse, Teun Frieszo, with whom he enjoyed an equally long and special friendship after a long love affair.

It was an austere gathering, partly because of the corona pandemic but also because it was what Frieszo had wanted. Music by Bach is played on the organ, husband Jochem Tims speaks, as do three of Teun's former lovers, and the church bells ring. There is a double row of mourners, observing the social distancing rules of 1.5 metres, which lends the scene something of a contemporary dance performance.

More than forty years earlier, Erwin and Teun had met while out on the town. Erwin had had a few casual boyfriends, but they had never amounted to much. For him, it was a case of 'no sex without love', he noticed. 'I only enjoy it when I'm really in love.' In the summer of 1978, during a night out, Erwin (19) suddenly set eyes on Teun (28). 'I stood as if nailed to the ground.' Teun's hippie-like appearance made an impression. 'Long-haired, skinny as a rake, a big, angular nose and broad chest, but something amiss, all the same,' he described him in a letter. 'I kissed Teun for the first time in the middle of the street, after a night out. With my trousers down to my knees, somewhere on a bridge in Utrecht.'

In addition to being his great love, Teun would become a mentor and teacher in a variety of fields, from sex to modern art and dance. Teun took Erwin to exhibitions and to dance performances by Lucinda Childs, Rudi van Dantzig and Hans van Manen.

Still, it had all been quite complicated, Teun Frieszo told me not long before his death, speaking about their relationship. He was ill by then, but not yet too weak to

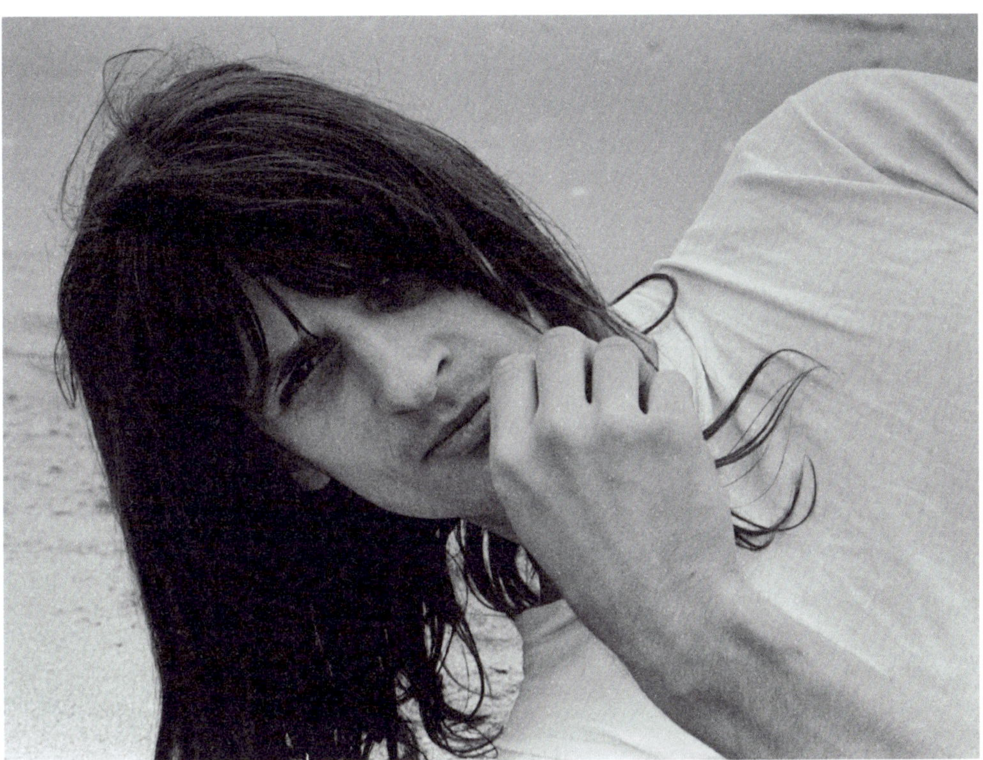

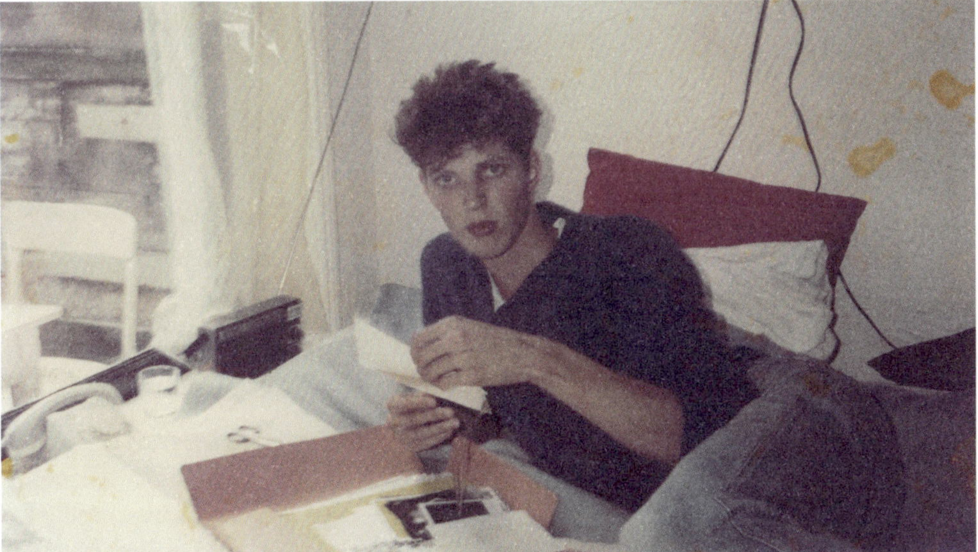

Top: Teun Frieszo's hippie-like appearance made an impression. 'Long-haired, skinny as a rake, a big, angular nose and broad chest, but something amiss, all the same.' Bottom: Erwin at home, Nieuwe Oostenburgerstraat 18hs, 1979.

elaborate on the genesis of a love story that would last nearly a quarter-century.

Not only did Teun have a long-term partner when he met Erwin, but moreover, they didn't, at first glance, seem like a perfect match. While Teun had been fascinated by that 'effeminate boy' at the time, he also found him incredibly irritating, a 'shrieky faggot' who wore high 'après-ski boots' in the height of summer and a big wool sweater. 'It was as thrilling as it was terrible. In short, the perfect recipe for falling in love, only I didn't realise it myself right away.' Nevertheless, Teun made the first move, or at least that's how Erwin remembers it: 'I was terrible at flirting. Being flirted with, that's where my talent lay.'

Teun, nine years older than Erwin, was an academic with Orthodox Christian roots and a passion for the church organ, who hailed from a very different world. While Erwin's young party friends wondered what on earth he saw in the 'old hippie', Frieszo's own acquaintances also had their opinions on his relationship with Erwin, namely, 'What do you see in that faggot?' But Teun's annoyance was soon supplanted by fascination and infatuation. 'Erwin was completely authentic; he was special and essentially different from everyone else. He was totally aware that he was "weird" and an "exceptional case".'

The way Teun saw it, his steady relationship did not preclude a new love: this was the 1970s, after all. Monogamy was not considered a badge of honour and certainly not in homosexual circles. It would be almost another quarter of a century before the legalisation of gay marriage, AIDS was still unknown, and most of the queer community at the time railed against bourgeois moral values and heterosexual ideals, such as suburban bliss. Still, Teun's unilateral decision to be polyamorous cast a shadow over the fledgling relationship. 'To protect Erwin a little, I had immediately warned him: don't fall in love with me because I've got a boyfriend.' A candid confession that lay at the root of many arguments. 'I meant well, but because of that proviso, Erwin long accused me of depriving him of the chance to find real love.'

The flip side was that Erwin also pursued other relationships in addition to their own. As he wrote in an undated note to Teun Frieszo: 'You're the horniest, sweetest, most beautiful and exciting man in the world, should I finally have to make the ultimate choice. Until then, I'll have fun with people, which I learnt from you! But you never cease to lumber me with a delicious helping of guilt.'

Meanwhile, Teun led him by the hand and broadened his horizons. 'Bach, the Holland Festival, difficult French films, German painters from the interwar period.' Teun marvelled at Erwin's unorthodox journalistic ambitions. In those days, and in those circles, journalism was nothing if not left-wing. Erwin may have been left leaning – he would always obstinately and sometimes grudgingly vote for the PvdA (Labour Party) – but he lacked intellectual aspirations. As he succinctly put it, 'Once you know that life can be a ball, why work and study?'

Yet Teun discovered an ambition as unfocused as it was burning behind his new lover's seemingly breezy superficiality: 'Erwin longed to be famous, he just hadn't worked out how.' He wasn't smug, however, as evidenced by one of the lists of good intentions that he still made with some regularity.

The reason: 'Only when I tell people that life's great, do I start to believe it myself. I'm not going to lose myself in drink or drugs anymore and will only drink or smoke when I feel good.'

1. Drinking: 2 beers a night, max.
2. Drugs (soft): only when feeling upbeat and happy.
3. Drugs (hard): never again.
4. Cockiness: in the next six months, to stop playacting and to feel free.
5. Lusting after interesting people or experiences and bragging about them.
6. Knuckle down to a career, perhaps as a model but not in an arrogant way.
7. Work hard at school, not sure how.
8. Don't go out too much.
9. Become confident enough to stop this idiotic list making (?)
10. Invent a new handwriting.

Relating his resolutions to Henny, he added, 'Guess what, I've quit smoking. I only smoke a pack and a half of filter cigarettes a day now, good huh?' He could joke about it then, but that smoking would still bother him considerably.

It was considered sacrilege at the left-wing journalism school – where there were clear boundaries between what was acceptable and what was not – but no one was really surprised that Erwin ended up doing his internship at the richly illustrated weekly magazine *Panorama*. It wasn't his first choice, but after finding out there were no placements at *Muziekkrant Oor* (a music magazine), it was the last remaining option. Writing for *Panorama*, which then had 350,000 subscribers and a thirty-five-strong editorial staff, was not done in left-wing circles.

'Bit of typing, bit of looking around, not much was going on in my head.' Still, Erwin did get a chance to distinguish himself at *Panorama*. In Rotterdam, for instance, he was sent to interview Bryan Ferry, whose band Roxy Music had just released the album *Flesh and Blood*. The interview was ostensibly about Ferry's recent divorce from model and actress Jerry Hall, who was now seeing Mick Jagger. But fame – 'other people's fame' – and celebrity had never been a huge source of interest. 'My opener was: I don't want to talk to you about Jerry Hall. "About what then," Ferry asked. To which I replied: have you seen *The Damned*? Visconti's film, which had recently made a big impression, turned out to be his favourite.'

The entire interview, which overran the allotted ten minutes and lasted a full twenty, was dominated by that dark film about a doomed German family of industrialists who collaborated with the Nazis. Jerry Hall didn't get a look-in and, as a result, *Panorama* held the interview back.

In his second year at college, he decided to turn his life around after his 'brain had been on pause for 12 months'. He knew he was susceptible to social control, as he wrote in the final report. 'I've always been terrified that cliques will talk badly about me or accuse me of being a good-for-nothing or a big-head.' To put those fears to bed, he decided to start collaborating more with his fellow students.

As a result, a teacher finally noticed him. Not only did he genuinely see something in Erwin, but he also expected him to deliver. Along with his colleagues and a bunch of students, Dirk van der Spek produced the school newspaper *Zipitaja*. And he also taught photography. 'Dirk was a free spirit. He picked you up, shook you out and stimulated you. But he also allowed you to fail.' Van der Spek involved him in the school newspaper. Erwin considered it to be a pivotal moment. His first piece was about a disco with Amsterdam's DJ *du jour*, Eddy de Clercq. 'I took a late-night picture of Harrie Wildeman, the future party monster, but very striking even then.' Snapped on a Polaroid in the dead of night, it wasn't a great photo. But thanks to that image, Van der Spek invited him to join his beginner's photography course.

The school newspaper also gave him an opportunity to get involved in design. 'Form has always been very important to me and now I could express my ideas to an admittedly small but select audience.' He complained that the school neglected graphic design at a time when journalism, in his view, was becoming 'hugely visual' – and had been for quite some time. For an entire term, Erwin, Jan Eilander, Moos Engels and others threw themselves into producing the paper. 'I had my work cut out for me every day: interviews, writing, making layouts, meetings. In short, a huge, human existence, and I loved every minute of it.'

When Herman Brood was due to play Utrecht, he decided to interview the singer for *Zipitaja*. Brood had just released the album *Shpritsz* with the single 'Saturday Night' and was at the top of his game. Marline Williams and Moos Engels accompanied him to the concert.

Brood, who was passing through the venue ahead of the gig, came and sat next to them, and they shared Erwin's joint. 'When I told him I was a student journalist and wanted to interview him, he invited me to his dressing room after the concert.' After singing along at the front of the stage, 'I just can't wait / I just can't wait / For Saturday night,' Erwin's bravura deserted him ahead of the scheduled interview, and it all went downhill from then onwards. I didn't dare mount the stairs to the dressing room. Marline, Moos and Herman Brood were hollering for me to come on up, but it only made things worse. I fled down the long corridor and out to the canal. I was mortified.'

'It's a shitty picture, kind of a failed paparazzi photo'

As the last generation of an anarchist period, the students treated the teachers as equals; hierarchy was a dirty word in these newly democratised times. Consequently, the *Zipitaja* crew often went round to Dirk van der Spek's house and sometimes stayed the night, or in his country cottage. On the way down, they played Kraftwerk at full blast on the car's cassette player. At Van der Spek's place, David Bowie was permanently on the turntable. 'We all slept there on mattresses, and we belted out "Five Years"' Jan Eilander recalls. 'And one day, Erwin came to me and said, "Bowie's in the Netherlands. And I know where".'

David Bowie was performing at Ahoy in Rotterdam during his Stage World Tour in June 1978. Erwin had discovered that he was staying at the Amstel Hotel in Amsterdam. Armed with a tape recorder and, on Dirk van der Spek's advice, also a video recorder and a camera – 'it was love at first sight: the weight, the cool metal in my hand' – the two headed to Amsterdam. Bowled over by the huge and, in their eyes, sophisticated hotel, they slipped past the doormen, parked their belongings out of sight and stole through the building 'like Indians'. Eilander asked a chambermaid if he could see the room list and there it was in black-and-white: Suite 7, D. Bowie.

They were convinced that, upon meeting their hero, they would become friends for life. All they had to do was knock on the door of Suite 7, behind which music and laughter could be heard. 'I stood there, my clenched fist a hair's breadth from the door, but I didn't dare bring it down,' Erwin recalled. 'Once again, I froze at the *moment suprême*.' Shaking with nerves, he suggested that they first have a drink in the hotel lounge.

Upon entering the bar, the boys were taken for thieves and ejected from the hotel. 'There we were, standing in the street before the Amstel Hotel,' says Jan Eilander. 'Erwin with the school camera and me with my notebook. But we refused to be defeated.' After a long wait, David Bowie finally left the building. The pop star laughed at the sight of the duo, and just at that moment, Erwin pressed the shutter: he'd taken his first press photo. Bowie waved politely as he got into the waiting limousine, which glided off down the street.

The interview hadn't happened, but they did have the photo – Erwin, nerves on edge, only printed it once. He was devastated. 'It's a shitty picture, kind of a failed paparazzi photo,' he concluded. 'Well, it's kind of glamorous; he gets into the car with sunglasses on. In a recalcitrant mood, I stuck a cellophane sweet wrapper on it and never printed the photo again.'

Their mission was an unmitigated disaster. 'I don't have many regrets in life, but not knocking on that hotel door in the Amstel is one of them.'

According to Erwin, Bowie's power lay in 'wanting to be unique – and, thanks to his flair for new trends – succeeding'. In his view, Bowie was 'on the one hand, afraid of being counted among the masses, and on the other, scared of failing before those very same people. These twin fears drove him to the heights of perfection. This perfectionism became ever more extreme because he didn't want the masses to steal a march on him.'

Erwin also shared his love of music with Moos Engels, a 'deeply mysterious' girl with good Amsterdam connections. 'We were both quite extravagant, me as a punk and Erwin as gay,' Engels recalls in her Amsterdam-Oost home. 'And we were attracted to one another.' Engels's best friend at the time was Arjan Ederveen, who studied at Amsterdam's Kleinkunstacademie (theatre and dance school) and became an actor and television director. 'Erwin went with me to Arjan in Amsterdam to have his hair cut, because Arjan did everyone's hair.'

During their first meeting, Ederveen saw a 'shy and insecure but hilarious guy' who was fiercely ambitious and skilled at articulating his ideas. It marked the beginning of a lifelong friendship.

They partied – increasingly in Amsterdam, especially at De Schakel, a 'gay disco' on Korte Leidsedwarsstraat. 'De Schakel was my first introduction to exuberance.' With Rudolf and others, he also went to DJ Eddy de Clercq's disco parties. It was the pre-AIDS era: the disease had already claimed its first victims, but nobody then knew that it was a deadly and sexually transmitted infection. The early days of gay emancipation were still being fearlessly celebrated.

Erwin's lover Teun, left behind in Utrecht, listened to ebullient tales from Amsterdam. 'For example, Erwin ended up at one of Eddy de Clercq's disco parties, of which he said: you can't believe your eyes, people in the water, flashing lights on their heads, decked out in see-through vinyl outfits, people fucking in the wave pool.' Erwin felt perfectly at home, and later still, the legendary pool parties were a source of inspiration for his own gatherings. But after just four parties, the music stopped: it had become too extreme, even for De Clercq himself. 'It was too much Sodom and Gomorrah. There was a latex-clad woman, charging through the water in vertiginous heels, pulling a naked man on a dog leash behind her. People were tied to the railings, candle wax dripping all over them. There were areas for group sex. The lifeguards came to protest that it was surely getting out of hand.'

After their unsuccessful rendezvous with Bowie, Erwin and Moos Engels embarked on another mission to photograph a pop star. They decided to try and capture Iggy Pop, who was performing in Rotterdam. A group of journalists had convened, and Engels was granted exclusive access. 'Erwin had to stay outside with his camera. And it transpired that Iggy Pop selected me because I was wearing a tiny coke spoon around my neck. When Iggy realised that I couldn't score any cocaine, I was ejected without

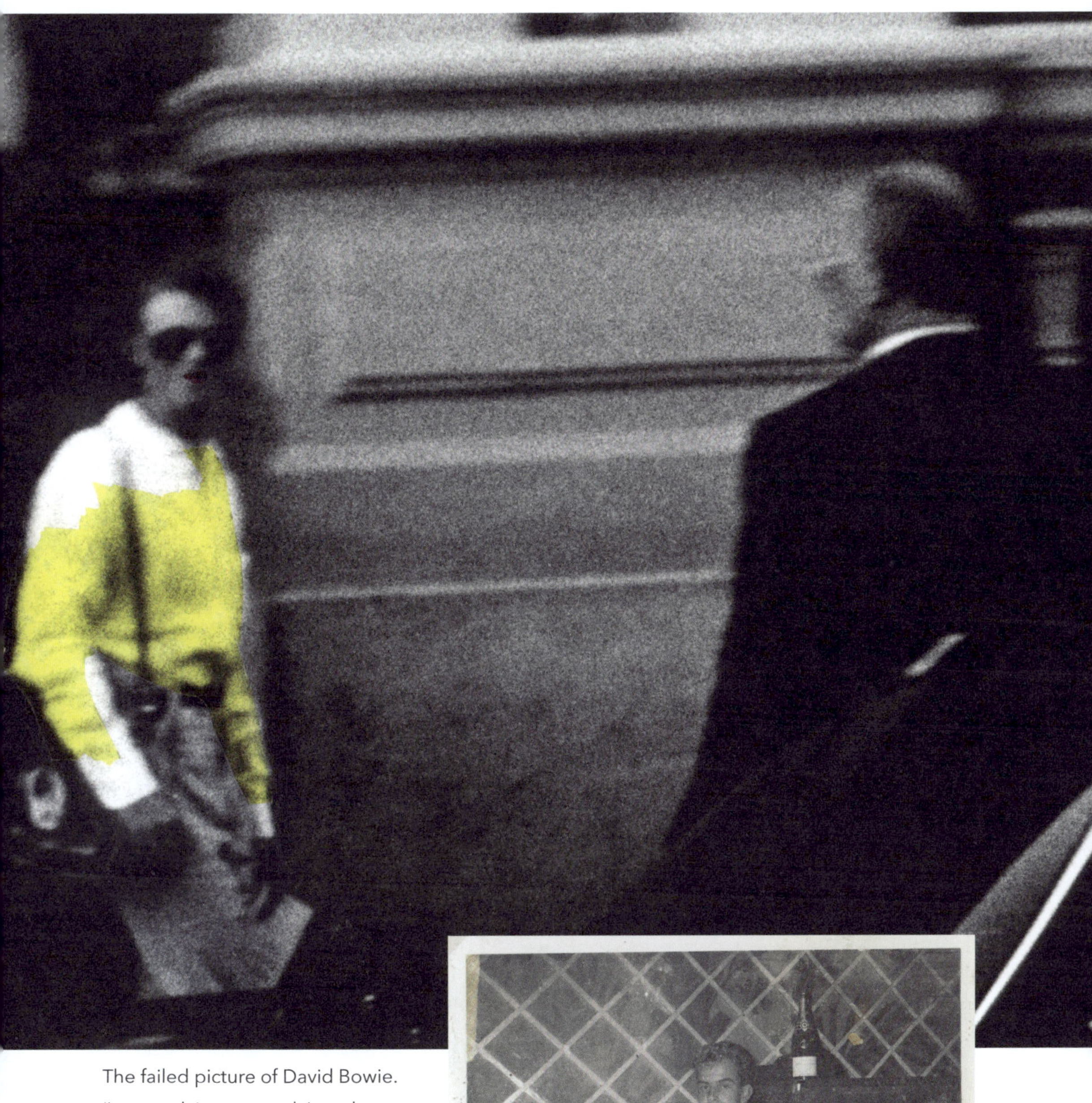

The failed picture of David Bowie. 'In a recalcitrant mood, I stuck a cellophane sweet wrapper on it and never printed the photo again.' Right: Harrie Wildeman on roller skates at Eddy de Clercq's disco at De Brakke Grond, Amsterdam, 1978.

having elicited more than a couple of words, and he pelted me with gnawed chicken bones on the way out.' Disillusioned, the two boarded the train back to Utrecht.

'The smell of chemicals, the brownish-yellow light, the temporary solitude'

These were formative events. 'That crappy photograph of Bowie intrigued me. I was very fond of it. From then on, I wanted to decide for myself whether a picture should be sharp or blurred. I wanted to make the métier my own. In a way, just a little bit, it's all to do with Bowie.'

Erwin's lack of aptitude for journalism had not escaped his lecturers, who had been aware of the fact for some time. In December 1979, when he asked if he could extend his degree by a year, extending the course from three years to four, the lecturers gave him some telling advice: 'You need to give some serious thought as to whether it makes sense to remain at the college.'

Erwin was livid, resolved not to let himself be written off so easily, and started his final assignment with gusto. For this, he had to interview the hip painter, Marte Röling, who had boldly declared elsewhere in print that 'having a cunt has nothing to do with my work'. Erwin was in awe. 'I thought that it was such a golden statement. Marte Röling captured the imagination; she was larger than life.' The interview turned into a five-hour conversation about art, cars, vanity and journalism, interrupted by the artist unceremoniously going to the loo on a chemical toilet that, because her house was being renovated, sat bang in the middle of her living room.

The interview marked a breakthrough. Not so much because of the text, which was returned with 'a few thousand crossings out', but because, on Dirk van der Spek's advice, he had taken a series of grainy, black-and-white portraits of the cigar-smoking Röling. His father, Siem, gave him 1,000 guilders (approximately €500 in today's currency) for a camera, which he spent on a Nikon FM. They had a heart-to-heart about his future. Siem backed Erwin's plan to pursue photography and to get a job after graduation, work for a year and save, after which he would travel for 'as long as possible' through North and South America.

It was a defining moment, as he would later write to his New York friend and gallery owner, Bill Hunt. 'Van der Spek's enthusiasm and the idea that I didn't have to be slaving away behind a desk all week, writing, changed my life forever. I felt at home the moment I set foot in the darkroom. I loved the smell of the chemicals, the brownish-yellow light, the temporary solitude and the privacy. But above all else, I was enchanted by an image slowly revealing itself on the paper, mere seconds after placing it in the developer. That was the moment that I knew photography was made

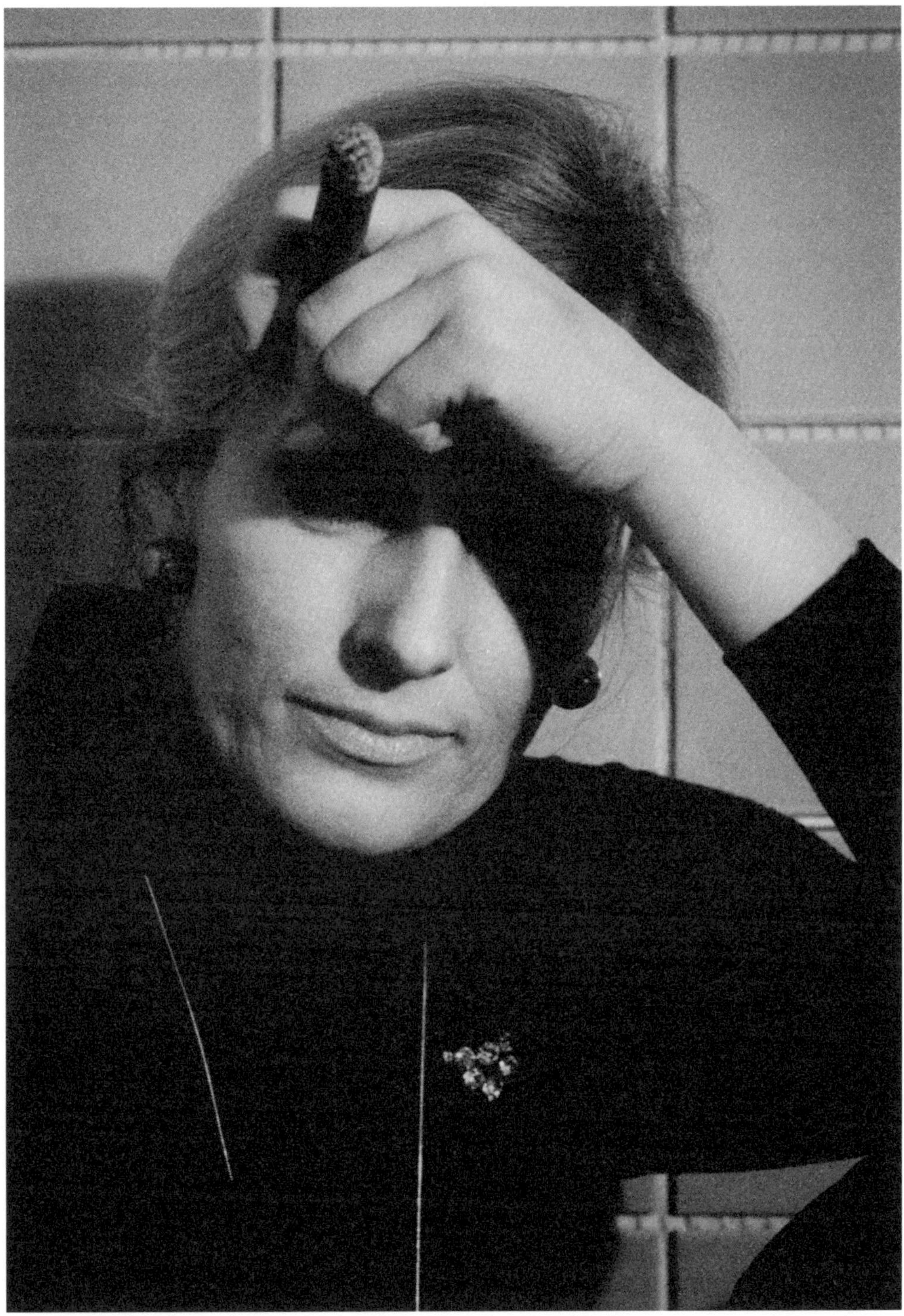

Erwin's black-and-white portraits of cigar-smoking artist Marte Röling secured his breakthrough.

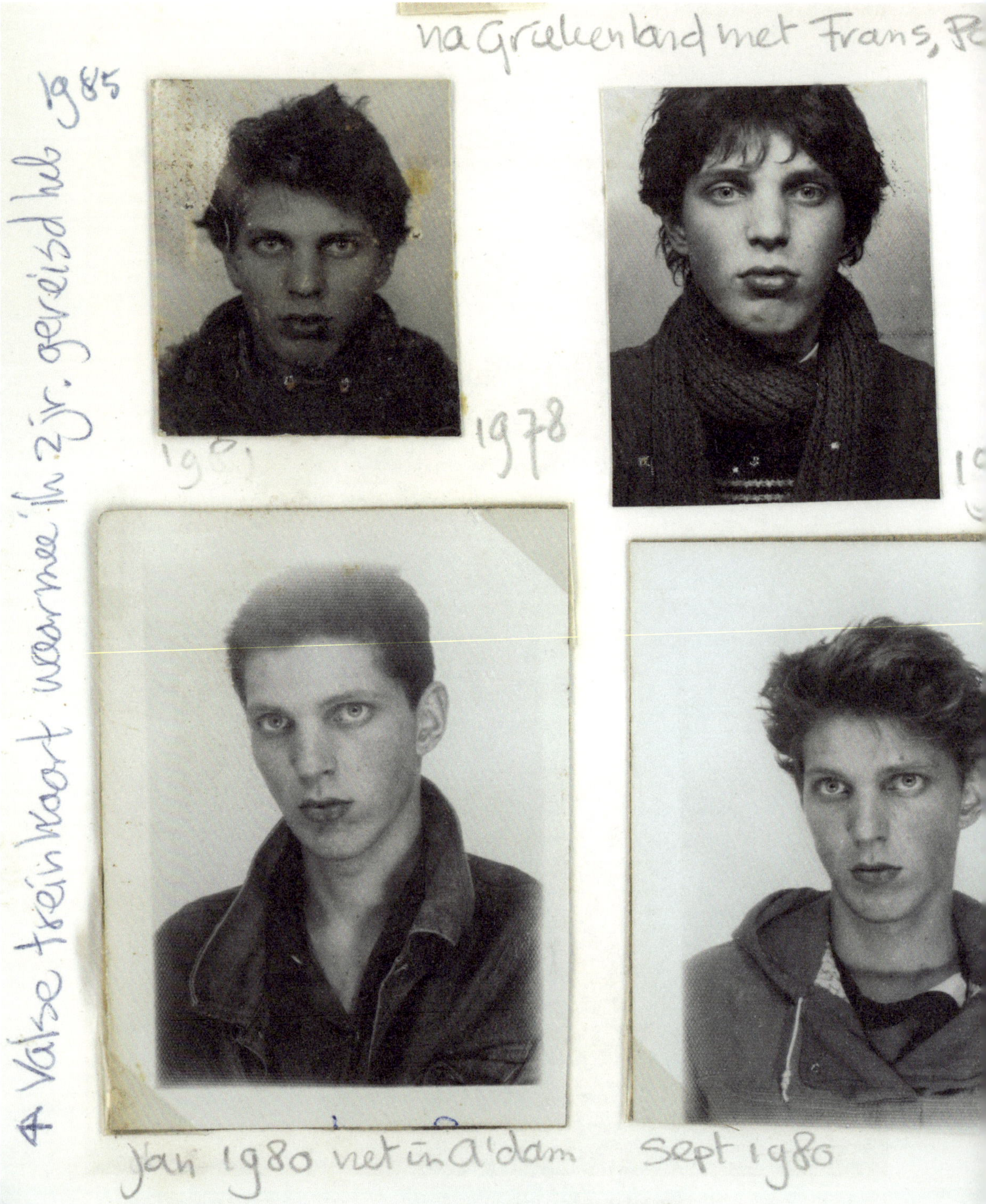

na Griekenland met Frans, P

Valse treinkaart waarmee ik 2 jr. gereisd heb 1985

1981

1978

Jan 1980 net in A'dam

Sept 1980

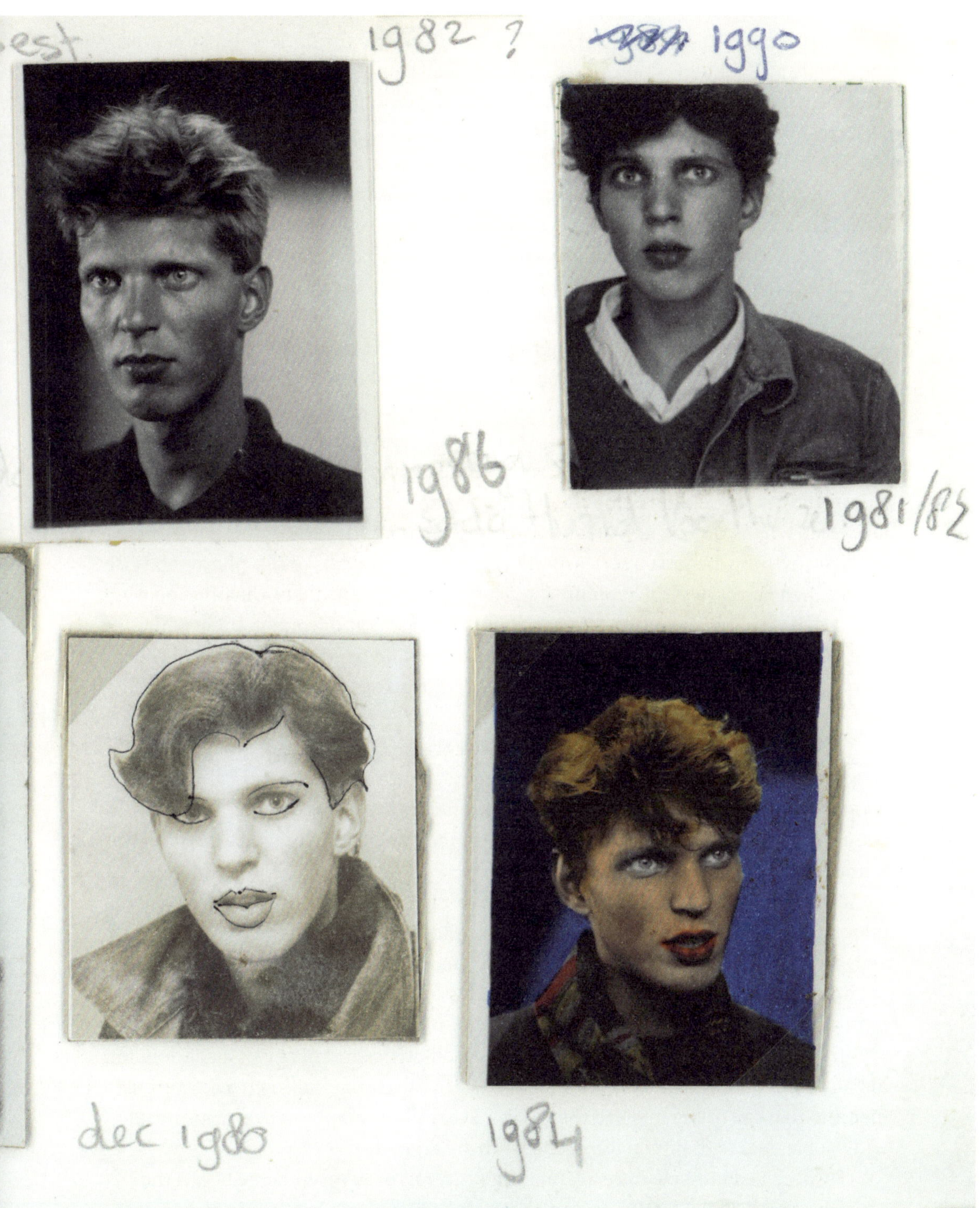
est
1982 ?
1990
1986
1981/82
dec 1980
1984

for me. There was an image, good or bad, a bit too grey or too dark; it didn't matter; these were all problems that could be solved. I had something to grasp; I was getting closer to the final thing. It was the opposite of writing, which was an endless struggle. That was the moment when I fell head over heels in love with photography.'

Upon receiving an assignment entitled 'What is normal?', he went to photograph people with learning disabilities in a psychiatric institution. It was his first foray into social reportage, and an eye-opener in terms of the subject matter. 'I found these gloomy wards, totally isolated, in far-flung corners of the complex. They contained violent self-harmers. People were strapped to their beds. I can see it like it was yesterday. A girl had gouged her eye out with a nail. A boy was tied to a chair to prevent him from compulsively banging his head on the table. The things that I saw and heard on those wards affected me deeply and, without a shadow of doubt, helped make me who I am today.'

He found it 'absolutely shocking' that the 'mentally handicapped', as they were then called, were capable of openly demonstrating their passions. 'They had psychiatric issues, but it didn't stop them falling in love. That you still know how to love, even when you're crazy, was a very confusing thought.' After promising not to publish anything, he took a series of photographs. The results of his 'photo safari', to use his own words, were disappointing. The negatives were dusty, the films poorly exposed. He had photographed the inpatients from afar and from on high, which, he says, comes across in his photographs as a superior and fearful attitude. In his own words, he had photographed 'harmless fools', who looked 'incredibly comical with their open flies, snub noses and jug ears'.

Just as he perceived his entire journalistic training to be one big failure, he also denigrated this photo series. 'I was dishonest with myself because what I really wanted to do was to make pictures that demonstrated my belief in mentally unwell people being equal, while I still abhor people who don't conform to my image of the human race.'

That unsuccessful experiment marked, in a peculiar way, the start of his photographic journey. He discovered that a camera allowed him to enter a nonconformist world, populated with people who, just like himself, were not 'normal' and who lived outside the box. 'They're my kind of people. My photography is a way of reaching their realm. At the same time, that camera kept me out of harm's way.'

In his final report, one endless stream of self-criticism, there was also room for his 'Vision of Photography'. He commenced with a warning, calling it a dangerous medium that can easily mislead the viewer. Every photographer does his utmost to win people over to their version of the truth, he argued.

He deceived himself, once again, in the autumn of 1979, when he began the series *Jongens* [Boys] – featuring only the most beautiful models. 'Every picture was characterised by this erotic tension between me and the model. Reason: I was horny.' He has since realised that he wasn't photographing reality, but his vision of it. 'And also, viewers have to know that they are not looking at the truth, but at *an idea* of the truth.'

Finally, on 18 June 1980, he graduated as a journalist following a public interview. His father, Siem, was absent due to illness, but his mother, Lida, was in attendance. Just as she was preparing to return to Amersfoort, Erwin introduced his beloved Teun to her at the very last minute.

It hadn't taken Teun Frieszo long to realise that Erwin's future lay not in journalism, but in photography. For that, too, Erwin thanked his late friend during the funeral service on that February day in 2020. Apart from his teacher, Dirk van der Spek, Teun had been the very first person to have recognised the photographer in him and had encouraged him to follow that new direction. Teun would become his first muse, one of his most amenable models, his ever-critical observer and, finally, his diehard fan.

In the winter of 1980, a journalist friend asked Erwin what he was planning to do, since he had graduated and could officially call himself a journalist. Erwin answered truthfully, 'Nothing, I'm unemployed.' Teun's reaction was of great significance, Erwin recounted when saying goodbye to his first great love. 'Teun said, "No, you're wrong to say nothing. You're taking photographs." That was an important sentence.' Not only because Teun's firm words made him realise what he really wanted to do in life – photography – but also because the conversation had a very practical consequence. Dick Hollander happened to know a photographer who was looking for an assistant. Which is how it all began.

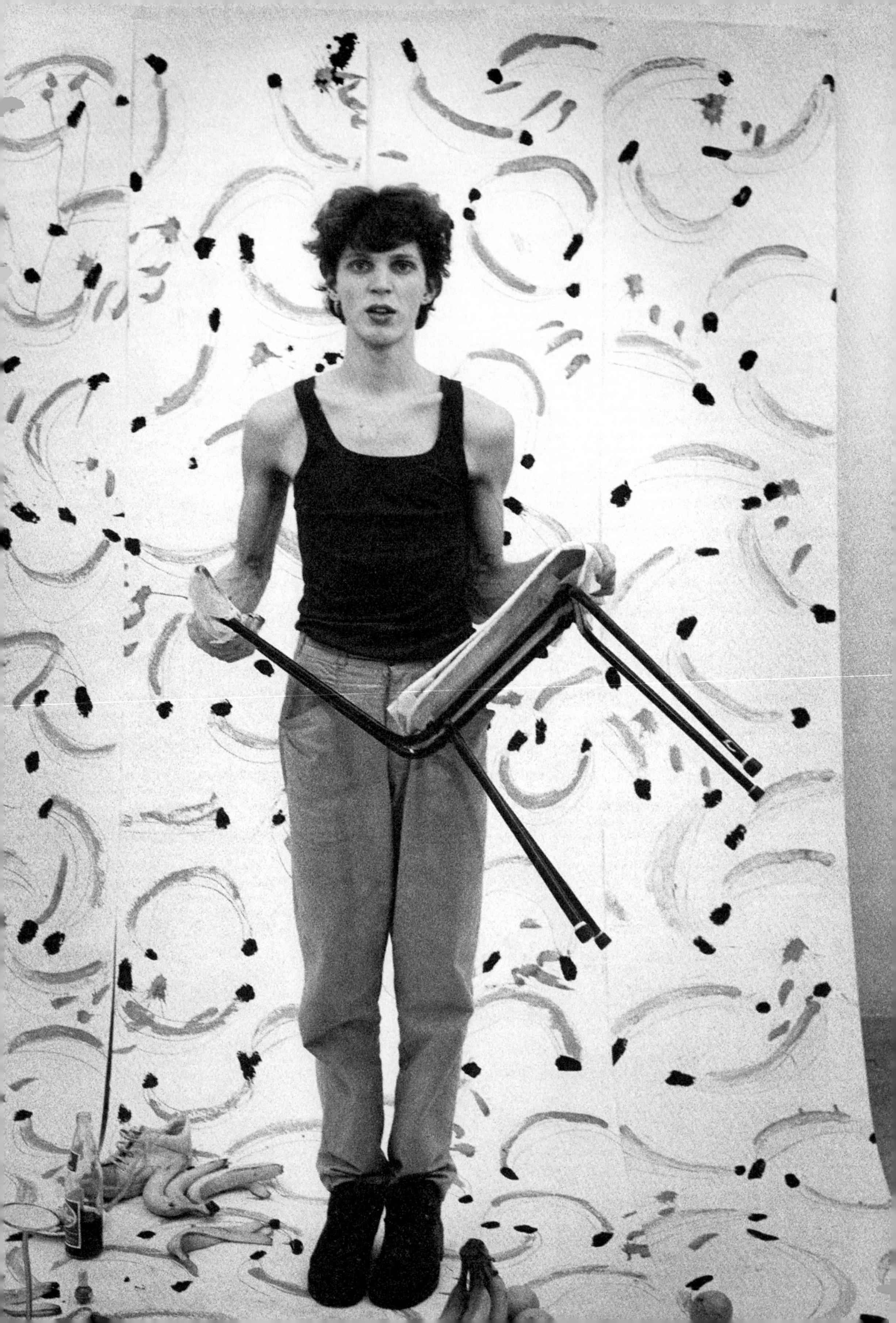

3 LEARNING THE ROPES (1981–1985)

'I want to be recognised and famous, and if I stay with you, it will never happen'

RUIGROK'S DARKROOM

Every day, Erwin and his team eat together at the long table in the studio's kitchen-dining area. The Surrealist-style decor was painted by his childhood friend, Frans Franciscus. He loves his team, many of whom have worked at the studio for years. He also cherishes his apprentices, most of whom are from photography schools. 'Many people tend to look down on vocational students, but I appreciate their eagerness and drive. They're always full of energy, eager to work.'

The downside of having an eight-person studio, Erwin sighs, is that it can't close its doors. 'I need to keep the money coming in.' He'd like to take some time off to recover, but he can't afford the 'luxury of a sabbatical or burnout'. 'Sometimes I fantasise about letting my staff go and returning to the basics, only photographing nudes.' However, he recognises that the two sides of his career are inseparable and mutually dependent. He is both a businessman and an autonomous artist.

Occasionally, he reflects on his postgraduate years in the early 1980s, filled with amazement at his own achievements. During that time, life primarily consisted of wild parties and drug use. Such a lifestyle was completely incompatible with employment, and job opportunities for freshly minted journalists were scarce.
He was lonely and unhappy in his dark, simple apartment on the ground floor, which lacked natural light and a bathroom – to shower, he used the local public baths. He missed his friends from Utrecht.

On 5 October 1980, he created a new list in his red-and-black notebook: 'From 1977 to 1980, I used the following drugs: 1. hash 2. weed 3. poppers 4. speed 5. cocaine 6. heroin (3 times) 7. purple haze (once; unpleasant, no hallucinations, insomnia yes).'

About three weeks later, he was already feeling more positive. He had started therapy at the end of August. After a discussion about depression, Erwin's doctor had referred him to a mental-health clinic. The talking therapy seemed to be working and the near-constant 'vicious thought circles' started to diminish.

Additionally, he'd found a job to supplement his weekly benefits of around €200 (in today's currency). He worked four nights a week on the reception and door of the Flora Palace, a spacious and fashionable nightclub. There, he saw live shows, bingo nights, mud fights and roller discos. The venue was a source of inspiration for the even more extreme parties that Erwin later organised. On Mondays, it was 'Gay Night', advertised across the city with slogans like 'Hey, are you gay? Join us on Monday! (At Flora Palace).' His early photographs of the flamboyantly dressed clientele eventually found their way into his debut photography book.

Despite his lack of writing skills or patience, he still rated journalism over photography. 'For me, it's all about concentration, that perfect moment when you know, "That's it!", then click, you capture it. A story or a book, however, is never truly finished. You constantly refine every sentence, every word.'

Therapy helped him, but he still had low self-esteem. 'I feel like a depraved scumbag, unscrupulously making my way through this vale of tears. (Oh God, I beg you, rid me of this writing style).'

His introduction to photographer André Ruigrok in Landsmeer, near Amsterdam, through Dick Hollander, freed him from his remaining literary ambitions. Now he was really going to learn the trade. And get paid for it too, although his assistant's salary was only a fraction more than his welfare benefits, which he complained about at length in his letters.

They got on well. André Ruigrok had overcome his severe stutter as a young man. It was this that made him so sensitive to feelings of exclusion in others, he realised later, including in Erwin. 'Let's get right to it. He was gay, and the rejection from a significant part of society affected him deeply.'

'I quickly realised that he was superior to me,' Ruigrok acknowledges. 'He was full of potential, and I noticed it immediately.' What exactly did he possess? 'The determination to get to the bottom of things. Staggering ambition and drive.'

In September 1981, Erwin began developing films, making contact sheets, and printing the shots that his mentor had marked. 'André taught me to print by the kilo. One day, I printed 1.5 kilos. He used a postal scale to measure everything, and I loved the thrill of it all.'

Ruigrok had developed a distinctive style, which was influenced by Ed van der Elsken's work. He passed this technique on to his assistant. 'It was a matter of adjusting the light using dodge-and-burn techniques, so that it highlights the focal point.'

Erwin proved to be an enthusiastic student. 'Interestingly, when he began exhibiting, people kept saying, "Hey, André, your prints look just like Erwin Olaf's!" But, of course, it was the opposite way around.'

Besides learning to print, the experience taught Erwin how to look. 'You have to distil the story,' Ruigrok explained. He preferred using a 28 mm lens because it forces you to get closer to your subject. To do this, he said, you must learn to become an invisible photographer.

He is reluctant to talk about it, as they are just simple tricks, after all, but there is more that Erwin retained from his apprenticeship, says Ruigrok. 'For instance, I frequently asked models to take a step forward and would press the shutter just as they began to move. You can see this technique in the series of portraits that Erwin took of the royal family in the Dam Square Palace.'

What stood out the most about his previous assistant? 'Erwin was extremely pure. He was clear and sincere in both his thinking and his outlook.'

Upon first encountering the tasks at Fotostudio Ruigrok, Erwin, a young man who wanted to conquer the world, may have found the work to be a humbling experience. However, he understood that mastering the craft of photography required dedication and hard work. His time spent in the darkroom honed his technical skills and fostered a desire for perfection. Additionally, he joined the studio's reportage missions, carrying the necessary equipment, including the Hasselblad case, flashes, lamps and aggregates. Ruigrok also took educational photographs for the Algemene Bond voor Onderwijzend Personeel's [General Education Union] weekly newsletter, and other trade union publications. In a photo he took of his assistant while they were working on a school report in 1981, Erwin can be seen looking down from a skylight, his eagle-eyed gaze surveying the playground, SLR camera at the ready.

Erwin quickly surpassed his teacher. 'I ran from education strikes to gay protests, captured lesbian motherhood and squatters' riots, sat for days at conferences on men's and women's issues, and witnessed crass blokes pelting queens with eggs during Pink Saturday in Leiden.' Dick Hollander, the editor-in-chief of *Het Schoolblad*, received the photos stamped 'Studio Ruigrok', but he immediately knew which images were Erwin's and which belonged to his employer. While Erwin had much to learn from André on a technical level, his images were already brimming with life. He truly connected with the subjects of his photographs. 'It's a shame that he didn't pursue photojournalism more. He was an excellent observer of people,' says Hollander.

In June 1982, André Ruigrok took him to see the Rolling Stones, who were touring that summer and playing three concerts in Rotterdam. 'I was taking pictures of four ordinary but incredibly sexy boys at the gig. Suddenly, out of nowhere, a blonde boy grabbed his mate's crotch, the latter of whom was wearing a string vest and sunglasses. I captured the exact moment on camera. I showed André the photo and bought

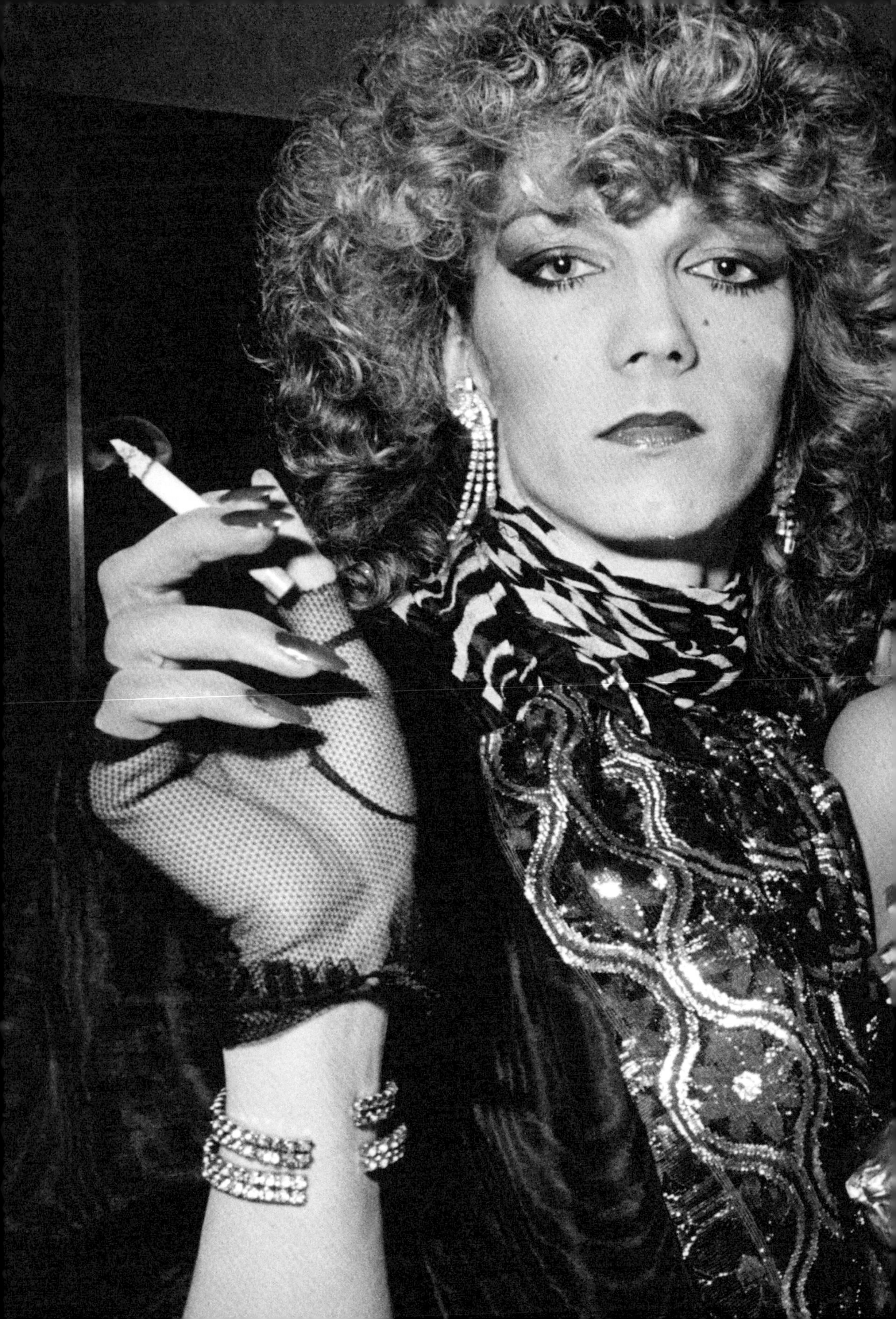

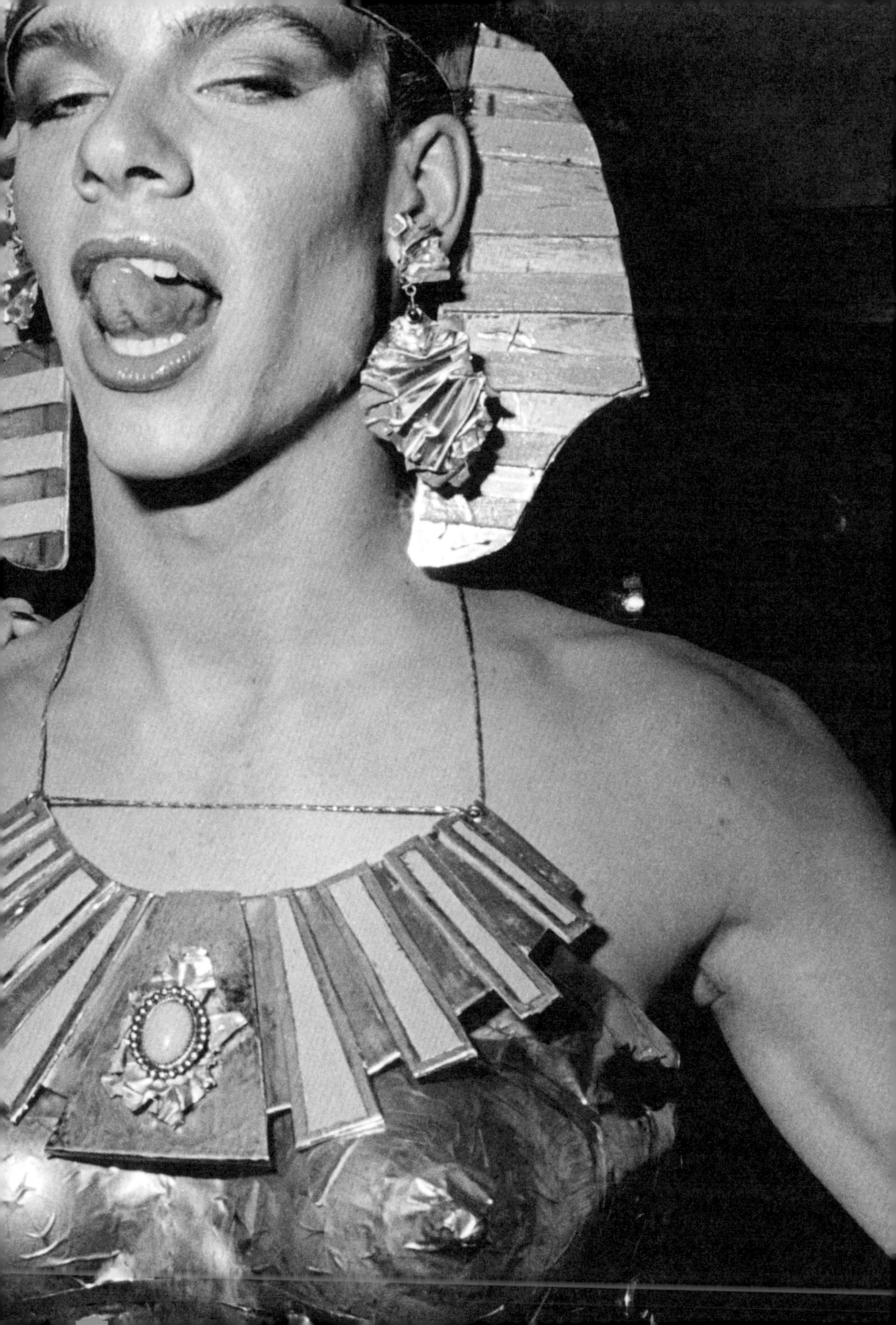

the rights to it from him. I paid off the debt with work.' It was Erwin's first non-commissioned photo to generate an income.

In the early 1980s, male bonding was a thing. Men explored their softer sides in dedicated discussion groups, stimulated by the second wave of feminism. The tension lay in exploring the boundaries between friendship and homosexuality. Erwin's photo of the boys was an instant hit and a covetable image, precisely because it illustrated the taboo-ridden area on the edge of eroticism and friendship.

When the picture editor of the French gay monthly *Gai Pied*, founded three years earlier, saw the photo of the four lads, he informed Erwin that he wanted to publish it as well. 'We'll make it a double spread!' The editors at the magazine also rang because they needed a credit line for the photo. But spelling his last name correctly presented a challenge: 'Springveld' proved to be quite a tongue twister for the French. Erwin then suggested that he drop his surname and use only his first and middle names. He chose Olaf as his new surname, which his mother had always told him meant 'son of a king'.

'I've always liked the cadence of two double syllables, with stress on the first, like "David Bowie" or "Gerard Reve". "Erwin Olaf" has a similar cadence, which makes it easier to remember. It has an exotic ring to it.' Additionally, a stage name allowed him to establish a clear distinction between his personal and professional life. 'In the twenty minutes between the studio and my home, as I pedal my bicycle, I transform from Erwin Olaf, the photographer, into Erwin Springveld, the private man.'

Gai Pied became one of his first regular clients. Additionally, he received a request from the *Gay Krant* to document their inaugural 'Mr Gay Krant' beauty pageant. He sent Henny a full debrief. 'I shot a sort of beauty contest last night, but with men,' he wrote. 'It was tacky, but it was a lot of fun. It was well paid. I was on a contract and given exclusive access. I could capture things that I would never have been able to photograph otherwise.'

As soon as he entered the tiny hotel where the pageant was taking place, he revealed himself to be a photographer-cum-voyeur and 'I was flabbergasted and couldn't believe my eyes!' It was a brand-new world, cruder but also more exciting than his usual one. 'I'll never forget that night. Since then, I've seen countless dicks, but the pageant organiser's brazen disregard for political correctness was a breath of fresh air in those divisive times.' Magazines such as *The Advocate* (United States) and *Gay Times* (United Kingdom) would eventually follow in the footsteps of the *Gay Krant*.

Indeed, photography was initially a way for him to explore his own homosexuality and to connect with the men he found 'attractive or thrilling'. He created his own reality, which also included less-refined images. Sometimes he suggested shots that others might want to see, as when he wrote to *Gai Pied*, 'Two swimmers in a

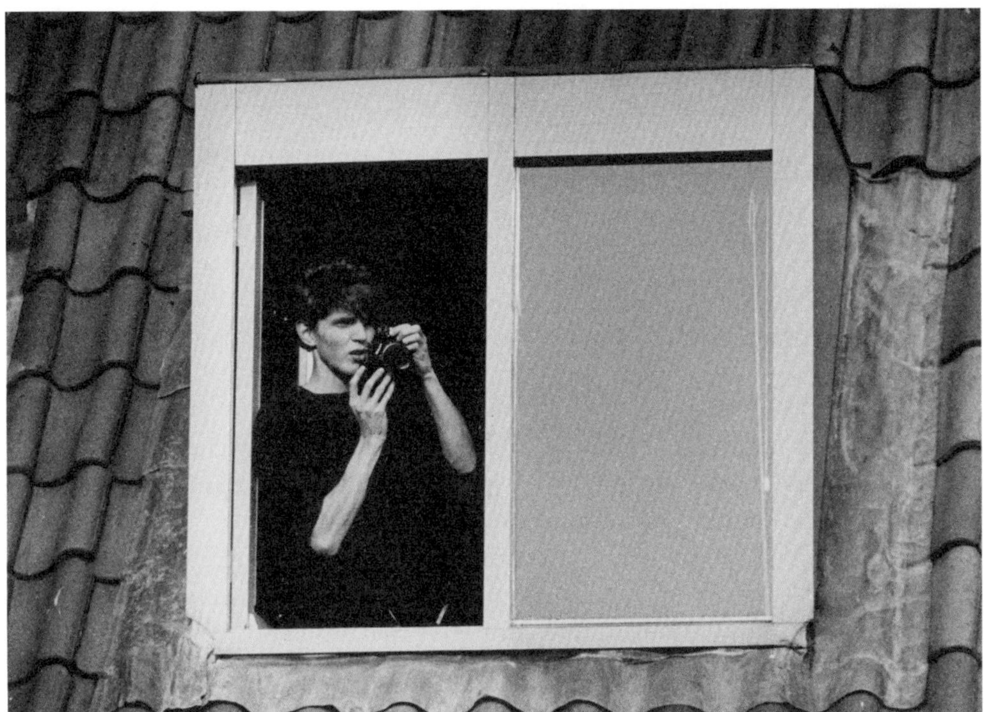

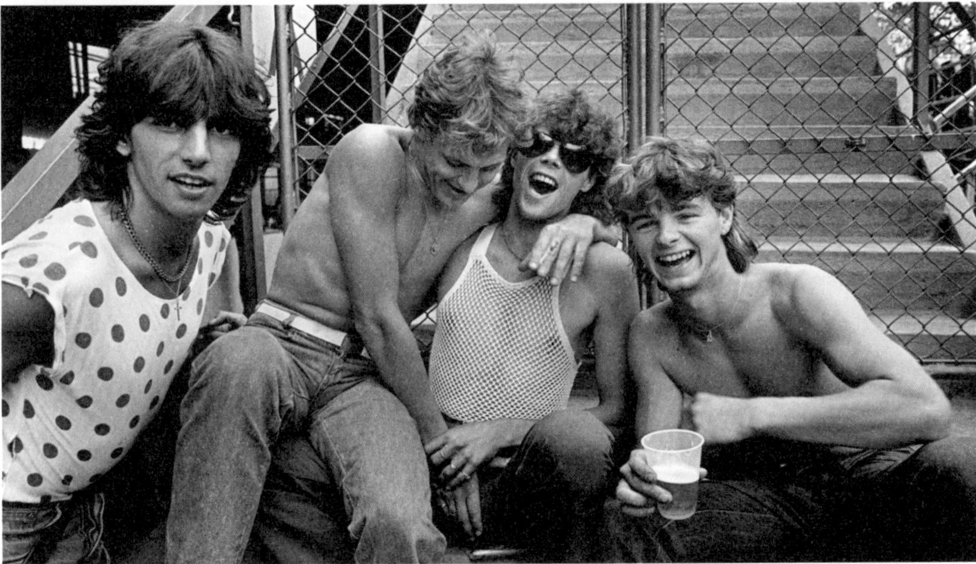

Top: Erwin as an assistant during a school reportage in 1981. Bottom: Stones fans at De Kuip stadium in Rotterdam. 'Suddenly, out of nowhere, a blonde boy grabbed his mate's crotch, the latter of whom was wearing a string vest and sunglasses. I captured the exact moment on camera.'

Previous photo spread: *First Aids Benefit, Club Flora Palace, Amsterdam, I, 1983*.

Photo on page 58: Self-portrait in his first studio in a squat, Kromboomsloot 55, 1981.

shower. One is raping the weak one. The guys will wear water polo outfits. Plenty of steam so the reader has something to fantasise about.'

He sent new pictures every month to the French gay magazine. 'It was the soft porn of the day,' says Teun Frieszo. For their first vacation, Erwin and Teun went Greek island hopping. On Naxos, they passed a ruined farmhouse and Erwin suggested that Teun pose nude in one of the windows. 'One of the photos features Teun with an erection, seated against a crumbling wall,' Erwin remembers.

While Erwin was gaining experience as an independent photographer, such photos provided him with valuable additional income. Later, when he wanted to dedicate himself to more serious work, he stopped publishing these sorts of pictures.

Ruigrok gave Erwin access to the photography studio during his free time. It was there that he created the first 'vintage Erwin Olaf' images, with Teun as the first model. Frieszo draws attention to this series, featuring two men dressed as sailors. 'This is pure Jean Genet,' he remarks. 'At first glance, it seemed unremarkable, but Erwin had to master lighting techniques. It's an historical moment.' In this studio, Erwin captured a dual portrait of his first nude subjects since the picture of Frans Franciscus. The models were Marlies and Ruth Louz, two sisters of Dutch and Surinamese descent, whom he'd met on the bus while they were doing their makeup for a night on the town. Erwin immediately pointed his camera at them and pressed the shutter, before inviting them to the studio.

Desiree Aben, whom Erwin met in high school, also posed for him. 'Erwin once told me about the moment when he first saw me,' she recalls. 'It was a beautiful summer evening. He thought my friend was very young and attractive, and later commented: "You looked absolutely stunning. Everyone else stepped back; it was like a wave parting." That was his first memory of me.'

Desiree has modelled in several photo series, often naked but always unrecognisable: 'Everyone knows my breasts, but nobody knows me.' She also became a protagonist in *Tadzio*, the short, lavish feature film that Erwin and Frans Franciscus made ten years later. During their initial studio session, she brought along her closest confidante, Suzanne Venema. 'We did everything Erwin asked of us. It was improvisation, or at least that's how it felt. He gave us both a leather pilot's cap and said: "OK, you're naked except for the headgear." We didn't hesitate to grant him anything, and we didn't feel the slightest bit awkward. Everything was casual back then, and Erwin was just Erwin. You never hesitated to take off your clothes in his presence.'

While Erwin learnt about love and photography, the outside world was far from cheerful. The 1980s were marked by high unemployment among young people and a lack of affordable housing. The economy hadn't recovered from the oil crisis. He noticed it on the streets, where he saw an increasing number of 'freaks'. 'Insensate, violent junkies with sticking plasters, sores and shit hair at the drug addicts' shelter on Prinsengracht, where an experiment with free smack was being conducted. Damstraat and the area in front of the Central Station were populated by addicts, alcoholics and emaciated queens wearing flimsy satin shorts and revealing, billowing blouses. ... How right-wing I seem, no, how right I am, when it comes to public order. I can't help it, and the streets sometimes make me feel nervous. The decline of people from lower socioeconomic backgrounds and those who are financially illiterate saddens me. If I was slightly more left-leaning, I might cry with rage.'

The prospects for many young people in the 1980s were bleak, with no housing or employment opportunities and significant cuts to welfare benefits. None of Erwin's friends had a job, and they had no dreams of a future. The Cold War and the fear of the bomb dropping only added to the despair and hopelessness of the era. Young Dutch people turned against the prevailing order and became activists.

The movements for peace and ecology gained traction, as did the anti-nuclear power movement. Squatters seized vacant properties from speculative real-estate owners. Erwin had his convictions, but as a photographer, he preferred to be an observer.

In November 1981, he marched in Amsterdam's massive demonstration against NATO's and the Warsaw Pact's deployment of cruise missiles. He did so, however, with some reservations. In a letter to Henny, he wrote: 'I have never participated in such a protest before, and I am not completely convinced. However, I think it is important, because I don't want to fight, I don't want to die, and I am afraid. I would feel guilty if I just gave up.'

His job at André Ruigrok eventually came to an end. 'My contract isn't being renewed,' Erwin wrote to Teun. 'I'm a victim of cutbacks.' He was ready to start working independently and was keen to get going, 'but on the other hand, I don't know what to do. Have I got what it takes?'

Despite his insecurities, he was filled with ambition. According to André Ruigrok, he didn't mince his words in his exit interview: 'I want to be recognised and famous, and if I stay with you, it will never happen.'

Erwin saw a silver lining in his unplanned departure, as it motivated him to act. He landed a lucrative position with Freddy Valks, the owner of the gay bar Boys Club and a procurer of gay escorts. Erwin took a picture at the latter's brothel, but Valks found it 'too chic'. He preferred to be in the pictures himself, along with his companion, pretending to be clients at the brothel, surrounded by a group of young men offering their services. Erwin used the 1,000-guilder payment from this job to buy a flashlight and a second-hand 28-mm lens.

Around the same time he moved to the Jordaan, with the help of a loan from his parents. This change improved his emotional state. And after relocating to the much

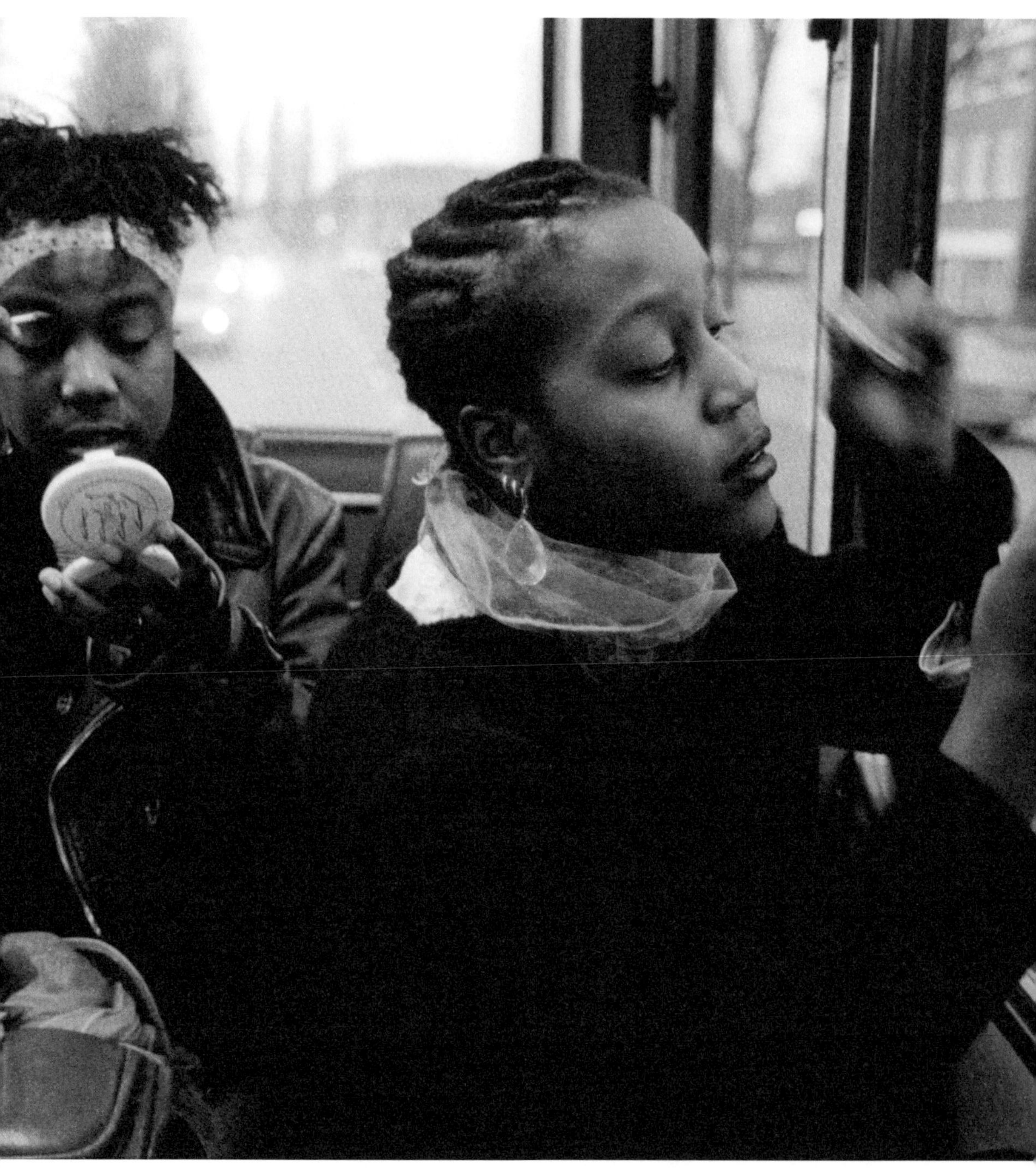

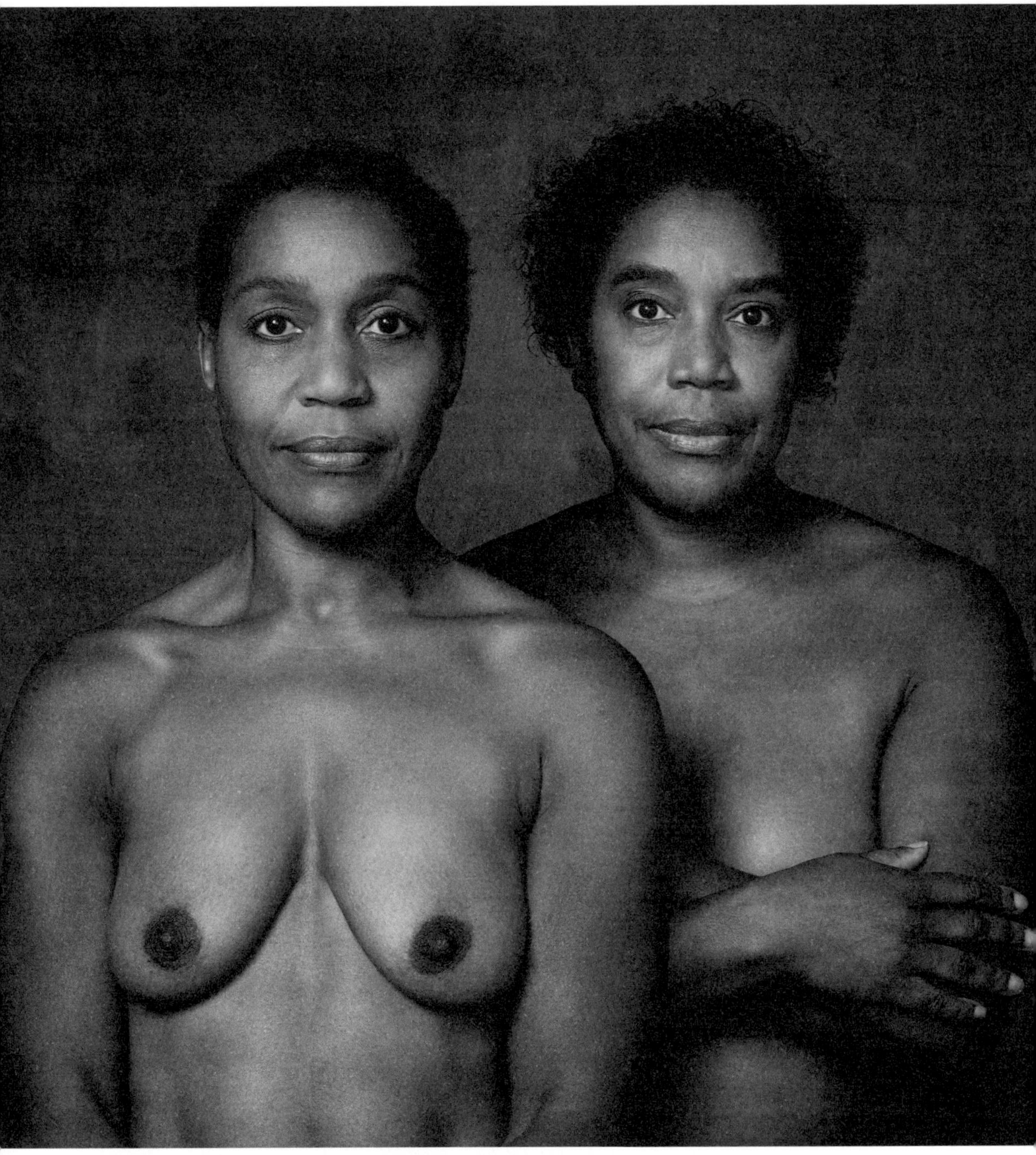

Left: Ruth and Marlies Louz in 1981 on the bus from Amsterdam to Landsmeer.
Right: Marlies and Ruth Louz photographed in 2021 at the IJselstraat studio for the *Muses* series.

brighter upstairs flat on Lauriergracht, he was able to discontinue therapy within a month.

He eventually managed to get off welfare, which had always been distasteful to him. 'Living on benefits was anathema to our family; it saddened and worried my parents.'

To make ends meet as an independent entrepreneur, Erwin determinedly pursued new opportunities. His goal was to capture unique images that hadn't been captured before. However, to support this aspiration and make ends meet in the meantime, he accepted any job opportunities that came his way.

'I'm not comfortable being naked, and I don't like my body

HONORARY NICKNAME – PORNOGRAPHER

On this weekday afternoon in March 2021, Hans van Manen's sleekly decorated apartment in Amsterdam-Zuid is in a state of chaos. His longtime friend Erwin Olaf is photographing him and his partner, Henk van Dijk. The immaculate dining room, adorned with art and ceramics, is upended by a softbox, lighting diffusers and other photography equipment. Erwin's assistant, Piotr Owczarzak, and an intern are currently engaged in the task of fine-tuning the lighting in this temporary studio.

Van Manen wears a tailored suit. He slips an imposing gold ring next to his wedding band and recalls his first photography session with Erwin in 1984. *Sek*, a gay magazine, had wanted to interview Van Manen, who at that time was both an acclaimed choreographer and a photographer. However, during the interview, a 'pleasant young man' unexpectedly appeared at the door. 'It was Erwin. He'd come to take the photos, but we immediately started talking about photography.'

It was the start of a lifelong friendship. They still meet up regularly, with their respective partners, at performances or for dinner. 'I've rowed with Erwin,' Van Manen admits. 'We're both very impulsive, but you can get away with a lot in a friendship. You can't really insult someone who's your friend. And if that happens, then you're a bit lost.'

Today, after many years and countless photo sessions, it is almost routine for them to take pictures of each other, although in recent years, Van Manen has only been in front of the camera. He complies by standing on the spot marked with a yellow sticker. However, beforehand, he requests a photograph in his dark sunglasses, black Borsalino hat and matching face mask. It's just for fun – otherwise, the choreographer says nothing. 'We're both directors in our own way, but in this moment, it's

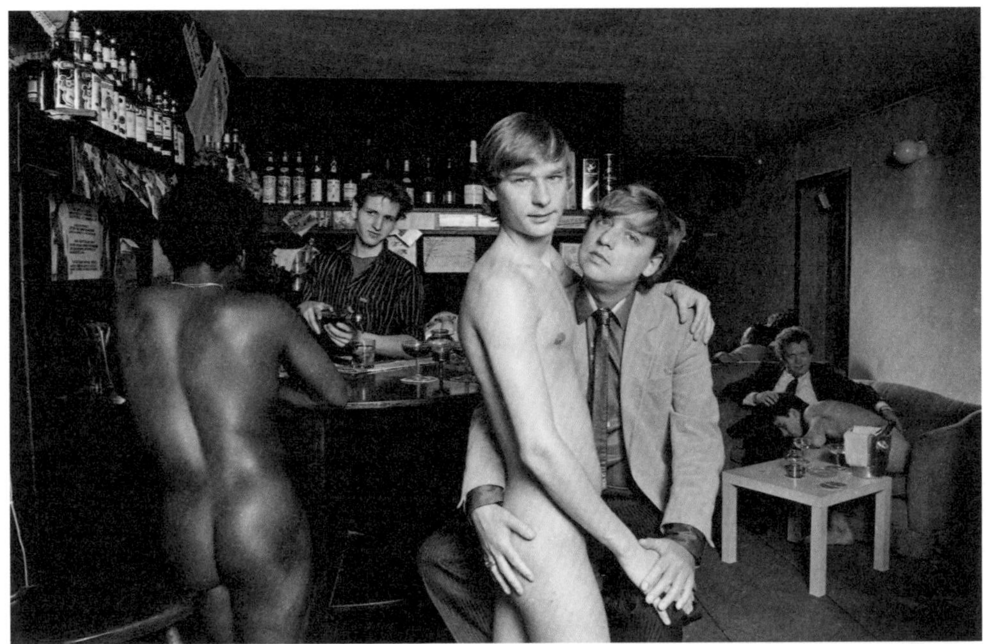

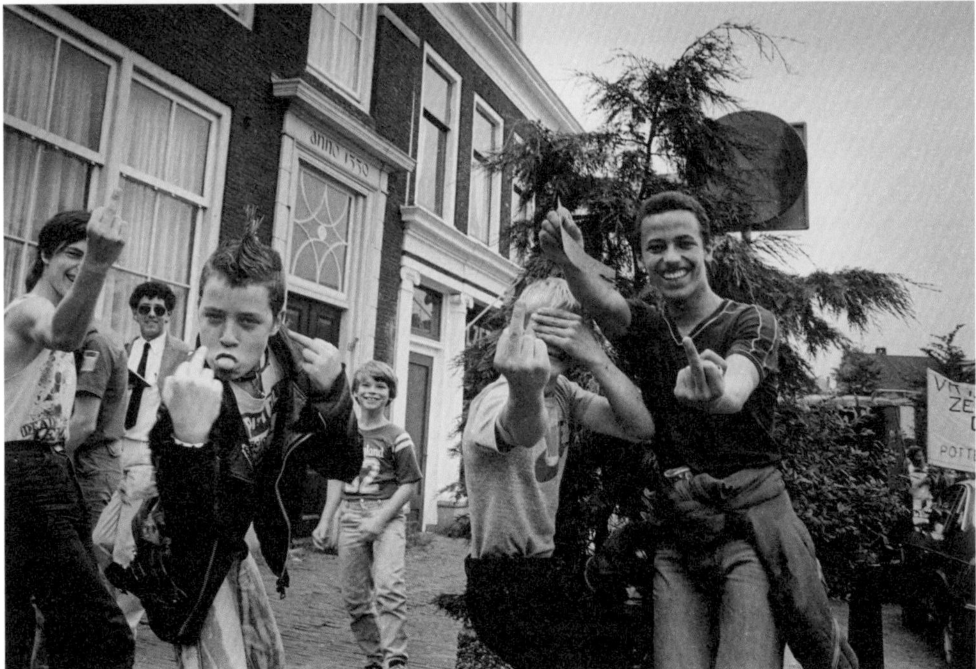

Top: Freddy Valks's brothel, with the owner of the gay bar, Boys Club, as the 'client'.
Bottom: Erwin's photo of Pink Saturday, Leiden, 1983. It didn't get out of hand, as it had the previous year in Amersfoort.

straightforward. When Erwin is taking my photo, I keep quiet and do what he says. I'm never worried; I know perfectly well that everything will turn out brilliantly.'

Erwin, meanwhile, gives orders: 'Nice Hans. Very nice. One, two, click.' Now, just turn slightly. Then put your hand like this. Indeed, you tend to lean forward. If you could just tilt your head slightly forward, that would help. Click. Lift your nose slightly, just a bit. The nose, it's the key to everything. One, two, click. You can remove your hand now. That's perfect.'

Back when they were taking the *Sek* pictures, Van Manen had shown his younger colleague his photo studio in the ground-floor flat. Erwin spent the entire afternoon there, before returning to be photographed himself – as a reclining nude. 'At first, I thought, "What am I supposed to do? This guy is photographing naked boys. I'm not comfortable being naked, and I don't like my body. I was nervous about going back, but Hans was so nice. He made me feel comfortable. The picture was gorgeous."'

Van Manen took Erwin to see his art collection. 'We spent hours looking at everything. and the scales fell from my eyes. I was thrilled to be able to see and study so many works of art at close quarters.'

In the early years of their friendship, Erwin was like a sponge around Van Manen. His own stunning photography, as well as masterpieces by Paul Blanca, Robert Mapplethorpe, George Platt Lynes, Joel-Peter Witkin, and artists such as Rauschenberg, Liechtenstein, Struycken and Dibbets, were all tastefully displayed throughout the house. A home where about six to ten people gathered almost every night to discuss – sometimes heatedly – dance, visual art, photography and politics, interspersed with raucous laughter, sexual banter and a healthy dose of gossip.

Van Manen introduced Erwin to his artistic circle of friends, including his husband, Henk van Dijk, a filmmaker for the National Ballet. Other acquaintances included theatre designer Keso Dekker and painter Jean-Paul Vroom. It was Vroom who had suggested that Van Manen purchase a camera. He initially took holiday snapshots, but soon switched to nude photography, mainly of young men. 'A body becomes sexy through exertion. I captured a boy as he caught his saliva in his hand, a moment that I found visually striking. And erotic, yes, that too.'

Through Van Manen, Erwin became more familiar with Mapplethorpe's work. He first saw the artist's photographs – which some considered obscene – in 1979, at Rob Jurka's gallery. 'I wasn't yet twenty when I first encountered Mapplethorpe's work, which struck me as overpowering and radically honest. I was stunned when I left the gallery; it was a resounding slap in the face.'

The dining room has been re-illuminated. Out of shot, a portrait of the royal family by Erwin Olaf hangs on the wall, taken in the Dam Square Palace. Van Manen comments, 'The royal family slowly advancing towards the camera. I have never seen a painting as strange as this photograph. That's why I absolutely had to have it. You'll only see the insanity of it a decade from now.'

Next to it hangs *Julius Caesar 44 BC*, a photograph of a crouching youth with a dagger plunged deep into his back, from Erwin's *Royal Blood* series, together with a fierce portrait of Hans van Manen by expressionist German painter Jörg Immendorff and a self-portrait of Paul Blanca. Van Manen donated his collection of twenty-four works by Robert Mapplethorpe to the Rijksmuseum. 'These days, it seems as if Robert was always famous, but he only became famous after he died.'

Van Manen also saw Mapplethorpe's exhibition at Galerie Jurka in 1979, a European first. 'At the time, I asked Robert if he would take my portrait. He was very keen. He came to my house and exclaimed, "You have a George Platt Lynes!" This photographer was a role model for him, so he knew immediately that he was in the right place.'

They developed a close relationship, meeting up regularly, mainly in New York. There, Mapplethorpe introduced Van Manen to David Hockney, Diana Vreeland and Bianca Jagger. 'Nobody believes it, but Robert was an absolute sweetheart. A modest and shy man. I learnt a lot from him. Literally, I took things from him. The best people never keep secrets from one another. I will never be able to capture images like he did, but he was a dear friend, an extraordinary individual.'

On another occasion, when Mapplethorpe stayed with Van Manen, the latter organised a slide show for him. At the time, Hans was still shooting in colour on 35 mm film and presented almost an entire roll of images, thirty out of the thirty-six frames. The pictures were all much of a muchness and could have been better. The American suggested, 'Hans, you need to be more discerning. Get rid of your 35 mm camera and use a Hasselblad instead.' The respected photographer's opinion carried weight, as Van Manen would tell Erwin Olaf years later. All under Picasso's alleged motto that 'good artists copy, great artists steal'. For Van Manen, imitation was a necessary part of his artistic development. 'When you understand how someone works with light and composes a shot, only then can you attempt something yourself. Anyone who claims that they don't need to imitate is being very foolish.' The importance of making decisions became a guiding principle for both Van Manen and Erwin. 'The choices you make define you as a photographer. And as digital cameras have become more prevalent, the importance of selectivity only increases.'

Van Manen's aesthetic nudes, and later Erwin's own, were often labelled as glorified pornography. A few years after their first meeting, in 1986, Erwin discussed the issue with his mentor during a radio programme entitled *Art and Porn and the Distinction Between the Two*..

Erwin Olaf: 'Why does nudity captivate you so much?'

Hans van Manen: 'I think everyone finds nudity intriguing.'

Erwin Olaf: 'Is it the muscle definition or the eroticism that draws you in?'

Hans van Manen: 'It's a mix of both. Of course, I'm also a choreographer, so I work with the human body. I often notice with dancers, even though they're always wearing clothes, that there's a lot going on inside their bodies that you wouldn't see if they were dressed differently.'

Erwin Olaf: 'It's a mean question, but what turns you on more, a naked or dressed body, when you're behind the camera?'

Hans van Manen: 'I can't tell them apart, because I'm always excited, whether I'm taking pictures or choreographing. I've never had an erection while shooting, but I'm always excited, because photography is inherently thrilling. However, sexual arousal is not a factor.'

Later, they discuss the distinction between 'serious nude photography' and pornography.

Hans van Manen: 'I see the people in front of the camera as performers. But in pornography, the focus is on selling something, not on the people. The photographs are taken for one reason, and one reason only: erotic arousal. However, if my images happen to be alluring, it is because I'm trying to convey a different message. An erection, per se, is not pornographic... But I don't object to porn, the only thing that matters is whether it's good or bad.'

Mapplethorpe's dismantling of the 'porn' accusation was liberating, as Hans van Manen recalled during the photo shoot with Erwin. 'When a man in a gay bar inquired about Mapplethorpe's occupation, he replied, "I'm a pornographer". I was so moved that he crowned himself with the very slur that had been used to drag him through the mud. And it became a kind of moniker for us too.'

'Mapplethorpe's photographs opened psychological doors for me that I hadn't dared enter'

'With Mapplethorpe, it was always about the body. About sexuality, about aggression. Whether it was fisting or a floral still life, he photographed everything in the same static way. I joined the ranks of that photographic movement.' The young American's influence was visible in Erwin's pictures from the moment he commenced studio photography, as he well knew.

However, Mapplethorpe's impact was even greater. He freed photography from its straitjacket, proving that it could also be considered fine art. In the 1980s, more and more photographers abandoned street work and returned to the studio, influenced by Mapplethorpe, but also by Cindy Sherman and Peter Hujar.

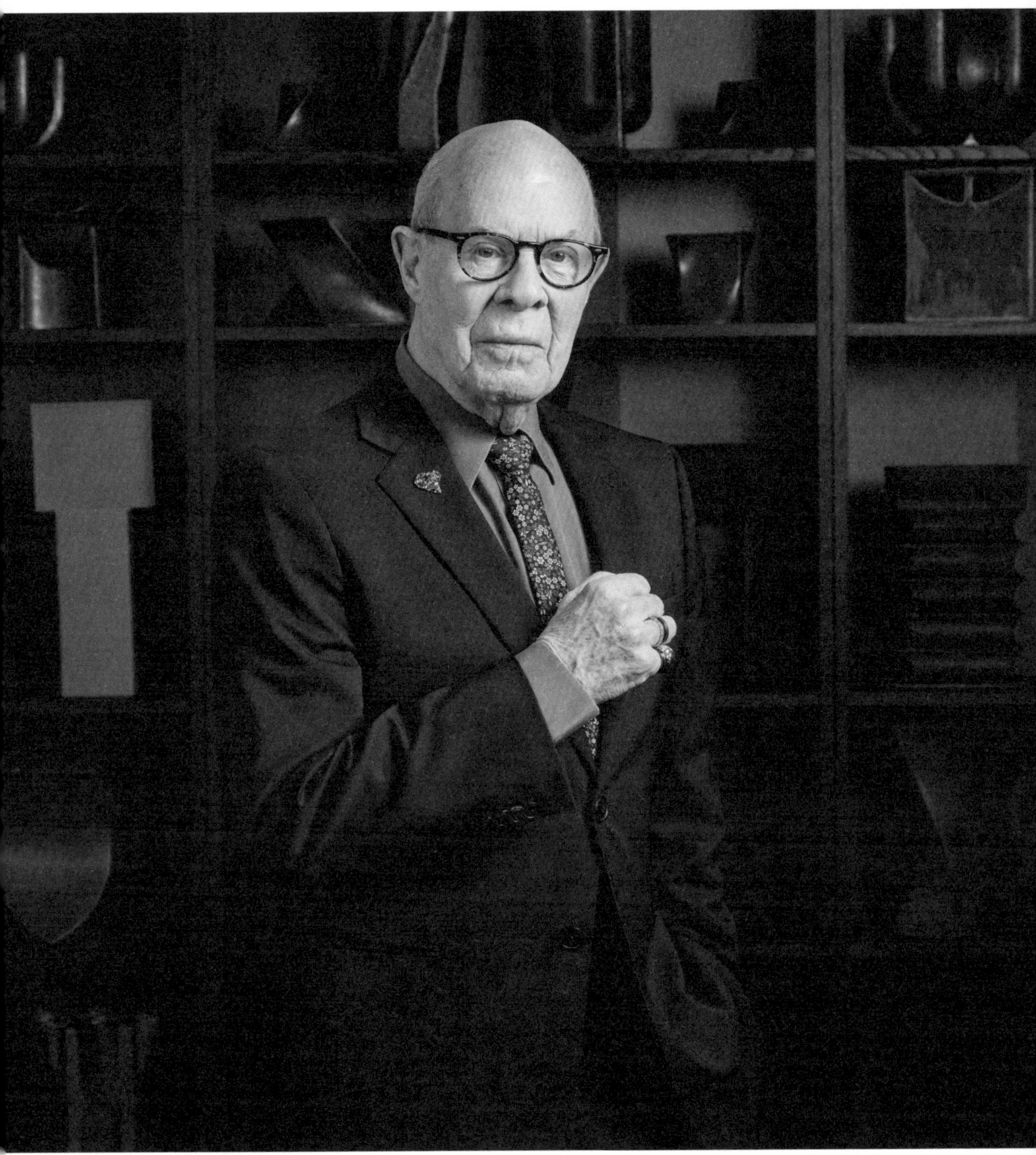

Portrait of choreographer and friend Hans van Manen, 2021.

In the Netherlands, photography primarily served documentary and journalistic purposes for quite some time. Erwin Olaf's contemporary Paul Blanca was a photographer and amateur kickboxer. Van Manen had met and cast him in his 1982 choreography *Pose*.

Erwin recalls their three-way collaboration. 'Blanca didn't seem too enthusiastic about me, and I found him to be fierce and intimidating. I responded to his rather overbearing personality by retreating further into my shell. For the first two years, I was often filled with fear and bewilderment. But I then discovered his stunning nudes and self-portraits, which elevated photography to the realm of art. In my opinion, Paul Blanca was out of my league.'

Before Van Manen, Blanca had already switched to a Hasselblad with square 6x6 negatives. Erwin benefited from their combined knowledge. He also bought a Hasselblad, but since it was exorbitant new, he bought a second-hand one – but he had no idea how to use the device. 'I was sure that my first picture with the new camera would be a masterpiece. But the photos were awful. Hans van Manen was my saviour; he showed me how to use it.'

They both hated the horizonless backgrounds common to mainstream studio photography. The supposed 'limbo' set was created for advertising stills, and we were determined to consign it to oblivion. Hans had a backdrop in his studio with a horizon line. They had a conversation about the art of photo retouching and their disdain for the overly grainy style that was popular at the time, as exemplified by photographers such as Ed van der Elsken and Willem Diepraam. 'Hans was a stickler for precise composition and the use of light and shadow to create a perfect image. The intensity of the shadow, whether it should be black or grey; the areas you illuminate with aluminium foil; and the technical distinction between a white sheet and a mirror in terms of reflection.'

As far as Erwin knew, studio photography required an entire battery of lights and several assistants. Van Manen, on the other hand, worked alone, using the simplest possible tools, such as one light and a few mirrors. 'I've always admired that approach. A lamp, a camera, and a back room with those sliding doors.' Erwin realised that he could imitate Van Manen's style. 'You certainly don't need twenty lamps, three assistants, a cacophony of screaming and screeching, and forty films. You can take a fantastic picture with just two films and a lamp. I adopted the technique directly from Van Manen.'

They found their models in bars, nightclubs and on the street. They posed extensively for each other. Forty years later, some of these images are still being sold as posters and postcards. Hans photographed dance aesthetics and compositions of the body within the Hasselblad's square format. 'A black, grey or white wall, a shelf, a lamp, and a few nudes were enough for him. It was captivating. With Paul Blanca, it was less about the composition and more about the idea.'

They honed their printing skills by exchanging techniques and refining their craft. Blanca was the first of the three to have his own darkroom. The details became all important, such as the size and type of paper, the depth of the white border, and the placement of the signature. Mapplethorpe's advice to ruthlessly edit and limit yourself to one photo per subject became a guiding principle.

Besides their appreciation of Mapplethorpe – 'always a discerning composition, perfect black-and-white nuances, never an element too many, no frills, something that I can still have trouble with myself. Every image is in absolute harmony' – they also shared a fascination for the work of Joel-Peter Witkin. Like Witkin, Erwin was also attracted to deviance. 'The nocturnal aspect, the Baroqueness of his work, his staged and utterly unique world – it was incredible. I found it thought-provoking rather than shocking. However, *The Kiss*, which depicts the bisected head of an elderly man who appears to be kissing himself, left me speechless.'

In comparison with Witkin's dark images and post-mortem photography, Erwin's tone was considerably lighter, especially in his early days. As Paul Blanca wrote in his review of Erwin's first studio portraits: 'The most striking thing about the series is the humour. Erwin Olaf describes Hans van Manen as a photographer of aesthetics, Blanca as one of emotion, and considers himself to be a photographer of jokes, even when deadly serious.'

Eroticism and physicality consistently played a leading role, just as in Mapplethorpe's work. 'Mapplethorpe's photographs opened psychological doors for me that I hadn't dared enter. Upon seeing a stunning, rock-hard penis captured in a photograph, my initial reaction was to wonder where the light source was. Hans occasionally invited attractive men over, whom he photographed in the nude. Although I found it mildly arousing, I was reluctant to admit it to myself.'

At first, he usually photographed more women than men. He often met his subjects in bars or nightclubs, but sometimes they approached him, as he once told a friend: ' You'll never guess who telephoned me yesterday afternoon, asking for a portrait: Mathilde Santing! The Netherland's most famous pop star, no less! Proof that I've hit the big time, and no thanks to anyone else!'

Paul Blanca wrote, 'Olaf, being a queen himself, finds it more challenging to persuade men than women. He claims that women are less inhibited in front of a camera and are less concerned about undressing. They are more willing to show themselves off directly.' Erwin believes that he was more hesitant than Hans van Manen. 'Hans photographed his muse, the ballerina Rachel Beaujean, without permission, while she stood with one leg on a chair, pulling on her tights. It meant you were looking straight at her pussy. It took me a while before I worked up the nerve to ask my models for such audacious poses.'

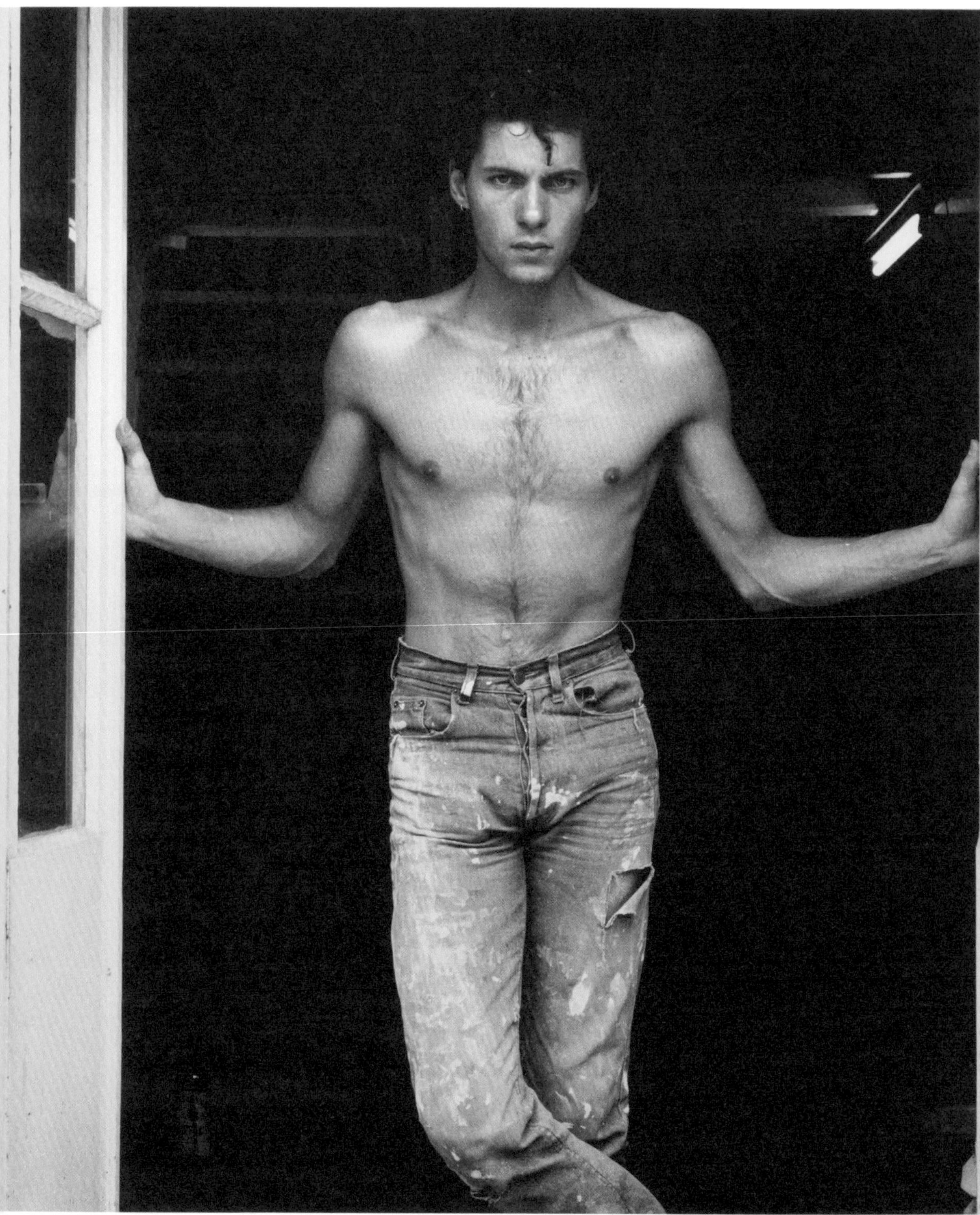

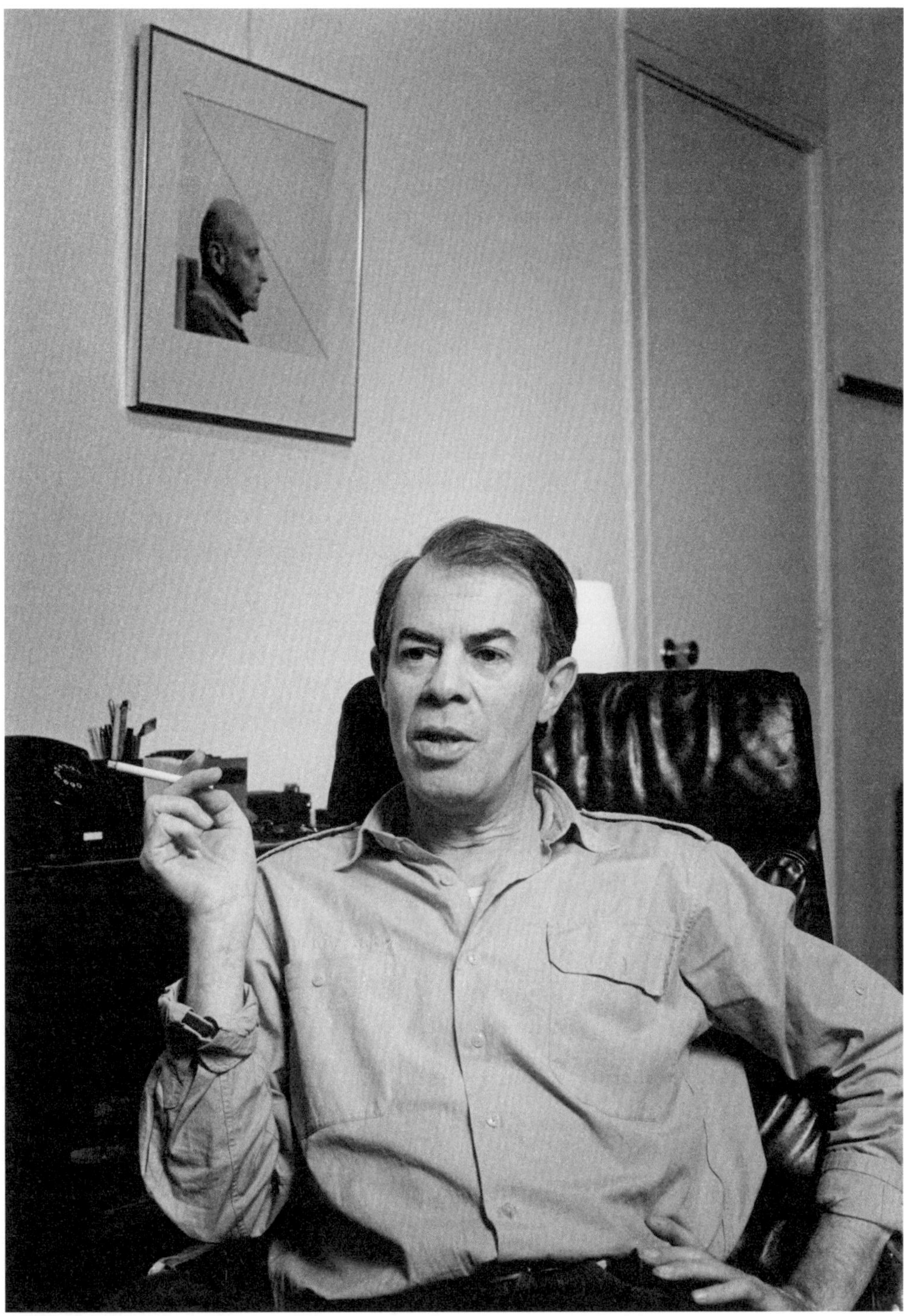

Left: *Marnixstraat 199*, 1983. Paul Blanca photographed by Hans van Manen.
Right: Hans van Manen photographed by Erwin Olaf for *Sek,* 1984.

Van Manen was a late bloomer in the field of photography and only worked professionally in this field until 1991. He noticed that his former apprentice Erwin was outperforming him so decided to concentrate on choreography. He said, 'All three of us went our separate ways. I packed up my camera and never looked at it again.' Erwin was the studious one in the group, while Paul Blanca was the angry young man.

Blanca and Olaf were inspired by similar sources but soon diverged. They were never truly close. Erwin's personal reservations, however, did not diminish his respect for the work. 'Paul was the most talented of us all,' he said. 'Plenty of *Sturm und Drang* and 1000% talent. I learnt a lot from him, and I always aspired to reach that level.'

His discussions with Van Manen and Blanca about art filled a void. Erwin had learnt a lot from Teun but he still lacked a solid art historical background and was eager to learn. Later, he started incorporating quotes from painting into his work. Forty years after their studio meetings, he acknowledged his debt to Mapplethorpe, as well as to Van Manen and Blanca. In a major retrospective of his work, Erwin displayed their pictures in his gallery of photographic icons at the Kunstmuseum Den Haag.

Meanwhile, on that weekday afternoon in March 2021, as Erwin photographs Hans van Manen at home, the lighting in the room has been recalibrated. Van Manen once again poses for his old friend. Having smoked a 'very nice' pipe of hash during the break between sessions, and now stripped of sunglasses, face mask and Borsalino, he willingly complies with the photographer's requests. Very occasionally, he expresses a reservation: 'Will I still be sharp enough, Piotr?' One, two, click. 'Once it gets to three in the afternoon, my focus starts to wane. I must stop, in fact.' Click. 'Piotr's got a very good eye. The power of youth. Click. 'How about the reflection? Isn't it better?' Click. 'Put your hand in your back pocket, then turn it down. That makes the light better.' Click. 'How about this pose where you're wearing sunglasses? Tilt your head slightly toward the light.' Click. 'Now pull the "who am I to be doing this" look, Hans.' Click. 'Ha, ha, ha. Yes, that's him; you've nailed it perfectly.'

They examine the screen side by side, meticulously analysing the results. Van Manen is thrilled with his own image. 'We're both vain. Except when we're working. Then it's not about us but about the art, and all vanity goes out the window. As one approaches ninety, people constantly inquire about one's thoughts on impending death. My usual response is, "I haven't got a clue." However, regardless of what happens to me, Erwin's photos of me today will endure for years to come.'

'We are, and we will always be, middle-class boys. It's something you can't shake'

RECIPE FOR SUCCESS

At the start of 2019, as he flips through the contact prints of his earliest work, Erwin explains that he only wants to show some of his photos from his early years with a line through them or an explanatory caption. 'I have always been transparent, and I'm determined to continue addressing topics that matter to me. I don't mind speaking up, even if it leads to unfair criticism online or being cancelled. Some of my photographs have obviously hurt certain people, and I respect their feelings, even if I don't always share them.'

That he would make it to a retrospective seemed an improbable dream in late 1984. 'I'm flat broke,' Erwin reported to his French client at the end of that year. After leaving André Ruigrok and coming off welfare benefits, Erwin had been able to experiment freely. However, his money problems, including unpaid student loans and rent, soon became overwhelming.

Despite this, he managed, with great effort, to pay off a debt to his father on time. 'My compliments! This proves once again that I can trust all three of my sons,' his father wrote, apparently having been uncertain about the matter until that moment. 'Mama and I are proud of you for this.' He went on to give business advice, telling his son to consider all the waiting around when pricing jobs, before wishing him 'love, good health, and less worry'. And with a playful yet slightly bitter allusion to Erwin's extensive interactions with his mother, which excluded him, Siem suggested, 'If you ever encounter a plump lady who seems depressed, and she introduces herself as your mother, please convey my warmest regards. I rarely get to see her these days.'

Erwin heeded his father's advice and soon took his newfound status as a self-employed individual seriously. He even enrolled on an accounting course.

Erwin looked for new photographic benchmarks and found them mainly in Richard Avedon, the fashion-turned-documentary photographer who published the photo book *In the American West* (1985). 'Avedon elevated his portraits to a dreamlike level, imbuing them with a fairytale-like air.' Qualities to which he also aspired.

Photographers like David Bailey and Jean-François Jonvelle served as further inspirations. Their portraits and nudes were less provocative than those of Mapplethorpe or Blanca. 'There's an entire universe to be conquered when it comes to photographing the male nude,' Paul Blanca remembers Erwin once saying. 'He's interested in photographing men because, as a genre, male nudity has never really been developed. The work that does exist tends to either be heroic or romantic. The camera angle is slightly lower, which broadens the shoulders and accentuates the pecs.'

He was experimenting with form, breaking away from his teacher, Van Manen, who, he claimed, had been taking 'terribly' bad pictures for some time. 'A roster of horny young men.' He continued pursuing the path he wanted to take with his photography: 'Played (ever so carefully) with the lights. I want theatre in my photographs.'

His first significant success as a photographer was limited to small circles, but it heralded progress. The booklet *Stadsgezichten* [City Faces], which included an introduction by Hans van Manen and a text by writer Guus Luijters, led to a presentation and modest exhibition at a bookstore on Leidsestraat. Erwin's hopes were high; there would be an ambitious 'leap forward' with this book, he noted. 'The child is whining again, and it's incredibly spoilt.'

Erwin wanted his artwork to transcend the gay community. 'Now I need to break into the hetromarket [*sic*]. ... It must be a sensation or at least a high-profile publication,' he wrote to his friend Frans Franciscus, who was painting in Berlin.

He remained very close to Franciscus, commenting on the world, techniques, idleness, vanity, fame, honesty, guts, the subject matter of his work, and shifts in the art world. They also discussed what was in and what was out. Despite the difference in their artistic media, they both created narrative and figurative works. 'We don't nail a turd to a board. Nor do we hang three wires in a corner. We want to show what we can do.' They realised, looking back, that they both came from backgrounds where 'high art' was not an option. 'When we were young, nobody ever encouraged us to talk endlessly about philosophical matters,' Franciscus explained. Erwin concluded, 'We are, and we will always be, middle-class boys. It's something you can't shake.'

Erwin had met Guus Luijters on the *Panorama* editorial board, and it was Luijters who had proposed the idea of *Stadsgezichten*. He had bumped into Erwin on the street near his studio, who happened to mention his initial steps in photography. When he showed his pictures, Luijters decided immediately that a small book was in order. 'We have to make this book right now, in double-quick time, because before you know it, you'll be too famous,' he said.

Luijters reached out to the small publishing house De Woelrat, which Frenchman Michel Vassallucci had established to publish 'homosexual literature'. *Stadsgezichten* presented an opportunity to highlight a queer artist's perspective while offering a contemporary and intimate glimpse into the gay community.

To adorn the back cover of the book, Erwin created a set of dual portraits featuring himself and Guus Luijters. They are both naked, wearing nothing but white socks.

Erwin invited his friends and relatives to the exhibition opening. Siem Springveld was unable to attend due to a recent stroke. Erwin was 'scared witless' when he heard

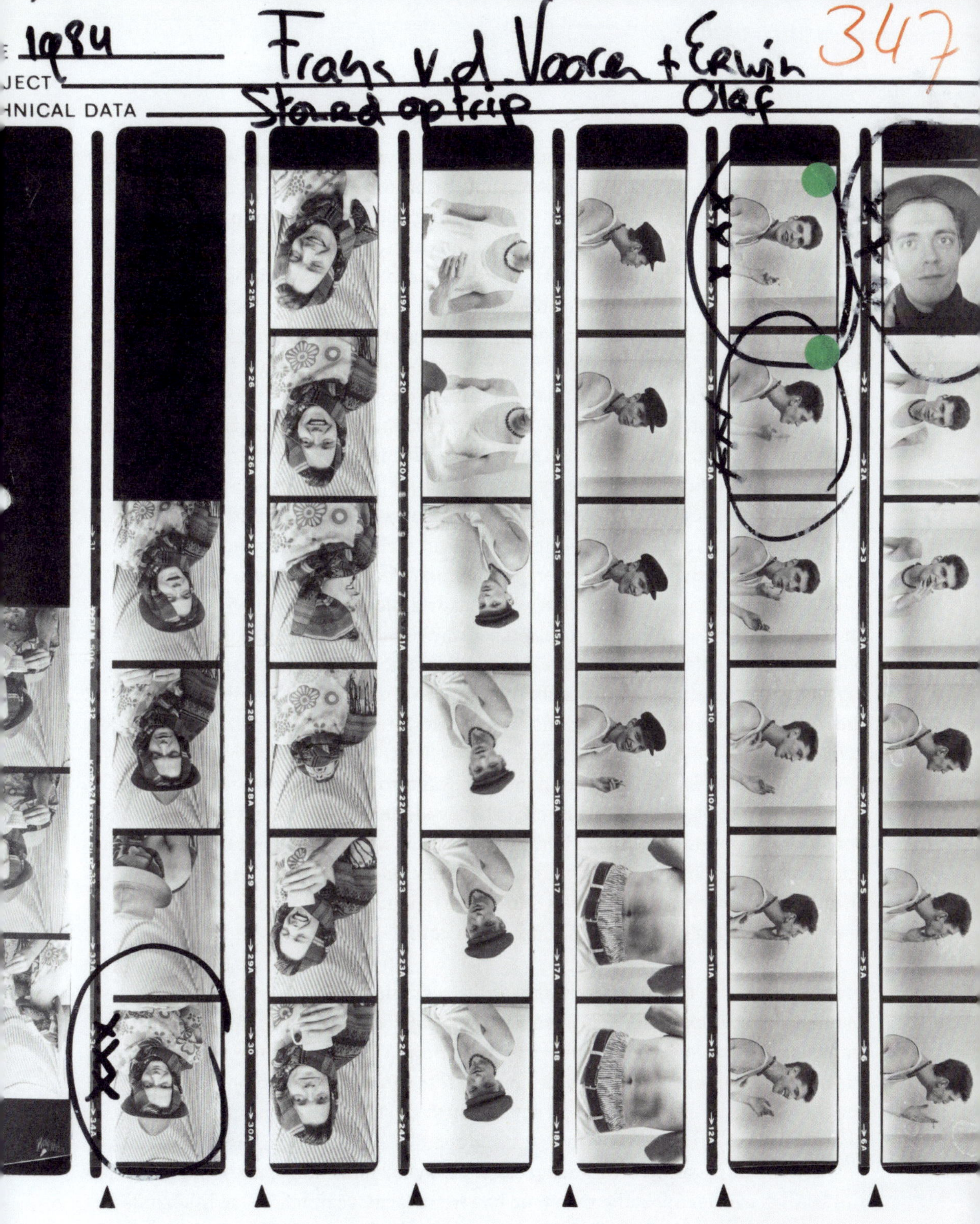

Contact sheet: 'Frans van de Vooren (Frans Franciscus) and Erwin stoned on a trip', 1984.

the news and called his mother immediately, during which he 'almost wept', so moved was he by her grief. 'My father looks terrible, his face is lopsided, and my mother can't stop crying. I kept her company one evening and confessed to smoking dope. "So long as you don't get addicted," she said. Of course, I am. But I said, "No".'

Erwin perceived his mother's 'suppressed panic', yet his emotions towards Siem were predominantly anger, stemming from all that he was putting her through. Nevertheless, he sent an invitation to his convalescent father, on which he wrote that he was 'terrified', about the forthcoming exhibition and his 'constant financial woes'. 'I sometimes wish that I was old and past caring.' He closed with a rallying cry: 'Work hard!' Two words that his father loved to hear and which, for all the parties and other distractions, would remain Erwin's personal motto. 'I owe my work ethic to him, really. *Ausdauer* [endurance] is everything.'

Siem Springveld recovered on this occasion. His relationship with his middle son gradually improved. At the same time, Erwin realised that he owed his father a lot, and that, in some ways, they were very similar. And not just because of their work ethic and frankness. Erwin's brothers, Jos and Ron, along with their wives, Gemma and Conny, attended the exhibition and became regular attendees at all subsequent openings. They joked about the 'Great Erwin Olaf Show' (according to Jos), because Erwin demanded more attention than he gave to the rest of his family. However, they adored him and appreciated his artwork, despite it taking some getting used to at first.

Lida Springveld, ever the proud mother, was also at the opening and carefully examined the photographs, one by one. She loved the double portrait of herself and her sister, was amazed by the weight-lifting picture with Jacques and Rudolf, and upon reaching Erwin's self-portrait, she asked her eldest son, Jos, 'Why is there water all over Erwin's face?' 'That's semen, Mum,' Jos replied. 'Oh,' Lida responded. Says Erwin: 'I think that's a perfect response, don't you?'

In the photo book, Erwin followed the twin tracks laid out by his two mentors, Van Manen and Ruigrok. In the *Binnenkamers* [interior rooms] section, studio photography; and in *Buitenkamers* [exterior rooms], reportage. He had taken these early photos in Hans van Manen's studio. Later, he moved into his own photography studio, a roughly 20-square-metre room in a squat, which he shared with another budding photographer.

Erwin also began writing about photography for *Focus* magazine, which was run by Dirk van der Spek, the man who had first placed a camera in Erwin's hands all those years ago. And apart from international gay magazines, he also hit the road for *Amsterdam in je kontzak* [Amsterdam in your back pocket], a city guide for queer men to what was hailed as the 'gay capital of Europe'. During this project, he captured images within the Wijers complex in Amsterdam, the largest squat in the Netherlands.

He knew the building well. He had previously staged a kind of art project there with his friend Rudolf Pfalz, an acrobat and dancer. He called it his 'first and last live performance'. In the somewhat chaotic squat, he created a makeshift studio for a blend of performance and portrait photography. 'Erwin had hung floral wallpaper in a corner and positioned a halogen lamp,' Pfalz recalls. 'There was a plinth, on which you could stand and have your picture taken in high heels. Price: 25 cents. And I danced around the space in the meantime.'

The city-guide photos taken in the Wijers led to problems. One of the squatters sued him for 5,000 guilders in compensation, plus destruction of the entire edition. This is equivalent to about €2,250 in today's currency. Erwin's lawyer argued, based on a full set of contact prints, that the squatter in question was desperate to be in the pictures. Erwin further stated that the photograph was not only an image of contemporary youth culture but also a 'homo-social' one.

In so doing, he aimed to highlight the fluidity of the line between heterosexuality and homosexuality. 'As a photographer, I'm captivated by this ambiguous zone. This does not mean that when I capture same-sex interactions, that I want to suggest homosexuality.' Ultimately, it was decided that the remaining prints would be altered to make the image unrecognisable.

This was not the only instance of a legal dispute with a homophobic slant. Another individual was offended by a photograph taken on a nudist beach that was used in a recruitment ad for *Gai Pied*. The complainant's lawyer stated that it could be worth around 3,000 guilders (about €1,300 in today's currency). Full of anticipation, Erwin expressed the hope of 'one day taking photos for which I can charge the amount you assume'.

The legal disputes had an important impact. 'One of the reasons I went to the studio was to get away from all that negativity.'

'I'm too jealous, too proud, too beautiful, and too independent to acquiesce'

Erwin's initial success and the surge of commissions coincided with an emerging backlash against homosexuality, which was not yet widely accepted.

Erwin's partner Teun and his brother Job came from a devout Christian family, but they had rejected the church's teachings. They danced demonstratively and kissed other men in discos and on the streets. Many people found it offensive.

Teun, who was assaulted by a tennis racket-wielding boy for allegedly staring at him in the middle of the day, decided to train in the Chinese martial art of Shaolin

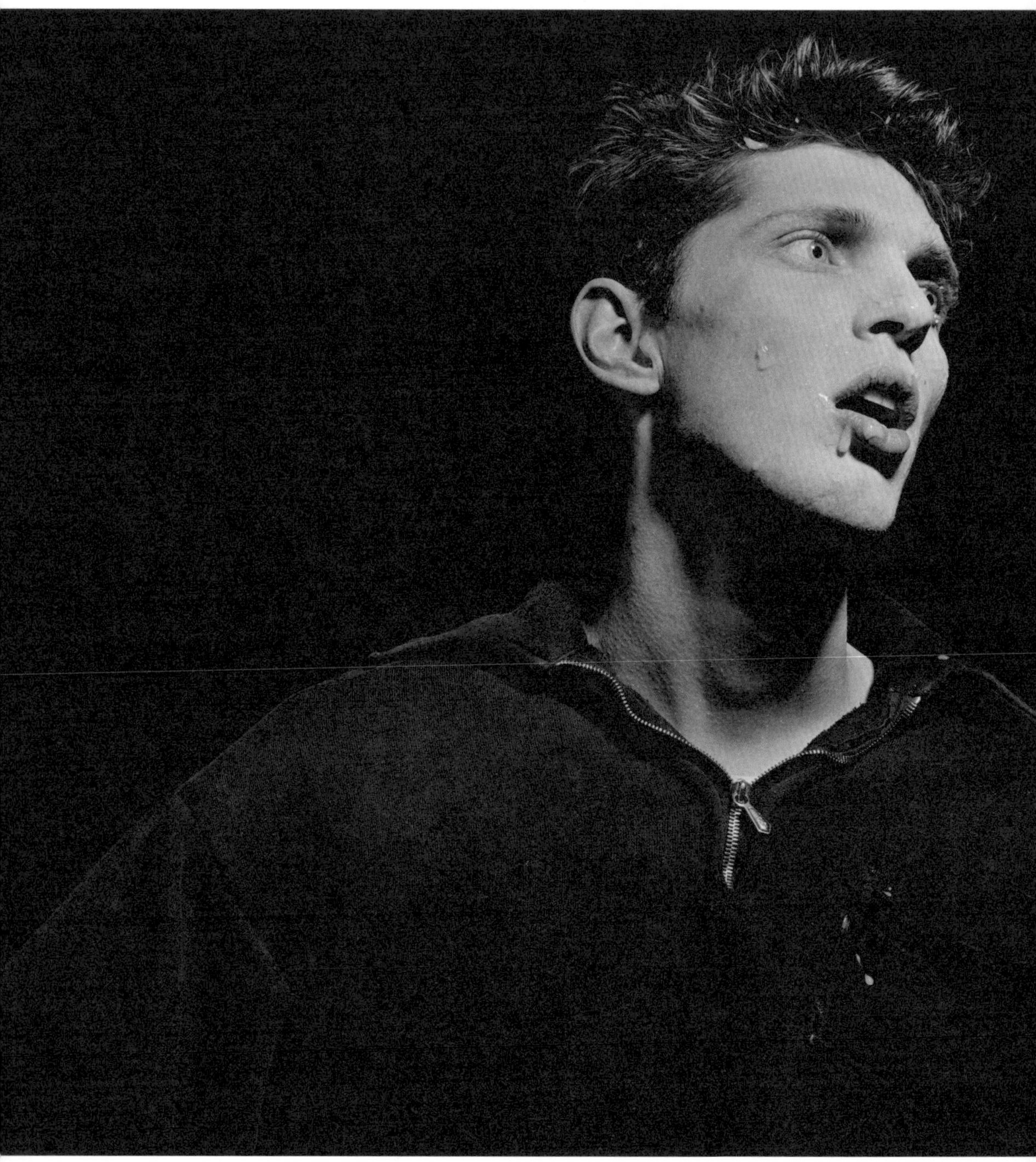

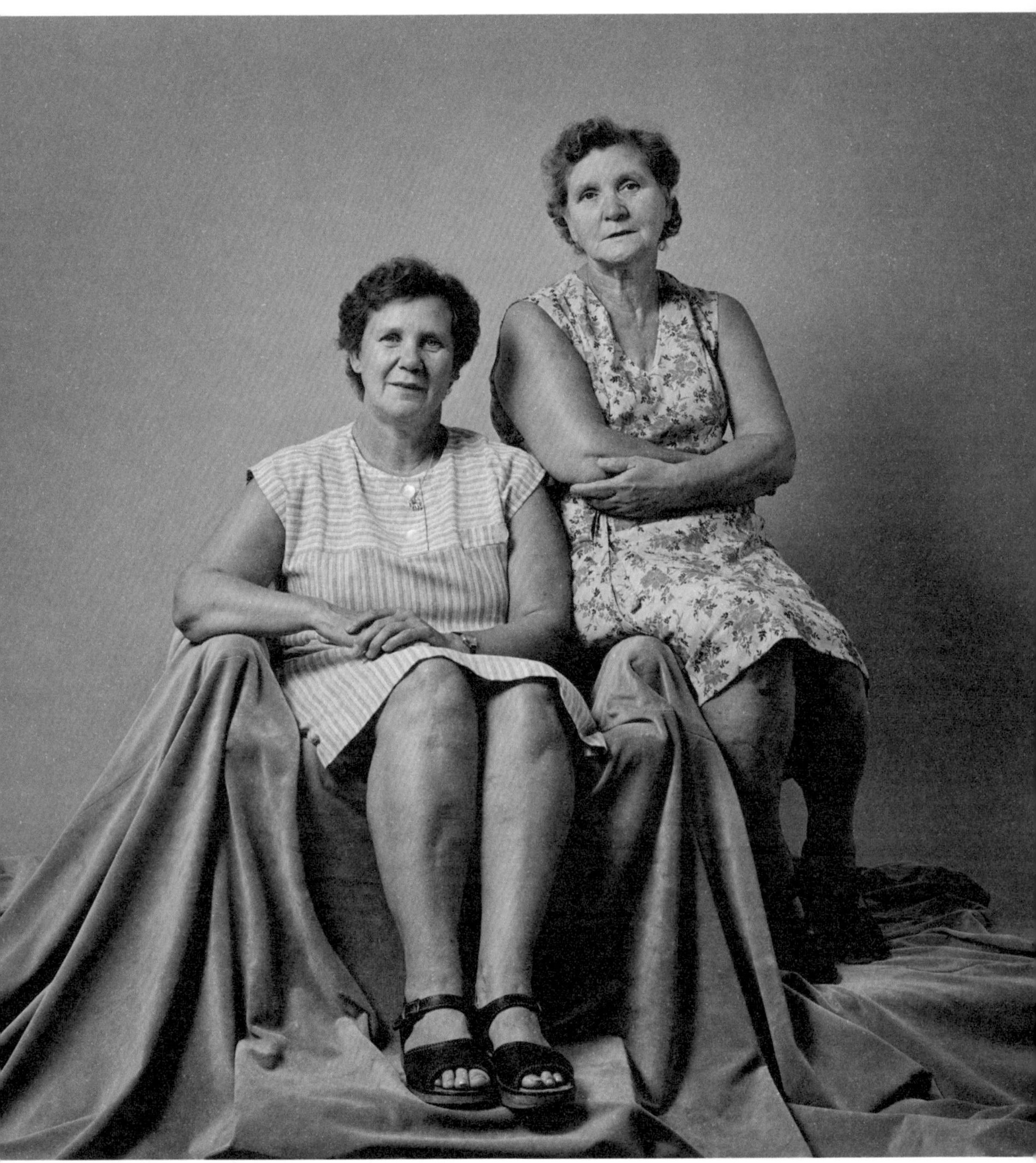

Left: *Cum, Self-Portrait, 1984*, from the *Squares* series. Right: *Sisters, 1985*, from the *Squares* series. Double portrait of Erwin's mother Lida and his aunt Jannie.

Kempo. He eventually taught the sport and joined a gay vigilante squad, the 'Fight Group', and became a co-organiser of the Pink Saturday demonstrations. These marches were intended to highlight the gay cause, while the 'Fight Group' would respond to attacks on homosexuals.

Erwin was happy that his partner was involved in these causes. He often went with Teun or other friends to demonstrations. He didn't brandish placards and wasn't drawn to the 'Fight Group', but he did capture everything on film – forever the outsider.

The Pink Saturdays played a pivotal role in the acceptance of the LGBTQI+ community. In 1984 it became illegal to classify homosexuality as an 'aberration' in medical textbooks. However, the most painful times were yet to come. Just as the straight community began to tolerate homosexuality, the gay community would be thrown back on itself by the emergence of the deadly AIDS epidemic.

Erwin's later activism, in which he leveraged his fame to combat all forms of discrimination against the gay community, was inspired by the more militant Teun. He was also motivated by his own experiences of homophobia, both at school and in later life. 'Erwin was very obviously gay and was constantly targeted, he was goaded far more than me,' recalls Teun Frieszo. 'He didn't take up martial arts like I did, but he fought back just as hard. I've witnessed him lashing out with a bike chain and thought, watch out, it could end very badly. Erwin is a street fighter.'

Against all the odds, they managed to maintain their relationship after Erwin left for Amsterdam. But Teun continued to put his ideals into practice, and this was a source of conflict. He wasn't just involved with Erwin. He continued seeing his 'No. 1' and began a third serious relationship. 'I fought endlessly with Teun about the third boyfriend.' Erwin devised nefarious plots to get rid of the rivals, proclaiming, 'Three is one too many,' but it was all for nothing. Pressure didn't help, and Teun simply refused to choose. Even after 'No. 3' disappeared from Teun's life, Erwin remained unsatisfied, unable to accept being the 'second partner'. He wrote in his red-and-black notebook, 'I'm No. 2 and I hate it. I said I would never accept such a thing. I'm too jealous, too proud, too beautiful, and too independent to acquiesce.'

It became an obsession, and they argued relentlessly. 'Someone needs to take Teun down a peg or two,' Erwin wrote jealously. Mostly in vain, and out of revenge, he also experimented with cheating. 'I failed again last night. ... No one gave me a second look.' Something had to change, because 'I must at all costs avoid conflating my self-esteem with my pictures'.

Decades later, Erwin reflects on those words. They seemed like fate at the time. 'The way others perceive me is deeply influenced by my photographs, and it is quite intoxicating when people consistently praise my oeuvre. If I stopped, my fame and recognition would probably slip away. I'm indivisible from my work.'

Alone at home, he has always been Erwin Springveld, a man who likes to surround himself with photography, but principally the work of others: three punks from Max Natkiel's *Paradiso Stills* series hang prominently in the kitchen-cum-dining room. Paul Blanca's self-portrait with his mouth sewn shut, Anton Corbijn's acclaimed portrait of Miles Davis, and David LaChapelle's *Amanda Lepore as Andy Warhol's Marilyn* are all on display in the living room. Nearby are Eva Besnyö's *Boy with Cello Near Lake Balaton* (1931), Roger Ballen's work, and Hans van Manen's portraits of Blanca and Erwin (as a reclining nude).

'I deliberately chose not to display any of my own work.' But in the hallway, you can see the transition between Springveld and Olaf. A passage. I must admit that I'm getting tired of this Erwin Olaf guy. He's inescapable now. People's perceptions of me are directly linked to my work, and my self-esteem is bound up in it as well.'

The fact that he was able to capture Teun with another man, despite their ongoing arguments about other lovers, made him feel 'very weird'. 'I photographed them as sailors. They're extremely attractive, I hope. They remind me of *Querelle*. My photos really turn me on right now. It's not really about sex, though. I must be careful, however. But I'm not really looking for sex or a raunchy night. I don't think I'm particularly horny myself.'

Photography was also a way for them to affirm and capture their love in meticulous detail. The resulting images played an important role in *Stadsgezichten*. The spunk on Erwin's face in the opening image of the *Binnenkamers* section, which had so perplexed his mother, was Teun's. It was the result of a session that was as intense as it was humorous.

Teun was serving as a stand-in for Erwin as he prepared his camera and lit the set. 'I took a seat on the stool while Teun began to masturbate. I was getting impatient, so I told him, "Alright, you need to come now." He had to squat behind the camera, as it was his responsibility to press the shutter button. I sat there, thinking to myself, "Hurry up, for goodness' sake!" A large drop of semen was sliding downwards, and I don't particularly like cum on my face. But for a self-portrait, you need to expose yourself and reveal something personal. Real or supposed. You've got to let go of your vanity. And I'm very vain. But there's no point in being all statuesque in a photo.'

He also took a joint portrait with Teun. Erwin, trousers around his ankles, and Teun, naked and on his knees, face averted and pressed against his lover. Just before Teun's passing, over three decades later, he reenacted the scene in a poignant reiteration of the artwork. The likeness of the two lovers appeared in *Stadsgezichten* alongside a formal portrait of his mother and aunt. 'A photo of my mother and her sister only becomes entertaining when it is surrounded by "unusual" pictures,' he explains. 'Just as a series of housewife photos would be dull and monotonous.'

He firmly dismissed his longtime friend Henny Dinklage's queries about his enduring fascination with unconventional subjects. In Henny's opinion, his portraits of ordinary individuals were just as compelling. 'Are you willing to introduce me to one of these "normal" people? And when you do, could you share what makes them so photogenic?' He would be asked the same question repeatedly, and both the amateur and learned public's insatiable appetite for documentary photography would wear on him.

Although he had many criticisms of *Stadsgezichten*, he was mostly proud of the book. Van Manen's concern, as expressed in his introduction, was that 'it's hard to earn money from this type of photography'. Erwin decided to continue working on his documentary photos for the time being, since these were the only ones generating income. Here, too, he combined business and pleasure: his fascination with extraordinary people in extraordinary circumstances.

As Paul Blanca perused Erwin's recent images, he noticed a departure from journalistic photography and a potential transition towards studio work. He used the unconventional portrait of singer Mathilde Santing as an example. In this image, she is seated on a chair, her back to the viewer, a silhouette. Her head and a hand holding a smouldering cigarette are all that can be seen.

'Be bold, charming and tenacious'

A collection of harsh reviews only deepened Erwin's doubts. 'Since the debut of *Stadsgezichten*, I've barely touched my camera.' He compiled a new list. Recipe for success:

1. You need specific, tangible ideas, not vague ones.
2. Be bold, charming and tenacious.
3. Call people you think might be interested in your ideas, but don't let them steal them!
4. Look attractive, and make sure your clothes and hair are good – but don't be too run-of-the-mill.
5. Learn new things. Get reading!
6. Profile yourself! Don't think that everyone else (whoever they may be) is better than you.
7. Develop new initiatives.

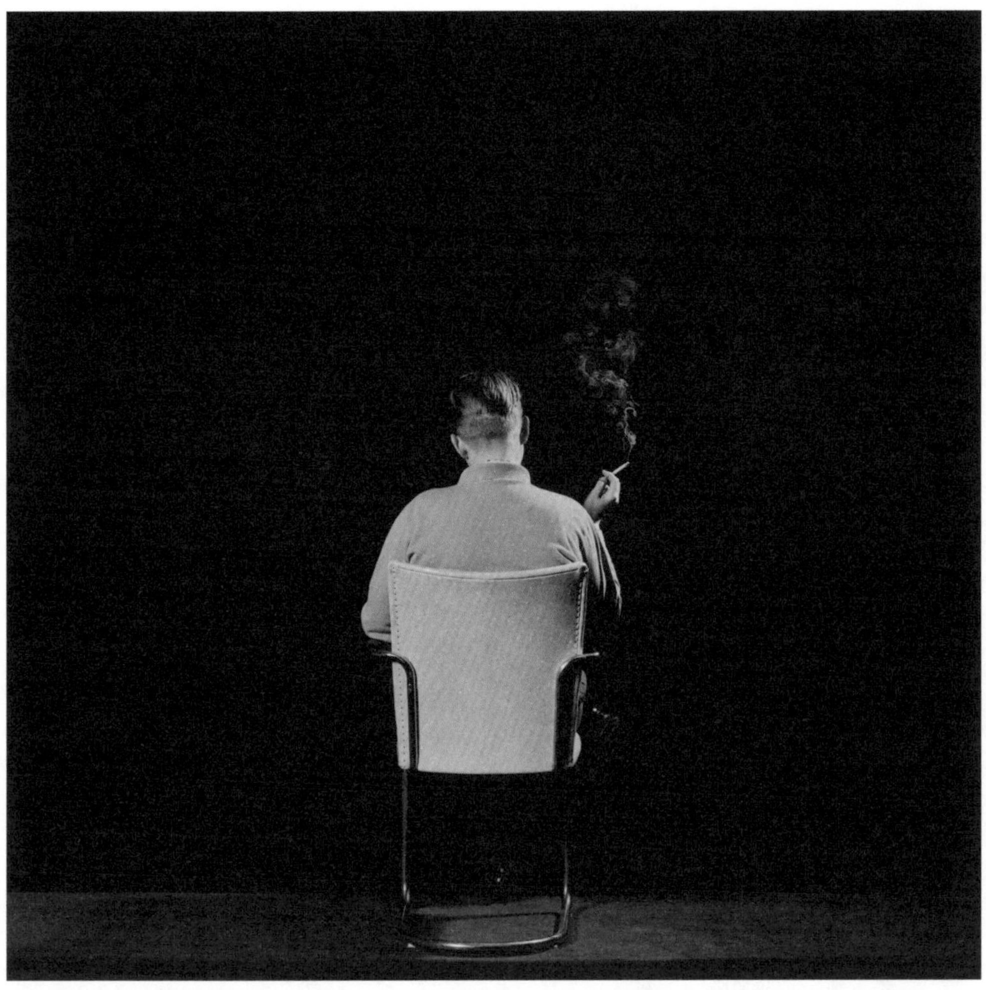

Portrait of singer Mathilde Santing from the *Squares* series, c. 1985.

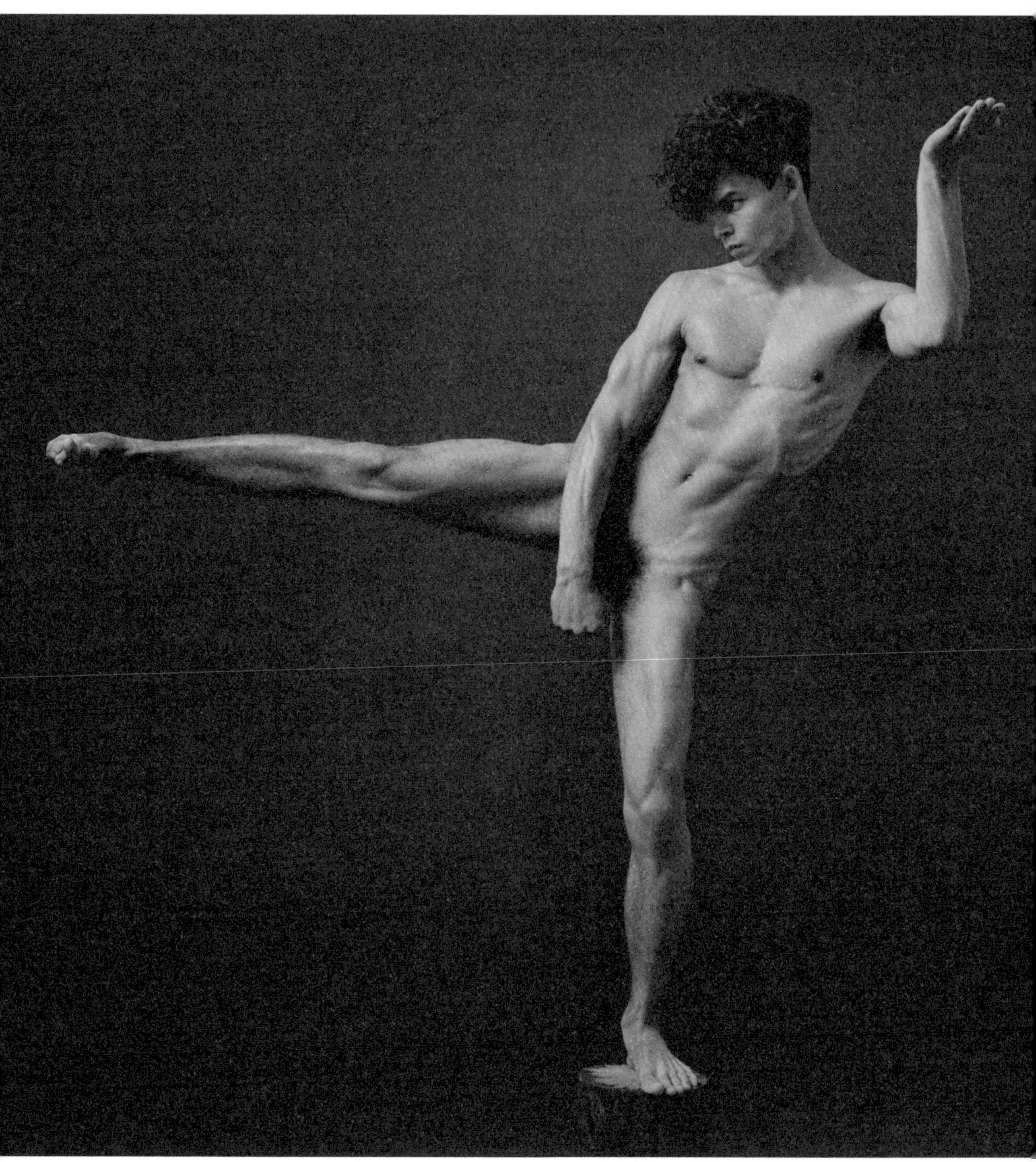

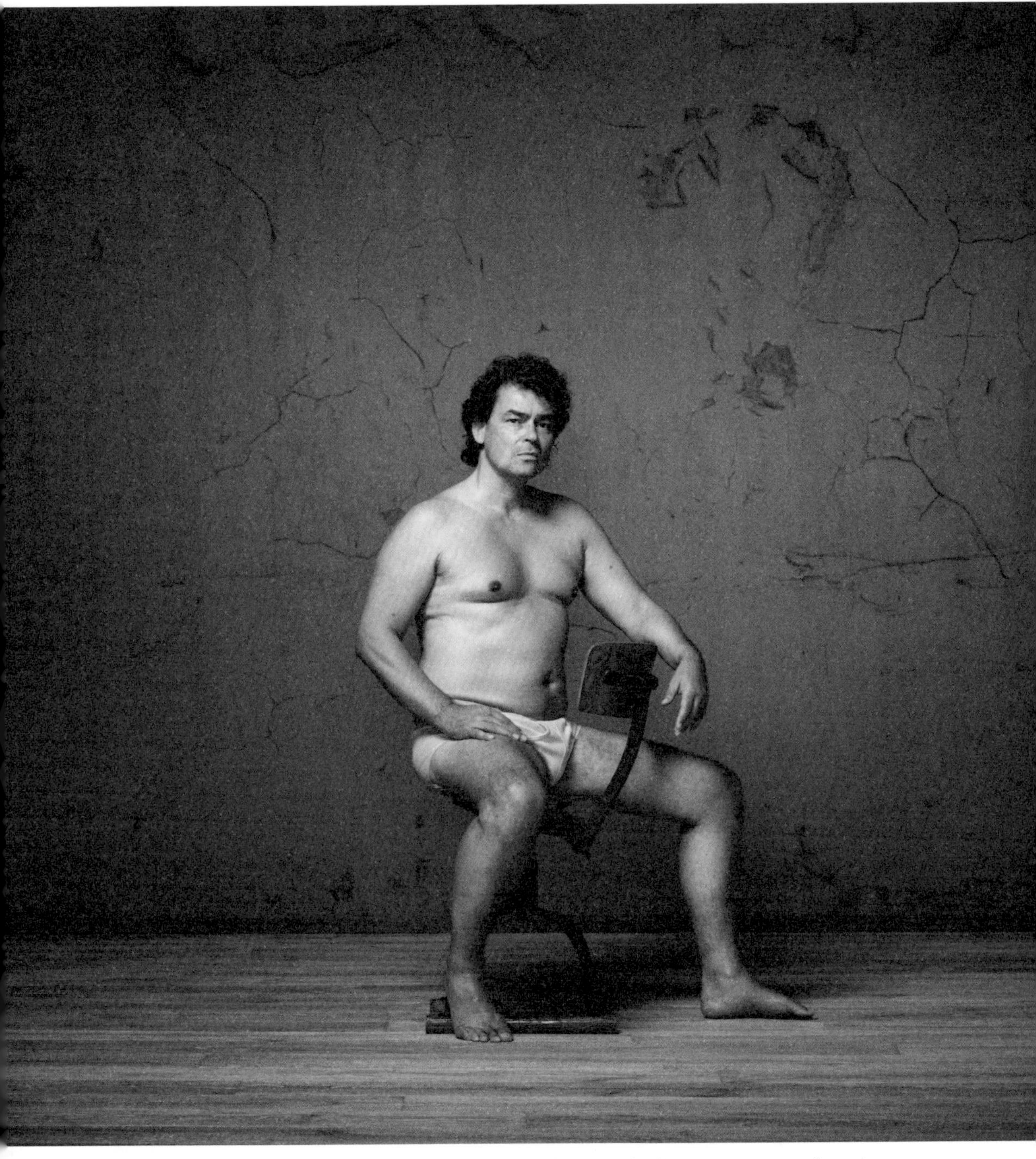

Left: Erwin Olaf, *Pencak Silat II, Squares, 1984*. Right: Rodrigo (Rodriek) Lutgens in 2022 from the *Muses* series.

And he literally made a name for himself as a photographer through publications and exhibitions of his work, which featured celebrities and semi-celebrities. From the beginning, his fame was bolstered by the controversies surrounding his photography. The criticism sometimes came from unexpected quarters.

One of his first group exhibitions was *Foto '84*, the first photography exhibition in the Netherlands to treat the medium as an art form. It was the talk of the town, and not least because one of the posters featured Paul Blanca naked, posing *en profil* with his newborn son.

Erwin had submitted five photographs of his bodybuilders for display, but when he arrived at the gallery just before the opening, they were nowhere to be found. The Italian curator, who had insisted on total nudity, had removed them. She didn't like the fact that Erwin's bodybuilders were wearing micro shorts. Enraged, Erwin contacted the press, and all hell broke loose. This experience taught him that the media often view art as news, especially when there is controversy involved. On this occasion, Erwin Olaf became famous not for his photographs, but for their absence.

His studio photography could be just as incendiary as his reportage work in terms of provoking controversy, such as the bodybuilders series. In the photograph *Self-Defence, an Answer to Hans Van Manen*, a naked young man performs a karate kick in midair, with his foot just centimetres away from the belly of a blindfold pregnant woman standing on a plinth, her hands tied behind her back.

Too shy to approach potential models, Erwin settled on Rodrigo Lutgens, a practitioner of the martial art form, Pencak Silat. He approached him and asked if he'd pose for a photo. After Erwin took a picture of Rodrigo performing a karate kick, Van Manen also invited him to be his model. Van Manen then captured Rodrigo as he kicked a designer vase filled with flowers.

'That picture, entitled *Attack*, is heartbreakingly beautiful. But I was furious because Hans had stolen both my model and my idea,' Erwin recalled. 'And I, in turn, wanted to outdo Hans by having the same guy kick out at something even more fragile than a vase. I approached Kaja, a Surinamese friend who was pregnant at the time, and asked her to serve as a model and wear a blindfold.'

As with his earlier pictures, Art Unlimited soon issues the image as a postcard, only to receive a flood of angry letters. One individual expressed their disapproval, stating, 'Your photograph seems to convey misogyny, and even more disturbingly, it targets a woman of colour.' Or: 'Kicking, in my opinion, equals hatred. Causing a black woman to miscarry – how does it differ from Mengele's treatment of Jewish pregnant women?'

An anti-fascist group, seeing the card as a clear symbol of the oppression of women, demanded that it be contextualised or removed from circulation. Erwin was shocked. He had never even considered hating women or black people. Radical queer and squatter movements, with whom he generally identified, were colour-blind. Racism was unknown in his milieu; discrimination was non-existent. 'I love all skin tones, and I adore photographing their every nuance.'

He refused to comply with the request to remove the card from circulation. 'It smells like book burning to me,' he said. 'People need to open their eyes and look at the image. I demand nothing less. To the left, you see a handcuffed and blindfolded pregnant woman, standing on a plinth. To the right, a young kickboxer. The woman's posture is as straight as a die; she's not afraid of the guy. He makes a futile attempt to kick her, fully extending his leg but still several centimetres away from her vulnerable stomach. He defends himself but fails in the process.'

A woman of colour stands on a white plinth. There's no hidden meaning, he emphasised in his defence. The Indonesian and Surinamese heritage of his models is insignificant; they happen to be his friends. He couldn't afford professional models for his studio work, so worked with people he knew. The fact that some of the models are people of colour has no deeper significance. 'I hope this clarifies why I don't view the image as a representation of racism or sexism.'

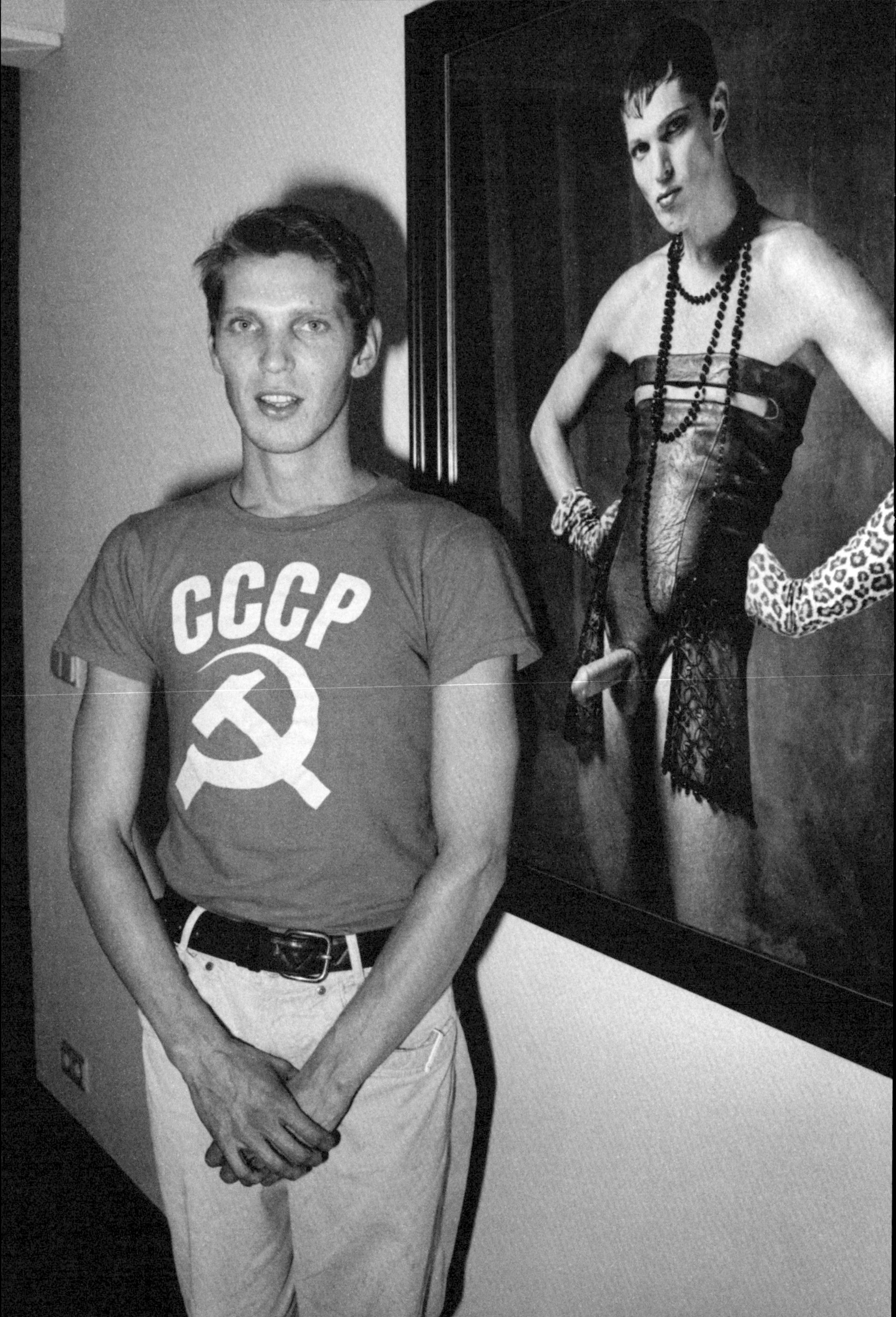
CCCP

4 PARTY (1985–1990)

'Even in the studio, you're dependent on that one magic second'

TRANSFORMATIONS

A balding man with a moustache is seated at the dining-cum-meeting table in the Studio Erwin Olaf canteen. He politely introduces himself: 'Jacques Elia Wolters, pleased to meet you.' Yes, it's really him: the incredible strongwoman from one of Erwin's most famous early photographs. Wolters is one of the 'muses' from the 1980s, whom Erwin has invited back to the studio to be immortalised anew, almost forty years after the initial shoot.

Erwin had first directed Jacques Wolters and Rudolf Pfalz in the summer of 1985, during a session in his small studio in central Amsterdam. Standing on a plinth, wearing nothing but a pair of stilettos, Jacques dangled an equally naked Rudolf upside down, like a trussed hunting trophy. Then she held him aloft with outstretched arms – but only briefly.

A few days later, Erwin wrote to Frans Franciscus, 'I'm satisfied with this series. Worked yesterday from 2 to 8 on the picture of the big woman holding a guy aloft. Unfortunately, everything – absolutely everything – went wrong. Hasselblad broken, cut through the only good negative (in the dark), so not much yet. Still, it's going to be one of my most beautiful photos. I can feel it.'

At the follow-up session a fortnight later, he invited stylist Harrie Wildeman and his friend to lend a helping hand. They lifted Rudolf, placed him in Jacques's raised hands, and stepped aside so that Erwin could capture the scene. The result was an iconic image that would be printed on postcards and magazine covers: the archetypal strongwoman. It also marked an end to simple staging *à la* Van Manen, lit with a single lamp. 'I now want to start working with depth of field, light and composition.

I want to start experimenting with big shadows and multiple lights.'

At the time, Erwin's work consisted of slightly erotic photos with a humorous twist, which did well as postcards. 'Spunk on my face, women gazing at each other's arses, boys with giant carrots and foaming champagne bottles,' he summarises succinctly. He didn't necessarily make them *pour épater les bourgeois*, but rather as a form of self-therapy, he explains before re-photographing Jacques.

'Looking back, there was a part of me that I hated, right up until the millennium, and I struggled to come to terms with my sexual orientation. The conventional wisdom is that you truly accept yourself when you come out, but that wasn't true in my case. There was a deep scar on my soul; it seemed to be etched into me that my preferences were wrong.'

Although he presented himself as a fellow gay activist, it would be a long time before he was at peace with his sexuality and body. But in so doing, he was eventually able to dismantle the defences of exaggeration and humour that he'd constructed around himself.

In the crisis years of the 1980s, his models were twentysomethings who found his studio not through modelling agencies but via personal networks. Sometimes he would place an advert asking models of all shapes and sizes to get in touch. Those 'muses' are now approaching old age against the backdrop of a very different crisis: the Covid-19 pandemic.

Time has left more than a mark, and the series will therefore culminate in a self-examination of the photographer, who will have to face his own deterioration through his lens alongside the decay of his generation. 'The decline on the other side of the camera says a lot about me.' Each one sadder and wiser yet proud of themselves and their art of survival, the models from the 1980s are ready to be rephotographed all these years later.

Marc Verhey, another of the muses, had first met Erwin while manning the cloakroom at DOK, a gay disco on Amsterdam's Singel. 'He was straight, but he sure knew how to look hot.' Celebrities such as Freddie Mercury, Eartha Kitt, Grace Jones, Rudolf Nureyev, Elton John and David Bowie would also occasionally show up. It was one big party, Marc Verhey recalls. He looks back on that time with a certain wistfulness – perhaps simply because it coincided with his youth. 'It was the carefree and tolerant 1980s. Now, I sometimes think we're heading straight back to the Middle Ages.'

Erwin is much less nostalgic. 'I never yearn to go back to those days, although I have fond memories of them. You're more ignorant in your twenties and think everyone's like you. You've just flown the nest and are ready to take on the world – full steam ahead and with a devil-may-care attitude.' All things considered, he believes tolerance has increased in recent years. 'You can be more yourself now than in the

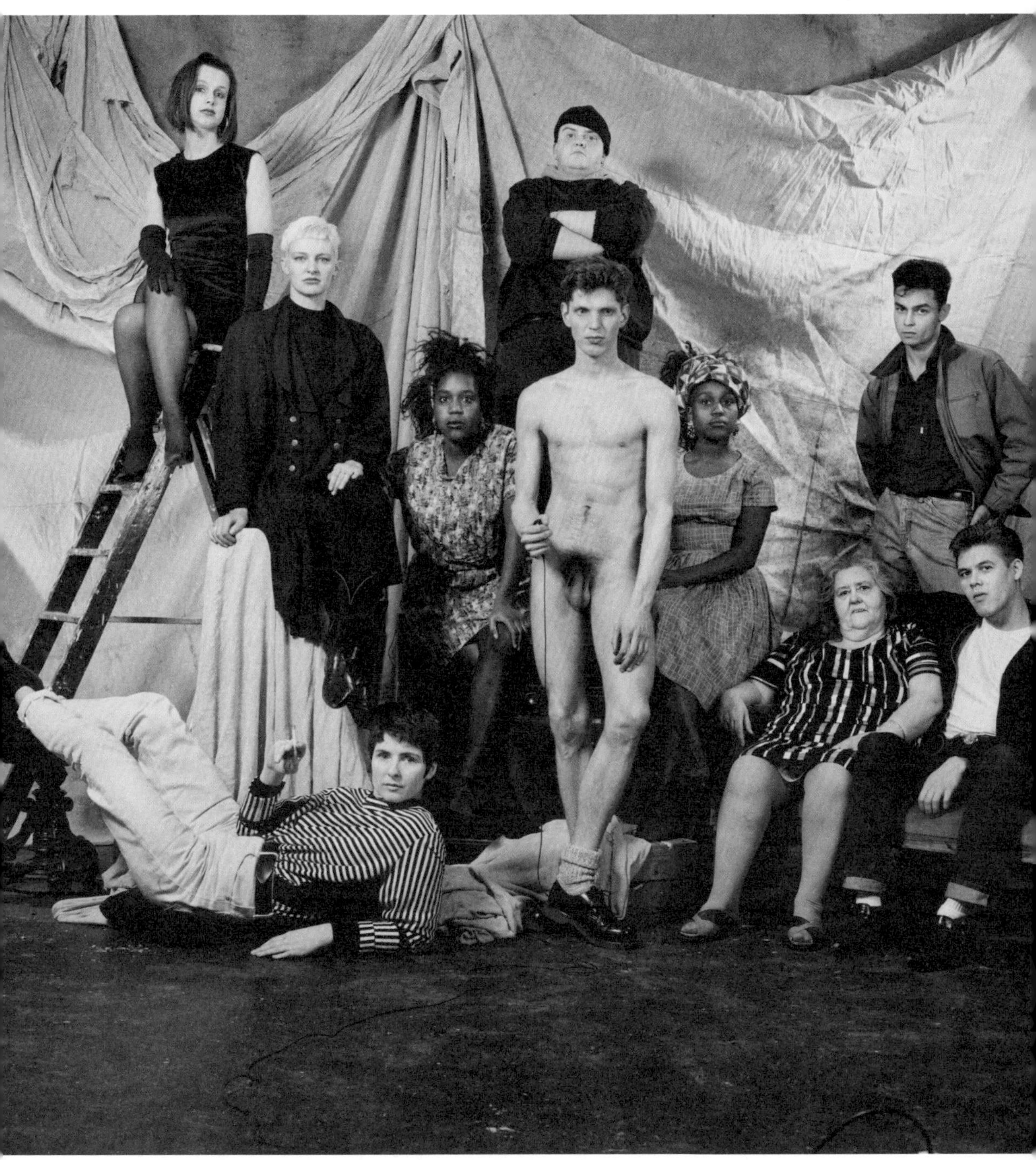

Team Erwin Olaf in 1987: Front, reclining, model Nelleke Strijkers. Back, from left to right Suzanne Venema, Sabien Jilesen, Ruth Louz, Jacques, Erwin, Marlies Louz, Marie de Nooyer, Rodrigo Lutgens and Marc Verhey. Photo on page 96: Erwin and *Self-Portrait, 30 Years Old, 1989*.

1980s. Albeit not in every neighbourhood. And the provinces seem to be more accepting than the cities nowadays.'

Erwin had asked Marc if he wanted to pose for a photo in *Gai Pied*. It was the beginning of a collaboration that lasted several years and culminated in the iconic photo *Joy*, which shows a naked Marc clasping a frothing champagne bottle before his groin.

First, there was an unsuccessful shoot where they raced through a bottle or ten – Erwin kept pressing the shutter too late. It was the era of analogue photography, and only in the darkroom did he see that the image looked 'more like pissing than ejaculating'. At the next session, they emptied another five bottles before the foaming, but eye-catching, result was achieved on the sixth. 'What it proves to me is that, as a photographer, you don't just wait for the decisive moment in journalistic photography, but that – even in the studio – you're dependent on that one magic second.'

Erwin couldn't afford to pay his model, and Marc Verhey, for his part, participated for the fun of it all. He received a dedicated print and a one-off fee of 595 guilders (about €270) from publisher Art Unlimited, who reproduced the image as a postcard. A pittance in retrospect, Verhey thinks, especially since the card quickly racked up a quarter of a million sales.

Strolling around Paris with his lover Teun Frieszo a few years later, Erwin discovered that someone had made a template of *Joy* and used it to spray the image onto walls. It felt like his first international recognition, and he proudly stood next to the graffiti while Teun took a photo.

But Marc did earn something else from *Joy*: he was allowed to assist Erwin for a period and ended up receiving champagne bottle postcards from all over the world, each bearing a myriad of flattering messages. 'I too was famous in a way.' Offers for commercials and a US video followed, which he turned down – afraid of ending up in the porn industry.

In his studio on IJselstraat in Amsterdam's Rivierenbuurt district, Erwin keeps things much simpler for the *Muzen* [Muses] series than he did in the 1980s. With one exception: the models are now expertly groomed by make-up artist Ineke Brugman. But he photographs his old muses in a documentary and unvarnished way. 'Now guaranteed without Photoshop,' he cries mockingly, referring to the criticism he once levelled at journalistic and documentary photography, where post-production editing was long considered taboo.

Today, it's Jacques Wolters's turn in front of the camera. Back in the day, Jacques was one of Erwin's favourite models because of his physique and willingness to adapt to the composition. They haven't seen each other for ages, but the connection between the photographer and his model is still strong. The result will be confrontational for both, Erwin thinks, and he stresses that Jacques should speak up if he doesn't like a picture. 'Would you like to see it, Jacques? The scars near your nipples are very visible. I like it, though; you're literally scarred by life.'

Erwin first met Jacques through his eccentric stylist Harrie Wildeman, who was full of anecdotes about his friend. As a young man, Jacques Wolters had fished Harrie out of the gutter in Arnhem and put him up for a while. Legend has it that Jacques had single-handedly taken on a gang of rowdy blokes who had jeered at him in a bar while he was out with two girlfriends. The assailants lunged at Jacques with bar stools, but by his own account, he ended up thrashing all five of them.

Erwin saw a picture in that story – 'I often get ideas from things people tell me, or tales I've heard about others.' He envisaged a strongwoman lifting a man over her head like a dead animal, and he knew it could be Jacques. When he initially proved untraceable, Erwin placed an ad in the newspaper: 'Jacques Wolters please call Erwin Olaf.'

'Erwin was a pretty insecure guy whose talent and ambition gave him a bit of confidence,' says Wolters. 'A sweet guy with a lousy little studio and a black curtain. With a clapped-out camera that constantly broke. Then he'd hurl things around the studio; he could get terribly angry. But when he was taking photographs, he was very serious and an almost obsessive perfectionist.'

That self-doubt of the early years – 'I'm always so insecure and therefore paranoid,' said Erwin in a letter – may have disappeared, but his perfectionism hasn't diminished, as the new session with Jacques shows. However long it takes, Erwin's historic muse does what he is told without complaint.

'Much prettier when your hands are hanging. Head tilted. Nice, tilt back slightly. Nose a bit more in that direction. Chin slightly down. Nice. Nose slightly up. Try some kind of strength in your eyes, yes. That one is nice. The one before that is very nice in terms of face. Relax your forehead. Pure confidence. Yes, that's nice. A little more to the top. Close your eyes. Nice. Open. Wow, that one's beautiful.'

Wolters has led a tumultuous life and is grateful that he met Erwin Olaf. Jacques was born intersex into a Jewish family where the prevailing belief was 'God is infallible' and 'men are men and women are women'. His father, a soldier who had always wanted a daughter, forced his child to adopt feminine characteristics via medication and inculcation.

At the age of fourteen, Jacques realised that there was something wrong with his upbringing and ran away from home. He developed an identity crisis. Later, when he was among the first people to register at a new gender clinic, he was referred to a psychologist. They advised him that he could either become very famous, which would permit him to do whatever he wanted without compunction. Or, as a form of self-exploration, he could embark on something radically confrontational, which would allow him to discover his identity.

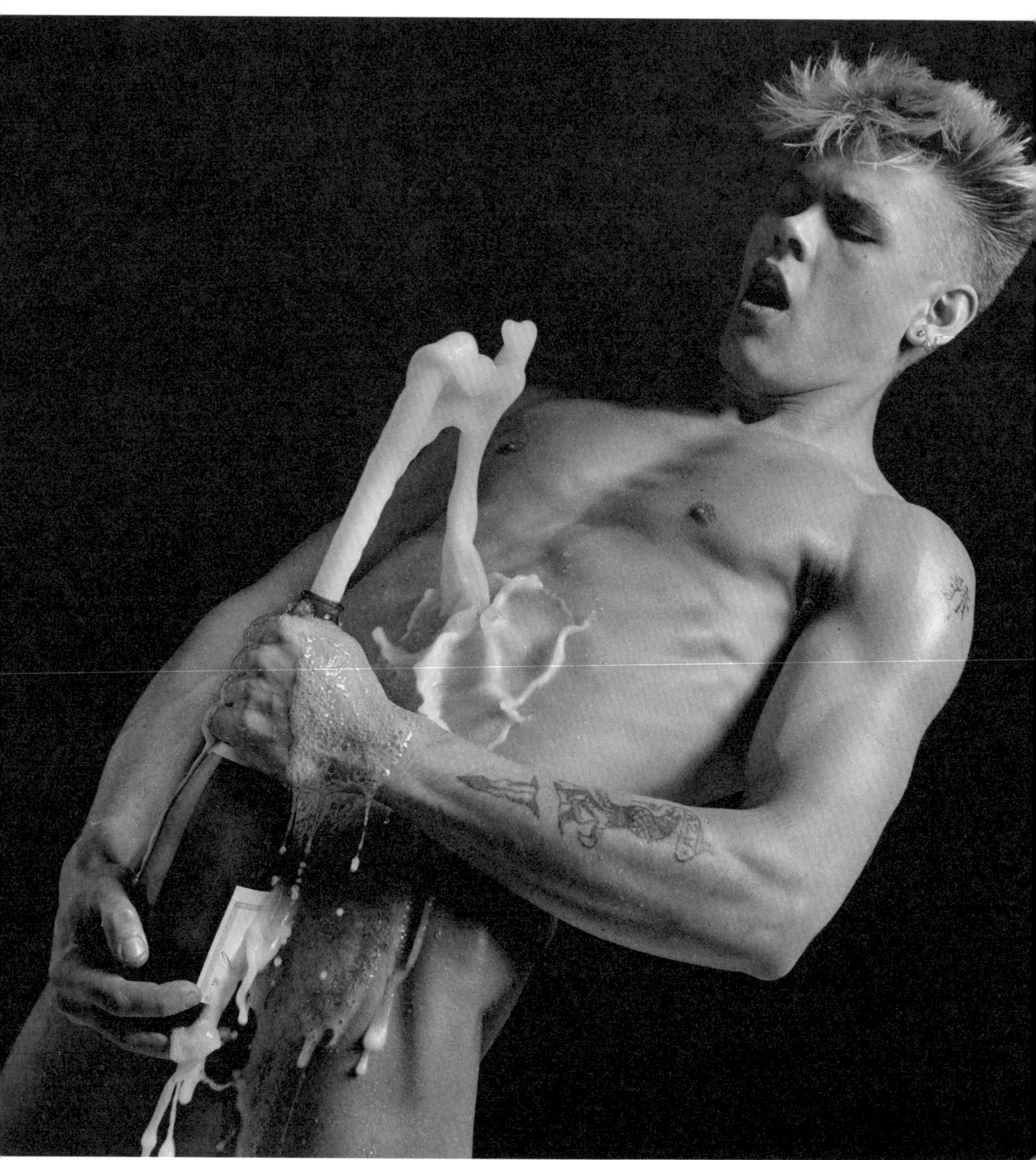

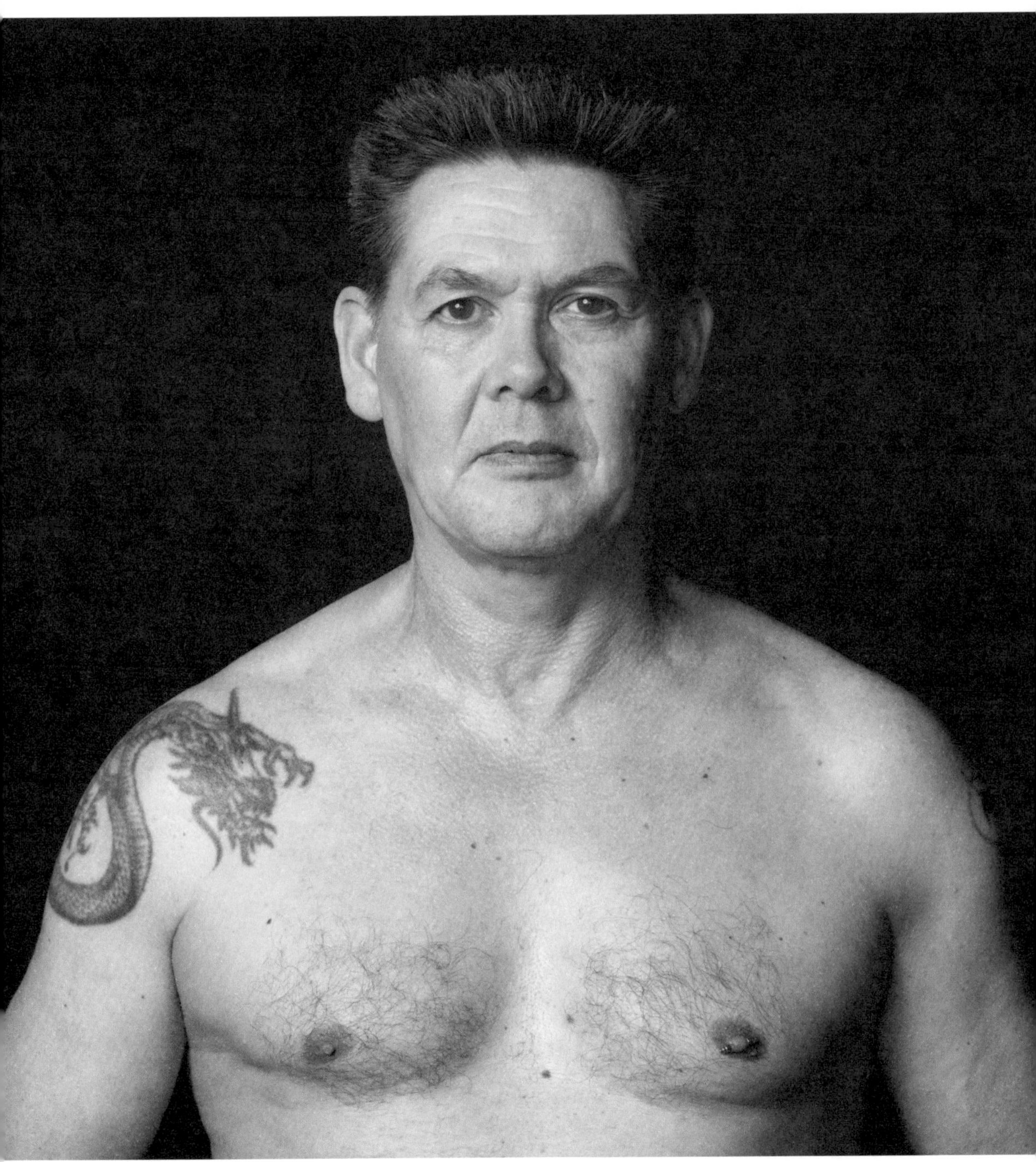

Left: Marc Verhey in *Joy*, 1985 from the *Squares* series. Right: Marc Verhey in 2021 from the *Muses* series.

Erwin's call came at an opportune moment. Jacques saw his chance to strip off in front of a photographer for the first time. 'Since Erwin didn't have any money, I suggested that he just give me a print. I thought, once I've got my hands on that nude photo, I'll know which way I want to go, male or female. I told Erwin: I'll pose naked in heels, or not at all.'

When he saw the image of himself as a weightlifter alongside the diminutive Rudolf, Jacques had an instant revelation: 'No way is this woman me! She's my ugly sister.' In a flash, he made up his mind to take the plunge and undergo hormone therapy at a gender clinic. He mused, 'In part thanks to Erwin's photograph, I am now known as Jacques, rather than Jacqueline.'

The promised print never materialised. And the more Jacques saw his hated female self, the more annoyed he became. The muse, feeling taken advantage of by the photographer, penned a letter to Erwin, expressing his dismay. 'Enough is enough, Erwin,' Jacques wrote. 'You keep ranting about these photos but stop exploiting me. It was meant to be private and exclusive.' He was grateful that the image hadn't already been plastered on margarine tubs. 'The pictures are starting to haunt my parents and me (they haven't wanted to see me since the postcard; well, tough, that's their problem').

Erwin and his muse Jacques Wolters enjoyed a long and happy working relationship, but it was not devoid of antagonism. They once had a 'massive row' about Jacques's transition, for example. Men who identified as women and subsequently underwent gender affirming treatment were a familiar topic. However, Jacques was a man in a female body, which was unfamiliar to Erwin. 'At first, I thought, Jacques is bluffing again. Because he could be quite theatrical. We once had a vicious argument in the studio that was so loud it could be heard on the street. When someone tried to ring the bell, a group of local thugs warned them, "Keep out! They're killing each other in there!" That was Jacques and me. But we quickly reconciled.'

There's no rancour, says Jacques. 'Not financially nor otherwise. I'm just grateful for that photo, which served as the spark for my transformation.' The true reward was the successful surgery, and its scars are still visible today as a reminder of the journey.

Erwin has changed tremendously and for the better, Jacques says a little later, while Erwin and assistant Piotr pause to deal with a faulty Softbox. 'He's become much more approachable,' Jacques explains. He used to say, "No, darling, I'm far too busy right now." He only paid attention to you when he needed something.'

Erwin wraps up the almost three-hour-long session with a declaration: 'Guys, I've got it, I think it's a fantastic series. Do you want to look, Jacques?' Together, the contemporaries scroll through the black-and-white images on the monitor, critically but also with some compassion on the photographer's part. 'This is absolutely me,' says Jacques. 'I've never seen myself like that before, so close, so beautifully exposed.

This is truly a fine old masculine head, with no drooping lips or anything. And then, somewhat moved: 'And the eyes... the eyes are incredible. I see my mother in them and my father, too.'

'I often photograph out of aggression; I've still got scores to settle'

LOOK AT ME!

This morning, Erwin is heading to The Hague to meet with Wim van Sinderen, curator of the Fotomuseum Den Haag, and his team at the Haags Gemeentemuseum (now Kunstmuseum Den Haag) to discuss his forthcoming major retrospective exhibition.

He is looking forward to his jubilee year, 2019, when he'll turn sixty, when all eyes will be on Erwin Olaf and barely any on Erwin Springveld. 'It tickles my vanity, and I get to shoot the breeze with journalists and gallery owners, but I'm so over myself. At some point, you become your own product. It's hard for me to overcome.'

The fact that he is one of the few Dutch artists who, from the 1980s onwards, has not only continually pushed the envelope, but also constantly reinvented himself, has never erased his basic insecurity. 'I am just a photographer. My trade has miraculously allowed me to earn a living since 1985, as well as for my studio staff. That's great. But it doesn't make me an important public figure. I don't have such pretensions.'

Preparations for the major exhibition in The Hague are in full swing. Van Sinderen is the driving force behind the project. He's been a fan of Erwin Olaf since the beginning, but it doesn't mean that they don't disagree about the hang.

They sometimes argue, but Erwin trusts Wim van Sinderen, a former picture editor at the pop magazine *Vinyl*. Van Sinderen has introduced Erwin's work to all the museums where he's worked, from the Kunsthal and Fotomuseum to the Haags Gemeentemuseum. This was a form of recognition for Erwin's artistic achievements. 'The rest of the art world hated me. Those arty people were disgusted by me and my work. I just don't get it. Sometimes, I think: Jesus, Erwin, you really tested them. With so many shit photos, so over-the-top, so provocative.'

Erwin didn't just start his artistic career in the 1980s. He also made increasingly commercial and semi-journalistic work. As a trained journalist, he was a perfect fit for the anti-establishment magazine *Vinyl*. In the early 1980s, inspired by hip English-language magazines like *The Face* and *Idea*, Van Sinderen wanted *Vinyl* to cover not only pop culture but also lifestyle, fashion and design. 'I was keen to turn a dingy punk magazine into an achingly hip *Avenue* for young people. I was an outsider

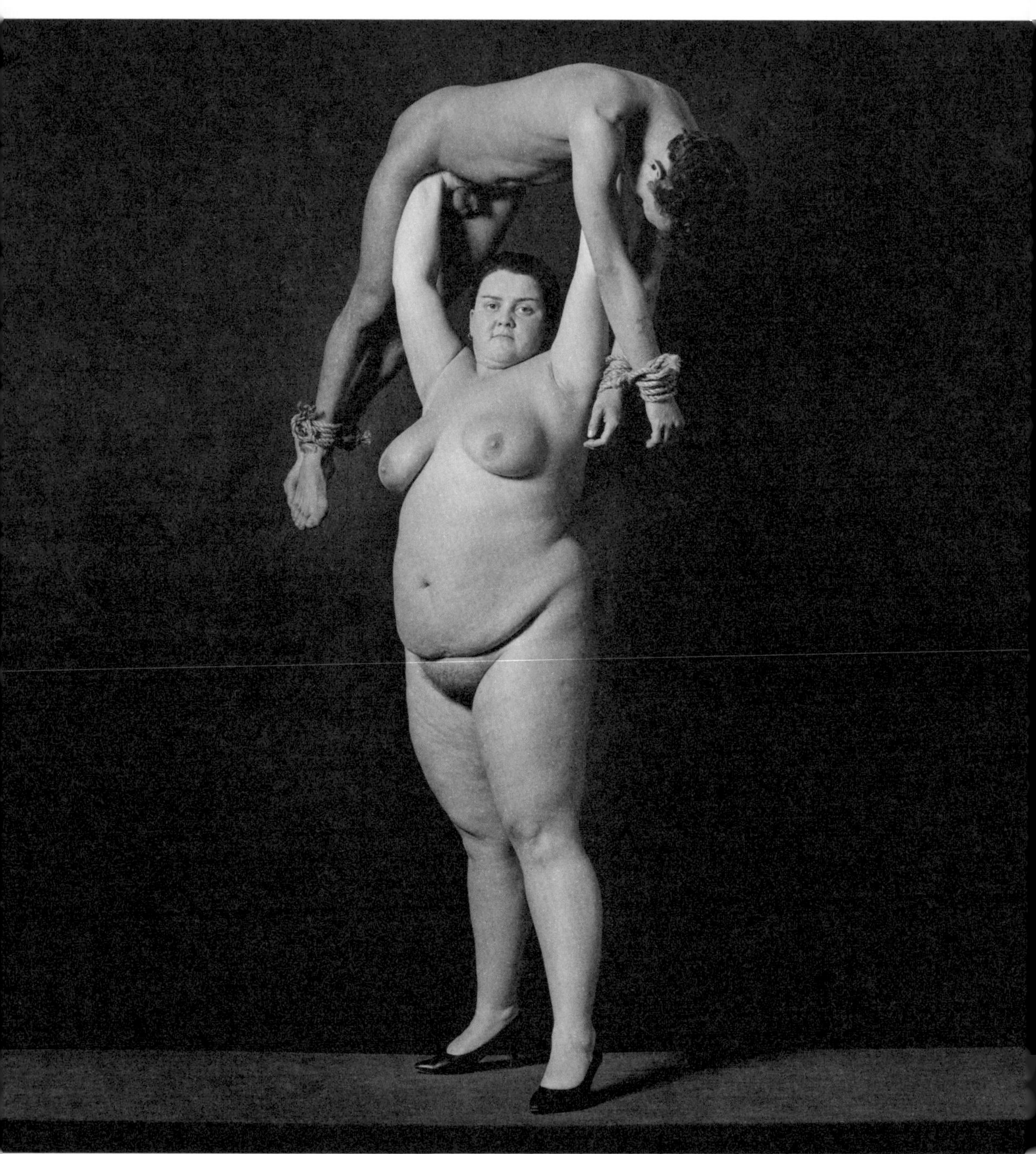

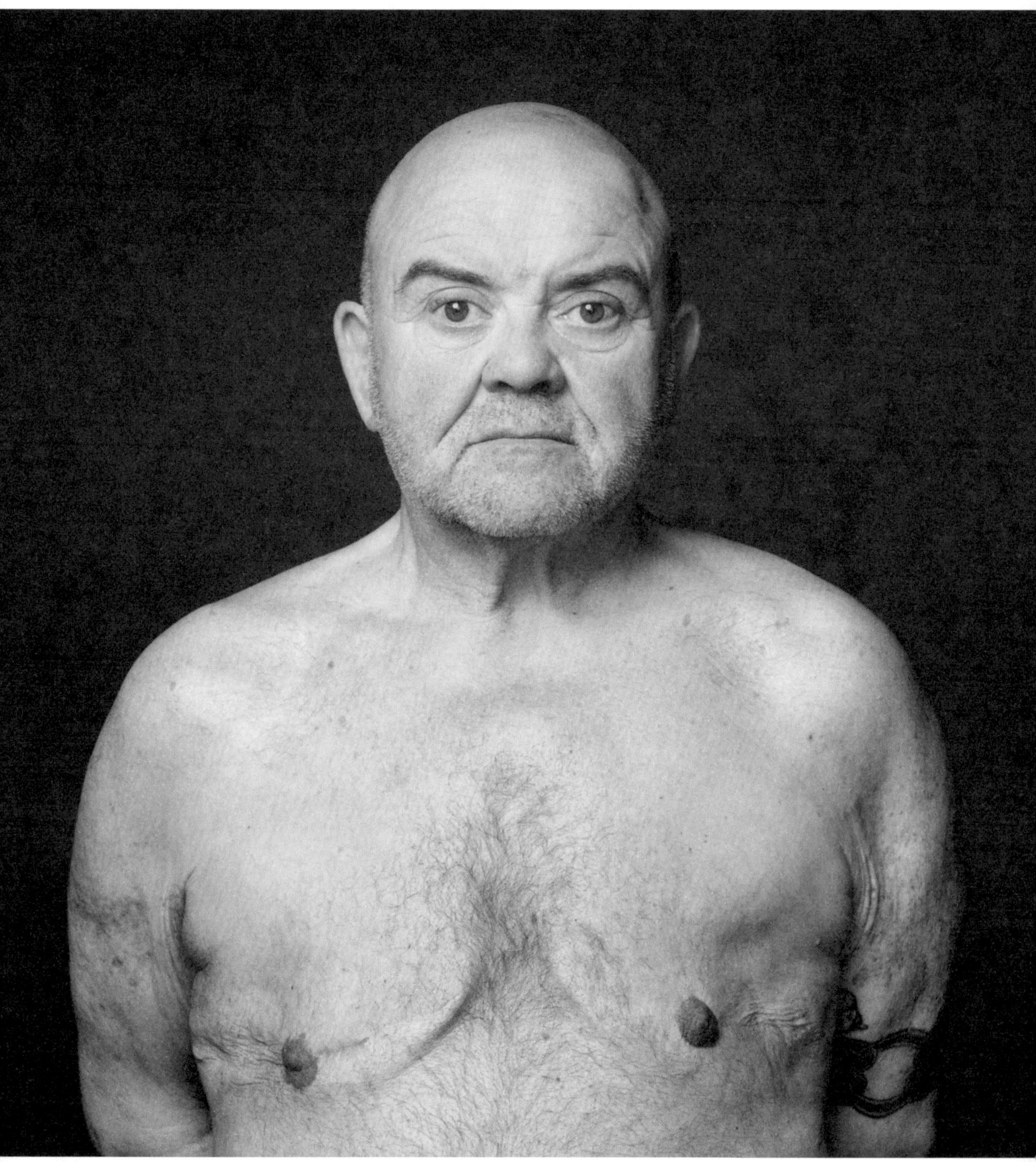

Left: Jacques Wolters in *Powerlifting I, 1985*. Right: photographed again in 2021 for the *Muses* series. 'And the eyes... the eyes are incredible. I see my mother in them and my father, too.'

in the editorial team, and Erwin was an alternative to a true pop photographer such as Anton Corbijn, who photographed for *Muziekkrant Oor*.'

Erwin Olaf met Van Sinderen through his former teacher, Dirk van der Spek. Erwin saw potential in the collaboration: he loved pop music and fashion. Van Sinderen had also positively reviewed *Stadsgezichten* and published *Powerlifting*, the photograph of Jacques Wolters and Rudolf Pfalz, across a full page. 'I was a huge fan of Erwin's early pictures for their clarity of style. And Erwin is very open about his influences.'

In the 1980s, the Hasselblad 6x6 returned in a big way, monumental and stylish. 'Peter Hujar was another photographer from that period, alongside Mapplethorpe,' says Van Sinderen. He describes Mapplethorpe as 'a rather unscrupulous careerist'. In 1976, Peter Hujar published *Portraits in Life and Death*, which included pictures of Fran Lebowitz, Susan Sontag and William S. Burroughs, among others. It is now considered one of the most important photography books of the twentieth century.

Erwin continued to photograph in that same vein and became a successful loner. Van Sinderen: 'He went all the way with it, and who wouldn't wish anyone that kind of reach and career? He created his own infectious world, not through careful planning, but through natural passion and determination.' He speaks with pride: 'The same man who now takes portraits of the royal family at the Palace on Dam Square photographed a girl regurgitating pearls for a fashion report in our magazine over thirty years earlier.'

Erwin Olaf's take on Vermeer's *Girl With a Pearl Earring* will be prominently displayed in the section of the exhibition dedicated to his early work. Van Sinderen and Erwin immediately agreed on this point. Singer Sabien Jilesen happily held a pair of long pearl earrings in her mouth. Erwin explains, 'It happened spontaneously. I found it more aesthetically pleasing than seeing the jewels on the ears.'

Erwin asked Jilesen, with her pixie haircut and mesmerising blue eyes, if she could adopt a 'lifeless' expression for the photograph. She had to stay motionless for half an hour as he meticulously adjusted the lamp to perfectly reflect in the centre of her pupils, highlighting the whiteness of her irises. But it was worth it. The work would triumphantly stand the test of time and was even acquired by the Stedelijk Museum.

Hripsimé Visser, who served as the Stedelijk Museum's photography curator for many years, still considers this to be a 'powerful image' and a 'brilliant' composition. 'It possesses a certain audacity and exaggeration that are typical of the period. It's related to fashion and advertising but transcends both thanks to its strong visual impact. That's clever. A masterpiece.'

Erwin was not part of Amsterdam's artistic circles. He describes them as 'cliques of men with winklepickers and thinning hair, cut in punky styles, conversing about

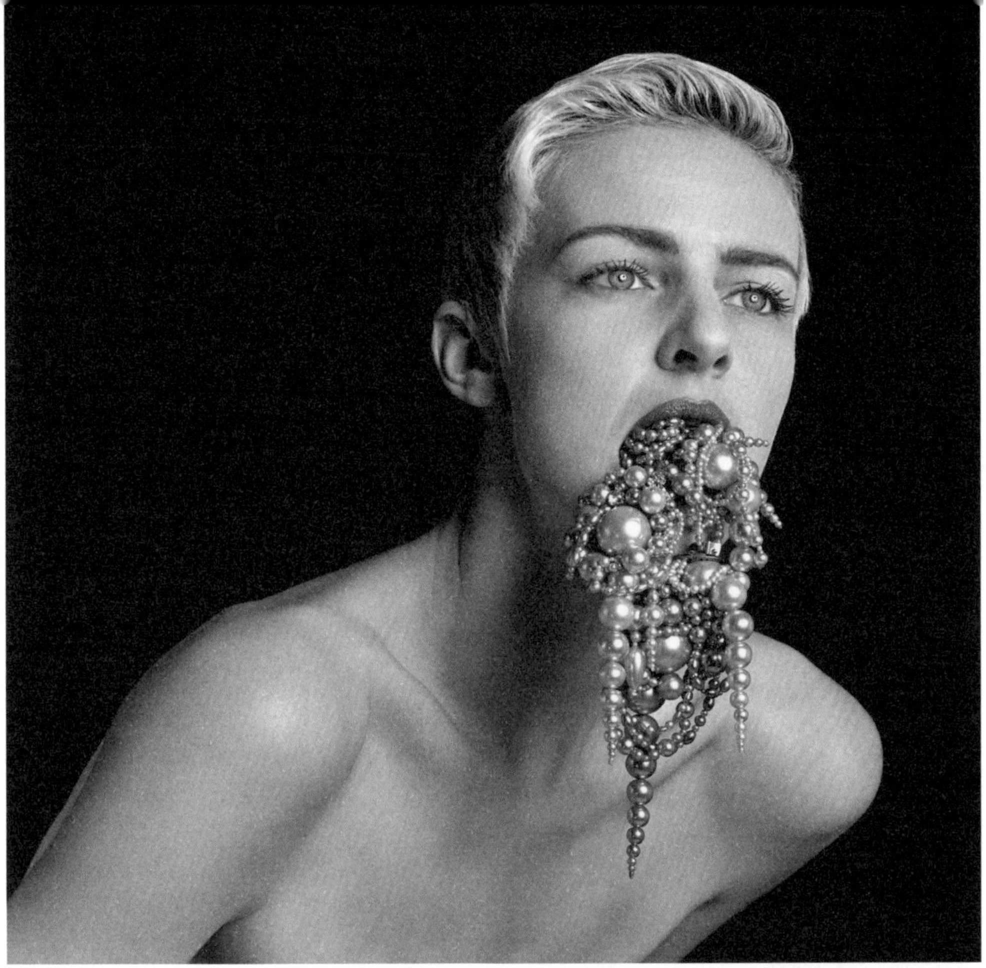

Top: Sabien Jilesen in *Pearls, 1986*, from the *Squares* series. Bottom: Photographed again in 2022 for the *Muses* series.

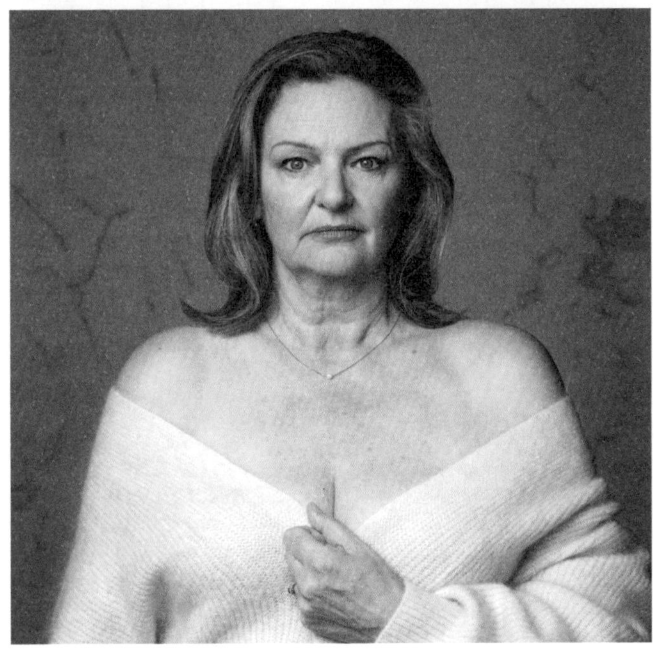

the Fine Arts, capital F and capital A. They consider themselves progressive and enlightened, yet it's all a sham. My goal is to expose their hypocrisy for what it is: worthless posturing from individuals who, when push comes to shove, turn their backs.'

He became a staff photographer at *Vinyl* and started training his lens on pop stars. This gave him a chance to erase the memory of his early failed attempts to capture Bowie and Iggy Pop. For the *Vinyl* covers, Erwin switched from black-and-white photography to colour, a transition that many photographers were struggling with in the late 1980s. Back then, black and white often stood for 'documentary' and 'truth', while colour was associated with knee-jerk commercialism. Moreover, it was difficult to edit colour photos in the pre-Photoshop years.

Erwin had always felt comfortable with commercial photography. He had trained as a journalist rather than an artist, and he didn't consider commissioned work to be inferior to his creative output. From the very beginning, he financed the latter through fashion and advertising photography. According to *NRC Handelsblad*, he became the 'trend-sensitive Netherlands' favourite photographer' thanks to his 'brutal' photos.

He paid scant attention to the celebrity world of pop, preferring instead to seek out his own subjects: people who piqued his curiosity, whom he could place in scenarios of his own devising. 'Pop stars tend to be the most awkward, annoying and boring people, full of their own hype, and you always have to run around after them.' With fresh reluctance, he photographed international stars such as Joe Jackson, and Mick Hucknall of Simply Red. But it was the Beastie Boys who made him wait in a corridor for hours, which brought everything to a head. 'I thought, I must be out of my mind; I'm not getting paid enough for this. What, three pimply boys? So, I opened that dressing room door without knocking and started taking pictures.' Singer Mike Diamond was so irate that he charged at him. 'I legged it with the cameras round my neck and I knew, at that moment, that I'd never willingly subject myself to that kind of treatment again.'

When David Bowie was due to play the Paradiso, the temple of pop, as part of his Glass Spider Tour, Erwin and his older brother, Jos, saw a chance to make good on their previous and unsuccessful photography mission. From the moment that David Bowie entered the room, Erwin was captivated. He'd positioned himself in the front row, camera at the ready. 'Bowie asked the room full of journalists, "Does anybody have a question?" So, I volunteered, "Yes, me!" To which David Bowie replied, "What is it?"' Erwin, who by now had clearly transformed from a writer into a visual journalist, shouted, 'Look this way!' Just as Bowie spun around, Erwin pressed the shutter. 'So much for my chat with Bowie,' he thought.

Through *Vinyl*, he discovered the weekly *Vrij Nederland*, where he quickly gained an enthusiastic admirer in editor Ingrid Harms. 'His photographs were unlike any-

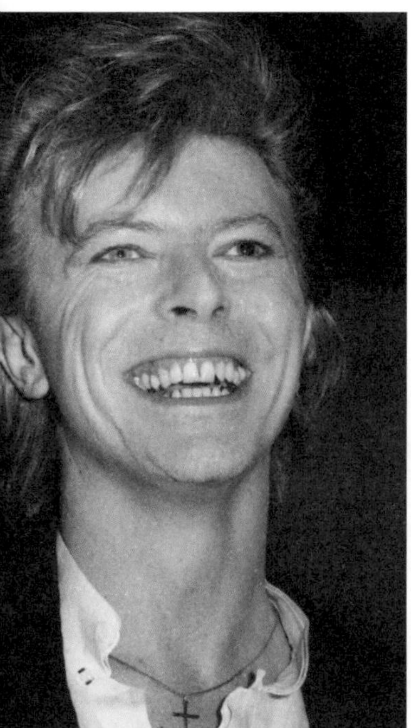

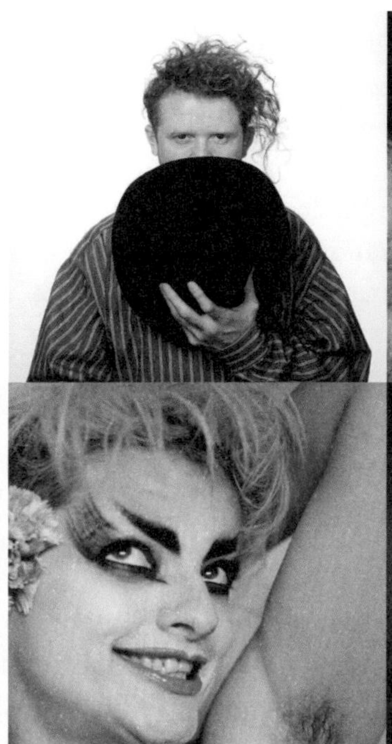

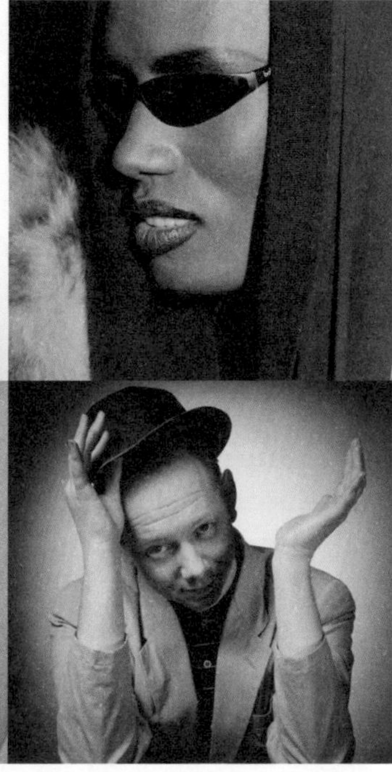

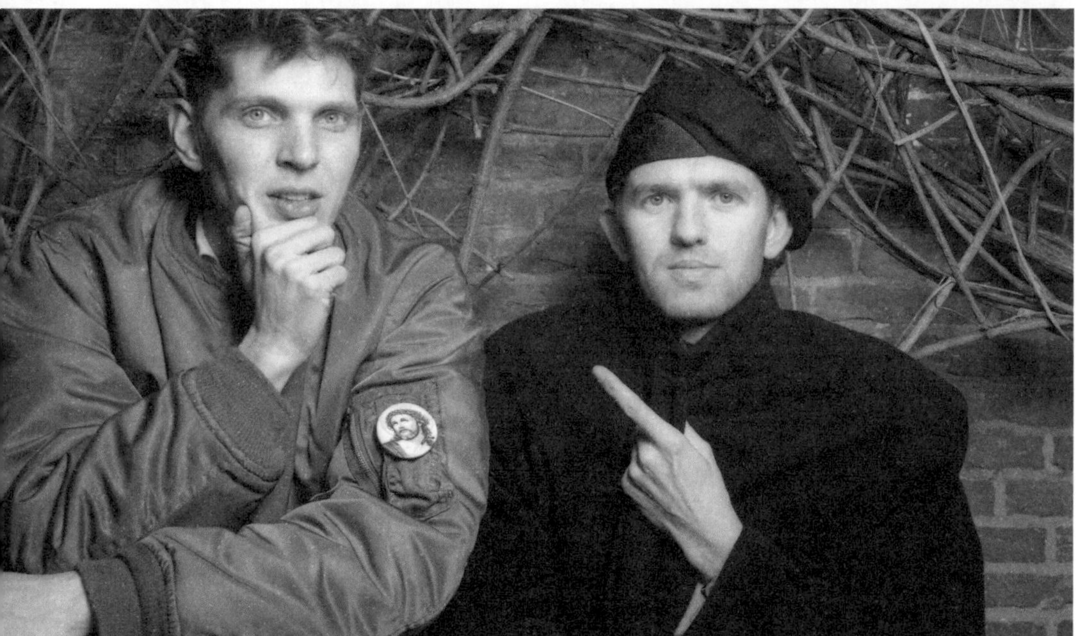

Bottom: With Anton Corbijn. Corbijn photographed for the music magazine *OOR* while Erwin did a stint photographing pop stars for *Vinyl.* Top, clockwise: Erwin's photos of David Bowie, Mick Hucknall, Grace Jones, Joe Jackson and Nina Hagen.

thing else at the time,' Harms recounted. '*Vrij Nederland* was all about social photography. Erwin chose the studio. His work was funny, glamorous and alternative – a touch androgynous.' She continued, 'He sidesteps the well-trodden path, is honest, doesn't look down on people and can be as sly as a fox, but he has a finely tuned antenna for humiliation and injustice.' A portfolio of Erwin's work appeared in the leading reportage and photography 'colour supplement' of *Vrij Nederland* (in August 1987). 'I'm fascinated by unusual people,' ran the headline.

'Photographer driven by aggression' was the initial strapline for *Vrij Nederland*. Erwin was initially taken aback by this headline, as the portfolio was supposed to mark his breakthrough into mainstream photography: 'I thought, what kind of bullshit is that?' He gradually realised that it was an apt description.

As a matter of fact, he'd confessed as much to his interviewer, Ingrid Harms: 'I often photograph out of aggression, I've still got scores to settle. I find it very shallow, but I'm still haunted by those boys who threw me into the bushes, and into those nettles that stung me, both inside and out.' Later, he would even come to regard the early bullying as something positive, a history that had made him go 'like a rocket' in his work. 'No one could trip me up anymore, as I'd already faced the worst. I responded in my own way. I didn't throw punches in the schoolyard, but I did in my career. And that's why I have a fabulous life now.'

Erwin regarded the *Vrij Nederland* article as a 'groundbreaking piece of journalism'. It not only reached a new audience but also resonated with the cultural elite. However, he was already contemplating a new series, a departure from his usual style. 'Erwin doesn't follow the beaten track,' said Ingrid Harms. 'He doesn't think, "This is running smoothly; this sells well; I'm in someone's good books now".'

'God knows, it was a hedonistic time'

Erwin had moved his studio to a spacious semi-basement at Swammerdamstraat in Amsterdam-Oost. It didn't look like much on the outside, but behind the shabby door on the somewhat dilapidated street was a large space that he shared with two of his Utrecht painter friends, Frans Franciscus and Suzanne Venema.

'It was all booze, drugs and photography, with Erwin's tantrums thrown into the mix. It was downright frightening at times,' Marline Williams recalled. Filmmaker Bert Pot, who once interned for Erwin, still recalls the chaotic atmosphere in the studio. 'When you locked your bike, you could hear Erwin laughing uproariously on the phone or erupting in anger. His explosive moods could be heard before you even

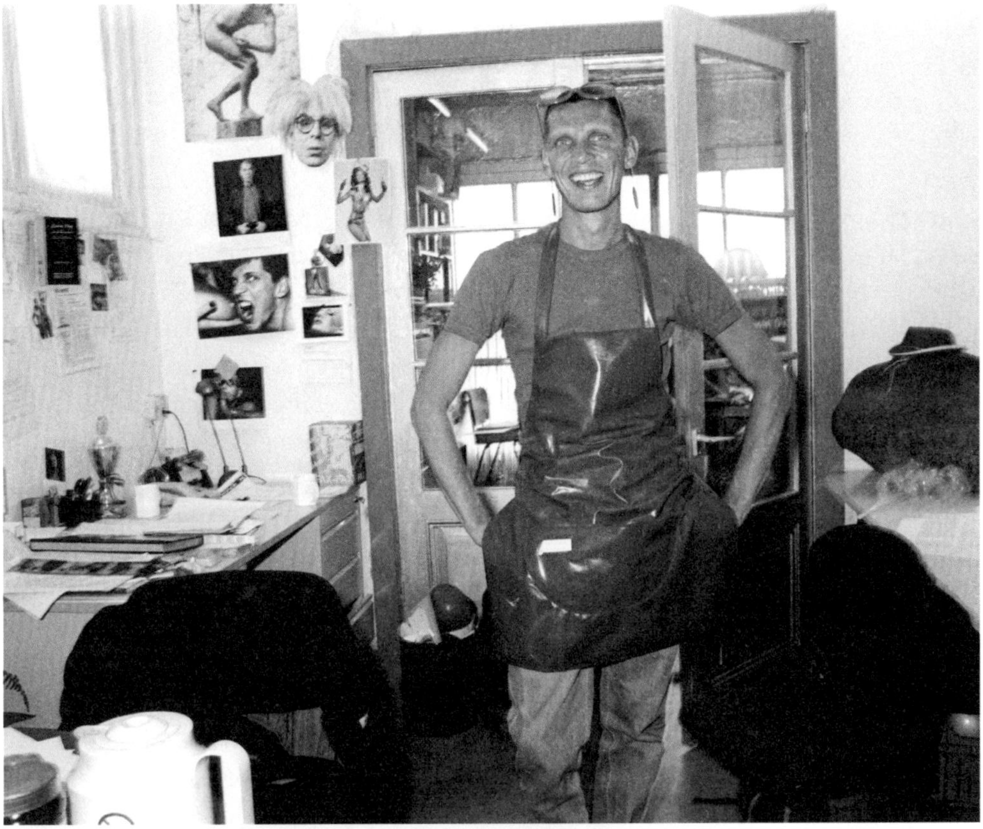

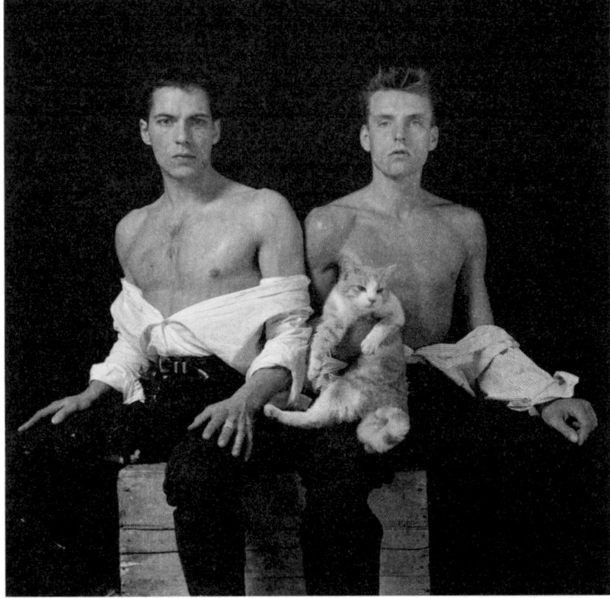

Top: Erwin in the Swammerdam-straat studio.
Bottom: Photographer Paul Blanca and poet Koos Dalstra.

stepped over the threshold. It was extremely intense, because, for Erwin, there was always something at stake.'

But there was also plenty of recreation, recalls Erwin: 'God knows, it was a hedonistic time. I was always high, and a badass woman with a coffee shop near the studio was our go-to dealer. ... Biodynamic weed though, mind you.' Photographer Thomas Manneke, who completed a six-month internship in 1991, recounts: 'Erwin told me: what happens in the studio stays in the studio. It was no secret that Erwin used cannabis every day; it made him cheerful and good-humoured. He did say, however, "If you catch me smoking while I'm still taking photos, grab the joint out of my hand".'

Franciscus noticed that his old friend was becoming famous not only via his work, but also through the Amsterdam club scene. 'One of the reasons that Erwin became so well-known is because he knew almost everyone on the clubbing scene. He raised his profile by going out a lot and organising his own events. In retrospect, I wish I'd done the same. That's how you build a big network.'

Rineke Dijkstra, then on the cusp of her own successful photographic career, admired her one-month-older colleague, who had already gained recognition through exhibitions, publications and interviews with esteemed interviewers such as Ischa Meijer and Theo van Gogh. 'We came of age in a wonderful era,' she said. 'There was so much strong, new photography that we could take as references. Black-and-white photography was giving way to colour, while we were still stuck in the monochrome age. You often have to produce both colour and black-and-white prints for commissions, but these are two completely different ways of looking which, in turn, determine whether you focus on colour or form and light.'

Erwin was not a role model for Dijkstra in terms of subject matter as his interests were very different. 'Still, I admired his work. It had a Mapplethorpe influence, but it was also very original. ... Here was someone who wanted to control everything. Just as a painter starts with a blank canvas, he creates his world from scratch using studio sets.'

Although they did not cross paths frequently, Dijkstra occasionally visited Erwin. 'Studio Swammerdamstraat was a time of great joy and happiness. ... It was so much fun, and everyone wanted to be part of that world. It radiated positivity and energy. You could really laugh with Erwin as he wore his heart on his sleeve. I was quite reserved, but he would tease me ever so gently. Yet we always held each other in high regard and respected each other's work.'

His star rose thanks to his weekly portrait series for *Haagse Post*, in which he photographed other ambitious contemporaries, such as the filmmaker Theo van Gogh, actor Thom Hoffman and presenter Paul de Leeuw. His true breakthrough as a photographer of artistic calibre was his *Chessmen* project, which earned him his first award in 1988: the German Prize for Young European Photographers.

After publishing *Stadsgezichten* and his photographs in *Vinyl*, Erwin started to experiment. His former mentor, Dirk van der Spek, had taken over the photography magazine *Focus* in 1985. Van der Spek was keen to collaborate on a book project. Erwin was initially hesitant due to a lack of material, but Van der Spek assured him that a book only needed to be sixty-four pages long. Which translated to thirty-two photographs with a white page opposite each image. Surely that would work?

That same evening, Erwin listened to a radio broadcast featuring renowned chess master and writer Hans Böhm. Böhm discussed his fascination with the strategic battle between the thirty-two pieces on a chessboard. Although Erwin had never been interested in the game, he was enchanted by the idea of a life-and-death struggle between two armies. Furthermore, the number of pieces matched the number of pages in Van der Spek's book proposal. Over the course of the following days, he read a classic textbook on chess. He swiftly advanced to the first round of shots.

'Of course there's a sexual element, but it's not as extreme as people think'

Erwin continued to socialise with Hans van Manen. He was a regular guest at his mentor's dynamic soirees, which were full of creative people: 'A bit of drugs, alcohol, intense conversations, sharpening each other's ideas, learning from the discussions, everyone adding something to the mix. I just sat there, as green as grass. Not to mention the mirrors and lines of coke that were constantly circulating. It was exciting, but I was terrified that I would sneeze or snort the whole pile in one go.'

He later regretted the drugs, as detailed in a letter to Frans Franciscus. 'If I decline, Van M. gets uptight or cross. I resolved not to take anymore, but four days later, I'm already bent over the mirror again (didn't look too bad). I don't know if it's from the coke or the stress, but I'm clenching my jaws all day. For weeks!'

The indefatigable Van Manen may have been difficult to keep up with in terms of narcotics, but his advice was golden. He suggested that Erwin call his new series *Chessmen: An Attempt to Play the Game*, rather than just a simple, one-word descriptor. The subtitle embodied the essence of the project which, in a way, was akin to a photographic warm-up exercise.

The shoot culminated in an ominous chess set with unrecognisable figures, including pregnant women and little people. Despite his continuing doubts, Teun, Hans van Manen and Frans Franciscus urged him to complete the series. He sometimes berated Frans for his tardiness: 'How do you like the pictures I keep sending you? I'm not paying for postage to hear nothing back! I want a reaction!' His chess match, dubbed 'the brutal clash between white and black', was variously described as 'innovative' and 'visually stunning', but also as 'veiled S&M' and 'luxury porn'. He had intended to create a code for making non-sexual photographs with sex toys, he explained. 'Unfortunately, it was misinterpreted. I thought people would see the horns as a joke. Alas, not. Of course there's a sexual element, but it's not as extreme as people think.'

His old friends had mixed feelings about the series. Marline Williams, in particular, was taken aback by its success, describing it as an 'awful battlefield' and 'heavy and ugly'.

Erwin was the first to downplay the series's quality. He admitted in an interview that only four of the thirty-two photos were truly successful. Which is understandable because, in his view, you could only really expect to produce four good photos in four months – the time he had allocated to the project.

He only rates four of the images: 'the woman pulling a boy along in a cart; the chicken skewered on a bayonet; the guy with the boulder tied to his back; and the pregnant woman with the little person.'

Erwin would only later articulate what the series was really about: his aggression, fears and inner struggles. It was only then that he recognised the perversity of *Chessmen*. It was less harsh than Mapplethorpe's work because 'that's not my kind of sexuality' and not as morbid as Joel-Peter Witkin's oeuvre. Yet both remained important sources of inspiration. Mapplethorpe for his subjects, as well as the simplicity and compositional strength of his images. 'He photographs a flower in the same way as an open arsehole.'

Unlike himself, Witkin took his work deadly seriously. He incorporated extreme elements into his photographs and deliberately scratched his negatives. Erwin's approach to photography was more carefree and impulsive. He often met unusual or unconventional people in clubs or elsewhere who, in turn, sparked his creativity or an idea for a scene. He preferred 'slightly strange people with beautiful flaws'.

Women whom others perceived as obese filled him with a mix of emotions. 'I did something scandalous with them: I bound their bodies or made them pull a chariot. But I lit them beautifully, so their skin looked gorgeous and soft.' Or he picked an angle that imbued them with heroism. He was captivated. And they were worthy. Strong women reminded him of his mother, 'and I still think she's the most amazing woman'.

It wasn't just the emotions, which he saw as akin to those invoked in Visconti's films, but also because of the photographic possibilities. The buxom female models, with their voluptuous and undulating forms, all light and shadows, weren't so different from the bodybuilders in his earlier work. He also felt a sense of solidarity with these models: they too were outside the norm. 'When I see how they must carry their weight, I'm incredibly moved. At eight years old, I expect they were bullied as much as me. They too were sidelined during gym classes. Always the last to be picked and I know that feeling well.' He advertised for nude models in *de Volkskrant* – 'over 100 people responded' – while Jacques Wolters also returned to the studio for *Chessmen*.

When he first met Marie de Nooyer, the former manager of the famous (and infamous) café De Nooyer in the Jordaan, it was love at first sight. 'The moment I saw her, in that big floral dress, with her glasses and her bun.... She came in and said, "Hello, I'm Marie." And at that moment, in the blink of an eye, I had a grandmother. Done deal! Really, such a fun woman, so easy-going, live and let live. Marie embodied liberation. A one-in-a-million woman. She taught me how to relax and enjoy life. Without her, I wouldn't be as famous as I am today.'

Erwin's early models played a vital role in the creative process. He didn't follow a set formula for creating and shooting scenes – that never worked. Instead, he collaborated with his models, who fed him ideas and were open to his bold suggestions.

The photographer's initial idea of photographing a constricted Ria Franken, 'tied like a joint of beef', was not so much his own fantasy, but the model's suggestion. Franken and her husband, Freek, had visited the studio and she wanted Erwin to photograph her for what she was: a masochist, a slave. She wondered why Freek, her dom, couldn't just tie her up as he did at home.

Ria Franken transforms into a voluptuous, horned woman in *Chessmen* – a semi-underground creature – who pulls a boy along in a cart. This image is also the result of her collaboration with Erwin. He explains, 'I can't invent something like that. The ideas flow while we're working. I need to see the person before me and, very often, they'll spark an idea. That's the difference with Witkin, who photographed his own fears. He constantly repeated himself as a result. You sometimes wonder if that story hasn't already been told. I realise people go through periods of despair, but you must find a way to eventually break free of those feelings.'

Although Erwin's photography was not documentary, he used it to show something he had encountered in reality. He wanted to erect a monument to the outsiders of this world, the true outcasts of the earth. 'Of Ria, and my other muses, I dared to ask the strangest things. And they trusted me enough to take the necessary risks. Marie de Nooyer, for instance, was willing to do anything, no matter how old she was at the time. No matter how crazy the idea, she always thought it was great fun. She was a true inspiration.' The same applies to the other models from this era, whom he thanked at length in *Chessmen*: 'The actors of the 1/125 second made it possible to photograph, with rare intimacy, a hidden people.' The photographs had emerged from a game of tender manipulation, wrote the brand-new publisher Dirk van der Spek. 'The models are captivating in their dignity, timeless, heads held high, and elusive in black and white.'

Erwin's liberal-minded models allowed him to tread new paths and explore the complex interplay of power and vulnerability. What accounts for people's submissiveness? Why do certain people strive for power at the expense of others? These two questions are ultimately the theme: the haves and have-nots of power. 'I'm angry at everything and everyone, angry at the Western world. A good-for-nothing like Reagan dresses up in a three-piece suit, yet still plays dirty. Thatcher also happens to be an impeccably dressed woman, yet she persecutes gays in England. And now we've got Le Pen in France, another well-turned-out man. Morals have vanished; it's all about the packaging.'

Dirk van der Spek's vision of a beautiful book came to fruition after a search for the optimal black-and-white print. Erwin, ever the perfectionist, discovered in the nick of time that the printer, on his own initiative, had slightly cropped his square-format photographs. As a result, the entire first edition had to be pulped. Van der Spek sold all 4,000 copies of the reprinted volume and ordered a reprint – a resounding success for a photography book.

While the presentation of *Stadsgezichten* had involved a modest celebration, the opening for *Chessmen* turned into an extravaganza. 'The most intense party I've ever experienced,' Van der Spek recalled. Amsterdam's Utrechtsestraat was blocked off and thronged with people. Jacques Wolters gave a speech, and publisher and gallerist Van der Spek noticed that 'all the queens' had dressed up in 'extravagant waiting staff outfits', with ultra-short skirts. The party spilled out onto the street and brought the tram to a halt – so the driver suggested the passengers disembark and watch the spectacle.

In his introduction, Van der Spek noted that Erwin Olaf had shot to fame. The press later reported that he had been 'discovered'. Before the making of *Chessmen*, Erwin Olaf had considered his photos to be somewhat disjointed. Whenever he presented work to gallery owners, they invariably stated it lacked 'a connecting thread'. Frans Franciscus, who was himself becoming increasingly recognised as a visual artist, discovered his friend's ability to develop himself into an idol 'from scratch'. Newspapers increasingly wrote about his meteoric success.

Erwin was beyond ambitious, and the more famous he became, 'the more he craved fame and recognition', as he acknowledged himself. The recognition did not bring out the best in him. He'd always been envious of other people's success, and the feeling hadn't dissipated. At the same time, he was the first to put his growing status into perspective. In the world of modern photography, he positioned himself in the middle ground and acknowledged the harsh reality that, 'If I die tomorrow, no one will remember my photographs.'

Moreover, he told film-maker and interviewer Theo van Gogh that being 'world-

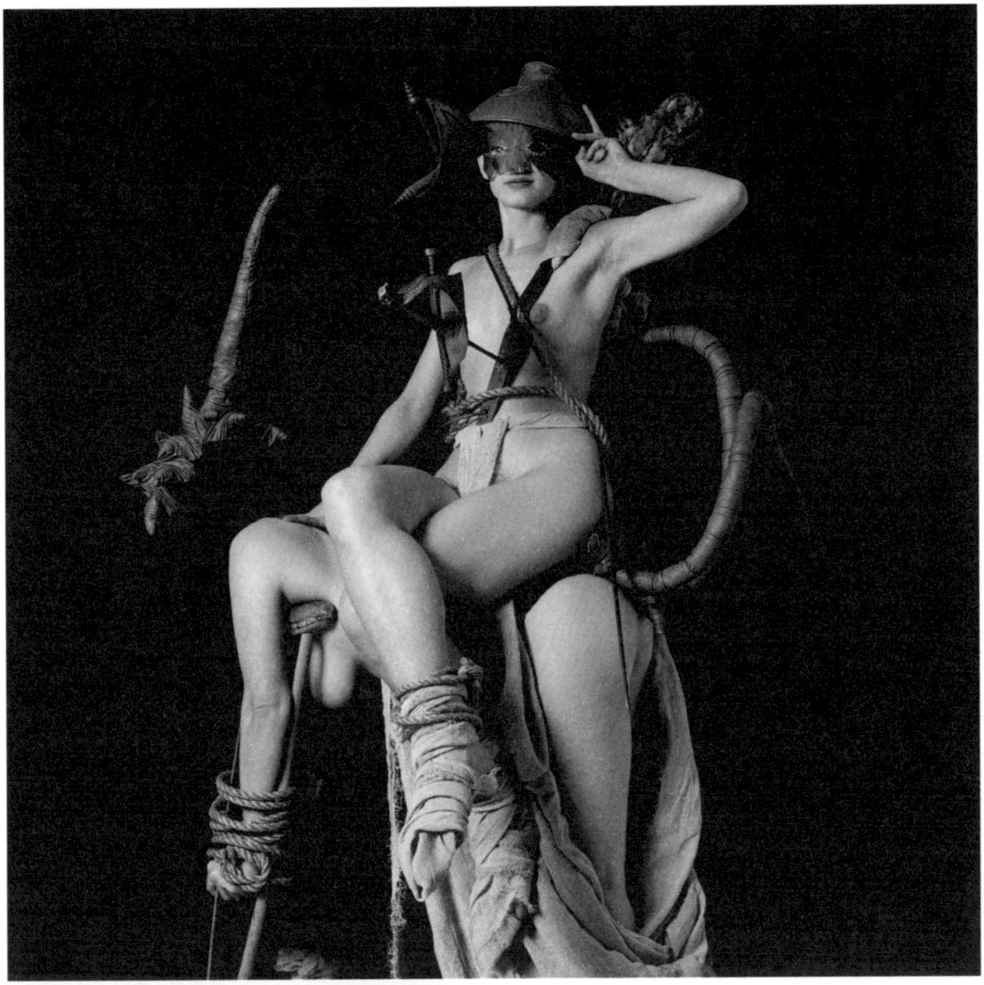

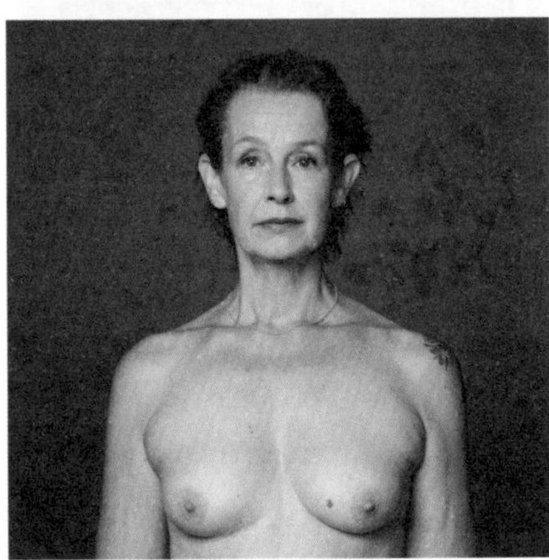

Top: *Chessmen XIII*, 1988, the first photograph in the series, taken in 1987 with the title *Knight 1* with Suzanne Venema on top.
Left: Suzanne Venema photographed in 2021 for the *Muses* series.

famous in Amsterdam' was not an unalloyed joy. 'You receive fan mail, a model offering herself, people approach you saying you make beautiful things. Ad nauseam. I'm insecure enough as it is and it's only going to get worse and worse and worse. And naturally, I'm a total scaredy-cat.'

A middle-class man captivated by other people's 'audacity' – as the antithesis of his own mundanity and because it made life a lot more interesting – was how he'd previously characterised himself. He hoped that his work would be praised for its beauty or written off as 'abysmal'. Which seemed to be the case with *Chessmen*, as even Theo van Gogh acknowledged that he'd managed to 'evoke the joyfulness of a concentration camp without the need for barbed wire'. Van Gogh, who shunned few taboos himself, felt Erwin Olaf gave his audience a glimpse of hell in *Chessmen*, showing his fellow human beings as 'insects under a paving slab'. He captured them in a frozen moment, either 'inflicting or suffering pain'.

If people saw his pictures as provocative, taboo-breaking, or even racist or sexist, Erwin considered it a positive sign. It meant that a spark had been lit, that an emotion had been elicited. At this time, he didn't worry too much about what the art critics thought of his pictures, claiming with bravado that 'I take criticism from four people: Hans van Manen, my friends Teun and Frans, and my mother. Everyone else can take a running jump.'

He wasn't surprised by the media's fascination with his new photographs. In a conversation about the American artist Jeff Koons, he identified the parallels in their work, noting that 'Koons only really became famous when he started messing around with La Cicciolina. That's the similarity between Koons's work and my pictures: cunts and dicks abound.'

According to Erwin, the sensationalist media naturally paid attention to his work, which they otherwise neglected. 'The entire journalistic community screams "woohoo" at the prospect of porn; it's an excuse to print a bit of tit. Koons knows how it all fits together, and at my level, I also understand the mechanics of it.' The *Chessmen* series not only made him famous, but it also continued to haunt him for a very long time.

'Nude photography is even more one-sided than regular portraiture'

THE ROXY YEARS

'It's been ages since you last photographed me, darling,' says Zu Browka International, all blonde locks, pouting lips and high heels. 'Do your other muses still look as ravishing as this after all these years?' On this glorious spring day in 2021, she stands before his camera in the darkened studio with green-painted nails and a bare torso. A golden necklace adorned with the letters 'ZU' dangles between her breasts, while her left arm boasts a huge tattoo of her surname.

Erwin guides Zu Browka, who long ago changed her baptismal name to that of her favourite vodka brand, towards a red cross on the studio floor. He understands that even a seasoned performer like her needs a compliment to feel comfortable in front of the camera. 'You look absolutely stunning,' he remarks, gazing through the viewfinder. 'After all this time. Despite all the partying.'

Just before the pandemic, in 2020, she received the 'Je Suis Zu' award, named in her honour, for her contributions to the city's nightlife. Mayor Femke Halsema praised her, saying, 'You represent the freedom, spontaneity and unconventionality that make us proud of Amsterdam.'

Many decades earlier, Zu had shamelessly let rip in Club RoXY as a stark-naked cage dancer or sex worker. In nocturnal Amsterdam, a decadent fairy-tale world was constructed, where Erwin Olaf felt at home. It was a universe of extremes that would inspire him for years to come. He was not so much bold as shy and nervous: 'When queuing at the bakery, I carefully examine my own reflection, afraid to place an order.' He enjoyed seeking out the company of the uninhibited. 'I'd say to a transsexual at the RoXY: I'd love to photograph your cunt one day. And then suddenly you're on your knees staring right up at it. What could be more beautiful?'

Some four decades later, Erwin is sitting in the studio canteen with Zu Browka during a break in the shoot. He has photographed numerous nudes over the years, but the process still puts him on edge. 'Behind the camera, you're in a strange position of power. Nude photography is even more one-sided than regular portraiture, which is already far from equal.' He acknowledges that the power imbalance may have led to erotic situations, but that it was never intentional.

Erwin notes that no #MeToo-like cases have landed at his door, even though he felt nervous when the Weinstein scandal erupted in 2017. It led to an onslaught of accusations against film producers, casting directors and photographers, with famous figures in the industry being accused by models of sexual abuse or harassment. 'You start to wonder: is there someone, somewhere, who still has a bone to pick with me or wants to pull a fast one? My business partner Shirley den Hartog and I thoroughly investigated whether anyone might come out of the woodwork, but we couldn't see any potential issues.'

Sex is also apparent in his later work. He therefore understands the relevance of the #MeToo movement. 'It makes sense, given that my models are highly vulnerable. The power imbalance can have an erotic aura, for both the viewer and the subject of the image. While you could say that I'm a voyeur in the professional sense, I am not a sexual one. I lose interest if the other person isn't aroused. The other person's arousal is what I find attractive.'

As a young man, he occasionally felt exploited. 'I had the idea that if someone gave me a drink and wanted to 'be with me', then I had to comply and go to bed with them. So, I have, on occasion, dragged myself upstairs against my will at so-and-so's place. I harboured a lot of naivety at the time, but I quickly realised my mistake.'

Erotic tension rarely emerged during photo sessions, but when it did occur, he would continue working, focusing 'coldly' on the composition or cursing a malfunctioning flash or incorrect shadows. Guys would occasionally hit on him in the studio. 'I talked to Hans van Manen about it once; we lacked courage. I've never had the nerve to approach those handsome men.'

Two exceptions, however, stand out. One of them goes by the name of Alandus Weertman. Erwin met him in 1989. 'Alandus completely blew my mind with his fluttering eyes,' he says. A photo shoot led to the creation of a striking portrait that appeared in the *Squares* series. The portrait shows a rake-thin Alandus dressed in a clingy, strapless dress, with stripes. The hem fans out at the bottom and is secured to the floor, left and right, by large nails. Weertman remains proud of the image, which he describes as 'so incredibly simple, lacking the ornate details that Erwin had become known for at the time. It's this minimalism that makes it so effective.' Weertman remembers that Erwin exuded confidence and control behind the camera but, in all other respects, he felt very insecure. 'He described himself as "just an obscure little photographer". I responded, "No way! You're extraordinary. You should be proud of yourself".'

During the photo shoot, sparks flew between the two men, marking the beginning of a long-lasting love affair that ran parallel to Erwin's relationship with Teun. Initially, the competition made Teun jealous, but he eventually developed a friendship with Alandus. Later, they could often be seen drinking champagne together at exhibition openings.

Apart from Alandus, the only other seriously erotic photo shoot was with a bisexual model in 1992. Pope Jerrod hailed from America but had recently moved to Amsterdam via South Africa and Paris, where he'd modelled for Issey Miyake. Erwin had met him backstage at the RoXY and went on to photograph him for the *Blue* series, among other works. Some of these images decorated a public toilet in Groningen. 'The guy deeply affected me, and we had a brief relationship. He was a womaniser, but I represented a rare exception, or so he told me.'

Erwin also occasionally posed for photos, sometimes semi-naked. In 1989, he created *Self Portrait, 30 Years Old*, for which he wore a corset-like dress with a hole for his erect penis. This did not constitute exhibitionism but rather a form of reciprocity. He wanted to demonstrate that he was prepared to be as vulnerable as his models, as a way of strengthening the mutual bonds of trust.

His mother criticised the way he presented himself. 'First, she asked if the penis was fake, and I told her that it wasn't. Then she replied, "Well, that's disgusting, then!"' But ultimately, Lida Springveld felt that Erwin had to make independent decisions in his life. She laughs: 'I couldn't just pull him out of his studio, smack him around the head, and order him, "Right, off home with you!"'

He eventually understood that his mother was right. 'In *Self-Portrait, 30 Years Old*, my penis is like a machine gun, a weapon that I'm aiming at the world in self-defence. ... It only gradually dawned on me that my obsessive vanity was a defence mechanism that I needed to relinquish.'

Erwin's assistant, Piotr, adjusts the lighting for the second session with Zu Browka, who is paying the price for her globetrotting performance antics in the form of a worn-out hip joint. She lumbers over to the green sofa in the middle of the studio and carefully arranges herself, fully naked. With this series, Erwin wants to show how the nocturnal creatures and avant-garde artists of yesteryear have aged. They comprise his peer group and, like him, they lived hard and fast in the 1980s and 1990s. Today, they are approaching retirement age. It is a documentary project, and he refuses to sugar-coat anything. However, he needs to ensure that his subjects feel at ease with, and even proud of, what he creates. He keeps emphasising this point.

'If you dislike something, then we'll scrap it,' he reassures Zu, who worries about the state of her chest. The almost sixty-year-old entertainer dreams of having the 'lumps' on her drooping breasts removed. She still celebrates the day she became a woman, which she calls 'my second birthday', but her prostheses, now thirty years old, desperately need replacing. But she can't afford such an expense.

Although Erwin wants to keep the *Muzen* series very simple, with 'staccato-like, face-on portraits, plus full-length ones, either seated or reclining', the session lasts an hour. Everyone works hard: the photographer, the assistants and, of course, Zu Browka herself. Faint muzak plays in the background, far removed from the RoXY's thumping acid house.

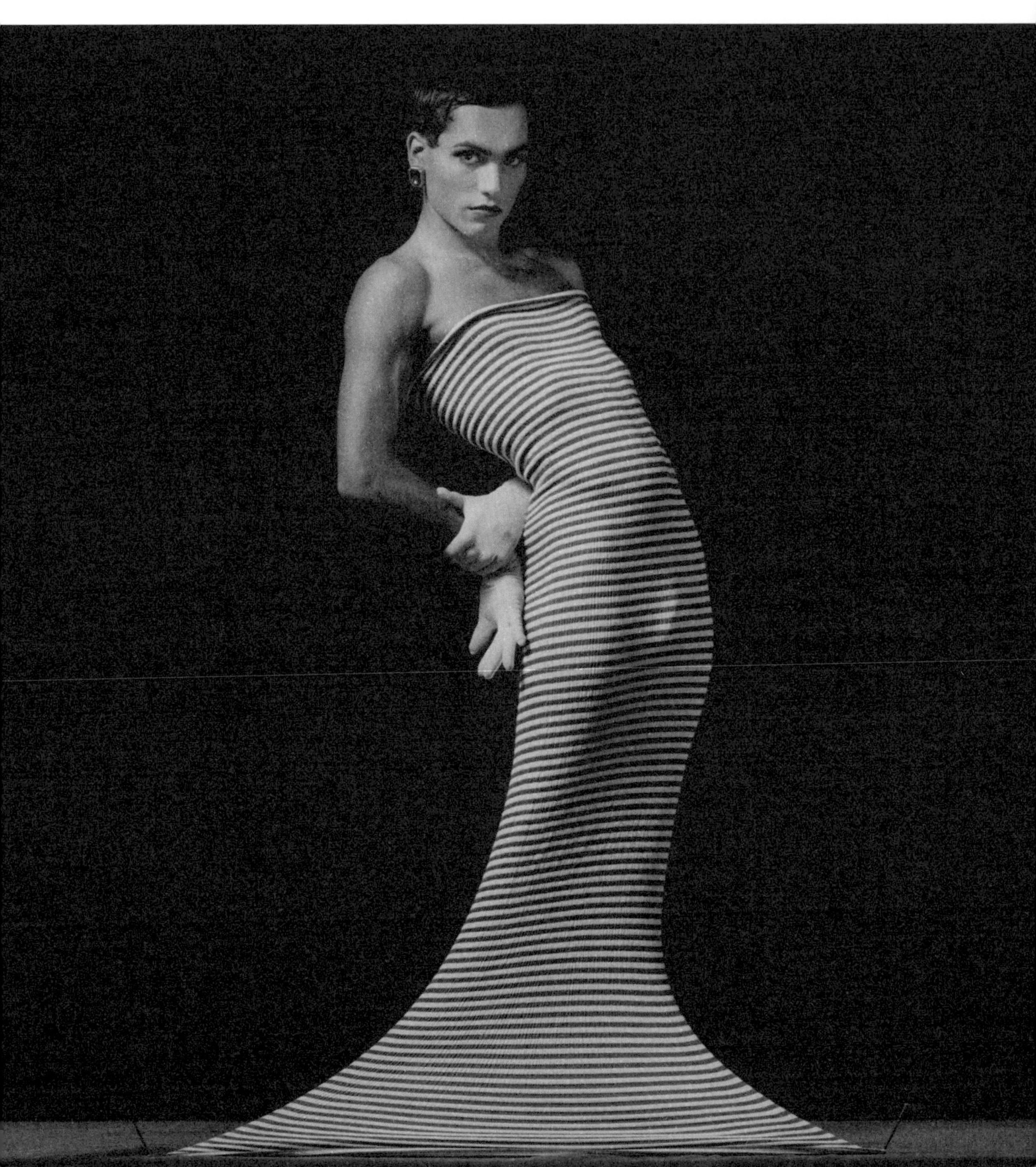

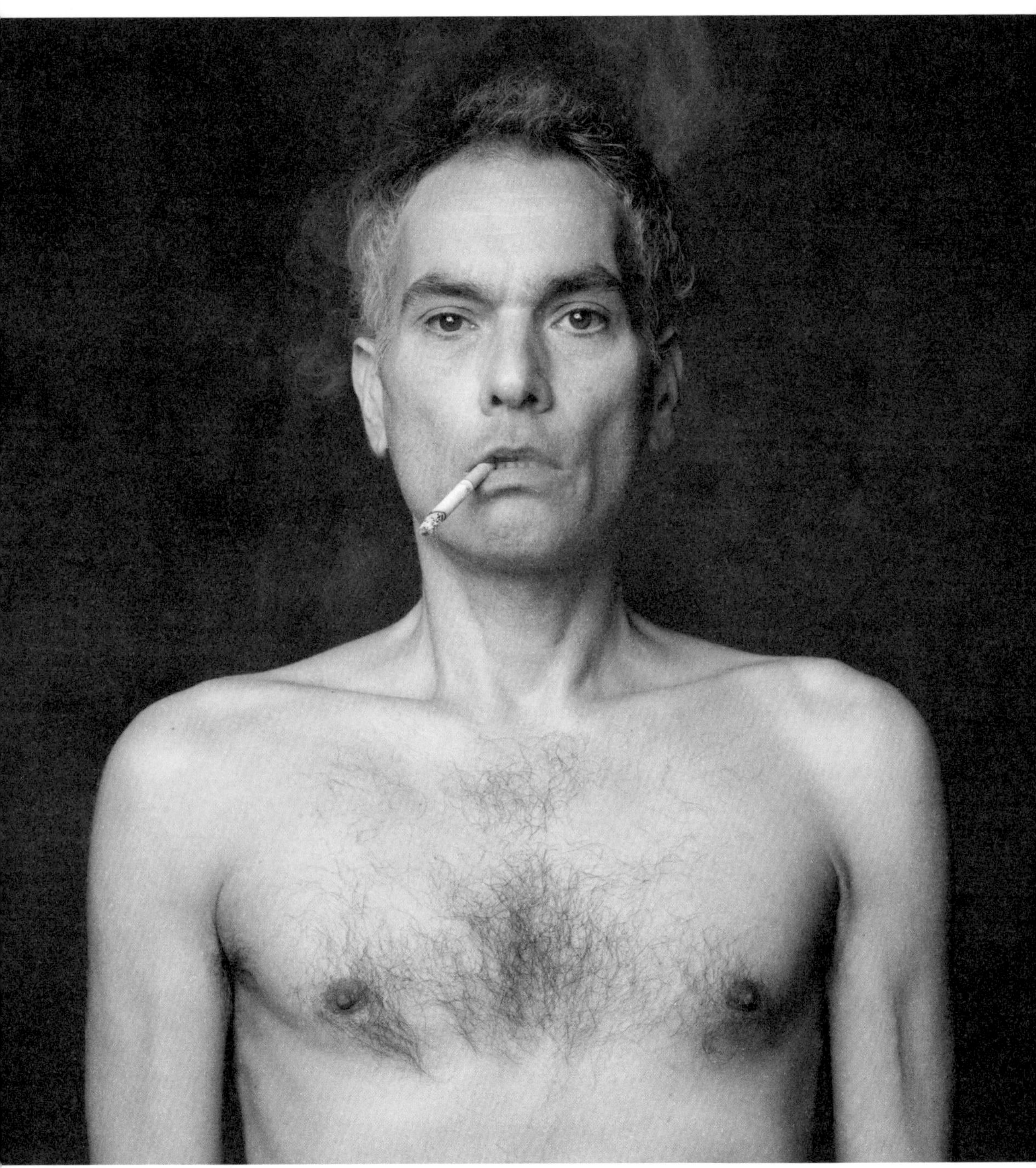

Left: *Alandus, 1990*, from the *Squares* series. During that shoot, sparks flew – the beginning of a long-term love affair. Right: Photographed again in 2021 for the *Muses* series.

'The RoXY quickly became my second living room'

It was at the RoXY that Erwin first encountered Zu. The venue had opened in 1987 with a launch party that presaged the extravagance and glamour that the founders envisioned. A five-tiered cake decorated with sparklers was lowered from the ceiling, filling the room with a fizzing, scintillating light.

The RoXY club, dubbed *a priori* 'legendary', represented a collaborative venture between Peter Giele, Arjen Schrama of *Vinyl* magazine, and DJ Eddy de Clercq. De Clercq was on the lookout for a new location to host parties after his extravagant celebrations at De Brakke Grond, the De Mirandabad and Paradiso. They were as creative as they were under-resourced: they lacked a building and money. Giele, whose motto was *ab igne ignem capere* [one fire lights another], lived a riotous life. He stumbled across a vacant property on the Singel, behind the old Roxy cinema on Kalverstraat and, in one fell swoop, solved one of their biggest problems.

They drummed up the money via an early kind of crowdfunding scheme: friends and acquaintances agreed to stand surety for part of a 50,000-guilder bank loan (€22,500). Erwin was also approached. 'The RoXY quickly became my second living room. I'd have lost my money if they'd gone bankrupt.' Insolvency didn't seem like an impossible scenario. Eddy de Clercq had imported the latest dance music from Ibiza – namely the acid house that was rapidly gaining popularity on the hip island – but he initially seemed too far ahead of the curve. The Netherlands, and even Amsterdam, weren't ready for the new music that facilitated hours of uninterrupted dancing.

De Clercq's acid house rarely attracted more than a few dozen enthusiasts to the dance floor during the early sets. The music wasn't Erwin's cup of tea, either. His musical tastes were quite safe, according to friend and DJ Joost van Bellen. 'I love seeing people let rip on the dance floor, but never joined them,' Erwin admitted. He sometimes regretted holding back and wishes that he'd been more outgoing in such an extroverted environment. 'I still feel a sense of shame, even when I'm alone. I've always felt as though several cameras are trained on me – that I'm under constant scrutiny. That shyness manifests as a superiority complex and an inferiority complex, all wrapped into one.'

In the summer of 1988, a year after its opening, the RoXY organised the Acid Gala in a desperate attempt to reverse its fortunes. Erwin was also involved. Zu Browka fascinated him because she performed nearly every week for almost nothing – 'they paid me a pittance, but yes, the drinks were on the house'. This is where their collaboration began. 'Erwin needed to submit a photograph for a weekly magazine, but he was stuck,' Zu reminisces. 'So, I audaciously declared, "I'm performing a show in a mud bath at the RoXY tonight. Take pictures!"' From that point onwards, she was one of Erwin's favourite subjects.

Zu Browka documented every aspect of her transition from man to woman, often naked and unfiltered, but always infused with humour. Shortly after receiving her new breasts, she sneaked out of the hospital to reveal them onstage that same night. When she finally got her vagina, she proudly displayed it for all to see.

The voyeur and the exhibitionist had found one another. In Zu Browka, Erwin saw a courageous woman who was willing to try anything – and he was smitten. And Zu saw Erwin as an appreciative observer and an eternal bystander, even on the wildest nights out. The latter's most outrageous attire was an Ajax football shirt bearing a photo of Johan Cruyff.

Jacques Wolters, who captured as much of the RoXY universe as he could on his movie camera, often had Erwin in the frame. Yet the latter remains inconspicuous in the otherwise vivacious crowd. 'Erwin rarely sought the spotlight. Like me, he's a voyeur of his life. He perceives reality through his camera lens, shaping it to match his desired perspective.' The film footage shows Erwin dressed in his other favourite T-shirt – this one emblazoned with CCCP (the Russian acronym for USSR, Union of Soviet Socialist Republics) – in the company of Zu Browka, or with a sign advertising an amusing and endearing offer of 'free sex with Erwin Olaf' with his phone number attached. 'Nobody called me,' he laughs. 'It's sad.'

The organisers had chosen Zu as Miss Acid Queen at the Acid Ball. People distributed bags of 'pills', which contained sweets, but the message came across loud and clear: a new party drug called ecstasy was on the scene. Erwin served as a judge, alongside former Shocking Blue singer Mariska Veres and Australian performance artist and fashion designer Leigh Bowery. 'Leigh was formidable – big and shaven-headed,' Erwin remembers. 'And he was a born performer.' Bowery often came to the club with his great friend Boy George, who was a performance in his own right. Leigh always wore a mask or heavy makeup, sometimes enveloped in a cloud of tulle. When he discovered clogs, he wore them out the very next evening – with high heels wedged inside.

The Miss Acid Queen beauty contest, which revolved around a battle between the delicate Zu and her Surinamese rival, the strapping Percy, ran over two nights. It came to a frenetic climax involving a pillow fight on a soapy beam above a mud bath. Erwin loved the elevated melancholy of it all, as 'Percy relentlessly pummelled Zu into the muck.' She was seething, and didn't show her face at the club for several months afterwards.

The Acid Gala at the RoXY marked a key moment in the success of acid house in the Netherlands. Once ecstasy became the party drug of choice, it was impossible to look back. It saved Amsterdam's extraordinary new epicentre. 'In those two months, a tiny pilot light became a raging inferno: the audience was converted.' Acid house's dominance also created the first celebrity DJs, according to Joost van Bellen. 'After all, these were faceless dance hits. It's the DJ who weaves the tracks into a musical narrative, and in so doing, they transport the audience into a state of ecstasy.'

The RoXY stood at the forefront of the Second Summer of Love, which the UK had declared in 1988. Steve Malenka, programmer of the 'Hard!' gay Wednesday night, described the RoXY as 'the birthplace of the love generation', saying that 'you could step inside and leave your heartache at the door'. The RoXY had already become a key meeting place for the queer community. Especially for those nights, Giele designed heavy faux leather curtains for the corridor to the toilets with crotch-height glory holes and circular openings. All manner of things could be inserted through the apertures.

Erwin didn't appreciate the gay-men-only evenings. In his view, your sexual orientation wasn't confined to certain times or places. Nevertheless, the extravagant décor chimed with his *Chessmen* series and S&M-themed assignment that he was working on for *Vrij Nederland* at the time. With his lifetime membership card, Erwin soon became part of the club's furniture. For many years, the RoXY was a sanctuary where he and his friends and girlfriends could be themselves. The club served as a meeting place for myriad creatures of the night, not to mention celebrities such as Diego Maradona, Prince, Elton John, Grace Jones, William Burroughs and Mariska Veres.

The smoke machines ran at full speed, the fire burned bright, while the fuel consisted of a generous selection of alcohol, poppers, ecstasy, amphetamines and cocaine, although the RoXY technically banned the latter drug. For Erwin, a natural observer, it was a feast for the senses. 'In the late 1980s, society became very hedonistic, and I reported on it in my own way. My work is highly personal, but I was also part of the zeitgeist and played a role therein.' The theatrical nature of the club scene influenced his photographs. 'Nightlife as theatre. Its baroqueness – it inspired me greatly.'

'In the clubs and in my pictures, everyone is celebrated for their scars, be they physical or mental'

His photography and the events he co-organised shared a common theme. 'You construct your own reality, which you have the power to mould and shape. You choose the angle of the light and can create an entire world out of cardboard. You think collectively: once you open the door, we're free. You can fully embrace decadence and strut onto the stage with a huge phallus. You can play with gender, sexuality and looks, all the while being in on the joke. You're valued, you're seen. The largest girls can even become the biggest stars. And people of small stature can still be worshipped.

In the clubs and in my pictures, everyone is celebrated for their scars, be they physical or mental.'

Influenced by his nightlife friends and the club scene itself, his photography remained relatively exuberant. He described it as having a 'big dose of humour as a way of drowning myself out'. He found 'fantastic' models at the RoXY and met his colleagues at the club. He brought collaborators, who often became friends, to the venue. For several years, starting in 1989, Cleo Campert regularly trawled the RoXY with two cameras slung around her neck. 'We felt that we were at the heart of the world, a select few. That we were witnessing something extraordinary, a place that evoked the spirit of legendary clubs, such as New York's Studio 54. We had to capture it in a unique way.'

Campert and Olaf had known each other for two years. Campert thought Erwin's pictures were 'cool', so she approached him to ask if he needed an assistant. 'I was terrified. I imagined him as arrogant and condescending. And I naturally tend to be shy. I didn't dare approach him until the early hours of the morning, but he responded incredibly nicely.'

Erwin saw Campert, the daughter of the renowned Dutch poet Remco Campert and granddaughter of the poet Jan Campert, whom the Nazis murdered, as a 'true Amsterdam socialite'. Her beauty and humour captivated him, and he eagerly wanted to make her his first real assistant. She joined Erwin in his studio and immediately got to work. 'I received benefits, and they paid me in kind, such as a Metz flash with a portable battery and a painting by Frans Franciscus. It proved an important apprenticeship. Afterwards, I launched my own career as a photographer.'

Cleo Campert performed everyday tasks and printed photos, but above all else, learnt from Erwin how to connect with people. 'It was one of his many talents. He had a very direct bond with his models, often people of all different shapes and sizes, big and small, or just different. He stood in their shoes, which put them at greater ease. "Oh yes, sure, I know the feeling." He did this masterfully, as if by instinct. It made the model feel like a vital component of a larger, extraordinary collective effort.'

Campert saw that humour played a significant role in Erwin's studio. It was often very extreme and self-deprecating, but also directed at others. However, it was rooted in a genuine affection for those around him. 'He doesn't do it if he doesn't like you, you just get ignored. I like this humour, very direct.' She spent a happy eighteen months working in the studio, setting up lights, winding film and filling cassettes. 'Until one day, Erwin said, "I'm having a blast with you, Cleo, but you've got to branch out on your own and start doing your thing".'

After work, they met at the RoXY. Cleo took pictures, while Erwin enjoyed the entertainment. Harrie Wildeman, Erwin's stylist, was also part of the crowd. Thanks to his outrageous clothes and lifestyle – he called his 'deviation' a 'pathological ostentati-

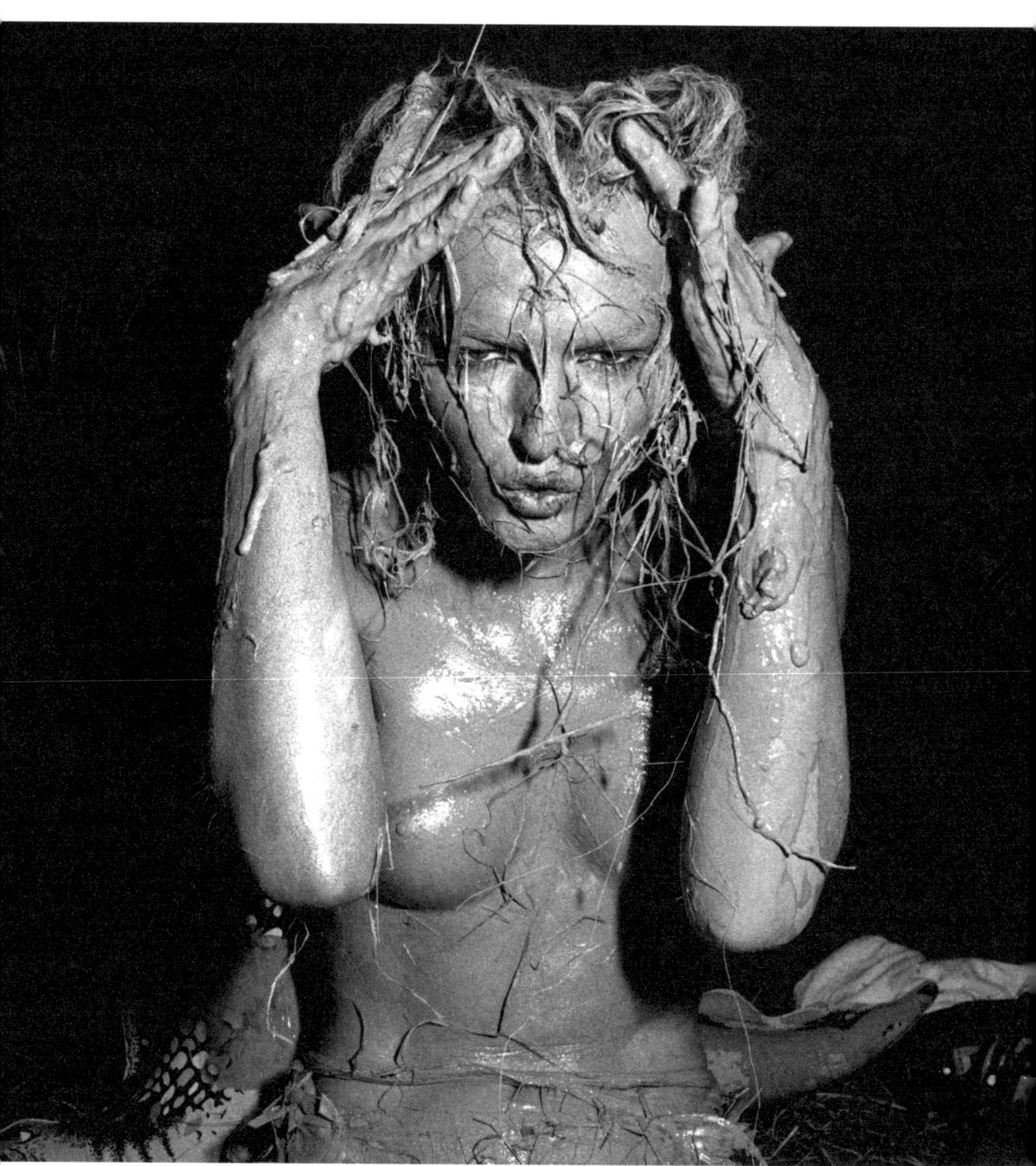

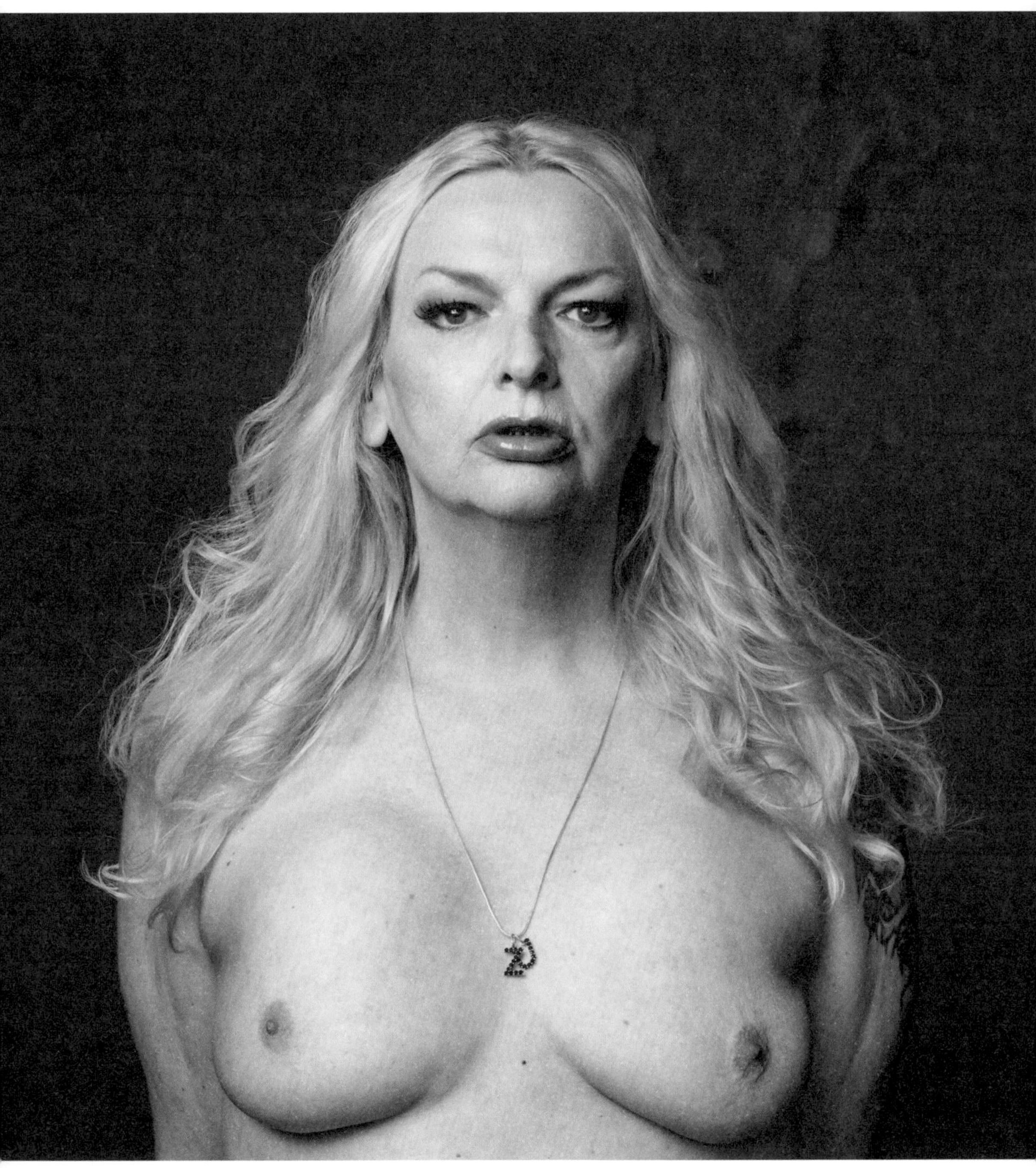

Left: Zu Browka in the late 1980s (photographed by Erwin Olaf during a mud bath at Club RoXY).
Right: Photographed again in 2021 for the *Muses* series.

on' – the flamboyant Wildeman became an icon of '90s excess. His motto – 'use your deficits' – resonated with Erwin.

At that time, Wildeman led a nomadic life. He often slept for months in Erwin's studio, on the streets, or in the RoXY's boiler room. He never wore the same clothes twice; he borrowed everything or 'forgot' to return garments after a shoot. And he served a prison sentence for stealing from the RoXY's coffers.

Erwin sometimes worried about his stylist, an original yet boundless spirit who continuously ravaged his body and who, far more than he himself realised, rejected conventions: 'Harry had something disturbing about him *à la* The Joker: always smiling but rather sinister at the same time.'

The RoXY and IT became Erwin's favourite places in Amsterdam, which was quickly developing into a global gay hotspot. The RoXY, specifically, represented a break with reality, a journey into a safe dreamworld that connected directly to the universe that Erwin cultivated in his Swammerdamstraat studio. Sometimes, the link proved literal. 'We got to the club at 1 a.m. and stayed till 5 a.m. We took ecstasy – but not too much because it made me sick. We smoked joints. Took devils. And a little coke, but it wasn't my favourite thing. Afterwards, we jumped in the shower and headed to the studio. We powered through and set to work, as we had an appointment. But first, a joint and a coffee. Our energy seemed limitless back then. Yet the nightlife did take its toll. 'I was off my face every weekend. It wasn't until three years later that I started wondering why I was often so depressed on Wednesdays.'

'It was devastating to see all those young people lying there, dying in the hospital'

A MAN FOREWARNED

'Sex was ubiquitous, the RoXY *WAS* sex,' Jacques Wolters muses, surrounded by Erwin Olaf's photographs in his Amsterdam-Zuid apartment. In addition to modelling for him, Wolters was a not untalented filmmaker, jack-of-all-trades and performance artist. 'I wore a leopard skin and carried Zu, an oversized infant in a baby doll cradling a giant bottle of milk powder, meant to evoke cocaine. I was so immersed in my character that I snorted the stuff.'

Wolters also roamed the club with his movie camera while collecting glasses. As an employee, he made sure, in passing, that the drug use didn't go too far. Coke caused the furore, not sex; everyone was at it, all over the place. 'My girlfriend at the time ran the coat check, and she had to turn away couples engaging in sexual activity.'

Sex never presented a problem. Until a deadly new sexually transmitted disease, which had just emerged in the Netherlands, started to spread like wildfire. The decadence of the nightclubs matched the hedonistic spirit of the post-Cold War era, but it also coincided with the harsh reality of the AIDS epidemic. Acquired Immune Deficiency Syndrome (AIDS) was first detected in the United States in 1981. The following year, the first Dutchman died of the disease. The impact of AIDS on the gay community became immediately clear.

Erwin was worried about the people around him and the life-threatening nature of the virus. Thanks to an early warning, he felt less concerned about contracting it himself. He was working as a photographer for *Sek* in 1983 when doctor and researcher Roel Coutinho, a pioneer in the fight against AIDS in the Netherlands, started to forewarn people about a 'gay disease' or 'gay cancer' – which is what it was called at the time, even by the left-wing press. 'On this occasion, it wasn't a case of my eyes popping out of my head. Instead, I pricked up my ears. I was among the first people to learn about the dangers of AIDS.'

'The common feature among the gay men who contracted the disease was that they had multiple sexual partners. I took the warning very seriously from the start. That's how I survived.' For the first few years he was very cautious, helped by his shyness. 'I wanted sex, despite the threat of AIDS, but I just couldn't bring myself to do it. I found myself involuntarily monogamous. Moreover, the fact that I'm always much more drawn to the front of a man's body saved me: his face, his mouth, his torso, a flat stomach with a bit of a six-pack, and his cock. His backside didn't interest me. Neither did dark rooms.'

After HIV was discovered as the cause of AIDS, testing became possible. This became a principled, almost political issue in the gay activist community. Teun Frieszo, who belonged to the radical wing, opposed HIV testing. He believed that taking a test would only increase stigmatisation. 'People don't know if they have cancer, so why should I be tested if I only have safe sex?' he argued.

The taboo surrounding the disease led to wild rumours. People were accused of being HIV positive, often unjustifiably, which made it harder for gays to get close to each other. If you had tested positive for HIV it felt like a death sentence, and you thought your sexual life was over. 'A blanket descended on the gay scene,' Erwin recalls. 'But at the same time, resistance emerged in the nightclubs. The epidemic provided yet another reason to dance on the edge of the volcano. Boundaries fell away, and dark room culture exploded at that very moment. 'In such circumstances, people rarely adopt rational reactions. What you find resembles the lawlessness and decadence of war, a form of nihilism.'

At the time, Erwin, along with his friends Jaap Hinten and Frans Franciscus, formed a 'club-world triumvirate'. Jaap and Frans decided to get tested, at the same time.

Erwin refused, citing his principles. Jaap's result came back negative, but Frans tested positive.

Afterwards, Erwin felt as if an iron wall had been erected between him and his closest friend, Frans. This is how Erwin recalls it: 'It was a sudden and complete breakdown in our relationship. Frans remained distant from me for a long time, filled with anger and disappointment.' Frans, on the other hand, has a different perspective: 'Erwin believed that I was abandoning him, despite my history of being his rock and a kind of free therapist. He also exaggerated the situation, claiming that I was "doomed". I was scared, but certainly didn't see it as a death sentence. Medication was already available; otherwise, I wouldn't have taken the test.'

In retrospect, the exuberant and euphoric expression of sexuality at the RoXY will forever be associated with the tragic disease that devastated the gay community. A link that soon became very noticeable. The RoXY and the Reguliersdwarsstraat, a bustling hub for the queer community when the sun shone, suffered greatly from the AIDS epidemic. 'We saw clearly that the illness primarily targeted the regular patrons of nightclubs and bars, the most extraordinary and captivating individuals. The most fabulous freaks, including drag queens, were among the first to perish, leaving a trail of disappearances.' The virus also claimed some of Erwin's friends and acquaintances.

The closet person to him to contract AIDS was Geert Vissers, better known as the drag queen Hellun Zelluf. Erwin visited him in hospital. 'A slattern and a volatile character who stood out for his shaved head, in the middle of which was an upright spike of hair, like an antenna. Despite his militancy, I saw his vulnerability, which created a bond between us.'

Hellun Zelluf featured in one of Erwin's 'Paassprookjes' [Easter fairy tales] for *Nieuwe Revu* and starred in Frans Franciscus and Erwin Olaf's short film *Tadzio* (1991). 'A sweet bitch, a highly politicised queen, and the only person I saw in one of the late stages of AIDS,' Erwin recalls. 'Hellun lay dying in the dedicated ward for AIDS patients. It was devastating to see all those young people lying there, dying in hospital. I only caught glimpses of the ends of the beds, which resembled cages draped with sheets – the slightest physical touch was agonising. By the time I reached Hellun's room, I was in pieces. I entered and saw a kind of rhesus monkey curled up in bed. I will never forget that heartbreaking image. And so ended the story of a vibrant, energetic and daring cross-dresser who'd embraced life to the fullest.'

Decades later, Harrie Wildeman, Erwin's longtime stylist and accomplice, would also succumb to AIDS. Harrie hid his HIV diagnosis for many years, struggling with substance abuse. In his words, 'I'm obsessed with drugs; they're a delightful treat. I sniff them like candy.'

The crisis affected Erwin's work like all other current events. However, he rarely,

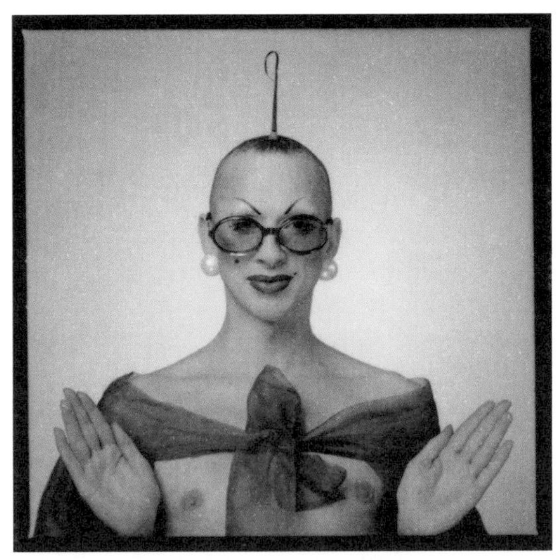

Top: Hellun Zelluf (Geert Vissers).
Bottom: Portrait of Martin Schenk, 1995. Image used in a campaign for safe sex in saunas and backrooms, with the message: 'Can I persuade you to practise safe sex?'

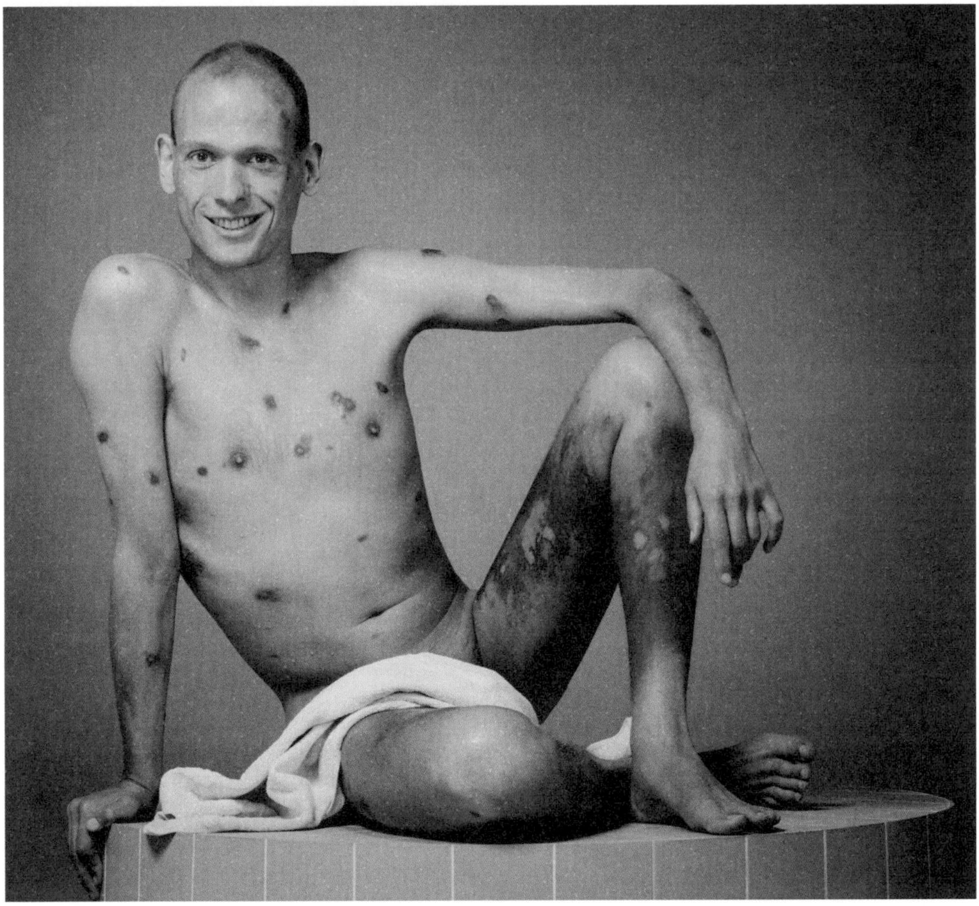

if ever, depicted AIDS directly. 'You won't see much death, misery or disease in my work. I am perhaps a bit self-absorbed, but it would be hard to focus my camera on that for an extended period.' He did, however, take Martin Schenk's portrait in 1995 for a campaign promoting safe sex in saunas and dark rooms.

'Martin was a kind, optimistic man. We depicted his Kaposi's sarcoma and his beautiful, smiling face. Clearly, he was about to die. There was no cure; there was nothing at all. The only thing we could do was photograph him, our hearts in our boots.'

The death and destruction caused by AIDS deeply saddened Erwin. He decided to symbolically end his relationship with sex, which he believed was the root of all his misery. 'At that time, I was convinced that we were on the cusp of a sexless society.'

Erwin thus organised 'The Last Season of Sex' at the RoXY. The party unfolded upstairs, and they placed two beds on the stage. This was where the World Fucking Championship would be won or lost. Participants: strippers Cynthia and Jonathan, and Zu Browka and her partner Jantje, the RoXY's ecstasy dealer. 'Cynthia and Jonathan were just pretending, while Jantje and Zu were doing it for real,' Erwin recalls with obvious delight.

The set designers had crafted a gigantic penis out of agricultural plastic. At the press of a button it would eject foam, symbolising the *moment suprême*. The crew was great – they knew exactly how to transform the club into a pinball machine, a flying saucer or a circus tent – but they tended to get stoned.

The party marked the beginning of many extravagant and exuberant events that Erwin would organise. The Supperclub, the RoXY, but especially the Paradiso – the temple to pop – served as frequent venues. He once contemplated releasing dozens of sex dolls from the ceiling, sending them cascading onto the dance floor. Teun Frieszo, his former lover, remembers: 'We went to a sex-doll wholesaler. A guy from Amsterdam showed us one of his many models. He said, "Here's one with all three holes." But Erwin replied, "We certainly don't need that many!"'

These parties drew him in with their extravagance, their campness, and the Fellini-like atmosphere. Freaks, acrobats, small people, drag artists and a man fucking sex dolls live on stage, and preferably all at once.

It wasn't always a ball, and not just because of AIDS. In April 1990, Marie de Nooyer, Erwin's muse and favourite model, suffered a fatal fall at the club. She'd been asked to devour an apple on the RoXY stage alongside three other women during the 'Nacht van Eva' [Eve's Night]. However, before she could fulfil her task, the naked De Nooyer needed workers to lift her from the dance floor to the stage using a freight elevator. Unfortunately, the manoeuvre went wrong, resulting in a fall that required her to be taken to hospital in an ambulance. She tragically succumbed to her injuries the following day.

Erwin called the accident 'gross negligence' on the part of the organisation. He would feel guilty forever, since he hadn't been there when it happened and couldn't prevent Marie from falling. 'Marie made a huge impact on me. I've always thought: I want to grow old with precisely her kind of open-mindedness and freedom of spirit.' Thirty years later, the Rijksmuseum hung the photograph of De Nooyer as *La Penseuse* (1987), from the *Squares* series, next to an engraving by Rembrandt, as a tribute.

On the final midsummer night of the twentieth century, a fire consumed the RoXY club. It was on 21 June 1999, the same day as the funeral for its founder, Peter Giele, who had suffered a brain haemorrhage. By then, the club had lost its status as the city's vibrant cultural hub, and Erwin hadn't set foot inside for years. The fire, caused by the pyrotechnics used at Giele's memorial, marked the end of an era of unbridled creativity and liberation.

The fire also brought the decadent *fin de siècle* in Amsterdam to a close. Innovative concepts swept across dance floors and stages, and nightlife excess was elevated to the status of art, thanks in part to Erwin's photography. After all the fatalities inflicted by AIDS on Amsterdam nightspots, the fire, as symbolic as it was all too real, razed their tolerant sanctuary to the ground.

'Religion and the far right collude against the body'

BODY PARTS

'We've become so ridiculously panicked about the body that it's regressive, completely backward,' Erwin fulminates during a photography-themed evening in Bruges in the spring of 2019. Earlier that day, he had struggled to drag his ageing body, which would turn sixty in a few months, from his hotel to the Concertgebouw. He had slowly navigated the narrow alleys and canals of the city. His hereditary pulmonary emphysema, which worsens with every passing year, required him to stop every 50 metres and lean on something to regain his breath.

Once on stage, however, he shows no indication of respiratory distress or poor oxygen saturation levels. Initially, the discussion flows smoothly. Erwin's tone becomes combative, however, when discussing the body's place in the puritanical era that we live in today. 'As human beings, we must accept our bodies, even if they're imperfect. This includes our genitals. It's strange that, in the public sphere, people are increasingly cloaking their bodies in shame, whereas penises and vaginas are all over the place in the digital world.' The audience might laugh, but Erwin insists that he's being deadly serious. 'Religion and the far right collude against the body. What's so special about a penis or a vagina? They're essential anatomical details.'

The free-spirited times are over, he said, as we headed towards the centre of Bruges. Take the series *Bodyparts*, which he created in the 1990s and for which he photographed the 'most beautiful part of the body, from the neck to the genitals, because that's all part and parcel of the whole'. He developed the idea while designing posters for the Zuidelijk Toneel, where Ivo van Hove had recently become artistic director. The first design was for *Het Zuiden* [South], a play by French-American writer Julien Green about two young men who fall in love on a plantation in South Carolina on the eve of the American Civil War.

Erwin had asked his model and muse, Olav de Graauw, who had 'wonderfully flawless' skin and an above-averagely sized penis, to join him at the studio on Swammerdamstraat. Olav, a performer and stripper on the gay circuit, liked working with Erwin. He saw his photographs as liberating as they shocked so many people. They matched with his worldview, he said thirty years later.

Erwin spent some time experimenting before deciding to smear Olav's body with a combination of oil and graphite. He then instructed him to cradle a bleeding (cow) heart in each hand, representing the unattainable love in the play. 'Olav casually held two hearts, one in each hand. His arms swung low, just grazing his groin, which revealed a fair bit of his cock. I found it rather appealing.'

Only later did Erwin realise that his design was not unlike the work produced by graphic designer Anthon Beeke, whom he admired. Beeke's poster for the Globe theatre group's production of *Troilus and Cressida* had caused quite a stir in 1981 and was one of the images that sparked Erwin's interest in staged photography. To use his own description, it was 'a black-and-white photographic detail of a naked woman's backside, saddled like a horse, slicked with oil and with a full view of her buttocks and vagina, ringed with hair, slap bang in the middle of the image. The fleshy thighs are tightly bound with leather straps.' Erwin was stunned, and instantly realised, 'I want this, too.'

The poster for *Het Zuiden*, which Erwin described as an 'unintentional tribute to Anthon Beeke's work', was not understood or appreciated by everyone. A critic for *Het Parool* lamented in a review: 'A theatrical poster used to be linked to the show it advertised. But this image is completely unrelated. There's nothing gory about the play, nor any blood or guts.' While one might interpret this as a form of substantive criticism, Erwin felt the objections stemmed from shame and prudishness.

A group of feminists in Amsterdam, along with the famous poster designer Gielijn Escher, provided a wave of much-needed attention. They defaced the posters with black paint or ripped them to shreds. Escher, a prominent poster distributor in Amsterdam and its vicinity, refused to use the design in the city, finding it to be 'unrefined, filthy and indecent'.

De Volkskrant contacted Erwin for comment, who relayed that he'd just returned

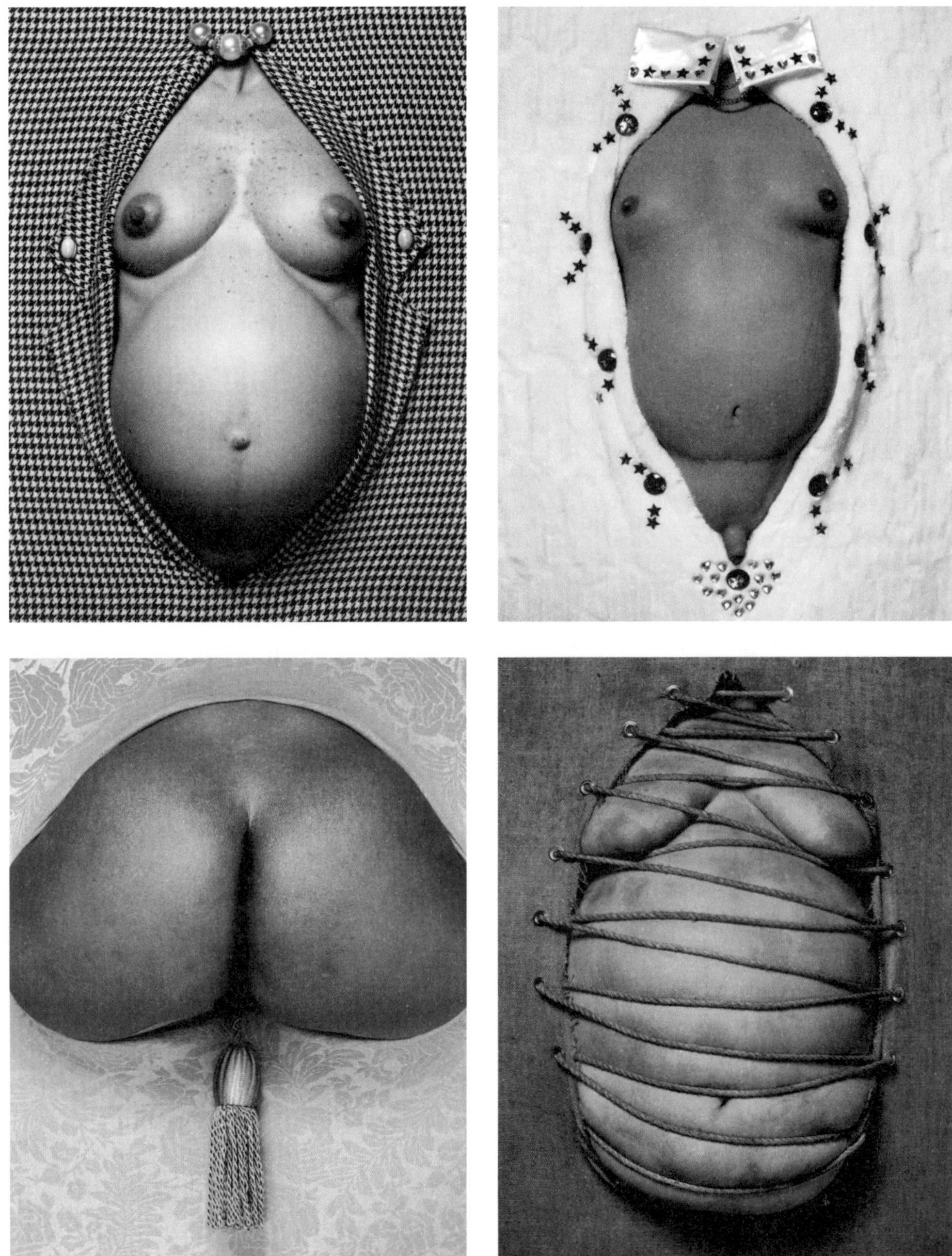

Five photographs from the *Bodyparts* series, photographed in front of the toilet doors at Club RoXY. The models were anonymous; the focus was on the body.

from a trip through the puritanical United States. He said that the situation in his supposedly progressive and liberal homeland had shocked him to his very core.

The criticism did not stop him from pursuing a new project based on the concept of the much-maligned poster. Like *Chessmen*, the models in *Bodyparts* were anonymous, with their faces hidden, which privileged their physiques.

This developed into a collection of nine photos for the RoXY's restrooms: five women in the men's room and four men in the women's. Thankfully, the clubbers were indifferent to the number of penises or vaginas on display. In the summer of 1993, it was rumoured that the series would be unveiled at a special event. Amsterdam's creative community gathered in droves, unaware that they would receive the cheapest supermarket cider instead of champagne, and that the toasts would be topped with cat food. The photos were printed so that idiots and collectors couldn't damage or steal them. They remained in situ for another six years before the fire consumed them.

'I don't understand the whole controversy around genitals,' Erwin states on Bruges's semi-deserted central square. All the restaurants are closed. He lingered after the performance signing the photo books presented to him by eager Belgian fans. Novice photographers admire him, while trainees offer their services, only to be gently declined. Collectors eagerly request autographs and present him with piles of vintage photography books. After the signing session, the discussion resumed, only now with a glass of white wine in hand. He then continued the argument at the side of a chip van, asking, 'What's the problem with a pussy or a cock?'

Thirty years later, he wondered whether he should include the series in his major retrospective in The Hague, given that people's tolerance for the work had declined.

One image in this collection depicts his young niece, Iris, at age four. It shows her naked, and he was struck by the purity and innocence of her body. However, he also noticed the increasing taboos surrounding child nudity, which made him want to question them.

In *Bodyparts*, he highlights various anatomical details, such as stomach, buttocks, breasts and penis. The rest of the figure is concealed by fabric. That same day, in his studio – 'very cosy, my sister-in-law, Gemma, was also there' – he hung a transparent piece of cloth. His niece, wearing Shirley Temple-style pigtails, stood behind it, illuminated by a single spotlight. As a result, she only appears as a shadowy outline, concealing her identity. Her naked body only appears through the torn section of the fabric. 'You could have ripped it above or below the genitals. I chose below, obviously.'

Gemma Springveld was caught off guard when she saw the results a month later. 'Erwin said he wanted to photograph Iris's belly, because he loved it so much. During the shoot, I couldn't imagine the final photo; it remained a mystery. All I knew was that my little girl felt cold after a long session. I just wanted to wrap her up in her bathrobe. A month later, we received an exhibition invitation, and guess who was on the front? I could have howled. I was incensed.'

On the advice of her mother-in-law, Lida Springveld, she called Erwin to discuss the situation. 'I told him: I wasn't informed, and I'm not okay with this. Can you retract the picture?' Unfortunately, Erwin couldn't accede to the request because it had already been published in a book. 'I was really pissed off, but thankfully, Iris herself was unfazed.'

Erwin thought his photograph was a 'super image', yet he was puzzled by the divergent interpretations that others had of the picture. He had intended to capture the purity of a child's body, which he knew people were increasingly viewing with suspicion and hostility. 'Once innocent creatures are metamorphosing into malevolent entities, a menace that needs to be eliminated. I wanted to document this transformation.' He contemplated displaying the picture in his retrospective at The Hague behind a discreet curtain as a statement. As a way of conveying that it belongs to a different time, a more tolerant era. By this point, he was convinced that he couldn't exhibit this photograph of his niece without some explanation, despite considering it one of his finest works. 'If people want to stir up controversy, and if they don't know the work's date, I'll be lynched immediately.'

The photo had previously appeared in his contemporaneous book, *Joy*, and in an exhibition of the same name at Kunsthal. It didn't receive any criticism at the time. Wim van Sinderen rejected Erwin's self-censorship, and the photo was displayed in The Hague without causing any negative reactions.

'We've all become a lot more prudish and it's not something that I can avoid'

Even after *Bodyparts*, Erwin continued to fight against the taboos surrounding the human body, skin and sensuality – both in the visual arts and beyond. He vowed never to succumb to the shame that he'd fought so hard to overcome, a battle lasting many years. As a young aesthete, he had primarily focused on what he disliked about his body. He slowly learnt to accept himself thanks to the free-spiritedness of the RoXY era and his muses' own lack of embarrassment. But it became clear that he still hated his physique, if indeed he'd ever stopped hating it, when *L'HOMO* commissioned him to photograph a series of male nudes in 2018. The concept was to depict sixteen men of different ages, ethnicities and physiques. Finding actors who identified as gay and had a typical physique presented a significant challenge. By 'typical', Erwin meant someone who looked like him: in a nutshell, once attractive, now seriously ruined and no longer chatted up.'

If such a 'normal' gay man wanted his picture taken at all, 'then not completely naked' was always the condition. Which was very different from the 1980s and 1990s. In those days, no one objected to being photographed stark naked. A further complication was that *L'HOMO* featured only real queers. Casting straight people wouldn't have been such a problem, according to Erwin. He believes that the demands that gays place on their bodies outweigh those of heterosexuals. As a result, they feel a stronger stigma about imperfections and the need to get rid of them: 'We often go directly from the closet to the gym.'

He has a theory about the cult of gay masculinity. 'The opposite sex arouses straight men, meaning that their partner must look perfect. Their flawlessness directly correlates to their sexiness. Obviously, with every conceivable personal aberration and perversion thrown into the mix. A gay man will fancy an attractive guy, but he will subconsciously or unconsciously project himself onto him, because, of course, he's the same sex. He looks in the mirror and thinks his muscles aren't toned enough; he needs to work on that. That's how the cult of masculinity in the gay community was born.'

Moreover, many gay men, like Erwin himself, were bullied in their youth. 'As a result, they strive for perfection, to make themselves as invulnerable as possible to their attackers.' This explains Erwin's sensitive eye for other people's strengths and weaknesses, a defence mechanism that helps him quickly pinpoint where to strike an opponent, should the need arise. A trait that has also helped him as a photographer. He has an immediate eye for imperfections when choosing models, yet also knows how to correct or sublimate them.

After discovering a first model who agreed to be photographed for *L'HOMO*, Erwin looked through the viewfinder and found himself distracted by the man's penis. He suspected that the reader would feel the same, so he asked the model to chastely place his hand in front of his genitals. 'He casually lowered his arms, and it worked. My attention settled where it should have been all along: on the skin and the eyes. These two elements have always represented the most crucial aspects of my photography.'

In the past, the primary objective of a photograph was to capture candid moments and reveal everything, as exemplified by the work of Robert Mapplethorpe and Hans van Manen. Otherwise, you weren't photographing the interaction of light and shadow on beautiful male bodies, but rather hiding genitals behind swivelled hips, hands, towels or white briefs. This time, it wasn't about power and powerlessness, as in *Chessmen*, or the raw provocation of his early pictures. Instead, the portraits boast a subtler complexity. 'My photography has become softer and less confrontational over the years. It is now more focused on the individual.'

He mused that the series has a peculiar quality: Erwin Olaf depicting men hiding their genitals behind their hands. 'The times they are a changing, and that applies to the Western world and no less to myself: we've all become a lot more prudish and it's not something that I can avoid.' His work is gradually becoming less extravagant and provocative. It is even beginning to resemble documentary photography, a genre that he had always rejected. 'I've moved a bit more towards the Rineke [Dijkstra] style of photography. I need less and less: a glance, a step to the left, a slight shift of a shoulder.'

Years ago, his 'Fellini years' could have led to his downfall as a photographer. Not due to excessive drinking and drug use, or lack of sleep, but rather to his unconventional promotional photos for parties and nightclubs, and his edgy posters for Ivo van Hove's plays, These choices positioned him well outside the artistic establishment. The cultural elite frowned on commercial and journalistic work, and he suspected that this attitude blocked his access to the world of museums and leading galleries.

Rather than conform, he agreed to design a poster for the film director Theo van Gogh. He considers him a 'sweet man' and 'the nicest straight man I know'. As so often happens, the result was born of chance. Erwin's best ideas often came to him while people-watching on a terrace or relaxing in front of the TV at home, ideally with a police series. In the case of the film *Loos*, which has S&M themes, one of his models, the dancer Louise Aarens, inspired him. Van Gogh described a scene from the film in which the lead actress, Renée Fokker, stands naked on her make-up case for hours. When Erwin asked Louise to do the same, she became unwell because of the bright blue horizonless background. Erwin later recalled that moment, describing how 'she bent over double and at that moment, in a split second, I saw the image I was looking for.'

Van Gogh wrote an enthusiastic column about the final result: 'The film's poster depicts a woman in stilettos, fishnet stockings and suspenders, standing on a toiletry bag, with a shapely derrière. The photographer Erwin Olaf created this stunning image. Her backside is attracting a lot of attention, undoubtedly because the soft, oblique light has elevated the shadow of her arse to art.'

Commercial commissions provided a valuable source of income and a fertile ground for Erwin's creativity, but they also prevented people from recognising him as an independent artist. He lacked the traditional art education that others possessed, which made him question his place in the art world. He observed that his peers, such as Rineke Dijkstra and Inez van Lamsweerde, who had indeed attended art school, were starting to make names for themselves. He felt neglected by the establishment, who seemed more accepting and encouraging of such photographers. Van Lamsweerde, thanks to the emergence of digital technology and software such as Photoshop, edited her images extensively. Dijkstra, on the other hand, created taut, documentary-style photographs.

Although Erwin counted both as friends, they represented the two photographic directions that he wanted to oppose. He disliked image editing at first, but enthusiastically embraced the technology some years later. Rineke Dijkstra's style of documentary art photography bothered him even more. He often ranted about the 'Becher-Schule' (School of Bernd and Hiller Becher). 'You see the same thing with all their followers. As if nothing happens in those lives – they keep repeating the same trick. They imitate reality, and then they imitate themselves and each other.'

At the beginning of his career, he was dead jealous of other photographers. He often questioned why they received prestigious photography awards while he didn't. At the same time, his envy frustrated him. Yet he refused to bend to art-world fashions and did not create a proper career strategy until many years later. 'I took a circuitous route, not the path you should choose if you want to gain appreciation in museum circles.'

As well as studio photography, he also kept a foot in journalism. He did this because he believed that good editorial work could encourage you to think differently. This led, in turn, to pigeonholing. He later tried to avoid this so as to be perceived as a serious artist by the artistic elite.

'Whether my interest is purely photographic or not is irrelevant'

S&M IN THE NETHERLANDS

Journalist Ingrid Harms recalls that, in early 1989, she was assigned to write a major story on sadomasochism for the *Vrij Nederland* supplement (published 1 May 1989). Erwin asked if he could take the accompanying photographs. He'd always found S&M fascinating, and Ingrid thought he'd make the ideal photographer for the story.

The magazine gave the journalist and photographer ample space, and the article occupied no fewer than sixteen pages: an in-depth look at the meaning of sadomasochism, in both words and images. Why do masochists crave humiliation? What background did the sadists come from?

Erwin viewed it as an exploration of liberated sexuality in the Netherlands, a matter of personal significance to him. 'I met such special and sweet, fun and crazy people who showed me that sex is just sex, no matter the form.'

He lacked a driving licence – 'failed twice' – but he hitched a cart to his bicycle, which transported his Hasselblad and photo lamps. Erwin often cycled past the people whom Harms had just interviewed. For out-of-town meetings, an intern drove him around in a dilapidated Fiat Panda.

Only Ria Franken and her husband, Freek, two of Erwin's long-standing contacts thanks to his book *Chessmen*, paid Erwin and Ingrid Harms a visit. They discovered

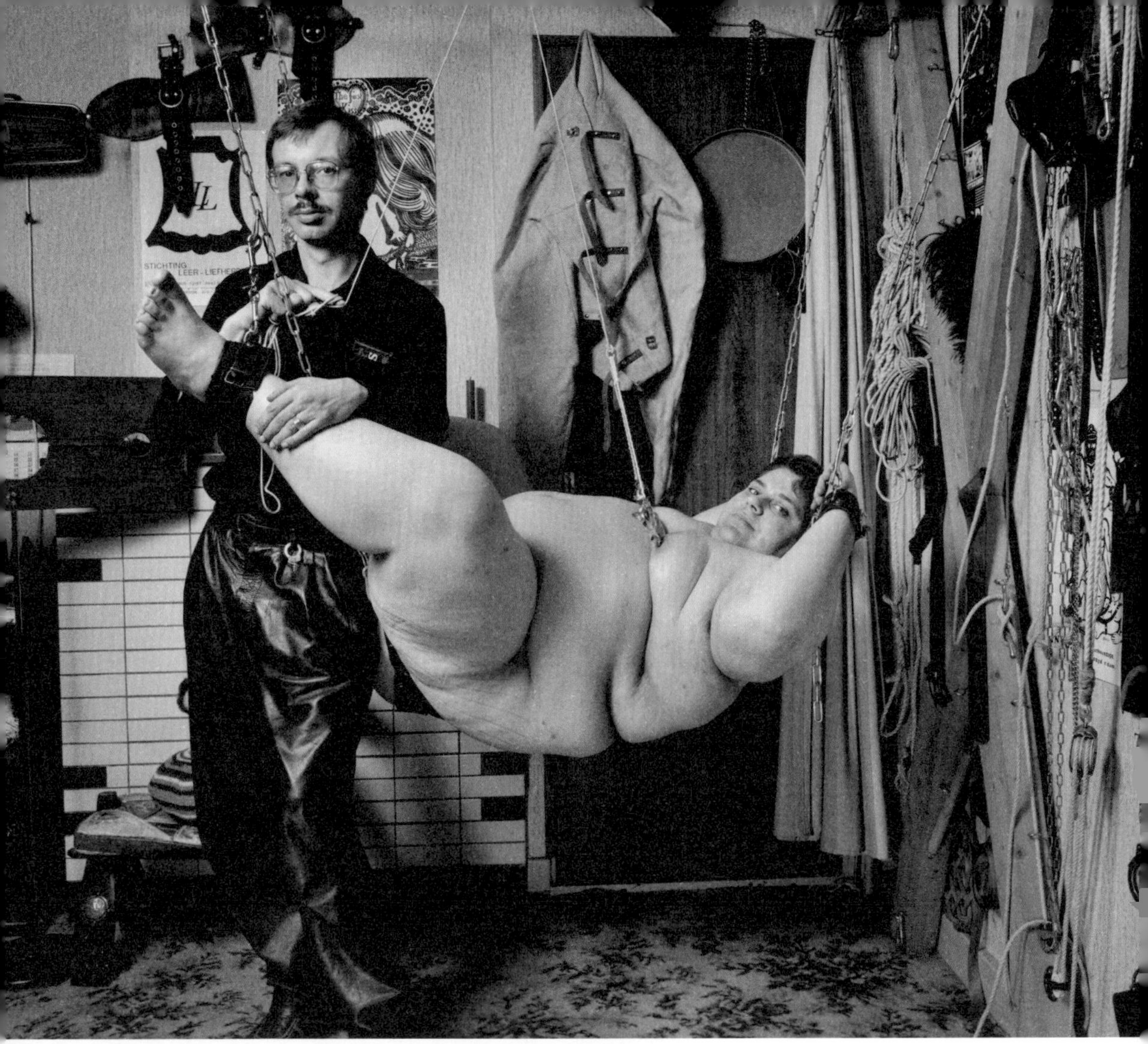

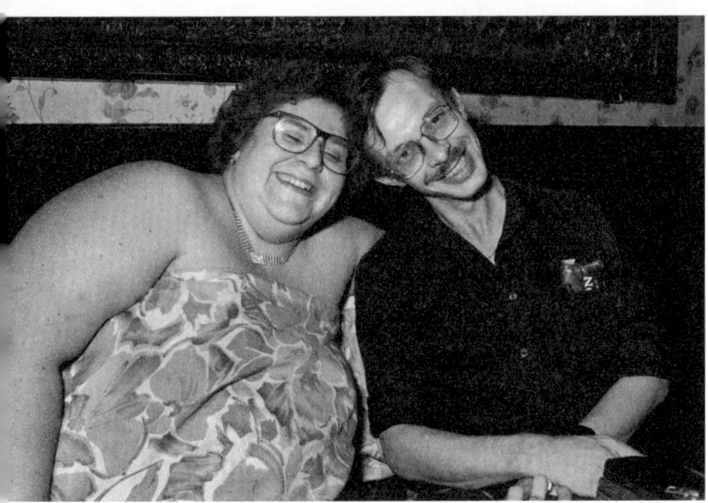

Top: Freek and Ria Franken photographed in 1989 for the weekly magazine *Vrij Nederland*. Bottom: Ria and Freek in May of the same year in Groningen, for the exhibition *Less is a bore* at the Groninger Museum.

that Freek had met Ria after placing an ad in *de Volkskrant*. Freek claimed that, despite being a dom, he was actually very gentle. He wouldn't hurt a fly in real life. Ria liked to be indulged. In the past, because of her weight, people often treated her cruelly: 'Fat equals stupid. I struggled for years to become who I am now. Psychotherapy, suicidal tendencies and a mental institution, I've had it all. I see S&M as my therapy,' she explained.

Erwin captured Ria and Freek in their S&M playroom. 'They were so uninhibited, amusing and tender. Who invites an unfamiliar photographer to capture such an intimate moment? I have always held a deep respect for anyone bold enough to agree. Leather-clad Freek stood next to Ria, who wore a harness and had nipple clamps.' Cuffs, straps, harnesses and masks were hanging on the wall. Ria and Freek struggled to understand and articulate their desires. Ria: 'Where does this come from? I'm not sure. Why do I want to grovel before my master?' Freek: 'I can't explain why I hurt and humiliate the woman I love. I sometimes think I'm mad.'

Apart from Ria Franken and Freek, another eight couples posed in all their gear and showcased the equipment they used. 'Photographing them was an extremely intense experience. One of the women in the series fainted in pain after her husband almost crushed her labia. It was also very typically Dutch: a cosy, cottage industry.' The sensational report in the weekly magazine was so popular that it sold out in record time. No doubt because of Erwin's photos, which allowed viewers to peep inside a secret pleasure garden.

Whether my interest is purely photographic or not is irrelevant, he declares as he flips through that decades-old copy of *Vrij Nederland*. 'I explore the boundaries of sexuality and create visually appealing images. Full stop. Whether it excites me or not is immaterial. I'm principled about this. I keep my deepest desires to myself, sharing them only with my lovers. I don't want to expose them.'

The topics of S&M and the *Chessmen* series continued to resonate with him for several years, until he became tired of it all. 'People saw me as the "bound woman" guy with a penchant for S&M. I wanted to shed that image. Initially, I was a queer photographer. Then a photographer specialising in obese women. Now, I'm an S&M photographer.'

Vrij Nederland continued to publish his work. He also made portraits for the rival *Haagsche Post* (now *HP/De Tijd*) and reportage for *Nieuwe Revu*. According to Erwin, his career took off from that point thanks to a few key factors: luck, keeping his word, and doing what everyone else did – but differently.

Nieuwe Revu gave him plenty of freedom. Editor-in-chief Derk Sauer, who had visited him on Swammerdamstraat after Erwin's photos caught his eye in *Vinyl*, had brought him on board. 'We had cleared pages in our Easter issue and the assignment to Erwin was: "just make something,"' Sauer recalls. He conjured up baroque scenes, obese people and small people in extreme positions; it was all-out Fellini – we'd never seen anything like it in the Netherlands. At that time, we bought hard news photographs, whereas his work was totally staged. Erwin's work was over-the-top, innovative, and just what *Nieuwe Revu* needed.'

According to Derk Sauer, Erwin lacked confidence, but he knew exactly what he wanted during a period of great financial and intellectual possibility. 'Erwin stands out and will continue to do so, as he didn't establish a school and was never truly copied or imitated. His work is inextricably linked to his unique imagination.'

In May 1989, museum director Frans Haks invited him to show his work in an exhibition on the Modern Baroque at the Groninger Museum. After that first meeting, Erwin began to wonder why he was even approached. Was his work Baroque? There must have been a mistake. His photographs possessed a technical simplicity and lack of adornment. He sometimes used fleshy models, which must have been why he received the invitation. But mistake or not, he eagerly accepted.

Three years earlier, Frans Haks had championed staged photography with the exhibition *Fotografia Buffa*. He believed that other museums unfairly overlooked this art form. His new exhibition *Less is a bore. Exuberance now – Minder kan het niet. Exuberantie nu* was all about showing the 'spiritual heirs' of repetition in art, a movement from the 1970s that emphasised decorativeness.

The phrase 'less is a bore' was first coined by Postmodern architect Robert Venturi. It later became the motto of the Memphis Group designers, including its founder Ettore Sottsass. Erwin Olaf's work embodied that spirit. Haks aimed to challenge what he saw as an artificial distinction between art and kitsch – an issue that would surface repeatedly in discussions about Erwin's later photography. Erwin was acutely aware of the debate. He feared that his highly staged style could easily tip into kitsch, and that he might end up like Rien Poortvliet, the Dutch artist and illustrator known for his gnome drawings and nature scenes, among other things.

The Stedelijk Museum in Amsterdam, which was concurrently presenting a similar exhibition entitled *Barock & Roll*, missed the mark, according to *de Volkskrant*: 'It's pure bad luck that the dwarfs, fairies, magicians, gnomes and angels – big and small – from Olaf's world haven't appeared at the Stedelijk.'

The Stedelijk Museum and Erwin Olaf would always maintain an uneasy relationship. Erwin suspected that he was not moving in the right circles due to his 'background and education'.

In stark contrast, his relationship with the Groninger Museum, particularly with its founder, Haks, remained strong. Erwin viewed Haks as his 'museum discoverer', admiring his 'sparkling' curatorial style and his courage in leading the team to explore new forms and ideas.

'Have you got a death wish?'

Erwin's former intern and assistant, Piek (Annemieke Kock), now established as a photographer, sits at the long table where the studio staff enjoy afternoon lunches. She can also use the IJselstraat studio for her independent projects, and her name appears below his on the doorbell. 'Erwin generously does this, but I don't want to be compared with him. I'll always be in his shadow.'

Piek arrived at Swammerdamstraat at the age of twenty-one in 1990. She recalls, 'With Erwin, I discovered true liberation for the first time. For instance, I could stop pretending to be more feminine than I felt.' It felt like coming home, and she could at last be herself, she says.

Piek documented the studio's everyday life in the 1990s with her own camera. She worked there as an intern, then as a permanent employee. However, she admits, 'I wish I had taken more photographs at the beginning. I lacked confidence.'

That same year, Jacques Wolters, who was well into his transition and had been riding a Harley-Davidson since he was sixteen, had been invited by the American Hells Angels to their annual meeting in Sturgis, South Dakota. 'I desperately wanted to go,' he recalls. 'But I didn't have the money. So, I suggested to Erwin that I had a subject he needed to photograph.' Wolters knew how to pique Erwin's interest: 'Hells Angels, Vietnam veterans who had lost their limbs... it's all very intense.'

They decided to take a gamble and go to South Dakota in the summer of 1990. It turned out to be an exciting journey, with serious repercussions. To begin with, Erwin lost all his equipment while transferring at O'Hare International Airport in Chicago, which sent him into a tailspin.

Once he arrived in the Black Hills, Erwin discovered that his inclination for extravagant models did not yet mean that he could also get along with rough-and-tumble bikers. They belonged to groups such as the Hell's Henchmen, the Outlaws, the Sons of Silence, or one of the many other biker gangs, and were hard to approach. Tens of thousands of Harley fans unsettled the mining town for ten days. It was 'born to be wild', but in real life, and the gathering led to over 200 drinking and driving fines, seventy-three drug arrests, 133 traffic accidents and eleven deaths.

In response to Erwin's desire to connect, they found themselves in a campground teeming with Hells Angels. The air was thick with the smell of petrol. 'I have never seen so many ugly, unkempt and hairy bikers (male and female) in one place before,' he wrote in a letter home. Wolters himself looked like half a Hells Angel, but Erwin felt that, once again, he was the duty outsider – even after he had removed his CCCP shirt at Jacques's insistence to defuse at least one of the dangerous combos of homophobia and communist hatred. 'I said, Erwin, listen, you're a faggot and in a

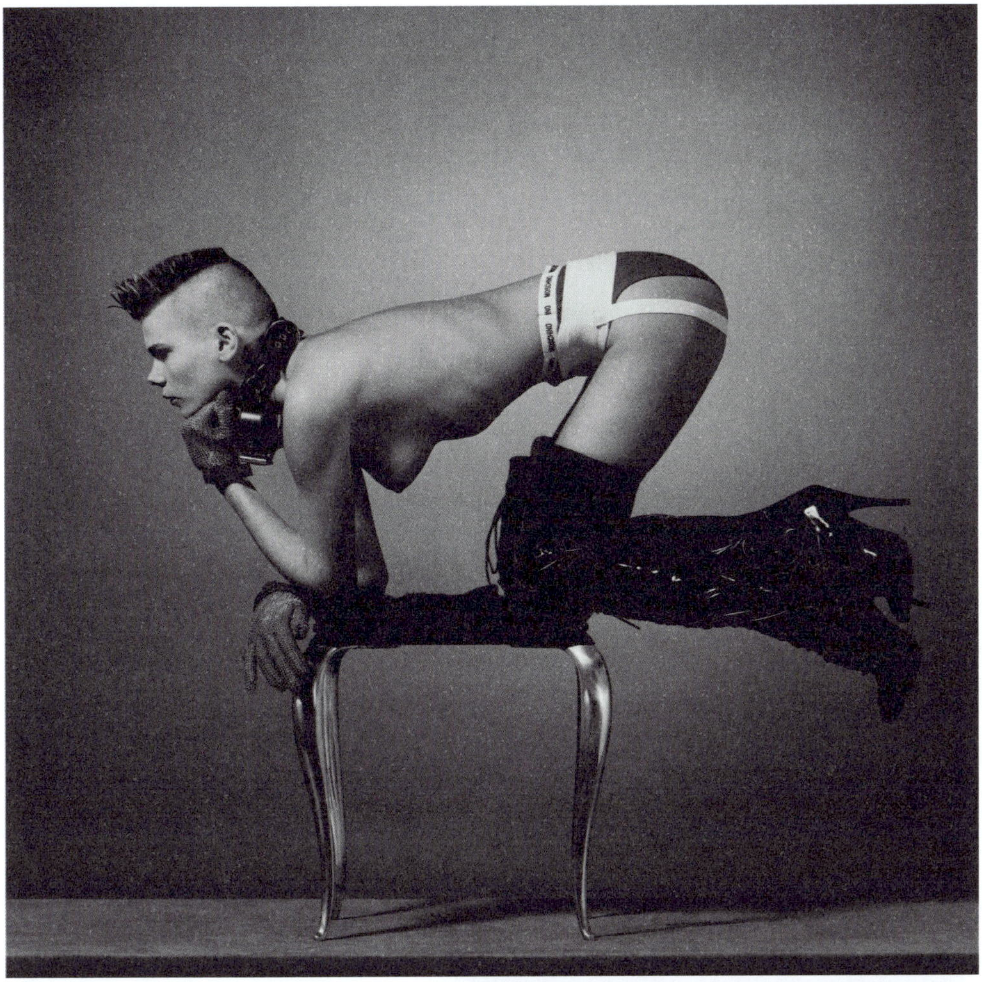

Top: *Piek on Philippe Starck, 1991*, from the *Squares* series. Bottom: Frans Haks, director of the Groninger Museum from 1978 to 1995.

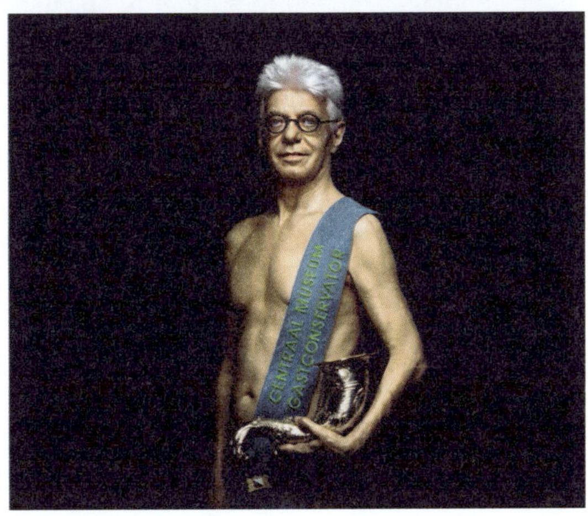

communist shirt. Have you got a death wish?'

Erwin's morning routine of showering also deviated from the norm. He always had the shower spray on his back, never the other way around. However, all those bulky, hirsute men were showering with their backs to each other. He approached and called out, 'Ja-a-a-acques, have you got the soap?' Wolters: 'Erwin stood in front of all those bikers and their bitches, fully exposed. Those startled women shouted, "I see dick; I see dick!" and the Angels were not amused. So, we fled to a motel.'

The first Gulf War was imminent. Watching the disturbing images on TV in their room, it seemed like World War III was about to erupt. The fear of war strengthened the feelings of nationalism and xenophobia within motorbike gangs and their circles. Erwin watched it from afar and with horror. 'Those Angels all bought a Yamaha, then they attacked them with iron bars, just because it wasn't American-made. I witnessed it first-hand, and all I could think was, "wow, these people are so weird".'

Wolters, who had bound breasts, sideburns, long hair and a black leather biker jacket, could have passed for a member of a Dutch motorcycle gang. He oversaw the locations and casting. Erwin wanted to create staged portraits in an improvised studio. He soon found a high white wall to use as a backdrop. Jacques arranged for the presidents of the Bandidos, the Nomads and the Hells Angels, and some Lakota Indians, the original inhabitants of the Black Hills, to be photographed. 'A renowned photographer would like to take a picture of you, your bitch and your bike. It will be in a very famous magazine.'

The entire thing failed. In just ten minutes, the first bulb blew, followed by the second. Then, the centre shutter on his Hasselblad's lens malfunctioned. 'That faulty Hasselblad caused me a minor trauma,' he claimed. Jacques's biker chapters, whether self-proclaimed Nazis or not, or 'white and proud', were captured on film with a 35 mm camera that the photographer hadn't used for ages.

His forays into reportage photography were also fruitless. His journalistic intuition, if it had existed at all, had evaporated completely. 'I then noticed everyone stampeding; apparently there was something to see, so I joined the throng.' The shocking thing turned out to be a biker bitch exposing one of her breasts.

After his return to Amsterdam, he managed, with some difficulty, to fill the allotted pages of *Nieuwe Revu*. The trip was a sobering experience from a photography perspective. It brought photojournalism to an end. Erwin retreated into the studio and made a resolute decision: he would henceforth have total control over his photography.

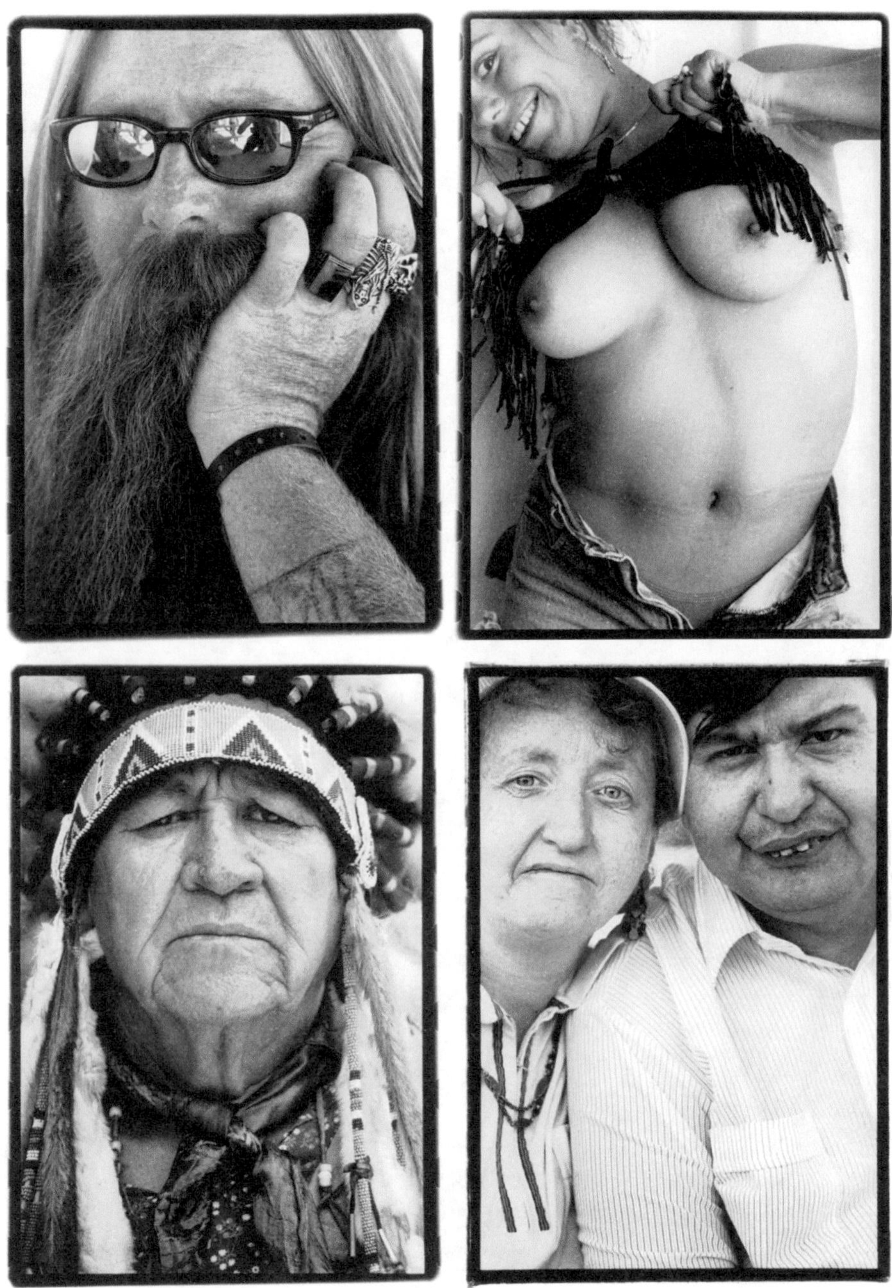

In Sturgis, Jacques Wolters approached members of the Lakota tribe, assorted locals and Hells Angels. 'A renowned photographer would like to take a picture of you, your bitch and your bike. It will be in a very famous magazine.'

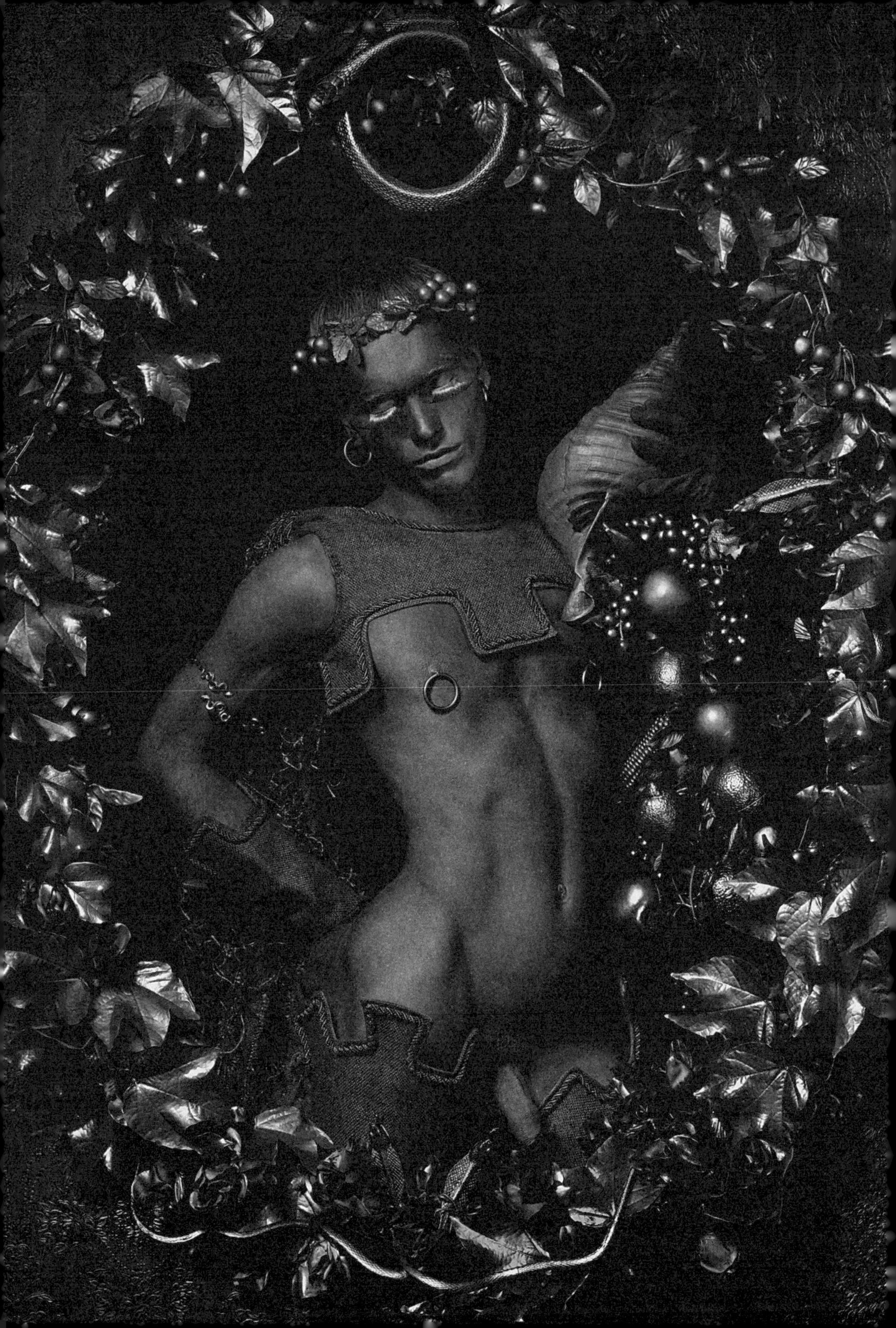

5 WORK AND PLAY (1989–1995)

'Blacks was photographed in a daze – I was totally stoned'

PAINT IT BLACK

Erwin's ex-lover Teun Frieszo points to a dark photo in a black frame on the wall of his Utrecht home. 'Erwin gave me this photo from the *Blacks* series. While it depicts genitals, it looks perfect over the dining table. You can't see very much anyway, through all that black.'

Robert Mapplethorpe's death was the initial catalyst for Erwin's black-on-black series of photographs. Frieszo explains that Erwin was due to meet the acclaimed photographer at a dinner hosted by Hans van Manen in early 1988. Mapplethorpe, who was showing at the Stedelijk Museum, was staying with Hans. But shortly before the appointed time, Van Manen called to say that Mapplethorpe was too unwell; the dinner was off. He died of AIDS the following year.

When Erwin heard the news, he asked Teun to take him to Antwerp. He'd seen ready-made fabric mourning wreaths in some of the city's shop windows. He bought one, sprayed it black and photographed it against a dark background. He elaborated further on that photo with *Blacks*.

Later that year, sitting in his living room on the Lauriergracht, Erwin was half-heartedly watching an episode of the TV art programme *Atlantis*. He'd recently been contemplating the series that he wanted to make as a sequel to *Chessmen*. Furthermore, he had been invited to exhibit new work at the Museum Fodor on Keizersgracht. He lacked a plan for his presentation and, despite all the publicity surrounding Chessmen, he was only partially convinced about his photography. The series' success hung like a millstone round his neck.

He'd forced himself to get clean and hadn't smoked a joint in weeks – also because he wanted to kick what had become a full-blown addiction. Erwin had graduated from 'nice little spliffs' to 'big fat joints' and, unlike with alcohol, cocaine or heroin, he couldn't live without the stuff. It took him many years to finally quit the habit, and only then for urgent medical reasons.

The imposing figure of Ben van Os – the art director on several of Peter Greenaway's most spectacular films, including *The Cook, the Thief, His Wife and Her Lover* – appeared on screen. Van Os – bald and stocky – was wearing head-to-toe black, including his scarf, hat and sunglasses. Impressive, thought Erwin of the art director who would later become a regular collaborator.

After switching off the TV, he smoked a joint and showered, with Janet Jackson playing on the living-room speakers. All his friends admired Michael, whereas he preferred the black R&B singers. Janet Jackson sang about black emancipation and other sensitive issues, things that Michael never touched upon. At the end of her politically charged album *Rhythm Nation 1814*, she speaks the following words on equality: 'In complete darkness we are all the same. / It is only our knowledge and wisdom that separates us / Don't let your eyes deceive you.'

Stoned as he was, he said to himself in the shower: OK, first Ben van Os in black and now these lyrics by Janet Jackson, it's a sign. I'm painting everything and everyone black; I will frame them all with black mourning wreaths, like the one I made for Mapplethorpe.

He stepped out of the shower and, without even towelling off, called his old friend and unofficial therapist Frans Franciscus. He had just one burning question: is this a great idea, or is it the drugs? 'Go ahead and make it,' Franciscus said.

Although Erwin felt far removed from the mainstream Dutch art world, it didn't mean that he'd abandoned his lofty cultural ambitions. Fodor served as an annexe of the Stedelijk Museum, a place that Erwin almost considered hallowed ground. A solo exhibition at the Fodor felt like an important advance in what was starting to resemble a bona fide artistic career. This was, after all, what he was still hankering after – no matter how much he mocked the shortsightedness of the great and the good in the art world, or behaved in a condescending manner.

The Stedelijk Museum's photography policy was supposedly under fire. The curator of photography, Els Barents, had resigned the previous year in protest at the lack of funds allocated to the medium. The Stedelijk Museum appointed art historian Hripsimé Visser as its curator of photography in 1990. She would stay at the museum until 2021 and, in Erwin's eyes, she was partly responsible for the Stedelijk never showing his work. Except on one occasion thanks to what Erwin himself described as a 'shortcut'.

Soon after completing the film *Tadzio* in 1991, Erwin and his assistant Rogier Alleblas travelled to Slovakia with the glass artist Bořek Šípek. Šípek had also participated in *Less is a bore* at the Groninger Museum. Afterwards, he'd approached Erwin to photograph the glass for his forthcoming exhibition at the Stedelijk Museum.

Erwin and Bořek got along well. 'A sweet, stimulating, atypical Dutch man, with his curlicues and flounces. Also, a partygoer. He's one of the people who shaped me,' Erwin claims. Furthermore: 'Bořek taught me to eat bull's testicles!' Czech-born Šípek suggested finding models, putting them in Eastern European Roma costumes, and photographing them with his glasses, bowls and furniture. Not a good idea, Erwin thought, far too flat. He suggested a reportage format instead: 'Why don't we travel to Czechoslovakia and photograph Roma with your designs?'

Working with natural light again felt strange to Erwin, his assistant Alleblas noticed. It made him nervous, so he took vast numbers of Polaroids to test the conditions.

Although they'd deliberately set out to capture the contrast between precious art and raw poverty, asking poor people 'to cradle a 5,000-guilder vase in their arms' [approx. €2,250] turned out to be a disconcerting experience. That the impoverished models were paid did little to assuage his guilt. 'You can smell and feel the poverty, the distress and the tension. You realise – this constitutes Europe too, but with different standards and values.'

Despite their good intentions, Erwin and Šípek both started to feel as though they were exploiting the Roma's poverty-stricken conditions just to make a splash, upon their return, with the Stedelijk Museum's privileged visitors.

When they were chased out of a village – before landing a single photo – it somehow felt like poetic justice. One family called them imperialist pigs. The translator warned that things might get out of hand. The team dived into the car and fled, tyres screeching.

'Forcing people to do things is futile,' Erwin concluded. But he marvelled at his professional aloofness, which undoubtedly came from his journalism training. 'I was shocked at my coolness. I could shrug it off so easily; I didn't lose a wink of sleep.'

This would count as his only exhibition at the Stedelijk Museum, much to his regret and chagrin. Over the next few decades, the institution's photographic policy focused mainly on documentary work, while he himself opted definitively for staged photography.

Like much of his oeuvre, the *Blacks, 17 Royal Portraits* series told a story while also testing new formal boundaries. Together with Teun Frieszo, he'd studied Jan van Eyck's and Jacob de Wit's grisailles. Both excelled at painting with light and shadow, using pigments to conjure up the illusion of three-dimensional figures, as though hewn from white marble. He wanted to achieve the same effect in his pictures. What would happen if he photographed everything black-on-black?

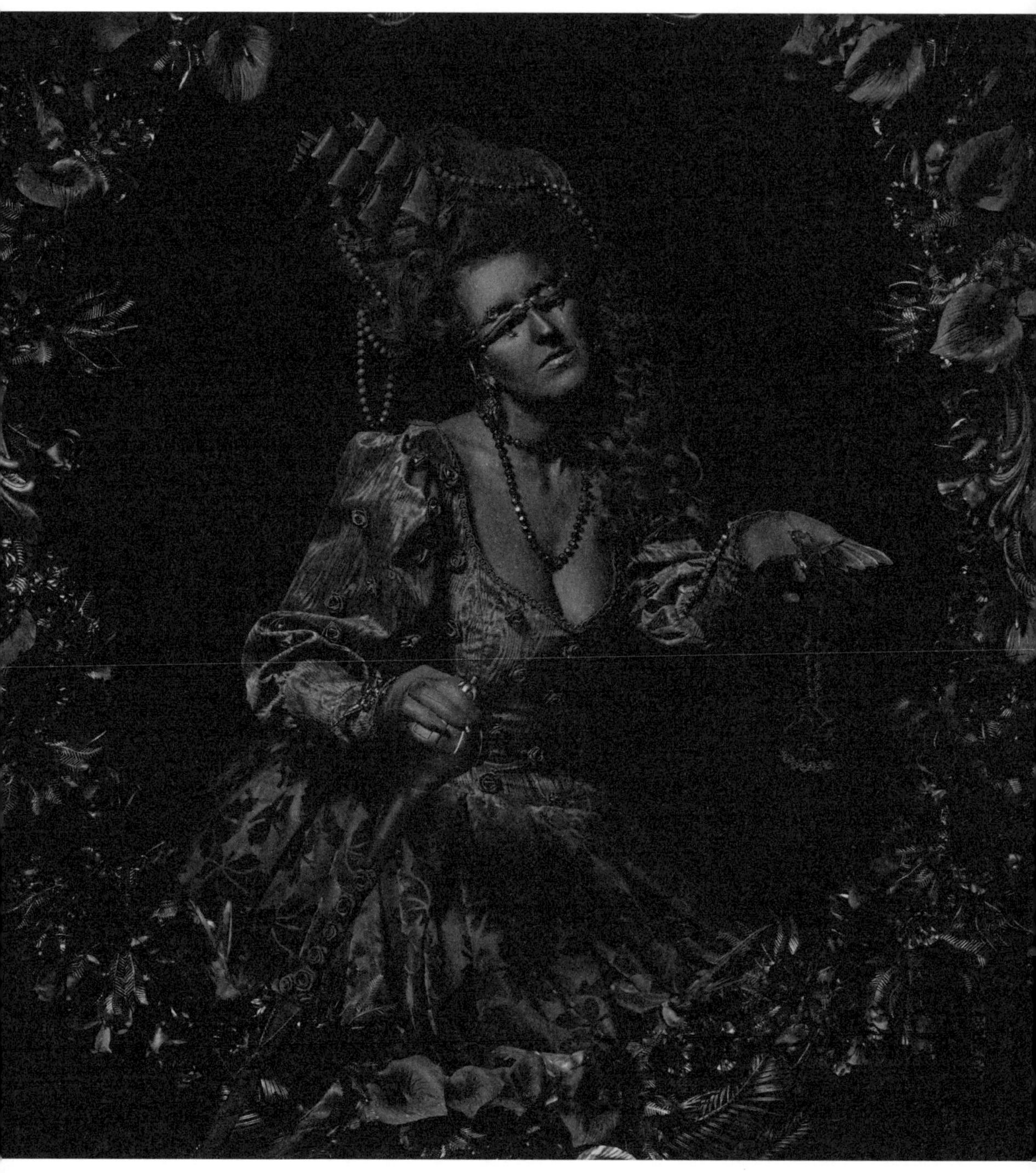

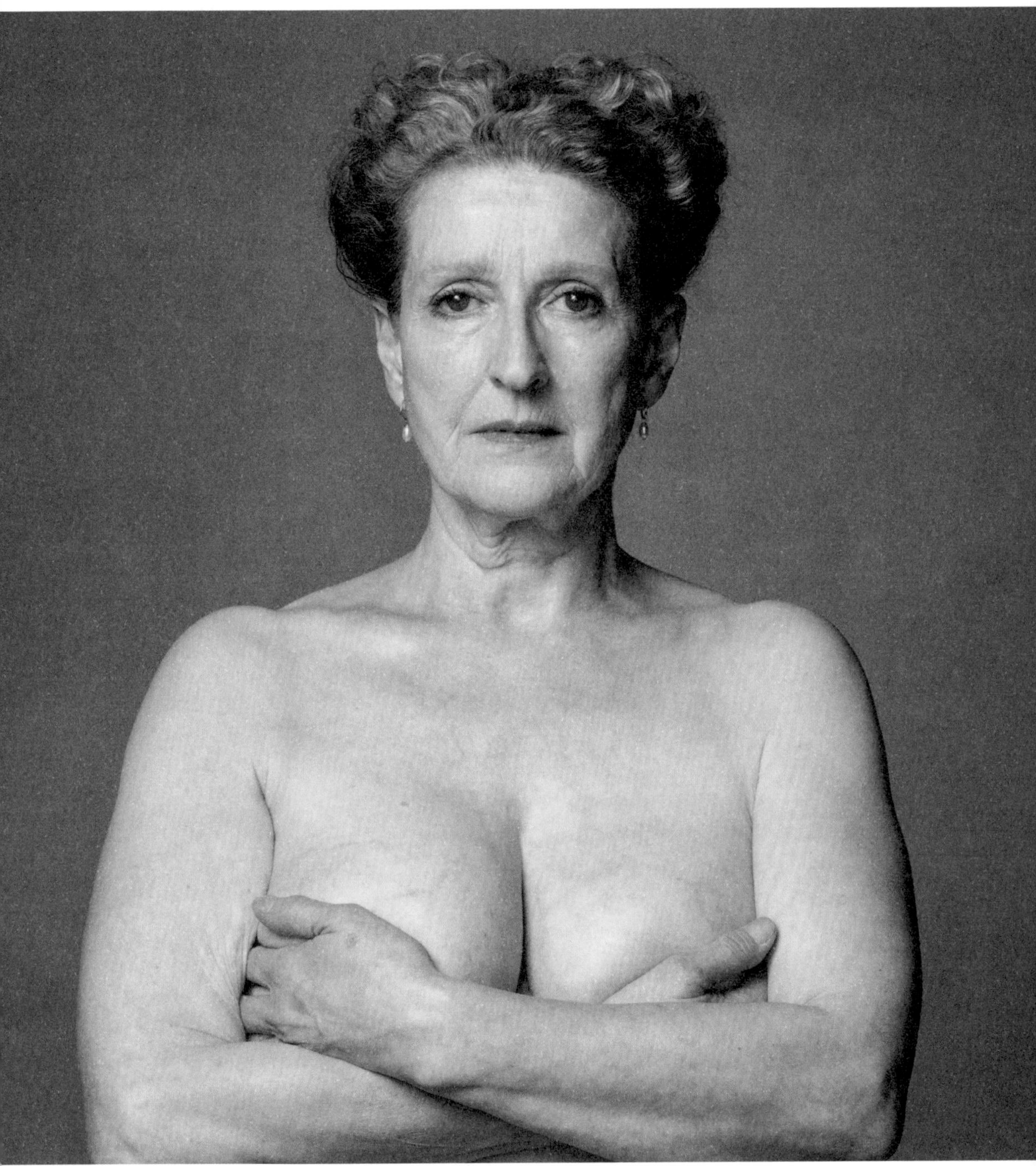

Left: Desiree Aben in the series *Blacks*, 1990, for which she also designed costumes.
Right: Photographed again in 2022 for the *Muses* series.
Photo on page 152: *Alandus, 1990* from the *Blacks* series.

For this series, Erwin was awarded his first grant. He found it useful: he'd long wanted to professionalise, but lacked the money.

All his previous models turned up at the studio on Swammerdamstraat and his paramour Alandus also came to pose. 'It took a lot of effort, but it went smoothly, and we were perfectly attuned as lovers,' Alandus recalls of the session. It marked Erwin's first experience of working not just with an intern but with a full team, including set designers, costumiers and stylists. His kindred spirits Harrie Wildeman and Jaap Hinten, better known as the designer duo Haute Couture Junkies, doubled up as stylists and models. He also collaborated with the designer Floris Vos, whom he'd met on the club scene.

Vos hammered and sawed the sets and sprayed the edges with polyurethane foam, while Wildeman made the wreaths that would say something about the fantasy figures portrayed. Jaap Hinten sewed the costumes, as did Desiree Aben.

The portrait series, which depicts people, painted black, against inky backgrounds, contains less aggression and sexuality than *Chessmen*. But like that earlier series, *Blacks* was embellished with extravagant props, following the postmodern adage of the 1980s, anything goes. The wreathed portraits included soft toys and dolls, along with tourist knick-knacks, kitchen utensils and musical instruments. Erwin was clearly under the influence while photographing: '*Blacks* was photographed in a daze – I was totally stoned.'

Erwin wanted the series to address gender inequality and racism, precisely because earlier pictures, such as the one of the guy karate-kicking a black pregnant woman, had garnered what he deemed unfair accusations of misogyny and racism. It isn't clear whether *Blacks* came across that way at the time – the series sometimes elicited interpretations as a reference to the all-pervasive fear surrounding AIDS. At the time, no one accused him of perpetuating a racist tradition by blacking up his models.

'We didn't think twice about showing the series,' recalls current Stedelijk curator Leontine Coelewij, who was then working at Fodor, looking back on the exhibition. 'But looking at *Blacks* through contemporary eyes, you can't help but think of this as blackface. It's unacceptable for white artists to paint people black and photograph them. Nor do you use a picture of a woman weeping before a photograph of concentration camp victims, as Paul Blanca did that same year... Back then, people considered it groundbreaking, and we loved the work. But times have changed, and you can no longer exhibit such images.'

He wouldn't make a series like *Blacks* now, Erwin agrees, although his intentions were far from racist. 'Indeed, the series was supposed to serve as a statement against racism. The term blackface hadn't caught on in the Netherlands, and I wanted to convey that everyone stands equal – in the spirit of Janet Jackson. Stereotyping black people is the very last thing I want to be associated with.'

Coelewij agrees. 'From the outset, Erwin portrayed people who deviated from the norm without belittling them, without turning them into exhibits in a cabinet of curiosities. He never ridiculed anyone; he included everyone, especially those outside the mainstream. Clearly, he never intended to denigrate people of colour in *Blacks*. But no matter how free-spirited we thought we were in the 1980s, we lived in a Western bubble here in Amsterdam, and that didn't change until very recently.'

The opening at Fodor in April 1990 was a true happening, one that saw Amsterdam's denizens of the night emerge into broad daylight, ferried across the canal on an American patrol boat. As Van der Spek, publisher of the book *Blacks*, remembers it: 'An ultra queer-party. As a publisher, you spend a fortune on drinks but still end up with a pile of untouched photo books at the end.'

Frans Franciscus dates the start of Erwin's artistic career to the black-on-black experiment. 'Before *Blacks*, Erwin didn't feel remotely like an artist. But this time, he had made a creative mark all his own.'

Erwin's dark mannerism received a lukewarm reception in the press. Film director and columnist Theo van Gogh, however, extolled its virtues. He praised the 'depraved' world that Erwin Olaf had created: 'His obsessions prove particularly distasteful.'

Van Gogh also wrote a foreword to a cahier published by the photography magazine *Focus*. 'The feeling, with a capital F, that emanates from these scenes – which are orchestrated down to the last millimetre – feels incredibly cold, as if the world comprises one huge, desolate ice plain,' is how he described the series. 'The beauty of *Blacks* is that it suddenly blinds people. The photographer is God and His wrath has descended upon us like a scourge, depriving His defenceless creatures of light.' He continued, 'That our world is bound together by sorrow is the least interesting observation. The beauty of Erwin Olaf comes from his merciless view: finally a photographer who refuses to compromise.'

Theo van Gogh was not a critic whose opinions carried weight, however, but a well-disposed artist. Appreciation from friends was all very welcome but it still stung that the professional critics ignored *Blacks*. Only *de Volkskrant* published a piece in which the reviewer cloaked his negative opinion in derogatory terms. 'Olaf, known – and in certain circles infamous – for his homoerotic photographs... painted some of his models black and framed them with leaves. The photographer dresses his models extravagantly and, here and there, lets a cock hang loose. ... The result is extreme; you either love it or loathe it; there's no middle ground. The models resemble naked chimney sweeps.' Years later, Erwin was still upset about the piece: 'I'm hardly ever reviewed seriously.'

Although people either disparaged or ignored *Blacks*, he nevertheless used the series to cement his own staged and Baroque direction. But before he could develop further as an artist, he needed to establish a business. Erwin wanted to professionalise, and consequently sought access to the world of advertising photography. By now, he had gathered a team of stylists, models and assistants around him, and he felt prepared for the advertising agencies with their generous budgets.

Golden years lay ahead and both he, and his posse, would share in the spoils. 'Things will change,' he enthusiastically announced to everyone who, hitherto, had always assisted him for free. Attractive, well-paid commercial jobs were on the horizon – but not before a surprising twist: he was given the chance to direct a film.

'Creating emotion on celluloid is fiendishly difficult'

VISCONTI A LA OLAF

Landhuis Oud Amelisweerd, a large country house in Utrecht, has a rich history. Until his self-styled abdication in 1810, Louis Bonaparte, King of Holland, had even wanted to make it a royal residence – but only ended up living there for nine days. Those illustrious years were all but a distant memory in 1991. The building had long stood empty, and it was as uncomfortable as it was cold. Portable electric heaters and real fires, which needed to be lit early enough, were the only sources of warmth. Only the original eighteenth- and nineteenth-century wallpaper still bore witness to the house's former glory.

A noisy and extravagant crowd rocked up at the estate on a bright spring day. The coach trundled up the driveway and a motley assembly of drag artists and other flamboyant types cheered as they alighted. Erwin Olaf welcomed Zu Browka, Jacques Wolters, Hellun Zelluf, Duck Jetten and others with open arms, having invited his friends and acquaintances from Amsterdam's clubs to star in his first feature film.

Staging photographs held fewer and fewer secrets, but Erwin still lacked professional confidence. He possessed, as he thought, no more than a 'limited' talent, but he knew how to exploit it to the maximum. 'I work from my weaknesses. What can't I do? This tells me immediately what I *can do*. Within those parameters, I come up with an idea. ... Actually, it's always the same: a face-on shot or a tripod on the lowest setting, one light and a couple of reflection screens.' Forever the same vantage point and angle – so it's hardly surprising that a story circulated about Erwin not using a tripod. It was rumoured that he habitually placed his camera on a concrete pole in his studio instead.

It was thanks to a commission from Els Hoek, curator of the Centraal Museum in Utrecht, that he directed his first film. She wanted him to make a short feature

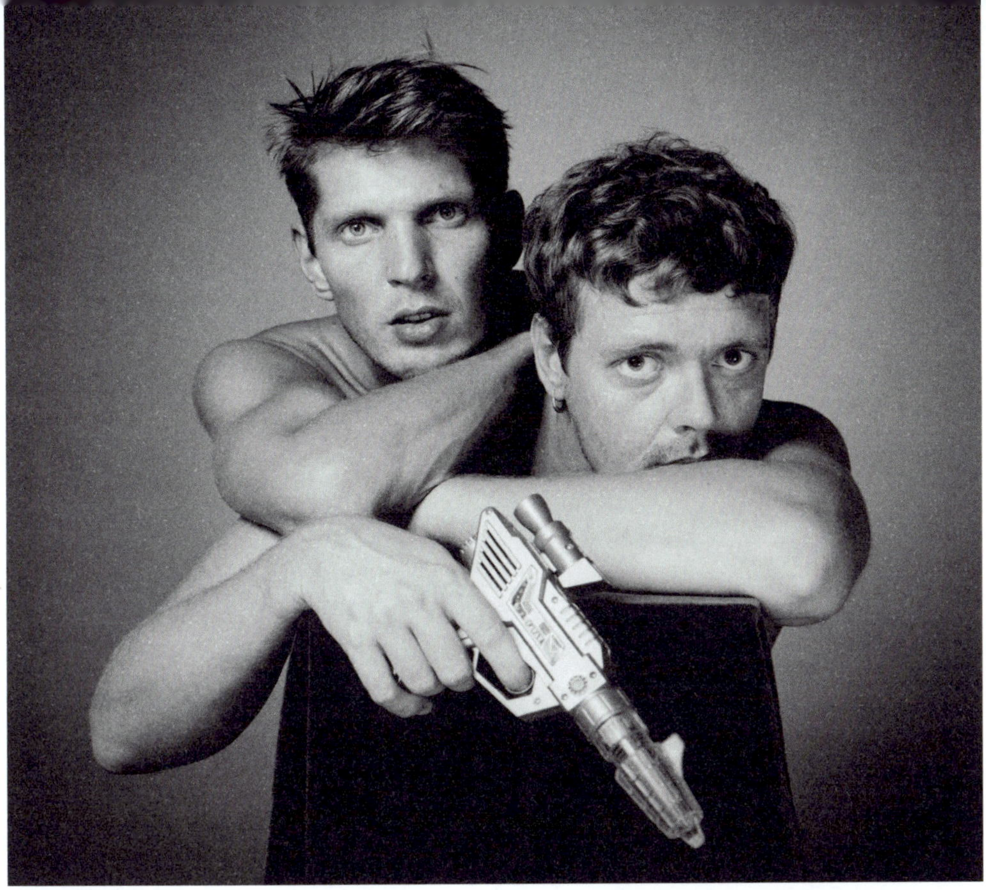

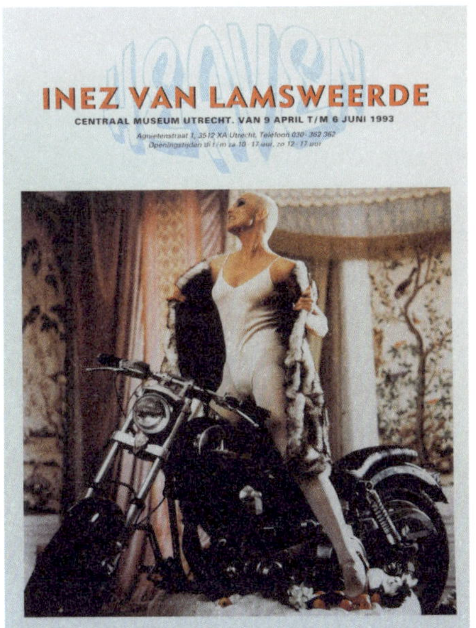

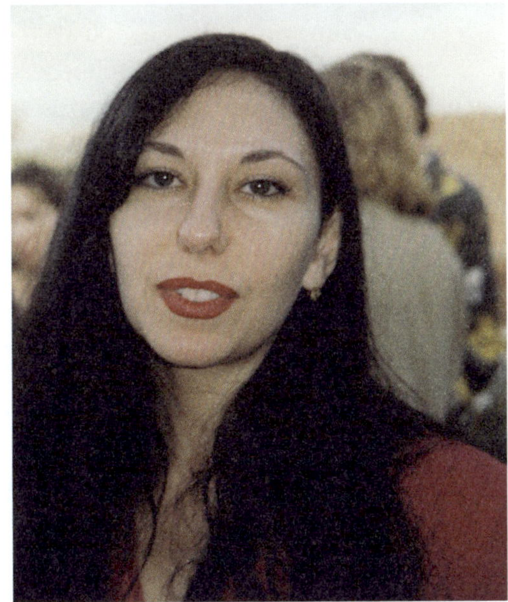

Top: 'Hey Frans, fancy making a film together?' 'Sure, why not.' Frans Franciscus and Erwin Olaf co-wrote and directed the short feature film *Tadzio* (1991). Bottom: Inez van Lamsweerde (right) captured the making of *Tadzio* in a series of staged film stills.

set entirely in the manor house: an open assignment with only two conditions: the film must result from a joint venture with another artist and showcase the historical significance of Oud Amelisweerd.

He had long been flirting with the idea of a feature film. Erwin and Frans Franciscus had previously collaborated on a children's science-fiction film, *Captain Tom*. It was supposed to concern Tom, a young boy whose grandmother is dying. When he discovers the 'Source of Eternal Life', he mends his grandfather's old rocket and sets off on a mission, with his grandmother, to find the 'Source'. *Captain Tom* never came to fruition. It remained a work-in-progress until 2007, when Erwin finally gave up on the project.

Meanwhile, he tried his hand at short films, such as six children's videos for a TV programme. Ben van Os served as art director, Haute Couture Junkies styled, and Desiree Aben designed the costumes.

Thomas Manneke, who later made a name for himself as a photographer, was an intern with Erwin at the time. He was impressed by Erwin's perfectionism and work ethic. 'Erwin went to extremes and persevered until he got exactly what he wanted.' The studio could be a stressful workplace, partly because the commissions offered little or no room for independent photography, which was where Erwin's heart lay. 'He seemed frustrated by it, but he never rushed into anything and always turned the commercial work into something special, something unique.'

Erwin's tantrums were notorious. 'As a young man, I was shocked, I wasn't used to that, and my personality is completely the opposite. He'd get irate, but he also knew how to atone.' During his internship, Manneke increasingly felt that Erwin's drive and ambition stemmed from the struggles he faced on an almost daily basis. 'He often used to walk into the studio and tell us about a taxi driver or street kid who, for the umpteenth time, had called him a poof or a faggot. I couldn't shake the feeling that his work was ultimately bound up with that battle.'

Erwin was charming and obliging to his models, Manneke observed. 'He had to be, because he demanded a lot from them: posing with a fish on their head, or naked, and in the weirdest positions.' The studio would resound with laughter, but the atmosphere was also incredibly focused. 'That's the most important thing I learnt from Erwin: to take everything you do as a photographer very seriously, always working with complete dedication. Never doing half a job.'

Thomas Manneke also assisted on 'Bello', the music video that Erwin made with the singer Mathilde Santing, as part of a tribute to poet and writer Annie M.G. Schmidt, best known for her children's books. According to the writer, the clip did not pertain to her work. 'It's a terrible shame. Just omit the song if you're not going to do anything with it. It makes no sense at all.' Erwin was upset about it for a while. While he'd never shied away from controversy, he wanted to please his audience, especially established artists.

As much as he wanted to put his name to a feature film after so many warm-up exercises, the prospect of actually making one was daunting. 'Photography is more like high school and film is university level. Creating emotion on celluloid is fiendishly difficult.'

Years ago, he'd written the synopsis of a semi-autobiographical screenplay. The main characters included himself, in a slightly different guise, and his parents. And he loved the idea of uniting his friends, models, collaborators and colleagues in a film. People who often didn't know each other personally but who all, each in their inimitable way, played a role in the screenplay of his life.

He'd sketched out a Warhol-like figure as the protagonist, 'a cool man or woman who belongs to the jet set'. The extended description made it clear that he modelled the fantasy figure on himself, at least in part. For it had to be someone 'stoned and therefore insular, but with a cohort of beautiful, charming, weird and strange people surrounding them.' A more succinct summary of his life, both in and out of the studio, is hard to find.

The film was meant to resemble *Blow Up* (1966), Italian director Michelangelo Antonioni's mystical thriller about a photographer. But it was also supposed to contain elements drawn from American director Tod Browning's film *Freaks* (1932), which had been banned in the UK because the vengeful characters were played by real disabled people.

Freaks had appealed to him because it stood up for the scorned minority, for the genuine outsiders, back in the 1930s. Erwin had always had an eye for them, according to his ex-partner, Teun Frieszo. 'Erwin has a soft spot for the extreme, for anyone who's been chucked overboard. This is the context for his interest in everything big, crazy, fat, thin, mentally challenged or weird. For its beauty. Certain people were shocked but he couldn't have cared less. Because that wasn't the goal, it was more of a by-product.'

He opted to collaborate on the film with Frans Franciscus, who had worked as a visual artist in Berlin for a while after graduating. Frans stimulated Erwin's creativity, and partly because of this, according to the latter, his imagination could 'run wild'. In the past, Frans had helped Erwin by introducing him to his gallerists, Claar Griffioen and Martin Rogge of Flatland in Utrecht. According to Griffioen, Erwin thought that people in the official art world didn't take him seriously. He saw Frans making a name for himself and he wanted that too.

'Erwin was warm and generous, and you could really have a laugh with him,' Griffioen says. 'A sharp mind that he could deploy humorously and positively, but also aggressively and negatively. He occasionally scolded me: that I didn't appreciate his work, that I was a straight cunt and so on.' Erwin had a complicated relationship with the gallery world. 'I can't tell you how often he said that gallery owners operated like racketeers with their ridiculously high percentages. Artists, he said, were being bled dry by people who, in and of themselves, represented nothing.'

Frans Franciscus witnessed at first-hand how his friend's unbridled ambition sometimes stymied his career, despite his increasing success. 'Erwin is a grafter who is prone to extreme jealousy. Success becomes addictive; you always want more and more, but it's never enough.' But it's precisely the dissatisfaction that makes you aim higher, Franciscus noticed. He knew instantly why Erwin had accepted Els Hoek's proposal. 'Erwin still hadn't ticked a film off his list, and for that reason alone he immediately said yes.'

'When I die, at least I can say: I've made a film'

Curator Els Hoek had a limited budget at her disposal, just enough for a fortnight's shoot, meaning that Erwin could not yet make the full-length feature film of his dreams. In keeping with the trend of Postmodernism, their script was a meta-story: a film about making a feature film *à la* Antonioni. Its title, *Tadzio*, alludes to the protagonist from Italian director Luchino Visconti's *Death in Venice* (1971), a film adaptation of Thomas Mann's homoerotic novella. Erwin was fired up by Franciscus's fascination with the classic Italian films by Visconti, Federico Fellini and Pier Paolo Pasolini, such as *Salò, or The 120 Days of Sodom* (1975).

'*Salò* didn't play in the Netherlands until 1978 and, as a nineteen-year-old, it was almost more than I could handle. I became utterly impassive. And the fake dicks annoyed me; they looked so obviously glued on. Frans and I had a bet with each other on who could sit it out the longest. Pasolini profoundly impacted my work: *Chessmen*, too, explores the themes of power and powerlessness, linked to sexuality. You can draw that line directly. With Visconti, Frans and I were looking at the grandeur, the kitsch and that "no expense was spared" atmosphere.'

Visconti's Tadzio is a beautiful youth, as in Thomas Mann's book. But Erwin, true to his fascination with the underdog, conjured up a new version for his film: a fourteen-year-old with Down's syndrome, played by 19-year-old Aat Nederlof with the same disability. He found Nederlof as Tadzio more intriguing than the pretty youths of his predecessors. And he deliberately wanted to make the part unappealing. 'I would like to upend all the clichéd images. That large people are jolly, homosexuals charm women, and people with Down's syndrome look cute: I want to demolish it all,' he argued as a justification.

Erwin's Tadzio arrives on a film set with his mother, a celebrated actress whose career is waning. While she awaits her lover, Tadzio wanders through the mansion with a toy gun. Behind each door he finds, as the director himself described it, 'all manner of absurdist little situations'.

Viewers therefore step, in the company of Tadzio, into a myriad of different worlds, populated by birds of paradise of every conceivable kind. Desiree Aben remembers the shoot as one big party. 'It was one huge, hysterical circle of friends, everyone was having fun, we were all incredibly driven. It provided a very safe environment, despite the blistering moments which were par for the course with Erwin.'

In the closing scene, after the credits, you gaze into Aat Nederlof's face, his nose pressed against a car window. 'To be continued' appears below, in Italian. Later, Erwin felt ashamed of that image. He knew he'd gone too far. 'Not good. It's so easy to make fun of people with developmental disabilities. Or portray them as pathetic or morose. And that's senseless.'

They had wanted to make a toxic and funny film, according to Frans Franciscus. Erwin could remain true to his way of working as a photographer because the film was recorded without sound. 'We were writing the dialogue as the camera rolled, translating it as best we could,' Frans Franciscus recalls. 'With a Prisma Italian dictionary close to hand, we were writing behind the camera.'

Tadzio premiered at the Dutch Film Festival to high expectations, but the critics were unconvinced. '*Tadzio* is something of a pastiche, somewhat camp and has less to do with Fellini than its makers may have wanted,' wrote *Trouw*. Erwin was long haunted by *de Volkskrant's* headline 'Photographer and painter dabble in film'. The piece continued: 'Beautiful, atmospheric and evocative photographic images that excite you until you discover they don't lead anywhere. Tadzio's last words are "*Perché, perché?*" Indeed, why this film?'

Looking back, even the makers' own enthusiasm had dissipated. They noticed that few people understood the work. Erwin had obsessed over the details; even as a filmmaker, he remained above all a photographer. In his eyes, the only successful scene is the one that prefigures the photographs he would make decades later, depicting a single, precise emotion. 'A close-up shows Desiree debating whether to sleep with her co-star. Those 30 seconds count as a triumph. The remaining 29 minutes and 30 seconds are a total failure.'

Still, Erwin's final verdict was positive. 'When I die, at least I can say, "I've made a film,"' he stated, looking back at *Tadzio*. 'That's already more than I thought I'd accomplish.'

'I work traditionally. I'm fascinated by the métier'

AGAINST THE SANCTIMONIOUS AURA

Filmmaker, photographer and semi-famous Dutchman, yet still an underdog – that's how Erwin felt. He managed to convince himself that he'd already been cast aside by Amsterdam's cultural elite. His long-cherished goal of becoming famous was finally in sight. But, as if to pre-empt the threat of decline, he claimed that his popularity consisted solely of hype. 'The gay avant-garde discovered me, but they dropped me long ago, when other celebrities arrived on the scene.'

He was referring to the critics who invariably likened him to his great role model: Mapplethorpe. 'Mapplethorpe is an aesthete, but his aestheticism only serves to expose the absolute truth of his reality, to the fullest possible extent. Compare Mapplethorpe's photographs with Erwin Olaf's cleaned-up decadence and you'll see that one homoerotic photographer is not like the other,' wrote *NRC Handelsblad*.

Erwin remained envious of his contemporaries Rineke Dijkstra and Inez van Lamsweerde. The former had broken through with the beach photos that secured her international reputation, while the latter had returned after a year in the US and, with her partner Vinoodh Matadin, was rising to prominence with heavily edited fashion photographs. He felt overtaken on both sides and relegated to old news before he'd even really begun. 'Inez is a chick with balls! And yes, my time is over. Of course, as a photographer, you can't stay young and upcoming all your life. Someone will have to succeed you at some point. So, I told Inez: "kid, I'm glad it's you!"'

His love life was also complicated. Teun Frieszo was still living in Utrecht and whenever they saw each other, arguments and tantrums followed each other in rapid succession. They made a conscious decision not to cohabit, according to Frieszo. 'It just wasn't done in those days – and it gave us plenty of reasons to fight.' He continued to juggle multiple relationships, as did Erwin on occasion. 'I preferred steady boyfriends; Erwin acted more casually. And what's more, we cheated on each other.' It led to clashes and angry letters: 'Teun, all I have to say is that I'm sick and tired of your twisting, lying and forgetting about shagging, boyfriends and horny guys. You now have everything the way you want it. Can't you at least try to be honest and spare me the jealousy? You often make me really sad. Bye, E.'

It was a wild time, and when things got too 'dramatic and disharmonious', Frieszo would promise to finally 'kick everyone out' and be eternally faithful. Yet Erwin always fiercely rejected the idea. 'He would say, "yes, you may have had your fill now, but I've still got a lot of catching up to do",' recalls Frieszo.

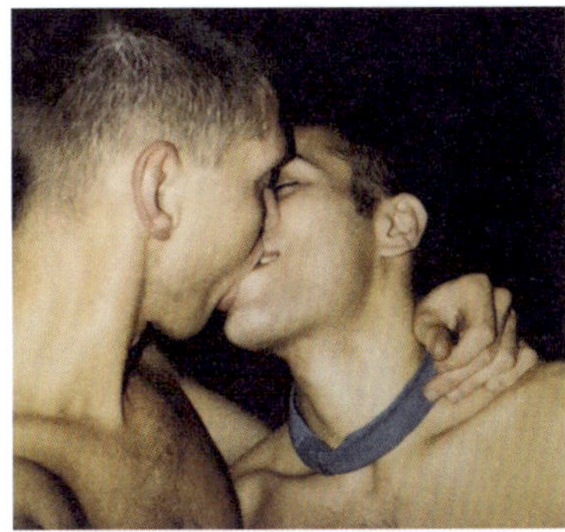

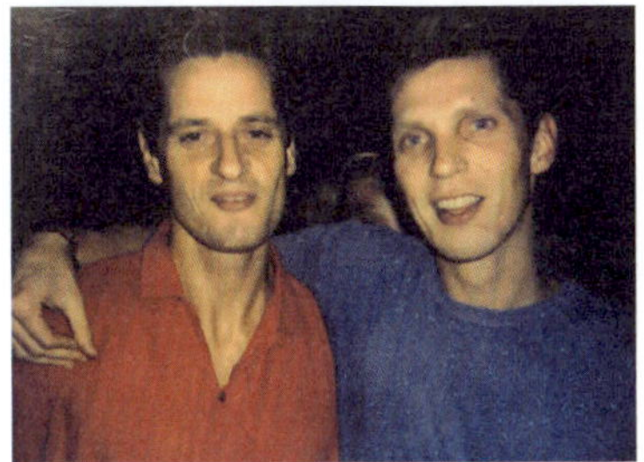

With Alandus (top) and with Teun (bottom).

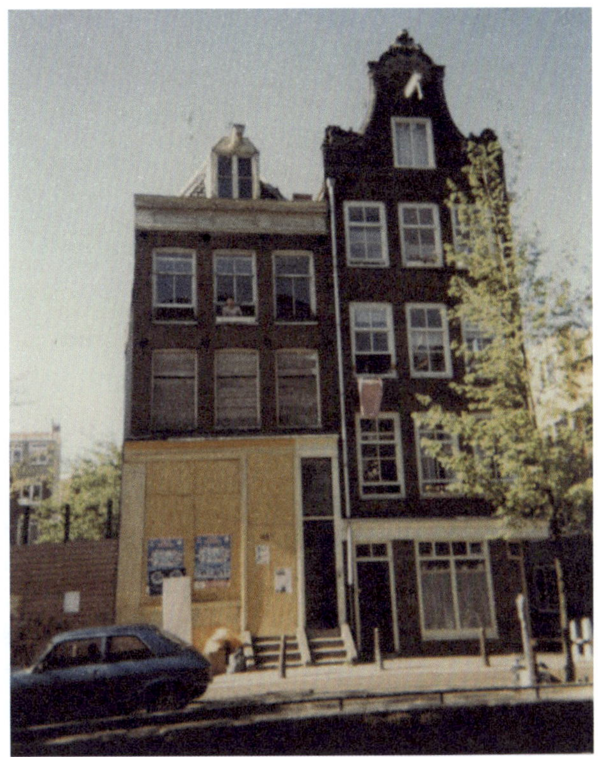

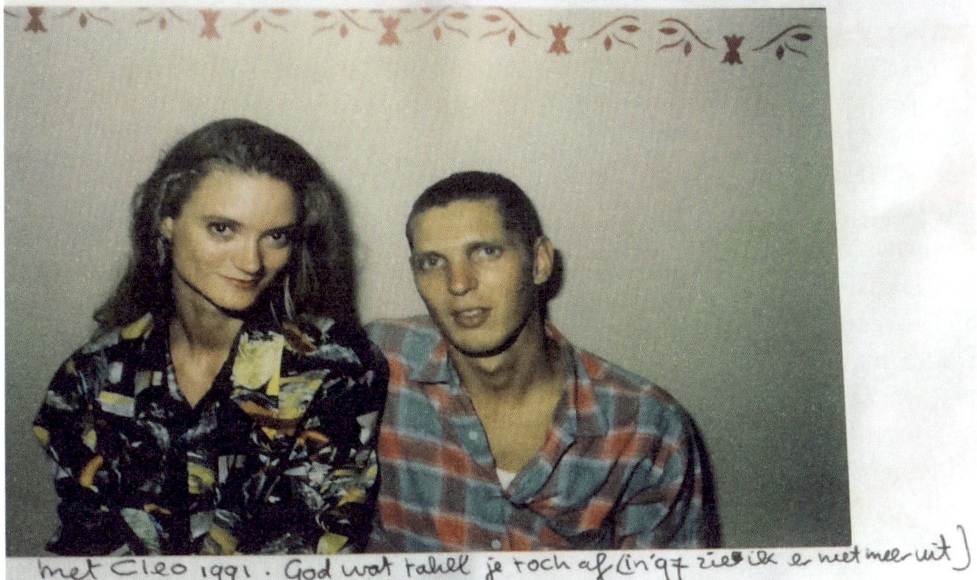

With Cleo Campert in 1991. Top right: Erwin standing at the window of the house on Lauriergracht, not long before it was demolished.

In short, they had 'unbelievable arguments', which Frieszo likened to a personality clash. 'Erwin always felt like he was under attack... Like all famous people, he has narcissistic traits, and these collisions affected him badly.' This held true in both the private and professional spheres. 'You can get a hundred compliments, and you throw them in your hat,' Erwin stated about the pressure of fame. 'But all it takes is for one person to say, I think they're crap photos, and that's what you remember.' His other great love affair was also in difficulty. Alandus had quit photography. He then thought his future lay in house music. That too proved unsuccessful. 'It's a bit like the story of my life: a jack-of-all-trades and master of none. Always never quite good enough.'

That disparity, combined with Erwin's ambitions and his perpetual insecurity, placed their relationship under considerable strain. 'We were both predisposed to unending drama.' It was a desperate love for someone with a very different character, although they did share a passion for recreational drugs, Erwin recalls. 'Alandus suffers from extreme shyness; he always thinks too much.' Alandus felt that Erwin projected his self-doubts onto him. 'When Erwin was in the doldrums, he could destroy me mentally.' Yet this did not weaken their love for one another. When Alandus reads back their cards and notes, it comes flooding back to him how 'infatuated' they were with one another. Erwin tended to be perfunctory. 'I'm so moved by this note, dated 18 February 1993,' Alandus says and reads aloud: 'On the train. This is a love letter to say that I love you in my own way, so, I love you. There. Now it's on paper.'

One reason that Erwin not only experimented with film but also pursued a more commercial path was his doubts about the lasting value of his photographs. He continued to produce work for magazines and for DJ Joost van Bellen's CD covers. And when *Playboy* invited TV presenter Monique Sluyter, who had also modelled for *Chessmen*, to be the playmate of the month for December (1991), he took the pictures. Erwin, who adored Christmas decorations, portrayed her as a female Father Christmas in suspenders. Such assignments bought him independence from the whims and biases of art critics, grant givers and museum bosses. He liked to provoke that world: 'Art comes with a gift all its own: hyperbole. Pictures are like thin air. It's ridiculous what a gallery makes someone pay for a photograph.'

In late 1992, he was awarded Groningen's annual photography commission. In autumn 1993, he presented the results: *De tafel van tien* [The Table of Ten], portraits of 'ordinary' Groningers in his familiar theatrical settings, with long, conical tin noses, tied to their faces. One of the subjects was the well-known painter's model Geke Hankel, who had gained fame for her voluptuous figure. Her body inspired him, as he preferred life models to the so-called perfection of their photographic counterparts. He depicted her in a variation of Man Ray's *Le Violon d'Ingres* from 1924. Hankel

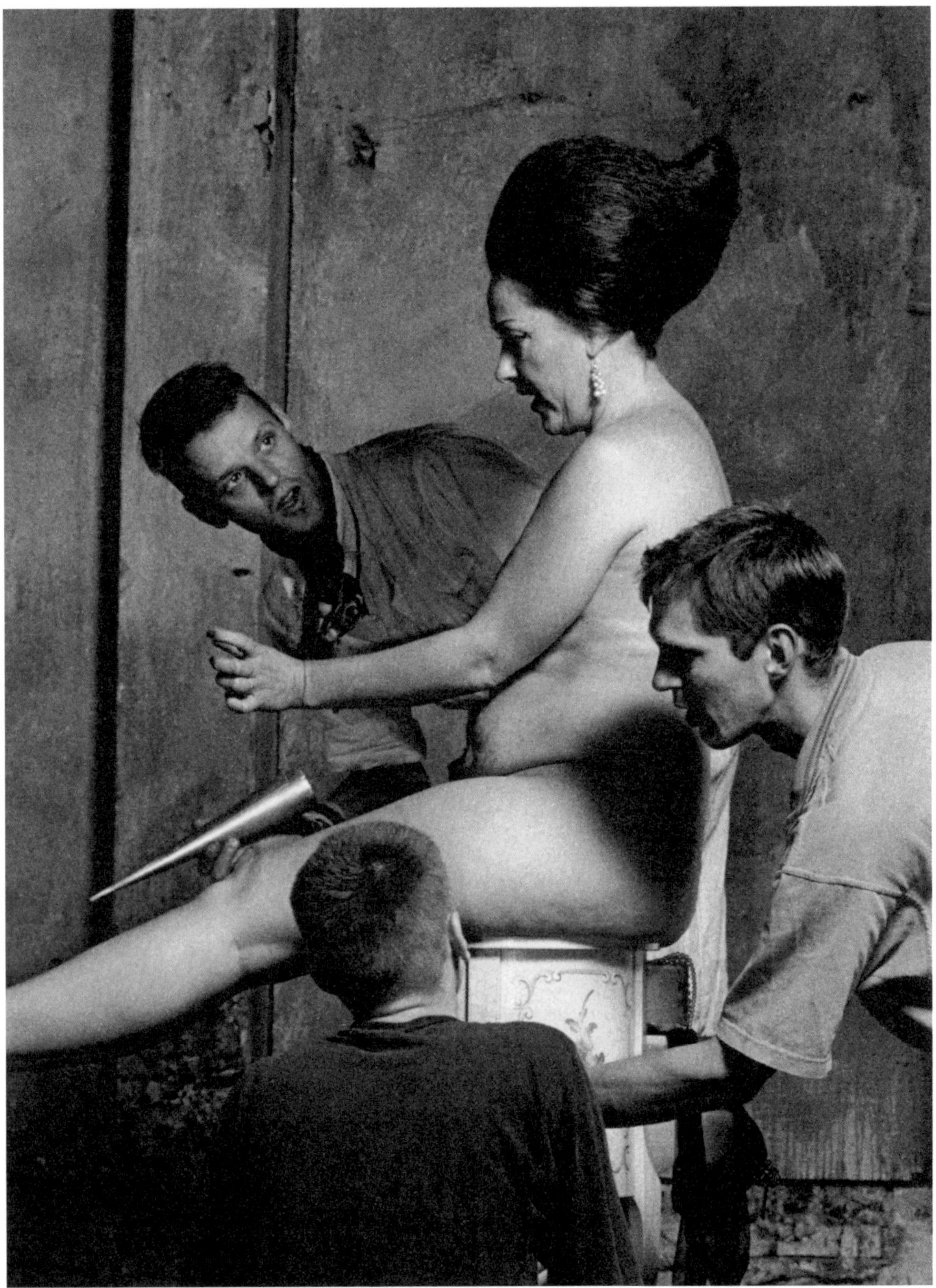

Working with Piek, Jaap Hinten and model Geke Hankel, 1992. They spent eight hours on a single photograph, which Hankel described as 'one of the most beautiful moments' of her modelling career.

considered the session with Erwin as 'one of the highlights of my professional career'. The picture was eight hours in the making. She was delighted with the final result: 'I like to call it one of life's gifts.'

With this assignment, he turned away from the sanctimonious aura surrounding visual art, but also the idea that photography belongs to its upper echelons. 'I work traditionally. I'm fascinated by the métier. I always use a direct eye-level camera angle and simple lighting. It's not part of some refined artistic processing. The photograph itself is the work.'

Around that time, Wim van Sinderen of the Kunsthal Rotterdam felt that a retrospective of Erwin's photographs was in order. He thought it absurd that people considered Erwin Olaf incompatible with the museum world.

For the people who stuck with him through thick and thin, despite the negative reviews, Erwin had a name: 'my people'. Besides Van Sinderen and publisher Van der Spek, this included the gallery owners Claar Griffioen and Martin Rogge. But he nevertheless harboured an uneasy, vague and unverifiable feeling that none of his faithful belonged to the inner sanctum of the art world. They, like himself, orbited on the fringes of that sphere, which was full of interminable jargon, an us-versus-them mentality and mutual backslapping. And its doors were firmly closed to outsiders. 'My people were not at the heart of modern art. And everyone involved in the latter turned their back on me. They were horrified the moment I walked into the room. Now they kiss my arse.'

'I want to force people to form an opinion about my photographs'

It was a huge honour for a 34-year-old photographer to have a retrospective at the Kunsthal. The exhibition *Joy* and the accompanying book felt like a form of revenge, and he also saw it as a chance to show the critics his true colours. 'Soon, a monograph about my work will appear. I want to force people to form an opinion about my photographs. I don't care if it's good or bad, so long as they have an opinion.'

The cover of *Joy* featured a photo from the *Bodyparts* series that had previously been used as a poster for Eugene O'Neill's play *Het begeren onder de olmen* [Desire Under the Elms] (directed by Ivo van Hove): a woman whose only visible body parts were her breasts, belly and pubic hair – the model was Desiree Aben. The image brought accusations of misogyny to his door.

Ivo van Hove ended their collaboration in late 1994, as Erwin's controversial posters strayed too far from the themes of the performances. Van Hove's argument was that Erwin was 'too much of an artist' and his work too forthright for these functional assignments. 'We worked happily together for five years. We fought vehemently sometimes, but always came out the other side,' Van Hove said. 'I'd rather stop now, when the going's good, than when things have gone too far.' Erwin was angry, but decided to leave it at that. 'Oh well, my pictures can live independently. The wheels keep turning.' Before concluding that, 'as far as I'm concerned, the entire theatre world can fuck off.'

Ninety photographs were exhibited at Rotterdam's Kunsthal, including all thirty-two pieces from the *Chessmen* series. The installation proved challenging, Van Sinderen recalls. Erwin disagreed with his idea for the presentation, namely the proposal to display the 100x100 cm square-format photographs from *Squares*, *Blacks* and *Chessmen* on a black background. 'When you can get as incensed as Erwin and still convey your message with clarity, you have my utmost respect,' says Van Sinderen. 'And I couldn't help but laugh at him; he has a sense of humour and he plays mean. But then again, not *too* mean.'

Erwin got his way and the scenography was praised in *NRC Handelsblad*: 'Olaf has transformed his sterile, corridor-like exhibition space into cabinets – long, intimate rooms in shades of dark blood red and one that evokes a moonless night, with an atmosphere of mock velvet and mahogany.' Hostesses, all named Joy for the occasion, welcomed guests at the Kunsthal vernissage. Hans van Manen and Frans Franciscus received the first copies of the book, which Erwin had dedicated to them. After which, a familiar spectacle unfolded: Amsterdam drag queens and other RoXY habitués thronged the galleries, copious amounts of cocaine were consumed in the toilets, and a polonaise was danced through the Kunsthal's restaurant.

Art historian Peter Weiermair – the director of the Frankfurter Kunstverein who had previously written about David Hockney and curated an exhibition with Robert Mapplethorpe in 1981 – wrote the introduction to *Joy*. This satisfied Erwin's craving for art-world recognition. According to Weiermair, Erwin's fantasy world differed significantly from Joel-Peter Witkin's 'bizarre necrophiliac' images. People often compared Erwin to the latter. Weiermair noted that Erwin played a game – albeit not always a subtle one – with the viewer's expectations, desires and insecurities. Lust was brought to heel in his pictures, Weiermair wrote, without it vanishing altogether.

He emphasised Erwin's fondness for artificiality and exaggeration and saw his oeuvre as 'camp', in the sense that Susan Sontag ascribed to the term in *Notes on Camp* (1964). Sontag had sought to collapse the boundaries between high and low culture. In so doing, she paved the way for artists like Erwin Olaf. He ignored such borders, if he recognised them at all, and felt perfectly at ease with all forms of culture, be it high or low.

Erwin saw a parallel with Jeff Koons, who had caused a furore with his exhibition *Ushering in Banality* at the Stedelijk Museum the previous year. Koons used banal images borrowed from consumer society, including porn, which therefore created new opportunities. 'Does Jeff Koons belong in the Stedelijk? Yes, because it means that I might get a place there too.' Koons's art was seen as shocking in some quarters, which made him laugh, since his work elicited similar reactions. 'Shocking isn't something that you can conjure up in the studio or from your easy chair, it just happens.'

Erwin felt a kinship with the American artist. 'His work hangs in a sacred building, a museum. I laugh my head off when I see one of those 4-metre-high cunts in there and people just walk up to it and scrutinise the details.'

Anna Tilroe, chief critic of *NRC Handelsblad*, did rave about Erwin's exhibition, which she said revolved around metamorphosis. 'This is where Olaf's secret lies: in the naturalness with which his characters portray transgressions, transgressions in terms of lust, aesthetics, sexual identity and bodily ideals.'

She was less fond of *Chessmen* on the grounds that it was 'irreverent'. On the other hand, she loved *Blacks*. 'The characters seem strange, yet the works resemble state portraits. The images seem to correspond to a reality. The only question is: which one? And this question is the most beautiful of all. It pertains to the scope of imagination, or our ability to think of ourselves as outside the norm. ... Erwin Olaf delights in everything that our society tends to call dubious, such as the ability to assume different guises.'

Back home in Hoevelaken, Erwin proudly showed his mother the full-page, 'posh' review in the quality newspaper. 'She read the piece standing up, bent over the kitchen table. Her thumb fixed over the spot where my self-portrait with an erection was printed.'

'Look at my place on the social ladder... it comes with obligations'

AROUND THE TABLE

A select company is seated at long, white-covered tables in Studio Erwin Olaf on IJselstraat. Mostly men: of the 70 guests, ten at most are women. 'For the invitations, I went through my diary,' the host explains. 'And I discovered, once again, that I'm very white and a very masculine homosexual. So I invited almost exclusively white queers.' The men he has plucked from his address file have all succeeded: as media personalities, fashion designers, doctors, lawyers and entrepreneurs – 'all faggots with money or influence', and often avid collectors of his work.

He has gathered his friends and acquaintances together in support of the organisation Human Rights Watch LGBT Global Circle, of which he is a member. He outlines the simple reason in his invitation. 'In the Netherlands, when it comes to gay emancipation, we've made great strides in recent decades. But internationally – and especially in the countries where the HRW is sticking its neck out with the LGBT programme – things look grim. Gay men's lives, and those of other sexual minorities, are being ruined, or have become impossible, to the extent that their lives are sometimes at risk.' The dinner is more about raising awareness than money, as he also noted in the invitation: 'It's not a begging campaign, although, of course, the LGBT Global Circle and its president, Boris Dittrich, could use the financial support.'

Now that he belongs to the establishment, Erwin believes that the role of outsider and eternal *enfant terrible* is finally behind him. 'Look at my place on the social ladder. But it was never a given, and it comes with obligations.' He remains as critical as ever, opposing injustice, although he admitted that fame sometimes causes him headaches.

In spring 2016, he had been invited to exhibit at the Pushkin Museum in Moscow. A few years earlier, in 2013, Vladimir Putin had signed the Russian anti-LGBT law, including a ban on distributing 'propaganda of non-traditional sexual relationships' to minors. It placed the gay community at extreme risk of prosecution. The consequences were dire, according to Erwin.

Like Marlene Dumas two years beforehand, he hesitated whether to respond to the Russian invitation. Intuition told him to decline. Not only was the introduction of the anti-LGBT law a new low point, but he also saw that 80% of the Russian population supported the legislation – which was a resounding slap in the face for all homosexuals. How should he react? Withhold his work or show as much of it as possible? A double bind.

After consulting an LGBT+ advocacy organisation, he finally decided to travel to Moscow to raise the gay issue on the spot, without concealing his sexuality. Marlene Dumas had chosen to show portrait drawings of famous gay Russians, such as Nureyev and Tchaikovsky, in St Petersburg. For Erwin, showing his own work sufficed.

His photographs resonated in artistic circles, but it was debatable whether they had made any difference to Russian homosexuals. He was fairly certain that his mission had failed and that he'd achieved nothing. Moreover, his stance towards Moscow wasn't unambiguous: if the invitation had come from Saudi Arabia or Nigeria, he'd have said no immediately. 'My kinds of people are tortured and killed there. If you live in this part of the world, you should thank God on bended knee. And no one more than me.'

He decided to boycott Russia until the situation improved, and made good on his

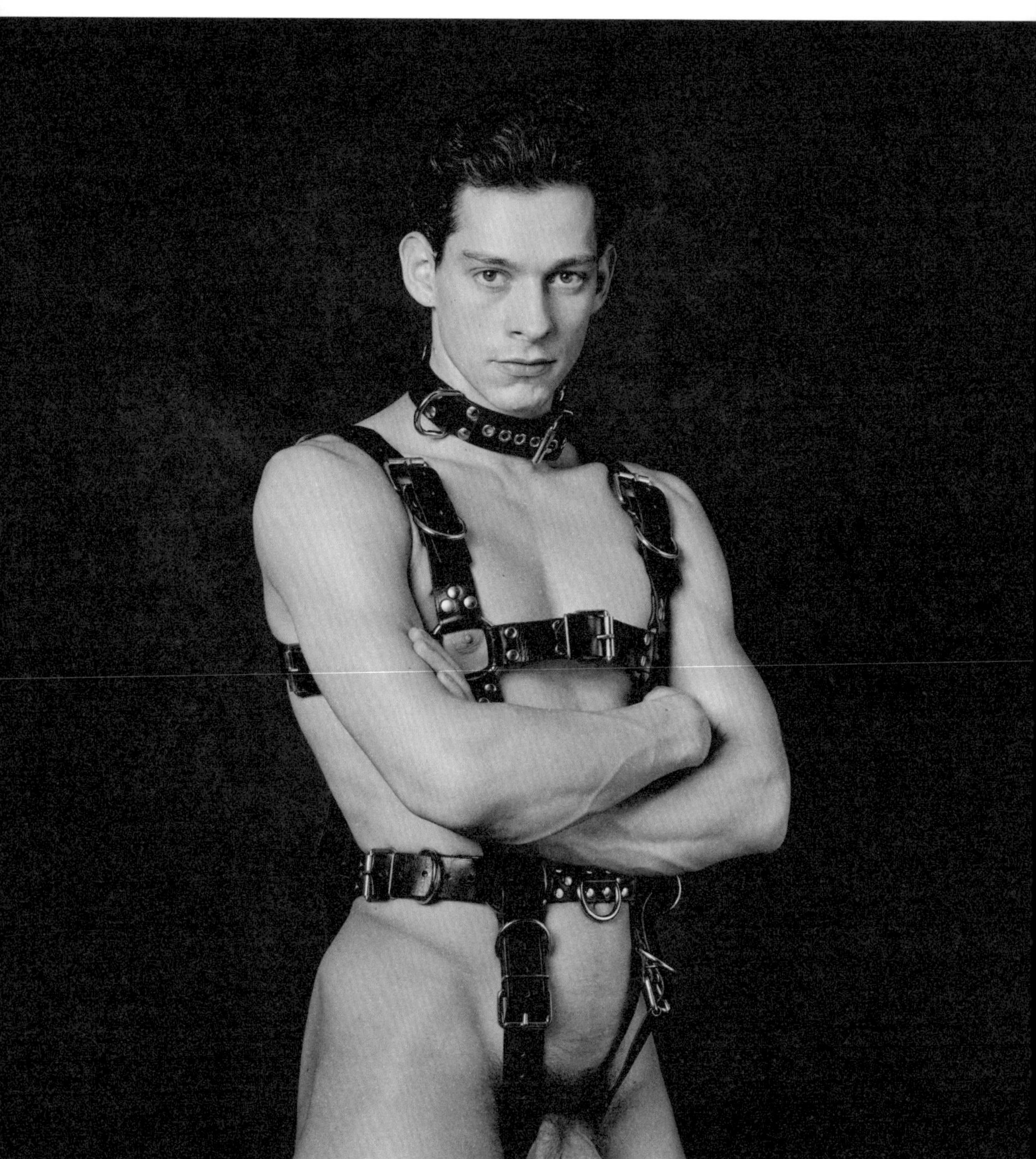

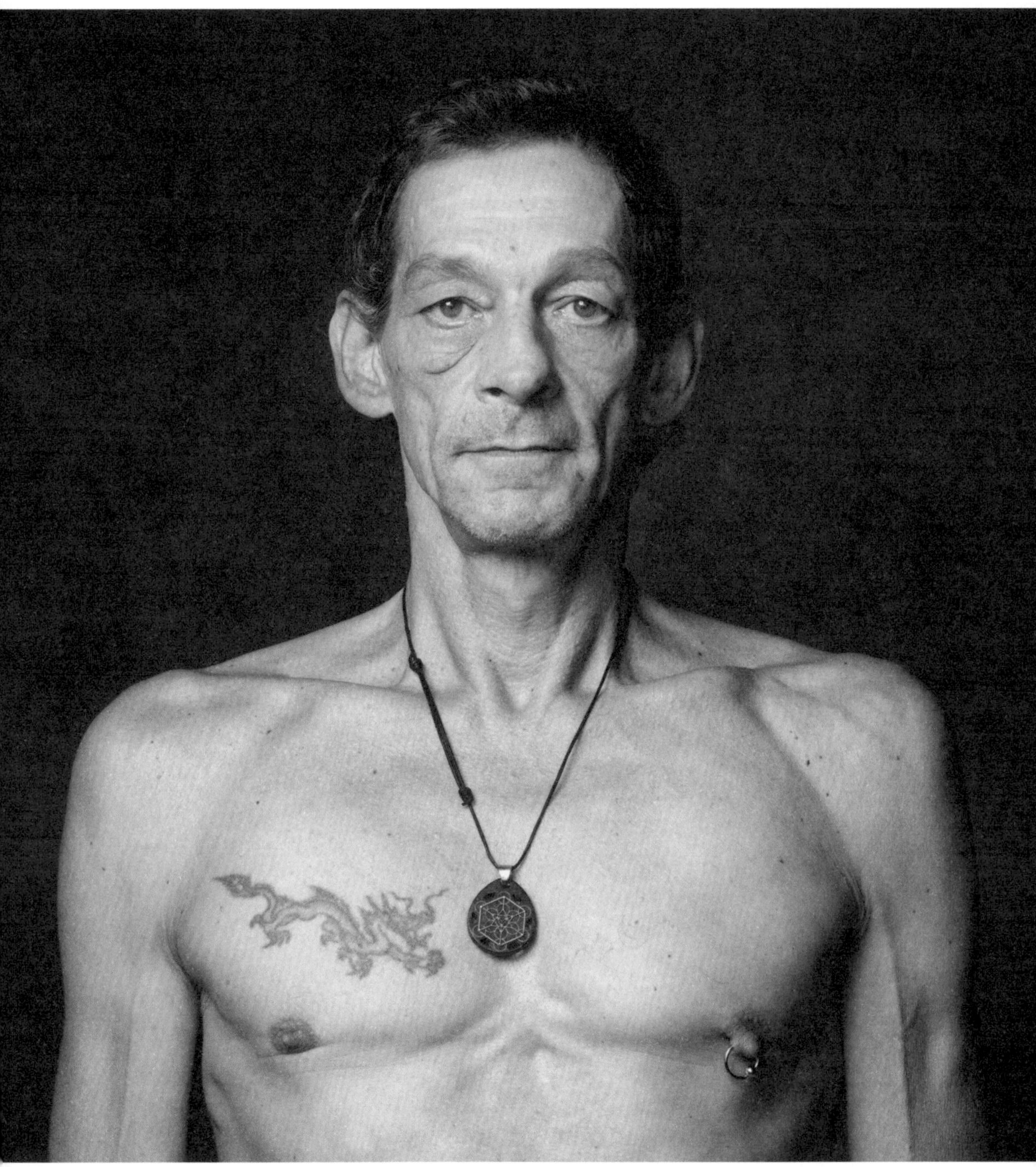

Performer Olav de Graauw loved working with Erwin and saw his photographs as liberating, precisely because other people labelled them shocking. Left: in 1986 in the *Squares* series. Right: in 2021 in the *Muses* series.

resolution by declining a further invitation from Moscow in May 2021. 'The current leadership is wilfully plunging legitimate political opponents, along with many innocent members of the LGBTQI+ community, into despair. I refuse to participate in this injustice in any way. My participation in an exhibition in Russia's current political climate would only add to the situation. It goes against all my convictions.'

'Can't we have some guidelines for such dilemmas? It's hard to maintain your integrity, be it personal or professional, when you're an artist,' said Erwin in 2016. 'I no longer know what I can and cannot do. I'm not allowed to work for the democratically elected [far right] political party PVV, yet it's OK to get involved with the Qatari royal family? A country that's responsible for over 1,000 construction worker deaths due to health and safety violations at the World Cup stadium sites (held in 2022).'

These days, he's more suited to public debates and charity dinners than vocal and opinionated talk shows. Upon watching his increasingly angry and out-of-breath television appearances, due to his lung disease, he realised: such a wheezy performance doesn't help the cause. So it's over with media activism, he decided. 'A grim old white man like me on TV; it doesn't work anymore. I've lost the magic.'

'I'd like to be Andy Warhol. Mind you, who wants to be bald with a grey wig?'

The early 1990s were lean years, even for art. In his bestseller *The End of History and the Last Man* (1992), political philosopher Francis Fukuyama pointed to the spread of Western liberal democracy around the world as the end point of humanity's ideological evolution. After the First Gulf War, US President Bush had announced a 'new world order'.

Meanwhile, unemployment was rising in the Netherlands and, for the first time since the end of the Second World War, Yugoslavia had become a battleground within the borders of the new Europe. The optimism that accompanied the fall of the Berlin Wall gave way to a minor recession, and the fear of AIDS and the fast-approaching turn of the millennium created a sense of doom and gloom among many young people. It was no coincidence, therefore, that one of the parties Erwin Olaf organised in October 1990 was called *The End of the World*. However committed he was, it was always about working hard and partying hard, preferably a combination of the two. He photographed for the club IT, organised parties at the RoXY, and presented his Ideal Dinners at the famous Supperclub in April 1994.

The Supperclub was a spin-off from a nomadic pop-up restaurant, but in early 1993, chef Thorwald Voss and his business partner Guda Stoop opened their establishment at a permanent location in Amsterdam's Jonge Roelensteeg. The concept anticipated a new trend – lounging – which chimed with the decadence of the *fin du vingtième siècle*. It did not follow the classic restaurant model; Thor aimed for a 'gallery for the art of cooking'.

Everyone who counted as hip and happening in Amsterdam showed up, along with all the Dutch celebrities of the day. Footballers, artists, actresses, politicians and CEOs frequented the venue – dining in decadence as the Roman Empire collapsed around their ears. Harrie Wildeman became an inevitable regular. For this reason, they gave him a starring role when the Supperclub invited Erwin to serve his Ideal Dinner on five nights in April 1994. Erwin had gleefully accepted the invitation. 'Manipulating a space and the people therein to create a fairy-tale world has always held irresistible appeal, as much in my photography as when organising parties and celebrations.'

He chose Andy Warhol, one of his heroes, as the theme. More specifically, the attack on his life. He was surprised to identify with the equally 'sexless' and world-famous artist. 'I'd like to be Andy Warhol. Mind you, who wants to be bald with a grey wig and ugly skin?'

Later, he inhabited the dual roles of Andy Warhol and Christopher Makos, who photographed Warhol's society magazine *Interview*. Makos had portrayed Warhol, who never openly presented as gay, as a woman. In *Self Portraits, 48 Years old*, Erwin photographed himself as a transvestite, both with and without a wig.

He had first heard of Warhol through his childhood hero, David Bowie, who references the American pop art artist on his 1971 album *Hunky Dory*: 'Andy Warhol looks a scream / Hang him on my wall. / Andy Warhol, Silver Screen / Can't tell them apart at all.'

Hans van Manen, who owned one of the famous *Flowers* silkscreens, taught him more about Warhol's work, and Erwin also saw the artist's retrospective in Paris. 'This art was about me and my time, that I understood. But I was also attracted to Warhol's androgyny and I devoured *The Philosophy of Andy Warhol (From A to B and Back Again)*. The book was simultaneously about everything – love, sex, food, beauty, fame, work, money, success – and nothing, like vacuous phone calls. I loved that tongue-in-cheek humour.'

Erwin had long admired Warhol's magazine *Interview*. A few years later, he'd let slip to Van Manen that he'd like to work for the publication. 'And Hans said, "That's bound to happen, dear." That's what I love about him. He believes in it, or at least makes me believe in it.'

He mirrored the Warhol phenomenon, and he saw it as a failure that he'd never permanently moved to New York. 'I genuinely thought that I had to be there to make it, but when push came to shove, I stayed at home. ... I can't ground myself anywhere else. I've suffered from homesickness all my life; even if I go away for a few weeks,

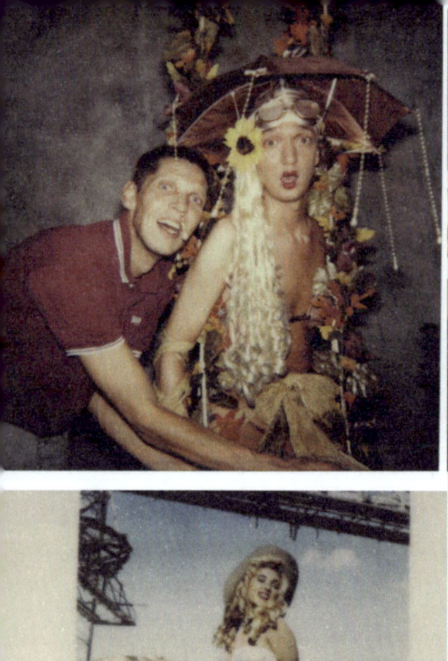

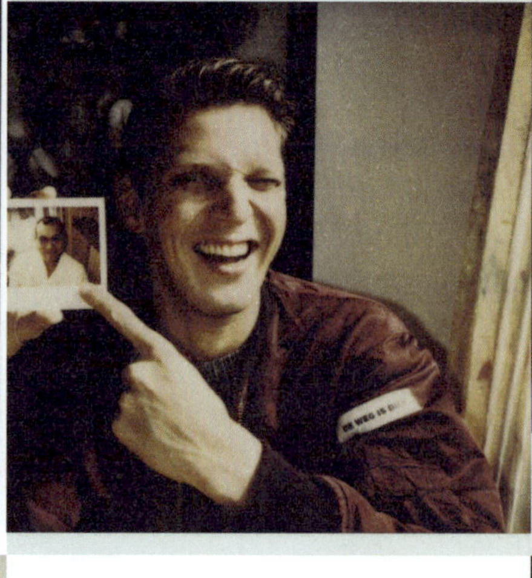

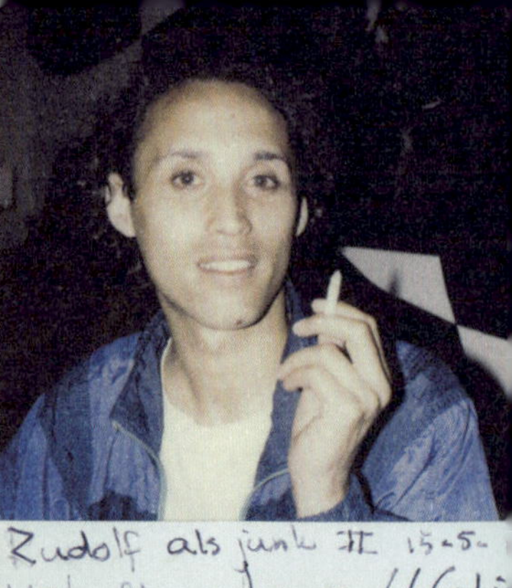

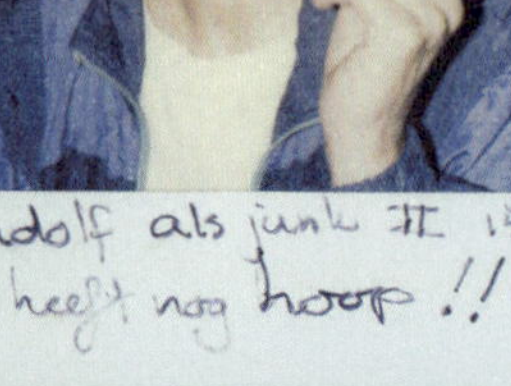

Rudolf als junk II 15-5-
Hij heeft nog hoop !! (al

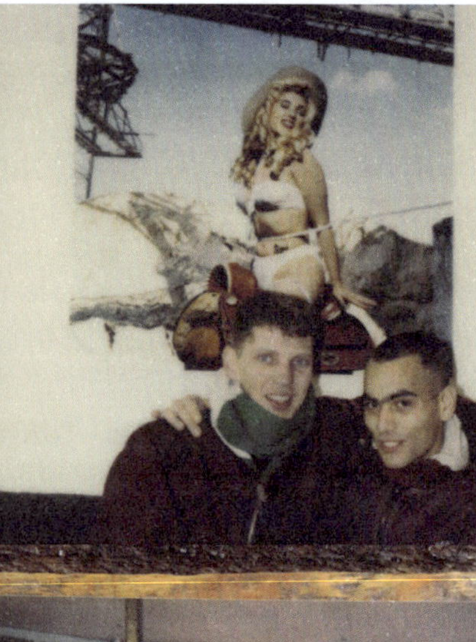

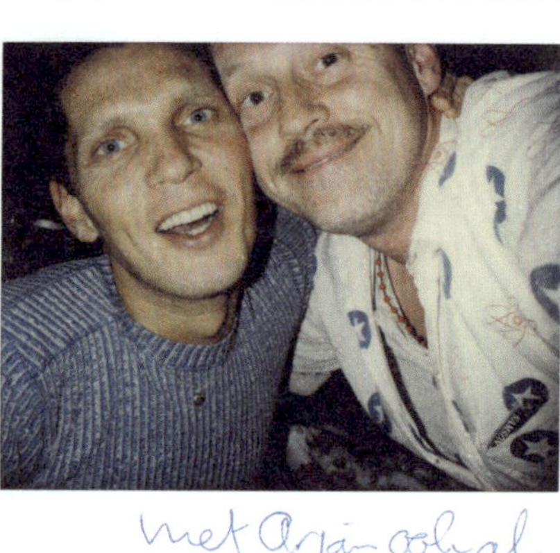

met Arjan ook al 40 jaar!

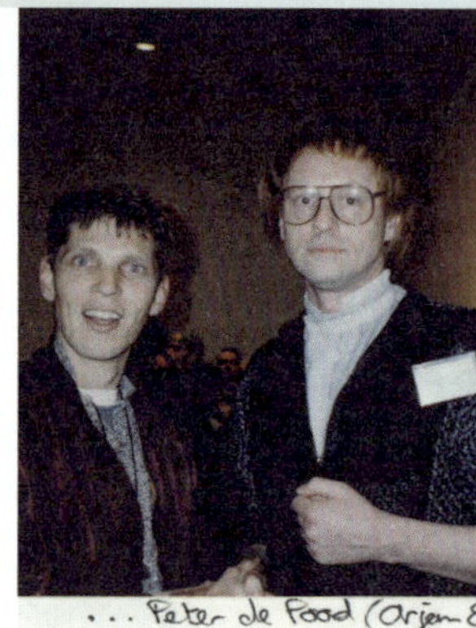

... Peter de Food (Arjan Ederveen
1995/94 (opening kreatief in stedelijk museum)

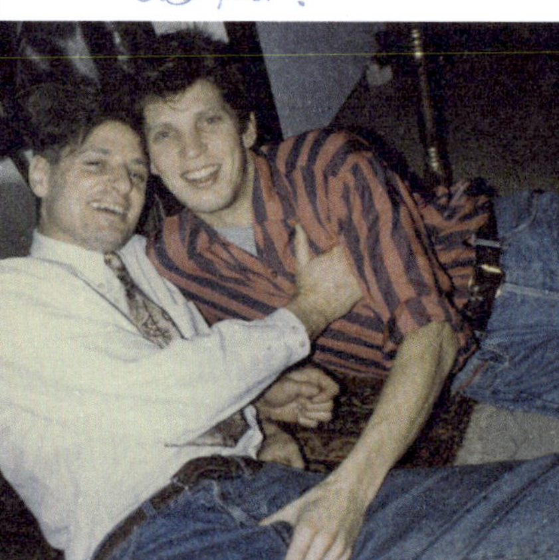

Oud thuis 89/90 Bij Dennis.

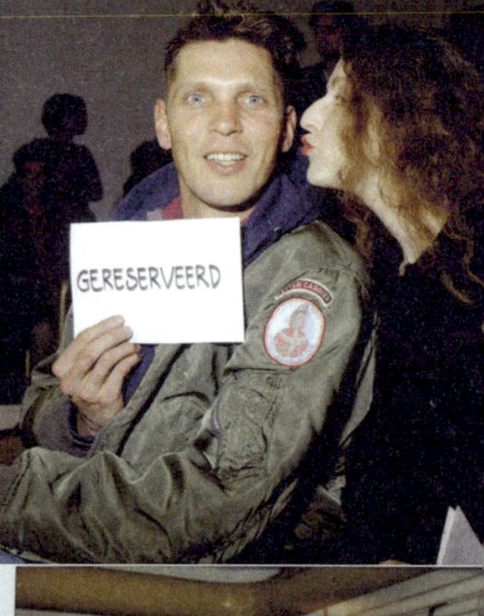

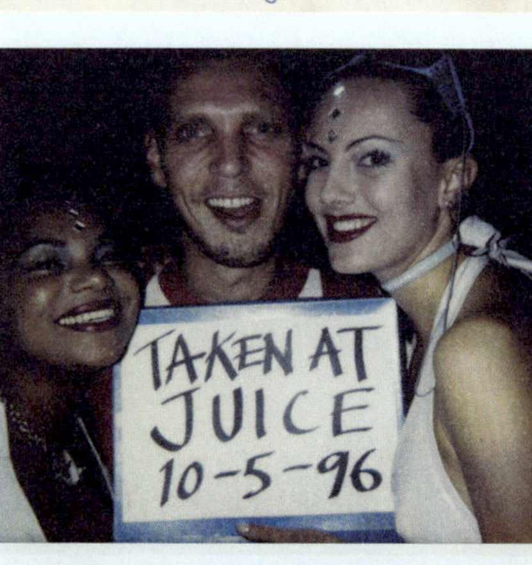

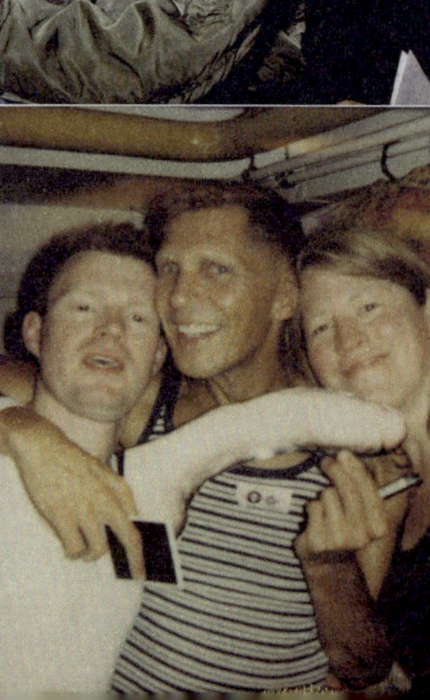

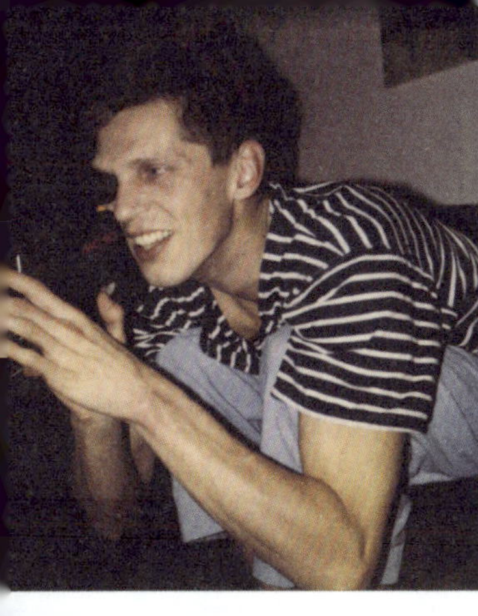

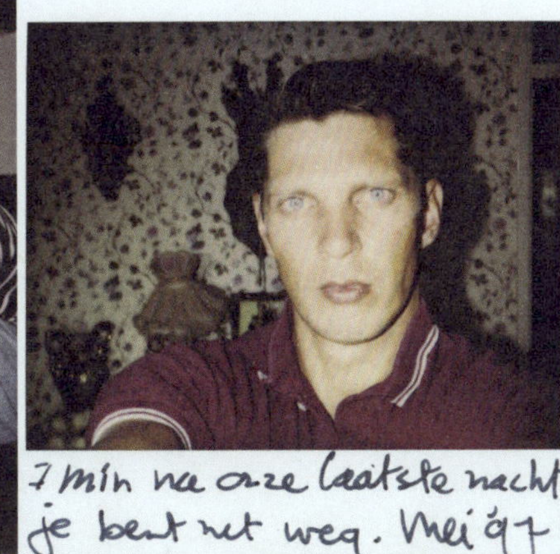

7 min na onze laatste nacht
je bent niet weg. Mei '97

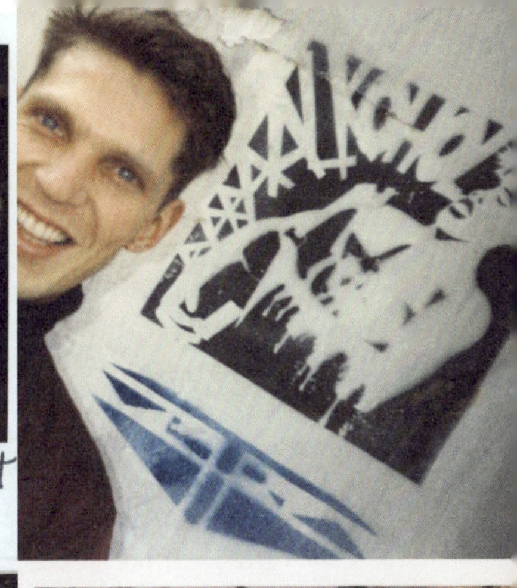

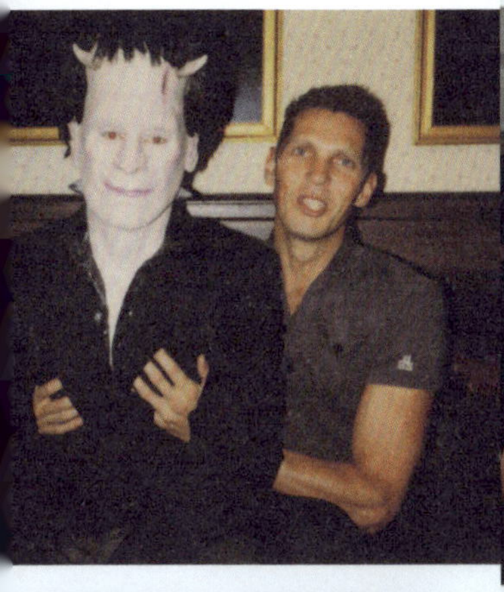

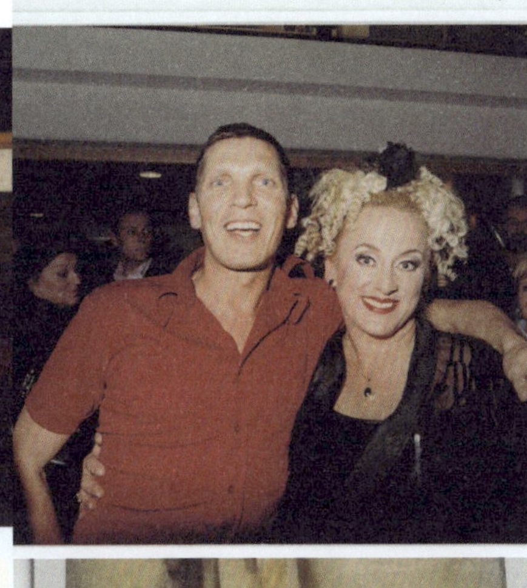

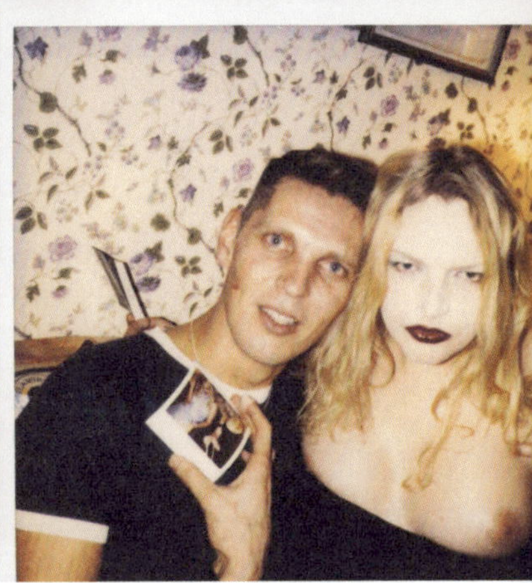

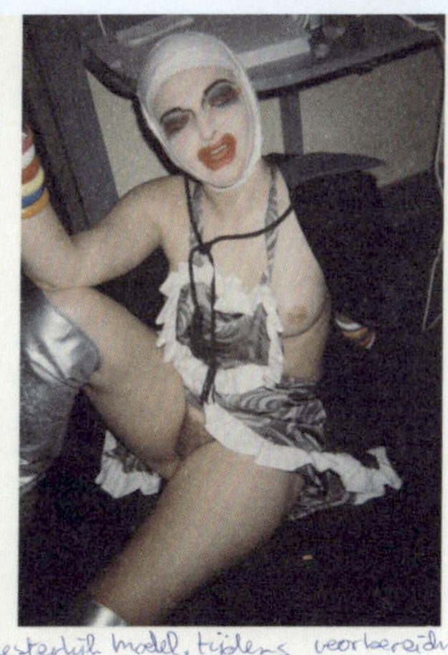

esterlijk model, tijdens voorbereiding

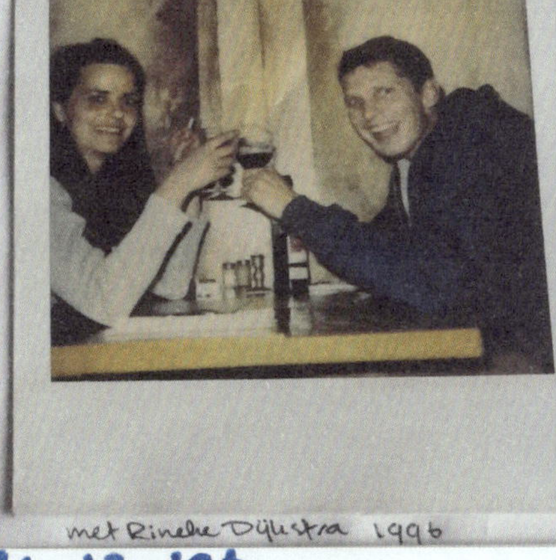

met Rineke Dijkstra 1996

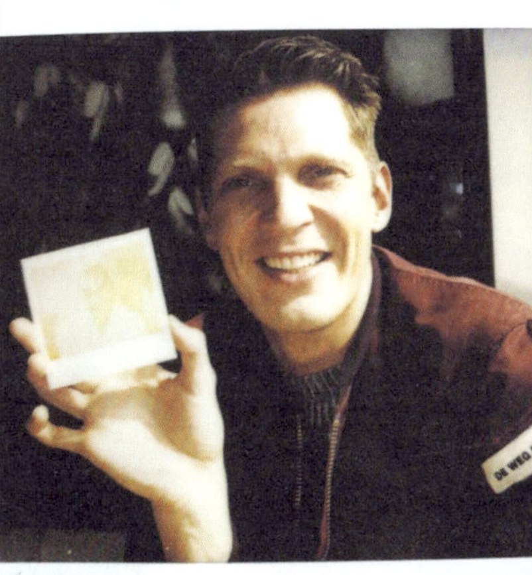

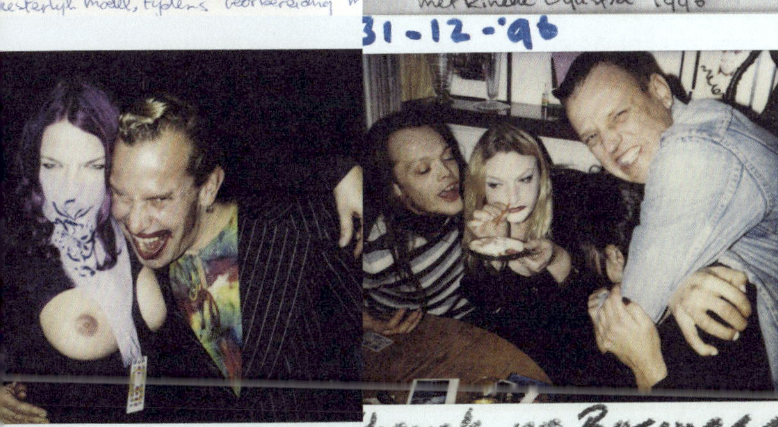

31-12-'96
here's no Business

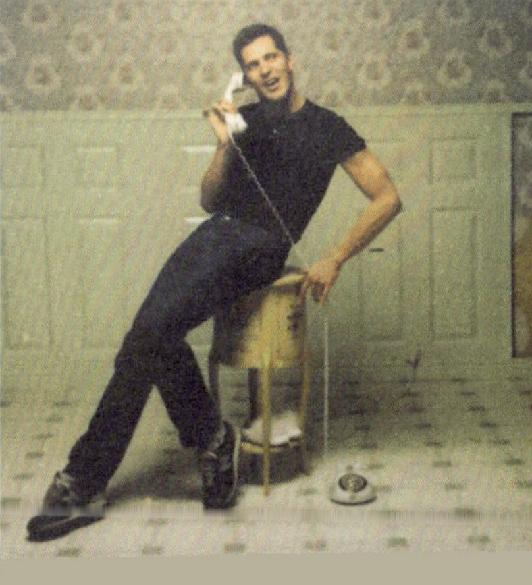

I long for Amsterdam again, for this part of the city centre, the quiet side of the Jordaan. I used to think that's why I missed out on a great career.'

Only recently did he realise that he hadn't missed out on anything by staying in the Netherlands. 'OK, if Warhol did something, it was in *The New York Times* and if I made or organised something, it was, at most, in the local newspaper, *Het Parool*. That's the difference. But whether it's Studio 54 or the RoXY, they're the same parties, the same decadence and emotion.'

'Only, unlike Warhol, I found myself surrounded by a valuable group of people. Warhol's loneliness filled me with dread; I thought it told a story of a lonely heart. He didn't choose love because he eventually showed Jed Johnson, whom he loved, the door. My love for Teun kept me here, too, and it was primal. And I was a mummy's boy; I needed to see my mother at least once every few months.'

But it turns out that global careers aren't bound to location because 'photography travels light', especially in the digital age. 'You can gain worldwide fame without leaving town.' Eventually, he ended up on the cover of *The New York Times* and saw his work hanging in the city's galleries. 'I couldn't have made what I made if I hadn't worked in the Netherlands. Here, I could photograph everything, say whatever I liked, and be myself. It heavily influenced all my undertakings. Because I bust a gut to test all the boundaries.'

Initially, Erwin's studio, like Warhol's at the time, served as a gathering place for artists. Moreover, it was modelled on his The Factory, decorated with silver foil, the 'silver screen' from the Bowie song. As a tribute, and because it offered theatrical possibilities, he wanted to serve up an exaggerated version of the attack on Warhol at his Ideal Dinner. In 1968, activist Valerie Solanas entered The Factory and shot the artist in the stomach. Warhol narrowly survived the assassination attempt.

Part of the Supperclub had been transformed into McWarhol. The 'poor people' – who gained admittance for a bargain price (19.94 guilders, €10) – sat behind fences. They could watch the spectacle unfolding at the tables through the chicken wire. The plebs were treated like wild animals. 'We had a deal with McDonald's and at one point the gates opened and the guys from the restaurant, in uniforms and caps, threw Happy Meals to the crowd.'

Meanwhile, the 'rich' – who paid 98.89 guilders (€45) – were seated at a long, white, U-shaped table. Film director Theo van Gogh described the evening in a letter. 'We ended up here in a parody of an orgy, with Warhol's mottos projected on the wall and slides of women making dogs pee all over them and so on. Whips struck those transvestite buttocks just as childishly as the flapping labia of a naked girl, who crouched over the table, holding her cunt like an oyster in front of a prim grandfather. I laughed my head off. Everyone was in high spirits, no one was aggressive.'

As they supped their soup – from Campbell soup cans, of course – the attack on Warhol replayed itself in front of the guests' eyes. According to Erwin, it was so realistic that a momentary panic erupted in the tent. After an S&M act by Olav and Louise and other erotic antics on the catwalk between the tables, Zu Browka emerged stark naked, painted silver, at the end of the main course. As a finale, two guys tipped tomato soup over her through a hole in the ceiling.

The guests were covered in red soup stains, the DJ hit the decks, and everyone piled onto the dancefloor. Meanwhile, in a small room, people watched Andy Warhol's films. An S&M afterparty kicked off in the basement.

Through the Ideal Dinners, Erwin celebrated life – as a game and with humour. But, like Warhol, he was steadily building his artistic career.

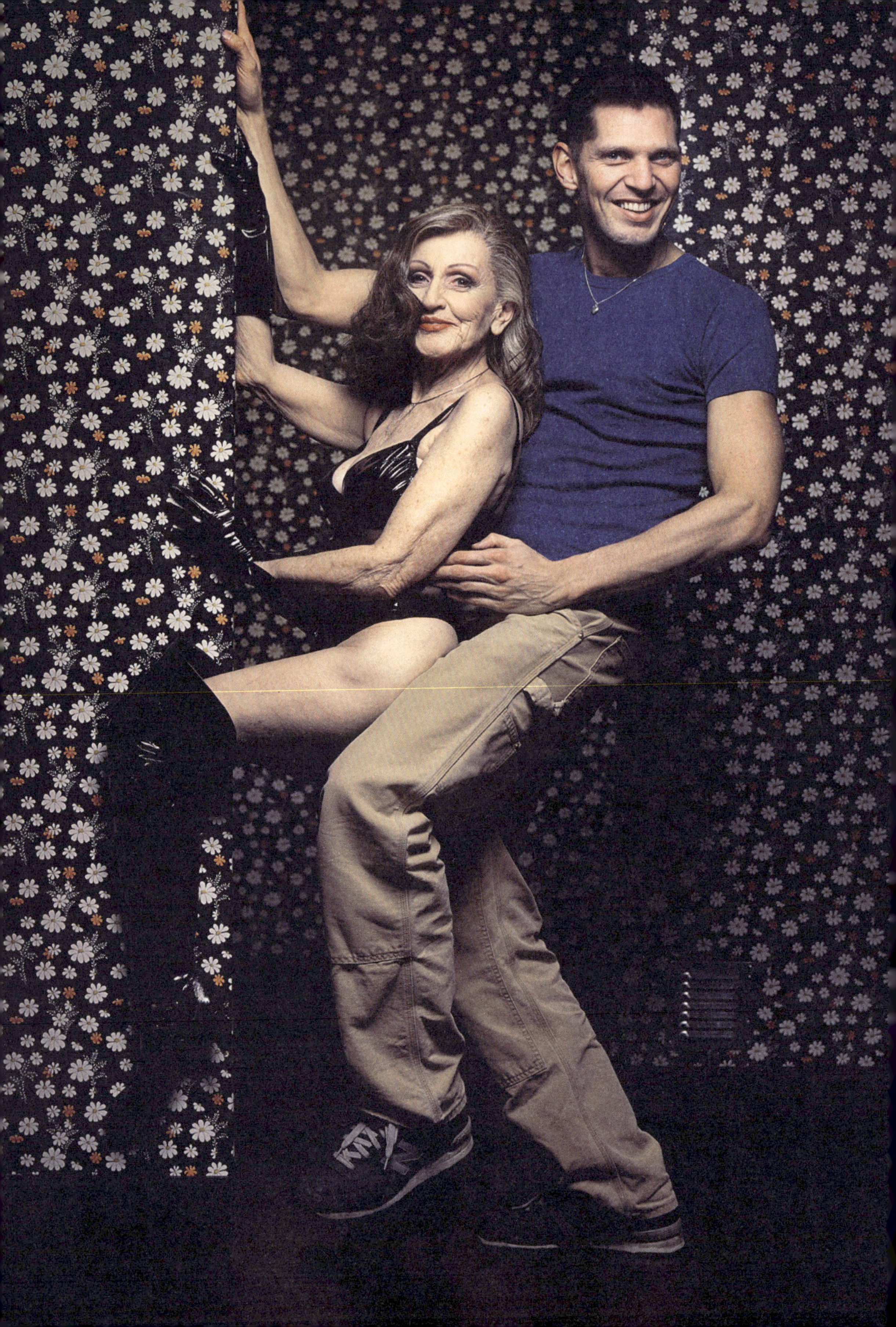

6 FULL STEAM AHEAD: ERWIN LTD (1996–2001)

'When you capture a great shot, it's like an instant infatuation. You forge a deep connection'

MIND OF THEIR OWN

'A wonderful idea to photograph children with Down's syndrome in such a glamorous and attentive way,' muses photo curator Hripsimé Visser in her upstairs office at the Stedelijk Museum in Amsterdam. 'In documentary photography, people who are seen as different are often portrayed in a pitiable way. I liked that Erwin turned it around with *Mind of Their Own* – he was fed up with the idea of the eternally wretched.'

Erwin had cherished the idea of photographing people with Down's syndrome since filming *Tadzio* – partly out of guilt for the final scene in which 'his' Tadzio, Aat Nederlof, is driven away in a car with his nose squashed against the window. He might have been exaggerating, but Erwin was still mortified by that image. He felt as though he'd made his protagonist look faintly ridiculous. And so he wanted to redo everything, with good scenography and greater respect for his models.

He asked for, and received help from a youth worker for people with Down's syndrome. 'She said, provided you don't just want to photograph cute-looking children, I'm in.' The studio sessions could be extremely moving, such as when he photographed Saskia, the girl on the book's cover. 'When you capture a great shot, it's like an instant infatuation. You forge a deep connection. I had that with Saskia. I asked her to lie forward. And she lay down and gazed into the camera with such devotion... I thought to myself: I can ask her anything; she's like putty in my hands. Gosh, that's so intense.'

People with intellectual disabilities had fascinated Erwin ever since his visit to a psychiatric institution for his journalism course. Like his contemporaries, such as

Rineke Dijkstra and Koos Breukel, he admired the work of Diane Arbus, the almost mythical portraitist of people on the fringes of society. Arbus's photographs of intellectually disabled people in festive costumes were initially controversial. One school of thought was that people with Down's syndrome or other intellectual disabilities ought to be hidden away rather than celebrated in 'cheerful' pictures, which is how Arbus presented them.

Erwin was impressed by Arbus's oeuvre and her photos informed his preference for 'unconventional' models. The question of what constitutes 'normal' – and an aversion to the very distinction itself – had long preoccupied Erwin, and Arbus had attempted to formulate an answer via her photography. In her words, she felt a 'mixture of shame and awe' when photographing her 'freaks'; for her, people with intellectual disabilities outshone so-called 'normal' people precisely because of their differences.

Yet Erwin took a different approach to Arbus. 'The people in her work are celebrating and they're happy. But even so, her images tend to evoke immense sadness.' What he wanted to do, instead, was to elevate his models by highlighting their independent characters, while also shining a light on their inner emotional worlds and their beauty. They were attended to by a team of hairdressers, make-up artists and stylists.

Other than being a response to Arbus, this glamorous series was also a reaction to photographers such as Marrie Bot, who had spent a decade photographing intellectually disabled people, and the work of Ad Windig. In the series *In het land der levenden* [In the Land of the Living], Windig combined still portraits of so-called mentally ill children with reportage photography. Erwin thought that her heavy black-and-white prints were full of beauty and integrity. But he wanted to demonstrate that staged studio photography could also be a source of socially engaged work – and not just in the style of the Dutch school of documentary social realism.

Mind of Their Own was shown at the FotoFestival Naarden in 1995. His submission was well received by the press. 'Erwin Olaf finds beauty where others dare not look. A study in innocence approached without irony, which adds to the sensitivity and endearment,' stated *Het Parool*. The reviewer saw none of the excess and mocking irony that had characterised the 'cabinet of curiosities' entitled *Chessmen*, nor the mannerism of *Blacks*. *De Volkskrant* observed 'children against a backdrop of almost psychedelic explosions of colour. Made up, with bare shoulders and perfectly styled hair, they pose in a manner usually reserved for pop stars and celebrities.'

Others called the work kitschy – an accusation that has often been levelled at Erwin over the years. A quarter of a century later, he can relate to the criticism. In an interview, and not without a touch of self-deprecation, he called himself 'the prize pig of visual kitsch', although he actually prefers the term 'Baroque'.

It wasn't so much the glamour that attracted criticism but the way in which the negatives had been manipulated. At the time, Erwin was still getting used to working with colour film. Unlike his black-and-white work, the prints couldn't be manipulated in the darkroom using post-processing techniques. He had yet to master digital editing but pursued new avenues with determination, driven by a single goal: to create completely novel work.

Earlier that year, as an experiment, he had heated the negative of a subpar photograph and achieved stunning results. 'It was crappy material and I thought to myself: I can rescue this by holding it over a lighter.' The plastic curled in the heat and he pressed the negative between glass plates, thereby creating charred fissures and random colour transitions across the 6x6 negative.
He used the same processing technique in the Down's syndrome series. The works were also a riposte to the beauty industry and the era's new-found mania for image manipulation. 'Look, this technique also works! You don't have to use Paintbox, like Inez van Lamsweerde.' Moreover, burning the negatives was also a form of social and artistic commentary.

'Unfortunately, *Mind of Their Own* didn't go down well in the art world and, even now, I still have my doubts about the work. But I'm very fond of those photographs. And I'm especially proud of them on a technical level. You can tell, simply by looking at them, that I always aspired to be original, that I was striving to make new and unprecedented work. I gave it my best shot, and I love that I tried.'

As was often the case, chance coincidences led up to that intervention rather than premeditation. 'It was an experiment to see how far you could manipulate classical photography without a computer. And how you might add depth to a portrait. I thought that a bunch of portraits of intellectually disabled people would be too thin, and then it would be all about the registration of a disability.'

The parents and carers of the subjects were thrilled with the results – it was the first time that anyone had thought to present this group of people in a glamorous light, as opposed to a sorrowful one. The eighteen models were also enthusiastic. 'I was so moved by this little nine-year-old boy,' Erwin remarks as he scrolls through the images. 'He never left my side: he fell head over heels in love with photography.' When Erwin won an award for the series later that year, he used the prize money to buy the boy a camera. 'I hope he's still taking pictures with it today.'

The FotoFestival Naarden was a milestone, but as ever, the perennial doubts returned. 'I carried my bouquet home, where I sat and ruminated: I'm chasing my ambitions, I want to prove that I'm capable of it all, so why do I still feel like I'm a six-year-old who's been excluded from the group? When you've had this kind of opportunity, and lived such an adventurous life, yet still feel like an outsider, well, you really need your head examining, don't you?'

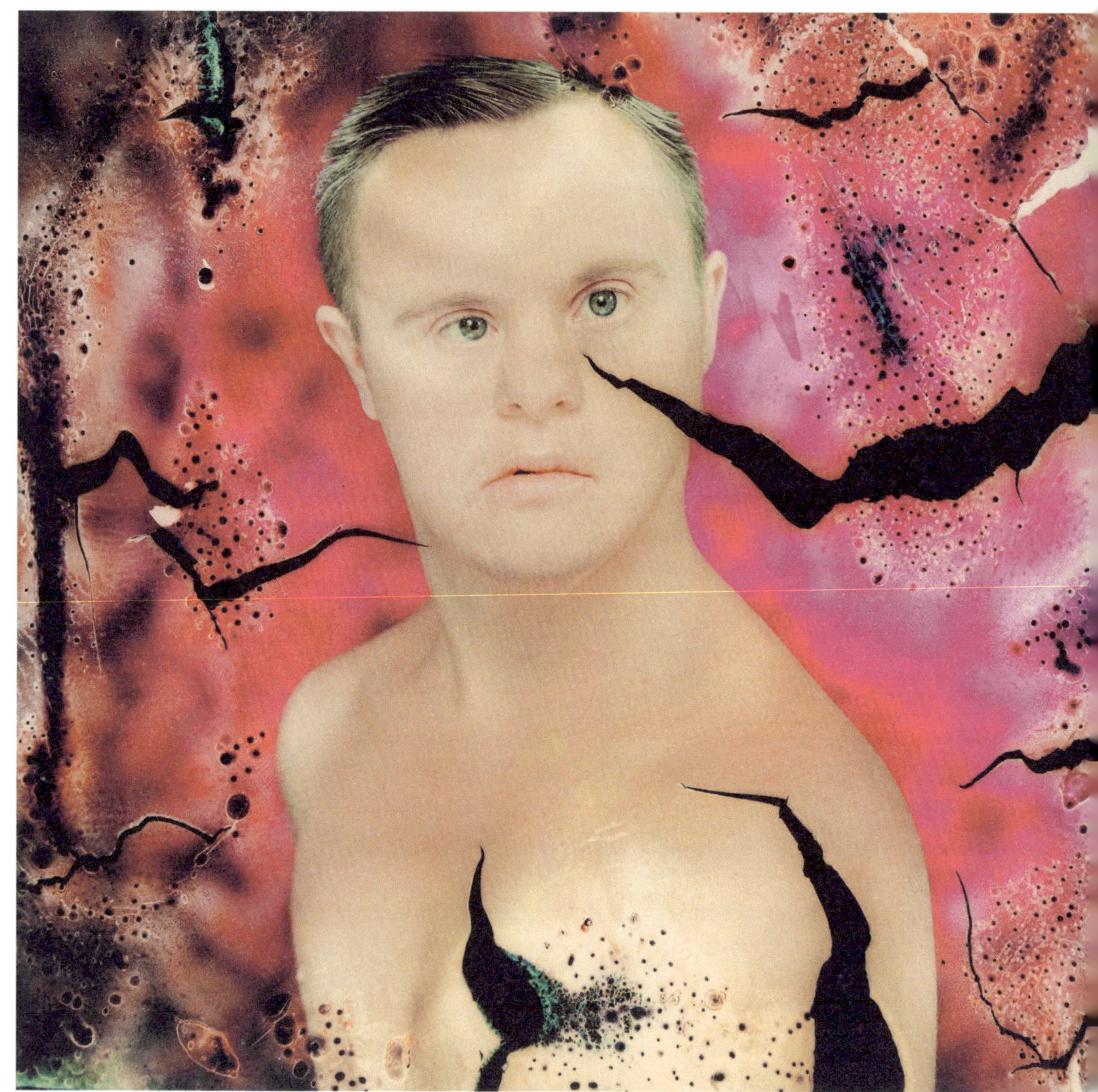

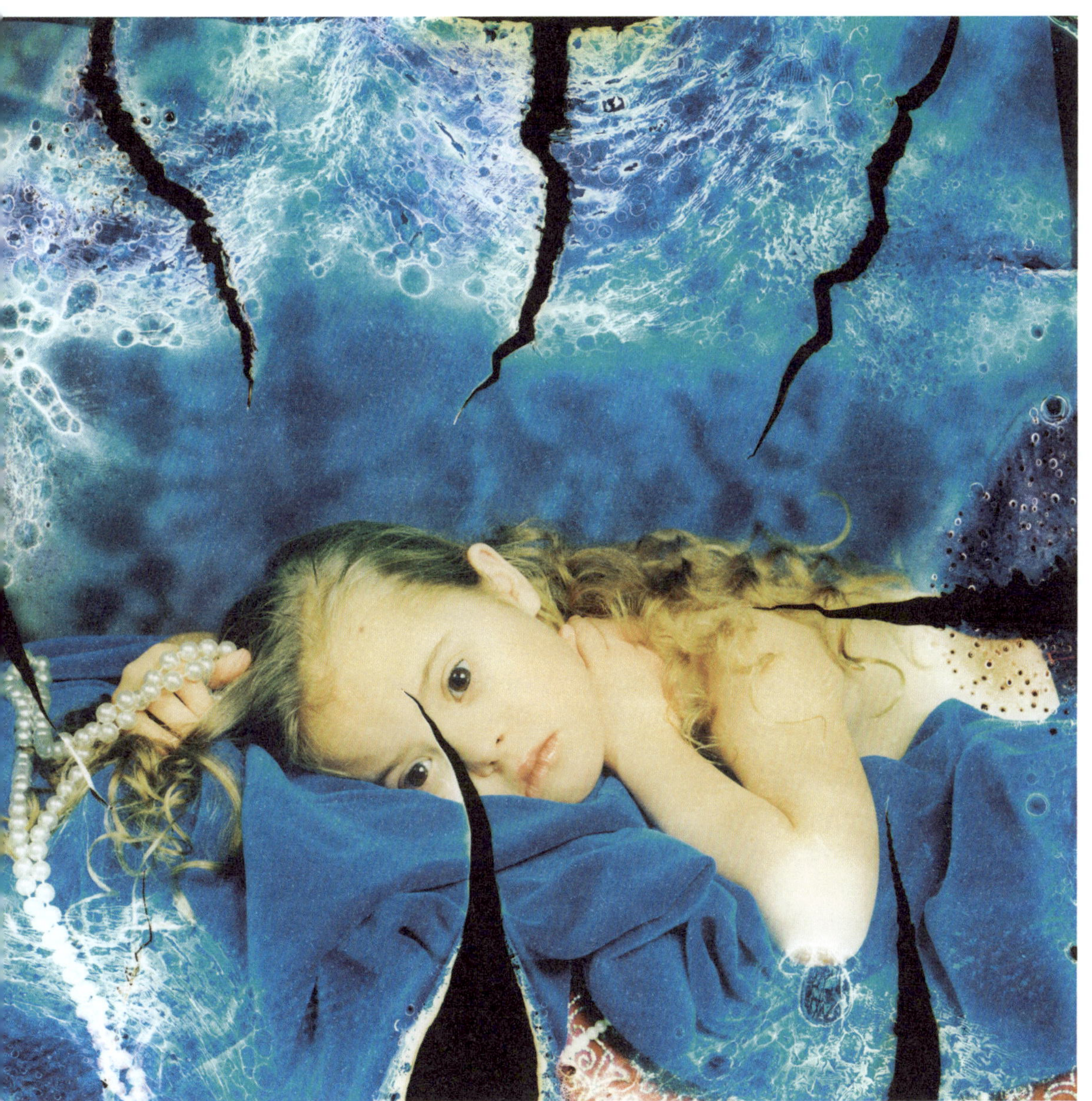

From the series *Mind of Their Own*. Left: *Aat, aged 24, 1995*. Right: *Saskia, aged 8, 1995*.
Photo on page 182: Erwin Olaf with model Kate M. from the *Mature* series, 1999.

Selling the photos of people with Down's syndrome also proved challenging – only relatives of the sitters purchased the works. Erwin finally realised that he needed to create a business, thanks to his assistant Piek's badgering. Like him, she was anything but commercially inclined and had put her own photographic ambitions on hold in order to learn and assist in the studio. Piek erected lights, loaded cameras and printed photos in the darkroom according to Erwin's strict instructions. She also helped build sets for special effects that would have been hard to achieve with analogue photography.

The studio was running better and better, but Erwin had little interest in contracts, copyrights and accounting. He decided to look for a business manager.

'Erwin's lateness set the tone when I came to apply and had to wait and wait,' says Mary Benjamins. 'I think hiring me scared him, as he feared losing his freedom. But it was essential. Erwin was brimming with ideas but he often couldn't implement them because the business was too ramshackle. He typed his invitations himself. He didn't have a computer, and personally answered all the phone calls. Henceforth, I sat between him and anyone who wanted something from him, often to the annoyance of the person at the other end of the line.'

Mary installed herself in a street-side office and set to work. 'Erwin ran a one-man business just before the tipping point. He was a well-known artist – if not notorious in some quarters – but the studio lacked structure and a back office. He needed money to take things to the next level, but all he really wanted to do was his independent work. It was a complicated balance to strike.'

To lay the foundations for building a studio, Erwin said yes to almost everything in those days, even the most uninspiring assignments, says Piek. 'You could call it adventurous, but it also lacked focus.'

He created several music videos, for example. Other commissions included a calendar featuring the clubbers and staff of the RoXY, promotional material for a fetish party and a controversial poster for Theo van Gogh's feature film 06. For this, a naked Louise Aarens perched on a toilet, legs splayed, holding a phone in one hand and masturbating with the other. The Reclame Code Commissie [Advertising Standards Authority] ruled that the poster violated the rules of decency and morality. 'It could be categorised as pornography.' Seven years later, a film magazine named it the second-best Dutch film poster of all time.

This was not the first instance that one of Erwin's posters had been called offensive and it would not be the last. In 1999, he created a design for the performance *Lang genoeg jong* [Long Enough Young] by his old flame Robert Long, depicting the singer flanked by two men, one old and one in his prime. People were scandalised that it also featured a penis.

That same year, he also produced a horror film for an anti-piracy campaign, focus-

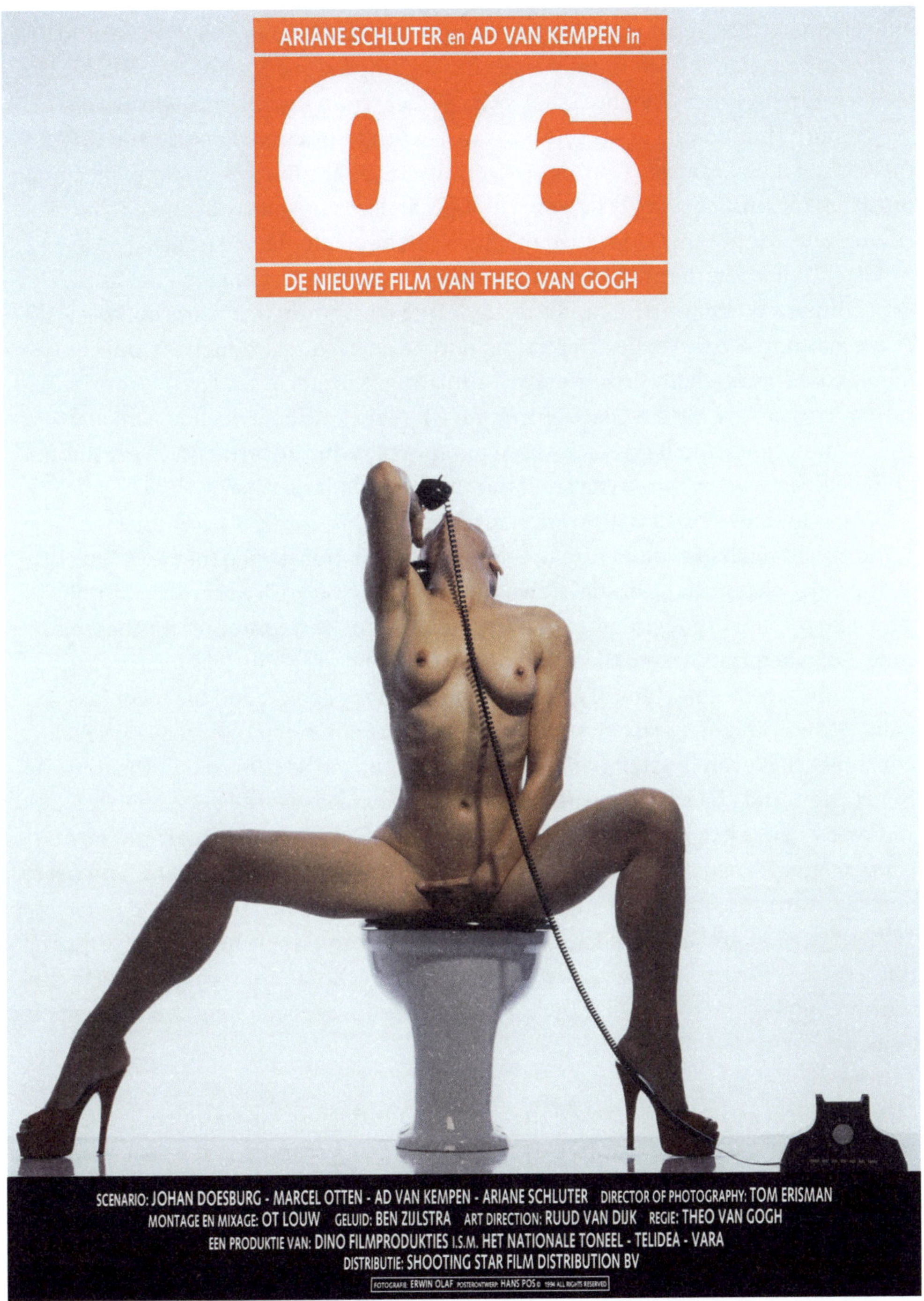

Louise Aarens on the poster for Theo van Gogh's film *06*. The Advertising Standards Authority (ASA), or Reclame Code Commissie, stated that the photo contravened public morality codes and 'could be classified as pornographic'.

sing on music CDs. It too came under fire from the Advertising Standards Authority. In the infomercial, the lips of musicians Ilse de Lange, Guus Meeuwis and Barry Hay (Golden Earring) are sewn shut – borrowing freely from Paul Blanca, who sewed his own mouth shut for one of his self-portraits – with a big, curved needle and thick thread. The message read: 'Don't stop the music. Start thinking, stop copying. United musicians against copying.' The Advertising Standards Authority deemed it 'horrifying' and 'frightening' and ruled that the clip should not be broadcast.

Piek and Mary, the studio's two permanent employees, witnessed the growth of the commercial assignments, and the mounting frustration that came in their wake. These jobs only tended to be interesting in financial terms, although art and commerce could occasionally be mutually stimulating. As Peter Weiermair wrote in his introduction to Joy, 'Erwin Olaf deliberately blurs the line between his personal work and commissions, and between fashion photography and advertising. Every photograph bears the artist's unmistakable stamp. The boundaries dissolve.'

Assignments occasionally went wrong, such as his Coca-Cola commission. The soft-drink brand had wanted him to make a sexy variation on the theme of 'pretty girls drink Coke from the bottle'. 'It was a prestigious job with a correspondingly large budget, and I thought great – it will allow me to use a computer for the first time. But when I submitted the result, it was rejected: the photo was *too* sexy!'

Erwin saw this as a typical example of a 'too many cooks spoil the broth' assignment. He was known to lash out at art directors on commercial projects, says Piek, but sometimes even his staff bore the brunt of his anger. 'It climaxed in the mid-1990s. Mary and I had an agreement that if Erwin exploded, we'd extract ourselves and grab a coffee in a nearby café. He simply wasn't used to having staff and no one pointed out to him that we were stressed out by all the screaming.' Benjamins: 'I never took his tantrums personally but then again, I'm also a trained psychiatric nurse.'

His need to prove himself and his aggression were at their most intense during this period. A frustration that was fuelled, in part, by the lack of recognition. He constantly complained that his work was either unacknowledged or viewed in a negative light.

Meanwhile, Erwin also monitored the counter-cultural movement's newly acquired rights and the acceptance of minority groups. In 1997, as Amsterdam prepared to host the Euro summit – where the Treaty of Amsterdam would be signed in October, simplifying decision-making within the European Union and expanding its powers – the authorities temporarily cracked down on drug use. The city needed to be sanitised for the international media.

The authorities specifically targeted the nightlife zones and less salubrious parts of Amsterdam, prompting Erwin Olaf to join the protests against the 'cleaning up' of the city. He told the press that he had 'a friend on heroin. And right now, thanks to the authorities, he's suddenly being targeted as a dealer in the Red Light District. And that's the Euro summit's fault.' He hoped that the city's nightlife would soon return to normal. 'The old Amsterdam simply bounced back after the summit. I wouldn't be surprised if half the city wasn't partying away and back on the pills and booze.'

That addicted friend was Rudolf Pfalz, who had gradually turned from a recreational user into a junkie. Erwin's drug use had remained confined to weed and pills, smoking heroin on a couple of occasions and snorting coke, although he tried to limit his use of the coke. 'Two lines: a great night out. Three: total paranoia. Also, I'm terrified that I'll have a brain haemorrhage. It's because my father had two strokes.' As for hard drugs, he didn't use them very often, but was open to experimenting. And just as Hans van Manen invariably passed around the mirror with lines, Rudolf couldn't escape the heroin in his own home. 'It was one big heroin den. And when you're surrounded by people using a gram a day but you're only taking a quarter, then you think you're doing alright. That's the trap into which Rudolf fell, and it was utterly tragic.'

Rudolf's floor was painted black, Erwin recalls. 'Once, when I visited, they were chasing the dragon, with a woman and baby in the room. They asked if I wanted in, and I said yes – I got off on the thrill of buying and using drugs. But the vapour went everywhere and I couldn't inhale it properly even then, with my bad lungs. Everyone gathered around the flame and inhaled it with me. They were shocked that I was wasting their gear. It was so depressing... I fled down the stairs without even saying goodbye.'

His work during this period lacked focus. He filmed a documentary on theatre diva Karin Bloemen. He made photographic artwork for a new prison. And he designed a public toilet in Groningen with architect Rem Koolhaas and his firm OMA, incorporating the series *Blue*, featuring models of colour including Pope Jerrod, who had once posed for Erwin, fig leaf and all, as Adam. 'You can see me at the entrance and over the urinals,' Jerrod recalled during his flying visit to Amsterdam from Cape Town to be photographed for the *Muses* series. 'You can stare at my bum while having a piss.'

The misinterpretation of the work underscores the challenges Erwin increasingly encountered as a photographer working with models of colour. 'A quarter of a century later, I read on social media that the toilet photos are considered racist. I hate it. Black skin is absolutely stunning; that's one thing. But, in this instance, I wanted to create something that resembled Delftware, and I also called the series *Blue*. Dark skin reflects blue light so beautifully.'

Now that the studio was running on commercial or subsidised commissions and Mary Benjamins had curbed the chaos, it was time for new independent work. Aus-

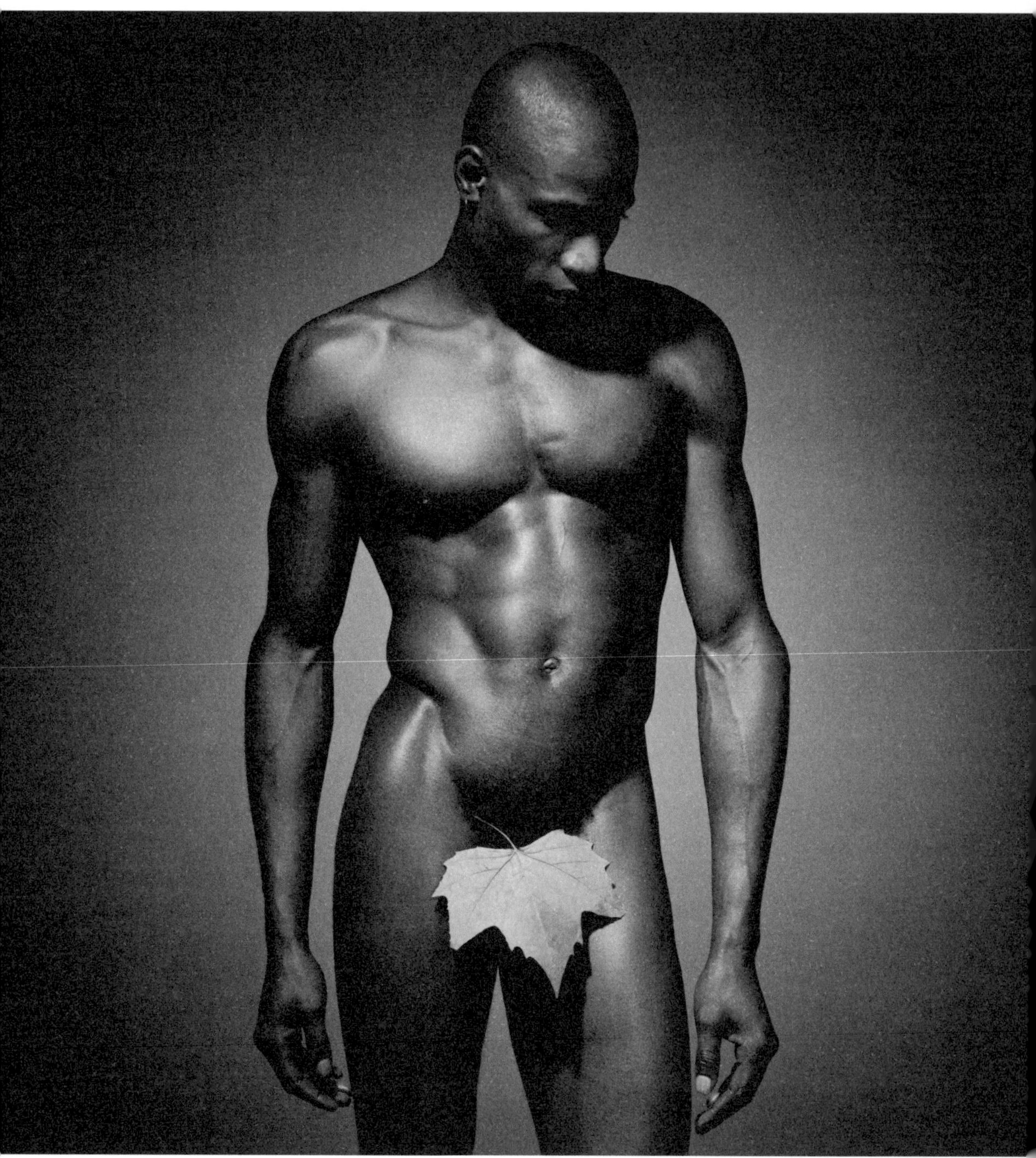

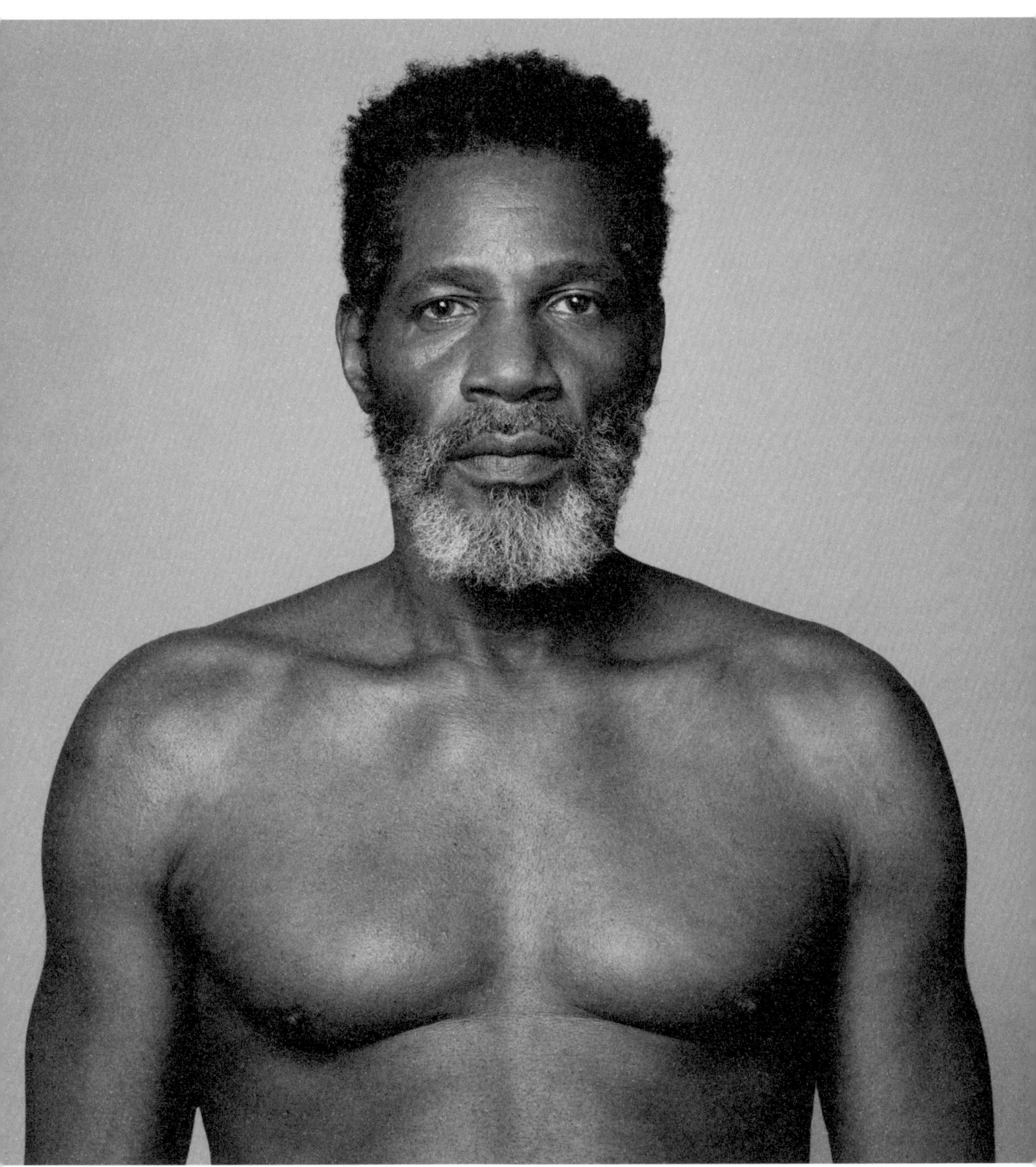

Left: Pope Jerrod in *Design by Nature, 1992*. Right: Photographed again in 2023 for the *Muses* series.

tralian curator and art critic Jonathan Turner, who discovered Erwin's oeuvre in the late 1980s, was fascinated by the rise of staged photography in Europe. As Turner says, 'I called him and said I wanted to discuss the merging of Surrealism and Realism in his work. He invited me to visit his studio in a fairly scruffy street off Wibautstraat. In that small, dark and dank workspace, Erwin managed to create the strangest and most surreal settings for his photographs.'

Turner wrote about the work for the New York magazine *Art News* and showed Erwin's work at two exhibitions in Rome in the early 1990s. 'I saw Erwin as an artist in the Pop Art tradition,' says Turner. 'I was intrigued.' Erwin was flattered by the attention and hoped that Turner would catapult him onto the international stage by way of Italy.

Like the other artists that Jonathan Turner admired, such as Andy Warhol, or those he worked with, like the French duo Pierre et Gilles, art and life were intertwined for Erwin. 'With these kinds of artists, contemporary art goes beyond what you can see in a museum; their whole life is one huge artwork.' The same could be said of Erwin at the time. The parties and festivals mattered as much as photography. Erwin was a cultural phenomenon, someone who transcended every conceivable category, who could make a statement in a gallery or disco, a museum or a pop temple. Life and work were intertwined, especially in the 1990s. His models were his friends and acquaintances, not professionals or celebrities.

Turner shared Erwin's sense of humour and his sardonic view of the art world. 'We both enjoyed jokes about the highfaluting pomposity of it all,' he claimed. But they also liked one another because Turner brought a non-Dutch perspective to Erwin's work. 'It annoyed Erwin when people labelled his art as being 'typically Dutch'. He found the pigeonholing too restrictive and appreciated that I situated his work within an international context.'

Unlike many others in the art world, Turner did not disparage commercial productions and also exhibited them in museums and galleries. 'Very unethical,' he says of his browsing in collections and indiscriminate visual combinations.

'Erwin was a fledgling artist in the mid-1990s,' Turner recalls. 'He hadn't started digitally manipulating his work yet, so was in a transitional phase and exploring new avenues. Back then, he didn't think that his small autonomous output would last in perpetuity.'

Erwin later distanced himself from much of the work that he made in the 1990s. Nevertheless, Turner saw him as 'a great artist', even then. 'I caught him early; it took the Netherlands much longer to embrace him and see him as a cultural figurehead.' Erwin slowly came to the same conclusion. He also did the sums: how many people might have already seen his work in galleries and museums? Other well-known figures that he'd met had been caught off-guard by their first big success. This now applied to himself: much to his surprise, he'd already attained a figure well in excess of 100,000 viewers – and it was only the beginning.

'You can spend a few years making shitty work in the name of experimentation and trying something new'

A NICE COUGH

Erwin Olaf sighs deeply at the sight of all his second-, third- and fourth-rate works. He is standing in his studio in Amsterdam-Zuid before a pile of carrier bags, rubbish bags and plastic crates that are overflowing with negatives and prints. Illness and age have spurred him on and he is keen to separate the wheat from the chaff. And 2019 is full of chaff. Which is only to be expected, 'after all, you need shit to grow flowers'. He will soon have his estate in order, he claims, and he wants a much easier life. 'And not just because of my illness but, to be brutally honest with you, because I've already done enough.' Not that he's truly convinced, by the way.

He has long been refining his choices so as not to burden posterity with inferior image edits, failed projects and 'stupid assignments' from around the turn of the millennium. It demands a ritual bonfire or, at least, a phone call to an archival shredding service. 'I want to turn it into a proper event, a happening. We've got to make an occasion of it, because a huge part of my life is about to disappear forever.'

Shirley den Hartog, who succeeded Mary Benjamins in the late 1990s and holds a 50% stake in Studio Erwin Olaf Ltd says: 'We're digitising the entire archive and disposing of what Erwin no longer wants to see. Amongst those works, we sometimes find extreme, never-published photos. Sex series that I hadn't seen before, and which never saw the light of day. Erwin cares deeply about his legacy as a photographer. The selection process has been going on for years now – it's insane. But the fact that it's happening sets his mind at rest.'

The goal is clear: a compact oeuvre must endure. Letting go is an art in itself – amid such a wealth of images, even those relegated to the C and D categories, hidden gems are bound to appear. He occasionally hesitates as he rifles through the archive boxes: 'Have I gone too far? I really need to sort through it all again, one more time, just to be absolutely sure.'

The A-category is reserved for photographs that, in his view, belong in an exhibition or museum. Most of these have already appeared in one of the many books published in the Netherlands and abroad. The B-selection is more of a reserve – after all, you never know when a newspaper might request a striking portrait of a particular artist. 'Just look at this – it's the fashion designers Viktor & Rolf. I must have shot about twenty rolls of film, so surely there's at least one great photo among them.' Somewhere between the A and B selections is *Mind of Their Own*, the series in which the Fotomuseum Rotterdam has expressed interest. 'They would like to acquire the negatives, and I honestly think that would be tremendous – it would place the work within a historical photographic context.'

In the mid-1990s he produced little autonomous work. 'To build the kind of professional studio I had in mind – one that would give me the greatest possible freedom from subsidies and financial stress – you have to keep earning. So you take on more commissions. Sometimes they're interesting, but sometimes it's just advertising junk.' Those commissions, says Erwin, fall into the C and D categories, as he demonstratively tears one photograph after another in half. 'This one was for the Asian market. Get rid of it. Everything about it has been totally Photoshopped.' Rip. 'Here, Volkswagen – and a dated jeans campaign.' Rip. 'These are a wealthy couple's kids – a failed group portrait.' Rip. 'This one is for Virgin Mobile.' Rip. 'And if you really want to see something worthless, take a look at this campaign for the French meat industry. I had to photograph people eating huge slabs of meat.'

Brands would occasionally offer him creative freedom. 'They would ask if you'd like to make something "very free", but, of course, you instantly know that's an illusion. In my independent work, it doesn't matter how charming or unlikeable the model is, or how pitted their buttocks. The emotion lies in precisely those details. Those so-called free commissions were always riddled with restrictions. Now look – this is clearly commissioned work; it needed to have an oriental and mysterious vibe that would appeal to wealthy ING savers.'

He found satisfaction in commercial work – beyond the income that ensured his independence – through technical achievements. 'Look at this, for Audi Asia! I can't quite believe I managed to create that light – it's astonishing!' He also pursued a double agenda, consistently trying to introduce diversity through casting. 'I worked a lot for Virgin Mobile – always variations on popular stories and fairy tales. I would not cast a pretty boy as Peter Pan, but someone who stirred me in some way, and I'd convince an African girl to play Tinker Bell. And for *Snow White and the Seven Dwarfs* I picked an Asian woman for Snow White. A black guy played one of the dwarfs.'

He fishes a picture out of the box of C and D prints. It shows a seated, blindfolded man, strapped into a leather harness holding a huge dildo in his left hand. It's a more commercial spin on the *Chessmen* series and was taken for a sex toy catalogue. 'It might actually find its way into the B category; it's not a bad picture. I like the light and the composition, but even so, you can't help but feel that this image – which was commissioned – says nothing about me at all. Still, I'm not going to chuck it away. I'll just have to accept the risk that it will end up on the walls of an exhibition somewhere, ten years after my death, and be considered a bona fide Erwin Olaf.'

After some hesitation, the studio switched to digital imaging in the mid-1990s, says former assistant Piek. At first, they mainly manipulated photos for commercial assignments, which made life a lot easier. 'On my first commercial job, I had the larger-than-life-sized letters of the brand name painted gold,' she recalls. Finally, after staring at the Polaroids for an age, the art director said: no, upon reflection, the letters need to be black. Image manipulation meant not having to do things twice over.' They acquired an Apple Macintosh, a scanner and some software – initially Paintbox, and not long afterwards, Photoshop. 'It wasn't all plain sailing. With some effort, you could edit a digital photo on your computer. Exporting it was a different matter altogether. These were the days before e-mail and DVD burners. All we had were floppy disks, but they didn't have enough memory for these kinds of edited images.'

As the studio transitioned into the digital era, Erwin began experimenting with the same software that he used for commercial assignments in his personal work. These images no longer pass his own self-critical standards, and he prefers to 'hide them away a bit'.

Three series, in any case, will not make it into the collected oeuvre. 'Just take a look at this – it's a really shitty series. Portraits of people blinking – a nice experiment but not all that interesting.' Yet expectations for the series had been high, as it was the first to involve computer processing. 'Inez van Lamsweerde shot to the top thanks to Photoshop, and I wanted a bit of that too,' he recalls. He also wanted the series to poke subtle fun at this kind of image manipulation, which he still saw as lazy and something of a cop-out. 'But I can only make beautiful things when I'm passionate, not when I'm driven by negative feelings, so the series didn't amount to much.'

The Lorena Bobbitt Boys was loosely based on the real-life story of Lorena Bobbitt who made headlines in 1993 by cutting off the penis of her sleeping husband, John. As she drove away, she tossed the severed organ out of her car window and called 911 to alert police to its location. Surgeons managed to reattach it. At her trial, Lorena testified that she had suffered years of emotional and physical abuse and that she had been raped by her husband. She was declared insane, while John was acquitted of rape.

The Patrick Bateman Girls was inspired by the eponymous serial killer and rapist from Bret Easton Ellis's novel *American Psycho* (1991). Erwin was a fan of the American author's work. 'I went wild. People had sawn-off legs and other blatant amputations. It was way too Baroque and, in terms of costumes, an overly literal translation of the club scene. Anyway, you can spend a few years making shitty work in the name of experimentation and trying something new. And if you can fight your way out the other side, you start to flourish again.'

'Looking at them now, *The Patrick Bateman Girls* and *The Lorena Bobbitt Boys* series look more like illustrations than art,' says Jonathan Turner. 'But at the time, they led the way in terms of image manipulation. This was creative and original work – the like of which we'd never seen before. The advertising world has long since assimilated this type of imagery, making it much more commonplace.' Turner's enthusiasm led him to take Erwin to Australia. The exhibition – featuring several videos and sixtyeight photographs, including works from *Chessmen* and *Mind of Their Own* alongside the new series – marked the first solo presentation of 'leading Dutch artist' Erwin Olaf in the southern hemisphere, according to the accompanying text. Reviews were not universally positive: the *Bateman* series was criticised as misogynistic, while *Blacks* led to accusations of a 'colonial attitude'. One 'visually offended' reviewer even stormed out of the gallery.

Jonathan Turner saw it differently, using the invitation card to describe 'striking images that raise questions about sexuality, violence and consumerism in contemporary society', but also the 'unadulterated pleasure' they exude. Pleasure is precisely what Erwin remembers most about his stay in Sydney. Turner had invited him for a major exhibition at the Roslyn Oxley9 Gallery during Mardi Gras – the annual celebratory freedom parade organised by the LGBTQI+ community, which attracts over 300,000 visitors and is the largest event of its kind in the world. It marked the start of a 'six-week rollercoaster', during which Erwin marvelled at the many drag artists who had flocked to Sydney – a colourful crowd from across the globe.

Only one thing annoyed him about Sydney: his persistent cough. 'I was introduced to one of Jonathan's friends, Sandra, a flamboyantly dressed socialite with a huge smile. At that very moment, I had a violent coughing fit and Sandra, a cigarette in one hand, extended the other and said in her heavy Sydney accent, "Nice cough."' He laughed at the time, but after his eight-week stay in Australia, even Piek noticed that he was coughing more than usual.

He had been feeling unwell for some time and was permanently exhausted – even cycling to the studio felt like an uphill battle. *The Ausdauer* [endurance] his father had always insisted on had vanished. He put it down to overwork and the blurred line between his personal and professional life. At the time, he was also using a lot of recreational drugs, mostly pills, and spending marathon nights out with Harrie Wildeman and Jaap Hinten, fuelled by copious amounts of ecstasy and alcohol. But Piek feared there was more to it than just overwork and smoking too much dope. 'You should see a doctor,' she urged.

After a series of tests in Amsterdam, he received the devastating news on a Friday in October 1996: he was suffering from a hereditary and chronic disorder, alpha-1 antitrypsin deficiency (AATD). This liver abnormality has a disastrous effect

k heb longenfyseem
ers ziekte +
felijke aanleg)
ben in juni 97
oor 4 nachten
t Leidse AZL
iekenhuis ingegaan
voor het eerst
van m'n leven.

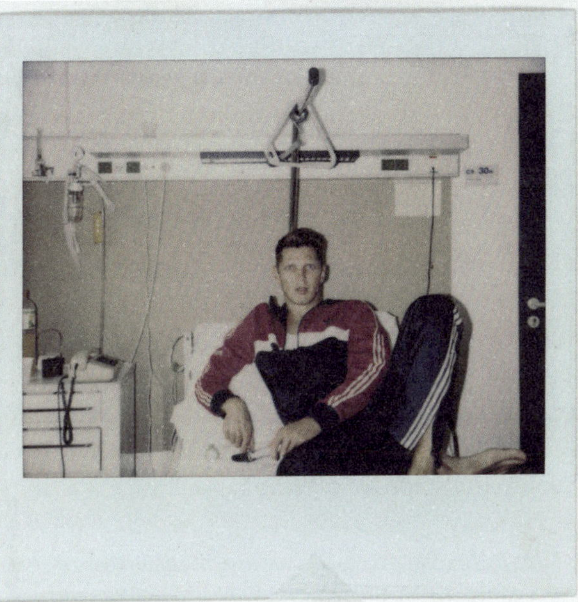

Overdenk het laatste
half jaar:
Ik een ongeneeslijke aandoe
Frans sero.positief
Alandus sinds 1½ mnd uit
m'n leven.
Teun net genezen van een
dubbele longontsteking.
Gelukkig gaat het tussen
Teun + mij beter dan
ooit: Dit jaar 9 jaar
bij elkaar!

Toch 4 dagen de tijd voor
meditatie!

Top: In Leiden, Erwin was examined by pulmonologist Jan Stolk, who would remain his consultant physician until just before the lung transplant. Tests revealed that he had the hereditary and chronic condition alpha-1 antitrypsin deficiency. Bottom: With Teun in hospital.

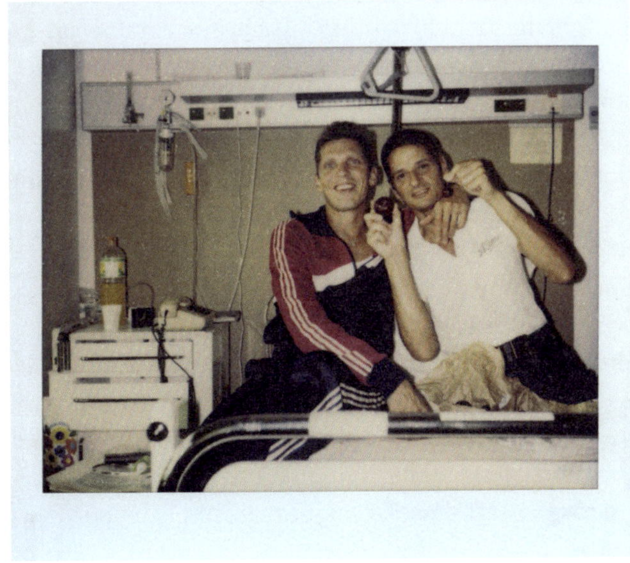

on the lungs, destroying the alveoli responsible for absorbing oxygen after inhalation and expelling nitrogen and carbon dioxide during exhalation. AATD is a degenerative and incurable disease – sufferers deteriorate progressively and ultimately die from the condition. The lungs enlarge while their capacity steadily diminishes.

Although the disease has a strong genetic component, Erwin's nicotine and cannabis addictions had both triggered and accelerated its progression. 'I remember that day like it was yesterday, mainly because the specialists warned me, "If you don't stop smoking immediately, you'll be in a wheelchair within five years."' Cigarettes and dope had been his crutch since high school. He had tried to quit. As he once wrote in a letter to Teun: 'Quitting smoking is going very successfully so far. No longer coughing and not grumpy.' Nothing could have been further from the truth – he had kept smoking and hadn't even contemplated giving up weed. All of this – combined with years of inhaling chemical fumes in the darkroom – had caused the disease to manifest at least a decade earlier than expected. If he didn't change his lifestyle, his lungs would become increasingly congested, and he wouldn't have long to live. 'It felt like I was doomed to suffocate.'

That same Friday afternoon, he boarded the metro, defeated. 'I was distraught, and I said to myself: I've got to stop with the cigarettes and joints. I'm not going to let those high-school bullies win – that's why I started smoking in the first place. I won't smoke myself into a wheelchair, followed by a coffin.' Until that day, he had always thought of himself as immortal, but the alarming diagnosis gave him a sharp sense of his own mortality overnight.

That weekend, he went out for one last hurrah – fuelled by joints, fags, booze and pills. Afterwards, on Sunday night, he sat at his dining table by the window on Lauriergracht with a hangover. 'I'd just rolled my biggest joint ever. I glanced out of the window while smoking it, and caught my reflection with this massive spliff.' Piek, who had stopped smoking the year before, had told him: when you quit smoking and give up the dope, you should have a good old cry. That show of grief helps you say goodbye to your addictions. 'I realised that I'd smoked my last joint. Of course, I followed Piek's advice and wept.'

It took a few more years before he felt truly free of his addiction. Not wanting those 'high-school arseholes to win' remained his driving motivation for years. 'I did not want to put on weight, so I didn't stuff my mouth with anything extra. And I had used Labello [lip balm] for years – I was pretty much addicted to the stuff. For the best part of a decade, I shouted it from the rooftops that quitting cigarettes and dope was my greatest achievement, the greatest work I'd done. It's more important than any series or picture. Later on, it changed again – by then, I thought that simply being alive at all was my biggest achievement.'

'I tried to kill my sexual embarrassment with humorous pictures'

SHIRLEY AND THE A-LEAGUE

Shirley den Hartog strides down the street. Erwin Olaf's business partner is making her way from Galerie Rabouan Moussion in Le Marais, near the Picasso Museum, to the Danysz gallery, a little further down the road. Together, these two galleries form Erwin Olaf's foothold in Paris – just as he has permanent anchors in Amsterdam, New York and London. Galerie Rabouan Moussion hosts regular solo exhibitions, such as the *Palm Springs* show in spring 2019. Erwin is curating the exhibition alongside gallery owners Jacqueline Rabouan and Caroline Moussion, with whom he has worked for many years.

Danysz also has a branch in Shanghai, providing a bridgehead to a new world that is ripe for discovery. Shanghai, says Erwin, has the energy of a burgeoning metropolis that threatens to overwhelm the individual. 'I initially had the idea: we're portraying the New York of the future with Shanghai. The USA is on the decline – it stopped being the New World long ago; now it's China. But when you begin a series, nine times out of ten, your original idea starts to shift. That's happened here too. In any case, it was already a problem that homosexuality is not accepted in China. Mind you, you still see quite a few gays strolling the Bund in Shanghai.'

The final series is about loneliness – mainly female – and the pressure of the masses. By Chinese standards, Erwin cast 'atypical women' as models: 'Nice independent girls, tall, pretty, mostly single.' He also had to hire two Chinese state workers for every European crew member. 'A whole battery of men sat behind the camera, idly watching. And the woman who stirred the most desire on set wasn't one of those strong, independent women, alas, but a meek 24-year-old doll-like creature who, after thirty-one rounds of plastic surgery and interventions, looked more like a fifteen-year-old. All those men soon perked up!'

Furthermore, Erwin's Western gaze did not always align with what China most wanted to present. 'We insisted on photographing a construction site in the middle of an old neighbourhood. It only happened after a great deal of effort. At first, we were told: "You won't find any." The demolition of those houses has changed the living pattern from horizontal to vertical. In low-rise, horizontal buildings, people get to know one another – that happens much less in tower blocks. The residents of the demolished neighbourhoods were in so much pain. We wanted to try to capture something of that past, although Chinese people generally prefer to look towards the future.'

At the Paris gallery this spring, Magda Danysz is presenting a high-profile

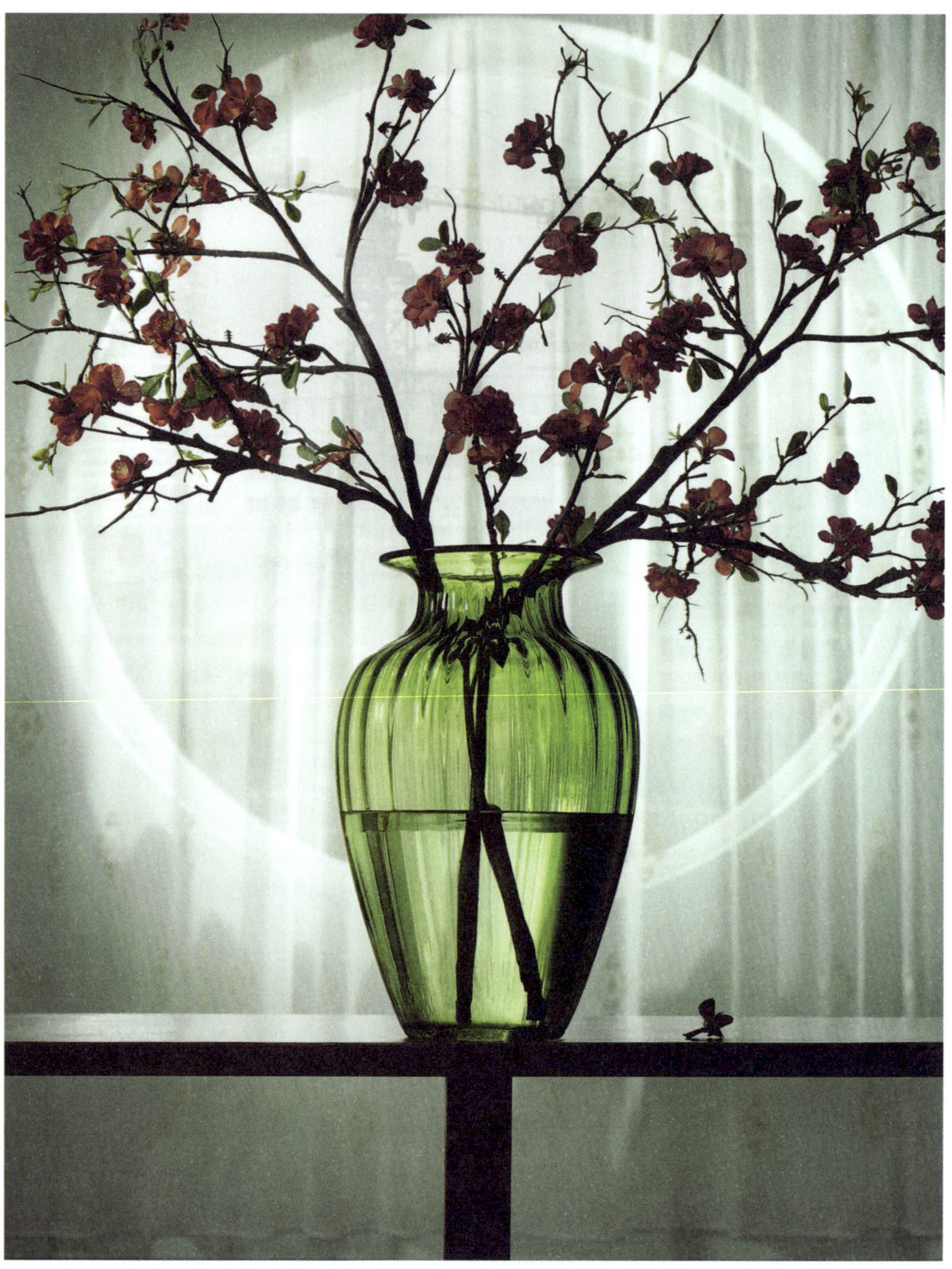

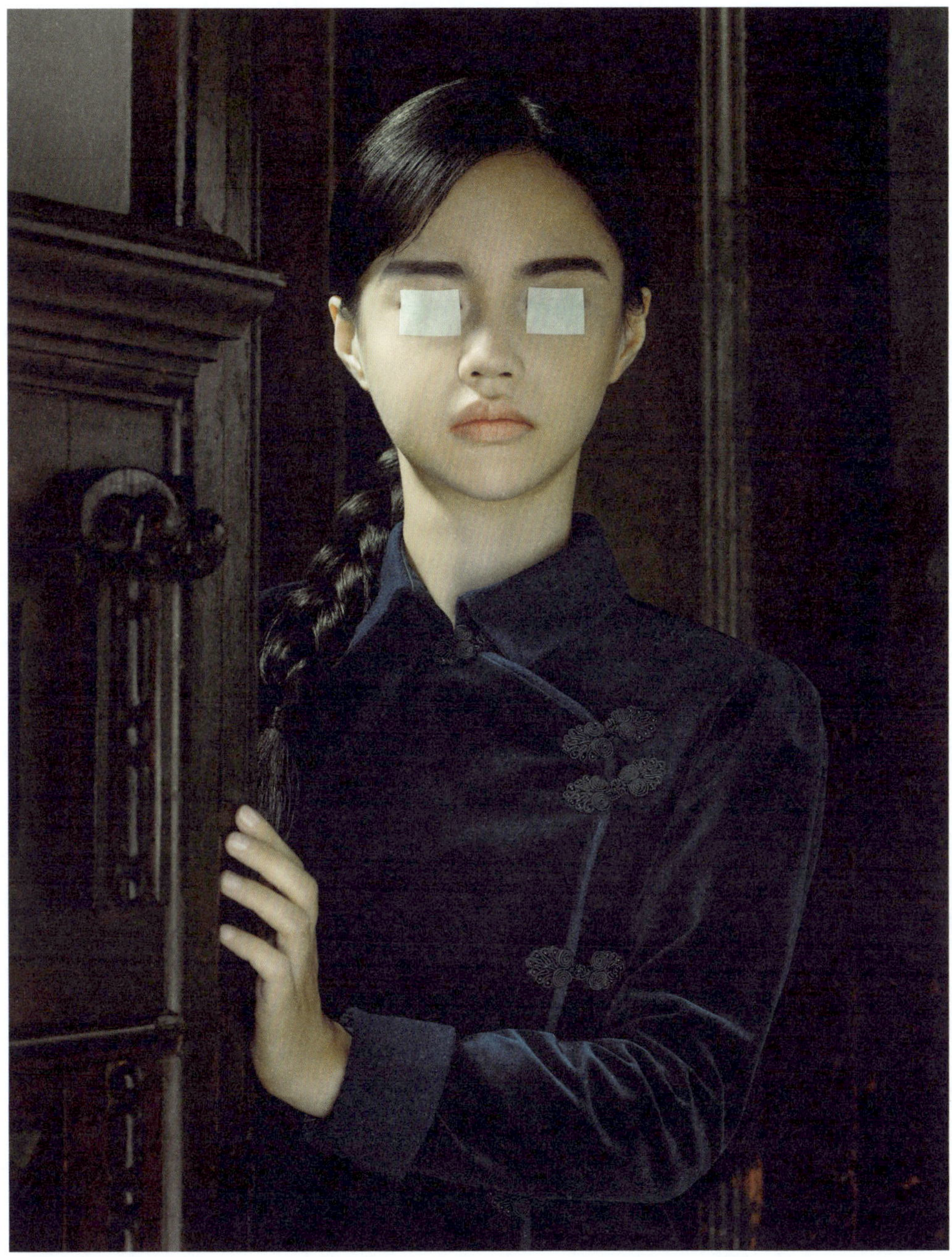

Left: *Huai Hai 116, Still Life, 2017*, from the *Shanghai* series. Right: *Fu 1088, Portrait 01, 2017*, from the *Shanghai* series.

exhibition of feminist video art, including the videos Erwin made in Shanghai. In a series of short films, five women turn to the camera and say things like 'Listen to me', 'Love me', or 'Touch me.' The French audience is divided: critics focus on questions of dependency and whether such material belongs in a feminist exhibition.

'A little fuss isn't a bad thing,' says Shirley den Hartog of the controversy, as she tries not to stumble over the narrow pavements of the Marais. 'But when Erwin asked the Chinese model to say, "touch me", she was shocked and felt rejected. She said, "A Chinese woman can't say such things." Erwin explained to her that the taboo made it all the more important that she did utter those words. Please tell me why that isn't feminist.'

Erwin had just received his life-changing AATD diagnosis when Shirley – or the 'red-haired monster', as he affectionately calls her – started working with him. Den Hartog, at least as driven and ambitious as the photographer himself, soon became the studio's business and strategic brain. Their stories have been inextricably linked ever since. There is no Erwin without Shirley.

When Shirley needed to choose an internship, she ended up at the Swammerdam studio with Erwin, Piek and Mary Benjamins. 'Mary was trying to create order because the studio was a mess. Money was rolling in, but no one knew how it was being spent.' Benjamins provided structure and began training Shirley.

Erwin's most important lesson – which Den Hartog has applied with unwavering discipline ever since – was a simple one: 'Everyone who calls the studio receives the same treatment. Whether it was one of Erwin's friends, a lady from Assen, or the queen.'

Not long afterwards, when Benjamins decided to leave the studio, Den Hartog submitted an analysis that she had written for her course, somewhat self-consciously noting that Erwin Olaf needed a manager. She added that he should focus more on art and waste far less time on commissions. 'I loved *Chessmen* and especially *Blacks*. I couldn't help but think: if you're capable of making such powerful work, why bother with such lame commissions – for CD covers, posters and the like?' she says. 'It's a very brutal analysis, reading it back now.' Perhaps that was why Erwin Olaf quickly picked up the phone and said: 'I've read your piece. Come on over.'

It soon became clear that they clicked. 'I laughed a lot with Erwin right from the start – what a crazy, original mind. And strangely insecure about his work.' They were both outsiders to the art world; they had no network and had yet to master the academic jargon of art historians and critics, let alone the thieving parlance of hip gallerists. But they were both determined to conquer the art world.

Den Hartog followed up her letter to the studio with a written plan for moving steadily up the artistic ranks. 'The steps I proposed back then are exactly the ones we're still following today,' says Den Hartog. 'It doesn't just sound systematic – it really *is* systematic. We never lose sight of our goal and take great pleasure in working towards it together.'

She has only recently shelved her plan to study sexology after nearly twenty-five red-hot years in the studio, Den Hartog says, while walking through Paris. She sees there is still plenty to achieve – and plenty to adjust. 'Aiming for the top inevitably means that other things have to give. We've often thought, we could take this exit now and just walk right in. But we've agreed to stick to the road map. We constantly remind ourselves of that and keep each other on track. You sometimes have to turn down lucrative assignments because they don't contribute to the bigger picture.'

That was never much of an issue for Erwin; he always preferred to keep away from anything directly related to money. He didn't know how much his pictures ought to sell for and paid little attention to how many prints were sold at his exhibitions. All that mattered – as he had learnt from his father, and especially from the bankruptcy – was that Erwin Olaf Ltd could show a healthy balance sheet at the end of the financial year, with income exceeding expenditure. 'Erwin cares about financial stability but not about money or material things,' confirms Den Hartog. 'At one point, I bought him a house in the Jordaan. I thought, you're living in a rented place on Lauriergracht, so it's stupid not to invest in your own home. Yes, I make those kinds of decisions on his behalf. He's had the same old car for years. He couldn't care less about designer clothes or expensive restaurants.'

The advertising world was awash with money in the late 1990s – enough to invest in risky projects. 'I wanted Erwin to be able to work as an independent artist, without having to depend on subsidies or third-party commissions – that was my ultimate aim. Even if things didn't turn out as planned, we needed a decent safety net. That's what I call the A-league: when you can make autonomous work without a specific audience in mind. That was my primary goal and, in the meantime, the commercial commissions were both a learning curve and a way to earn money.'

Den Hartog pushes open the door of Danysz, housed in a sleek, white-painted building on the edge of Paris's former Jewish Quarter, now a trendy neighbourhood. She has an appointment with gallery owner and art dealer Magda Danysz. In Danysz, she found an ambitious counterpart, and together they plotted Erwin Olaf's leap into China. 'We spent seven years working towards his entrée into China. We were warned: this is a country where it only makes sense to enter the upper echelons of the art hierarchy. If you start in the middle, you'll never reach the top.'

That pinnacle had seemed a distant dream in the 1990s – even in Europe – though the studio hitched a lift at a time when money was flooding the advertising world. Smirnoff became the studio's first international client in 1996; two years later, Diesel knocked on Studio Erwin Olaf's door. Diesel had previously worked with David LaChapelle, who had produced vibrant, Baroque images for the Italian jeans brand. Studio Erwin Olaf was expected to be a little darker and 'grungier', but was essentially given free rein.

Whereas Dutch advertising agencies always produced precise storyboards, complete with lighting plans, the English agency's drawings for the Diesel account were more like doodles – just a viewpoint and an overarching idea. Erwin would then make his own sketches and, once fixed in his mind, he refused to deviate. Fashion designer Renzo Rosso, Diesel's founder and CEO, once stopped by the studio to check on progress. After a quick glance and a nod of approval, he promptly left.

The Diesel campaign ultimately comprised five photos. One image shows four nuns in habits worn over jeans – three of them casting demure and downward glances at their rosaries, while the fourth looks meaningfully out into the world. A small chapel with a statue of the Virgin Mary stands in the background. The picture was entitled *Superior Cloth*, a reference to the Mother Superior. It was perfectly in keeping with a late twentieth-century trend: advertising that didn't look like advertising – unless you looked closely.

Another photographer might have chosen an imposing Gothic church for the shoot, but Erwin allowed his imagination free rein and selected his own distinctive location. His shoots resembled a film set, with Erwin directing the models like actors and experimenting with different lighting set-ups. 'From that Mapplethorpe-like light, I suddenly went to real film light – which was very difficult.' Staunchly Catholic countries, such as Italy and Ireland, banned the Diesel campaign over the jeans-wearing nuns. The brand had factored in the controversy surrounding the series – if not actively courted it – and it aligned perfectly with Erwin's autonomous work.

The image for *Different Fits*, which featured a bearded woman, a small man with amputated lower limbs and a giant, seemed like a nod to his favourite film, *Freaks*, and echoed his early portraits of outsiders. For *Workwear*, he created a sadistic universe, revisiting the *Patrick Bateman* series with its sawn-off limbs. In *Slim Fit*, a denim-clad doctor and two nurses perform liposuction on a helpless obese boy – an image that once again allowed him to vent his rage at the fat high-school bully who had sat on him.

For *Dirty Old Denim*, the young art directors had submitted a vague sketch of two elderly people on a park bench. What they hadn't included was a sexual act between the couple – although that soon materialised. Erwin found inspiration in Hans van Manen's 1981 ballet *Sarcasmen*, in which Rachel Beaujean grabs her dance partner Clint Farha by the balls, and developed the idea further for Diesel.

The Diesel campaign won a Silver Lion at Cannes and opened the door to advertising commissions from brands such as Levi's, Hennessy Cognac, Lavazza, BMW, Microsoft, Nintendo and Heineken. Erwin flew all over the world for clients who often

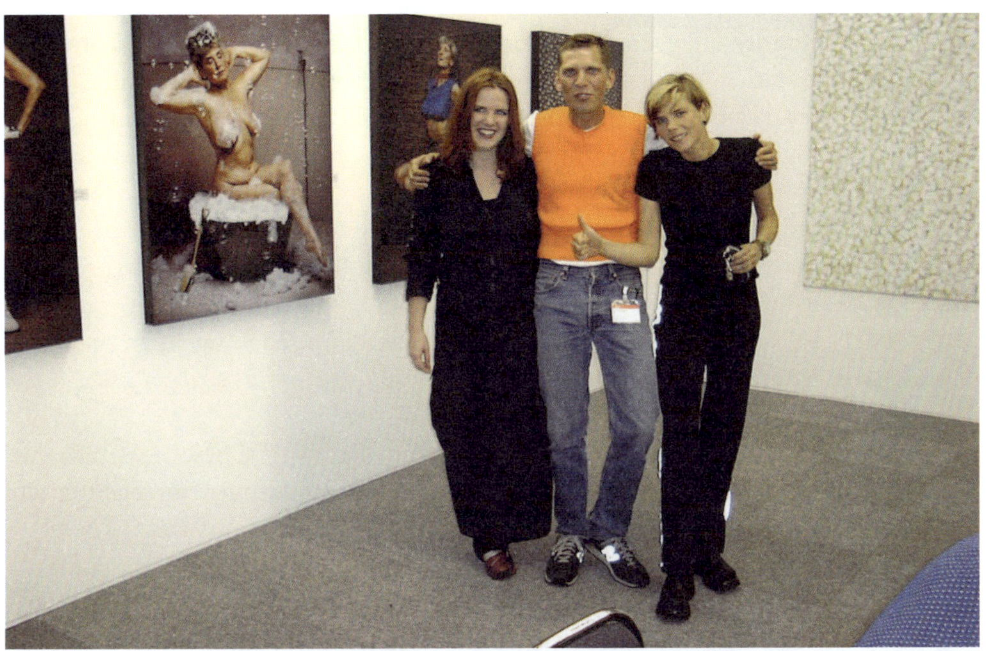

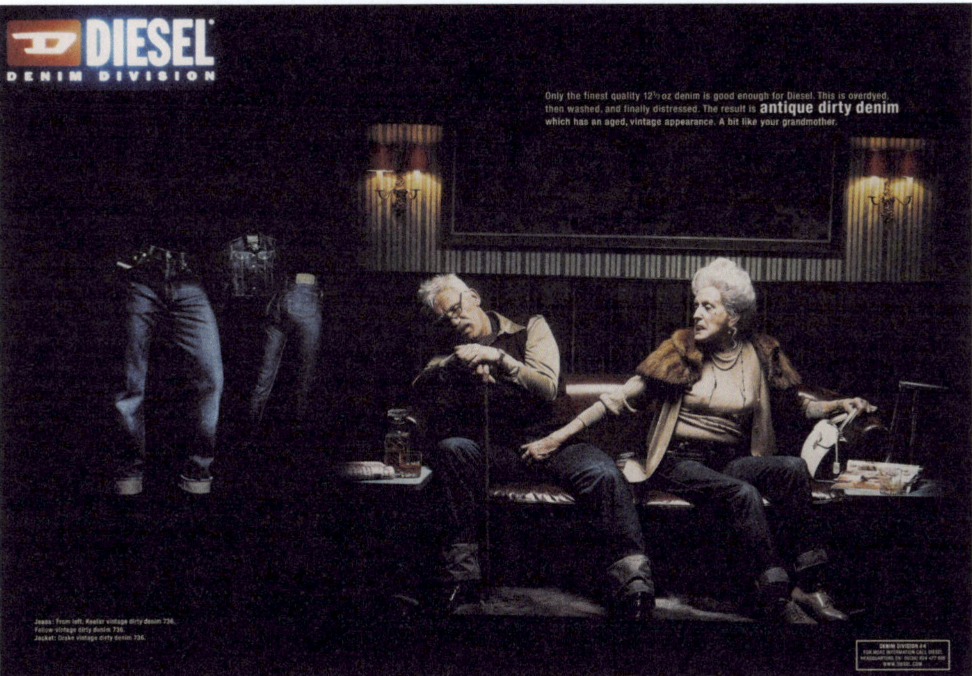

Top: Shirley, Erwin and Piek. Bottom: Erwin's 'Dirty Denim' advert for Diesel. The advertising world was awash with money in the late 2000s, and his studio was much in demand. Commercial work was also a catalyst for new ideas.

wanted 'dark, gloomy and grungy' campaigns. He also created images for Nicorette, in collaboration with art director Cameron Blackley – now at Saatchi Australia. They recreated entire aircraft and rented film studios to build the sets. These campaigns were shot mainly in Amsterdam, but also in London – for instance, with Posh Spice from the Spice Girls [Victoria Beckham].

According to Blackley, the budget for such an assignment could run into hundreds of thousands of euros. Photographing for Nicorette – a nicotine chewing gum that supposedly helps people quit smoking – was, for Erwin, a form of poetic justice against the tobacco industry that he blamed for his damaged lungs. Then again, he was not so principled as to turn down jobs for cigarette brands such as Silk Cut, Lucky Strike and Camel.

The Diesel series earned him a lot of money but also sparked new ideas and lighting schemes. Moreover, it marked his first foray into building complete film sets – albeit on a small scale – which would later define much of his free work. All good reasons to preserve the photographs as part of his legacy, although in his view, they haven't quite earned their place. 'Their commercial origins diminish my identity. At the end of the day, it's just not 100% me.'

Despite the Diesel campaign's success, Shirley den Hartog was not entirely satisfied. She had envisioned working with an artist but instead found a man who, in her eyes, sat passively waiting for new commissions. She felt that Erwin was producing what others wanted to see, rather than the images that fuelled his own imagination. 'I thought, if I'm going to be Erwin's artistic manager, then he'd better start behaving like an artist.'

Erwin, for his part, believed that a combination of both types of work offered the most possibilities. He knew he'd soon get bored working only on commercial jobs, but he couldn't survive on autonomous photography alone. It might work, Den Hartog thought – but the balance needed to shift.

Diane Hindriks-Van den Bergh, who had appeared in five of Peter Greenaway's films and was then over seventy, became one of Erwin's Diesel models. Her anecdotes inspired him to create the series *Mature*. In this body of work, he set out to portray ten older women – 'just short of a complete pin-up calendar' – in a provocative way. Thanks to Hindriks's adventurous dressing-room stories, he realised that many older women were still enjoying active and exciting sex lives.

He was approaching forty, but his illness made him feel twice his age. Erwin ultimately wanted his oeuvre to read like a diary: though not strictly autobiographical, it nevertheless reflected his life experience. It revealed him as a sex-obsessed twenty-something – or rather, in his own words, 'sexually frustrated'. 'I tried to kill my sexual embarrassment with humorous pictures.'

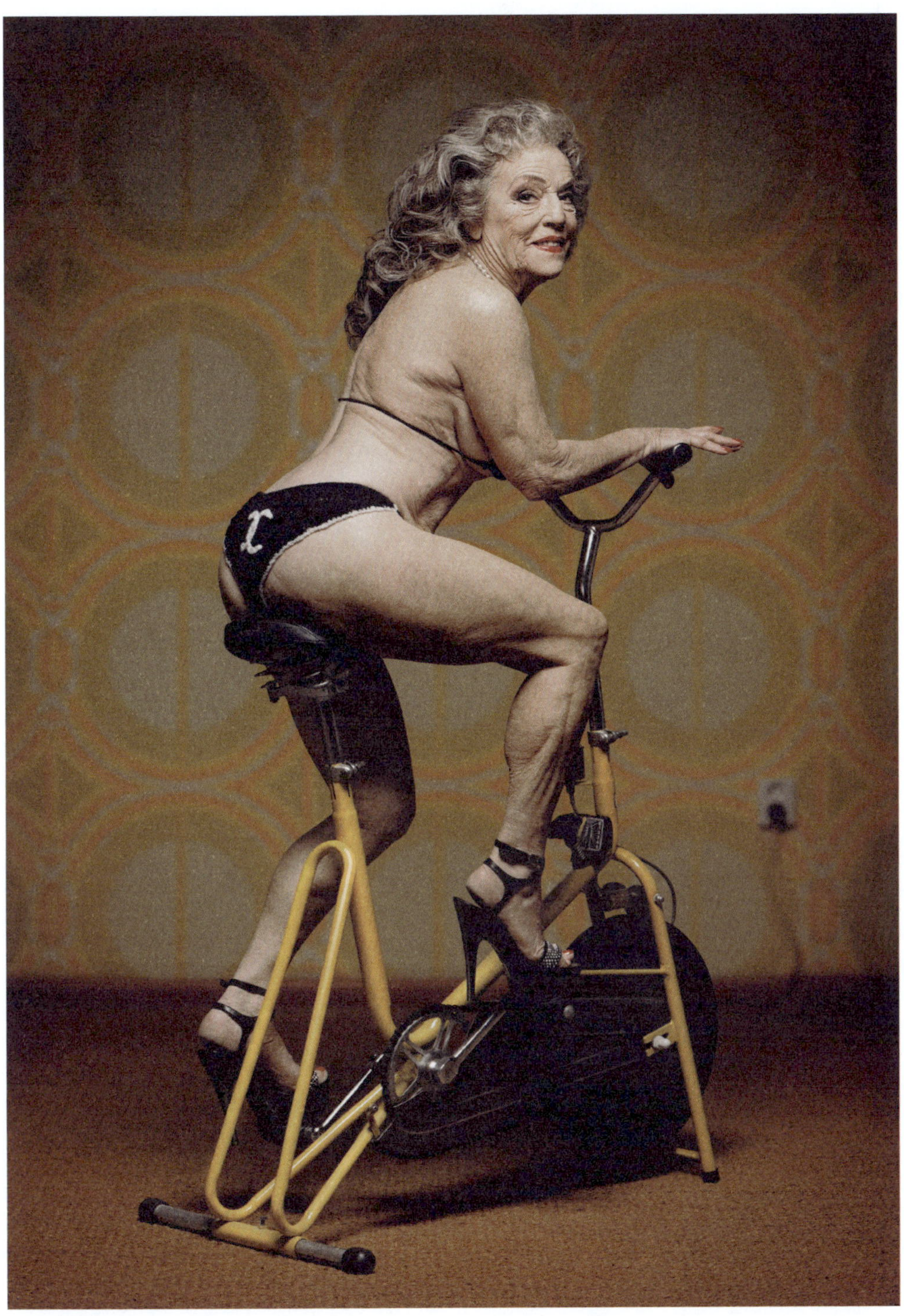

Cindy C., 78, 1999 from the *Mature* series.

In his thirties, he was aggressive and ambitious. He therefore felt the need to depict his forties as well: as a farewell to youth, allowing maturity to step in front of the lens. While commerce and aesthetics were equally important to him, his work was always accompanied by another constant – the need to question moral conventions, both in the fantasy world of his images and in reality.

As a result, he continued to work hard for the emancipation of the LGBTQI+ community – a group still referred to as 'gays and lesbians' as late as August 1998, when the Gay Games were held in Amsterdam. Erwin made the short film *De mooiste kussen* [The Most Beautiful Kisses] for the opening ceremony at the city's arena. In poignant close-ups, he portrayed couples making love: 'Newlyweds, two guys, the elderly, youngsters, two disabled people and two women. Later on, the two women extended their steamy kissing session on a movable stage high in the sky.' After this, the officials declared the Gay Games open. Amsterdam's mayor welcomed the participants and other attendees – including tennis legend Martina Navratilova, fashion icon Jean Paul Gaultier and Eurovision winner Dana International – to his city, which could now justifiably be called the 'gay-way to Europe'.

He also saw older women as a demographic ready for sexual emancipation. For *Mature*, he placed an advert inviting older models to contact the studio. Thirty women aged between sixty-one and ninety responded. He explained the idea as follows: 'It's playing with the 1950s pin-up idea. Imagine that I ask a woman to strike a 1950s pin-up pose before saying: hang on a moment, I'm just popping out for a pack of cigarettes. And then, fifty years later, I walk back into the room and nothing's changed. She's still standing there, and I say: you look marvellous. I take the shot, and it's printed. It's high time we looked at older women through different eyes. You can be sexy right up until the day you die.'

Mature was intended as a series of sexy portraits of older women, loosely inspired by the pin-ups of Alberto Vargas. 'What strikes me about women of this age is that they're not pathetic. When men lose their wives through divorce or death, they instantly become lachrymose. Not women. They keep on making something of their lives. You often see sexual catch-up in the process.'

Image editing, which Erwin had first used in *The Patrick Bateman Girls*, continued in *Mature*. The women had to look glamorous, but he also wanted to skewer the image that he always photographed 'sturdy' women. 'I used the computer to nip their waists in a bit and slightly elevate their tits, also to make the veins a bit more pronounced.'

That manipulation of photographs would become increasingly important from *Mature* onwards. 'I see myself as a director of still images, and I compare image processing to editing in film. I finish my photos with a colleague who looks at my raw material with fresh eyes. By sharpening and manipulating my photos, I can get closer to my thoughts – I can scrape along the inside of my skull.'

He also saw his new work as a commentary on documentary photography that shows the ageing process on the face. 'I do that more subtly. Only on closer inspection do you see the devastation.' He felt a sense of pride in the perfection of the styling, lighting – and above all, the direction – he achieved in *Mature*. 'That I can still get an eighty-year-old woman to let go and show her naked vulnerability.'

From the presentation of *Mature* onwards, he felt less like he had something to prove: the imposter syndrome was gone. As always, opinions were divided. At KunstRAI in 1999, the pictures – priced at 7,000 guilders (around €3,000) – sold easily, and galleries in Rome and Paris also saw potential in them. But the visitor who angrily turned to the gallery owner because he didn't want to look at those 'knobbly knees' reflected the views of many Americans, who were offended by the older models. Erwin's attempt to market the series in New York – and achieve a breakthrough in the United States – failed.

'My father became anxious. Little by little, you saw a beaten man'

DEATH SCENES

Erwin watches his model on the screen of his Hasselblad and nods with satisfaction. 'You're a top model. Gaze is nice, hair sits well – classic Duck, with all those kinds of nail polish and a bit of sloppiness here and there.' He had met Duck Jetten after she began her modelling career at the age of forty, following a modest career as an actress. From then on, he drew inspiration from her for years: Jetten was the first to call herself his muse.

He liked working with her because he could easily direct her as an actress, but also because of her fuller figure and 'that huge mouth and those big eyes'. Jetten had no issue undressing for him. 'I always feel very comfortable with Erwin. It's an interaction. When I'm with him, I feel good and that shows. In turn, that allows Erwin to take beautiful photos.'

With *Mature*, he had moved on from what he called the *Chessmen* era. That meant new models – he no longer needed to rely on his old muses.

It also led to a break with his archetypal muse Duck Jetten, as he stopped asking her to model – though she would still perform at *Fucque les Balles* and other parties he organised at Paradiso. 'I was going like a rocket – and then something like that happened. I was self-centred,' Erwin reflects now that he has brought her back to his studio after so many years.

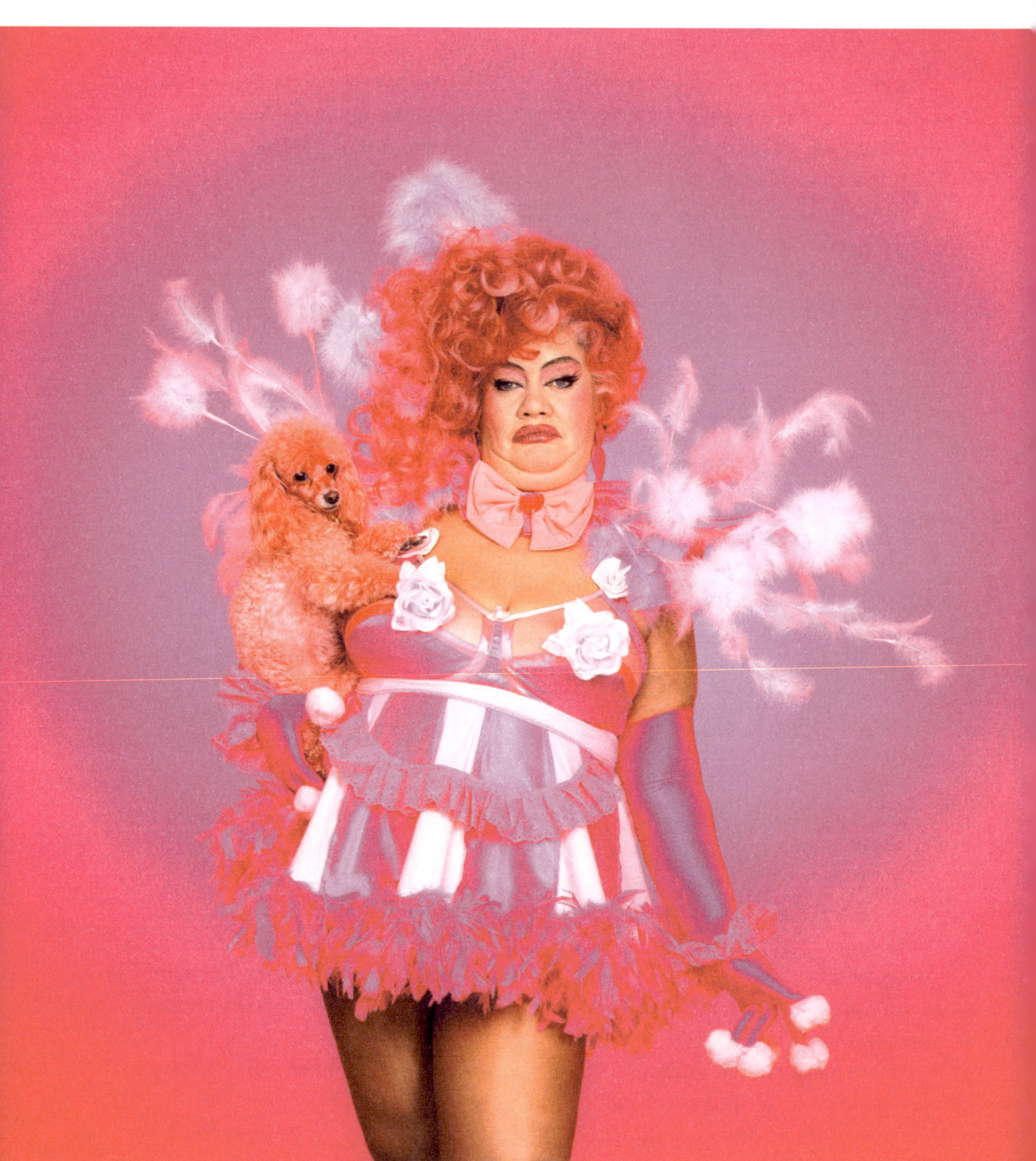

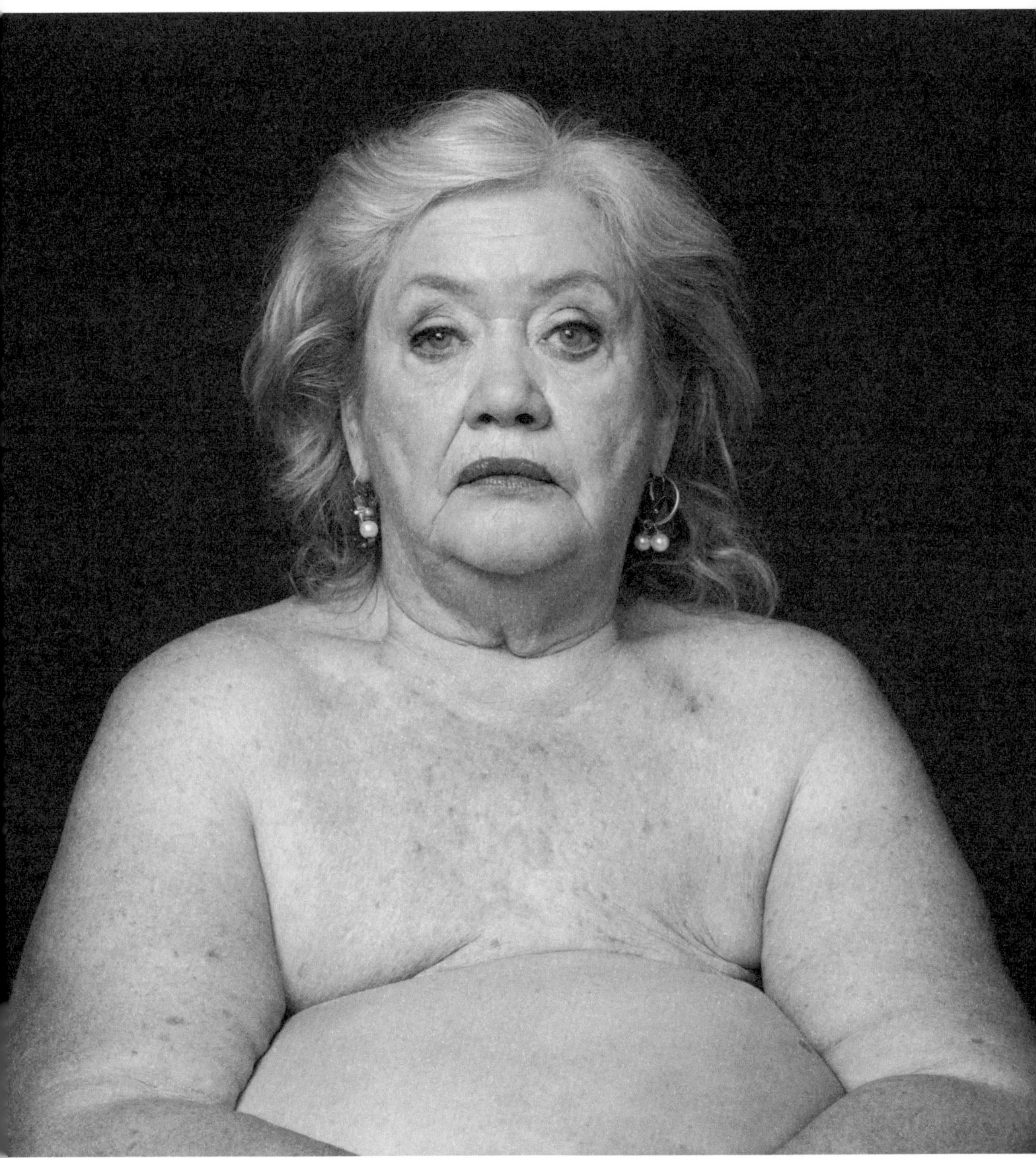

Left: Duck Jetten in *Shocking Pink, 1996*, for a Veilig Verkeer Nederland (Safe Traffic Netherlands) campaign. Right: Photographed again in 2021 for the *Muses* series.

They did not meet up again until twenty years later, when he invited her for the *Muses* series, which he began during the Covid-19 pandemic. Jetten – seventy-five at the time of the session – carries the scars of life, like many of Erwin's former models, and like Erwin himsel. She'd had a double mastectomy; she smokes like a chimney during the shoot, and an assistant soon heads out to buy bottles of beer.

After the session, Erwin Olaf is delighted with the result. 'You do see a bit of scarring, but such things happen; it's not about aesthetics anymore. We are all from that feisty generation of the 1980s. Some have stayed fresh and gossamer thin, others are ailing and heavy. But everyone still surprises me with their confidence.'

Jetten is also more than satisfied. 'I'm glad I got over myself and did it anyway,' she states after looking at the results of the photo session. 'How beautiful I am. OK, I may be old, but that's not a bad thing at all. And I'm proud of myself for posing with my fat belly and without those boobs. You're sweet Erwin, next time I'm going to give you a big French kiss.'

His career was on the rise both commercially and artistically at the turn of the millennium, thanks in part to the series *Fashion Victims*, in which he ridiculed the commercial appropriation of sexuality. 'I wanted to show the porn behind fashion photography. Those girls always look so whorish during fashion shoots, don't they?' It was mainly thanks to *Royal Blood* that his audience expanded even further. He pushed image manipulation to the extreme in this series on fallen royals, starring Princess Diana, who had crashed in a Paris tunnel in August 1997 while fleeing the paparazzi. In the startling image, the German car manufacturer's logo pierces her left arm.

Royal Blood – the first series Erwin created in his brand-new studio on IJselstraat – marked the transition from analogue developing and printing in the darkroom to digital image editing. For this, he initially worked with image editor Wieger Poutsma. His models and collaborators were now less often friends and acquaintances from the club scene. No longer seeing himself as an outsider, he chose fewer outsiders as models. 'At some point, you get bored of models that others label as "freaks". Extreme and deviant are ridiculous terms anyway: only 1% of humanity is exceptionally beautiful.'

Through his commercial work – which allowed him to hire professional models – he became fascinated by the 'unreal beauty' of the increasingly younger and thinner guys, and especially women, who offered themselves to him as models. 'The absolute and dangerous beauty of those young people – that's what I tried to capture in *Royal Blood*. In retrospect, it's the fascination of someone who feels the years are starting to catch up with him.'

Royal Blood also explored the glorification of violence and the fascination with royalty, emphasising the artificiality and manipulation of the images. He had now fully embraced the technical innovations he had once resisted – and was having a ball

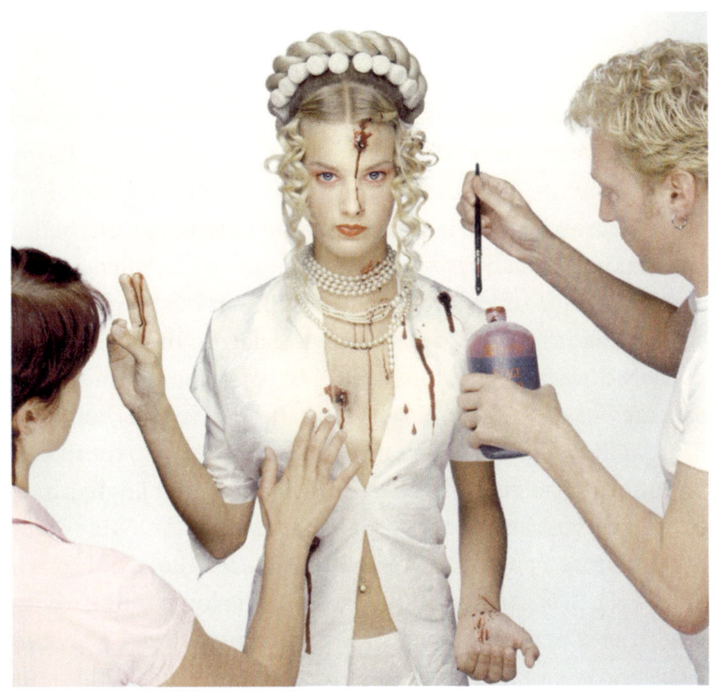

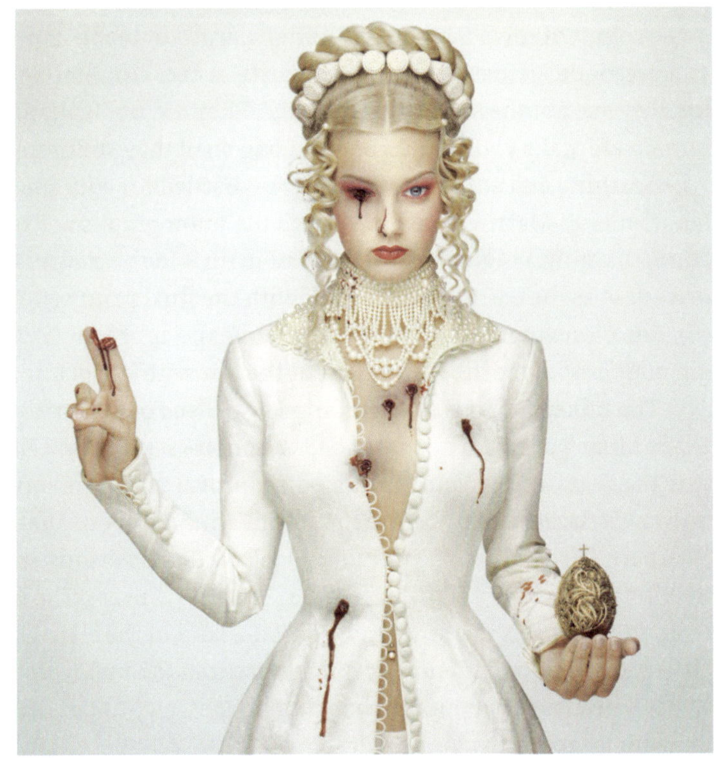

Tsarina Alexandra, 1918, 2000 from the Royal Blood series. The models were splattered with paint and the photos were edited and digitally processed.

at the computer. 'I wanted you to know: we are now looking at a new, fresh phenomenon. I enjoyed producing a very slick result.'

It was his second series on royals, following *Blacks*, subtitled 'seventeen royal portraits'. After the black-on-black of that earlier series, he now experimented with white-on-white. In addition to *Lady Di*, there was *Sissi 1898* – with the sharpened file in the heart with which Italian anarchist Luigi Lucheni had stabbed her to death. *Jacky O., 12:29 pm* and *Jackie O., 12:30 pm* were modelled on Jacqueline Kennedy – later Onassis – with and without the blood of her husband's assassination on her clothes and face. *Julius Caesar † 44 BC*, with the dagger in his back. *Ludwig II of Bavaria* supposedly drowned on 13 June 1886, but was probably murdered. *Tsarina Alexandra*, executed in 1918, *Marie-Antoinette*, beheaded in 1793, while the pregnant *Poppaea*, murdered by her husband Emperor Nero in AD 65, completed this tragic company.

Journalist Peter Brusse, a connoisseur of the English and Dutch royal houses, opened the exhibition *Violence and Passion*. 'Oscar Wilde died a hundred years ago, and he wrote a poem for Erwin Olaf, who was born only sixty years later,' he began his speech. 'Yet each man kills the thing he loves, / By each let this be heard / Some do it with a bitter look, / Some with a flattering word. / The coward does it with a kiss, / The brave man with a sword.' After quoting from Wilde's *The Ballad of Reading Gaol* (1898), Brusse continued: 'Erwin Olaf's victims are dressed in white, because white is the colour of royal mourning – and the drops of blood look all the more beautiful and decadent against the lily-white purity. ... Like contemporary saints hewn from ice, they stare at the spectators; abashed. They did not want to die – they wanted to remain eternally young and angelic. Long shall they suffer in glory.'

Loathing and admiration once again battled for supremacy in this series. Flatland Gallery's Martin Rogge presented the photographs at Paris Photo in November 2000, charging a high price for the first print – in the 'aggressive American' way. The price rose as the edition progressed, with the final print selling for 12,500 guilders (€5,600). One reporter observed that while the appeal of Erwin Olaf's 'bizarre kitsch glamour' resonated, he stood alone at the fair with his 'glamorous genre'.

The mixed feelings surrounding *Royal Blood* occasionally caused issues. Erwin Olaf's Milan gallery owner described the photographs as 'excellent kitsch'. Less amused was *The Times*, which voiced strong disapproval when the series was exhibited in Galway, Ireland, shortly before the fourth anniversary of Diana's death. Conservative Northern Irish politician Ian Paisley Jr also called it 'disgusting' that someone was making 'so-called art' at the expense of the late princess. The blood splashed on *Jackie O., 12:30 pm* was also poorly received in the land of the slain US president's ancestors. Gallery owner Maura Kennedy quickly assured the public that visitors would be warned in advance about the shocking images, and under-16s would only be admitted with an accompanying adult.

A few years later, *Lady Di* would spark yet another row when the image was exhibited in Australia. The Australian Monarchist League demanded that the Dutch government withdraw its support for the exhibition and apologise to Queen Elizabeth for this 'sickening insult'.

Erwin responded with surprise: 'A fierce, almost hateful, conservative wind has started blowing. I can only wonder at it – but I'm not going to adapt. And I realise more and more that I've created pictures that retain their power, that last for a very long time.'

On 3 March 2001, Erwin had to say goodbye to his father for good. He had always struggled with this 'strict, nationalistic middle-class' man with whom he had to share his mother. But over the years, he had come to realise that he had inherited his father's stubbornness, egalitarianism and temper. 'I'm temperamental, like him, and can damage people with words.'

He had told himself that no matter how much his father annoyed him, the arguments had to stop. More importantly, the bickering was terribly upsetting for his mother – which was something that Erwin wanted to avoid at all costs.

Springveld Sr, meanwhile, took pride in his middle son's success, despite his 'very peculiar photography'. He had apparently managed to earn a living from it – even establish his own business. 'Every year when I came back from the accountant, I'd show him my annual figures. He'd say, so, you did very well again.' In company, Siem bragged so much about Erwin that his wife would sometimes try to temper his garrulousness. Not that he saw all the photos: Lida kept the most extreme ones from him. He especially liked the commercial images and had hung one of Erwin's Heineken advertisements on the wall.

During the 1990s, things had continued to go downhill for Siem Springveld. He was paralysed on his left side after a brain haemorrhage, which led to years of cantankerousness. 'It caused a lot of distress for my mother and brothers, who cared for her – but the person who suffered most was him.' Siem Springveld's social life had ground to a halt due to his physical and financial decline. 'My father became anxious. Little by little, you saw a beaten man.'

Within the family, Erwin rarely showed up. On the rare occasions he did attend a party, everyone had to take cover, according to his sister-in-law Gemma. 'He'd arrive, cause a commotion for two hours, then collapse and leave. That's typical Erwin.' But celebrating Christmas together was sacred. Erwin would sometimes invite his brothers, sisters-in-law and cousins to his house in the Jordaan on 25 December. Jointly decorating the Christmas tree – preferably as manically as possible – was the highlight.

When Siem Springveld died in hospital at the age of seventy-four, his wife Lida and their three sons were at his bedside. In that moment, Erwin finally understood the importance of family, after years of not showing much interest in his brothers, their wives and children. 'Gay men don't typically have kids. I've got two brothers. Thanks to them, I have nephews and nieces – and suddenly it dawned on me: that's my base. That's where the core group of my life sits. Yet I only see them, at most, three times a year.'

He also only truly understood after his father's death how much his father had loved his mother. 'My mother, small and sturdy, had never been the confident model type. "There is no one left who loves me so much," she said after the funeral. For the forty-five-plus years of their marriage, he asked her daily: "Lida, have I told you today how much I love you?" And then he would stroke her hair.'

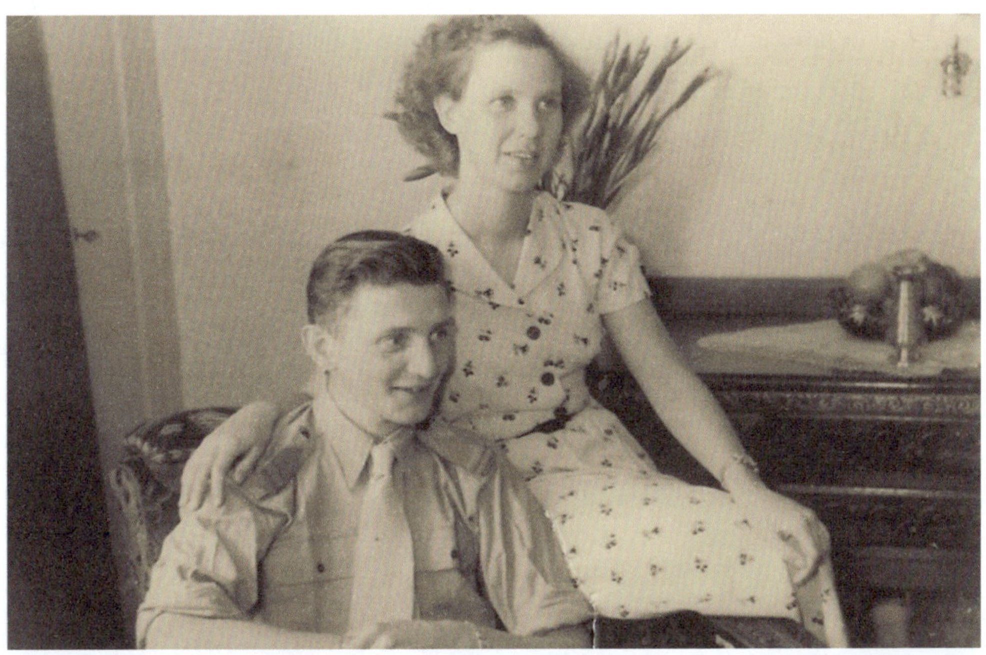

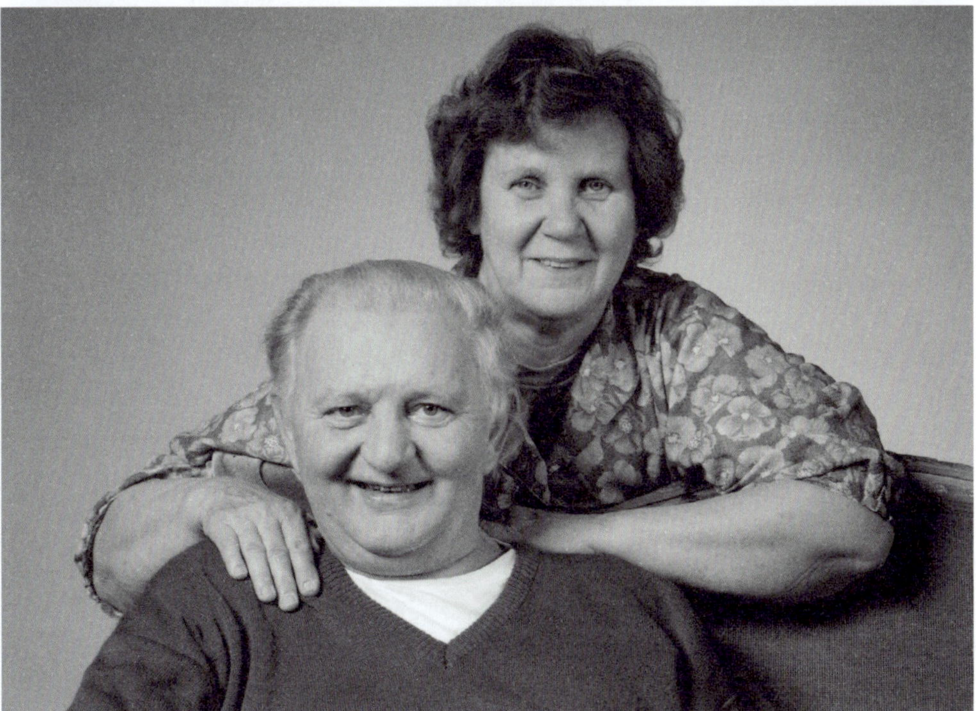

Lida and Siem Springveld in 1956 and in 1991. For the forty-five-plus years of their marriage, he asked her daily: 'Lida, have I told you today how much I love you?' And then he would stroke her hair.

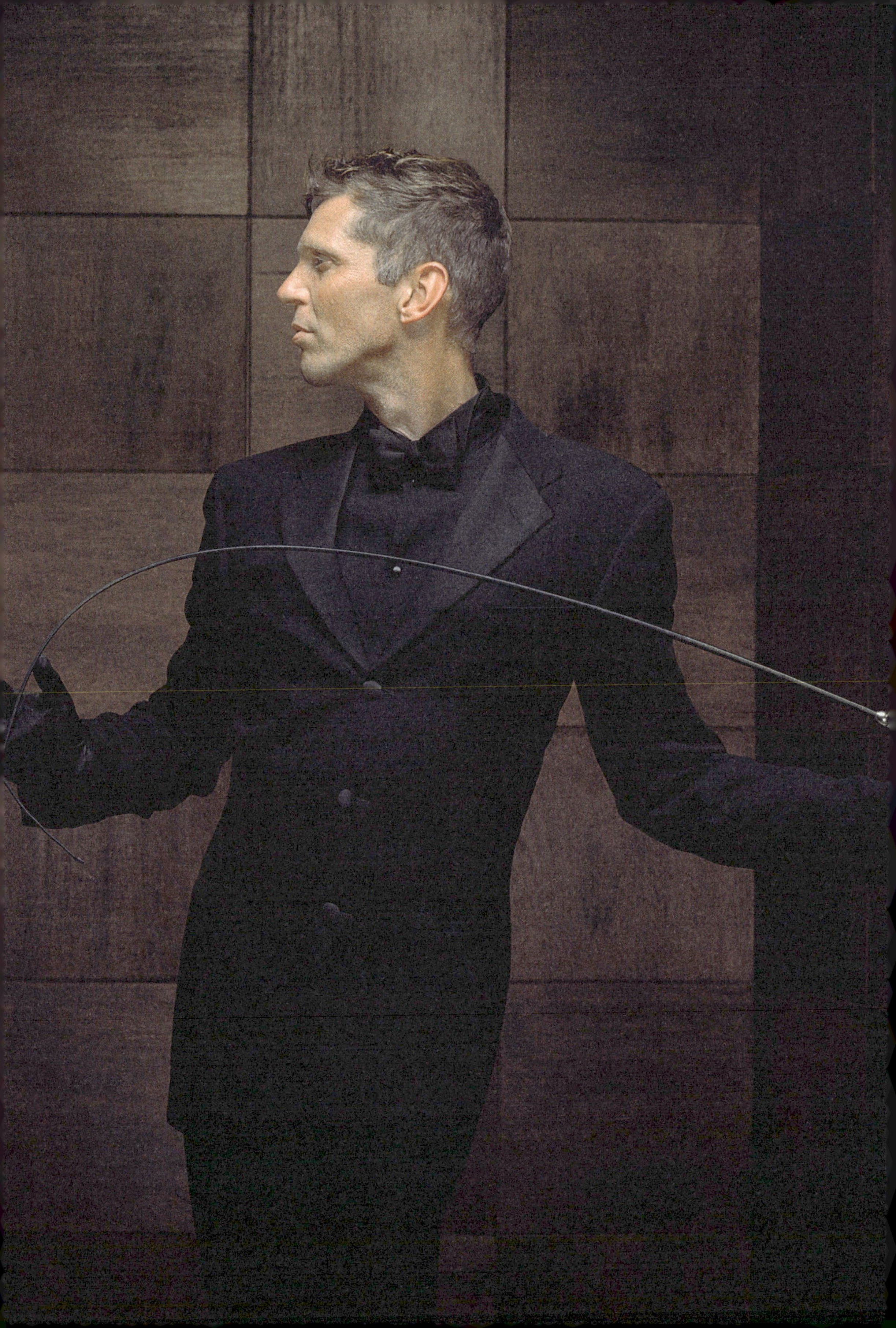

7 BEYOND *STURM UND DRANG* (2001–2010)

'Love is so hard. It's such a fight'

STREET FIGHTER

They had dined at the home of Teun's brother, Job Frieszo, in Amsterdam's Oud-West, and were walking back afterwards, Erwin recalls. He's seated at the round table by the window of his Jordaan flat – not far from his former residence on Lauriergracht.

Near the Lijnbaansgracht, he and Teun got into an argument, Erwin continues, though he can no longer recall what sparked it. While not a natural-born fighter, he lunged at Teun in a moment of sheer fury. It wasn't an especially rare occurrence – but this time, the blow landed hard. 'Teun fell into the canal and dragged me in with him,' Erwin says. 'We plunged into the water, more stunned than scared.'

The incident was emblematic of their long-fractured relationship. 'We fought constantly; it was a real case of *was sich liebt, das neckt sich* [lovers like to tease each other],' he says now, reflecting on a bond that was breaking down after nearly twenty-five years. 'Me: too aggressive, self-centred and stoned. You: too unfaithful, horny and taciturn. But I'll always be grateful that I got to experience such an indescribable and overwhelming sense of love,' Erwin wrote much later in an email to Teun.

On every level, their relationship was as passionate as it was extreme. 'The most intense love and sex – but more often than not, we'd be hurling pots, pans and Christmas baubles across the room.' According to Teun, Erwin often came out on top in these clashes. 'I could never win an argument with him. I was always quite rational and would try to argue my case. Erwin would accuse me of something, and while I was still working out a response, he'd already leapt ahead by three issues – and was ready to stab me in the back with a fourth. Erwin is a street fighter.'

No matter how destructive their relationship became, Erwin found it difficult to be with other men while Teun was still part of his life: he couldn't – and wouldn't – commit to anyone new. Alandus Weertman, too, had proved to be a desperate and hopeless love.

Unable to find solace with Teun, Erwin came to see their love increasingly as an unending struggle. 'Love is so hard. It's such a fight.' Fierce, mutual jealousy was one reason for the split – and for a long time, it hadn't been offset by any equally powerful desire for each other.

As the years of relentless work and heavy partying around the turn of the millennium began to take their toll, the distance between them only grew. It was an aggressive period, fuelled by drugs. 'Anyway, between the ages of 30 and 40, I was hyperdriven – like many people at that age. I was champing at the bit, everyone had to get out of the way, and you could see that in my work just as much as in my personal life.'

The commercial assignments were also intensely demanding, often requiring him to shoot three scenes in a single day – which meant building three separate sets and coordinating just as many casting sessions and styling teams. 'Actually, it was too much of a good thing, and I could be quite cantankerous after a long session.' This, combined with their still-relentless partying – Teun mostly in Utrecht, Erwin in Amsterdam – took a serious toll on their relationship. They saw each other less and less, and other friendships began to deepen.

One such friendship was with Erwin Venema, an apprentice photographer. Though it never developed into a full-blown love affair, the two Erwins bonded closely and often attended fetish parties together. They went to Snax several times – a massive biennial gathering for leather and rubber fetishists of all persuasions at the Berghain club in Berlin. The two would often show up wearing just jockstraps and sports socks – which counted as a fetish too, even if it wasn't latex.

Erwin Olaf wasn't nearly as free-spirited as his photographs might have led some to believe, and his interest in fetish parties was more visual than sexual. He observed them much as he had at the RoXY: from the edge of the dance floor, taking it all in. 'Close to the flames, great, but still at a safe enough distance. I love it when people live life to the full, because I'm too timid for it myself. When it comes to dancing, I'm the one who's swaying along. ... And I'm an inveterate voyeur, but not an exhibitionist. Always in the scene, but never centre stage.'

Berghain was a jaw-dropping experience. 'A latex outfit is visually stunning, and I revel in the perversion. I'm proud that people can enjoy that in Western society – that it has a place, and that we have the freedom to express it.'

His fascination with perversion had little to do with his own erotic desires. 'Leather is too thick, and latex scares me witless. That's not to say I'm not sexually adventurous – but just not in public, and not in a big group. I'm terrible at orgies. I immediately slip into host mode and start passing around cheese cubes and salami slices. "How are you doing? Everything OK?"'

He marked the turn of the millennium with a VPRO-commissioned short film, *Dancing With You*, in which Erwin Venema appeared. There was no leather or latex involved – just naked youths dancing into the new century. Venema hesitated before accepting the role. 'My mother warned me not to do it. She said: "don't – it's a nude film, and it'll haunt you for the rest of your life". I did it anyway, and I have no regrets. I explode at the end of the film, atomised into a cloud of crude pixels. Erwin was standing at the threshold of the digital age.'

Venema also appeared in the photo series *Paradise The Club* (2001), this time dressed as a clown. To bring his extreme fantasy world to life, Erwin recreated the basement of the pop temple Paradiso – graffiti and all. He took a no-holds-barred approach to Photoshop for the layered series; in this saturated, merciless universe, nothing retained its original form.

At the same time, Erwin also created *Paradise Portraits*, a series featuring the louche clowns from *Paradise The Club*. The idea came from Shirley den Hartog – since the clowns were already fully made up, she thought it would be a waste not to use them for something else. For this series, Erwin worked with a new studio lamp that made his own reflection visible in his subjects' eyes.

These works, created in 2001, marked a moment when Erwin's fascination with the club scene and simmering aggression intersected with the shock of the 9/11 attacks in the United States. 'The series grew darker and darker as it progressed, because I was very, very angry.' *Paradise The Club* evolved into a study of the struggle between good and evil – with the clowns representing the most disturbing and violent impulses, and the female nudes embodying innocence. The battle lines seemed to echo a broader cultural clash: Western civilisation, seen by some as decadent and amoral, versus radical Islam, which sought to impose its laws through force. 'People shouldn't interfere in other people's lives through their churches and mosques, or out of civic triteness.'

Erwin's formal inspiration came from a visit to the Prado in Madrid – specifically, Peter Paul Rubens's *The Rape of Hippodamia* (1636–37). 'This is what I want to capture in my work.' The painting portrays the dramatic wedding of Hippodamia to King Pirithous of the Lapiths, a fierce mountain tribe. The ceremony is violently interrupted by centaurs – half-man, half-horse – who instigate a brutal battle. At the heart of the chaos stands Hippodamia, half-naked and exposed, the vulnerable focal point of the scene. Though abducted by the centaurs, she is ultimately rescued by King Theseus of Athens.

Erwin's Photoshopped interpretation is a disconcerting, almost hysterical tableau of extravagant figures – clowns, bearded women and all manner of nocturnal creatures. It's an explosion of colour, where his anger over the attack on Western civilisation converges with his admiration for the radical self-expression of the club scene.

Another source of inspiration was the *Fucque les Balles* benefit parties – a kind of sequel to the Love Ball events Erwin had long been organising with DJ Joost van Bellen at the pop temple Paradiso. The first *Fucque les Balles* of the new millennium, held in December 2000, carried the theme 'Christmas Circus'. It was a dazzling spectacle, populated by night owls, drag performers, bearded women, go-go dancers, revellers in elephant masks, little people and many of Erwin's friends and acquaintances.

Conny Janssen helped organise the event. 'Erwin had the gift of transforming pure banality into sublime decadence. It was a whirlwind of a party – everything that could go wrong did go wrong, and that's exactly why it was such a roaring success.' Her job was to calm an overstressed Erwin while managing a twenty-strong majorette troupe of drag performers, including Zu Browka. 'It was a real baptism of fire. I'd just arrived from the provinces, green as grass, and most of the drag performers were totally bitchy and hysterical.'

Not long after *Paradise The Club*, Erwin parted ways with Jaap Hinten – the man who, in his eyes, embodied both the spirit of the series and the aggressive lifestyle he had lived throughout the 1990s. Hinten had long been Erwin's partner in crime, his go-to stylist for parties, photo series and commercial projects. Later, alongside Harrie Wildeman, Hinten formed the designer duo Haute Couture Junkies, which rose to prominence in entertainment circles and staged fashion shows at the RoXY.

Hinten had been the studio's regular stylist, but at Shirley den Hartog's urging, Erwin occasionally began working with other collaborators. As his photography became more cinematic and theatrical, he felt the need for a fresh perspective on set design. By then, Hinten had grown increasingly dependent on Erwin as a client, and the reduction in work may have caused a cooling in their friendship. 'We were very close; we did a lot of naughty and fun things,' Erwin recalls. 'But for me, the partying started to matter less and less and the work more and more.'

His relationship with Teun came to a definite end around the same time. According to Teun, it was mutual fascination and great sex that had kept them together for so long. 'We had a wonderful time, but it was never harmonious,' he said of the break-up. 'Eventually, I couldn't take the constant rancour anymore – and not just because of the shameless cheating, which I was certainly guilty of too. Erwin had a short fuse, and his mood could shift in an instant. The drama became harder and harder to manage, and in the end, I called it a day.'

'Erwin struggled to accept it but ultimately realised it was for the best,' Teun noted. 'It changed his work – and for the better. The rather bizarre series like *Paradise* and *Royal Blood* gave way to quieter, more introspective images. Before the split, it

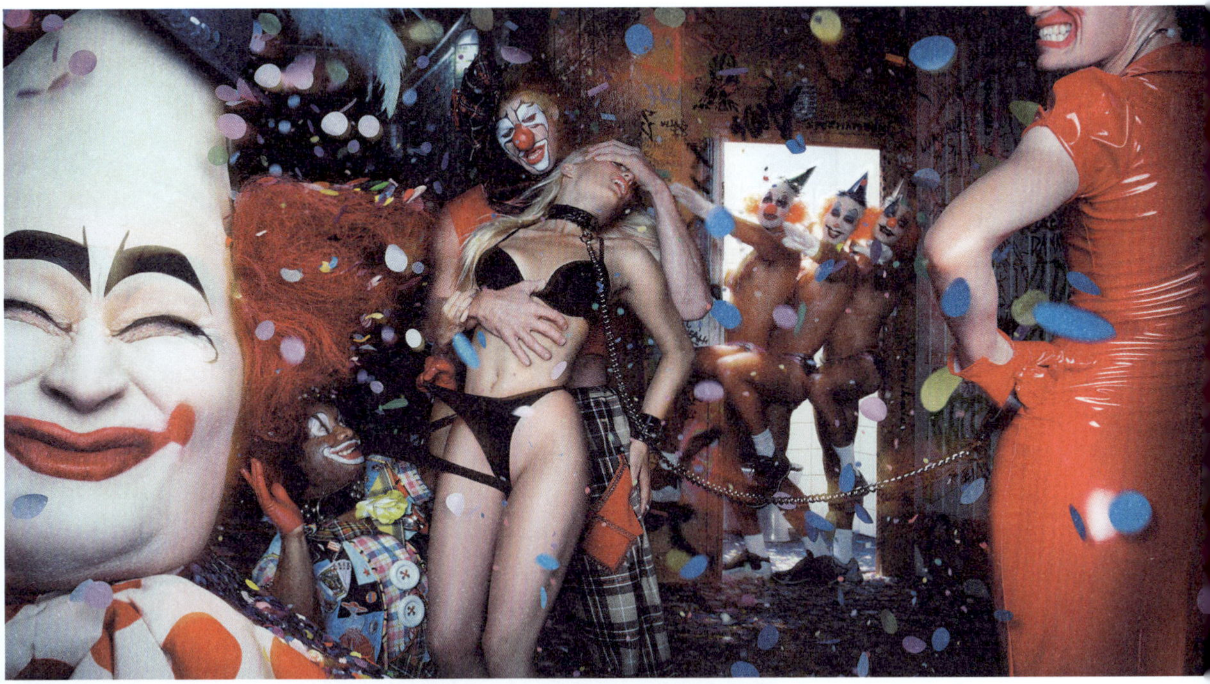

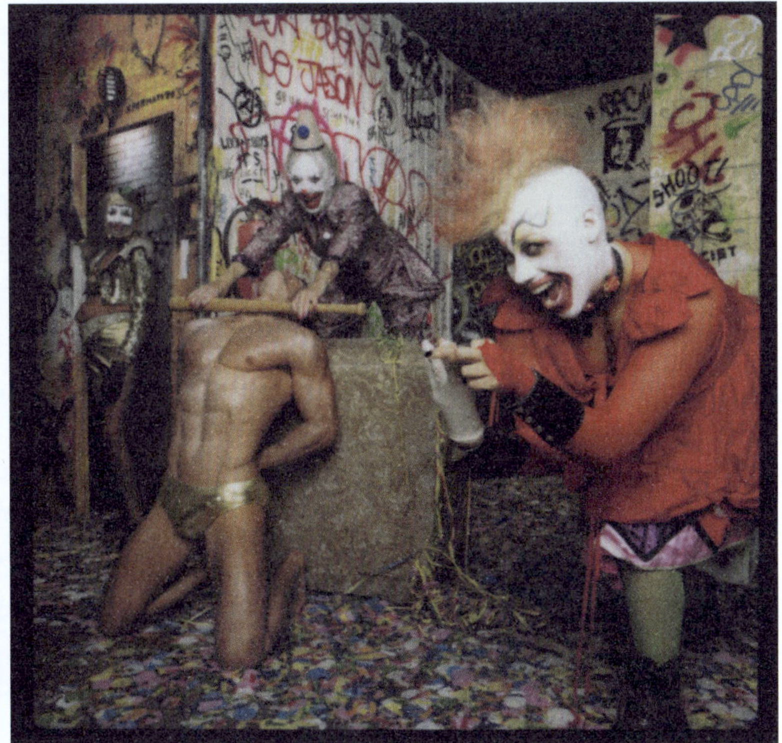

Dancefloor, 2001, from the *Paradise The Club* series. With Erwin Venema as the model (right) in red. Left: Polaroid taken during the filming of *Paradise The Club*.

Photo on page 220: *Yves Saint Laurent - Self-Portrait, 2000* from the *Fashion Victims* series.

had all felt like a game. Afterwards, his work became more serious, more consistent and, in my view at least, also better. Some of the post-breakup photographs are incredibly sad.'

Erwin's personal life had been shaken by the death of his father, the end of a close friendship, and his break-up with Teun – but in the wake of 9/11, the entire world seemed to be unravelling. In those dramatic times, reality felt stranger and more extreme than any fiction, including his own art. A sadder and wiser Erwin closed his most commercially successful years with *Paradise The Club*, sensing he had reached a turning point. He felt 'done with the expressive aggression and all the shouting from the barricades' and found himself beginning to 'abhor violence, which seemed completely inane'.

The new and more sombre series that emerged from this period was entitled *Separation*. Erwin struggled with the breakup and the loneliness that followed nearly twenty-five years with Teun. 'Coming home alone after important moments,' he said, 'was hard to swallow'. Another relationship seemed unlikely, though he did test the waters with a few potential partners. By his own admission, he could be quite demanding – a trait only amplified by the rise of online dating. 'You used to cycle endlessly to someone's house to get to know them. Nowadays, before you even make it to a first date, you already know whether he's got a six-pack, a long dick and whether he's house-proud. It's like getting sex out of a vending machine.'

But *Separation* was, above all, a farewell to Erwin's rambunctious years. For this new series, he searched deeply within himself and, as Teun put it, rediscovered 'the lonely, outcast boy from his childhood' – a figure who was also beginning to surface in his photography.

As so often in his work, the series was static and subdued yet unsettling, exploring a central theme – in this case, abandonment, exclusion and betrayal – while also breaking new formal ground. 'I wanted to compose an elongated, narrow image, with light filtering in from an upper window, and use close-ups – simultaneously. Extremely tricky, but I pulled it off. That was a thrill.'

It was the first time Erwin had constructed an entirely new world within his independent work. He built the sets in collaboration with Floris Vos, with whom he'd reconnected on the club scene after a long hiatus. Vos designed seven seemingly cosy living rooms, adorned with floral wallpaper. From that point on, the décor would become just as important as the models within the frame. 'Floris taught me to broaden my vision. He helped me realise it's not just about the people in the photos – I needed to examine everything around them, beside them, even behind them.'

In one of those décors, he placed a latex-clad mother and son – a shocking image. It was inspired by a gruesome story told by a fashion designer in the fetish industry who'd been commissioned to make a child-size latex suit lined with nails. The tale percolated around Erwin's head for several years before he decided to do something with it. Skin was the organ he focused on most in his photographs anyway, and he knew he could work with latex as a second layer. He envisioned the image of 'a desperate mother and her sad son, both trapped for eternity in their rubber suits'.

Only after completing the series did Erwin realise it had an autobiographical slant. 'The latex was a metaphor for my childhood loneliness, my vulnerability, the sense of exclusion, and all the frustration. Latex is an incredibly thin material, yet it creates a world of distance. The mother and her little boy can't reach each other and can't truly connect. Just as my own mother couldn't comfort me, couldn't come closer to me during those hellish years of being bullied at school.'

Looking at the doleful mannequin encased in its rubber shell, Erwin felt as though he were staring at his younger self – locked inside, unable to process his emotions. 'In that moment, I felt a powerful emotion leave my body; all my childhood sorrow seemed to escape from the studio. Since then, I've felt much stronger. I've moved on from my past, and I care far less about what others think of my work.'

The series marked a transitional moment and a significant learning experience. Not just because of the new importance given to the sets, or the addition of a short video – just under four minutes in length – alongside the photographs. More importantly, it was due to the presence of the articulated mannequin and Erwin's desire to communicate with the viewer through body language alone, in the absence of facial expression.

'I had to give that mannequin its own motor skills – kneading, pushing and pulling its limbs to express emotions such as sadness and shyness. Gradually, I discovered I could evoke a sense of loneliness or melancholy by gently lowering a shoulder, tilting the head, or leaning the figure against a wall. Laying him on the bed suggested exhaustion; shift him slightly, and he appears to be sleeping. Standing on tiptoes heightened the impression of yearning. This subtle, indirect way of communicating with the viewer felt like a revelation. I was mesmerised – it became an obsession: the study of emotion made visible through the smallest changes in posture and gesture.'

As *The New York Times* would write of the series, 'Even some of his most vexing imagery, such as his 2003 series *Separation*, depicting a mother and child clad in full-body black latex who can't quite reach each other, is a study of human vulnerability.'

'If I ever see her, I'm going to give her a giant kick up the arse'

CRITICAL NOTES

'What a fantastic year!' Erwin reads aloud from notes he jotted down at the end of 2003. He laughs quietly now, two decades later, knowing the summary wasn't entirely accurate. Still, one undeniable highlight was his major retrospective at the Groninger Museum, celebrating twenty-five years as a photographer.

Moreover, the catalogue, entitled *Silver* like the exhibition, was a weighty tome 'that you could smash over your favourite enemy's head and cause some serious damage'. He had chosen *Silver* because it was a short and snappy title that not only alluded to his silver jubilee, but also to the light-sensitive silver bromide in photographic paper.

For once, he was a major crowd-puller: over 45,000 people visited the Groninger Museum to view his work – a personal record. The exhibition included not only the new series *Separation* and *Fashion Victims*, but also his commercial work and journalistic photographs from the 1980s, including reports on gay demonstrations and the S&M series for the current affairs magazine *Vrij Nederland*. After all, everything was interconnected in Erwin's universe.

Soon afterwards, clubbers were sleeping on the street in sleeping bags to get tickets for his annual party, now christened *Fucque the Future*. The 'insanely dressed visitors' left the pop temple Paradiso shaking on its foundations. There was a Planet of the Apes disco, an open stage for air guitar, a Theatre of Hell, a Michael Jackson lookalike accompanied by a fire-breathing robot, a throng of Barbarellas, and a hulk. In short, it was a fantasy world – absurd yet familiar – where Erwin felt enveloped by the love of like-minded people and shielded from the prejudices of the outside world.

However beautiful it sounded, and however reassuring his recollections, the fact that it was a year to remember was also due to two articles in the leading newspaper *NRC Handelsblad*. On 26 September 2003, art critic Hans den Hartog Jager launched an attack on the hype surrounding photography, which had increasingly come to be seen as a fully-fledged art form. His critique had deleterious consequences. 'More than journalistic or documentary photography, "art photography" takes the rap, in which the photographer "through staging or manipulation" wants the viewer to reflect on the "visible world" in which he lives.'

Reality matters less and less to these photographers, Den Hartog Jager wrote, and 'the photographer's vision increasingly becomes the focus of the photograph'.

Moreover, art photographers, he argued, often crudely imitated fine art. Their goal was not to present reality, but to 'manipulate, distort and aestheticise' it – just

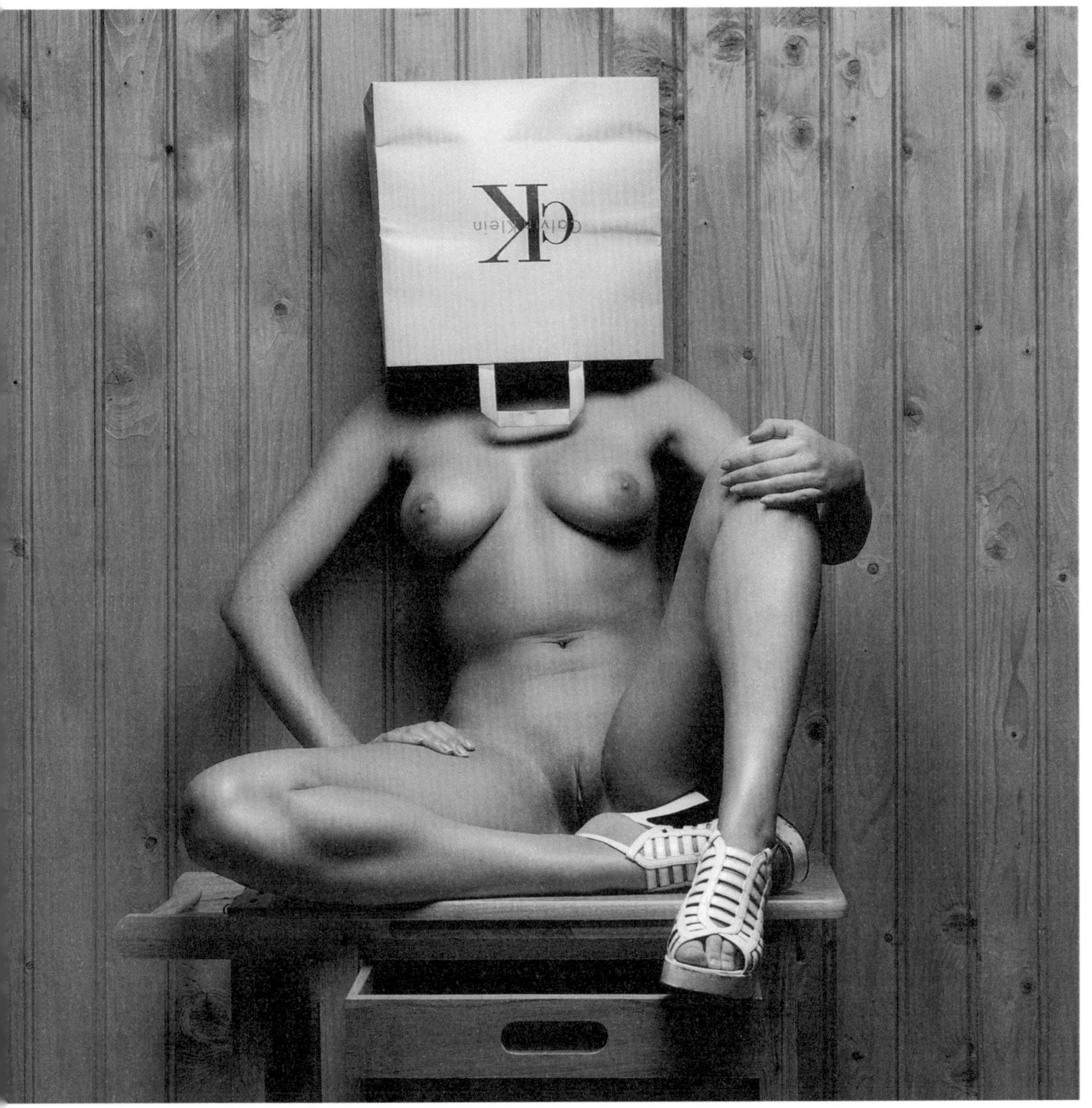

Calvin Klein, 2000, from the *Fashion Victims* series. Erwin offered a critique of the fashion industry in this independent body of work. Nevertheless, art critics viewed it as commercial photography.

like traditional artists. These days, the critic concluded, anyone with a Hasselblad and a working light meter could land a solo museum show.

Readers could easily interpret the piece as a harsh critique of Erwin's work. Yet the name 'Erwin Olaf' didn't appear once, which allowed him to brush it off.

But Janneke Wesseling's review of his Groningen exhibition – published in the same newspaper on the same day – was something else entirely. She dipped her pen in poison and wrote a piece that hit Erwin for six. It was a review he would remember for years to come and even cite in interviews.

The newspaper had followed his work for some time. Its writers had variously described his photographs as 'tender and refined' or 'pornographic and bizarre', while he himself was labelled either 'provocative and hip' or dismissed outright as a 'glamour photographer'. Erwin was well accustomed to the full spectrum of critical opinion from the esteemed paper. But Wesseling's take on *Silver* was positively vitriolic. She described the exhibition as being filled with 'blood and sex, quivering flesh, black boots and taut ropes, masks and latex, tits, buttocks and erections, transvestites... and Baroque costume balls.' That hit hard.

Erwin had embraced the idea of a silver jubilee exhibition at the Groninger Museum. It felt like a mark of professional recognition, of the kind that still eluded him in Amsterdam, and which he deeply craved.

For years, he remained deeply aggrieved by the Stedelijk Museum's rejection of his work – especially painful given his fixation on that bastion of contemporary art. The fact that the most prestigious museum in his own city dismissed him became a recurring grievance, one he aired repeatedly, like variations on a theme, in both public interviews and private conversations, with friends and adversaries alike – and well beyond the *Silver* period. Even the mere mention of the word 'Stedelijk' could set off a furious tirade against what he saw as its sanctimonious arrogance: a museum that celebrated his artistic heroes Joel-Peter Witkin and Robert Mapplethorpe, and championed his contemporaries Rineke Dijkstra and Paul Blanca as major talents, yet consistently ignored his own oeuvre.

That his work was welcome in the collection and galleries of the Groninger Museum, which had more or less specialised in staged photography, at least counted for something. 'Reviews of this exhibition will crack a few hard nuts. Go on then, judge me.' To which he trepidatiously added: 'It doesn't make me nervous, just vulnerable.' *Silver* included both Erwin's independent work and his advertising photography. He wanted to show that these different forms could coexist within a single oeuvre and even enrich one another. But it was precisely this blend of art and commerce that the reviewer loathed.

Surveying the Groninger Museum, she claimed to see no difference between Erwin Olaf's autonomous photography – 'as he calls it himself', she added with venom –

and his commercial images. 'He uses an identical strategy for both categories. ... It's fashionable to claim that there is no longer a distinction between free and applied art. A grave misunderstanding, for the simple reason that an autonomous artwork is not created for any practical purpose. Functionality is the antithesis of art's *raison d'être*. A work of art is altruistic. It has no need to please.'

In another quality newspaper, *de Volkskrant* (25 September 2003), reviewer Rutger Pontzen saw *Silver* as a runaway masquerade, a madcap fantasy in which Erwin Olaf – whom he characterised as a 'maverick' – went all the way. 'Excess can be detrimental, but not with Erwin Olaf. Exaggeration is his lifeblood. He swears by exorbitance. He is hyperbole incarnate – to such a degree that even extremism doesn't go far enough. Which is why we don't just see a naked little person walking through his set, but one in spiked sandals.' Erwin's 'brooding baroque' was unparalleled, according to Pontzen, who praised him as a trendsetter, a trailblazer and a champion of gay rights.

Those Baroque hyperboles seemed to be contagious. According to Pontzen, the exhibition was 'an orgasmic reckoning with the Dutch air of peat, sprouts and dank living rooms. It's clearly the work of a child of the 1980s – the decade that was actually brighter than suggested by the contemporaneous slogan, "No future". Olaf can bend the world to his will. And not just in terms of lighting and staging. There is also an infectious yearning for an ideal, in a social sense. Hence his homage to those in danger of being excluded in the process. ... His pictures scream – in no uncertain terms – that freedom belongs to everyone.'

The aforementioned reviewer, after some initial hesitation, had stepped into Erwin's fantasy world after all, whereas *NRC Handelsblad* had made mincemeat of it with a blunt axe. Janneke Wesseling signed off with: 'Olaf's work is uncritical. He's no Jeff Koons. His work lacks an ancillary layer. It's devoid of irony. It's one-dimensional and excludes the imagination. In this way, Olaf effectively shuts out the viewer. It doesn't matter whether it's a beer bottle or a person – these people are meaningless. They're reduced to objects.'

She ended with words rarely seen in visual art criticism: 'This is what makes his work so repulsive.'

Years later, the article still makes his blood boil. 'A fucking bitch [has] been viciously pelting me with shit. If I ever see her, I'm going to give her a giant kick up the arse. If an artist uses his imagination and fantasy, it's definitely not appreciated around here. No, photographing an overflowing ashtray... that's beautiful. So-called realism. It makes me sick to my stomach. I have to look at reality every single day. The fantasy in my photos is uniquely mine. It's impossible to fake. Try it – you won't succeed.'

As Wim van Sinderen, who had co-curated the earlier exhibition *Joy* with Erwin, remarked: 'It was cruel of the newspaper to send the queen of minimal art to review

Erwin's oeuvre. But it did send him in another direction, which is also very fascinating.' Indeed, *Silver* – perhaps partly shaped by that brutal review – would mark a true departure from his more extravagant photography.

Erwin Springveld managed to rein in his alter ego, Erwin Olaf, and steer him onto a new path. 'I said to myself: I'm over this incessant need to prove myself. You know how to photograph. Full stop.'

Things certainly had to change, but he wasn't sure what the next five years should look like. His handwritten notes about his goals don't tend to be well articulated, but they do give an impression of his associative thought processes in respect of photography and his business.

'Am I going to do the children's film this year or not, and if so, what does my lead actor look like? ... Can I teach myself, once and for all, how to use Photoshop correctly? Glow-in-the-dark photos? Have those light-blocking curtains arrived yet? ... And what about that feature film, then? No dialogues yet conjecturing that something is being said, theatrical acting, wordless, only sounds, theatrical sounds, long hair rippling with sadness, Visconti women? Rustling dresses, weeping? No, no blubbering! ... Whoosh, a red cape sweeps by, alone? Why am I haunted by the image of a burgundy cape in a milky white room? It's a scary cape. Milky white and padded, burgundy, velvet? Ruby? Is she crazy? Is it even a woman? Only females? Or a gender-neutral person? Or just a gender-neutral person, with a cape? No. No. Not a guy and no blubbering, or perhaps yes? Ten pictures? No, that's far too many, isn't it? And a video, panning out further than *Separation*, plus visual splendour – or will that be too expensive? Two videos? Need to land some big commissions: will Virgin Mobile come knocking?'

'I'm not interested in reality. I'm fascinated by the unreal'

NORMAN ROCKWELL'S DEPRESSED NEPHEW

No, Erwin rarely had a razor-sharp image in mind when he started a new series, production designer Floris Vos explains, in a café close to his studio flat in Amsterdam-West. Rain, the series on which Vos worked intensively and which marked the end of Erwin's period of *Sturm und Drang*, is a typical example of their collaboration. Such projects only tended to crystallise during the course of the session. Later still, such series acquired an overarching narrative, in conjunction with the other parts of the triptych *Rain*, *Hope* and *Grief*.

Erwin did not fixate on a concept but tried to search freely for new images.

He worked intuitively, only to realise, along the way, that his photos were not only semi-autobiographical, but also said something about others and even social reality. Yes, perhaps he was even a kind of philosopher, as he conceded, not without self-mockery, in an interview. Or, as he later phrased it: 'I'm naturally savvy and want to illuminate the universal in the minuscule. As an overarching theme, the preservation of freedom in the Western world, how our values and norms are at risk and how they must be defended.'

After *Separation*, a vague idea developed for a new series about the 1950s, when Europe still regarded America as a liberator and protector. He had just produced an advertising picture, commissioned by the German lighting designer Ingo Maurer, that was inspired by the paintings of Norman Rockwell, the chronicler of American culture. For almost half a century, Rockwell drew the covers of *The Saturday Evening Post*. During the Second World War, he painted iconic front pages featuring the Four Freedoms from US President F.D. Roosevelt's famous State of the Union address (1941): Freedom of Speech, Freedom of Worship, Freedom from Want and Freedom from Fear. But Erwin also recognised something else in Norman Rockwell: no matter how important the painter was to American culture, and irrespective of how many millions his paintings could command at auction, he was never lionised in highbrow art circles as an autonomous artist because of his realistic, somewhat sentimental images of American daily life and his work as an illustrator.

Erwin wanted to put his own spin on Rockwell's idealism as an antidote to the anti-Americanism behind the Twin Towers attack on 11 September 2001. He was outraged by the suggestion that America, as an arrogant and imperialist world power, had brought it on itself. *Rain*, together with the follow-up series *Hope* and *Grief*, charted his emotions in the years after his father's death and the split with Teun, but they also represented an escape to the past during those violent early days of Islamic fundamentalism and the subsequent war on terror.

The fantasised, bloody murders of *Royal Blood* became a reality with the 2002 murder of Pim Fortuyn, the populist, far-right politician whose bloody death had naturally shocked Erwin, even though he loathed his rhetoric. But the religiously motivated murder of his creative friend and contemporary, Theo van Gogh, made the most indelible impression of all. The well-known film-maker and columnist was murdered by a Dutch-Moroccan jihadist in November 2004.

Erwin had always got on well with Theo van Gogh, whom he found 'sweet but fierce', and for whom he'd designed a couple of supposedly offensive film posters. Van Gogh also gave Erwin a walk-on part in his feature film *Loos*. The two men had riotous times and they shared a vicious sense of humour. Both felt like outsiders. They enjoyed teasing one another but were known to quarrel; they also fell out for a time.

Erwin was travelling in South Africa when Van Gogh was murdered. Upon his

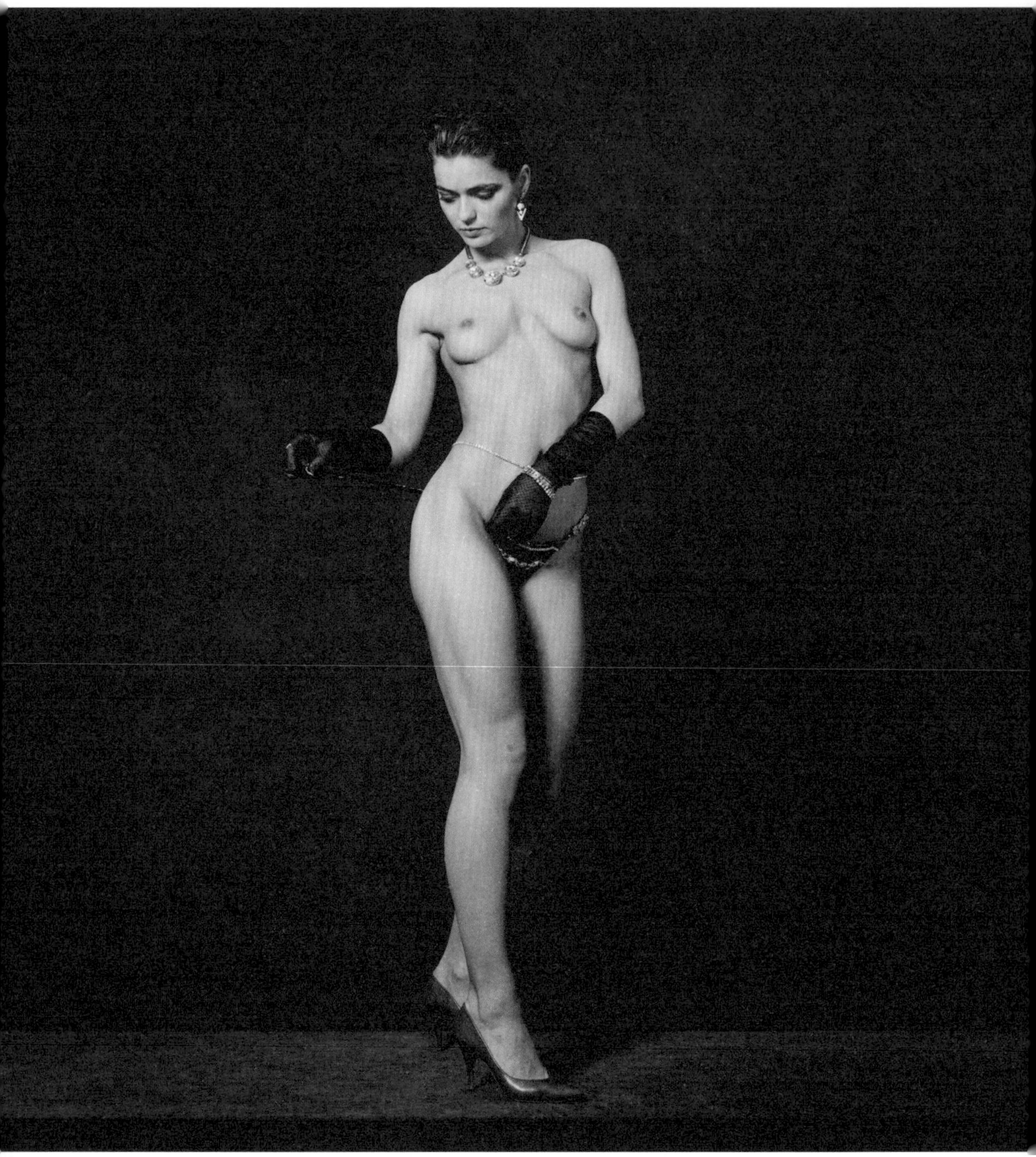

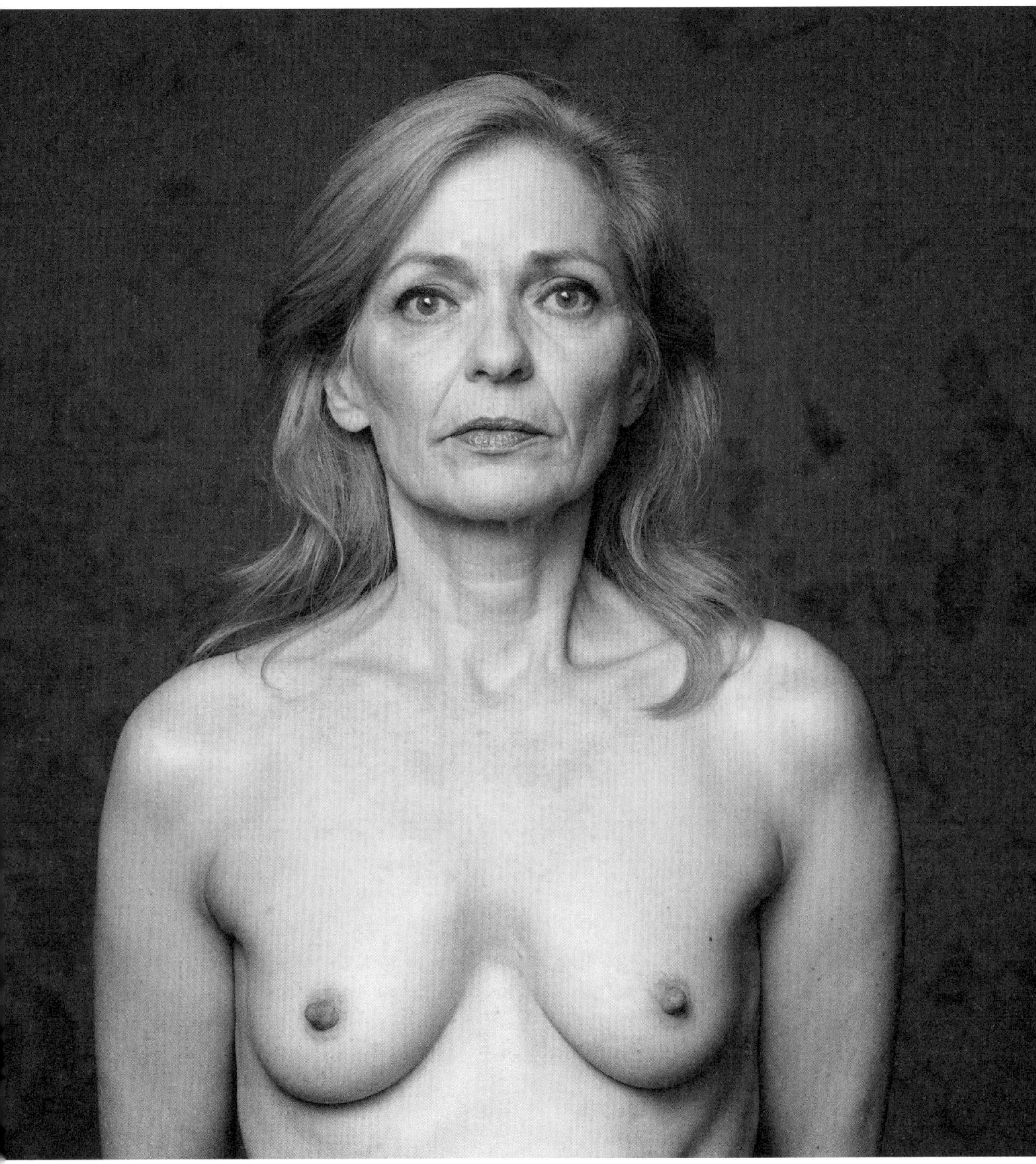

Left: Louise Aarens in 1986. Right: Photographed again in 2021 for the *Muses* series.

return, a new assignment awaited him: he'd been asked to photograph eighteen Amsterdammers of Moroccan descent for a major exhibition on 5,000 years of Moroccan culture. An awkward coincidence so soon after the murder. Erwin was shocked by the incident and his first thought was to cancel the project altogether. Instead, he decided to make his point another way: by having a trans person handle the exhibition communication. To his surprise, no one in the Moroccan community took offence. What had begun as a provocation ultimately proved to have an almost therapeutic effect. 'I wanted to let go of some of that anger.'

Like most Dutch people, Erwin was bewildered and, above all, outraged. He was incredulous when people said that Van Gogh 'shouldn't have had such a big mouth then'. Instead of solidarity and manning the barricades in defence of free speech, they 'simpered, hissed and wrote that the film-maker had asked to be killed'. As a 'huge fan of the royal family', he was aghast that Queen Beatrix had 'hugged local Moroccan mothers' following the murder but didn't visit Theo van Gogh's widow.

For Erwin, the ensuing years were dominated by the West's lack of resilience and that of the 'so-called progressive affluent class' which, in his view, had failed to defend free speech. He was convinced that the USA was a source of inspiration and a champion of democracy. He believed in the Four Freedoms – and he wanted his work to reinforce that image. Inspired by Rockwell, he sought to depict the happy and nostalgic side of the USA: the America of diners, cheerleaders, Lassie and Mister Ed. Moreover, using the book *Norman Rockwell's America* as a starting point for building the cinematic sets allowed him to combine his fascination with time travel and feature films.

Floris Vos was tasked with creating the sets. 'You have to evoke the period atmosphere from scratch. I started delving into that era, the United States in the 1950s and 1960s,' Vos recalls. 'And we began constructing the scenes. As we worked, the idea of using differently coloured spotlights for each set grew. Bathing everything in the washed-out technicolour atmosphere of the 1950s and 1960s.'

At the funeral of his friend and creative brother on 4 October 2019, Erwin paid tribute to the depth that Vos's cinematic sets had brought to his photographs, which had changed his work forever. 'From that moment on, the camera angle alone elicited greater curiosity. The possibilities of "looking beyond" the initial layer to a second or even third one suddenly became infinite. And the mystery of each picture was subtly enhanced.'

What had begun as a positive take on Rockwell's idealised, patriotic world turned into a melancholic and disillusioned staging *à la* Edward Hopper in *Rain* and later in *Hope* and *Grief*. The initial plan for *Rain* had received a working title of *Happy*, after the quote by gay African American writer James Baldwin (*Giovanni's Room*, 1956): 'What's the good of an American who isn't happy? Happiness was all we had.'

But even as he took the first picture, showing a dance school with black pupils, Erwin knew that his approach was doomed to fail: the happiness he was striving to capture was far from being his own.

The lost world he was so keen to portray felt more distant than ever in the early twenty-first century, he realised. 'There are moments in your professional career when you feel a lead weight in the pit of your stomach, and the first day of that shoot was one of them. The unhappier I am with my work, the more Polaroids I start making. Out of insecurity. I will scan the entire room for a light, an angle, a piece of furniture, a dress... The slightest thing that can make a difference. But, of course, it's never about details; it's about the overarching emotion.'

Floris Vos witnessed that desperation up close. 'Erwin is never difficult with me; he's simply demanding. He trusts you; that's important. First see what I come up with, then adjust if necessary. And, as with all good directors, he's usually right.' Erwin, for his part, listened to Floris's advice, which was informed by his cinematographic work: always think about the camera angle and 'pull it back' for greater depth in the image. Provided it was well argued, everything was negotiable – this is how Erwin remembered the experience of working with his 'very articulate, incredibly funny and intelligent friend'. 'Floris didn't suffer from an overinflated ego and it was always possible to deviate from the set path.'

Erwin's precise visions for his scenes often remained a mystery. He knew roughly what he wanted to say but struggled to translate it visually. More or less by chance, he discovered a way to make the 1950s imagery his own, noted Floris Vos. 'With the first set, the dance school, the picture was initially too crowded: it included a pianist and four students. Erwin didn't really know what to do with them all.' The image was bloated and the cheerful atmosphere the scene should have exuded was positively gloomy. 'I was distraught.'

The models milled around until Erwin had a fit: he asked them to stand stock still and quit the jollity. As was so often the case, he didn't know what he was seeking, but found it anyway through a sudden flash of inspiration. Now that the forced gaiety wasn't working, perhaps it would be better for the scene to express loneliness instead. He pressed the shutter, watched the image emerge on the Polaroid and saw that he'd found his story: the end of the American Dream.

His gaze had shifted from a celebration of American freedom to a record of its demise. An initially happy image had turned into one featuring two lonely, eminently sad people for whom the music had stopped – even though the practice steps were already marked on the dance school floor. A saddening image, he thought to himself. 'Society was paralysed, too lame to react.'

Apart from the dance school, Floris Vos built sets for a barber shop and an ice-cream parlour, among other things. The supporting colour was green – a colour

Erwin also owed to Vos. 'What Floris really opened my eyes to is his favourite hue: green, in all its endless variations.'

Vos built these fictitious worlds in the high-rise studio on IJselstraat. 'I sourced all the props, carpets, wallpaper, furniture and appliances, often collecting them in my own Volvo. You make sets for pictures that are going to cost a fortune, so everything has to make sense, not too many anachronisms, even if it's a fantasy. The sets were fun to make and I was delighted with the ice-cream parlour because I really had to get creative when meshing everything together. It was a replica of a non-existent Norman Rockwell, with that Boy Scout with a plaster on his knee.'

Floris and Erwin loved fine-tuning the details. The series was deliberately artificial. 'I'm not interested in reality. I'm fascinated by the unreal. And that imaginary world has to look as believable as possible.' You can take a good photo in ten minutes, Erwin knew; most of the time went into preparation. These were expensive and labour-intensive projects: a day of carpentry, a day of decorating, hours spent with the stylist. Afterwards, the series was extensively post-processed, which Erwin accomplished with his regular digital editor, Edwin Veer, 'an artist and my soulmate'. The investment paid off handsomely, not only in terms of success but also financially: just five years later, the Sir Elton John Photography Collection paid 25,000 euros for a print of *The Ice Cream Parlor*.

The grandiosity and clamour of his earlier work had been replaced with a subtler emphasis on details, poses and the choreography of emotions. '*Rain*, *Hope* and *Grief* concern the distance between two people. Is the hand on the table or lap, where's the phone, the depression in the sofa cushion: has someone just departed? I said goodbye to hard, direct and straightforward photography. My personal work until 2003 has that in spades... because I cut my teeth on posters and covers and advertising campaigns. The starting point was always: this is what I want you to see. But after that point, I just wanted to break it all down.'

The series was an instant success, especially outside the Netherlands. 'The interesting thing about Erwin Olaf is that he can be both classic and contemporary,' said Paco Barragán, curator of the Sydney exhibition that included *Rain*. 'His compositions are a portrait of our times, steeped in perverse elegance.'

Rain and *Hope* also provided a first breakthrough in the United States and won Erwin commissions from *The New York Times Magazine*. Whereas American audiences had previously failed to understand *Mature*, this new work proved to be just that. The series debuted at the Flatland Gallery's stand at Paris Photo in the autumn and, to Erwin's surprise, caused a sensation. 'You don't think, now we're going to do Norman Rockwell and it's going to secure my breakthrough. You trust your instincts. That *Rain* caught on in the US, in particular, was a huge surprise, even to me.'

One of the interested parties was New York gallerist, former actor and photo

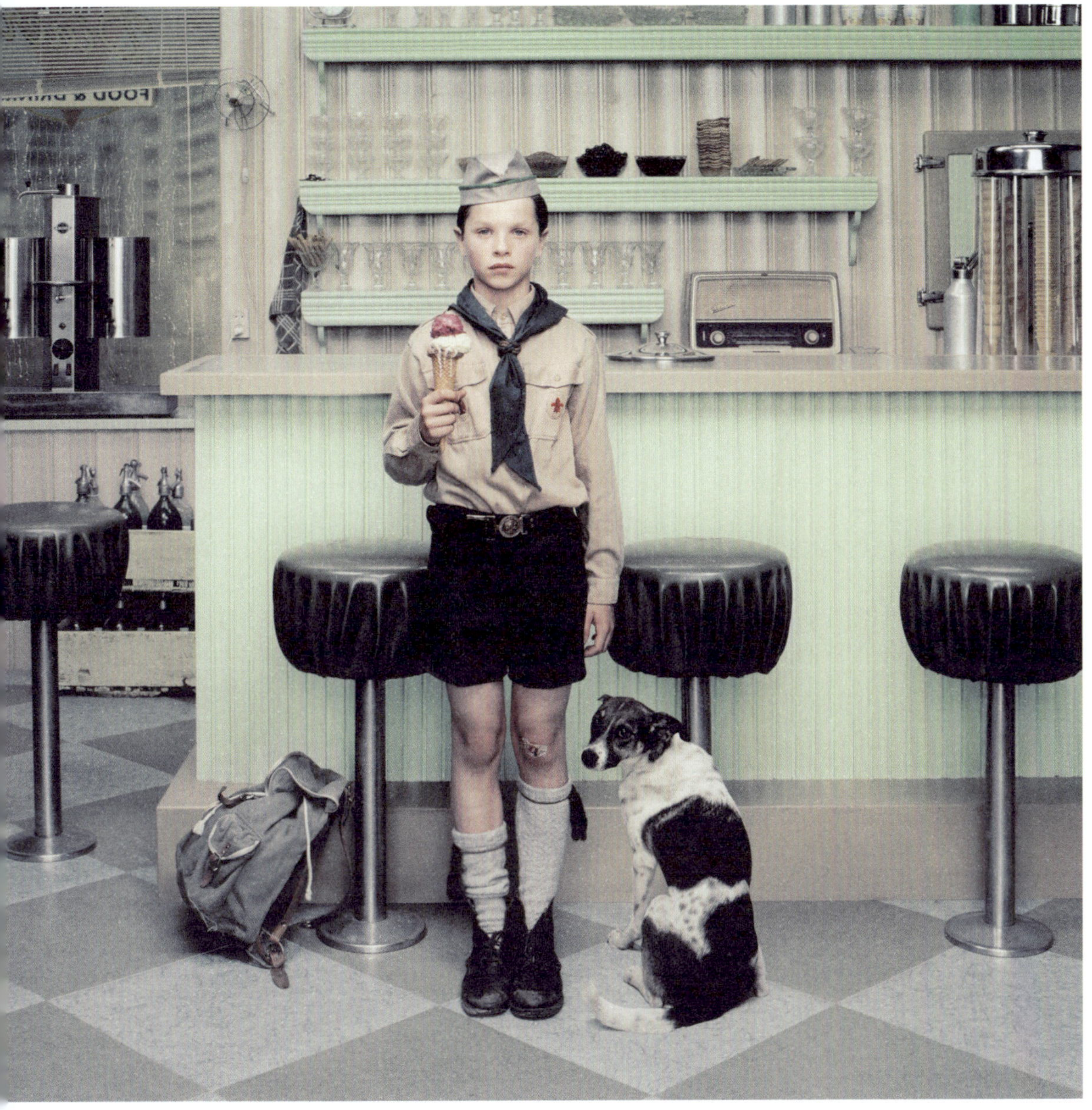

The Ice Cream Parlor, 2004, from the *Rain* series. 'I'm not interested in reality. I'm fascinated by the unreal. And that imaginary world has to look as believable as possible.'

collector Bill Hunt. Hunt had amassed a collection featuring work by all the most illustrious names in photographic history, from Joel-Peter Witkin and Richard Avedon to Diane Arbus and Cindy Sherman. He had previously dismissed Erwin's photographs as too extreme. 'I knew his early work,' says Bill Hunt in the lobby of Amsterdam's Apollo Hotel. 'And I didn't like those series. The early black-and-white work seemed derivative, like it was aping other, better photographers' work. And I found *Royal Blood* disturbing because I loathe anything to do with knives and stabbing. 'Finally, when I did go and look, there hung the *Rain* series and I said to myself, "Wow, man, this is really good!" I immediately started preparing a show of Erwin's work in New York at our Hasted Hunt Gallery.'

Why did this work appeal to him so much? 'I think because Erwin quoted from an American visual tradition and used it to tap into a nostalgic longing for innocence that, as an American, casts you back to the post-war period, to the 1950s. Keywords: Korea, Eisenhower, middle-class bourgeoisie, white, saccharine. But of course, it's an illusion; he effectively dramatises something that could have happened but never did – except in Erwin's imagination and that of the viewer.'

There are prejudices against artists who also make commercial work, but he himself actually saw it as a plus, Hunt said. Anyone who likes Erwin's photographs should also look at his commercial assignments, he says, such as his 2004 advertisements for Lavazza Espresso. 'They're close to the nocturnal *Paradise* series, but set in daylight. The compositions are crazy, the models are dressed in red-and-white leotards and it looks very fierce, but it's just an ad!'

Hunt, a former judge of the World Press Photo contest, feels that he and Erwin Olaf are kindred spirits. 'We're good together. Erwin is shy like me, but we also know how to master the feeling and how to behave professionally. Part of Erwin, the best part as far as I'm concerned, is a little boy around eight years old. He's truly innocent at heart. When we talk in private, we share a genuinely immature amazement at life.'

All well and good, but there was also money to be made. Did the new work also take off in the spoilt-for-choice New York art world? Hunt begins with a disclaimer: 'Art dealers never tell the truth about their sales figures.' The reaction of New York's art-loving public was initially reserved, but Hunt nevertheless managed to attract customers and, in the end, eighteen pictures were sold before the opening. 'I don't use a scattergun technique and try to be strategic. The first client to buy Erwin's work was a fish that I'd been trying to hook for a while, a rich and funny guy from the South who'd never bought anything from me before. He called and said, "I'm looking at this Erwin Olaf stuff you've sent and I've got to have this picture. Now!"'

As per Studio Erwin Olaf's strategy at the time, Hasted Hunt also implemented the multiples system whereby the lowest numbers in the print run are always the cheapest. The price then increases incrementally, which means the early birds are

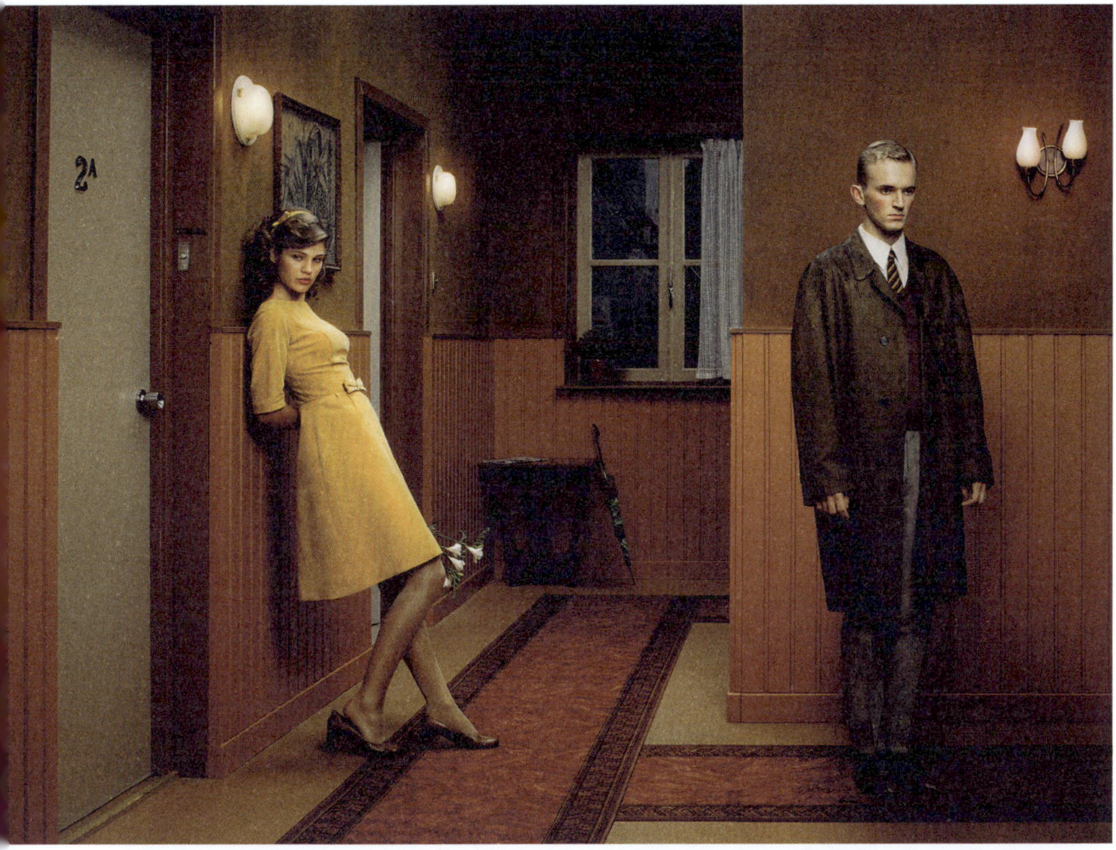

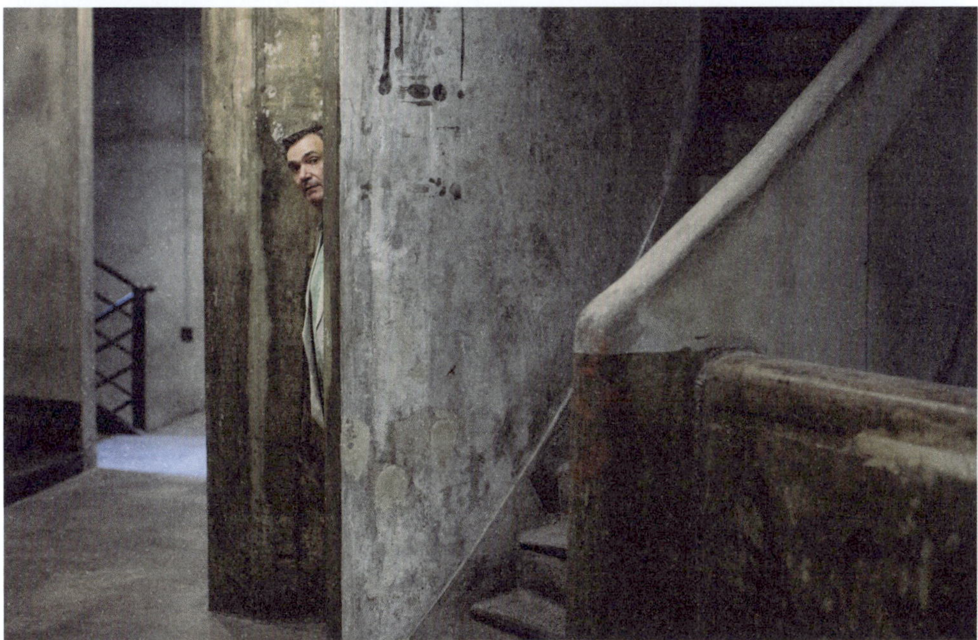

Top: *The Hallway, 2005* from the *Hope* series. Bottom: Production designer Floris Vos.

rewarded, Hunt says. 'This was the last, large-format copy of *The Ice Cream Parlor*, so duh!' The principle of prioritising quick deciders has since been abandoned.

Another success at Hasted Hunt – and one of Erwin Olaf's most sought-after works of all time – was *Woman in a Yellow Dress, Portrait #5* from the *Hope* series. (In 2009, *Portrait #5* fetched over 27,000 euros at Christie's, then a record sum for an Erwin Olaf photograph.) Hunt said he could have sold that photo 'as many as 500 times over'. 'I can see why people fall for that picture: it carries the promise of youth, beauty, simplicity and young love. Whereas the mackintosh-clad boy awaiting his sweetheart in *The Hallway*, another photo from that series isn't as immediately eye-catching. To give it a Freudian interpretation, I believe Erwin himself is closer to that inconspicuous boy in his brown mackintosh than to the flamboyant girl in her yellow dress. But taken together, the duo in *The Hallway* is Erwin to a T.'

It wasn't just Bill Hunt who developed a better understanding of Erwin's work after *Rain, Hope, Grief* and the subsequent *Fall* – the entire English-speaking world also started to see it in a new light. The exhibition was reviewed in *The New York Times* and he was introduced as 'a successful Dutch commercial photographer' as well as a film-maker. The reviewer discussed 'scenes that Norman Rockwell's mordantly depressed cousin might have painted'. He concluded by stating that, 'If Mr Olaf intends a social or political commentary on American culture, it is unclear what he is trying to say. But his best pictures are mysterious and touching.'

Erwin noticed that Americans preferred more understated and less spectacular works, whereas the Italians, for example, adored the over-the-top *Paradise*. These differences in taste became painfully apparent once more during a visit to the photo collection at the J. Paul Getty Museum in Los Angeles. Shirley den Hartog and Erwin were on their first joint business trip. They were welcomed by the curator of photography, Virginia Heckert, who provided a two-hour tour of the galleries and cold storage rooms for the photo archives. She then browsed through Erwin's portfolio, and when they reached *Royal Blood* she announced that she was about to say something 'you'll remember for a lifetime'. Heckert then uttered the words that Erwin would later frequently quote: 'A series like that, you know what we call it here? *Eurotrash*.'

That was tough. It cast a shadow over the whole US trip. Only back in the Netherlands did he manage to process the criticism. The incident did not change their plans to conquer America, says Shirley den Hartog. 'As an artist, you have to be thick-skinned, be convinced of what you're doing and be a bit naive too. You've got to be able to handle it when someone says: your work is shit. Although, fortunately, Erwin only hears 1% of those nasty remarks because he was smart enough to put me in the middle. And I'm convinced that Erwin's work will one day hang in the Getty Museum.'

Not long after opening the *Rain* and *Hope* exhibitions in New York, Erwin had lunch

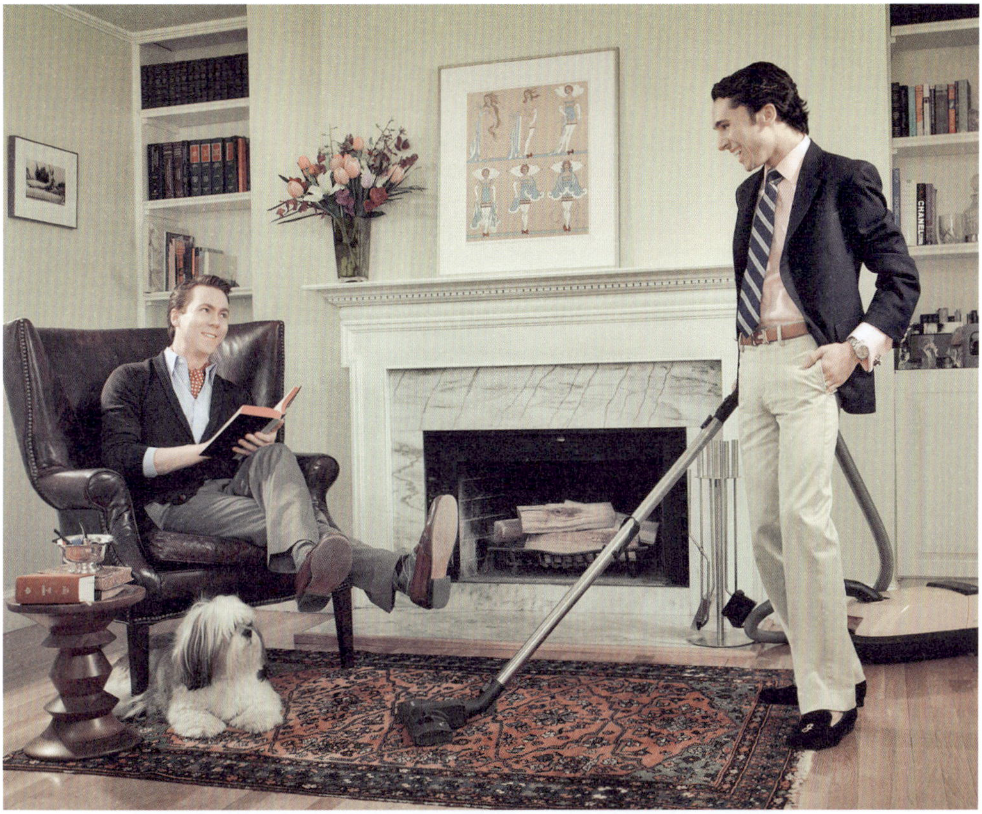

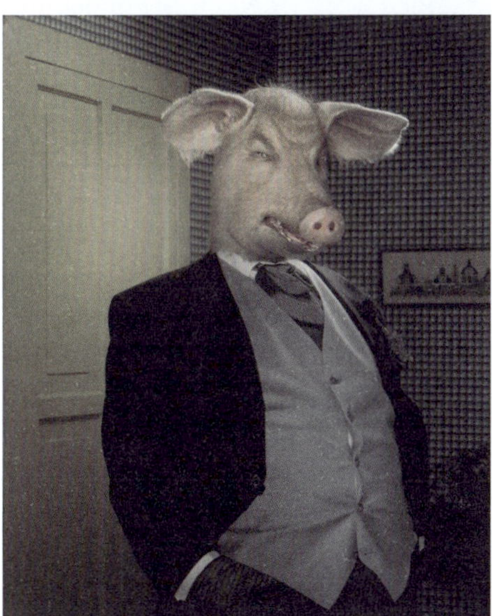

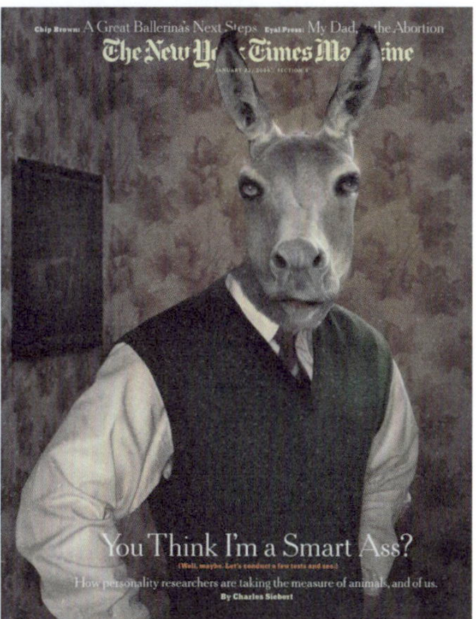

Top: *Livingroom, NYT Gay Couples, 2008*. Photo to accompany 'Young Gay Rites' in *The New York Times Magazine*. Bottom: Erwin makes his debut on the cover of *The New York Times Magazine* in 2006. Photo editor Kathy Ryan commissioned photographs to accompany a story on animals and emotions.

in Amsterdam with Kathy Ryan, chief photo editor of *The New York Times Magazine*, for which she'd commissioned photographers such as Sebastião Salgado, Nan Goldin, Gregory Crewdson and Rineke Dijkstra. Erwin was keen to be published in the magazine; after all, New York felt slightly more special than Rome or Paris, and as an ex-journalist, working for *The New York Times* sounded better than shooting for *Elle*. He wrote to Ryan and included his advertising photos for Dutch fashion brand The People of the Labyrinths. He suggested photographing famous Americans in the same style. 'As if they're Rembrandt's models, wealthy and timeless.' The celebrations surrounding the 400th anniversary of Rembrandt's birth (1606) seemed like a perfect time to publish the photographs.

While the aforementioned fashion series did come to fruition, he made his debut on the cover of *The New York Times Magazine* with a totally different image: a photo of a man with a donkey's head and the strapline, 'You Think I'm a Smart Ass'? Kathy Ryan had thrown him a rush job: could he take photos to accompany a story on animal emotions? 'Sometimes you pitch the idea and allow the photographer complete freedom. Erwin is insanely creative, so idiosyncratic. I told him to let his imagination run wild.' He took Ryan's call on the Monday and the deadline was the following Saturday. He photographed human bodies with animal heads: a sad sheep, a self-righteous pig, an angry donkey, a happy cow. Ryan was delighted with the results but, ultimately, it was still commissioned work. 'It was made under great time pressure and that influences my current perception of the work. I'm not going to chuck it away but nor does it really belong in the collected oeuvre, in my view.'

The New York Times continued to follow his work and he made several additional series for Kathy Ryan, including a particularly notable one featuring young American gay couples. The commission was to portray them in the style of Lucille Ball – ironically at a time when Erwin was single again following a complicated relationship with an artist twenty years his junior. Erwin enjoyed the ensuing 'appropriate solitude', living happily alone with his cat called Beauty. He could scarcely imagine cohabiting or getting married, as gay men in the US seemed to be doing younger and younger. 'The question was whether it's progressive, or a backward step towards the bourgeoisie of the past. Right now, it's essential to bring homosexuality into the open again.'

The somewhat surreal yet utterly truthful portraits of the newlyweds were shot in their own homes in Boston, without much styling and post-processing. Later, *The New York Times* could no longer afford to fly in photographers from Europe.

He preferred to use his time to strengthen ties with his mother, Lida, whom he took on a safari to Kenya and Tanzania. 'My father had died and my mother had difficulty walking. A safari was ideal in that respect because you didn't have to do anything.' Those trips provided at least as much inspiration as vegging out in front of the TV with a joint. 'You're sitting in front of one of those tents, watching Kilimanjaro while chatting to your mum and then a giraffe walks into view. You wake up to the fact that there's something else in life. Just something very different. Of great beauty.'

Grief, the third part of the triptych, was an exploration of grief and sorrow. He recognised the feeling of being alone in the world – and dying alone – that his mother always so aptly described as the feeling of 'sitting at home on the sofa and wanting to go home'.

But his illness also played a part, and this was discussed extensively in the publicity surrounding the series. Even in the documentary *On Beauty and Fall* (2009), which Michiel van Erp made about him, his condition was a common thread: 'It's made me very sad at times. And I've already decided what to do if it all gets too much. I'll end it. I'm not going to sit in one of those wheelchairs. No way.'

In *Grief*, Erwin explored the moment when your existential balance is torn apart by that one devastating phone call, by that one communication. He'd experienced this himself when receiving his diagnosis. But it also reminded him of his childhood. One of his earliest memories was linked to the Kennedy assassination, and he clearly recalled the Springveld family's neighbour in Hilversum being very ill. They all whispered about 'K'. 'Everyone was sad yet no one was crying.'

He selected models that looked as if they'd stepped straight out of 1960s photographs of the haute bourgeoisie, loosely based on Jacqueline Kennedy as a grieving archetype. Introspective figures standing by large windows allude to the colour photography of his early childhood, the 'Kennedy years', inspired by *Life in Camelot: The Kennedy Years* (edited by Philip B. Kunhardt). 'Photography was freer back then with the 35mm cameras and colour, and there was a reason everyone stood close to windows in those pictures – because it was the only place that you could shoot without a flash.' For this series, he worked for the first time with a digital model of his old, trusty Hasselblad.

The room sets for *Grief* were a challenge for Floris Vos, 'because they didn't require much, just a few odd walls and a fake window'. Each of the seven interiors had to be visually distinct, however, and have the chilly and luxurious feel of a hotel suite.

The final photographs were tighter and more personal than Erwin could have imagined and, once again, he had succeeded in taking his work in a new direction. Perhaps, in part, also thanks to the derogatory newspaper critic and the curator in Los Angeles.

In the meantime, he also rekindled his love of film. Under the pseudonym Franzy Millers, he made a couple of porn movies, *Revanche* and *Revenge*, for the Wasteland Festival. High and low culture as two sides of the same person. According to Erwin, the films were a response to the restrained aesthetics of *Grief*. Moreover, he wanted to demonstrate that pornography could also be stylised. The actors appreciated the fact that they were being properly lit for once. 'The protagonist was an English porn star who was assaulted by three women in Japanese school uniforms. The guy was fist fucking so I thought: let's shove a baseball bat in too. Those girls improvised like crazy; they went wild and we clustered around them with lights and a camera.'

The 1960s also left an impression on *Fall*, which featured a combination of young models and still lifes. The sets, once again designed by Floris Vos, recalled hotel rooms from the time of Erwin's childhood, especially in terms of the colour schemes. But the backdrops, which featured walls made of lathed plastic, reeds and cork, looked like they'd come straight out of a DIY catalogue.

What had once made perfect sense, for example in *Grief*, now seemed hollow. 'I disliked those photos until I stumbled across a close-up image, taken from a high vantage point, showing Kim Feenstra blinking.' That half-failed close-up, which any decent portrait photographer would have binned, actually stuck with Olaf.

The hotel room décor gradually vanished; the pictures became more intimate and enigmatic than originally intended. The uncertainty lingered. 'Because these days I only have the bare bones of an idea when I start working on a series. Sometimes, a heavy silence descends upon the studio. I feel like I'm drowning in quicksand. I have no idea whether I'm on the right track.'

After completing the series, he decided it was time to change course. He'd been working cautiously, aesthetically and modestly – except in those porn movies – for four years now, which was beginning to distress him: his work couldn't possibly become any more introverted. 'The other day, one of my pictures was in a charity auction: a brutal little experimental picture, a nude with a lot of pussy. A collector texted: "But what do you mean by such a shocking photo?" Then I knew: it's high time I started taking some beaver shots again.'

'A gyrating horde of militant, sweet, flamboyant and beautiful women, men and everyone in-between'

BLACK TEA

The banquet tables in the Netherlands Central Bank's top-floor reception room, overlooking Amsterdam's Frederiksplein, are draped in white linen. The attendees must wait just a little longer. On this November evening in 2017, the guest of honour and keynote speaker is Erwin Olaf. 'I'm going to read my speech because it will stop me blathering on and overrunning,' he begins. 'And the lungs aren't great. From time to time, my voice starts to falter – even though I'm NOT emotional.'

The event is a benefit gala for The Blue Fund, which supports projects to advance LGBTQI+ equality.

After an introduction on the acquired rights of the gay community, Erwin segues into a bleak description of recent attacks on homosexuals.

'There's something amiss, here in the Netherlands. No other demographic faces such violent discrimination. When a lesbian couple hold hands in central Groningen, they are verbally abused and beaten. In Amsterdam-Noord, an older married queer man is pulled off his moped and assaulted. A gay Polish man is stabbed to death while cruising in Oosterpark. A queer couple walking home after a night out are attacked by teenagers – one of them has his teeth knocked out.'

For non-heterosexuals, public displays of affection come with the risk of violence or verbal abuse – something he knew from bitter experience. 'A tender goodbye kiss, a passionate snog, or simply holding hands: any of these things will, at the very least, provoke insults.'

'It makes me so sad to think that I'll go to my grave without ever having been able, freely and peacefully, to show affection for the man – or men – I love in public. Not for a single hour, and this in my own city, my own country. It makes me deeply depressed, but also defiant. There's a real risk that, further down the line, all the hard-won achievements of recent decades will amount to nothing more than victories on paper – and that must never happen.'

He concluded his address by arguing that the gay community needs to stand up for itself more forcefully. Moreover, the message of diversity must be championed in schools. 'So that young people understand that a range of sexual preferences is the most normal thing in the world – and that it's neither threatening nor inferior. ... The fight against bigotry, racism and sexual discrimination calls for solidarity.'

It was an inspired speech, backed by a long personal history. By that point, Erwin had endured bullying and slander for over half a century. He confronted the issue directly and didn't mince his words, according to his longtime friend Hans van Manen.

'Erwin had a volatile temperament, and we all know that can have its downsides. At times, we rubbed each other up the wrong way. No, never about work – always about "political" issues. My husband Henk and I had just returned from Morocco, and tensions between the Moroccan and gay communities had worsened. Erwin felt it was unconscionable to holiday there. Enraged, he jumped to his feet during our Christmas dinner with ten friends, and we had a blazing row.'

A cool farewell letter followed: 'Hello Hans, as you've noticed, I don't intend to continue our friendship on the current footing. Our characters have proved too conflicting and friendship should, in my opinion, be based on equality. Unfortunately, there's no such thing. Your will and opinion are law. It remains for me to thank you for the friendship and professional support. I wish you all the very best and plenty of smoking pleasure. Erwin.'

Van Manen: 'As soon as I read the letter, I went running to him. It's the kind of thing that happens between us and it's always instructive, to be a bit pompous, so to speak. It's the flip side of the temperament that makes him so fantastically driven.'

Theo van Gogh's murder – and the hypocritical reactions to it – gave new momentum to Erwin's self-appointed role as a spokesperson for minority groups. In his view, the amorphous group he referred to as the 'cultural elite', with whom he had never felt aligned, turned a blind eye – and kept their mouths shut – when it came to religiously motivated violence. The progressive crowd, he felt, did little to actively defend freedom of speech.

While Erwin Olaf the photographer had become less aggressive, Erwin Springveld the homosexual remained as outraged as ever by the casual violence and abuse directed at him personally and at the broader LGBTQI+ community. Enraged, he published a piece in *Het Parool* on 30 May 2005.

Describing his anger as 'deep and hard', he also turned a critical eye on the gay community – and on himself. 'Where are we, where's our fighting spirit? It looks like the majority of us would rather get fucked in dark corners than take to the streets to show we're a force to be reckoned with. What is it? Are we lazy, or are we indifferent? Or maybe we're just cowards, full of self-loathing? We must unite and defend ourselves – now. We owe it not just to ourselves, but to the next generation of queers. We won't be driven out of this city like the sparrows and ducks!'

The Amsterdam police later conceded that gay hate crimes needed to be better recorded, and that both physical and verbal violence against gays and lesbians should be more closely monitored.

Before the year was out, Erwin was attacked again. Friends and acquaintances were taunted, and he was personally humiliated at Rotterdam Central Station, where a youth called him a 'filthy homo' and spat at his feet.

That spring, a zealous Erwin selflessly contributed to the 60th anniversary celebrations of the COC, the leading Dutch LGBTQI+ rights organisation. He created a series of double portraits of gay couples – this time without extreme models or any trace of hyperbole – to highlight the simple 'normality' of queer lives. The most powerful portrait, in his view, was of a Moroccan woman and her Surinamese lover. He found it both extraordinary and courageous that a woman from that community would so openly express her sexual identity.

It was another successful year for the studio. He shot campaigns for major multinationals including Nokia, BMW, Microsoft, Virgin, Lee and Heineken, while also contributing work for the COC and the Asthma Fund – a cause close to his heart for obvious reasons. Notably, it was the first year that he earned more from his autonomous work than from his lucrative commercial commissions.

Shirley den Hartog notes that, around this time, the prices for art photography skyrocketed. 'But the bubble soon burst. Not with us, because we never believed

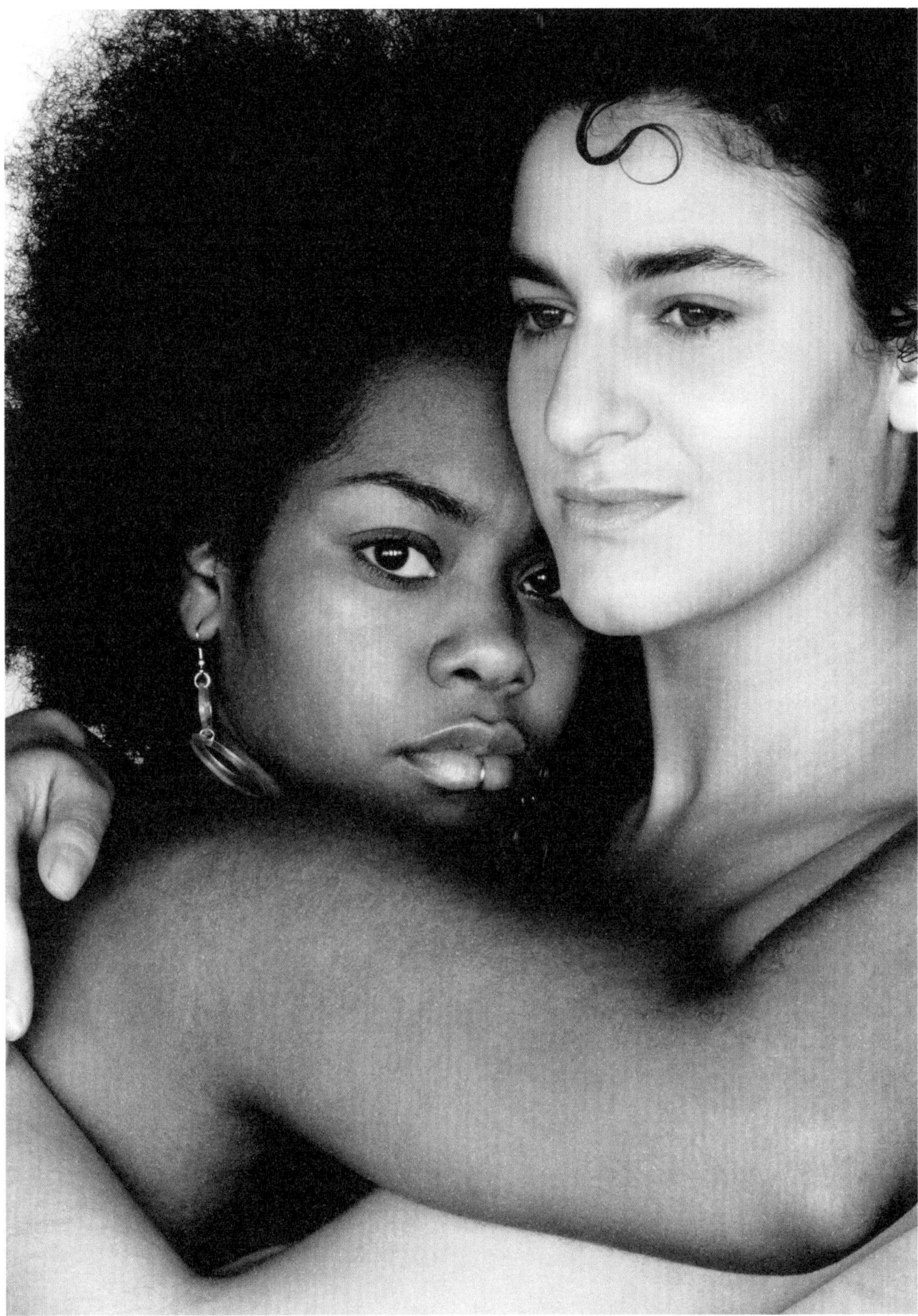

One of the double portraits commemorating the 60th anniversary of the Dutch LGBTQI+ rights group, COC.

in such extreme pricing. Gallery owners often urged me to raise our prices, but we always held the middle ground. We made a conscious decision not to join the race to the top. We didn't want to price ourselves out of the market.'

It could be frustrating to see other photographers' work fetching five times more than Erwin's, but Den Hartog stuck to the plan. 'It's easy to boast that a picture costs €20,000, but that excludes all the small collectors – and the Koreans or Japanese, for example, who might not know Erwin but like the work. And I've seen plenty of one-hit wonders charging eye-watering prices for their photographs, only to vanish without a trace.'

Erwin not only sold well, he was also the 'most visible artist' of 2006, according to *Kunstbeeld* magazine. In subsequent years, too, he would also top lists, either as 'artist of the year' or for smashing an auction record. And when the weekly *Vrij Nederland* concluded the first decade of the twenty-first century with a survey of 'the national art elite', he was naturally included.

That didn't stop him from being hassled in the streets – or from remaining just as militant. As the 20th century ended, the LGBTQI+ community had achieved unprecedented legal rights and broader acceptance. Yet Erwin felt that, after the Amsterdam Gay Games in 1998 and the legalisation of same-sex marriage in 2001, the emancipation movement had stalled.

'A poisonous mix emerged, fuelled in equal measure by the Christian and Social Democrats. With their calls for religious freedom, the Christian parties frustrate the school system. ... The Social Democratic party has long insisted: "Shush, this is light-skinned working-class people we're talking about – they haven't done anything wrong." Together, it's created a toxic brew for homosexuals and Jews.'

Several incidents in the years that followed underscored the lack of a political solution. In May 2010, a gay man was beaten unconscious by two Moroccan youths on the bridge over Keizersgracht, near the gay monument. Just a day earlier, the Second World War commemorative ceremony on Dam Square had been disrupted, leaving dozens injured. Erwin was deeply shaken by the news.

These events were fresh in his mind when, just after midnight on a Sunday in May, Erwin left De Trut, one of his regular haunts in Amsterdam. Right outside its doors, he witnessed a man – whom he described as Moroccan-looking – verbally abusing two twenty-somethings who were kissing.

He noted that the man, who later identified himself as Yugoslavian, wore a black leather jacket with a thick fur collar and a black cap. He was extremely aggressive. Erwin stood his ground, asserting that in the Netherlands, gays are allowed to marry – and therefore to kiss.

'The fur-collared kid squared up to me. I called the police and explained the situation to the operator. She urged me to calm down, but that was easier said than done.'

It all blew over but Erwin couldn't have been more shocked at the young clubbers' response to the situation, which was the opposite of his own. They dismissed him as a 'discriminatory, right-wing queer'. Times had changed, he realised, and young gay men are no longer willing to step up to the plate. There was no need for provocation.

As Erwin furiously pedalled home, he couldn't shake the feeling that he was no longer in tune with the zeitgeist. From that moment on, he decided, young gays and lesbians would have to figure it out for themselves. He wasn't going to get involved anymore – it was their fight now.

He soon announced his move to Berlin, where earlier that year he had filmed a video campaign in a luxurious suburb for the French online clothing company vente-privee.com (now Veepee), owned by art collector and tech billionaire Jacques-Antoine Granjon. Erwin's script featured a handsome delivery man who draws the attention of bored women in a villa district, each anxiously awaiting a package from vente-privee.com – or perhaps something more. The campaign's bright, clean imagery echoed Mondrian and Edward Hopper. The payoff line read: Desire is good, but nothing beats satisfaction. It felt worlds away from the homophobia he'd just experienced on the streets of Amsterdam-West.

One of the highlights of 2010 was Erwin's appearance on *Zomergasten*, an immensely popular Dutch television programme in which notable figures curate their ideal evening of viewing and discuss a selection of clips.

It offered Erwin a national platform, and he made the most of the opportunity. He came across as an ambitious artist. When asked by the interviewer whether he had already reached 'the top', Erwin replied: 'No, first division. There's one more floor to go.'

At the same time, he appeared to be someone yearning for greater peace and privacy. 'I'm a little bit tired and would like a quieter life. I feel something of an Erwin Olaf overkill, so after this broadcast and a couple of outstanding assignments, I'm going to sit on my arse for six months. I'm tired of Erwin Olaf. I want to rediscover Erwin Springveld.'

He was a telegenic activist who not only won people's hearts but also had an announcement to make: a massive party at the pop temple Paradiso. At first, he had wanted to celebrate sparrows – his favourite bird – which had all but vanished from Amsterdam. But in the end, he chose a Black Tea Party theme. Under the slogan 'I'm Outraged!', the event was intended as a celebratory condemnation of homophobia. Erwin's press release promised an all-out celebration of racial and sexual diversity.

'Life's a ball, and all thanks to the diversity of skin colours, religions, sexual preferences and gender traits. Thick, thin, small, large, gay, straight, pitch black or lily white, transvestites and transsexuals – they're the salt of the earth. And this should be celebrated, not decried.'

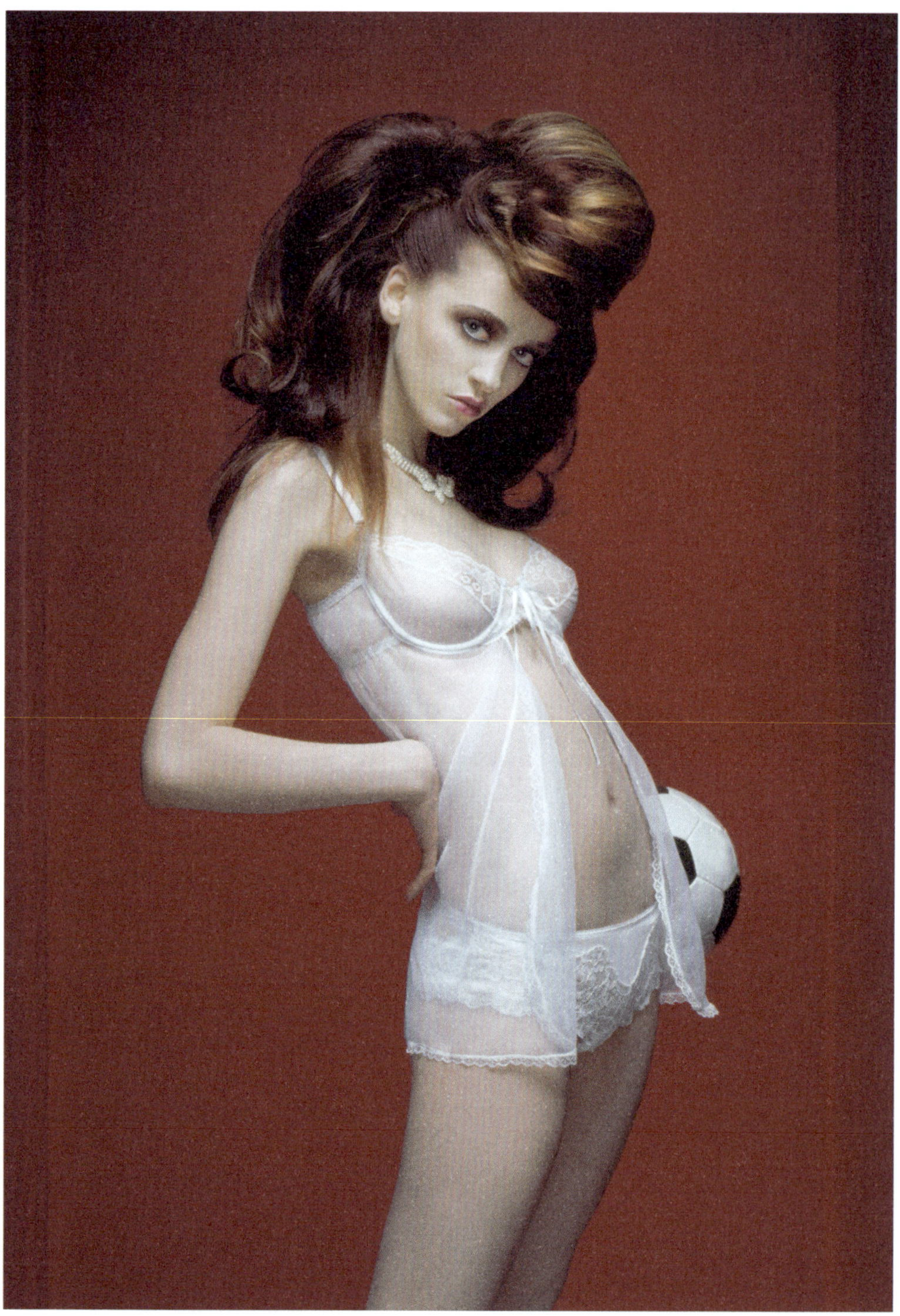

Girl from the *Rouge* series, 2005.

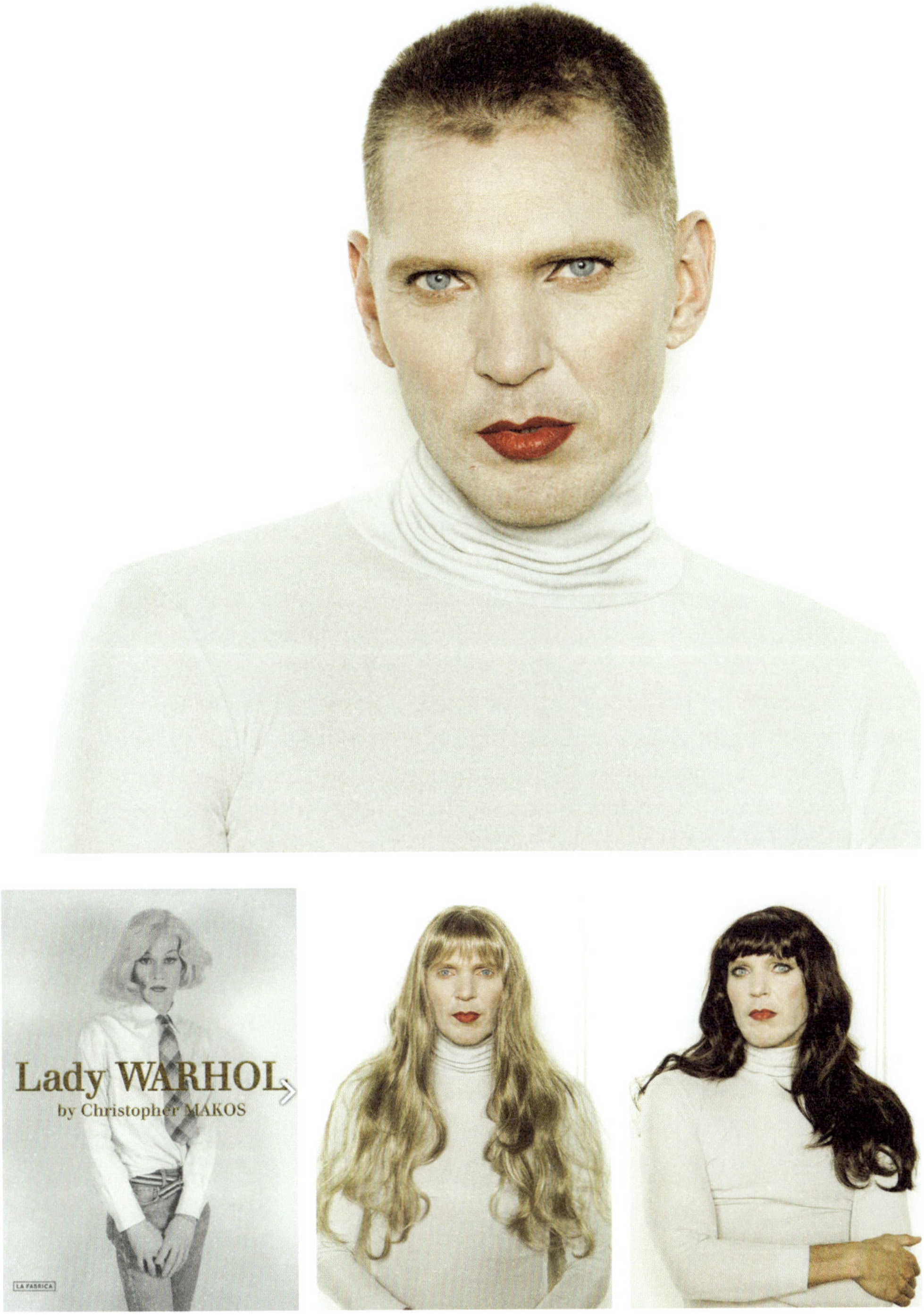

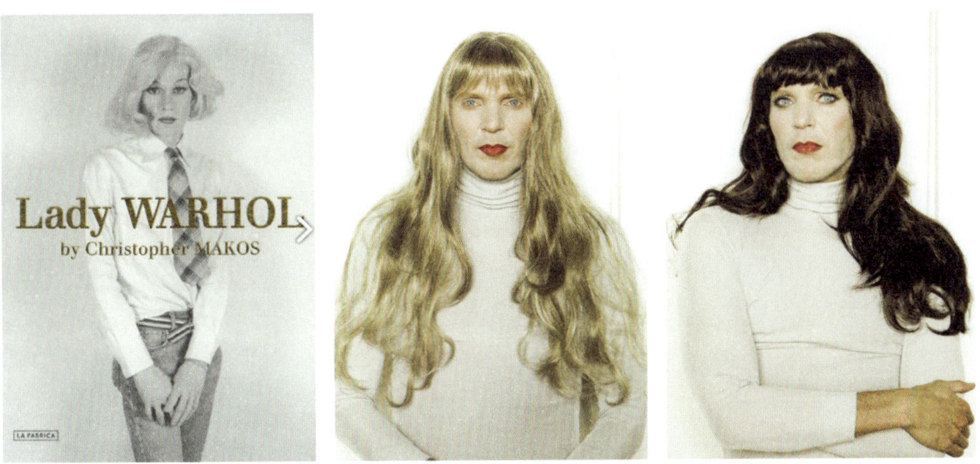

Self-Portrait, 48 years old, No. 4, No. 1, No. 3, 2007. Bottom left: Christopher Makos, *Lady Warhol*, with pictures taken in 1981 by Makos and Warhol for the project *Altered Image*.

The Black Tea Party was a masked ball with black as the dress code: a symbol of mourning for more tolerant times, and a statement about how unsafe the LGBTQI+ community felt in the city. But it was also an upbeat dance extravaganza. 'We, the new Dutch citizens – gays, transvestites, transsexuals, little people, big people and heterosexuals – stand as one, and we all have to get along in this tiny city.'

Supportive messages flooded Erwin's inbox. Friends and acquaintances sent congratulations. *Zomergasten* had been a turning point: it made Erwin – despite his desire for privacy – into a bona fide Dutch celebrity.

More importantly, his message reached political ears. The mayor of Amsterdam quickly invited him to a meeting with the city councillors.

The Black Tea Party became 'a gyrating horde of militant, sweet, flamboyant and beautiful women, men and everyone in-between. Clubbers queued on the pavement, and the venue was packed to capacity – all in the name of freedom and acceptance.'

'Amsterdam's best traits converged at pop temple Paradiso,' recalls Erwin's friend Marline Williams. 'The city belonged to us – all the outsiders who deviated from the norm. Paradiso was our palace, where we held court. It was an indescribable feeling – made all the sweeter because it started with a party.'

The Black Tea Party was rooted in the idea, infused with a 'hint of the flower power spirit', that Amsterdam is too small for discrimination. The basement of the Paradiso was transformed into an Arabian lounge; the small space became a 'transvestite tea room'; the larger one hosted a hetero fetish act; a bearded woman and little man poured the champagne. Erwin screened a video in which a moped-riding 'Moroccan lad' and a 'faggot' with a lapdog get into a fight but end up embracing.

He knew that his party had set something in motion within the gay community – it had become a catalyst for greater visibility. The 'insanely emotional' Black Tea Party had sparked a new kind of energy, he observed. 'We rediscovered something we'd unthinkingly lost, something fundamental: our sense of self.'

Erwin had firmly established himself as a gay-rights advocate, a role for which he would receive an award just a few months later. He was, in short, successful and 'to some extent happy, but also a bit glum' – mainly because he was still single. 'All I need now is a kind and beautiful man!' he wrote to a friend who had emailed to say that, after *Zomergasten*, he was adored by 'the whole of the Netherlands'.

'Because of the lung damage, my career, and my personality, I've been withdrawing more and more,' he confided in a letter to his brother Jos.

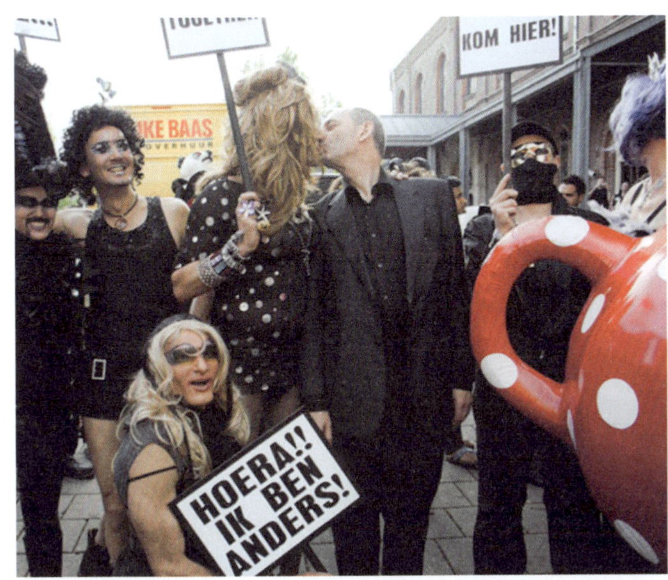

Job Cohen, former mayor of Amsterdam, kisses drag queen Jennifer Hopelezz during the Black Tea Party at Paradiso. Bottom: Eberhard Van der Laan, former mayor of Amsterdam, sitting on the lap of his predecessor, Cohen, at the pop temple Paradiso.

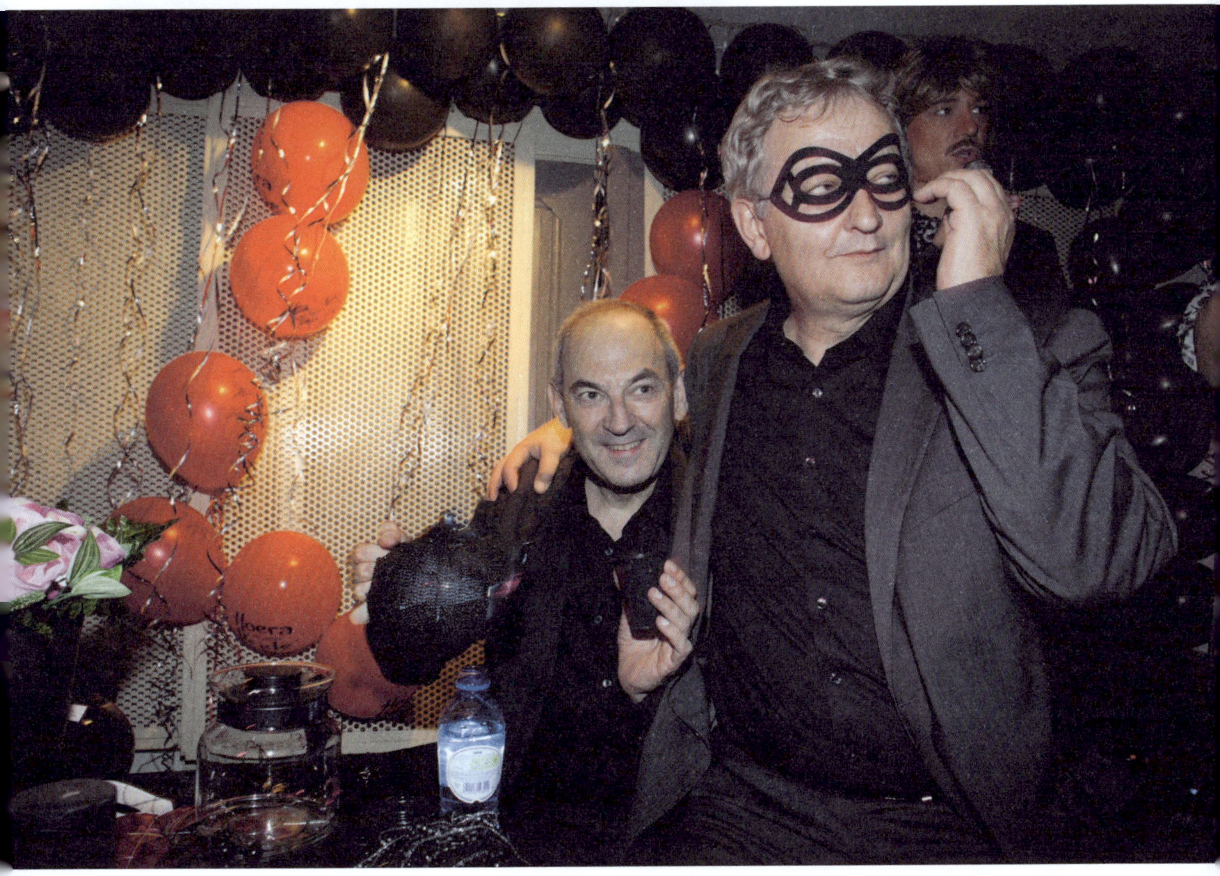

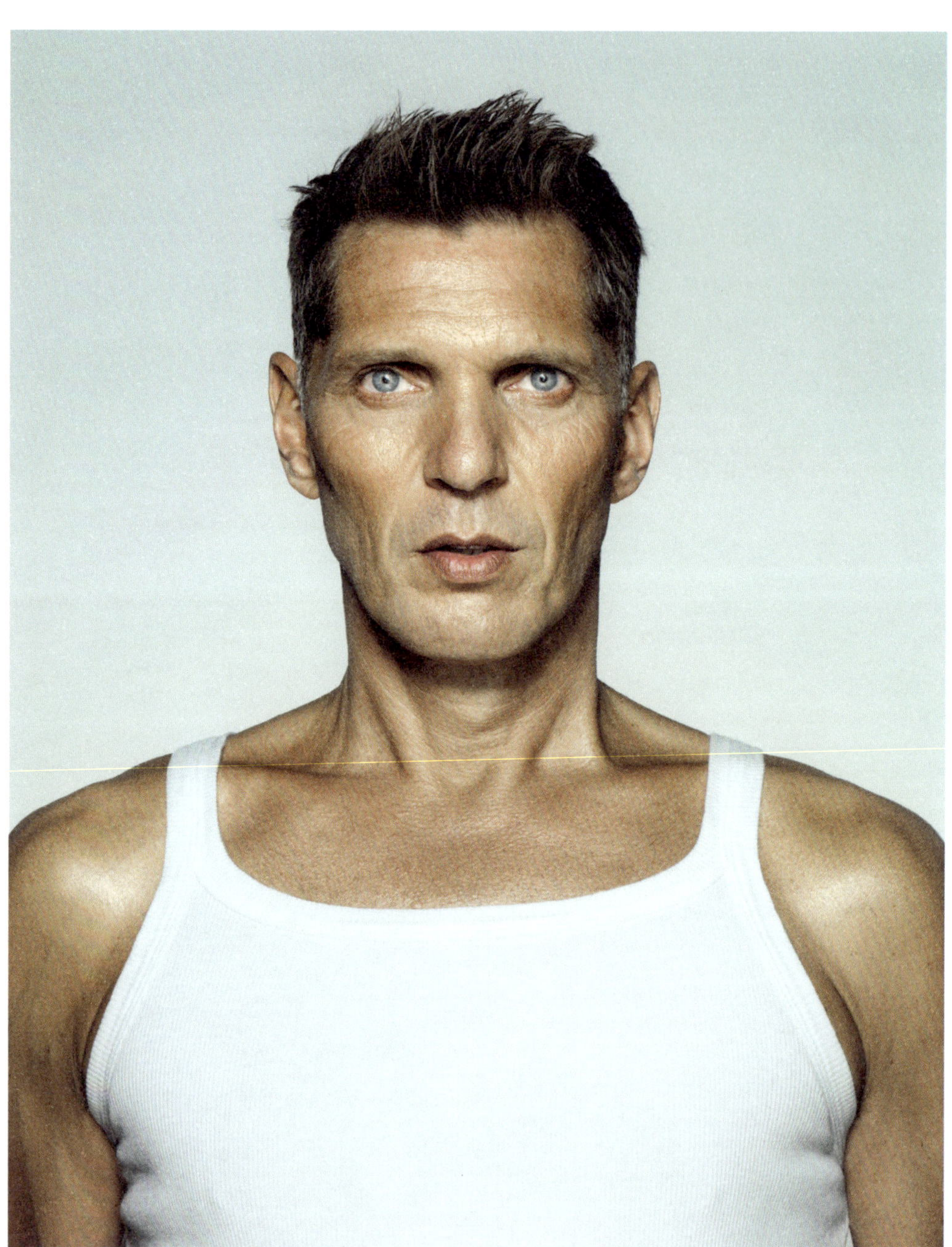

8 GOLDEN YEARS (2009–2015)

'With the most beautiful things, nothing really happens'

AUTHENTICITY IN A FAKE WORLD

As he cycles to his studio in Amsterdam's Rivierenbuurt district on a beautiful spring morning, Erwin's phone rings. Late for an appointment, out of breath and pedalling briskly – despite his compromised lungs – he picks up and hears the sonorous voice of former professor Victor Halberstadt. As president of the judges for the 2011 Johannes Vermeer Award, the influential economist is calling with good news.

After Halberstadt tells him that he's been awarded the national prize – only the third recipient after theatre director Pierre Audi and film-maker Alex van Warmerdam – Erwin's first thought is: 'Great, I've vaguely heard of it, but it's less than 2,500 euros, so there's no way I'm going to stop cycling.'

When he tells the jury president that he feels incredibly honoured, Halberstadt replies that whilst honour is one side of the coin – and certainly not an insignificant one – 100,000 euros will also soon be transferred to his bank account. Never before had Erwin dismounted his bicycle so quickly. He needed to recover from the emotion, he recalls.

Used to feeling misjudged by the art world, he found compensation elsewhere – such as the special edition of photography magazine *Focus*, marking the departure of his 'discoverer', Dirk van der Spek. Although they hadn't spoken for a long time, Van der Spek had published four photo books of Erwin's work, starting with *Chessmen*. As guest editor-in-chief of *Focus*, Erwin shared some of his own work in the magazine and also invited several of his former assistants – including Piek and Cleo Campert – to contribute.

Winning the Johannes Vermeer Award was undoubtedly an accolade, but the

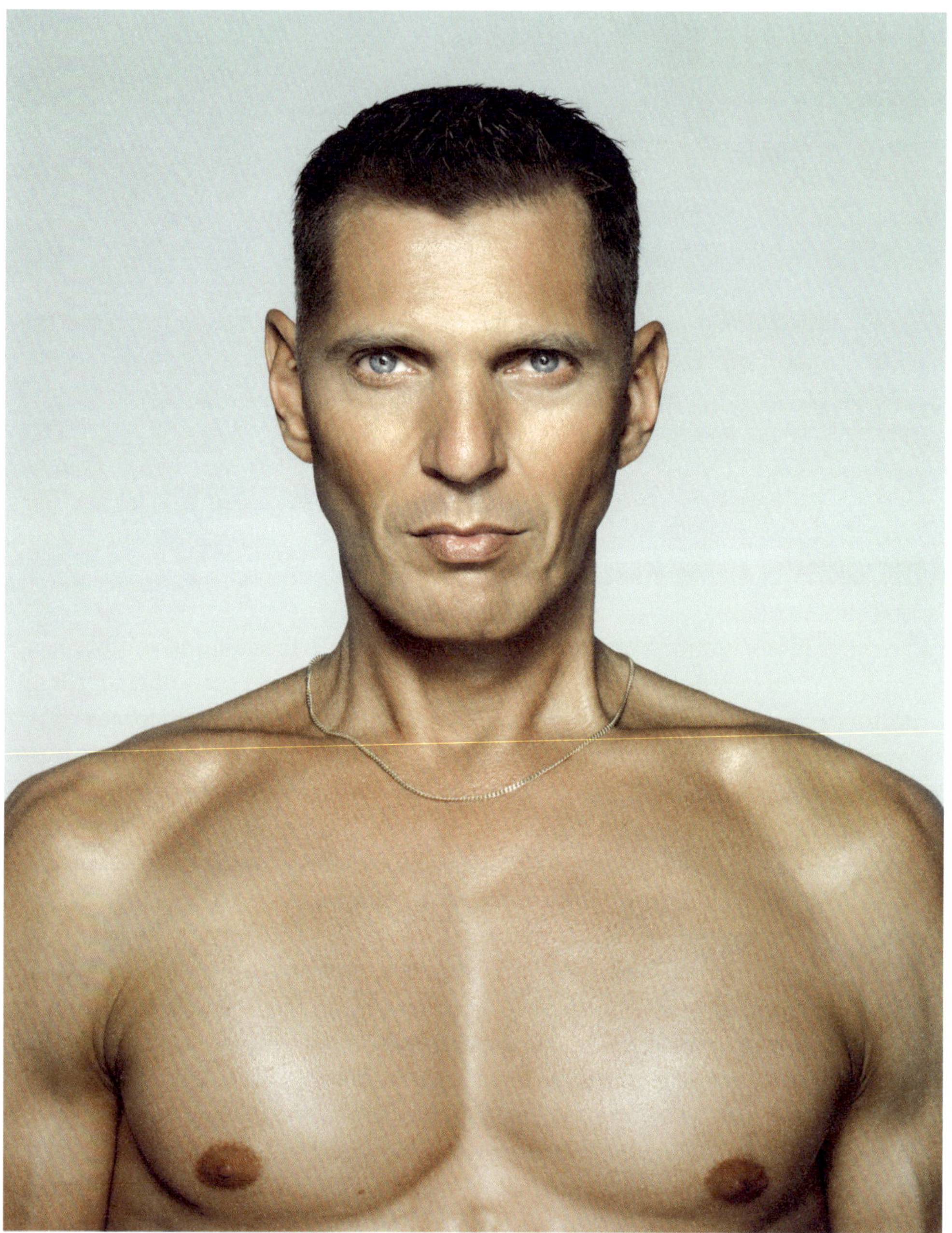

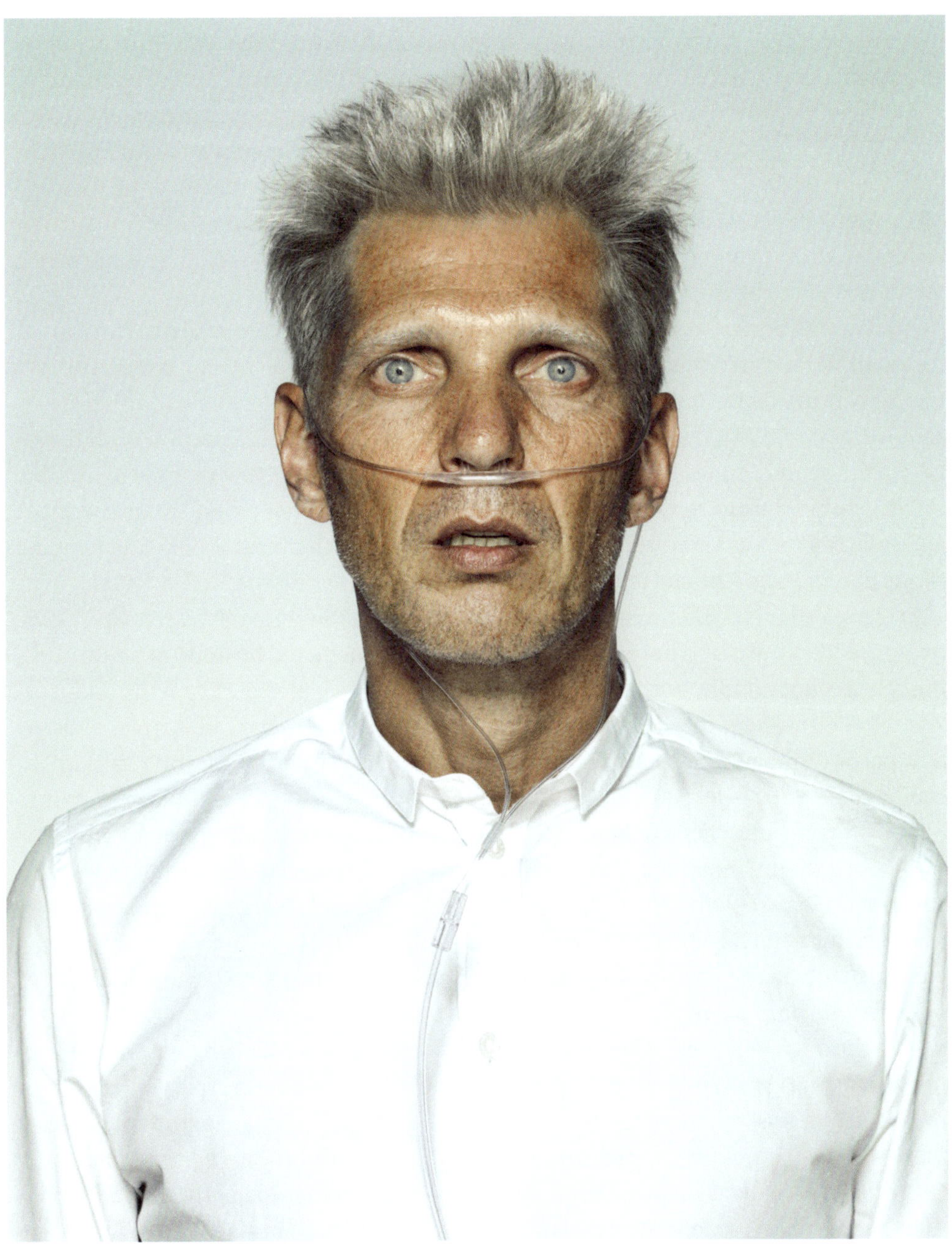

Left: *I Wish, 2009*. Right: *I Will Be, 2009*. Photo on page 256: *I Am, 2009*.

perennial doubts continued to gnaw at him, especially when a *de Volkskrant* reviewer once again wrote that his photography illustrated 'how difficult it is to abandon something that was once successful, but now threatens to become a gimmick'.

The prestigious award was a boost and, on top of that, the money would certainly come in useful. He was allowed to spend one third of the sum however he liked – 'I'm going to get an eye lift to stop me looking like an old dog and some liposuction around the abs. Then I won't have to train to get a six-pack,' he joked. The other two thirds needed to be invested in his work.

It was the perfect arrangement. As always, Erwin had numerous plans. He wanted, for example, to experiment with classical nudes and carbon printing – a slow, nineteenth-century technique – and the prize would allow him to devote enough time to acquiring the skills. He also hoped to explore a long-standing fascination with the Weimar Republic and German artists of the interwar period. Now that his work was being exhibited from New York to London, and from Paris to Beijing – in museums and galleries such as Hamiltons in London, Hasted Kraeutler in New York and Rabouan Moussion in Paris – he started to feel like he was outgrowing the Netherlands.

Fame and travel did not make him truly happy. In the series *Hotel* (2010), he captured the loneliness and boredom of hotel-room life, depicted by nude or semi-nude models in photographs with titles such as *Kyoto Room 211*, *Moscow Room 168* and *Hotel Winston-Salem Room 304*. 'I increasingly loathe travelling. It's part and parcel of being famous but, at the same time, it's meaningless. You travel the world, you're a "big star", and yet you're always alone. What's it all for? Why? Sitting in another crap room, waiting for a meeting. Just to be able to tell my mother that I'm in Tokyo once again?'

But Germany remained almost virgin territory. The idea of relocating to Berlin – to shoot on location with the entire studio team – suddenly became feasible thanks to the prize money. His failed American adventure with the Hells Angels in Sturgis was well and truly in the past and he was eager to start experimenting beyond the safety of the studio once again.

Earlier that year, he'd taken the entire studio to Leiden. Working without sets felt liberating. For three days, he directed thirty-five models and extras – plus a dog – in Leiden's Pieterskerk for his largest-ever staged photograph. This monumental history piece – measuring 2.5 x 3 metres and intended for the exhibition *Vrijheid! Leidens Ontzet 1574–2011* – was inspired by *De gebedsdienst na Ontzet Leyden* [The Prayer Service After the Relief of Leiden, 1861] by Jan Hendrik van de Laar. He also spent a long time studying how Rembrandt had arranged the riflemen in *The Night Watch*.

The picturesque light in the Pieterskerk raised the spectre of kitsch – a label that often loomed over his work. 'There's a wafer-thin line with kitsch. I sense that with Gregory Crewdson's work, a photographer who is firmly in the staged photography corner.'

As a counterpoint, Erwin based his picture on recent scientific research. Malnutrition – and especially the Black Death – thus acquired a more prominent role in his historical *tableau vivant* than in its nineteenth-century antecedent; his version is much darker and rawer.

Alongside stuffed crows, pigeons, a half-skinned dog and a cat, he also incorporated anachronistic elements into the image – an iPod shuffle, flip-flops, a Sensation wristband and an S&M harness. Typical, Erwin Olaf jokes – it had to be spelt out to the good viewers that it's not an 'objective' representation but a personal, twenty-first-century take on an historical event.

The story of the successful fight for liberation from the Spanish, as depicted in Van de Laar's painting, aligned with his belief that Freedom is the Netherlands' most important global export. It was fundamental to his very best work – as he well knew. Ironically, just a few months later, some of his most explicit nude photographs were plastered with black squares in an exhibition catalogue for a show in Dubai. It was blatant censorship and ran contrary to his instincts and principles – yet he let it stand. He later reproached himself for not complaining about the degradation of his work.

The Pieterskerk photographs were reproduced in the retrospective publication *OWN*. Flicking through the huge book, he realised once again that his collected oeuvre could easily be interpreted as autobiographical. 'It's a diary. The early years, with those robust women and those little people, reflect my struggle with my sexuality. I was ashamed. I felt ugly.'

Given all the plans – in addition to Berlin, a short film and a new book were also in the works – the Johannes Vermeer Award was more than welcome. It was also a gesture of recognition for the genre of staged photography, especially since the prize bore the name of the painter from whom he had learnt a great deal. Teun was not the only one who sometimes compared him to Vermeer for the luminosity of his work, saying, 'no one else has that light of yours.'

Erwin's response was characteristically modest: 'That painter is far more virtuoso; I just push a button.' Yet he was undeniably influenced by Vermeer's use of light and his compositions. Like the Delft master, he 'caught the light, manipulated it and bent it to his will', as Mattie Boom, photo curator of the Rijksmuseum, observed. He had also borrowed the narrative quality of staged scenes from Vermeer. As Hans van Manen put it, 'Erwin tells stories with his pictures. He doesn't make theatrical photos; he makes theatre. Like a theatre-maker.'

Erwin admired Vermeer for his combination of beauty and restrained emotion – a quality that he himself had recently started to specialise in.

'I want to capture that honesty while I'm in a totally fake world. But the painter

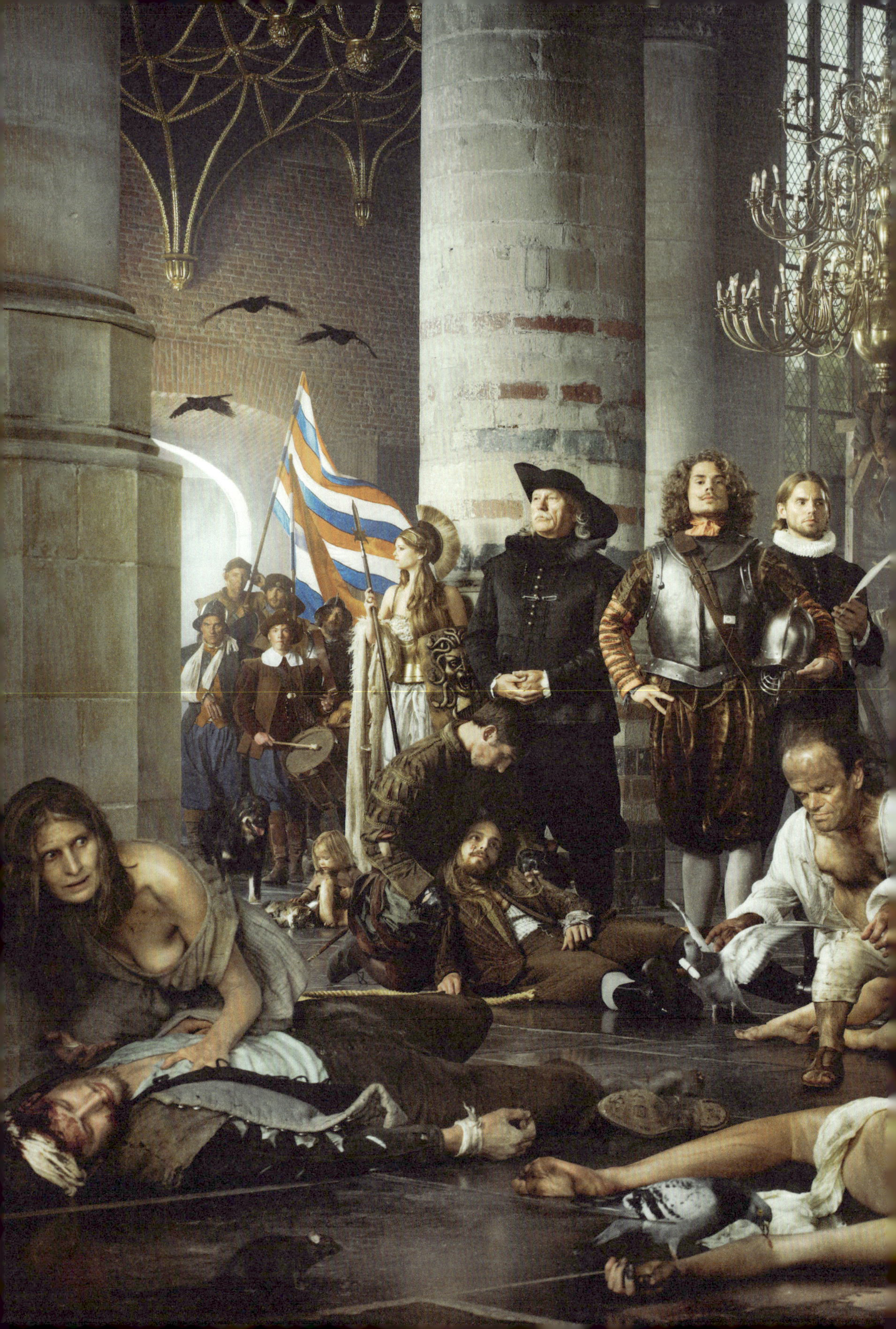

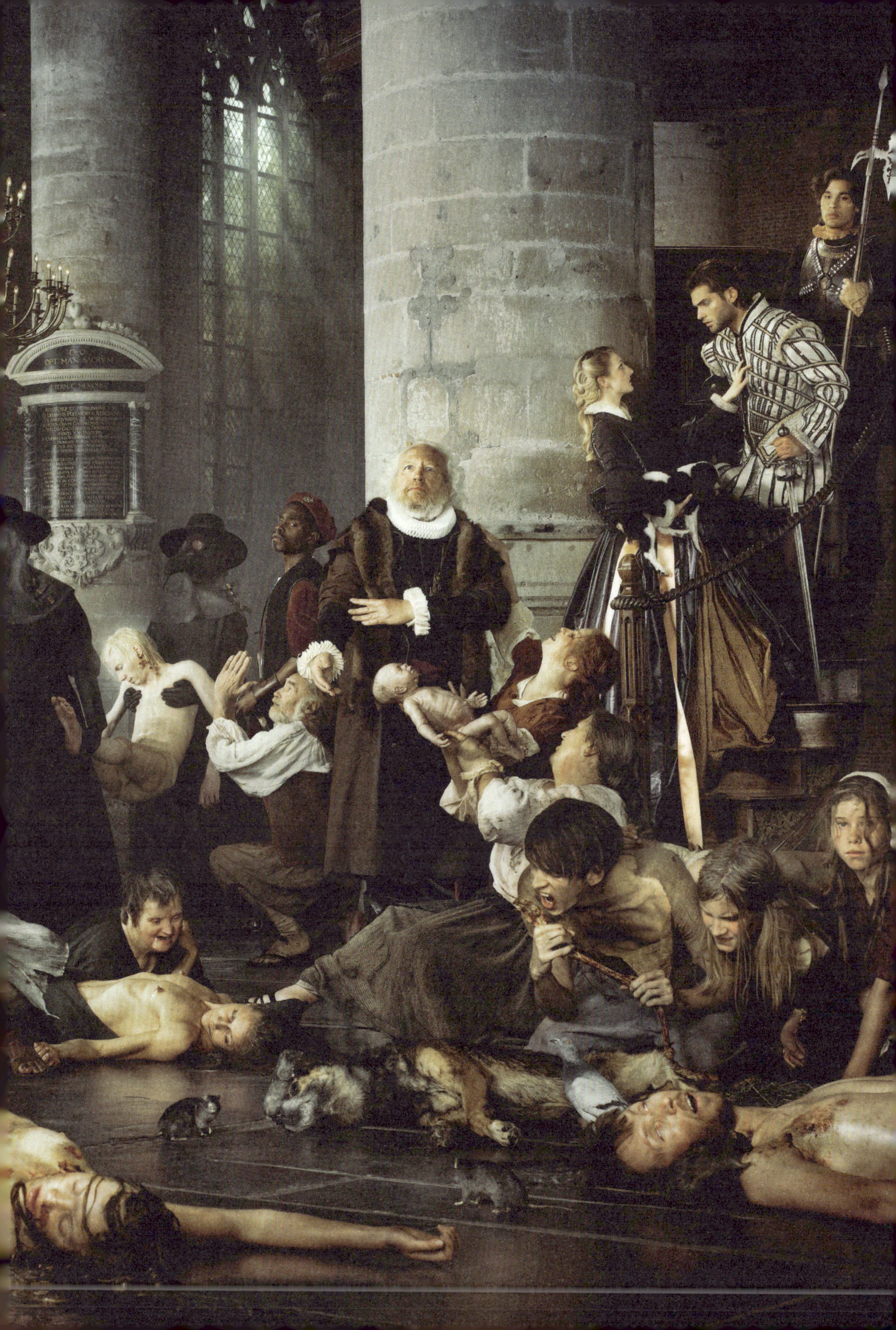
DEO
OPT MAX SACRVM

was too. He also positioned that girl by the window. He probably also used a primitive reflector, because that shadowlessness is impossible. That sparse, transparent shadow did not spring from his imagination. He must have seen it. That's what is funny about these kinds of photo. It's the same with those paintings. Nothing really happens. That's what you can learn from the art of painting. Sitting, standing, looking. What is a girl reading a letter?... With the most beautiful things, nothing really happens,' he said in the documentary film *Views on Vermeer* (2009).

This was not that different from the woman in his own series *Hope*, who sits at the table in her red American 1950s kitchen, alone with her inscrutable thoughts. What he had also learnt from Vermeer was that 'something distressing is rendered most beautifully when it is very restrained, almost invisible but just tangible. Everything is carefully staged, like a chair pushed away that reveals there is someone else in the room. No phone just sits there and everything in the fruit bowl is contrived.'

Crafting the creator's imagination, as he himself defined his genre, has recently received more attention after years in which documentary work had predominated. In his acceptance speech for the Johannes Vermeer Award, and not without a hint of exaggeration, he described how the stores of Dutch museums were overflowing with photographs of 'genuinely sad-looking girls in front of neutral backgrounds, on which we can just make out an electrical socket, as a clue that what we're looking at is real'.

While he grumbled about those random electrical sockets, he also included them in his own staged work, using them to bring a semblance of reality to his fantasy. The audience might have taken the 'electrical sockets' as a veiled critique of his friend and colleague Rineke Dijkstra, who occasionally left one visible if it happened to be there. But it was not intended as criticism; in his speech, Erwin named her among the 'world-class' artists he admired. Alongside Rineke Dijkstra, he cited Rem Koolhaas, Marlene Dumas, Inez and Vinoodh, Pierre Audi and Viktor & Rolf as examples.

Erwin cited these illustrious names to make a point to the art world during the ceremony. At the time, the then State Secretary for Culture, Halbe Zijlstra, was proposing sweeping cuts to the arts, and the cultural sector was in uproar.

Erwin was disinclined to weep alongside the artists who, in his view, could apparently not survive without state support, while he had built his career under his own steam. He had rarely extended his hand, and he was proud of that fact. Though still a social democrat at heart, he was also an entrepreneur who recognised the value of market forces in the arts. Besides, he mused, perhaps there were simply too many artists – and too many art schools. In some museums, he claimed, numerous curators were 'listlessly waiting' for new buildings that were never completed. This was a pointed jab at the Stedelijk Museum in Amsterdam, with which he had a notoriously complicated relationship. The fire service had closed the museum's building on

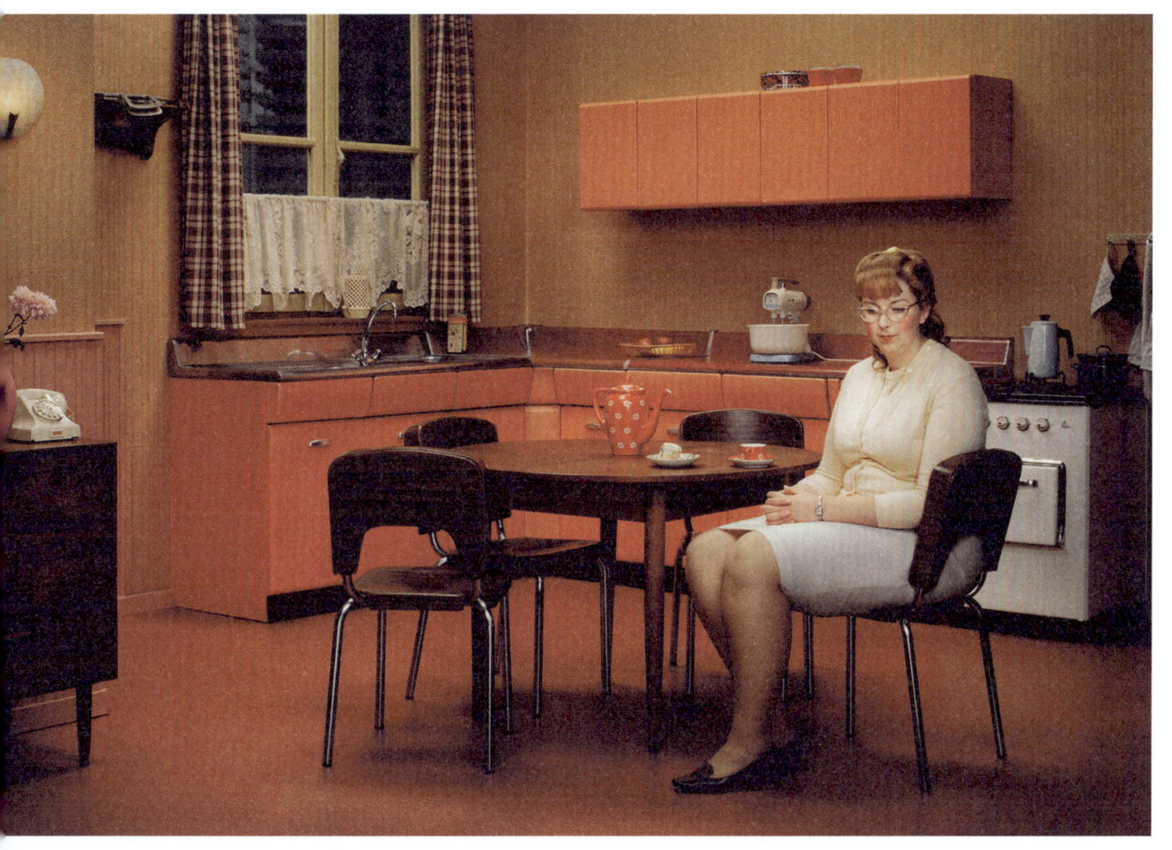

The Kitchen, 2005 from the *Hope* series. Previous photo spread: *Liberty - Plague and Famine During the Siege of Leiden, 2011*, commissioned by Museum De Lakenhal and Leiden University.

Museumplein in late 2003 and, eight years later, it was still being renovated.

But just as his acceptance speech seemed to endorse the Secretary and his assault on the art world, Erwin made a sudden volte-face and urged Zijlstra to lay down his blunt axe. Who, after all, had done more to put the Netherlands on the international map than its artists? Their creativity, liberal spirit and willingness to act were rare and vital qualities in a world ruled by servitude and unyielding capitalism. Even the most celebrated artists had once received government support and, while it had helped them, the Dutch state had reaped the rewards twice over – financially and in terms of cultural prestige.

With the prize money, Erwin planned to go to Berlin to create a series outside the studio and make short films. He had first visited the city in the mid-1980s, when it was still divided into East and West. At the time, his artist friend Frans Franciscus was establishing a career as a painter in the German capital. During the trip, Erwin sent a postcard home to Lida Springveld: 'Dear Mum, Berlin is weird. That Wall is so final. I threw snowballs over it in the hope that someone would throw one back. No luck. Tomorrow we go East.'

He now found Berlin to be a 'pleasantly reliable and democratic' place, and even considered buying a flat in the city. He'd departed on this reconnaissance trip with a new flame, Kevin Ray Edwards. Instead of immersing themselves in the nightlife, they spent much of their time walking – including through the nineteenth-century Botanical Gardens. It was there that Erwin fell in love with Kevin, partly because of his endearing love of plants. 'I feel much more comfortable in my love life,' he wrote in an email to a friend.

'It feels like an interwar period, and a jet-black cloud is on the horizon'

Berlin was a logical choice for his first major series outside the studio. While studying in Utrecht, Erwin had read Susanne Everett's *Lost Berlin*, which captured the interwar period in Germany's capital through a blend of photographs and text. 'You can see how free, civilised and raucous that period was..., but also how difficult. With all those people who had returned from the war maimed and impoverished. All those parallel worlds, in that huge, exceptional empire. Then suddenly, all that freedom and decadence melted like snow in 1933.'

He drew parallels with his own time. 'We live in the richest part of the world, can party to our hearts' content, and are drowning in luxury. I've always been terrorised by that thought. When will the bubble burst? I've no idea where it comes from, but I've had that feeling since early adulthood.'

In any case, he admired the critical German artists of the interwar period, such as George Grosz and Otto Dix, and had previously referenced a work by the Berlin graphic artist and Dadaist John Heartfield (born Helmut Herzfeld) in his *Chessmen* series. Hanging in Teun Frieszo's toilet was a reproduction of a photomontage by Heartfield – a cynical image of a dove of peace impaled on a bayonet, accompanied by the text *Niemals wieder!* [Never Again!]

Erwin had admired Grosz and Dix ever since visiting the *Paris-Berlin* exhibition at the Centre Pompidou in 1978. He felt a particular affinity with Dix, drawn to the fusion of theatricality and reportage in his work. In the cultural and sexual freedom of 1920s Berlin – oblivious to the impending world war and Holocaust – he saw an 'obvious' parallel with his own time. He also experienced a personal sense of liberation in the German capital, not unlike that experienced by homosexuals during the Roaring Twenties. 'In Amsterdam, it often feels like my wings are clipped. I hardly dare fly. In Berlin, I can be the swaggering faggot. Footloose and fancy-free.'

He shot in locations where traces of the Weimar years – and the period following the Nazis' rise to power in 1933 – were still visible. He also worked at Rathaus Schöneberg, where John F. Kennedy delivered his '*Ich bin ein Berliner*' speech, and where, after the fall of the Wall, Willy Brandt and others had also addressed the nation. With camera in hand, Erwin climbed the so-called '*Führertreppe*', which the architect had constructed to give Hitler direct access to the balcony from which he delivered the opening speech to the 1936 Olympic Games.

The self-portrait on those stairs became popular with collectors of his work – despite, or perhaps because of, the location's obscure history and the photograph's simple composition: 'a piece of cake', as Erwin himself put it. That was another lesson. 'Climbing the stairs, that was all it involved. With my back to the camera. Yet the impact was huge.' Even for Erwin, the image – in which he ascends towards the light with a camera dangling from his hand – held special meaning, according to Shirley den Hartog. 'Erwin said to me: "Remember, this will be my farewell photo."'

That ending increasingly preoccupied him. A few months earlier, in December 2011, he had put his ideas for a living will down on paper, including a euthanasia declaration and a donor card. Those ideas would be implemented almost exactly as written more than a decade later, although he never did, as he had foreseen, end up in a nursing home. So he never moved into the imaginary 'home where homosexuals reside, preferably in the Jordaan area of Amsterdam', where he had hoped to grow old 'proudly', despite everything. In his eyes, the tragedy of ageing lay not so much in physical decline, but in the loss of dignity and the sense of being cut off from one's past and loved ones.

Whether it was due to the tightness in his chest or not, Berlin was increasingly becoming a city of stairs for Erwin. As the location scout led him around, taking him up and down countless steps, he suffered from his emphysema. Every photograph in the series features stairs. As does the photo *Clärchen's Ballhaus, Mitte, 2012*, photographed in the ballroom ('since 1913') where Nazi officers and their sweethearts danced in the Second World War and where Quentin Tarantino had filmed scenes for *Inglourious Basterds*.

Whether the staircase represents a descent into hell or an escape from suffering, Erwin lets the viewer decide. In this image, he made his indebtedness to Otto Dix and other artists of the interwar period abundantly clear through an almost literal – albeit mirrored – reference to Dix's painting *Der Salon I*. The work depicts prostitutes sitting around a table, waiting for customers. After a disillusioned return from the First World War, for which he'd confidently enlisted in 1914, Dix began to paint the fall-out from the conflict and the seedy underbelly of the Weimar Republic. War invalids, alcoholics and downtrodden women populate his canvases.

Erwin had long searched for models to embody the three elderly prostitutes. A trio was essential – not only because he wanted to reference Dix's composition, but also because he considered three a 'magic' number: 'With three, you have conflict and a good composition.' He is ecstatic about the woman on the left: 'She was eighty-nine and very liberal. The worse we made her look in the photo, the more she liked it.' To the woman in the middle, he'd said, remember your youth – 'hence, perhaps, the melancholy smile'. He transformed the woman on the right into a geisha-like character. A dissolute figure appears in the background – of the kind that is frequently seen in Otto Dix's work.

Like the children who occupy a central position in the *Berlin* series, the girl on the right symbolises the power of youth. Light enters from the right, and she appears to be leaving the Old World behind – with hopes for a better one to come. She is not innocent – after all, she too has been sitting at that table with the old prostitutes – but she has stood up and distanced herself from the decadent old world.

Yet it was questionable whether so much salvation could truly be expected from youth – the young protagonists in the *Berlin* pictures carry a distinctly dangerous air. And rightly so, according to Erwin: 'Children seem innocent, but they have unprecedented authority. The roles have been reversed. It's not the adults who rule the world, but the children.'

In Berlin, he once again created his own dream world – or rather, a semi-prophetic nightmare. He had never entirely shaken off the doom-and-gloom mentality of the 1980s, the era of his youth. The Western world danced on merrily at the start of the twenty-first century, oblivious to the looming threat. 'We live in the richest part of the world, but it feels like an interwar period, and a jet-black cloud is on the horizon. We're devouring the entire planet – crunch, crunch. And me as much as anyone else,

I'm certainly no saint. You make your charity donations and move on. What are we doing? When do we reach the tipping point? Where are we heading? I don't have children. I can think: *Après moi, le déluge*. But it doesn't make me happy.'

'We can kiss on every street corner, in front of every café and beside every bus stop'

KISSING KEVIN

Saturday, 11 August 2012. A balmy summer evening. Erwin and Kevin Ray Edwards are dining at Razmataz, a restaurant in Amsterdam-West, near Erwin's home in the Jordaan district. They're celebrating their first anniversary. As the beautiful evening draws to a close, a painful new chapter is about to begin.

Four years earlier, Erwin had tried to hit on Kevin Edwards, a much younger man from Rotterdam. 'I thought he was a cute guy with glasses.' Kevin was dancing with a friend on Zeedijk during a week of festivities in Amsterdam when Erwin saw him through the window of the queer bar, The Queens Head, and tried to get his attention. 'Then Erwin came outside, grabbed me, sat down on the windowsill, and pulled me onto his lap.'

That was all for the time being. Kevin wasn't interested in this twenty-year-older, slightly wheezy man, who turned out to be a well-known photographer that he had never heard of.

He held his ground for months, while Erwin persisted, calling and texting. It wasn't until two years after their first encounter that they finally went on a date. And during the trip to Berlin, love blossomed.

When Kevin had to prepare for his taxi exam and couldn't study in peace at home in Rotterdam, Erwin offered his house as a quiet space. 'I wanted to return the keys, and Erwin said: keep them.' They soon started living together. Erwin's relationship with Kevin was his first real love affair since Teun and Alandus.

After those previous break-ups, Erwin had partied and indulged himself for years, and in every imaginable way – with the exception of cigarettes and dope. In matters of the heart, he'd acquired a protective layer of indifference, and often used his razor-sharp humour as the first line of defence.

He'd developed that humour in secondary school as a survival mechanism: a joke or cutting remark had to land instantly and lethally. Whenever he entered a room, he could – along with spotting the nearest escape routes – instantly detect everyone's

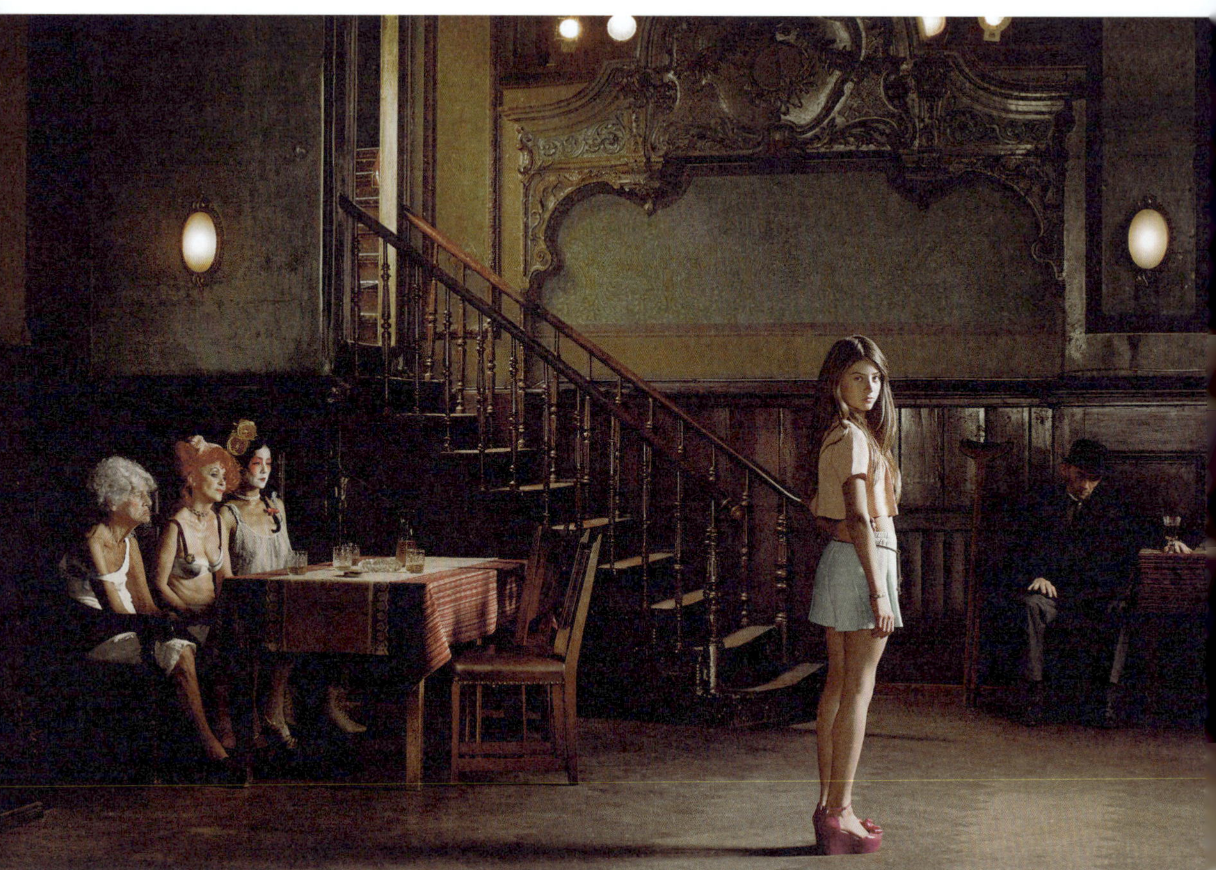

Left: *Clärchen's Ballhaus, Mitte, 10 July 2012*, from the *Berlin* series. Top right: Otto Dix, *Der Salon I*, 1921. Bottom left: *Chessmen XXVII, 1988*, from the *Chessmen* series. Bottom right: John Heartfield, *Niemals wieder! 1930–1932*.

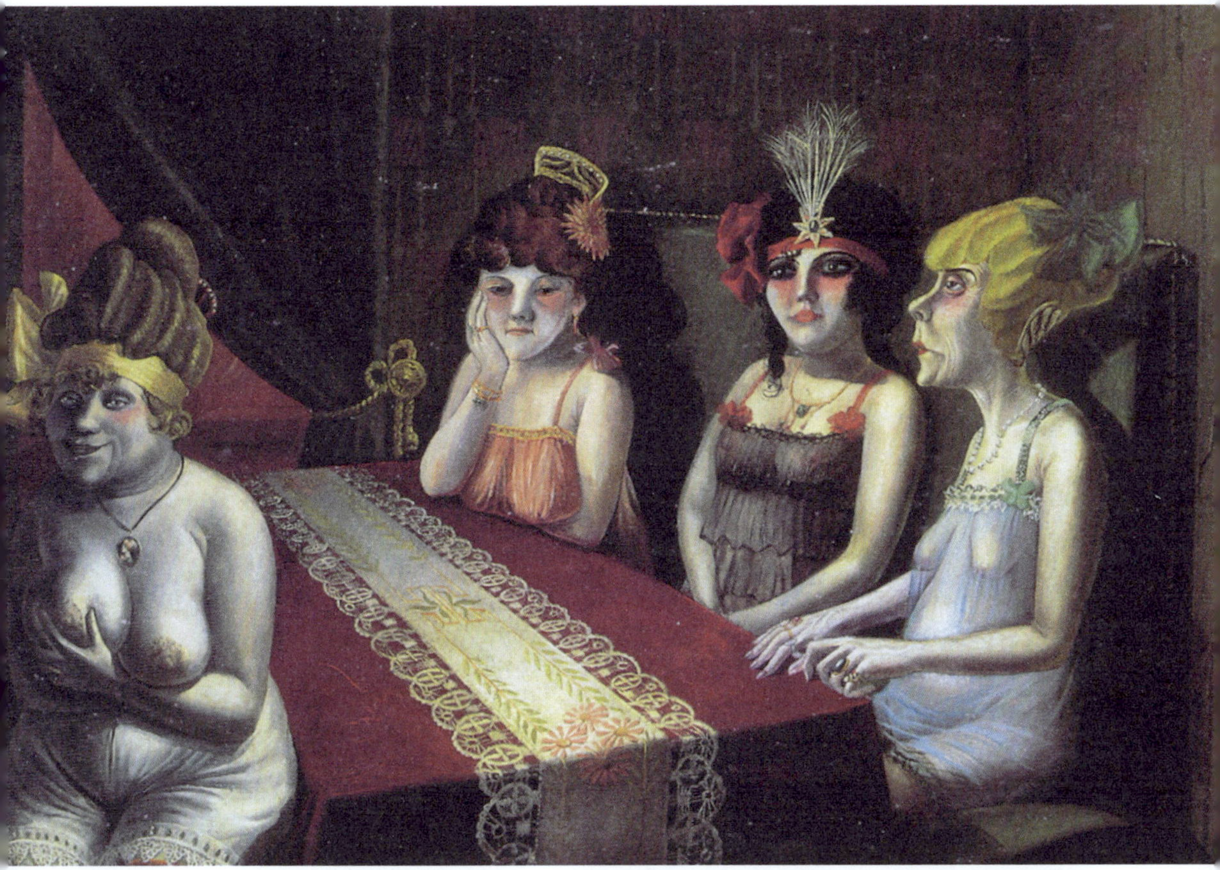

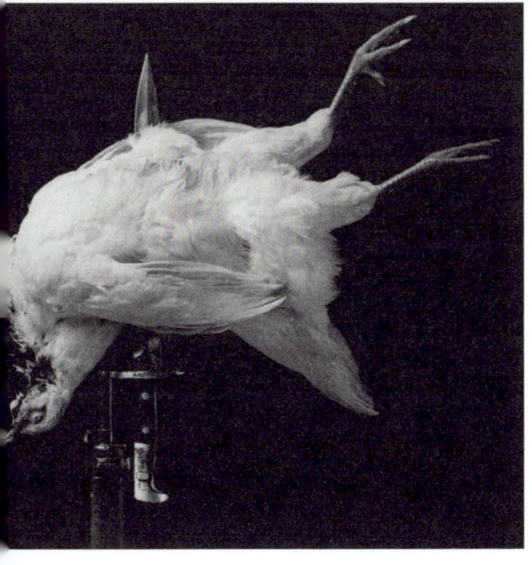

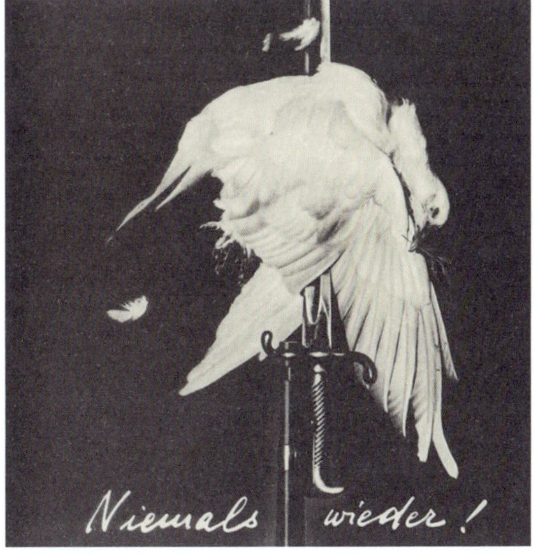
Niemals wieder!

weak spots, whether physical, stylistic or personal. He became a master of observation – a skill that would serve him well in his photography career.

His eyes and his mouth were his only weapons against the bullies; it was a matter of watching and striking before being struck – all while concealing his own vulnerabilities as much as possible. That bullying lay at the root of his struggle with self-acceptance. Even in his forties, he still loathed himself and the fact that he was gay.

Despite being a militant gay-rights activist, it was only around the age of fifty that he gradually began to lower his guard and felt that he could admit – on a near daily basis and with genuine conviction – that 'it's great to be gay'. He adds that if he were to be reincarnated, it would 'absolutely be as a queer again, but only in contemporary north-west Europe, because it's still far from safe for us everywhere'.

Acerbic jokes were a powerful weapon, but they also led to loneliness. They kept everyone at a distance – including those you wanted to draw closer. Erwin knew that many gay men struggled with this kind of humour.

Great jokes, no problem – you laughed yourselves to death together, so it could also have a unifying effect. But the underlying bitterness was ultimately corrosive to friendships and eroded mutual trust. You had to stay on your guard, because you knew: the moment you turned your back, you'd be the butt of the next joke.

Although he wanted to reign in those cynical jokes, he never quite succeeded. His keen eyes defined him as a photographer, and he couldn't resist gently mocking other people's weaknesses – whether it was a stuttering assistant, a lanky intern or an insecure model. He remained, as his old friend Marline once put it, 'as honest as the day is long, to an almost relentless degree', and those around him had to put up with it. His tantrums had lessened, however, after his business partner Shirley den Hartog issued an ultimatum: either he took an anger-management course, or she would walk away. Erwin, wisely, chose the former.

After all the quarrels with Teun, his first great love, and the difficult, sometimes desperate relationship with Alandus, Erwin had finally found stability with Kevin Edwards. He noticed that Kevin was a 'William the Silent', someone who had no interest in histrionics or caustic queer humour. 'Erwin was really vicious back then,' Kevin recalls. 'I said to him: why are you acting like that, why are you talking about others in this way – they're only human. I think that helped make him sweeter and pulled him back from that fake campness.'

It was a new kind of love: no less intense than his two previous relationships, but far less complicated. Kevin didn't mind that Erwin was always the centre of attention, and he accepted without hesitation that his new partner was terminally ill. 'I'll take care of you anyway,' had been his spontaneous response when Erwin told him about his progressive lung disease.

In Erwin's eyes, Kevin was exceptional in his ordinariness – a no-nonsense Rotterdammer who preferred not to make things more complicated than they needed to be. In other words: above all else, never complain. If Erwin wanted to splash out on an elaborate meal, it was Kevin who reminded him of the leftover macaroni in the fridge.

In Rotterdam, Kevin had worked transporting mentally disabled people to and from their care facilities. In Amsterdam, he at first became a waiter on a canal boat, and later ended up behind the bar at the artists' society Arti et Amicitiae – but otherwise, he had little to do with the art world.

Erwin and Kevin shared a love of parties and celebrations – the sanctuaries of life. They were also very good at doing nothing together, lazing on a beach in Mallorca or Thailand.

That night at Razmataz, they had lingered over dessert, discussing love. From his time with Teun, Erwin had retained the belief that love and monogamy were totally incompatible. Back then, Teun was the older and more experienced one. This time, the roles were reversed – and the situation was mirrored when it came to views on fidelity. Erwin had learnt from Teun that flirting with others shouldn't be off-limits and that mutual freedom should be respected – prohibition, after all, only led to misery. He was too restless by nature for a monogamous relationship, although his lung disease made him less sexually active than he would have liked. Still, he told Kevin he could have other lovers – he was young and handsome, after all.

A few years later, even after they were married, Erwin continued to defend that view. He loved Kevin deeply and would stay with him forever, but that didn't mean he would never sleep with someone else. 'Look, there's a big difference between climaxing and thinking, where's the exit; and making love, after which you lie blissfully in each other's arms until you fall asleep. To be honest, I don't have much of a jealous gene. Kevin is twenty years younger than me, and I don't want to be a millstone around his neck.'

Discussing love and monogamy that evening at Razmataz, they didn't see eye to eye and agree to disagree for the time being. At 10.30 p.m., they pay the bill and head for their bikes. Before mounting, they hug and kiss each other. Then they hear a shout: 'Stop that.' It's the thirty-something Turkish guy from the adjacent kebab shop.

They walk up to the snack-bar owner, who becomes even angrier and reiterates that there will be no kissing on his doorstep. According to an eyewitness, Erwin launched into 'a tirade'. He shouted that he was sick of strangers accosting him in public and interfering in his love life – something he'd endured for decades. To drive the point home, he kissed Kevin again, eliciting rapturous applause from the Razmataz terrace. Finally, they hopped on their bikes and rode away from the square.

The day after the incident, Erwin posted an appeal on Facebook: 'Why don't we hold a mass kiss-in outside the same snack bar next Wednesday evening, 15 August, at 8.30 p.m.? As many people as possible – gay, straight, bi, transgender and all our allies – passionately kissing each other. To demonstrate that, after the legalisation of same-sex marriage, we're free to show affection – but apparently not here, in the Netherlands.'

He had taken the idea from a recent protest in Berlin, where the owner of an ice-cream parlour had objected to two young guys greeting each other with a kiss. In response, 500 couples – both straight and gay – had staged a kiss-in at his shop.

A day after his appeal, Erwin reported on Facebook that he had been overwhelmed by the number of responses. A columnist in *NRC Handelsblad* quoted the snack-bar owner: 'To Erwin, who felt discriminated against, I'm quite willing to apologise. But it's six of one and half a dozen of the other. I wasn't the one at fault.' And: 'He's a well-known Dutchman. I'm already one-nil behind.' He even claimed that Erwin Olaf had urged him to 'go back to his own country' – something Erwin denied online.

'We shook hands and I apologised for my tone of voice,' Erwin wrote on Facebook, 'but not for what I said.' He admitted that he may have been too vehement, but he still wanted the kiss-in to go ahead.

He expressed hope for a 'fun and peaceful' gathering, but it wasn't to be – the well-intentioned action backfired. Shirley den Hartog was not around to calm him down on this occasion; she was on holiday. 'For the first time in all those years, I'd resolved to turn off my mobile,' she later recalled. 'Until my companion suggested that I might like to check the Dutch news. I was shocked when I turned on my phone.'

It started beautifully but ended badly. The square was packed with hundreds of people: couples, journalists and 'city bobos', as the popular conservative newspaper *De Telegraaf* put it. Erwin shook hands with the kebab-shop owner and said he was glad the event had become a positive action rather than a protest. The latter remained wary: 'There are lots of people – but are they here in support, or out of hate?'

As Erwin began his speech, dark storm clouds gathered over Amsterdam-West. 'What am I actually worried about?' he began, just as the first raindrops began to fall. 'If I want publicity, it's for my photography – not because I'm agitated about a violation of our collective freedom. Bisexuality and homosexuality were decriminalised decades ago – and it was a democratic decision. Ever since, it's been permissible to have a one-night stand or fall passionately in love until death do us part – and everything in between. An amazing achievement and it should be the norm all over the world – but this is not the case, alas. Fortunately, on this tiny patch of earth, it is! These are hard-won rights – people were imprisoned and persecuted, jeered at, spat on and ridiculed.'

'Marriage has been open to same-sex couples in the Netherlands for more than a decade. I am immensely proud of this fact. But what is still far from possible is to express our affection, sympathy or passion in public. … If we can get married, then we can kiss on every street corner, in front of every café and beside every bus stop. … My big dream is to grow older and older and one day, without fear, to be able to shuffle down the street arm in arm with my boyfriend, stopping now and then to kiss – without anyone batting an eyelid. That's why I'm here, and I hope you are too. So, as we head towards that future, let's begin right now with a minute of snogging, embracing, group hugging, kissing and tender touching. It doesn't matter what, as long as it's loving. On the count of three, the music will start – and you can get stuck in!'

Everyone started kissing. Moments later, the heavens opened, and people ran for cover. Most had disappeared by the time reporter Tom Staal from the website *GeenStijl* arrived. He was accompanied by Zimra Geurts, voted Playmate of the Year by *Playboy* readers. At the time, she was also a temporary reporter at *GeenStijl*.

The journalist urged Geurts to snog Erwin. Erwin refused. 'For the camera, no,' he replied politely. 'I'm not a performing monkey.' After further prodding, a rattled Erwin gave Zimra Geurts a five-second kiss.

The reporter's goading echoed the bullying Erwin had endured during his school days: the pretty girl used as bait to provoke the homosexual, to highlight his supposed 'abnormality' – or perhaps even 'cure' him. He knew the playbook all too well. He felt humiliated, but this time he wouldn't let them get the better of him. Erwin struck back immediately. He spat in Staal's face – 'I still had her saliva in my mouth, and then I spat it onto that journalist.'

Interest in the kiss-in evaporated. The journalist's behaviour was overlooked – he was praised on the *GeenStijl* website and even beyond. The conversation had shifted from gay rights and tolerance to 'the spitting incident'. The negative media attention led to a barrage of death threats. Shirley den Hartog shielded Erwin from them as much as possible – he was deeply shaken by the violent backlash. He decided to quit social media. Den Hartog notified the police of the threatening emails and online posts.

Ironically, Erwin Olaf had been appointed 'municipal ambassador for civility' just the year before. At the Lowlands music festival, he'd delivered a somewhat resigned address on the subject: 'I must be getting old because I'm here to make a plea for greater courtesy. … Unfettered egoism is starting to disrupt public life in Amsterdam. … One of my employees, for example, was grabbed by the crotch in the Vondelpark because she looked too immoral in the perpetrator's eyes. It's high time we began showing more mutual consideration. Politicians and journalists must set a good example.'

After the spitting incident, there was cross-party support on Amsterdam city council for Erwin's immediate resignation from his honorary post as civility ambassador. The alderman summoned him to account.

He was particularly incensed by the attacks from newspaper columnists. 'Those people are so clever, I'm always going to be on the back foot. If I want to make a statement, I'm better off doing it through my work than by sounding off.'

One source of solace, however, was the esteemed Dutch author Arthur Japin. In his 'Hollands Dagboek' ['Dutch Diary'] for *NRC Handelsblad*, he wrote: 'Anyone who is prepared to weather the storm in the fight for gay rights, like Erwin Olaf, is my hero.' He also emailed Erwin with words of encouragement: 'Willingly or not, you've become a symbol of courage, strength and love. Countless people admire you and your deeds. So do I. You do things from the heart. That's what matters. That's what enrages the playground bullies and makes them jeer.' Erwin welcomed the support; troubled by the personal attacks, he was suffering from insomnia.

The kebab-shop owner also reflected on the furore. In ten years of doing business on the square, he had never encountered any problems. It was his home from home, he believed. 'But I made a mistake.' Perhaps so, his wife remarked. 'From one day to the next, you no longer feel like you belong.' He considered returning to Turkey. 'Thanks to Erwin thingamajig.' His wife completed the sentence: 'Olaf. I'll never forget that name.'

During a forest retreat with Kevin, Erwin made a key decision. He would bow out with dignity and step down as ambassador for civility. The spitting incident had made him realise that he first needed to reflect on his own behaviour. With the benefit of hindsight, he realised, once again, that he'd been too quick to charge into battle. It was time to leave the fight for gay rights to a new generation – one that favoured acceptance over provocation. A generation which, in the words of the gay youth magazine *Expreszo*, no longer identified with the actions of someone like Erwin Olaf, who 'blows things so far out of proportion that it becomes a caricature'.

'I couldn't possibly have the queen sit on such an awful toilet bowl'

LETTER TO THE KING

A strong breeze whips the wide steps of Noordeinde Palace in The Hague, the working palace of King Willem-Alexander and Queen Máxima. As the already somewhat unruly group gathers for a photograph, the wind buffets them further – sending dresses, ties and hair flying in all directions. On this particular Monday, Erwin Olaf's friends and family have assembled outside the palace with the photographer. The purpose of the visit remains unclear, although Shirley den Hartog has wracked her brains trying to work it out.

Erwin had received a phone call: could he attend the palace on 13 March 2023 – the king and queen wished to thank him personally. 'I thought, we'll have a cup of coffee, I'll present a bouquet.' But it turned out to be something much grander: he was allowed to bring twenty guests. Erwin travelled to The Hague in a rented minibus with his family, friends and studio assistants.

Alongside Kevin, his family, Shirley, and both current and former studio employees – fondly referred to by Erwin, both ironically and affectionately, as his 'dream team' – were Frans Franciscus, Marline Williams (in a vivacious green outfit), Arjan Ederveen, Hans van Manen and his partner Henk van Dijk, Erwin Venema, Piek and several old friends. Only Rudolf Pfalz was absent – his lungs too weak, the journey too strenuous. Erwin himself had only made it with great pain and effort; it was one of his first public outings with a nasal cannula for oxygen.

He was ashamed of his now visible impairment, but finally had to acknowledge that the future image he had once sketched for himself in the series of self-portraits *I Wish, I Am, I Will Be* (2009) had come true. 'The first portrait, *I Wish*, is a kind of joke. A young man with a beautiful torso who is always in the gym. I'd think, I long for that kind of physique. So I asked him to pose for me and then Photoshopped my head onto his torso. The middle portrait, *I Am*, is me – no Photoshop, no nothing. The third image, *I Will Be*, gets to the heart of the matter – especially the oxygen tubes.

At the time, he'd wanted the images to invoke his future as a lung patient. 'I did shed a tear when I looked in the mirror while taking the picture, but it was also a relief. I thought: OK, this is what awaits me. The image helped me come to terms with that.' In so doing, he referred, once again, to Rineke Dijkstra's self-portrait in the Marnix swimming pool for the 'documentary' effect. 'The light and shadows are much less staged than usual, and I used an identical, nondescript background. You can see the vulnerability in my eyes. These photos offer a glimpse into my emotional world and are far removed from how I used to gaze into the lens – unyielding and inaccessible. Rineke and I are on different planets in photography terms, but this is something I learnt from her.'

Dijkstra saw it too. 'Erwin discovered his vulnerability through his lungs, just as I was confronted with mine when I broke my hip. This could be a parallel – vulnerability as a departure point. But then again, the difference is that I like to go out into the world and be surprised. I love it when I'm working and the unexpected happens. I think Erwin lacks that – on the contrary, he knows, in his mind's eye, precisely what he wants to create. He's a director of photos and is very good at it.'

As he waited for the inevitable, he reflected on the monarchy – which he'd always supported. Even back in April 1980, when he'd only been living in Amsterdam for a few months, he'd watched in bewilderment as police charged at protesters seeking to disrupt Princess Beatrix's coronation.

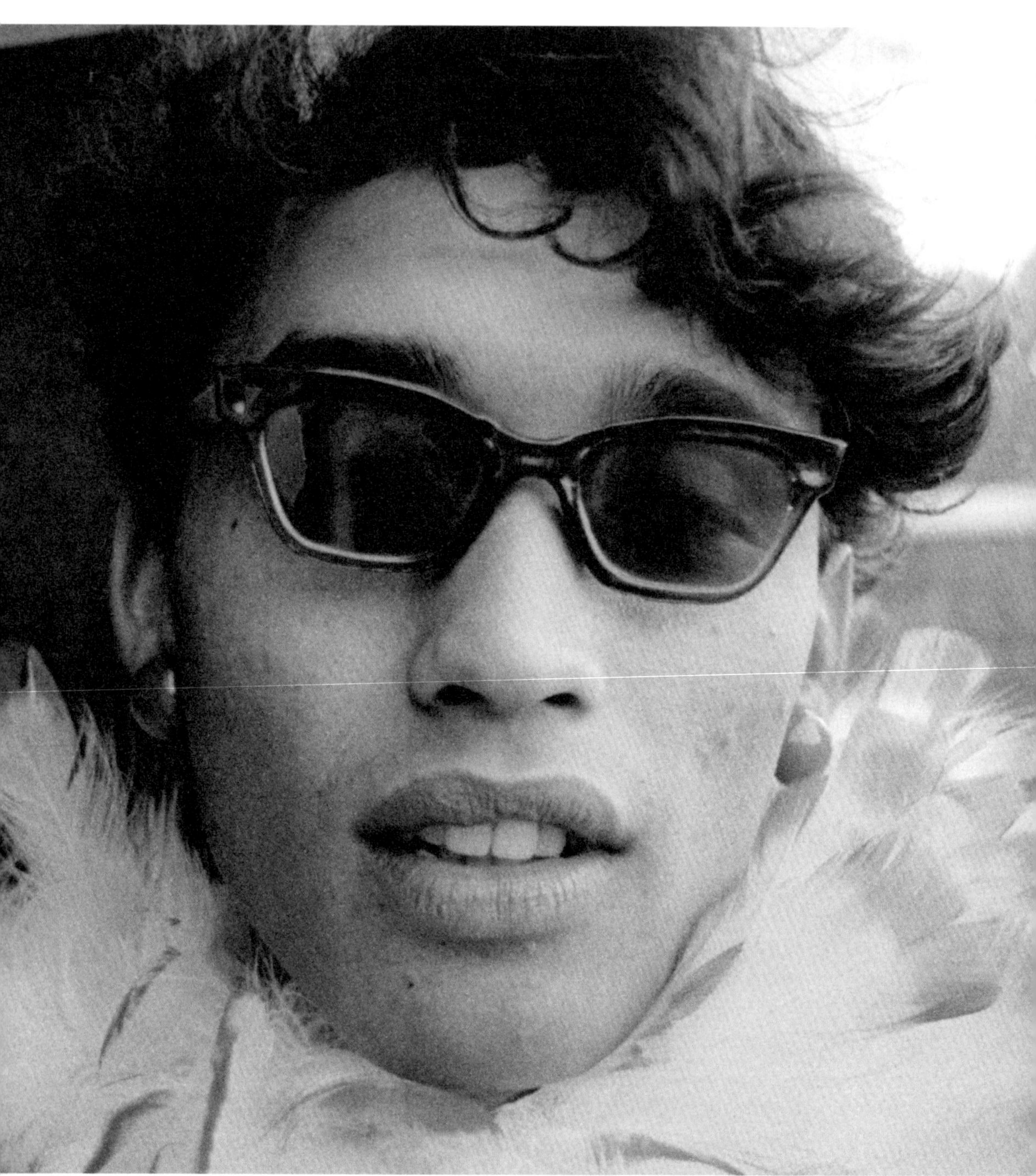

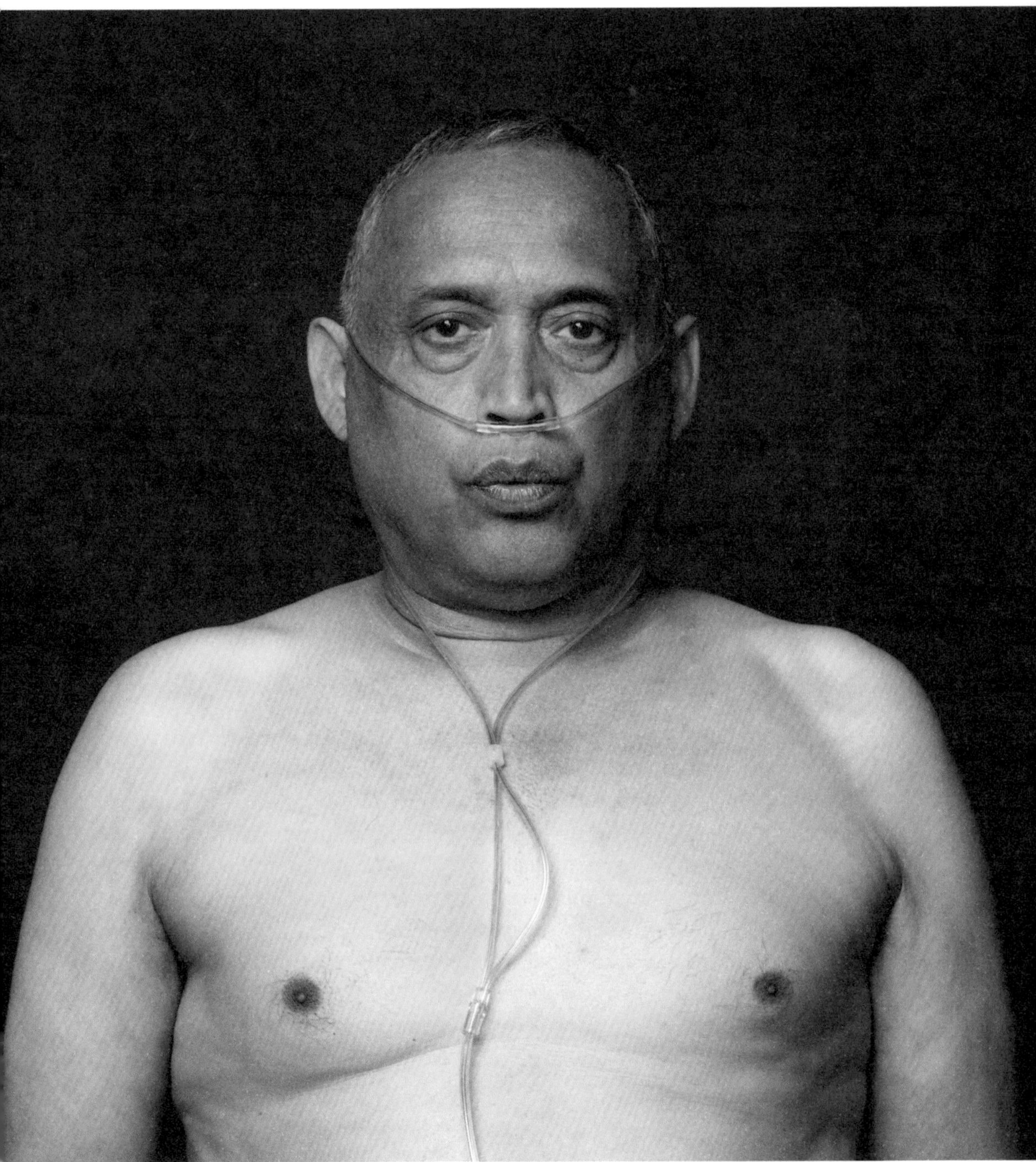

Left: Rudolf Pfalz in Erwin's first published photograph, in the magazine *De onderste steen*, 1977–1978. Right: Photographed again in 2022 for the *Muses* series.

Erwin was attuned to the symbolism and theatricality of the royal family. 'It's a newfangled fairy tale, and I love fairy tales; I create them myself. I love being able to shape an imaginary world.' He believed that 'two crowned heads, supposedly above us', were preferable to 'a dopey president'. 'And if we've agreed to have a monarchy, I say in for a penny, in for a pound. If we're going to celebrate them, let's do it to the max.' He was proud of the Dutch royal family – 'the most undemocratic instrument through which to defend our democratic values'.

He was certainly honoured to know that Willem-Alexander and Máxima had visited his exhibition *Rain, Hope, Grief & Fall* in The Hague in 2009, outside official opening hours. But that didn't stop him from being sharply critical of Willem-Alexander's demeanour and appearance a year later, during a lengthy interview on the television programme *Zomergasten*.

'He means well,' Erwin began his critique. 'But I don't feel like I'm looking at a future king. It's very strange. I think he should gradually start to take matters in hand. If I might be so bold as to offer some advice: whiten your teeth. Treat yourself to a nice pair of expensive gold-rimmed glasses – you'd look much better. Because, let's face it, he wasn't first in line when they were handing out the beauty genes. He needs to spruce himself up a bit. We live in a media age, in a world of images – especially when it comes to the international monarchs of this planet. You've got to keep up appearances, and the minute people start grumbling, you're toast. So you really have to focus on your image.'

After some prodding from the interviewer as to whether he would accept a commission for a royal portrait, he replied, 'I don't know, I'd have to think about it.'

Following a conversation about a film about top photographer Annie Leibovitz's photo shoot with Queen Elizabeth II – 'she took four masterful portraits' – and the necessary display of modesty – 'I'm not much of a portrait photographer' – he did have some sound advice for Willem-Alexander and Máxima. 'Hire Mario Testino, who has already taken marvellous portraits of you for *Vanity Fair*. Because Leibovitz's images worked wonders for the British royal family.'

His style advice fell on fertile ground, apparently, because the following year he was commissioned by the newspaper *AD* to photograph Máxima on the occasion of her fortieth birthday. He was allowed, as he later put it himself, to 'help build the image of the princess, as she was then'. Apparently, Máxima didn't mind being portrayed by someone who had critiqued her husband's appearance.

While working on the project, he sent a photo of himself with the princess to his mother. 'Hello Ma, here's a picture of Princess Máxima and myself, it's not quite finished, but it's quite nice. Don't you think so? I do look a bit angry, but it's the only photo to date. Bye for now, Erwin.'

Erwin didn't comment further on his palace visit, although he later described the shoot with Máxima as 'magical'. 'My relationship with my sitters is private. Because I feel it's a very intense relationship. For those few minutes, I always feel an intense infatuation between me and the model. Everyone is exhausted at the end of the session – my six studio staff, the model, and myself. If I'm not tired, then there's something very wrong.'

His portrait of Máxima was even likened to the Mona Lisa by some of his peers. He had already said on a television programme that, over the years, he had learnt you didn't need to photograph in a radically different way to produce something special. 'I used to think you had to completely reinvent the wheel, but I've since discovered you need to do exactly the same as everyone else – just a little differently. It's invisible.' That he had achieved something unique with a small intervention was noted by Vincent Mentzel, himself a well-known figure at the court and for many years Queen Beatrix's house photographer. 'Photographing Máxima from a low level – like a surprised child looking up at someone – was a stroke of genius. 'Bloody hell,' Mentzel thought, 'I should have done that at least once with Queen Beatrix.' Although Erwin often manipulated his photos – a hallmark of his style – he took these photographs *after nature*, as it's called. The princess hadn't been turned into a Barbie; you could see she was forty. She had the occasional, beautiful wrinkle. He cleverly maintained that balance.

In 2013, Erwin then had the opportunity to put some of his royal style advice into practice. Alongside eleven others, he was invited to submit a portrait of Willem-Alexander for the new Dutch euro coins. 'My first reaction: why the hell are they asking me?'

He began the project nonetheless, but gradually became disheartened. It wasn't his cup of tea. That all changed, however, when he was cycling through Amsterdam-Zuid and caught sight of Hildo Krop's sculptures. He realised he needed to work in a more abstract way – that he had to create something three-dimensional.

He submitted two designs and won the competition. He had aimed for a 'powerful and strong look', befitting King Willem-Alexander. It could be abstract, since for Erwin the head of state was, above all, a symbol of 'unity within diversity' – hence the portrait was composed of several facets. He also wanted to depict him as a modern monarch, a king at the heart of society.

But how could this positive view be reconciled with his earlier criticism? The question arose as he was about to be formally presented to King Willem-Alexander. Erwin composed a letter to the king, belatedly apologising for the critical remarks he'd made more than three years earlier. 'This worries me a little bit,' he wrote. Playing the clip back, he was struck by the 'brusqueness' of his speech. 'Although I tried to express my opinion as constructively as possible, given my professional background, I think that I was crass and hurtful. It bothers me, and I would like to apologise.' He emphasised how much of an honour it was 'to be able to contribute in a modest way to the image of the modern Dutch monarchy, to which you and your wife add a splendid lustre, and with great élan'.

The king appeared to have moved on from Erwin's 'brusqueness', and Erwin's relationship with the royal family deepened further when, a few years later, Queen Máxima considered having herself photographed with her daughters as a gift for her husband's 50th birthday. 'Erwin queried, "Why are you asking me? Family portraits aren't my forte. I'm mainly a fantasy photographer – or at any rate, a photographer of fiction,"' Shirley den Hartog recalled. 'Sometimes I could kick him in the shins.'

The queen and the three princesses were dropped off at the studio on IJselstraat on a Tuesday in April. Erwin had sent suggestions for their attire. 'I'd said: bring white shirts or blouses. Unfortunately, their stylist had brought frumpy dresses and some kind of white batwing robes – not very flattering. In the end, only a fraction of the collars were visible, and the results, in my humble opinion, were spectacular.'

He had prepared thoroughly, on several fronts. 'When the appointment was confirmed, I took a critical look at my three old toilets. Really, men's loos. I couldn't possibly have the queen sit on such an awful toilet bowl. So I had a new one installed. I stuck a little crown on the door. Princess Ariane noticed it immediately: "Hey, a crown." I said: "yes, if a princess comes to visit, I take it very seriously."'

Via a mood board, he'd suggested making close-up portraits of all four with their hair blowing across their faces. 'As a result, there's a kind of "oomph" in all those photos.' He intended to display the individual prints side by side in a two-metre-long frame. He found the queen impressive. 'A very sexy, attractive woman. A true lioness – albeit a friendly one. The huge diamond earrings felt appropriate. You could see at once: this is royalty. Afterwards, I said to her: Your Majesty, I believe I've just photographed the new stamp.'

At the earlier session with Máxima, when she was still a princess, the make-up had taken four hours and seven assistants managed the seven sets she moved between. This new portrait was a secret – a surprise for Willem-Alexander – so time was of the essence. 'The children finished school, then they raced to my studio in double-quick time, we took the photographs – bam, bam, bam. Then they hurried home before the day was even out.'

The result was a series of close-ups in which Erwin explores the threshold of proximity within a portrait. 'With Máxima there was a genuine click – she really understands my style of photography, she has the right degree of assurance, and she knows I'm not out to undermine anyone. We have a similar mindset. The queen is also someone with a very liberal outlook.'

Erwin selected the prints, which the Royal Household then either vetoed or approved. 'I'd opted for a slightly more pleasing version, while they chose a more

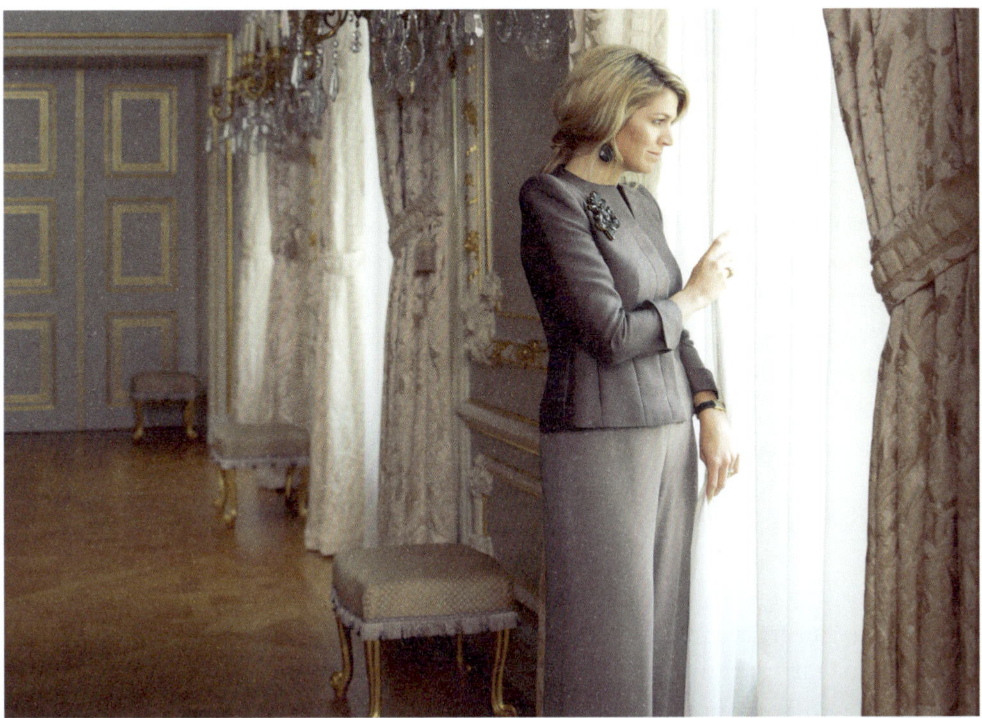

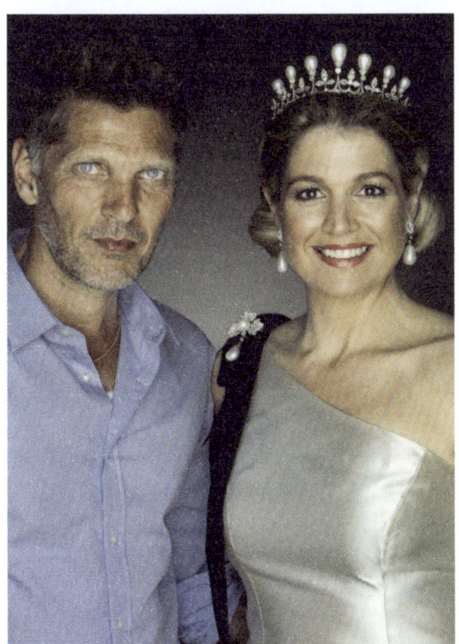

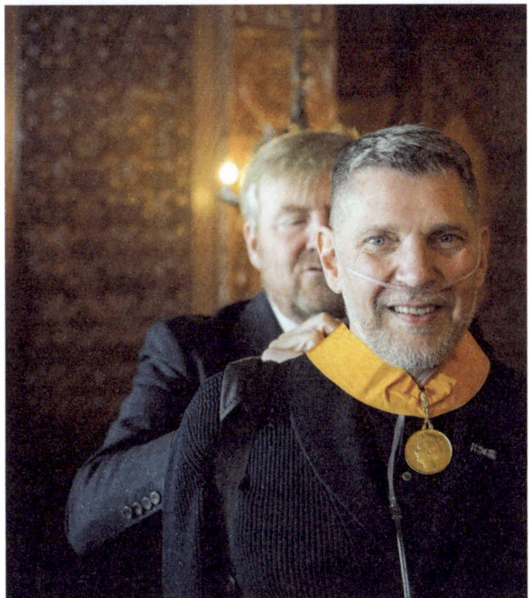

Top: *Her Royal Highness Princess Máxima of the Netherlands, Portrait 6, 2011*. Bottom left: With Princess Máxima in 2011. Bottom right: King Willem-Alexander presents Erwin Olaf with the Medal of Honour for Art and Science from the Order of the House of Orange, 2023.

confident one. The youngest, Ariane, has an open-mouthed smile. Alexia has just the hint of one. Amalia looks timid. And Máxima watches over her cubs like a lioness.'

That same year, in 2013, *Vanity Fair España* used his portrait of Máxima as its cover image. 'Do you know what I love more than anything else? The Spanish newspapers published online galleries of my early photos – like the frothing champagne bottle and the picture of the naked man with an erection and a Gucci bag on his head. And next to them all was Máxima's portrait. That we can do such a thing in this part of the world – isn't it amazing? Because Willem-Alexander and Máxima obviously know how extreme my photography was in the past. And they didn't have any issue with the work.'

'You notice that the people around the king are as sensitive as dragonflies'

Through the queen and princesses, he finally fulfilled his dream of meeting the king: 'Fame and celebrity are overrated, in my opinion. But if they ask me tomorrow to photograph Willem-Alexander, I won't say no. For that matter, get me Harry and William as well, pronto. And, please, let's have Harry naked.'

In March 2018, after almost five years on the throne, Willem-Alexander wanted to be photographed with his family at the palace on Dam Square. Peeping Toms from the media – as with Annie Leibovitz – were excluded. 'You notice that the people around the king are as sensitive as dragonflies.' The final result was the photo of the royal family that Hans van Manen insisted on hanging on his wall because 'you wouldn't see the insanity of that picture for another ten years'.

As a kind of final chapter in his work with the royal family, Erwin was now, in March 2023, being ushered into Noordeinde Palace with Kevin, Shirley, his brothers and sisters-in-law, his mother-in-law, and his close friends and associates.

Kevin and Erwin introduced everyone to the king and queen. 'The king then commenced his speech – very touching and sweet.' Willem-Alexander praised Erwin's 'irresistible lack of airs and graces' and described him as a 'boyish *éminence grise*'. He spoke of Erwin's loyalty to old friends, his support for vocational education, and the value he placed on craftsmanship in his profession.

Erwin was momentarily taken aback when the king mentioned *Zomergasten*. 'That stung for a moment, but then I thought: how lovely that the king shares one of my traits – he holds on to negative things for a long time.' Shirley den Hartog added: 'The king also said: "You prefer unconventional characters – and in that regard, I'm delighted to be of service."'

The speech was followed by an official ceremony. 'Then it was pinned onto me, the medal of honour.' Erwin had previously been appointed a Knight of the Order of the Netherlands Lion, so he wasn't overly dazzled. Over drinks, he and Máxima discussed art, science and music. 'We briefly touched upon dancing and I mentioned that Kevin is a wonderful dancer – he'll even start twirling in the supermarket. And I think Máxima loves it too. I suggested they should be dancing partners.'

On a more serious note, they also talked about the recent royal visit to Slovakia, during which Willem-Alexander and Máxima had visited the gay bar in Bratislava where two men had been shot dead in October 2022. In a speech to the United Nations shortly afterwards, the king had expressed his support, stating that he was glad to see 'the equal rights of gays, lesbians, transgender and other minority groups' increasingly being enshrined in law across the world. 'The fight against overt and hidden discrimination must continue on all continents,' he declared.

That, Erwin thought, as he left Noordeinde Palace with his family and friends, was exactly why he continued to support the royal family, despite everything. 'They use their symbolic power to stand up for minorities.' Shirley den Hartog: 'And then we all drove in the minibus to the Chinese.'

'Only time will tell whether my work is seen as kitsch or enduring. But... I'm going to do my bit to help'

RETURN TO THE DARKROOM

On a long table in the studio lie prints from the *Royal Blood* series: Lady Di with the Mercedes logo embedded in her bleeding arm, Sissi, Jackie O., Julius Caesar and other blue-blooded figures who met a violent end. This was the series for which Erwin traded his darkroom for digital imaging nearly a quarter of a century ago. The technical perfection he attained in the black space, enveloped in chemical fumes, has long since been replaced by collaborations with digital photo editors.

For several years now, however, the IJselstraat studio has again housed a darkroom. Fellow photographer and studio collaborator Feriet Tunc uses it to process his black-and-white prints, which – for better or worse – Erwin always likes to appraise, before giving the final touch by cutting them down to size. Tunc, who joined the studio as an intern more than twenty years ago, has since become one of its mainstays and a master of the darkroom.

Today, Erwin is consulting with printer and digital imaging specialist André Beuving about a new technical shift they've been experimenting with for the past few months. Their collaboration dates back to the *Royal Blood* days, and after a quarter of a century, they are entirely in sync – able to finish each other's sentences. 'And André has a very good eye'.

The issue at hand is the transition from digital printing to inkjet, and consequently, to a different kind of paper. It is a sensitive matter. Erwin and Shirley jointly determine the edition numbers of his photographs. Special prints are made for exhibitions, which are either destroyed afterwards or kept in storage. In addition, several *épreuves d'artiste* or artist proof copies are usually available: prints made for the artist that are numbered separately from the main edition, but generally produced at the same time.

This does not mean that all series and sizes are printed in advance and available for purchase. The photographs are printed individually. When someone orders a print the following year, it must be identical to the earlier ones. The trick is to get as close to the original as possible.

At the outset of his career – or rather, before it had even begun – Erwin described how, in his view, a photograph's finish was of negligible importance. In an account of a 'photography for beginners' course at the School of Journalism, he noted that a photograph 'is the result of the creator's vision and not his actions'. Technology played a role, but he also knew: 'Even with the best equipment, a bad photograph will never become a good one. Whereas you can take the most effective shots on a cheap Polaroid camera. Just think, for example, of *Andy Warhol: Photography and Andy Warhol's Exposures*.'

In young Erwin's eyes, a photograph had to demonstrate 'how the photographer thinks and feels when he presses the shutter and communicates his view on the event or person'. He could subsequently adjust that vision a little in the darkroom, 'but basically the click of the shutter is always the decisive moment'.

Later, after beginning to master photography as an apprentice to André Ruigrok – for whom he made prints by the kilo and whose perfectionism he adopted – he came to appreciate the importance of working in the darkroom. Since then, he often found himself 'completely obsessed' with whether a print was perhaps a little too grey or slightly too dark. Although the press of the button and the photographer's gaze remained paramount, his love for the artisanal side of the métier never faded, and he has since been able to pass it on to his own trainees and assistants.

As an example, Piek learned to print during days-long sessions in the darkroom on Swammerdamstraat. When working outside the darkroom, she would sometimes hear Erwin 'shouting and ranting' when yet another print had gone wrong – or just at the radio if he'd heard something bad on the news.
Erwin taught Thomas Manneke and Rogier Alleblas, now fellow photographers, the

laborious technique of printing on Baryta paper. Alleblas recalls spending entire days printing just two negatives. 'I was bloody nervous when Erwin reviewed my first prints for *Blacks*. They were displayed on a cloth in the studio; he walked past them and said of the last one, "This one is starting to look like it." Followed by, "all rejected" – and then ripped my prints in half. Very relaxed and resolute, not to put me in my place, but simply because they were unusable. "No problem," he said. "Just start again."'

Bert Pot, now a cameraman and documentary maker but once a trainee, recalled: 'I already felt like a good photographer until I started printing with Erwin. There was a protocol, a very clear manual, and an outline of what to print and what to hold back. And that's what you tried to imitate. He was always incredibly precise. He's a man of extremes, and he could get irate when things went wrong. But his mood could change in the blink of an eye, and then he'd be joking around and all cheerful again.'

Erwin himself sometimes longed to be a hermit again, ensconced in the darkroom, where he had occasional fits of anger but also good laughs. The place where he was often slightly or totally stoned, communing with the prints he was perfecting. 'Nothing is more delightful than going from tray to tray in the dark with some music playing. Then, at the end of the day, noticing: oh fuck, they're all a bit too grey. When I was still smoking joints and, from time to time, didn't know whether I was coming or going, I could print for days on end, non-stop. Because of that, I've accumulated a great stock of vintage prints. I'm so glad about that today; they're part of my pension.'

The vintage prints are rare, require careful monitoring, and are always limited in number. 'You have to be 100% reliable on this front, and cheating is out of the question: the photography world is far too small.' He initially struggled with the restrictions. 'In the 1980s, I thought: surely I can just make another print? Why can't you keep printing ad infinitum? That's what I find so liberating in the visual arts: democratisation. Everyone should be able to afford my art. But at a certain point, you have to say: OK, I can pour my heart and soul into my work, but if I want to earn a living with it, then I have to abide by the rules. That's the deal: sold out is sold out. Otherwise, your credibility goes down the drain, along with your market value.'

During his first trip to the United States in 2006, Erwin became fascinated by the nineteenth-century process of carbon printing. At the J. Paul Getty Museum in Los Angeles, Virginia Heckert had critically described his *Royal Blood* series as 'Eurotrash', but she had also explained the fragility of contemporary photographic techniques compared to the perfectly preserved nineteenth-century carbon prints. The 'modern' prints by photographers such as Thomas Struth and Andreas Gursky were sensitive to temperature changes and sunlight, and housed in special climate-controlled cases to prevent discolouration and fading. Yet when Heckert lifted a selection of carbon

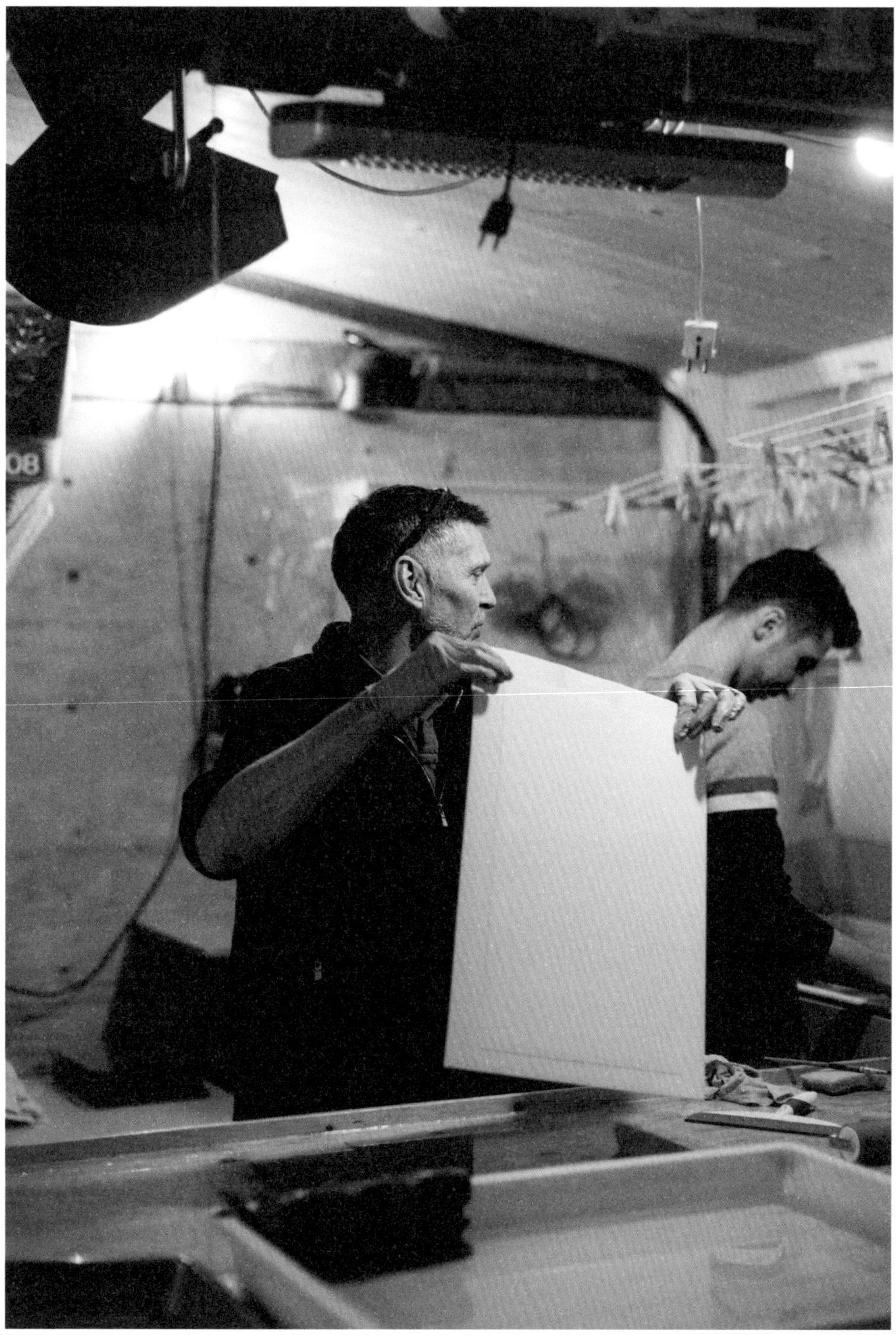

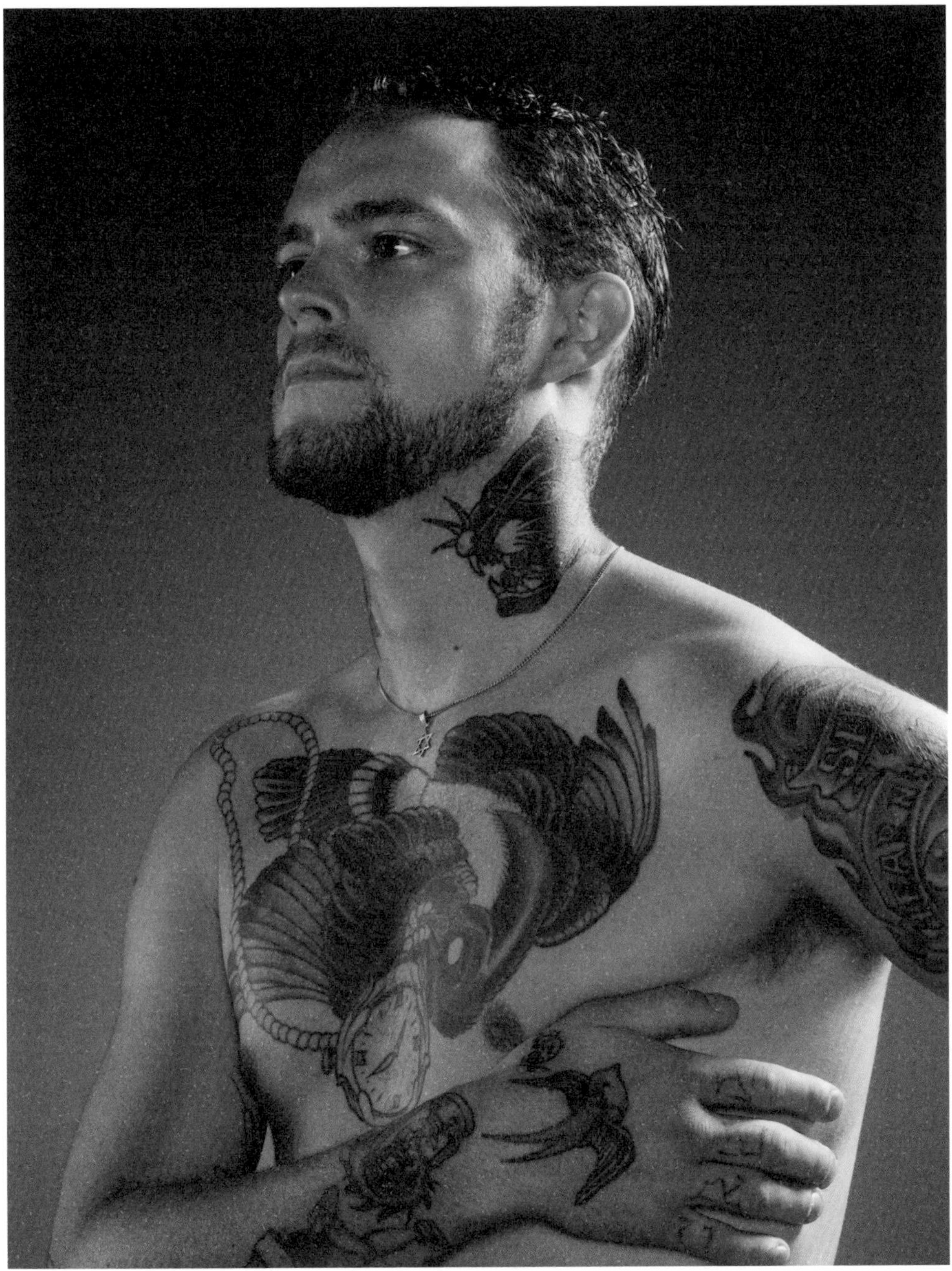

Left: Erwin in the darkroom printing his series on Jewish Amsterdammers, together with his assistant Piotr Owczarzak. Right: *Modern Jewish – Benjamin, 2013*, from the series *Joods* [Jewish].

prints from a drawer – small photographs more than a century old – they seemed as if they had only just been printed.

Their technical brilliance and timelessness captivated Erwin. He saw the potential in returning to analogue work while retaining the advances of digital imaging. 'If you look at photos by Ed van der Elsken today, they have a beautiful atmosphere. But secretly you can recreate it all digitally and even augment it. I don't think we'll reset the clock. But we can use contemporary techniques and supplement them with the reintroduction of historic ones. That leads to something unique.'

Erwin had always been open to influences – from other photographers' work to cutting-edge techniques, says Wim van Sinderen, former curator of the Fotomuseum Den Haag. 'Unlike Anton Corbijn, who likes to maintain that he invented everything himself, Erwin is quite open about his sources of inspiration. At a party for the fashion brand The People of the Labyrinths, who collected Erwin's work and commissioned him, we admired a book by American photographer and publisher F. Holland Day. It contained reproductions of his carbon and platinum prints. At the time, Erwin had no idea those processes even existed. But not long afterwards, he began to learn carbon printing – not because it was trendy, but because he was curious about its potential. He wanted to experiment, and started working in a smaller format.'

And, as always, there were further sources of inspiration, such as an extraordinary black-and-white still life with roses by Bernard Eilers.

In 2012, a particularly hectic year, Erwin drove from Amsterdam to Middelburg every six weeks to study the delicate method of carbon printing, far away from the hysteria of Amsterdam. 'Few believe in the longevity of current printing techniques. I always say that only time will tell whether my work is seen as kitsch or enduring. But, whatever the case, I'm going to do my bit to help.' His tutor was photographer and designer Kees Brandenburg, who specialises in restoring historical photographs and is, according to Erwin, 'a gentleman who lives a quiet life and is very calm.'

In an interview, Erwin described the labour-intensive printing process. First, a layer of gelatine mixed with black powder is applied to a support. This is exposed and transferred, while submerged, to a new sheet of paper. After rinsing in tepid water, the image is transferred to the new sheet. 'The rinsing takes half an hour, three quarters of an hour – as long as it takes. And, in the meantime, you have to stay relaxed. ... There is charcoal, gelatine, light-sensitive material, a sheet of paper and a negative, and those nineteenth-century techniques can be unpredictable. Even talking introduces too much movement and the gelatine washes away – then you have to start all over again.'

Erwin's penchant for the artisanal side of his craft – a dialogue with photography,

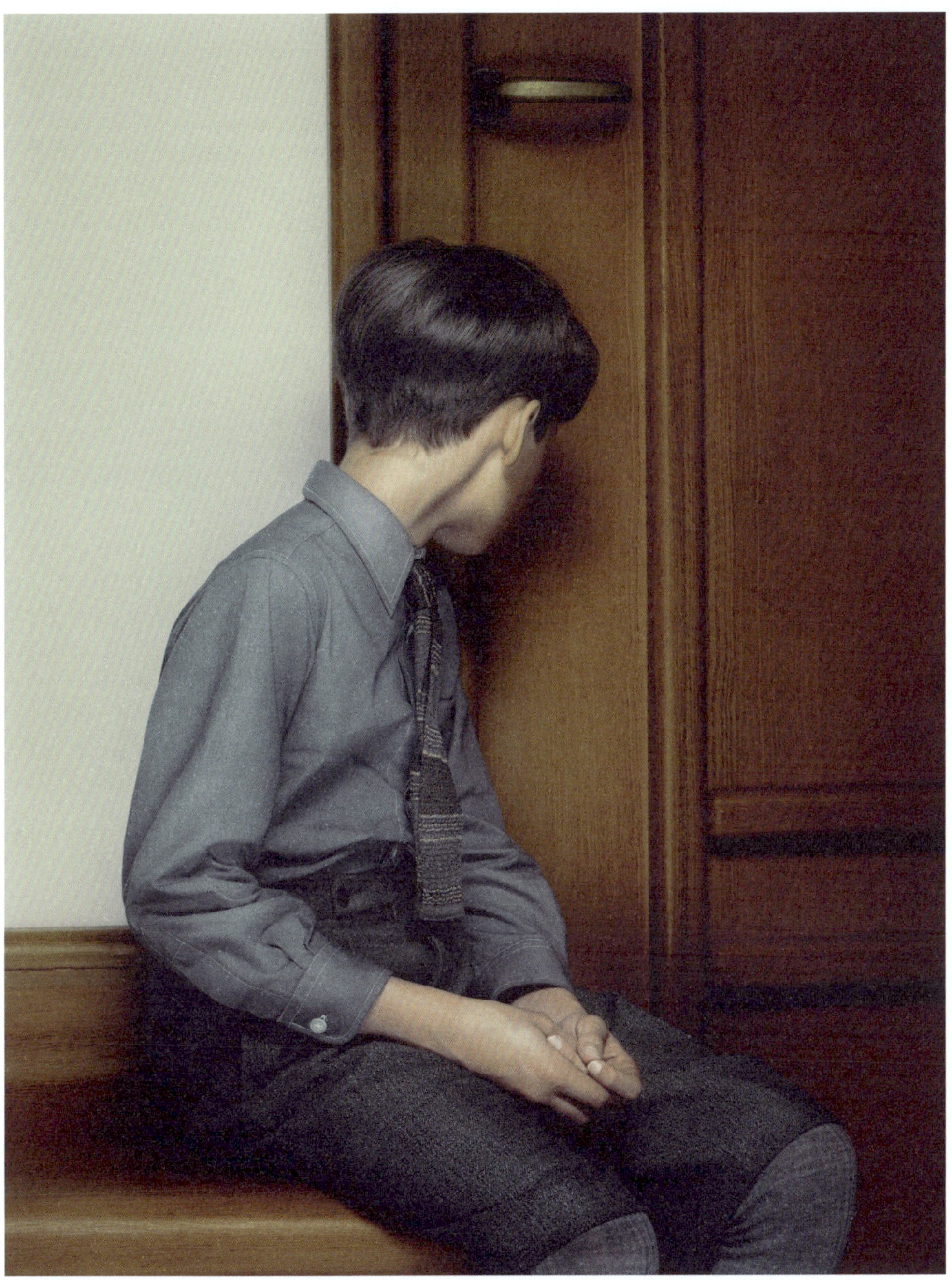

Keyhole 1, 2011 from the *Keyhole* series.

as he called it – was also related to ageing and his need for introspection. After his wild *fin-de-siècle* years, he sought stillness and longed to return to the simple pleasures of the darkroom, where he could create 'miniature jewels'.

When, in 2013, he was asked to create work in response to Fotostudio Merkelbach's archives, where many Jewish Amsterdammers had their portraits taken before the Second World War, Erwin produced sixteen studio portraits, entitling the series *Joods* [Jewish]. It featured residents of the city who identified as Jewish – whether ethnically, culturally or religiously. He portrayed his models slightly from below, tightly and austerely lit in an isolated studio setting. He printed eight of the portraits using the same time-consuming carbon-printing technique that Jacob Merkelbach had employed to print his glass negatives. He considered the process ideally suited to the subject: 'There was symbolism in the decision to use that delicate but imperishable technique because Jewish identity is under pressure.'

Erwin immersed himself in the subject – about which he knew little beforehand – but it was already self-evident that Jews fell within his concept of excluded minorities. 'I've been taunted my entire life because of my identity. Jews too. Being gay doesn't mean I'm automatically all sorts of other things. The same goes for being Jewish. You're reduced to one aspect of your existence and tormented, ostracised – and worse – on those grounds. All it takes is for the wind to change and it becomes a toxic soup for homosexuals, Jews and other minorities.'

The Jewish series marked a temporary departure from digital photography and seemed to herald a foray into documentary work, which he had previously criticised. He was slightly bored with staging and the huge sets. 'Why does that camera always have to be so far back? Simply to prove that I'm capable of lighting such a big space?'

Appreciation came from unexpected quarters. According to curator Hripsimé Visser, the series demonstrated that Erwin Olaf is an 'incredible craftsman' who works with 'enormous precision', she says, at the Stedelijk Museum's new building. She does not see it as a switch to a more documentary approach. 'I don't know if these pictures are all that realistic. Carbon printing also creates a certain densification; the photos are very layered. Jewish history is inextricably linked to the city of Amsterdam, and it's very legible in these photos.'

Visser regards this layering and subtlety as 'exceptional' within Erwin's oeuvre. 'His early work, in particular, was rather in your face and perfectly captured the spirit of the 1980s and '90s. The series of Jewish Amsterdammers is especially beautiful because the photographs are both conceptual and documentary in nature. Moreover, their scale enhances this – the carbon prints are tiny. I've been longing for the return of small-format photographs for quite some time now – although I do appreciate that the work of certain photographers, such as Rineke and Erwin, actually benefits from a more majestic scale.'

Hripsimé Visser also congratulated Erwin on his Jewish series at the time. He wrote an effusive letter to his carbon-printing tutor, Kees Brandenburg, saying that Visser had paid him a compliment 'for the first time in thirty years', before adding, 'I'm absolutely thrilled.'

The increasingly large formats in art photography, for which Visser sought an antidote, stemmed from photography's recently acquired status as high-value art. Rocketing prices made collectors expect more for their money.

The period during which Erwin Olaf, Rineke Dijkstra and other photographers of their generation had come of age was also when photography had matured as an art form and, concurrently, became marketable. Walter Benjamin's fear that 'it was the final hour' for art in the age of mechanical reproduction had not come to pass, although photography's reproducibility now seemed infinite in the digital age.

Limiting print runs and emphasising the importance of 'owning' signed prints bolstered photography's economic and market value. For vintage prints by photographers in Erwin Olaf's category, tens of thousands of euros were readily paid. In the late 1980s, when he sold his first photographs, the few collectors of contemporary photography only parted with a few hundred guilders (at most). Press agencies and editors often simply discarded the prints after use, since new copies could always be made. The prints were merely temporary image carriers.

Contemporary fine-art photography only became a serious market in the early twenty-first century. In the 1970s, even prints by famous photographers went for a song. There was a very limited auction circuit, a small group of collectors, and those involved were true connoisseurs with an understanding of art history and materials. In just a few decades, a market developed from this niche world, and photographs became big business.

When photography was recognised as an autonomous art form, young photographers began outsourcing print work to photo labs using fast and cheap processes such as Lambda laser printers. These prints were not developed for the art market and were not designed to last indefinitely. Many colour photographs thus had a limited shelf life. Fading and discolouration were common problems, whether on the walls of private homes or in museum storage facilities. Cibachrome was the only process that could claim to be more robust – although even that depended on whether a photo was kept in a cold room or hung in a bright space. Yet colour photography's transience remained a taboo subject. From artists and galleries to buyers, nobody was keen to discuss the problem.

Erwin was often amazed by the sums lavished on photographs. Although, at the time, auction prices for his work were a mere pittance compared to those commanded by some other visual artists. 'Marlene Dumas projects a photograph and then paints it. That's a cool €1.3 million. That's wonderful for her, isn't it? You have to remember that there's only one painting, while I have an edition of ten.' If you wanted to sustain the market for photography, you had to offer quality, Erwin understood. And a historic and labour-intensive technique such as carbon printing seemed more authentic, closer to the maker than a perfect but smooth digital print.

In his early days as an artist, paintings were unique and exalted objects, whereas photography was considered an applied art, at best. Photography seemed to emulate and even surpass painting's status in the late twentieth and early twenty-first centuries – a development that stagnated following the introduction of the iPhone in 2007 and, shortly thereafter, the proliferation of filters. Mobile phone photography was here to stay. The commercialisation of photography was not unwelcome to Erwin, even if he himself received only a small percentage – through the artist's resale right (ARR) or *droit de suite* – of the ever-increasing sums paid at auction. 'Secondary-market works selling for a king's ransom don't make me sad. On the contrary, it pushes up the value of your entire oeuvre.'

Impermanence was an ongoing issue: there was something absurd about collectors paying a fortune for a unique print that was destined to fade or discolour once hung above the sofa. A 'vintage' print from 2023 needed to be more durable than its predecessor from a quarter of a century earlier, yet look identical.

Hence his discussions with André Beuving. They have spent months experimenting with different kinds of paper in order to make the switch from digital to inkjet printing. Today, they examine test prints together to decide on the next steps. For years, Erwin's photos were printed by exposing photographic paper to laser light – now an outdated technique. 'I could be the only one still using those old machines,' says Erwin, 'but they are falling apart from misery by now. I'm dreading it, but it's time for a change.'

The plan is to switch to inkjet, a process that has improved considerably in the last decade. 'It's a different world,' explains printer and digital-image expert André Beuving. 'You use pigment, as in oil paintings, only much less and much finer. Pigments are less sensitive to various external chemical influences and therefore last longer.' Now that the decision has been made, it's all about the paper, which should resemble the original Lambda prints in colour and texture.

For specialist Beuving, the various *Royal Blood* prints – indistinguishable to a layman – each tell their own story. 'Each photograph has its own character. If you switch to ink, then you have to try to recreate the same texture as in the original image.' Erwin Olaf: 'No one would notice, by the way. Until you hang it in an exhibition.' Beuving: 'Occasionally I have to put on the brakes: hey Erwin, it's a work from 2000.

Then you shouldn't print *à la* 2022.'

If a client calls to say a print is starting to fade, 'I'll immediately swap it for a freshly printed one. I'll keep doing that as long as I live. And afterwards, my heirs can continue: the printer's settings are fixed, so you can make identical copies of my work forever. Only it may no longer be called "vintage" when I'm dead. And, of course, there'll be no more signatures. So if you want to buy something of lasting value from me, don't wait too long.'

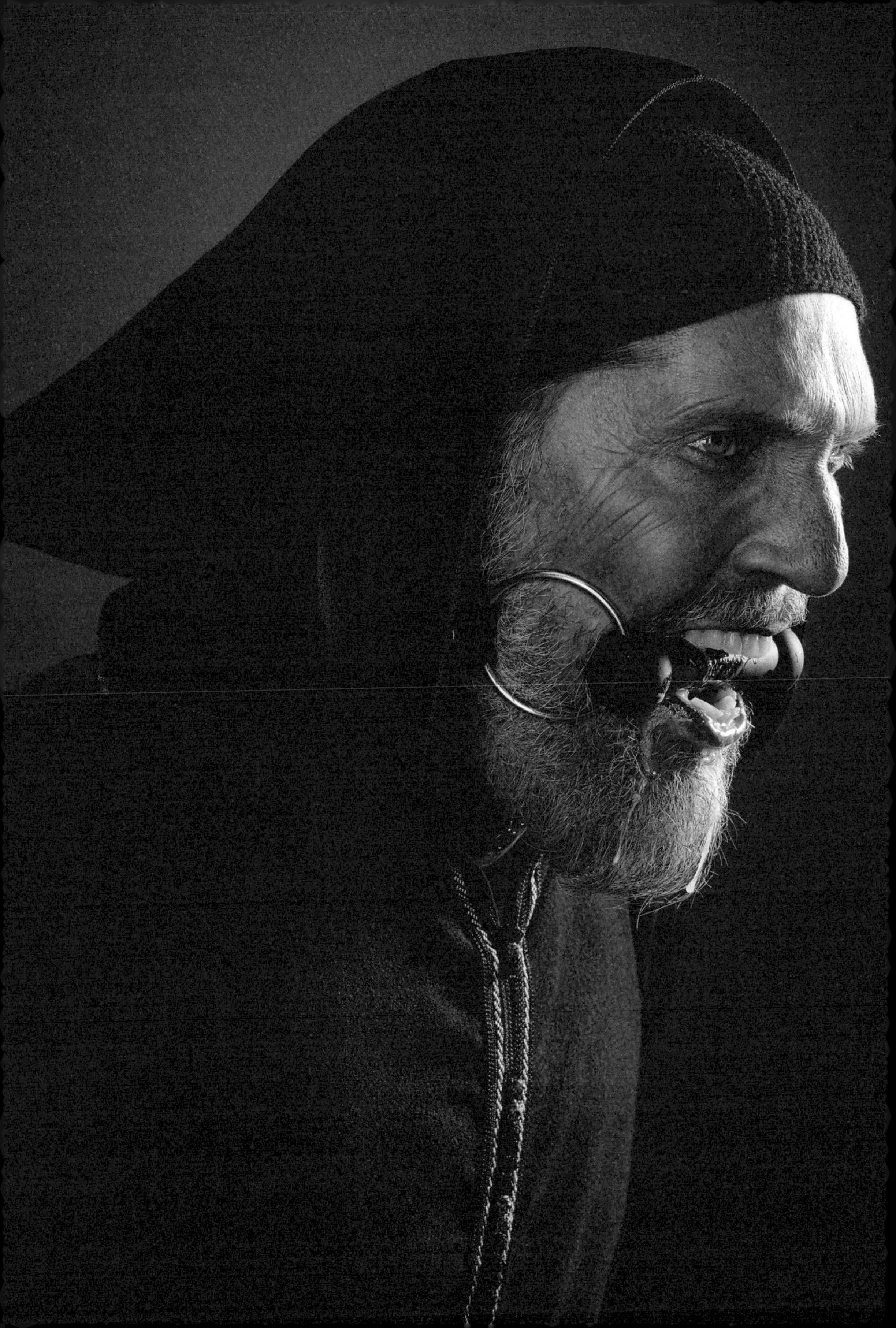

9 LEGACY (2015–2019)

'Let's pause our revelry on the edge of the volcano to remember all those who perished'

OUTRAGED AND GAGGED

'This will be my most political room,' Erwin remarks as he walks through the Haags Gemeentemuseum (now Kunstmuseum Den Haag). On this wintry day in early 2019, he is busy installing a major exhibition to mark his sixtieth birthday. For months, he has been meeting up with Wim van Sinderen. The photo curator, who has been following Erwin Olaf for more than thirty years, remains unabatedly enthusiastic. 'I see Erwin's openness, and the authentic self-discovery with which he has developed his oeuvre, as his strength.' Yet there are also points of criticism: 'He should loosen up a little – be bolder, more irrational. At times it is perhaps a little too reasoned, too contrived.'

They did not always agree, and Erwin would occasionally flare up, thereby disrupting the otherwise harmonious collaboration. When the dust had settled, the video work was given a place among the photographs, something that Van Sinderen disliked – 'moving images distract from the photographs' – but he had by then resigned himself to the decision (a win for Erwin). A separate exhibition on Erwin's photographic influences is opening at the Fotomuseum Den Haag, which is adjacent to the art gallery (a point for Van Sinderen). In addition to the black-and-white work from the 1980s and 1990s, the Fotomuseum is also showing the photographs that influenced and guided his 'thinking about photography'. In an earlier email to curator Wim van Sinderen, Erwin had compiled a list of twenty-one photographs that have been important to his work: 'I've critically reviewed the list and below are the works that shaped me as a photographer, made me think again, or pushed me in a different direction. And, even now, I'm still moved by these photographs.

1. Hans van Manen – *Pieta Self-Portrait*; 2. Horst P. Horst – *Mainbocher Corset*; 3. Pierre Molinier – *Untitled*; 4. Paul Blanca – *Self-Portrait Hand Nailed on Piece of Wood*; 5. Robert Mapplethorpe – *Self-Portrait*, 1980 (with cigarette in leather jacket); 6. Robert Mapplethorpe – *Man in Polyester Suit*; 7. Weegee – *Man arrested for crossdressing, New York*; 8. Helmut Newton – *Saddle I, Paris*; 9. Irving Penn – *Single Oriental Poppy*; 10. Joel-Peter Witkin – *The Kiss*; 11. Richard Avedon – *Marella Agnelli*; 12. Rineke Dijkstra – *Self-Portrait Marnixbad Amsterdam*; 13. Andres Serrano – *Piss Christ*; 14. Brassai – *Fille de joie Quartier de Italie*; 15. Christopher Makos – *White Trash Divine*; 16. Frances Benjamin Johnston – *The Hampton Album* 2; 17. George Platt Lynes – *Untitled* (naked man, in front of a hessian wall, with a hand in front of his crotch); 18. Henri Cartier Bresson – *Model Prison, Leesburg, New Jersey*; 19. Man Ray – *Noire et Blanche*; 20. Richard Avedon – *The American West, Beekeeper*; 21. Bernard Faucon – *Les Amis*.

Van Manen, check. Blanca, check. Mapplethorpe, naturally; and Avedon, Newton, Penn. Rineke Dijkstra received an email requesting a small print of *Self-Portrait Marnixbad* (1991). 'Now, there's invariably one of your photos that has given me a significant push... This image really made me think, both then and now. I still partly model my self-portraits on this image. I'm still impressed by the power in that vulnerability and its apparent simplicity. I would love for your work to hang among all this macho violence.'

The new *Palm Springs* series hangs in the first room; there is a separate 'royal cabinet', and at the back, the 'most political' room presents Erwin's explicit responses to some of the extreme events of the 2010s. He may no longer be a journalist, but he has never lost the urge to engage with current events. LED screens display his responses to the attack on the Bataclan concert hall in Paris in 2015. In the same room hang the self-portraits that he took after the attack on the editorial offices of *Charlie Hebdo*, together with a wooden sculpture addressing the New Year's Eve assaults on women in the city of Cologne, and a commentary on the covering of classical nudes in Italy following Iranian President Hassan Rouhani's visit in 2016. Several photographs from the *Joods* series also appear here because, as Erwin notes, 'anti-Semitism is unfortunately on the rise again'. He combined this series with black-and-white portraits from the *Morocco Project* (2004) – 'because they have to live side by side'.

Over the years, he had not only responded to anti-gay violence and other abuses via letters and advertisements, but had also reflected social developments through photographs and installations. When creating series such as *Chessmen*, he had not yet articulated what he would later elaborate in catalogue texts: namely, that the work revolved around 'human sexual-power games' in response to 'the homophobic rhetoric of politicians such as Ronald Reagan, Margaret Thatcher and Jean Marie Le Pen'. Yet his advocacy of inclusivity and self-determination was already evident in his early work.

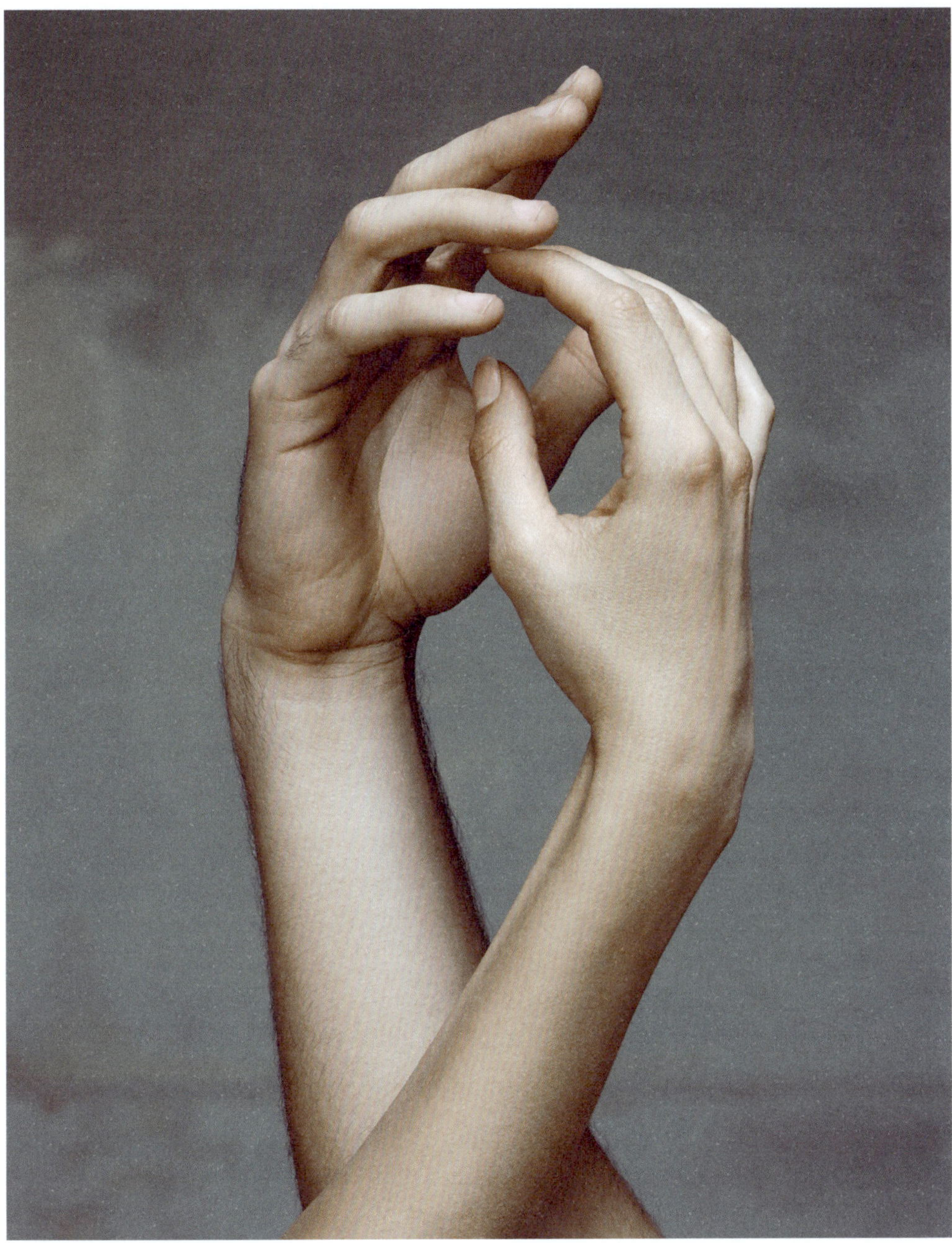

After Rodin VI, Cathedral, 2016 from the *After Rodin* series, photographs of the Dutch National Ballet commissioned by the Groninger Museum.

Photo on page 296: *Anger, Self-Portrait, 2015*, from the *Tamed & Anger* series, created in response to the assassination of the editorial staff of *Charlie Hebdo* on 7 January 2015.

At the parties he organised he gave free rein to his imagination, true to the one-liner he often repeated: 'If I want to see reality, I'll look out of the window.' At these events, as in his work, it was not so much aesthetics as his often less-than-subtle humour that took centre stage: 'I always laugh my head off at my own jokes.' Ultimately, the parties were about creating a sanctuary for 'birds of all feathers', a place where they could freely indulge their fantasies. 'That freedom, that enthusiasm, that diversity. I think there's a place under the sun for everyone. And I want everyone to feel like a star.'

At the Milkshake Festival in the summer of 2014, for instance, he presented the *Fat Brats*, men who derive pleasure from being 'squashed' by obese women. To heighten the revelry, he included bondage acts – some featuring 'latex-clad women', others with 'men and women in leather' – as well as erotic cage performances and 'live wax play'.

At the opening of the festival, however, the mood was far less upbeat. The news that a Malaysia Airlines Boeing 777, flight MH17, had been downed – as it would later emerge, by a Russian Buk missile – was only a few days old. Erwin asked festival visitors to observe a minute's silence for the 298 victims, including 196 Dutch nationals. Among those who perished were professor and AIDS researcher Joep Lange and several fellow epidemiologists, who had been on their way to an AIDS conference in Melbourne.

Visibly moved, he addressed some 2,000 extravagantly dressed ticket holders: 'Let's pause our revelry on the edge of the volcano to remember all those who perished. Among those innocent victims are men and women who have been pivotal in the decades-long fight against AIDS. They have helped slow the spread of this global scourge and, as far as possible, brought it under control. Without them, many of us here today would not be celebrating so joyfully.'

Art and celebration were inseparable from current events. In the years following that speech, Erwin's social engagement became ever more evident in his work. Homophobia was his primary preoccupation; it had become intolerable to him.

He spoke out against the homophobic language of certain Amsterdam columnists. 'We're always denigrated and made to feel like second-class citizens; we're judged on our sexual preference. When push comes to shove, as a gay man, I'm the lowest of the low.'

In Erwin's eyes, however, the growing influence of religion on ideas about homosexuality was an even greater threat than homophobia among the cultural elite. As a white man, he may have been privileged, but as a gay man, he was castigated by the majority of religions. 'What is preached and interpreted in the various scriptures is often the height of murderousness when it comes to homosexuality. I don't trust orthodox Jews and strict Protestant congregations one bit in that regard either, but radical Islam certainly sees us as the lowest of the low. It's a doctrine that can have dire consequences for me personally and for the wider gay community: people see us as lower than dogs and pigs. And they think we should be trodden underfoot, stoned or thrown headfirst from tall buildings.'

His vigilance had its origins in an incident years ago, when he was verbally abused outside his former studio – a manifestation of religious fanaticism and violence, according to Erwin. But the barbs never ceased. On one occasion a taxi driver signalled for him to cross the street, only to lurch forwards as Erwin stepped into his path. The driver shouted that 'gays have no right of way'. 'And recently a man hurled insults at me for several minutes: "Dirty, dirty homo, with your filthy, filthy, thin homo fingers, stick them in your dirty, dirty homo arse…"… I have to fight every day not to become bitter. The Netherlands can be very beautiful, but even here we live on quicksand. The most commonly used insult is "homo". Is anyone surprised, then, that gay schoolchildren are five times more likely to attempt suicide than other schoolchildren?'

The dangers of conservative Islam were, in Erwin's view, gravely underestimated. With his comments on the West's lack of resistance, he sometimes skirted uncomfortably close to radical right-wing theories that the 'self-hatred' and 'oikophobia' of the 'progressive West' would once again lead to its downfall. 'It would be great if we didn't keep pointing the finger at ourselves and stopped draping the cloak of love over everything.'

Film-maker and columnist Theo van Gogh's murder had already shown that, even in Europe, hatred was not confined to words. This was horrifically confirmed on 7 January 2015, when terrorists Saïd and Chérif Kouachi murdered twelve people in an attack on the Paris office of the satirical weekly *Charlie Hebdo*. Erwin's studio, along with the rest of the world, was aghast. Shirley den Hartog had never seen Erwin so distressed as on that day.

He felt compelled to respond directly to the events through his work, as this massacre of journalists and cartoonists was intended to silence artists, reporters and satirists alike. Erwin stood before his own camera as the model for the stark self-portraits *Tamed & Anger* (2015), a diptych in which he appears bearded and dressed in a homemade costume that referred to a strict religious dress code. In the images, his arms appear to be bound behind his back and his mouth is forced open by a bar gag, a BDSM device that renders speech impossible.

By portraying himself as both outraged and gagged, he sought to make viewers feel 'uncomfortable'. 'Am I defeated, or am I angry? I'm not a crusader. I believe in freedom of worship. However, leave me alone. Don't concern yourself with my sexuality. Don't obstruct my freedom of expression.'

It was time to reveal his activist side and make a direct political statement. '*Anger* comes closest to the fury I felt when I had just heard about the attack. *Tamed* reflects the feeling I have now: everyone picks up where they left off and things settle down again. Slowly but surely, a different set of standards is being imposed on us.'

Erwin's work had always engaged with social and political power relations, whether explicitly or indirectly, and he recognised that political content could come at the expense of art. The days when he photographed gay protest marches were long behind him. Yet he avoided the potential criticism of delivering an overly simplistic message by emphasising the ambiguity of *Tamed & Anger*: 'The older I get, the more I appreciate the absence of unequivocal answers. Which also means no unambiguous self-portraits.'

Unlike far-right politicians, he did not wish to target an entire demographic but only the extremist minority. When he attended the 'Amsterdammer of the Year' nominations a week after the attack, several students from a 'black' vocational college asked to be photographed with him. 'Very funny, I had a *Charlie Hebdo* T-shirt and that's how I had my photo taken with those girls wearing headscarves. Everyone always focuses on the negative. Anger fuels my work, but it's OK to be positive sometimes. I love that photograph: it shows everything I stand for.'

Later that year, again in Paris, it became even clearer that soft power was not working. On 13 November 2015, terrorists stormed the Bataclan theatre on Boulevard Voltaire. Eighty-nine music fans were killed during an Eagles of Death Metal concert. Shortly afterwards, the Palais de Tokyo invited Erwin – along with Anish Kapoor, Matthew Barney and Bret Easton Ellis, among others – to create a public artwork for the *Nuit Blanche* in Paris, an art walking tour scheduled for October 2016.

Seeking inspiration, he perched, as he often did, on his favourite Amsterdam terrace – Koh I Noor on Westermarkt – and watched the passers-by. 'Inspiration often strikes.' Sitting at his outdoor table, he realised that Paris was a 'beaten city' and that Museum Night would be extremely fraught. 'You then start to think: what do I want to say?' He decided to use the opportunity to make a statement about the Paris attacks and devised two video installations for the Hôtel de Ville, the town hall in the 4th arrondissement. On the top fifteen windows – each five metres high – he projected images of white faces with red lips in ever-changing expressions, through which he sought to convey 'the pain and emotions' of the terrorist attacks 'on innocent people who were making the most of their civil liberties'.

At the same time, he expressed 'the strength and flexibility of the open and therefore vulnerable democratic society' by presenting videos of fifteen naked people of varying ages and backgrounds. As a sign of their vulnerability, they slowly rise to their feet and raise their right fists, only to bow again. As always, both form and content played a part in the work. By morphing the portraits – *The Troubled* (the initial reaction of dismay to the atrocities) – and then, by filming naked people standing up and raising a fist in slow motion – *The Awakening* (a free person's response to terror) –

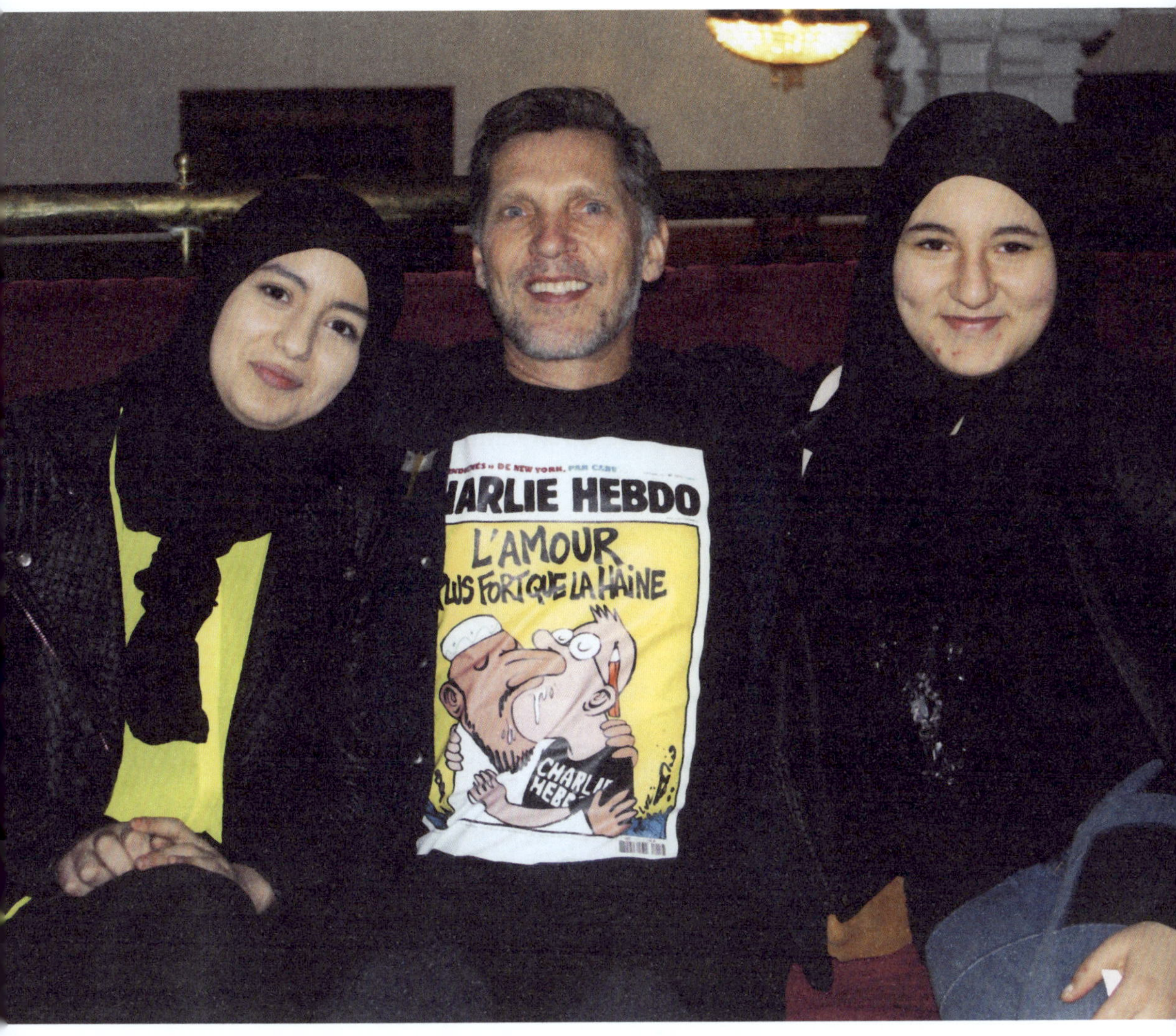

With pupils from the Montessori College Oost, 2015. 'I love that photograph: it shows everything I stand for.'

he wanted to explore the boundaries between photography and film. But above all, it was an intense response to the attacks. 'It's a three-minute cycle that reveals our vulnerability but also says: no matter how many times we're attacked, we're not going anywhere; we'll always get back up again.'

He called on new models and old muses, among them his childhood friend and fellow artist Frans Franciscus. 'Casting was crucial. I had a girl from Morocco, someone from Azerbaijan, a heavily pregnant woman, gay, straight, the whole shebang.' The video was filmed in Brussels with a camera that could stretch eight seconds to three and a half minutes with no loss of focus.

'There were fifteen of us; we had to undress, bend down and slowly rise again,' Franciscus recalls. 'Erwin rebuked me harshly on several occasions,' he laughs. 'As he also did when making a 3D statue of me after Rouhani's visit to Italy.' That statue, too, arose from anger over a current event. When Iranian President Hassan Rouhani made a state visit to Italy in January 2016, white plywood boxes were placed around the Capitoline Museums in Rome to cover centuries-old nude statues, as the president might be offended by the nakedness. Such a measure was not without precedent: a few months earlier, one of Jeff Koons's nudes had been covered during a visit to Florence by Abu Dhabi's crown prince.

Erwin's series *Skin Deep* (2015) is a straightforward homage to the naked body and to the skin itself. He sought to celebrate the human figure by linking it to painting. *Reclining Nude No. 1*, for example, refers to Gustave Courbet's *L'origine du monde* (1866). 'When you see that painting, you immediately say, that's fine art. But when I photograph the identical thing, it's seen as porn. I take great issue with that distinction.'

The covering of the nude statues in Rome was, in Erwin's eyes, not only a rejection of Western cultural values but also a personal affront. In protest against the free West's act of self-censorship, he resolved to create a nude sculpture of his own. This time it would be in three dimensions and in marble. He was furious – not only at terrorists and homophobic Muslims, but also at himself and at his fellow Europeans.

His statue was not intended to embody perfection but, on the contrary, to depict a rather ordinary middle-aged man whose physique leaves something to be desired. Frans Franciscus was once again asked to pose. The figure was to stand 140 centimetres high and be carved from marble. 'I had to stand naked and look upwards in anger,' Franciscus recalls. 'A guy with a 3D scanner circled me, capturing me from head to toe.'

Erwin sent the scans to Carrara, the Tuscan centre of marble extraction where, some half a millennium ago, Michelangelo ordered the stone for *David*. There, Frans Franciscus was mechanically hewn from the rock; details were added by hand, and the sculpture was polished to perfection. Erwin did not have to concern himself with

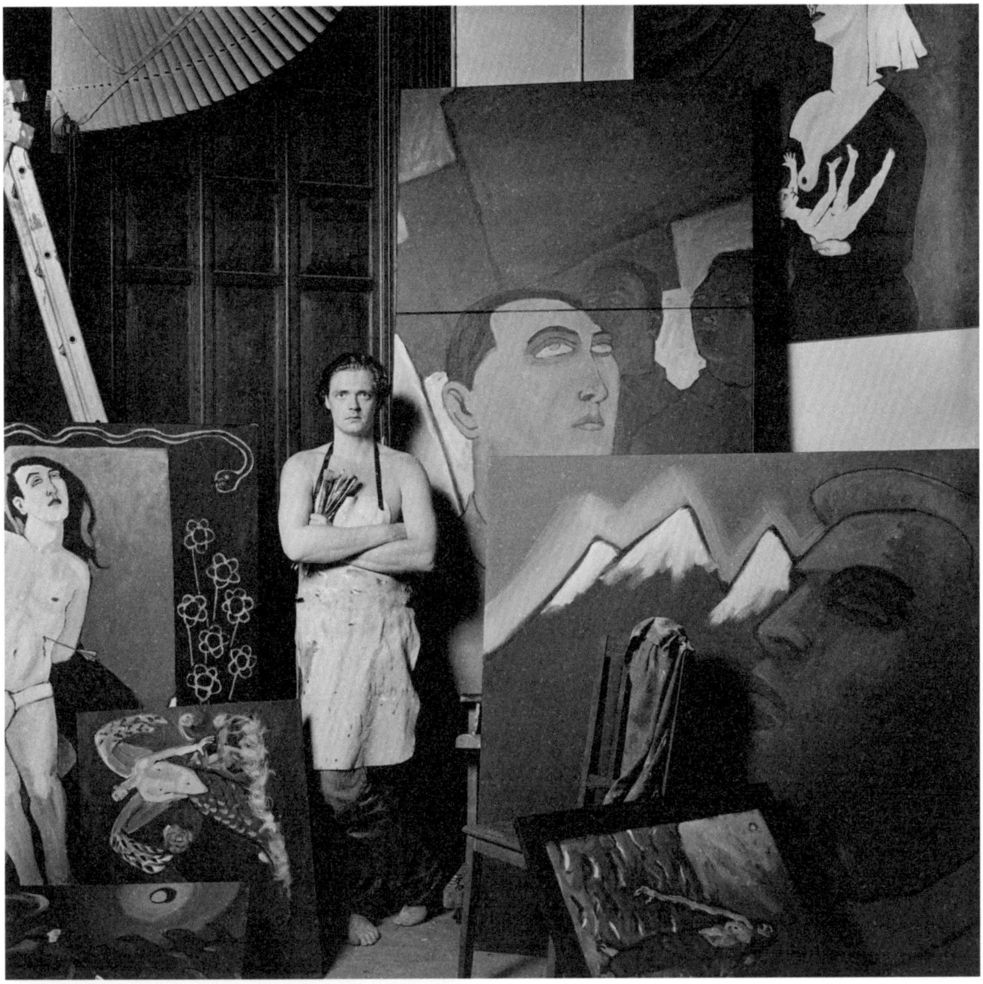

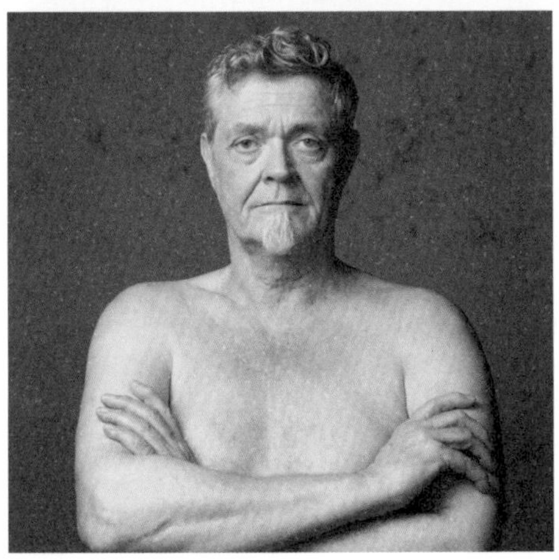

Top: Frans Franciscus in his studio on Plompetorengracht in Utrecht in 1985. Bottom: Photographed again in 2023 for the *Muses* series.

the process – much as Jeff Koons has his sculptures executed by others according to his instructions. 'Erwin has the ability to experiment – and then he sells those experiments,' says Franciscus. 'Most of the time, that is. Because it will be a hard sell this time round. Honestly, who wants that kind of work: a marble sculpture of a fat, naked, furious bloke in flip-flops?'

Erwin looked at Frans with different eyes: 'Perfect bodies are extremely boring to work with, to touch, and to appreciate. Frans, who is my friend, is a beacon of hope for us all. He stands tall, proud and open to the world: he is at peace with himself and with his own naked body, just as he is.' According to Franciscus, this was more a flight of fancy on Erwin's part than a reflection of reality. Be that as it may, the only copy of the sculpture ever produced, entitled *Rome, The State Visit, 2016*, would never be sold.

Erwin made another politically motivated, Koons-like foray into the three-dimensional world at around the same time: this time with a 2.5-metre-high wooden sculpture based on a 3D photograph. It was another satirical comment on the lax attitude towards those who, in his view, failed to acknowledge Western values. The work was prompted by the events in Cologne on New Year's Eve 2015, when a gang of young men targeted women celebrating at the train station. That night, 1,580 charges were filed for theft, violence, rape and assault in and around the station square.

The mayor of Cologne – who, as recently as October 2015, had been stabbed by a right wing fanatic because of her support for Chancellor Angela Merkel's refugee policy – responded to the outrages with advice on how women should behave. At a press conference, she stated that women should 'keep strangers at arm's length'. In Erwin's view, the subtext was clear: it is the victim, not the perpetrator, who is held responsible for the crime.

His outsize Rubenesque woman, carved from limewood, wears nothing but a bra – 'vulnerable, which is why it's such a strong image' – and stretches out her arm to keep her attackers at the safe, recommended distance. After exhibiting the sculpture several times, Erwin decided to burn the work and film this act of destruction. The video of the conflagration seems to allude to historical witch burnings. From that moment on, the video and the sculpture together formed the artwork entitled *Eine Armlänge Abstand* [At Arm's Length].

What had begun as a commentary on the events in Cologne soon transcended current affairs and, from then on, came to symbolise women's rights to respect and self-determination. In this, his response diverged from that of the far right. In Germany, the right-wing AfD party sought to make political capital out of the fact that most of the perpetrators had been identified as North African. It was viewed as a failure of Angela Merkel's policies, who had responded to the large influx of refugees in August 2015 with '*Wir schaffen das*' ['We can do it'].

Erwin, as a 'die-hard social democrat', did not want to be driven into the arms of

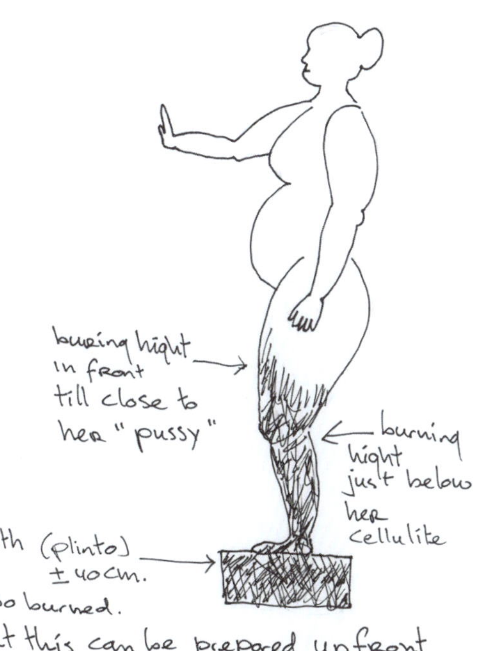

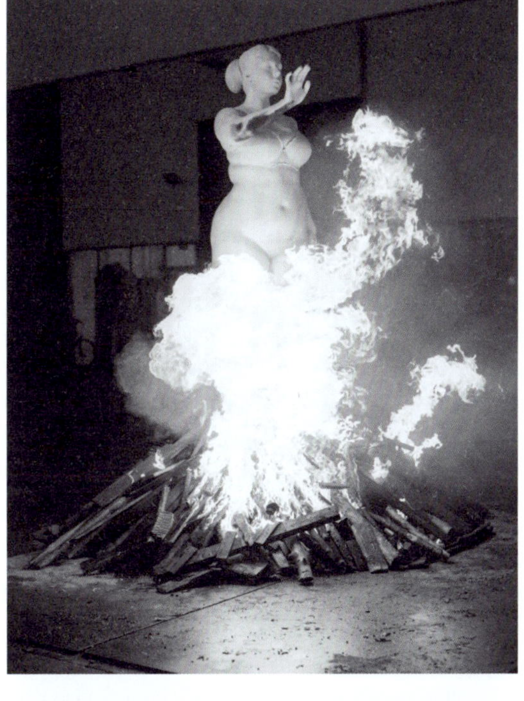

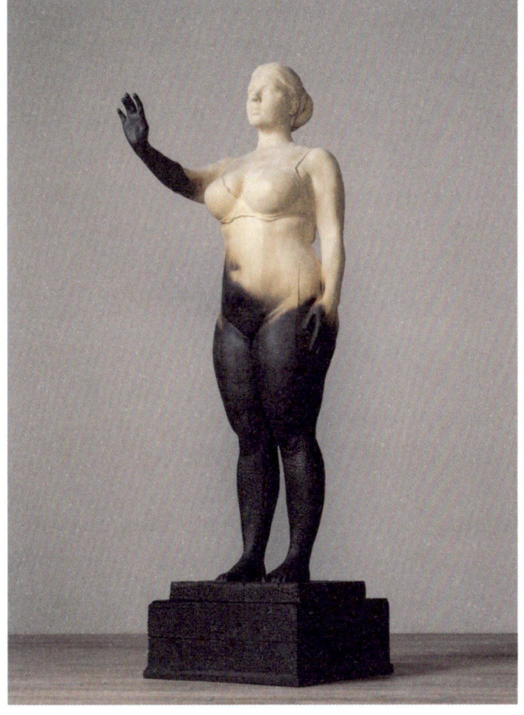

Preliminary design, burning and the finished work, entitled *Köln, Eine Armlänge Abstand,* 2016, [Cologne, At Arm's Length] created in response to women being sexually assaulted in Cologne on New Year's Eve 2015 and the mayor's response to the situation.

the far right. At the same time, the left seemed to turn a blind eye to his fear of radical Islam. 'I'm angry because, even when we've laid out all the facts, we never stare the monster in the face and say: this is happening, and this is how we'll respond. We've been trying to run with the hare and hunt with the hounds for far too long. We need to spell it out: anyone who comes here must accept society's soft side and abandon the machismo.'

He reached for the 'paid advertisement' weapon again that year, after a man armed with a semi automatic rifle and a handgun opened fire on patrons at an LGBTQI+ nightclub in Orlando, Florida, in June 2016. The gunman, a security guard born in the US to Afghan parents, allegedly killed in the name of ISIS. Fifty people died, including the perpetrator himself. The motive for the massacre was never established. Homophobia was suggested, but the nightclub – where the gunman was known to have made homosexual contact – might also have been randomly targeted. Erwin was convinced of the former: 'Someone walks into a gay nightclub and shoots as many people as possible while shouting *Allah Akbar* – what's so confusing about that, exactly?'

Again, there were critics who felt he had been too harsh and was wrong to drag religion into the debate. A spokesman for an LGBTQI+ advocacy organisation said: 'We will not allow ourselves to be set up against peace-loving Muslims or Christians.'

The anger of those years never left Erwin, even as he became increasingly ensconced in the establishment from which he had once liked to keep his distance. Together with colleague Anton Corbijn and other leading writers and artists, he joined the newly founded and prestigious Akademie van Kunsten [Academy of Arts], created to ensure that the voice of the arts would be heard in Dutch society and politics. The Rijksmuseum had also expressed an interest in acquiring part of his oeuvre.

Down-to-earth Rotterdamer Kevin Ray Edwards, with whom he tied the knot on 17 September 2016, proved a calming influence. Erwin had proposed to Kevin four years earlier from the sofa at home, while his fiancé stood in the kitchen over a pan of Brussels sprouts, which – in that heady moment of love and emotion – ended up spoilt and in the bin. From that day on, they wore necklaces bearing each other's star signs: Erwin a fish for Kevin (Pisces), while Kevin wore a crab for Erwin (Cancer).

For years, Erwin had introduced Kevin as 'my fiancé', until they finally stood in Amsterdam town hall, with his childhood friends Frans Franciscus and Marline Williams as witnesses on Erwin's side. The wedding, conducted by Amsterdam's social-democrat mayor Eberhard van der Laan, was reported in a news article. Erwin was amused by the fact that a gossip magazine also ran an illustrated piece about the union: at last, his mother's neighbours could read all about him.

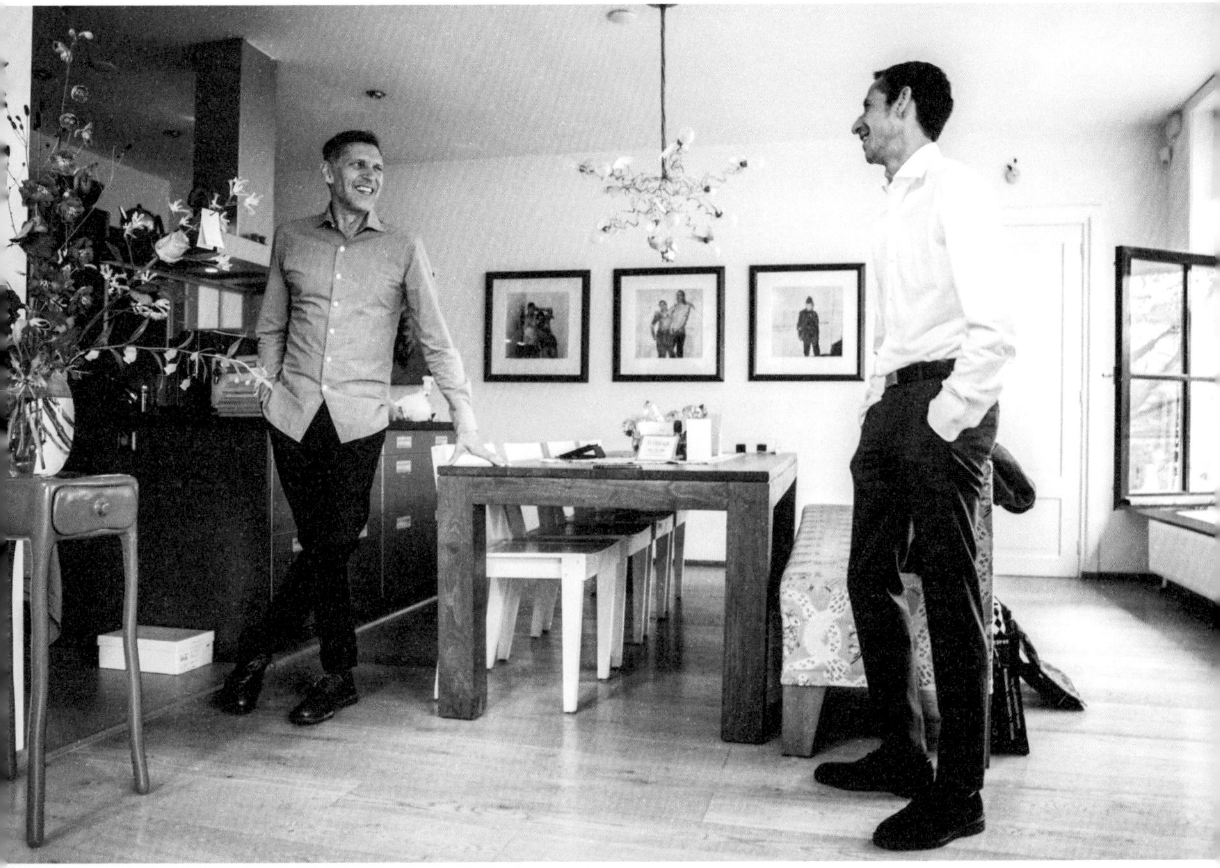

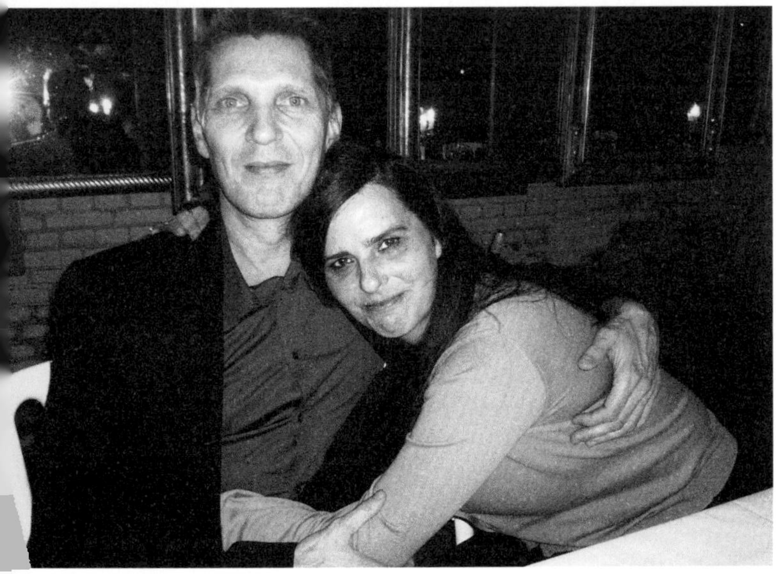

Top: Erwin Olaf and Kevin Ray Edwards at home on the Egelantiersgracht on their wedding day. In the background are photos from Max Natkiel's *Paradiso Stills* series, 1986.

Bottom: Erwin Olaf and Rineke Dijkstra in 2012.

'My mother taught me not to discriminate: everyone scored a perfect ten in her eyes'

AN OLD MAN IN HIS GLAD RAGS

Atop a mountain near Los Angeles, Erwin steps off the bus that has carried him and his crew to the summit. He walks about ten metres and collapses. For a moment, he fears he will take his last breath far from home, in California. It is autumn 2018, and he has travelled to the United States to create a new series. The final frames were to be shot in the Californian mountains, where fierce forest fires were raging at the time. The ash from the charred oaks and pines choked him; it was blisteringly hot, and the air at 1,800 metres above sea level was exceptionally thin.

Looking back on that moment from his sanctuary in Amsterdam, he chokes up once again at the memory of that day. 'I kept repeating to myself, "Erwin, keep calm." I went into survival mode and was panting like an old dog, unable to move forwards or backwards. I felt desperately ill, and my first thought was: I'm having a heart attack.'

He realised, with a jolt of shock, that his illness had entered a new stage and that he could no longer trust his body. His lungs couldn't supply enough oxygen and, as a result, his heart was unable to function properly.

The acute breathlessness was brief, but it was only one of many obstacles that threatened to derail the US sessions. Despite his meticulous preparations for the shoot, the entire fifty-strong team – the size of a modest film production, and about half the number of people who had accompanied him to Shanghai – was caught off guard by the announcement that Lida Springveld, Erwin's mother and his greatest supporter, had died at the age of eighty-five. Everyone was distraught.

Erwin and his mother were like two peas in a pod. He liked to call himself a 'mummy's boy', while Lida Springveld described herself as a 'protective mother hen'. She had always stood unconditionally by her son, no matter what he did or how extreme his work sometimes became. 'I inherited her creativity. And there was no evil in my mother, only pure love. She taught me not to discriminate: everyone scored a perfect ten in her eyes. I took that from her – although, in my case, the needle could drop to one in just a few seconds.'

Just a few years earlier, Lida Springveld had become dependent on a wheelchair. From being a strong woman with a sharp sense of humour, she had turned into a needy senior citizen, angry at her allotted fate. It changed their relationship. 'The wheelchair came between us, and I could only walk behind her for half an hour, talking to the back of her head.'

Before Erwin's departure for Palm Springs, his mother's condition had worsened.

He sought and received permission from his mother and brothers to photograph her on what would become her deathbed. He captured her surrounded by flowers and wearing her gold necklace – 'so much vitality, alongside that dying face'. During a visit to her care home, the petals fell from a bunch of peonies by her bedside. The symbolism did not escape him.

Back in the studio, he built a tent and photographed a vase of tulips in stop motion, taking a frame every minute for ten days, to visualise impermanence. The result was a black-and-white video of flowers blooming, wilting and dropping. He put it into a loop so that the process repeated endlessly. 'My mother's final weeks and the making of this work were synchronous. I didn't think much of the film at first. One evening, the camera failed and a lamp broke. And I just loathe watching something that isn't right. But once I'd ironed out the glitches, it became perfectly clear: this is what I want to say about my mother's death.'

Lida did not believe in euthanasia – on this, she was adamant. Erwin, true to his atheistic upbringing, did not believe in anything at all. 'I can't believe all this fuss about the afterlife. Do shrimps and amoebas have a life after death? My mother was afraid of dying, and she knew there was nothing on the other side. That seems disturbing enough.'

When the news of her death reached Erwin in America, it was not wholly unexpected – but nevertheless, it came as a profound shock. 'She was always on my mind – at least when I wasn't at work – because once I'm behind the camera, I forget everything and everyone.'

After the initial grief, he felt supported by his crew and experienced a surge of energy. Deadlines were tight, and his creativity soared as a result. In ever-sunny Palm Springs, he longed for a slightly overcast day – and he got it. The light acquired an almost mystical quality. 'There was an angel hovering over our heads in Palm Springs, and I like to think it was my mother.'

The plan for the series was not unlike the one he had devised for Berlin: move out of the studio and into the world, and then, in his own unique way, capture its zeitgeist. In Berlin, he drew parallels with the interwar period – democracy under threat, but also liberal morality. In Shanghai, he was struck by the vitality of China as an emerging world power but, on the flip side, also by the omnipresent power of the state. He saw how women and minority groups were oppressed and how many people lived in loneliness.

In contrast to China's economic boom, the United States – once the promised 'land of opportunity for all' – seemed to be in terminal decline. He chose Palm Springs for his American series because of its architecture and the lingering atmosphere of the 1940s and 1950s, the period in which the desert city became a haven for the old Hollywood stars.

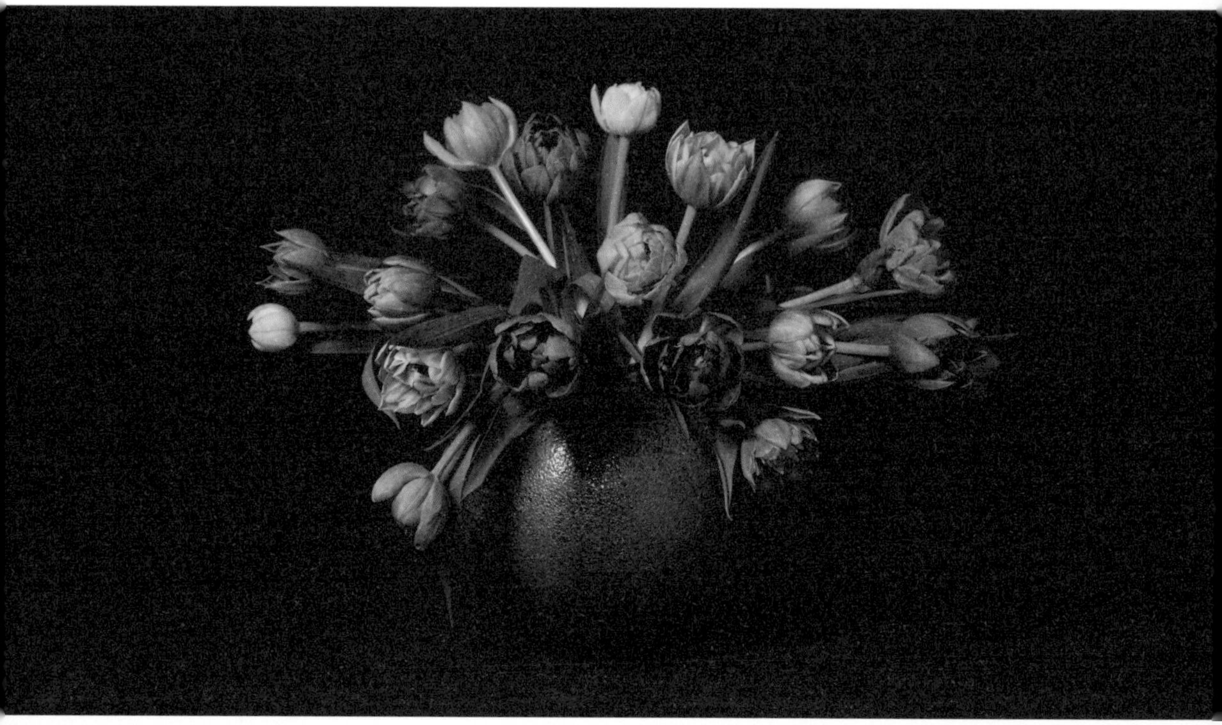

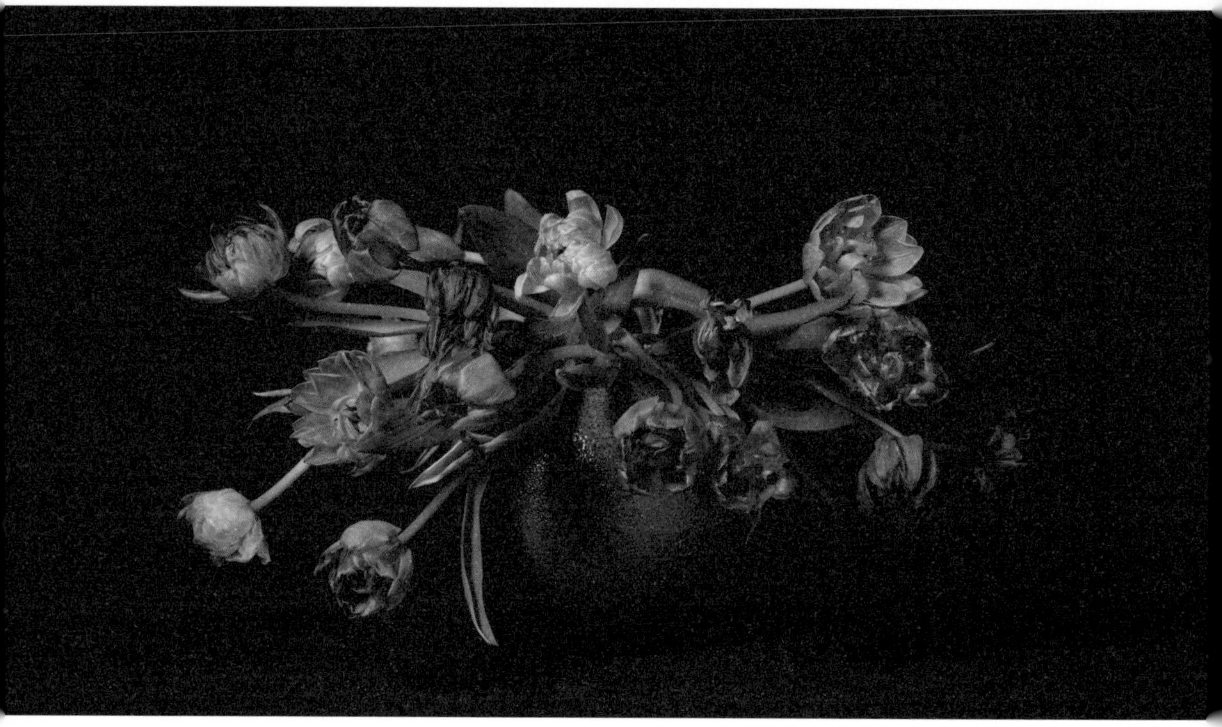

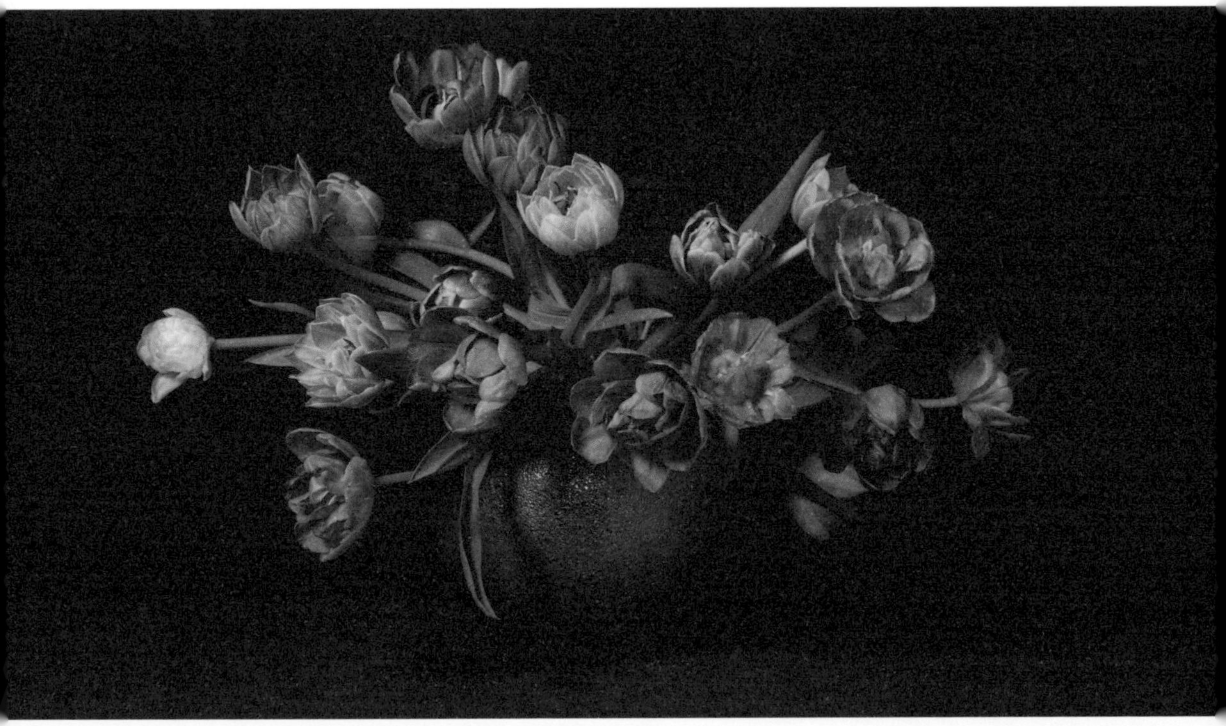

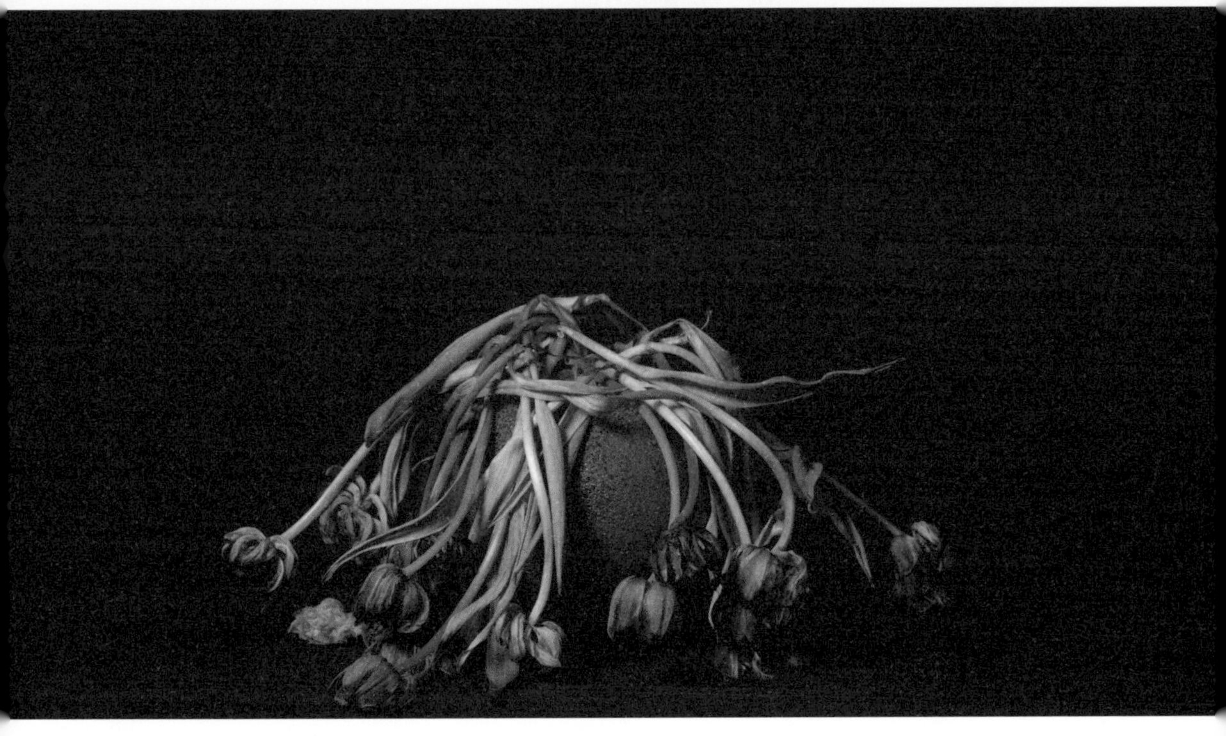

Stills from the video installation *Life – For Mom, 2018*.

'I love the dialogue with another time. The optimism and extreme artificiality of that strange city in the desert took me by surprise. First of all, there are the green lawns and swimming pools, but they soon give way to endless sand and desert.'

'I want to show an unattainable kind of beauty – the longing for the person you used to be'

Despite mourning his mother, Erwin was exhilarated to be working in Palm Springs. 'All the different techniques you need outside the studio were sending my work in a new direction. We immersed ourselves in the lighting methods of the 1950s and 1960s, when vast amounts of location work were shot with flashlights.' Whereas he had once sought out the limitations of the studio, the interplay between interior and exterior settings now added a new dimension to his work.

Current affairs occasionally found their way into the frame. See, for example, the picture of a girl on a green couch, entitled *The Family Visit, The Niece*. The gold crucifix around her neck refers to an abuse scandal in the Catholic Church of Pennsylvania, which had just come to light at the time. Children wore such crosses to signal that they had fallen prey to abuse. 'I wanted to tackle religion because it is so ubiquitous in the USA, and I was keen to photograph this girl, Jordana, because she seemed to carry this kind of secret with her.'

Meaning seeped into the photographs almost of its own accord – as is often the case, the theme of the series only became apparent to Erwin during the shoot. Orchestrating and fine-tuning the image from behind the camera – that was the real work. He would make impulsive, wholly intuitive decisions. 'My imagination collides with reality, and what emerges is often something I could never have predicted. No matter how well I prepare in advance, a great deal ultimately rests on chance. I don't start with a preconceived plan; that wouldn't interest me at all.'

He only realised during the photo shoot in the 1950s villa that the two boys – one white and wearing swimming trunks, the other black and dressed in military uniform – could never have swapped roles. 'When I made the sketches, I thought: I'll decide later who wears what. But back then – and actually still today – a black youth would never have been a credible cohabitant of such a vast villa complex. At most, he might have been employed as staff.' He positioned the boys with their foreheads touching, just as he'd previously photographed Teun and his new lover Jochem. Erwin said: 'it's a universally recognised sign of love, but also something distinctly masculine, like the locking of antlers, as opposed to a gesture shared between a man and a woman.'

In the spring of 2018, he'd written to his ex-partner Teun Frieszo, who was by then seriously ill, suggesting a double portrait with Teun's new lover, Jochem. But his real request was the idea of remaking *Getting Close* (1985), the double portrait with Teun, 'in which you partly hide your head behind my legs and I press the self-timer. It seems like the most beautiful way to capture time and decay.'

The idea had come to him while watching *Call Me by Your Name* (2017), a film that not only affected him deeply but also reminded him of his special relationship with Teun. The film had 'felled him emotionally', he wrote to his former love. 'I sobbed for hours, and merely writing this has reduced me to tears again. Over the film, of course, but even more so over my own experience of love – of which you've been such a big part. I suddenly realised how grateful I am for what we shared. That, like the amazing young protagonist, I experienced an all-encompassing, overwhelming infatuation – with you. Although we ended up fighting far too much, when I look back, I'm so incredibly happy that I had the chance to share this indescribable and overwhelming sense of love with you.'

He was pleased with the result of the remake, although, as always, he remained critical of his own appearance. He cared little about his attire but was mildly preoccupied with his physical decline. 'Just the other day, someone told me that almost every man eventually becomes a potato on a pair of skewers. I'm starting to reach that stage now.'

Realising that his grief for the irretrievable past was part and parcel of ageing and growing frailer, he lamented: 'There are things that I will never experience again.' With that zest for life uppermost in his mind, he stepped out from behind the camera in Palm Springs and into the frame for a variation on David Hockney's 1972 *Portrait of an Artist (Pool with Two Figures)*. 'In my self-portrait of the photographer, I want to show an unattainable kind of beauty – the longing for the person you used to be. You can put on your glad rags, but it doesn't change the fact that you're a clapped-out, sixty-year-old man, standing within the walled garden of paradise.'

On closer inspection, that paradise is disappointing: where the background in David Hockney's work is a lush green, in Erwin Olaf's you see desiccated, yellowed grass and a barren mountain. 'The production team wanted to spray the grass green. It's incredible that people are prepared to do that kind of thing for you, but it's exactly what I didn't want. The scorched grass lends beautiful poignancy to the contrived and artificial world of Palm Springs. It adds an additional layer, one that alludes to the climate crisis.'

This was once the playground of Frank Sinatra, who in the late 1940s built his villa – Twin Palms – in the resort. It is now available to rent for parties and holidays. 'Everyone had a pool, but the desert was extremely hot and arid. And this has only intensified over time.'

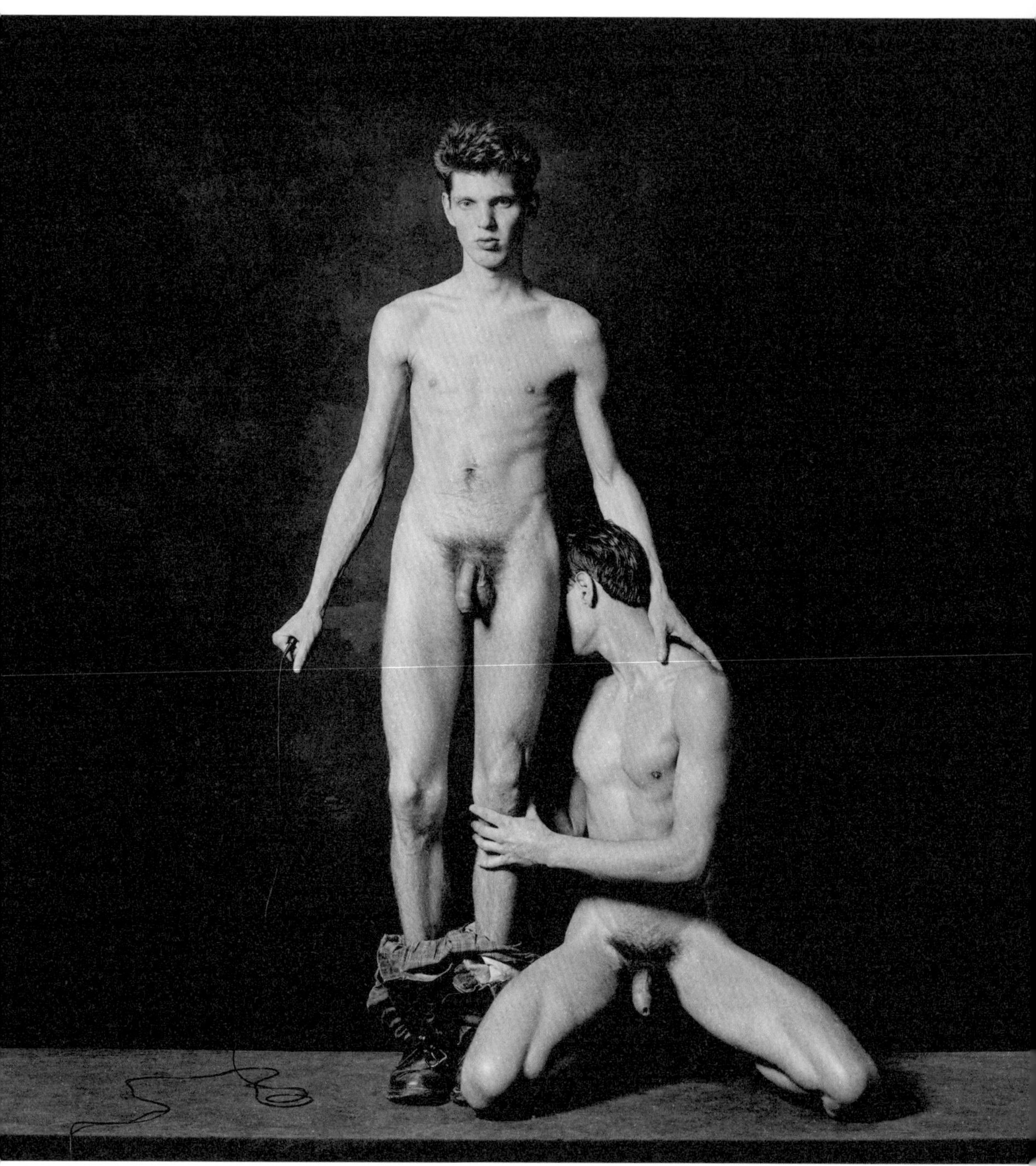

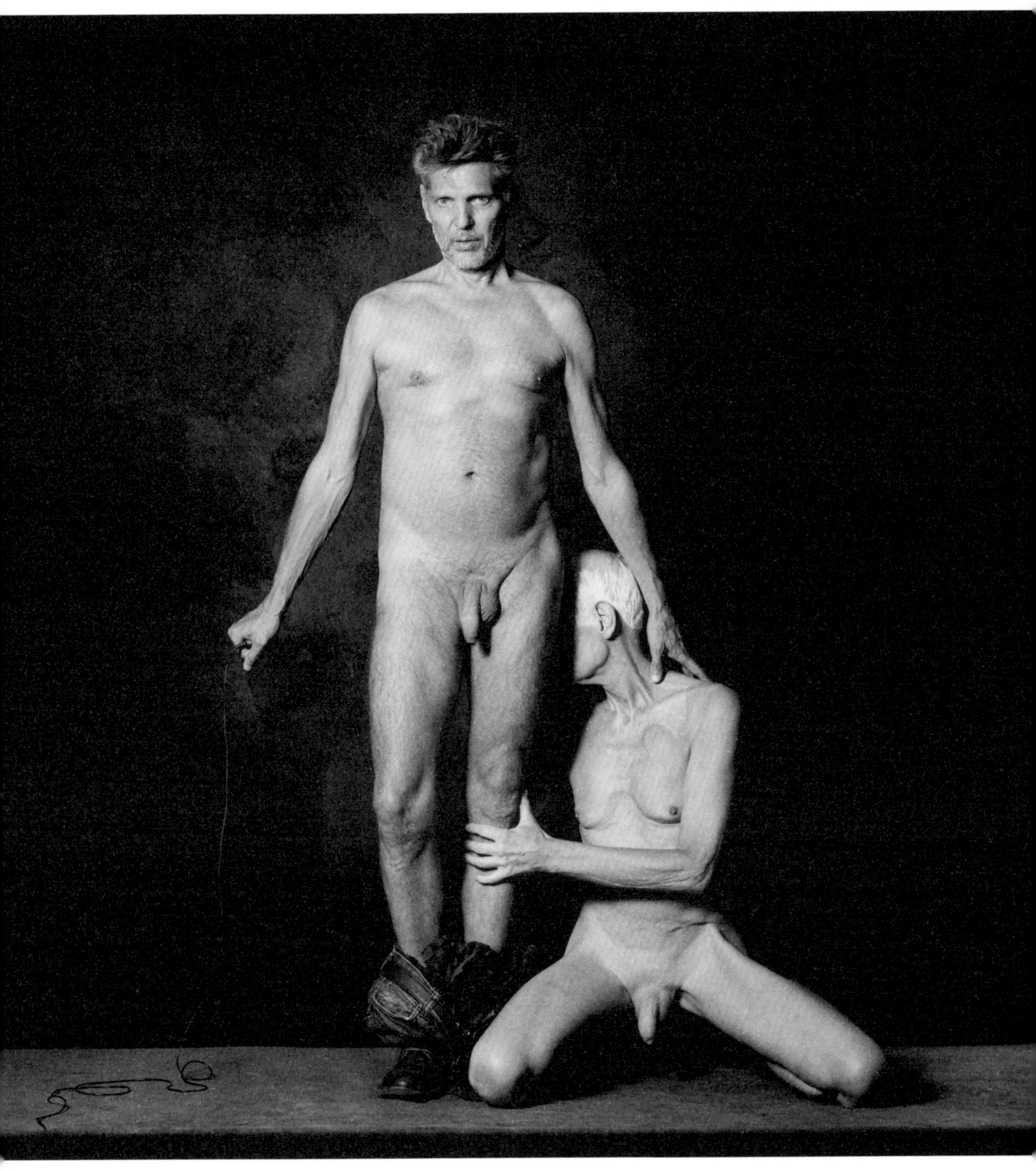

Erwin Olaf and Teun Frieszo in *Getting Close, 1985* and *Getting Close Again, Self-Portrait with Teun, 2018.*

'You only have to make one shitty film, and the faux pas will stick'

Before starting work in Palm Springs, Shirley and Erwin had visited Los Angeles to discuss Erwin's first feature film – an adaptation of *Een schitterend gebrek* by the renowned Dutch author Arthur Japin [published in English as *In Lucia's Eyes* and filmed as *A Beautiful Imperfection* in 2024, dir. Michiel van Erp].

It had been a struggle to find investors, but the final round of financing was almost complete. Everything seemed to be falling into place, and distributors in Germany and England were queuing up.

Erwin and Arthur Japin had met years earlier, when Erwin took Japin's portrait. 'Erwin's gaze is like his camera lens – large and questioning, open and searching. His studio reminds me of a seventeenth-century painter's studio,' Japin wrote in his diary. He later collaborated on a book about one of Erwin's series and, even then, was suitably impressed. 'If you embrace Erwin, you feel his steel biceps, but at other times you also sense his rapid breathing – short, laboured breaths. He folds his arms across his chest and raises his head as if gasping for life in a higher stratosphere.' (Arthur Japin, *Geluk, een geheimtaal, dagboeken 2008–2018*, De Arbeiderspers)

In January 2012, Erwin photographed Arthur Japin with his lovers, Benjamin Moser and Lex Jansen. The starting point was Peter Paul Rubens's painting *The Four Philosophers* (1611). In his diary, Japin described the sitting: 'I can't see Erwin's face, only his silhouette against the huge light box behind his back and, in front of it, his raised hand. A hand that hardly moves yet conveys exactly what he wants from us. The wrist sways smoothly, the fingers fanning like sheaves in the wind. Like a puppet, my head follows every movement. I respond to him and he to me. It's a dance – very clear, hypnotic – between us and the man behind the camera. For hours we dance.'

After the session, they discussed Japin's 2003 novel *Een schitterend gebrek*. Erwin was eager to film the story of Lucia, the first lover of the famous eighteenth-century womaniser Giacomo Casanova. Disfigured by smallpox, she used her deformity to her utmost advantage. Lucia dovetailed perfectly with his earlier work, which had often focused on misfits, exclusion and how to cope with it. 'I can't discuss *Een schitterend gebrek* without getting emotional,' Erwin told Japin. 'All my life, I've been concerned with people struggling with their appearance. I'd like to make one feature film in my life. Let me know if Stephen Fry re-releases the rights to your book.'

Erwin had observed how Anton Corbijn had successfully transitioned from photography to feature films, and since *Tadzio* – which had been only a modest success – he'd always felt the need to have a second stab at directing a feature film, because, as he put it, 'Photography is schooling; film is university.'

After Japin had agreed to the film adaptation, for which he himself would write the screenplay, Erwin soon began to have misgivings. Was a multi-million-dollar production not too much for him? How was he to keep his studio running in the meantime? How could such an undertaking be reconciled with his longing to retreat ever further into the peace and quiet of the darkroom? And above all, wasn't photography his true medium? 'With photography, you can tell the consummate lie. Everything can be staged, and the emotion I seek only needs to be visible for 1/100 of a second.'

It felt like a crossroads. He had to decide one way or the other, while also factoring in his illness and the limited time he would still be able to work. 'If something like this is going to take two to three years, I need to do the maths: how old will I be?' Moreover, it was a project fraught with risks. 'You can quickly shoot yourself in the foot with a new medium. You can spend a quarter of a century photographing the stars in the sky, but you only have to make one shitty film, and the faux pas will stick.' To premiere a film only to be written off in the media after two years of hard work – as had happened to Tadzio – was a galling thought. 'It's relatively easy to recover from a bad photo shoot. You feel rubbish for three weeks, then you think: I'll get my own back. And you eventually make even better work. After a lousy film review, you languish in the doldrums for what seems like an eternity, and it makes it much harder to get a new feature film off the ground.'

On the other hand, he still wanted to film *Een schitterend gebrek*, which he considered a masterpiece. He planned first to take a short directing course in Los Angeles; after all, directing actors was completely different from photographing models. He realised that, in the past, he had sometimes been overwhelmed by the power of actors and actresses – a feeling he needed to overcome. The film weighed on his mind during the Palm Springs project, and his anxiety mounted. The tightness in his chest was already hampering his ability to manage a week-long session with a large team. How on earth would he cope with a three-month film shoot in one of the hilliest and hottest parts of Italy?

After pressing the shutter for the last time, Shirley, Erwin and the team drove straight to the airport – they needed to reach the Netherlands in time for Erwin's mother's funeral. 'I landed and slid the door of the production bus closed. I looked at Shirley and she looked at me. We both thought: I've got something important to say.' Erwin was the first to unburden himself: 'I'm not going to make the feature film.' Shirley replied: 'I was just about to tell you not to do that film.' That sealed the deal.

Back in the Netherlands, he notified all the interested parties. While at the producer's doorstep, he phoned Arthur Japin to impart the bad news. 'It's not going to happen. Our film. I can't do it, my health ... I can't make *Een schitterend gebrek*.' He felt wretched about abandoning the film. 'Six years of our lives! And we've come SO far! The money, the script, the goodwill – everything is in place. We're ready to roll.

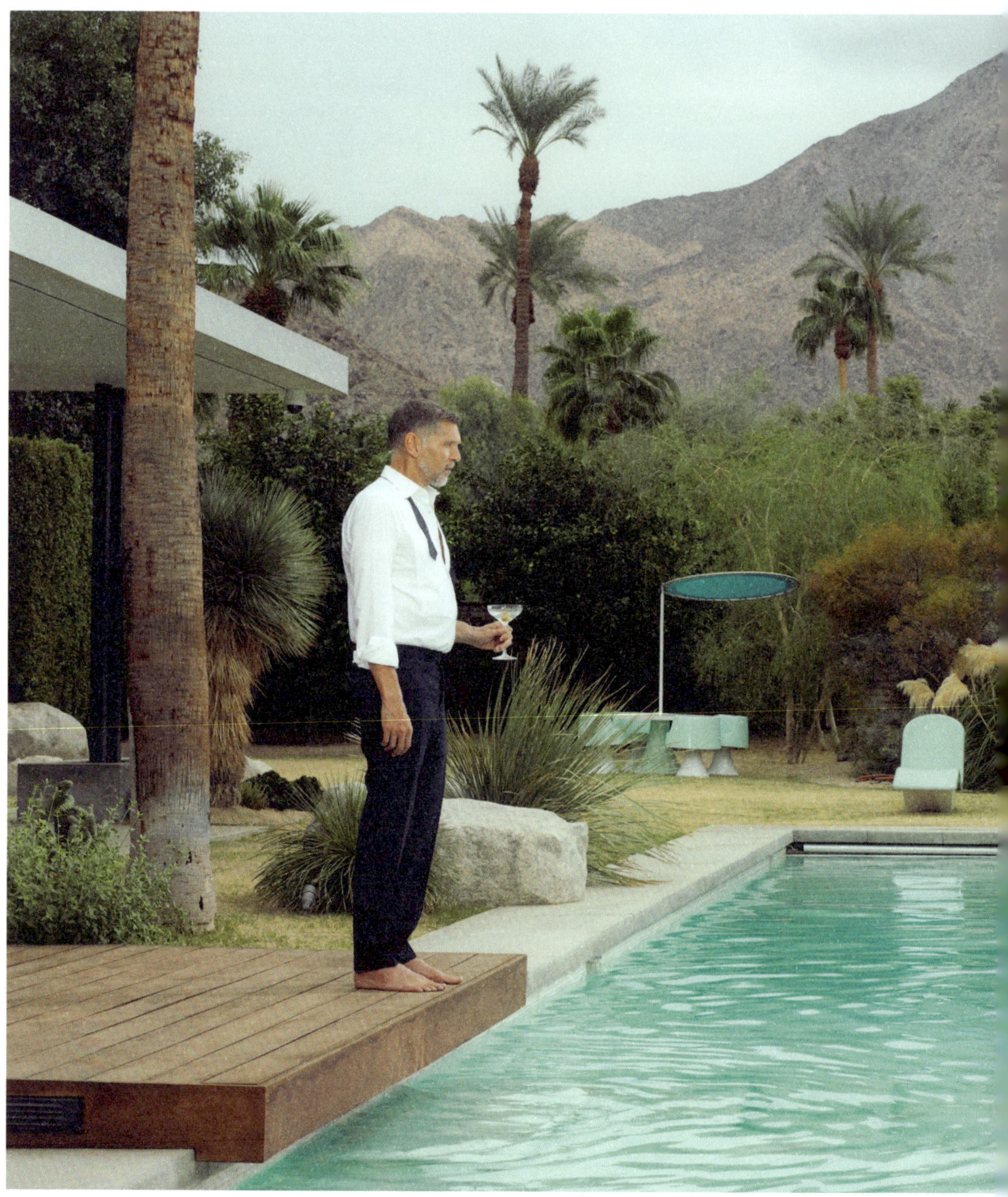

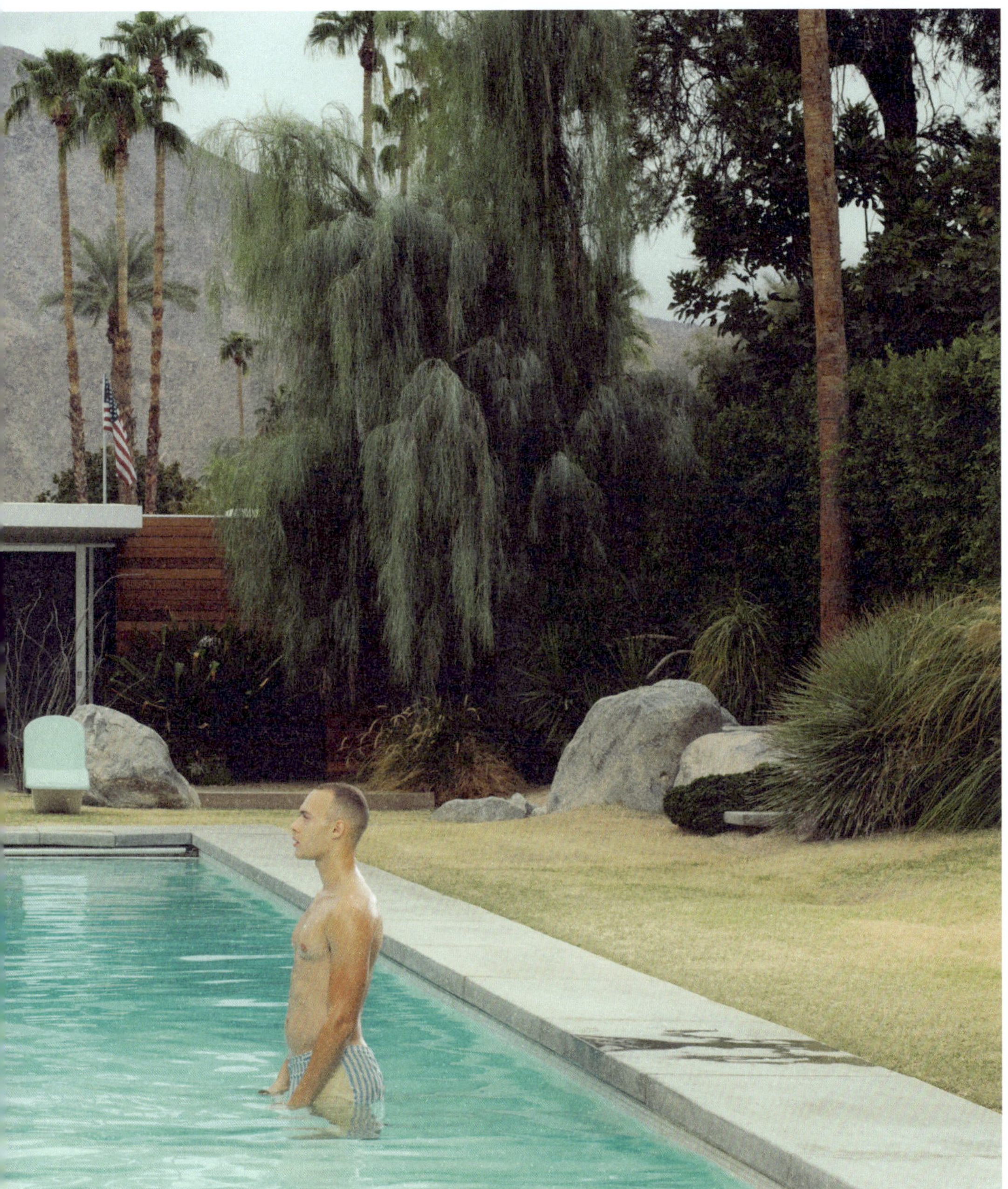

American Dream. Self-Portrait with Alex, 2018, from the *Palm Springs* series.

But you know how things are, Arthur; I know what I'm up against.' Japin had long dreaded this moment, he wrote in his diary. He did not blame Erwin at all; on the contrary, he felt sorry for him.

Erwin was conflicted. In the past, his professional decisions tended to revolve around others, but now he realised: 'This decision is not about anyone else; it concerns me. About how my life fell apart while I was dreaming about the film. After imagining you'll live forever, it's a devastating thought.' No one tried to persuade him to press on regardless. 'Because I've never exaggerated my illness, not for a nanosecond, and everyone knows the true extent of my condition.'

In one fell swoop, he also cancelled a major commission from Citroën. The assignment involved visiting seven countries over the course of two months. 'I'm really a sick guy now. I'm not going to stop working, but on the other hand, I ain't seen nothing yet, my body is going to suffer even more. I have to start making plans.'

At Lida Springveld's funeral – 'she left us after a difficult struggle', read the death notice – were the three brothers, their partners and five grandchildren. It was a beautiful, sunny day and a sober gathering.

Erwin asked his brothers and sisters-in-law for permission to exhibit the tulip video and the photographs of Lida on her deathbed. The video *Voor Ma* (2018) [For Mom] posed no issue, but the brothers struggled with the idea of showing Lida in her final stages of life. Erwin decided that the withering and blossoming tulips were significant enough: 'This is my mother. Much more so than the photos of her deathbed.'

After the funeral, Erwin received, not for the first time, a serious warning from his lung doctor. He would not survive a bout of pneumonia and henceforth needed to avoid winter in the Netherlands. Erwin first travelled to Vietnam with Kevin, trying to outrun his illness. Back in the Netherlands, he called his staff together to tell them he wanted to tread new ground, which would have consequences for the studio: it had to downsize drastically. 'My body says: stop,' he told his team. 'And reconciling myself to that decision brings me peace of mind – even though I'm staring into the abyss.'

'The Rijksmuseum... is the opposite of having your work disappear into the rubbish bin after your death'

JUBILEE YEAR

The streets around Studio Erwin Olaf on Amsterdam's IJselstraat are crowded with fans and bargain hunters. Through a side door, they are admitted, one by one, into the inner sanctum, where a huge sale is underway. In late October 2019, a jubilee year had come to an end. The exhibitions in The Hague and at the Rijksmuseum had closed – and Erwin had, for the time being, stopped complaining that his work was always overlooked.

But after a tsunami of accolades and publicity, he had crashed back to earth and was manning a market stall in the middle of the studio. He was touting his wares in the company of Kevin, Shirley and assistant Ruben. They were surrounded by stacks of books, his photographs and volumes by Norman Mailer (*Marilyn*), Bill Brandt and David Salle, among others. Also on sale were all the props – drums, footballs, lamps, an axe, and a dildo – that had accumulated in the studio over the years. The proceeds were earmarked for a 'super decadent' Christmas meal with the staff.

There is a strategy behind the clearance. 'We've agreed to keep going for another five to seven years,' says Erwin. 'I want to make sure Shirley and Kevin are well looked after. The rest will manage.'

Erwin wants to break new ground with a clean slate and in peace, to enjoy more freedom, with Shirley as the business anchor. Although he does not feel he has anything left to prove, stopping completely is not an option either because his physical decline seems to go hand in hand with a surge of creativity. 'It feels miraculous. My pictures are sold worldwide – from Seoul to Paris, from Amsterdam to Shanghai – and, more recently, at my new gallery in New York, Edwin Houck.'

Erwin had yet to celebrate his sixtieth birthday in grand style. He had postponed the huge party at pop temple Paradiso due to his faltering health. The idea had been to use it as a fundraiser for the victims – whether homosexual or simply outside the norm – of school bullying. 'I'm going to put my nose to the grindstone because I know, from personal experience, how much bullying hurts. You're scarred for life.'

The postponement was only a minor hiccup in the year 2019. After the major exhibition in The Hague, Michiel van Erp's documentary *The Legacy* and the Dutch postal service's series of stamps featuring his photographs, the opening of the Rijksmuseum's exhibition on his birthday was the final highlight of the year. 'Without a shadow of doubt, this has been one of the best years of my life', said Erwin.

After the exhibition in The Hague – with 328,000 visitors, by far the best-attended Dutch photography exhibition of all time – it was now the Rijksmuseum's turn. For three months, a selection of twelve of Erwin's photographs was shown in 'a very chic, modest exhibition', to use his own words. His work hung in the galleries – the presentation was not so modest in reality – alongside works by forefathers such as Jan Steen, George Hendrik Breitner and, above all, Rembrandt van Rijn.

Erwin had a long history with Rembrandt. When he was eleven or twelve, he visited the Rijksmuseum on a school trip. The young boy admired *The Night Watch*, but it was Rembrandt's *Self-Portrait* from 1628 that made the biggest impact. Half a century later, his fascination remains undimmed. What continues to intrigue him, even after all these years, is Rembrandt's treatment of light and how shadow obscures the most prominent facial features – a technique not unlike a backlit photograph. The young painter's daring approach, according to Erwin, demonstrates his individuality and courage. No matter how many times he visited the museum, he could never resist stopping to look at *Self-Portrait*. In 1985, it had inspired his own – no less bold – self-portrait, *Cum*, from the *Squares* series, in which Teun's sperm drips down his face.

That twelve of his photographs were juxtaposed with the Dutch Masters in the museum's Philips Wing was an immense honour, but also akin to raising the middle finger at the Stedelijk Museum on the south side of Museumplein – that temple of modern art where he had never gained a foothold. 'Nothing is more frustrating than being ignored by the people from whom you seek recognition,' observed Martin Rogge of the Flatland Gallery. 'That dissatisfaction and thirst for recognition trouble Erwin, but at the same time it is also his driving force.' It had been an infuriating start to the year. Erwin was excluded from an exhibition in Zwolle, dedicated to the fifty most important Dutch artworks from 1968 to the present, whereas his peers, such as Rineke Dijkstra and Hans Eijkelboom, had made the cut. 'So much the better that other people do recognise him as a great artist,' Rogge said. 'And above all the Rijksmuseum, which, with an eye to the future of Erwin's work, is a more important institution than any other.'

Erwin's first professional contact with the Rijksmuseum dates back to 1996, when he took a square-format, black-and-white photograph of the outgoing director. Four years later, Erwin donated the *Blacks* series to the museum, which had only begun assembling a collection of mostly Dutch, French and American photography in 1993. The bond was further strengthened when, in 2010, Louis Vuitton donated the series of portraits of Dutch celebrities – Dick Bruna, Johan Cruyff, Janine Jansen, Hans van Manen and others – that they had commissioned from Erwin.

As he cycled through the passage beneath the Rijksmuseum, on his way from the Jordaan to the Rivierenbuurt, he mused fondly about the painters he most admired in the museum. Like those Old Masters, he did not set out to capture reality, but to

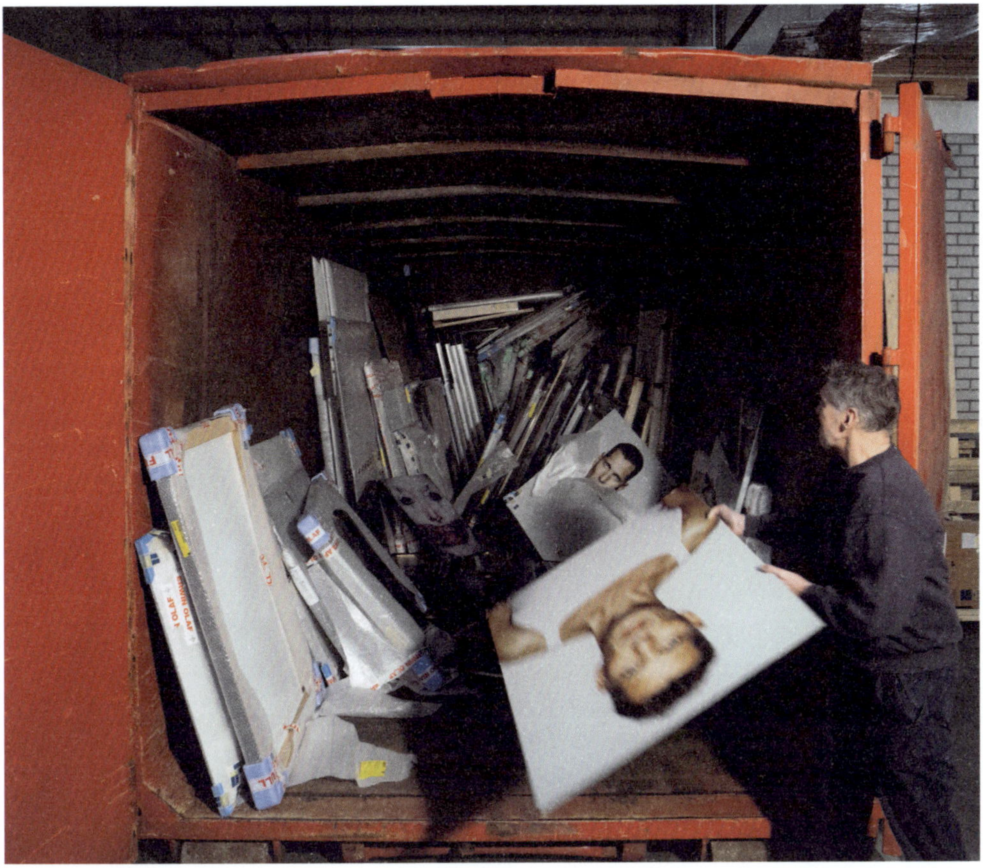

Reason enough for a clear-out: Erwin wants to start afresh and explore new avenues in peace and quiet. Bottom: The PostNL stamps issued in July 2019 with a print run of 95,000 copies.

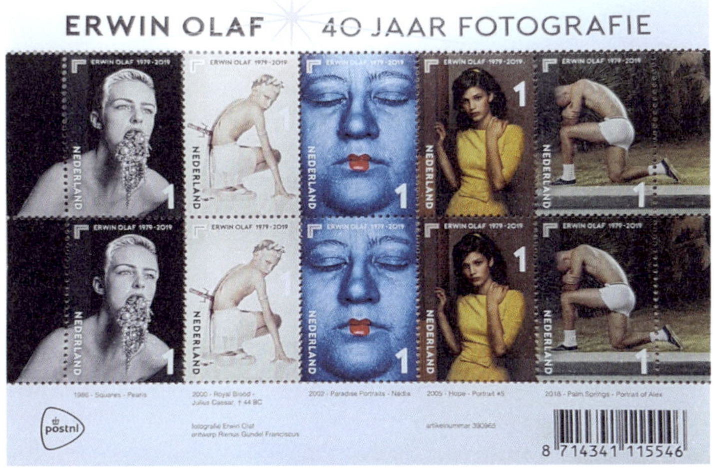

make tangible the image in his mind's eye. As well as Rembrandt, he had also learnt much from Vermeer, especially about light, composition and the narrative aspect of an image. He was keen for *Erwin Olaf Volume II*, published by US publisher Aperture, to be presented at the museum in winter 2014. He designed a temporary installation featuring photographs from his new series, *Waiting*, for the exterior of the museum and, for the interior, two video screens displaying the same images. The project was eventually cancelled by the fire brigade.

Two years later, the then museum director decided that Erwin would be the perfect curator for the fashion exhibition *Catwalk*. It became a quirky selection from the fashion collection of the past three centuries, displayed in an unusual installation – the catwalk was, for example, a reclaimed sushi conveyor belt. It seemed, Erwin humbly thought, that this was the furthest he could go 'as an ordinary, jobbing photographer'. Yet the idea of one day showing his work in the museum kept gnawing at him.

Then Taco Dibbits, who was to take over that same year, called round to sound him out about some form of collaboration. 'An exhibition sounds perfect,' Erwin said. But that was not Dibbits's primary concern – he wanted to discuss acquiring Erwin's work for the permanent collection; because, as he put it, 'I'm not talking about three months; I'm talking about 150 years minimum.' Only after the director left did Erwin realise the import of the conversation: if it happened, his photographs would become part of the national art canon. 'Which is the opposite of having your work disappear into the rubbish bin after your death.'

Dibbits's proposal aligned with Erwin's desire to demarcate his oeuvre and, from the hundreds of thousands of photographs he had taken, to keep only the very best examples. He had long been chipping away at the immense task, but was now champing at the bit – his illness and limited lifespan made everything seem more urgent. That the Rijksmuseum considered his work of national importance and wanted to add it to its collection of over 700,000 works on paper, including photographs, prints and drawings, was a welcome boost. Nevertheless, he recognised that it would be the art historians of the future who would decide whether his work should hang next to Rembrandt – or not.

He struck an honourable deal with the Rijksmuseum. He agreed to donate 412 photographs and seven videos, plus journals and books. These were artists' proofs with no tax value, since the Rijksmuseum is a non-commercial institution. In addition, the museum paid €200,000 for sixty photographs and three videos.

Hans Roosenboom and Mattie Boom, curators of photography, made the selection. In Erwin's company, they spent three years immersed in his archive – an intensive operation almost without precedent in the history of the photography department.

Through the deal, the museum acquired photographs that are more fragile and perishable than most paintings and prints, but curator Boom had no qualms. 'We're equipped for that: we have three photo conservators on the team and, furthermore, the prints are preserved at the optimal temperature in our underground stores – colour prints need to be kept slightly colder than black-and-white ones. When we receive a loan request, the lux hours are always calculated, because every time you exhibit photographs, you diminish their lifespan.'

On the day of the official handover, a white-gloved Erwin signed the prints from the *Grief* series. The atmosphere was solemn, as if everyone was only just realising that what had once been 'just a photograph' was now a bona fide artwork and part of the national patrimony.

Museum director Taco Dibbits was called upon to mark the occasion. Erwin's work fits into the Rijksmuseum's tradition, he explained of the donation. 'We show how our visual culture is created. Erwin is part of that tradition, but at the same time, he also redefines it. For an entire generation, he has determined, quite literally, the world of images: how we look, and how we photograph ourselves.'

The true issue is what exactly is being preserved 'for eternity', says curator Mattie Boom. After all, the original of the recent work is a digital file, while for the analogue photographs it is the negatives – and all that material remains safely stored in the vault on the IJselstraat. 'Erwin signs the contemporary prints, and this makes them unique,' says Dibbits. 'The vintage prints from the 1980s and 1990s are exactly that. When you look at them, you can see the passage of time. You can sense that these are older photographs, and this connects you directly to the period in which they were made. The donation includes some very explicit images, which are not just artistically important but also evoke the spirit of Amsterdam in the 1980s and, more generally, the wider Netherlands. Erwin is a seminal figure in this era and a prominent activist during the fight for gay rights.'

That might all be true, says Erwin, but he has also fought tooth and nail to prevent his work being categorised as 'gay' by the art world and cultural elite. Although he has never hidden his sexual orientation, and has stood resolutely on the front line of the battle for LGBTQI+ rights, he is adamant that this does not mean his work is 'queer art'.

'Then again, this is an image from a very recent series,' says Dibbits, as he unflinchingly points to *Barbara* from the series *Grief*, while Erwin signs the print. 'The staging evokes one of Rembrandt's greatest paintings, *Jeremiah Lamenting the Destruction of Jerusalem*. Both works deal with loneliness and grief. Taken together, a series like *Grief* allows us to see the paintings in our collection anew, through the prism of Erwin's photography.'

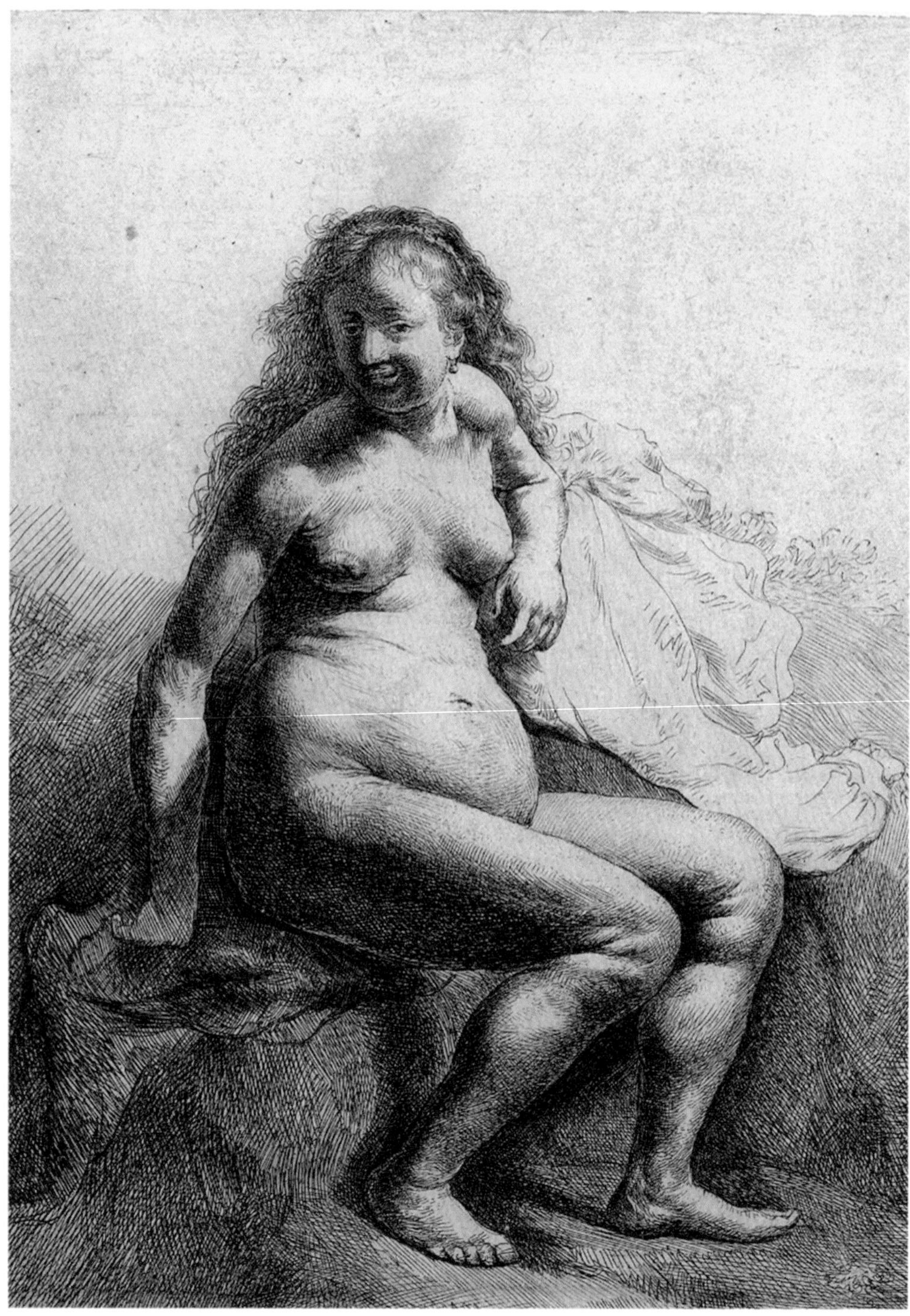

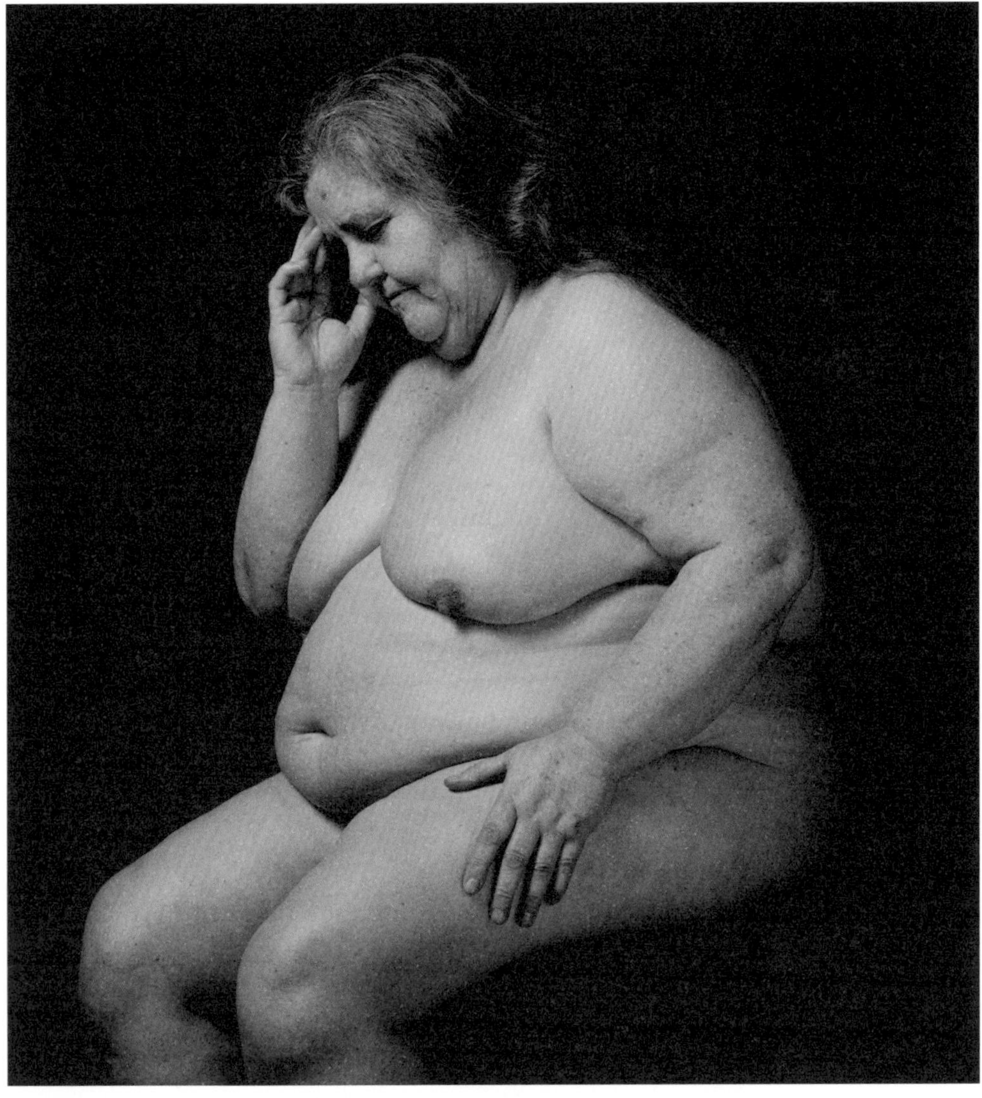

Left: Rembrandt van Rijn, *Naked Woman on a Mound*, c. 1631.
Right: *La Penseuse* [The Thinker], *1987*, from the *Squares* series. Model: Marie de Nooyer.

Erwin, meanwhile, signs *Troy*: a young man on his knees in a 1950s interior, wiping away a tear with his right hand. 'I have to retouch this one; there's a tiny blemish. Look, the interior needs to be more masculine in this work, so the overarching design is more angular.' Pointing to a flower painting on the wall in *Troy*, Dibbits says: 'It's extraordinary that you consider magnolias to be masculine, Erwin. And does that decanter on the cabinet contain whisky? It all seems so obvious, just as we know, almost without looking, that there's a loaf of bread on the table in Vermeer's *Milkmaid*. Yet nothing is accidental – the artist calls all the shots; everything is staged.'

More than six months after the ceremonial handover, Erwin, Dibbits and the museum staff reconvened to prepare the exhibition. Selecting from the donation was a difficult enough task without the added mission of combining the works with the Dutch Masters in the permanent collection. Erwin compiled a longlist. He was as excited as he was uncertain – 'this exhibition will probably be slated in the press' – but also looked forward to working with Dibbits. 'Taco has a vision, and it's wonderful to see how thorough the museum is in its approach.' What undoubtedly helped was Dibbits's publicity, describing Erwin as 'one of the most important photographers of the last quarter of the twentieth century' who, with this donation, 'has become part of Dutch cultural history'.

In Dibbits's office, the photographer and director play around with colour photocopies of works by Rembrandt, Ter Borch, Goltzius, Jan Steen, Breitner and others. The plan is to whittle the selection down to ten paintings. 'I like the fact that there's a limit, as this will determine the scale,' Erwin thinks. 'But eight is too few and twelve is unwieldy.' They eventually settle on twelve.

Erwin and Dibbits agree that café owner Marie de Nooyer, posing nude for *La Penseuse* from the *Squares* series (1987), will hang next to Rembrandt van Rijn's etching *Naked Woman on a Mound* (c. 1631), which was made some three hundred and fifty years previously. Both reference the past: the painting alludes to mythological women at their toilette, such as the figure of Bathsheba, while the photograph speaks to Rodin's *The Thinker* (1880). As far as Erwin is concerned, the etching and photograph both deal with the 'amorphous body' and how it catches the light or falls into shadow and, above all, these are real women, not idealised models. *Naked Woman on a Mound* had caught his eye a long time ago and reinforced his belief that Rembrandt was also fascinated by 'imperfections'. Says Dibbits: 'For Rembrandt, cellulite and sagging breasts are a cornucopia of light and shadow.' Erwin could not have agreed more. 'I see it exactly the same way. In addition to being like a second grandmother, Marie de Nooyer was, for me, a study exercise into the relationship of light to the body and skin.'

Shirley den Hartog, meanwhile, fans out the ten provisional combinations on the office floor. They all agree that *Portrait of a Girl Dressed in Blue* by Johannes Cornelisz.

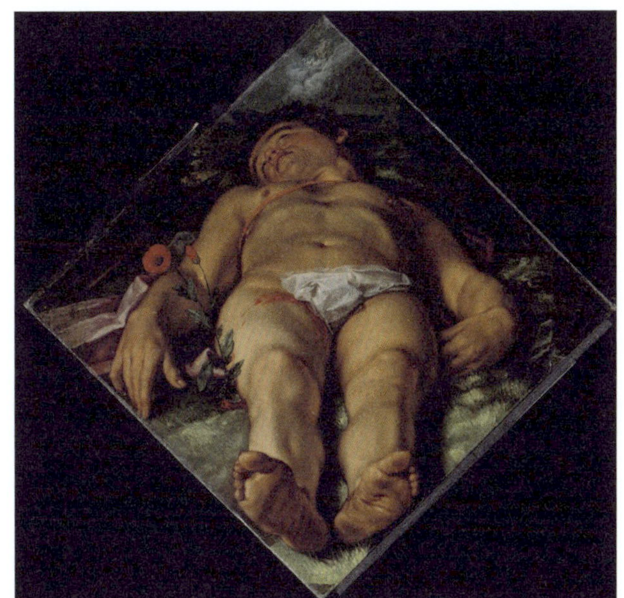

Right: Hendrick Goltzius, *Dying Adonis*, 1609. Bottom: *Reclining Nude No. 3, 2015*, from the *Skin Deep* series.

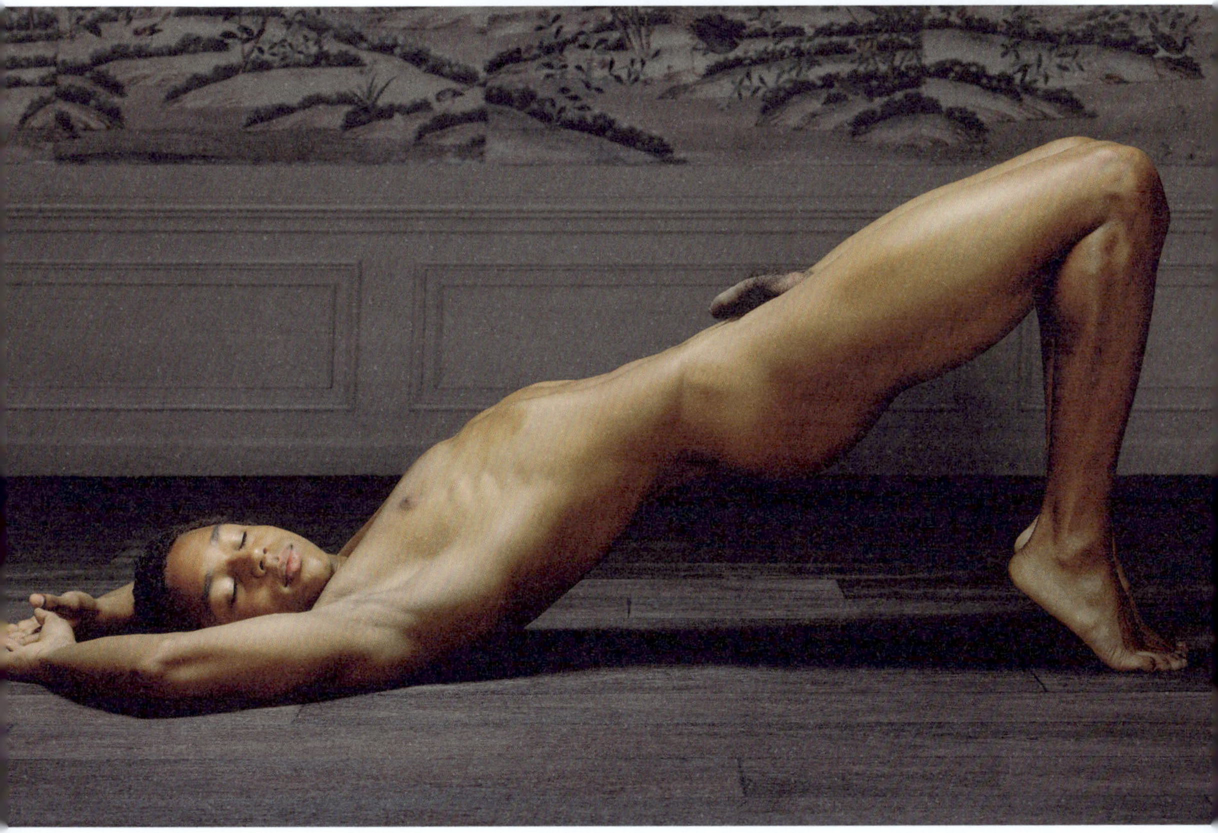

Verspronck should hang next to Erwin's *Hope, Portrait #5*, which shows a woman in a yellow dress. Dibbits sees the 'doubt, existential loneliness and resignation' in both portraits. After Erwin's death, as a tribute, the curator gave *Hope, Portrait #5* a temporary place in the Rijksmuseum's Gallery of Honour – the very first photograph to be included in the selection.

The installation only falters when Erwin suggests hanging *Cum* (1985) next to its source of inspiration, Rembrandt's *Self-Portrait* (1628). Dibbits's objection to the pairing is not so much that the young Rembrandt has a semen-free face – unlike the equally young Erwin – but that the photographer himself is overly prominent. 'Your early pictures relentlessly scream, "This is me!" The later ones leave much more space.'

Even *Reclining Nude No. 3*, the photograph Erwin wanted to combine with Hendrick Goltzius's *Dying Adonis* (1609), finds no mercy in Dibbits's eyes. 'For me, your picture is very much about a dick, which isn't a problem per se, but it has nothing to do with this Adonis. Do you understand?'

Erwin: 'I'm afraid that you're going to erase the male nude from the exhibition entirely when it's such an important part of my work – and in the history of painting, for that matter.'

Dibbits: 'The roots of our collection lie in nineteenth-century Calvinism, so it contains very little nudity – for that, you need to look to the sixteenth century. It's difficult, therefore, to find a correlation with that aspect of your work – which is why you're struggling.'

Erwin: 'That's precisely why the bleeding Adonis was such a discovery. Why isn't there a link with my own reclining nude, in your view?'

Dibbits: 'Goltzius tells a dramatic story, centred around a corpse, whereas your picture is the very antithesis of this scene. It's not the cock that bothers me but the fact that it is synonymous with vitality.'

Eventually – at Shirley den Hartog's suggestion – they agree that *Reclining Nude No. 5* – depicting Jack Wouterse gazing up from a mattress, naked apart from a pair of socks – will hang alongside *Adonis*. And *Hennie*, in one of the initial pictures from the *Ladies Hats* series, a body of work in which Erwin plays on gender, will hang next to its inspiration, namely Rembrandt's early *Self-Portrait*.

Friend and model Marline Williams reflects after the official opening. 'We all used to belong to the exalted fringes of society: we all deviated from the norm.' The credit, of course, must go to the photographer, she stresses. 'The praise is heaped upon Erwin, but it also trickles down to us, which almost elevates us as a group of outsiders. And in that precise and beautiful location, at the heart of the establishment, we gain the seal of approval in our dotage.'

After the speeches, everyone could make up their own minds as to whether Erwin's work could hold its own against the Old Masters. Following the large-format violence across the walls of the white cube that is the Kunstmuseum Den Haag, the Rijksmuseum's presentation is far moodier and more intimate. The photographs are not printed too large because Erwin did not want to 'blow the Old Masters away' in terms of scale. The exhibition feels, in the words of art critic Rutger Pontzen, like a 'triumphal march'. And despite the sombre walls, Erwin's illness and his solemn interment in the museum's collection, there was nothing 'funereal' about the presentation.

After all the highlights, the idea was to downsize: to clear out the studio, to ease off. But before long, it became clear that Erwin was once again brimming with new plans. He wants to continue directing rotating advertising hoardings – his very short films, moving portraits, inspired by the outdoor advertising he has recently and more frequently been producing. After the trips to Shanghai and Palm Springs, he is considering shoots in St Petersburg and Paris. 'In the short videos I made in China and the USA, all the models speak in the imperative. I envisage creating a huge room that people enter, where all the models on life-size screens turn and say, "kiss me," "look at me", "love me", "touch me", "feed me" and "teach me". Such is the world today – everything is in the imperative. Especially in politics, where it's all "do this for me", "do that for me" and "fix it for me". My next project will be a meditation on human interactions.'

He also placed his accumulated technical prowess at the service of his unique form of reportage, as he had worked so brilliantly in the series on Amsterdam's Jews. He was weary of staged sets populated by grieving or suspenseful models, and even more so of the explicit nature of his early photographs.

Returning to documentary work – at a time when museums were only just opening their doors to his own exalted form of staged photography – felt like the right kind of exit. He still regarded reportage as the 'mother of all photography' and, after all those years of staged work, he wanted to find a stylised hybrid between his fantasy and reality; for example, by exploring disappearing identities – religion, nobility and the circus. The latter idea arose after photographing a former 'sex contact', an elderly acrobat from the former East Germany – 'anyone who can fold himself into a glass coffin or suitcase is bound to be great in bed' – who advised him to visit Ukrainian circus schools to witness the death throes of the profession.

Meanwhile, his own body was failing. The emphysema had him in its grip. He could no longer travel to international exhibitions of his work without supplementary oxygen cylinders. He also felt like a burden on the much younger and fitter Kevin, who loved nothing more than to dance until the early hours. After prematurely fleeing a party at the Cipriani in Venice due to his extreme shortness of breath, Erwin confided to his friend Arthur Japin that he worried about his decline and the terrible toll it was taking on Kevin. Erwin noted in his diary: 'And that hurts me anew. Perhaps I'd prefer to go the final distance alone.'

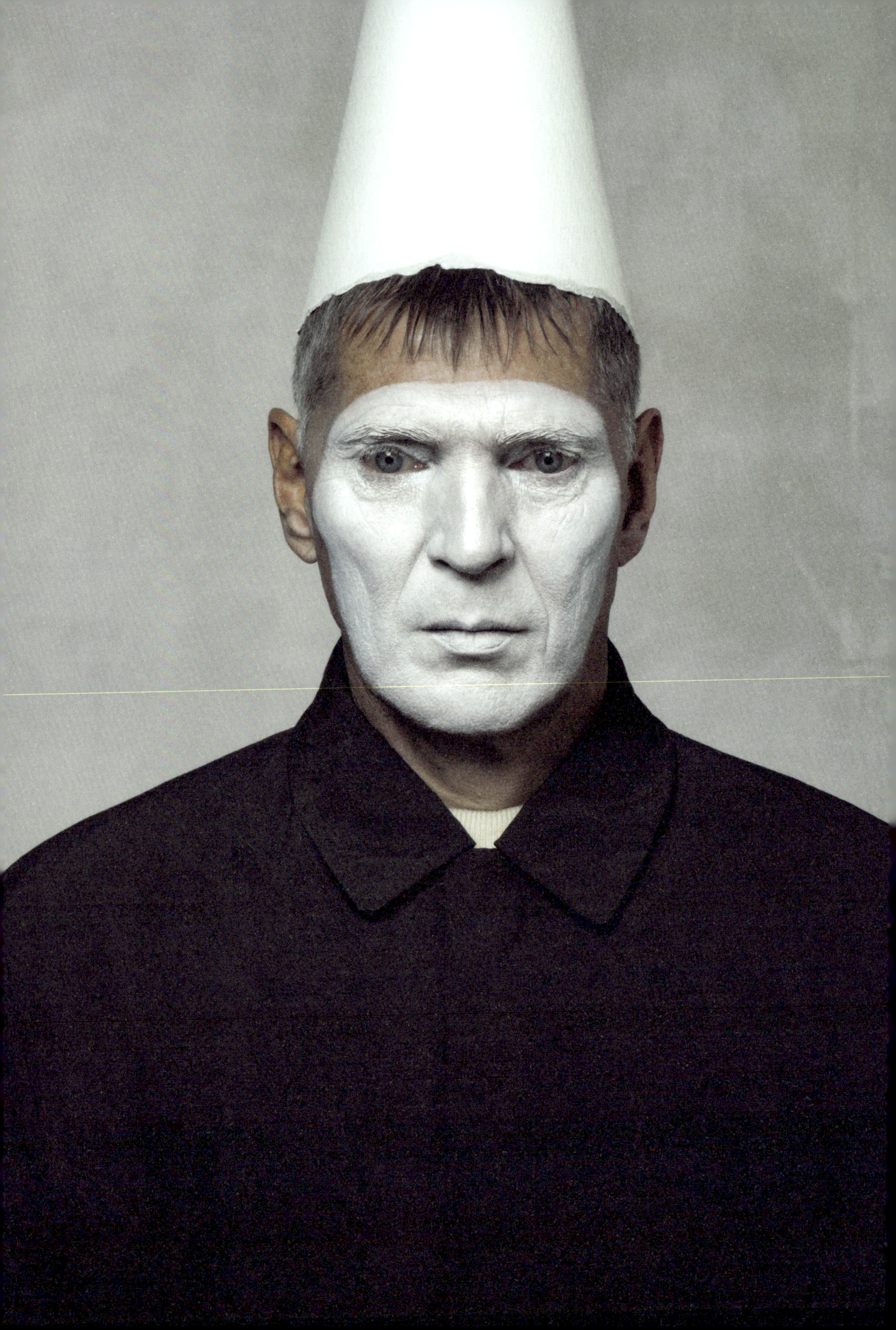

10 THE FINAL CHAPTER (2019–2023)

'I want to show human hubris in relation to nature. We devour everything and destroy everything'

LOST TIME

In the middle of the empty studio stands a small house, no larger than a student room, with a single door and one window. It is ringed by large lamps, cameras, scaffolding, chargers and mobile tripods. Everyone on the film set – for that is what the studio has become today – is wearing a face mask, except Erwin. Daubed in chalky makeup, he is dressed in a black mackintosh and a white pointed hat.

It is early June 2020. The world is in the grip of a pandemic; the Netherlands has only just emerged from its first 'intelligent lockdown'; face masks are mandatory on public transport, and the first SARS CoV 2 tests have become available. Fear has all but replaced the euphoria of 2019.

After wintering with Kevin in Thailand, Erwin had thought he would begin a new chapter with a clear mind.

'Our plane took off just as Bangkok went into lockdown. Once in Amsterdam, there was a brief spell of total silence and bewilderment. Then panic set in and the supermarkets were mobbed. Instead of clarity, I felt only exhaustion, anger and fear.' He belonged to one of the most vulnerable demographics: the coronavirus would wreak havoc on his lungs, and he had to protect himself.

It gave him time to build a fireproof vault for the vintage prints and to sign the accompanying certificates of authenticity that Shirley den Hartog had printed as a precaution. Pandemic or not, emphysema or not, her long-term plans – financial and, above all, artistic independence – had to remain intact.

Only a handful of the once eight-strong team remained attached to the studio.

Sales dipped in March at the onset of the pandemic, but in the months that followed, the anxiety lifted and the work began to sell 'like hotcakes' once more, she observed. 'Globally. People everywhere were longing for a return to normality, and that yearning also extended to the art world.'

Negotiations were underway with gallery owner Ron Mandos, who would announce Erwin's transfer to his gallery later that year. 'We've ended our collaboration with Martin Rogge's Flatland. We had some fantastic years together, and there are no hard feelings,' says Den Hartog. 'But a change like this brings a fresh burst of energy; it's a new beginning for all of us.'

Erwin Olaf and Ron Mandos – a professionally trained trumpet player who once owned a chain of flower shops – found each other in their shared ambitions. Both were outsiders in the often insular art world. Mandos admired Erwin not only as an artist, 'but also as a champion of the LGBTQI+ community'.

They knew each other because Mandos organised annual exhibitions of work by recent graduates. Erwin would occasionally buy a piece. They also crossed paths in the queer nightlife scene. Mandos could take a joke, and Erwin liked to tease him in the gallery by calling him 'flower man' while he was speaking to potential clients. They clicked professionally as well, since it was a win-win arrangement: collectors of Erwin's work were drawn to Mandos's gallery for the first time, while Mandos's international clientele discovered Erwin's photographs.

Erwin said that current events had given him 'a kick up the bum'; he wanted to respond to the absurd nightmare engulfing the world through his art. At the beginning of April, vulnerable or not, he and a handful of assistants set out early one Sunday morning to capture the pandemic on film in the empty capital. 'I was already walking around Dam Square with a team at eight in the morning, but it wasn't working. I was getting pretty desperate about the crappy photos I was taking. The sun so bright and, oddly enough, there were still too many people out for a stroll in the otherwise deserted city.'

After that failed attempt, he tried again later the same month, and in May 2020 he published his series of self portraits, *April Fool*. 'I've been gripped by fear and helplessness for weeks now,' he wrote in the caption accompanying the photographs. 'I feel like a tiny extra in a horror film with an unpredictable ending.' His fear – that the volcano on which he and the rest of the Western world had so long been dancing would finally erupt – seemed to be coming true. 'I wander around aimlessly, afraid of an invisible enemy. Waiting for the complete unknown.'

That fear also fuelled his creativity and ignited new ideas. For his next series, he envisioned 'a zombie clown' drifting through a desolate, post-apocalyptic world. The clown with a white-painted face and a pointed cap – 'stolen from an old amateur photo on the internet' – is reminiscent of the 'self-portraits as a clown' by Pablo

Picasso (*Au Lapin Agile / At the Lapin Agile*), Max Beckmann (*Selbstbildnis als Clown*) and Edward Hopper (*Soir Bleu*).

Erwin also saw it as the dunce cap of a little boy sent to the corner by his teacher. 'The virus is a punishment for our human folly.' He transformed himself into Pierrot, the white-faced and somewhat more solemn clown. He then assumed the role of court jester, the foolish outsider who speaks truth to power and warns his fellow citizens that 'the world is sick and the party's over. The house of cards is collapsing, and we're all fools.'

In the photographs, Erwin, his face ghostly white, pushes a shopping trolley past empty shelves in a deserted supermarket, only to find himself alone and disconsolate on a park bench. Over several days, he created the series in an Asian grocery store in Amsterdam-Zuidoost, 'as a kind of guerrilla operation'. 'It was a semi-journalistic project and also a form of therapy – never before had I managed to capture my feelings about world events so swiftly and directly.'

And now, a few months later, the pandemic continues unabated, and the shoot for the *April Fool* video is ready. More recently he has been working increasingly with video, seeking a 'dialogue between photos and moving images'. Erwin had come to see the limitations of photography, feeling that it elicits too little emotion. 'Music, literature and film have the power to move people, to the extent that they openly show their emotions, but I've never yet seen anyone cry over a staged studio photo.'

Hence the one bedroom apartment he has constructed in the middle of the studio. Its arrangement alludes both to the lockdown and to the invidious creep of the surveillance society. Some saw this as looming alarmingly close during the pandemic.

Trapped on the treadmill of solitude, the ghostly figure exudes a profound ennui. The theme was timely, so too Erwin's belief in loneliness as an existential force. 'I don't necessarily see it as a negative thing, but I've felt like this since childhood. I understood my mother's restlessness when she sat at home on the sofa and said she wanted to go home. And since *Grief*, I've often tried to capture that feeling in my work.'

The dunce arrives home with the groceries, paces the room and occasionally sits down at one of the two chairs placed at the round table with a transistor radio, a fruit bowl and a well-thumbed paperback of *Swann's Way*, the opening volume of Marcel Proust's masterpiece. A fitting presence in a world lost to lockdown and isolation.

The anonymity of the white-faced man in his tiny room stands in stark contrast to the presence of photographer and cameraman Bert Pot, once one of Erwin's interns some thirty years ago. Along with his crew, he records the limited existence of the man in the dunce's cap.

'This has to be a film that feels as though it's been distilled from CCTV footage – the kinds of images where you never see exactly what you want to see. Can the man be identified? And yet, you are spying on a lonely figure in a pointed hat. He comes home, and then what?'

Indeed, what do you do during a lockdown? What if you're at home alone, unable to see your friends and with nowhere to go? Finally finishing Proust – who did not have emphysema but did suffer from severe asthma – is one possibility. Erwin had been reading Julian Barnes's *The Man in the Red Coat*, a portrait of the cultural world of the French *fin de siècle*, which 'just like now, was a time of decadence and fatalism'. It was this that reminded him of, and inspired him to begin, *In Search of Lost Time*. In the final edit of the video, Donald Trump's voice can be heard through the transistor radio, further heightening the film's apocalyptic tenor.

Prior to filming, Erwin had gained first-hand experience of his protagonist's lonely predicament. Aside from this project, he had been preoccupied with his failing lungs. A fellow sufferer, who was also afflicted by alpha-1 antitrypsin deficiency (AATD), talked to him about his own lung transplant. 'By the time he was fifty, he was in a far worse state than I am now. He'd undergone a transplant ten years earlier and was now as fit as a fiddle. We arranged to have lunch, and he practically skipped into the restaurant while I arrived panting and stumbling. He showed me the scar on his chest and said: you have to do it. You really have to do it.'

It was a success story that held out the promise of a longer life, free from shortness of breath. Encouraged by it, he travelled to Groningen to be examined by the city's pulmonologists, who specialise in lung transplants.

Was he sick enough, and yet strong enough, for such a serious operation? Unfortunately, the former seemed to be true, while he had doubts about the latter. 'I've never been as tired as I am now; I've never felt so depressed.' Claustrophobic as he already was from his shortness of breath, he allowed himself to be placed in solitary confinement at the hospital – to reduce the risk of infection – and submitted to a battery of tests.

Spending a week in isolation gave him time to think deeply and sparked the idea for the one-room apartment he would soon have built in his studio. It also produced a wealth of medical data. The tests revealed that he was a promising candidate for a lung transplant – a dubious honour, for it meant his lung disease was already far advanced. If he signed up, he would be placed at the top of the waiting list.

According to Shirley den Hartog, Erwin was therefore 'jubilant and elated' at the prospect of a transplant and of regaining his old Amsterdam life. Of course, those new lungs would eventually become damaged as well, since the source of his AATD lay in his liver. But he was already thirty-six when the disease first manifested. 'So with my new lungs, I'll be well over a hundred by the time it really starts bothering me again,' he calculated. 'We'll cross that bridge when we come to it.'

A few weeks later, however, the jubilation had almost entirely faded. After the video session, still wearing the white pointed cap, he confessed that he was in two minds and had not yet put his name on the waiting list. 'New lungs – I still haven't

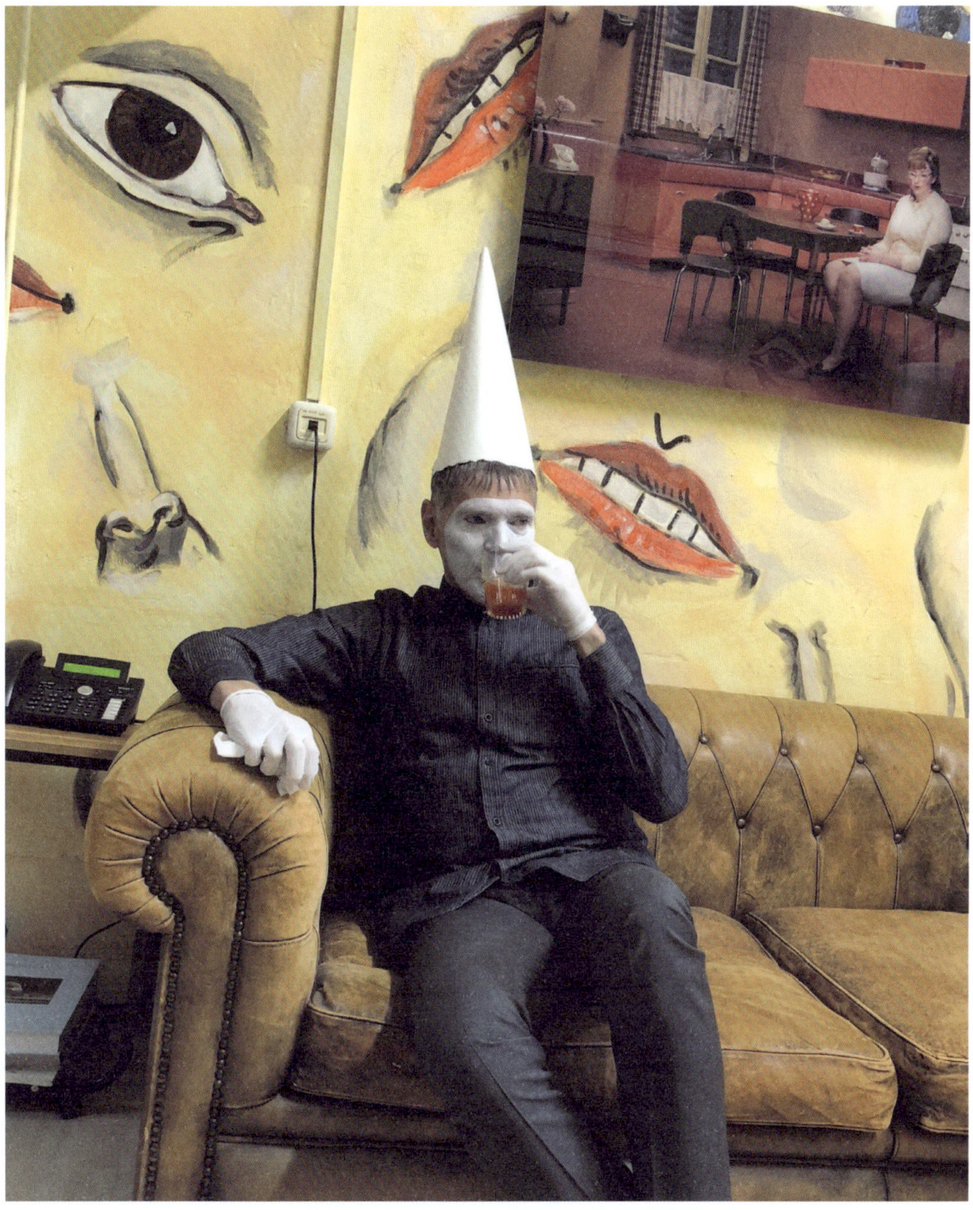

Break in the Studio Erwin Olaf canteen during the recording of the *April Fool* video, 6 June 2020.
Photo on page 334: *11.05 am, 2020* from the *April Fool* series.

computed what this really means. It takes an entire year to recover. And after that, there's a travel ban for another year. And taking twenty medications a day for the rest of your life. It's very hard to process.'

Furthermore, compared with other lung patients, he was doing relatively well – how appropriate was it for him to jump the queue for a new set of lungs? And, finally, why should one wish to stay alive at all costs? 'I count my blessings; I was born under a lucky star, a Sunday's child. But I don't want a second life, because that's what a transplant feels like. As far as I'm concerned, if I die tomorrow, I'll have no regrets. But I'm not ruling out the idea of joining the list.'

Back in Amsterdam, Erwin's shows in Italy, Toronto and Copenhagen were either cancelled or postponed because of the pandemic. A lecture in Palm Springs suffered the same fate. The exhibition *Parallel: Erwin Olaf* at the Shanghai Center of Photography did go ahead, but it had already closed by the time the pandemic emerged in China.

But Erwin was already turning his attention to new goals. He was eager to 'conquer' Germany, 'a very reluctant country to date'. Despite *Berlin*, the Germans had not yet embraced his work: 'You realise that you've arrived at the home of commercial documentary photography, the world of the photographers trained at the Düsseldorf Photoschule. The Becher School still wields immense influence.' The German art audience remained ambivalent about the dark, intergenerational fantasies of his *Berlin* series. The retrospective scheduled for 2021 at the Kunsthalle München held the promise of a breakthrough moment.

Despite his stifling Californian experience, he returned to the mountains to make *Munich*. 'Even though my condition practically precludes high-altitude photography.' Stubborn as ever, he was determined to see the project through. 'Oxygen cylinders at the ready, get set, go.' He felt an inner compulsion to show how 'human hubris has contributed to the climate crisis'. In the Black Forest, he found the vast, overpowering landscape he needed to illustrate the insignificance of humankind.

His guide in Germany was Roger Diederen, the Dutch-born director of the Kunsthalle München. Diederen had seen Erwin's exhibition at the Kunstmuseum Den Haag and had been struck by its quality. 'It was a weekday and the museum was packed. Not only was it crowded, but the visitors seemed to represent a broad cross section of society – it was very different from the usual museum-going crowd. Erwin knows how to grab people with his photographs. You don't need to know anything about art; you don't even have to like it, but you can't help lingering before those photographs.'

Diederen decided he wanted to bring Erwin to Munich. 'It was risky, because I realised that he was virtually unknown in Germany. When I mentioned his name to fellow museum curators, the reaction was always: never heard of him. I had to explain who he was and, for convenience's sake, I compared him to other artists working in the field of staged photography, such as Jeff Wall, Thomas Demand and David

LaChapelle. At the Kunsthalle, we depend on visitor numbers for our income, so it took some effort to convince my colleagues: out of the thousands of photographers you could exhibit, why on earth Erwin Olaf?'

Curator Anja Huber of the Kunsthalle, a former ballerina, travelled to the Kunstmuseum Den Haag to study the work in depth. 'That changed my opinion somewhat,' she said. 'Erwin turned out to be more of a camera-based artist than a photographer. In addition to videos, he also creates sculptures and installations.'

According to Diederen and Huber, his relative obscurity made it essential for Erwin to present a new German series in Munich in order to make his work more accessible to the local audience. 'When designing the exhibition, we left space for that new work, even though we didn't yet know what it would be – we were on tenterhooks right up until the last moment.'

Erwin did his homework and immersed himself in German history – 'terrible but also beautiful, from the ridiculous King Ludwig II to the genius of Wagner'. It became a journey of discovery, through art history as well, particularly the work of nineteenth-century painters such as Caspar David Friedrich and Arnold Böcklin. 'People in the Netherlands know almost nothing about Germany. We no longer learn the language, even though, after that horrific dark chapter in its history, the country has become the beating heart of European democracy.' He was equally fascinated by contemporary Germany. In Munich, he saw 'dirndls alongside niqabs, the nudist *Freikörperkultur* alongside picnicking immigrant families – a kind of diversity that we lack in the Netherlands.'

Ludwig II of Bavaria's hunting lodge can normally only be reached on foot – an impossible task in Erwin's condition. By special permission, he was allowed to drive into the mountains, where he discovered 'an incredible building in a remote spot. From the outside it looked like a traditional wooden chalet, but inside was an oriental salon. Absurd and fantastic.' The surrounding landscape was breathtaking: 'Romantic, but also dark.' Combined with nineteenth-century painting, it immediately sparked visions for a series to be staged in a documentary, almost journalistic way.

He let reality sink in and then translated it through his imagination, but this time without the retro elements seen in the series *Grief* and *Rain*. 'For me, it's about the here and now. That's done. I want to show human hubris in relation to nature. We devour everything and destroy everything. I also want to question my own mortality and my ego – what am I really all about?'

Erwin took his team and models into the woods and mountains, resulting in 'the gloomiest series I've ever made': *Im Wald* [In the Forest]. He left behind the studio, where he had total control over the world, yet still transported a huge fake boulder into the mountains, just in case, and sketched out every scene so as not to leave anything to chance – which did not always work. 'At the waterfall, for example, the wind

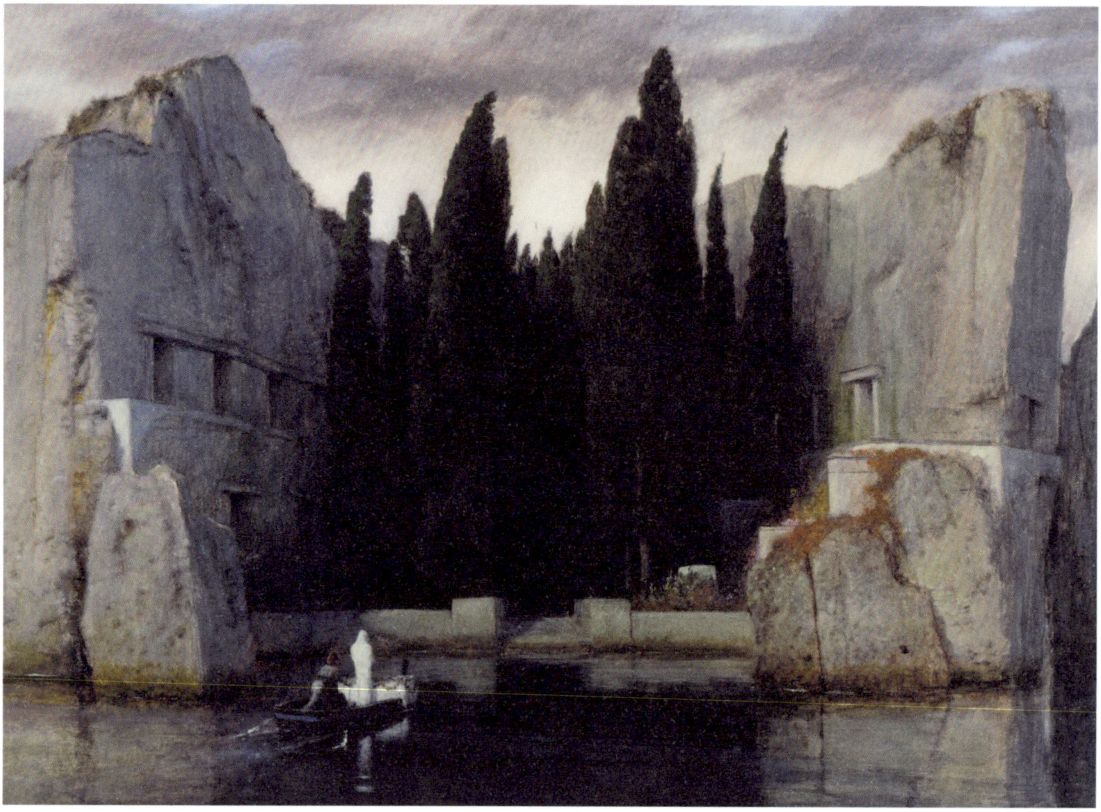

Top: Arnold Böcklin, *Die Toteninsel III* [Isle of the Dead, III], 1883.
Bottom: While photographing *Auf dem See* [On the Lake]

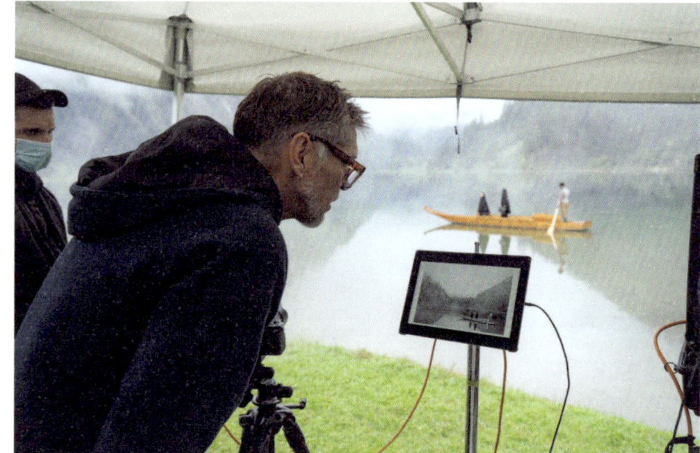

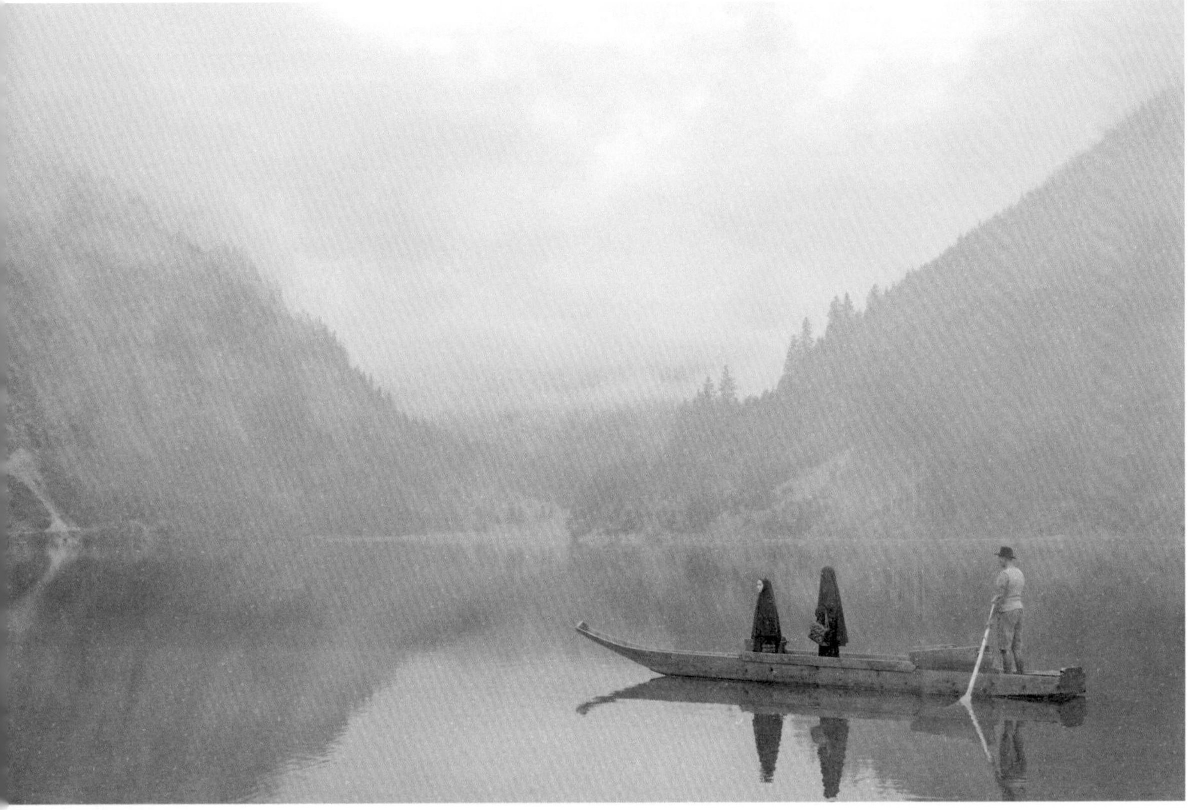

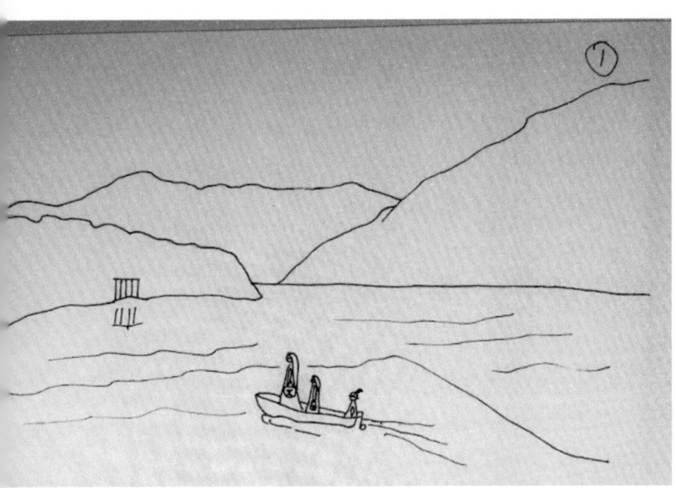

Top: Erwin Olaf, *Auf dem See, 2020* from the *Im Wald* [In the Forest] series. Bottom: Erwin sketched all the shots in advance.

was blowing in the wrong direction and my lens was covered in spray. You then have to find a new location while sixteen men and women are anxiously awaiting your instructions. I've never worked so hard in my life.'

'If only Im Wald *survives after my death – and perhaps* Rain *and* Grief *– that would be enough'*

Erwin's black-and-white photography also foreshadowed the approaching end of his own journey, lending it a further solemnity. *Im Wald* felt like a final chord – and a glimpse of the inevitable. Of course, death was present in *Auf dem See* [On the Lake], the photograph in which a Bavarian ferryman in lederhosen transports women dressed in niqabs across a misty lake. The man is covered in tattoos, like a contemporary Charon – a scene freely adapted from Arnold Böcklin's *Die Toteninsel III* [Isle of the Dead III].

But the photographs in which Erwin says goodbye to his husband Kevin in the depths of a dark forest, as in *In der Abenddämmerung* [In the Evening Twilight], also suggest an ending. 'He's twenty years younger than me and will soon have to learn to carry on without me.' For Erwin, it was one of the most meaningful images in the series, while Kevin understood, above all else, what it meant to be his model. 'Suddenly, I really had to listen to Erwin. He directed me and knew exactly what he wanted for that photo. He issued instructions, but without explaining the underlying reasoning. At one point, I stood motionless in the forest and I could hear him ranting and raving from behind his camera: "Keep walking! Goddamn it, just do what I say!" I thought, "And you can take a running jump!"'

In *Vor der Felswand, Selbstporträt* [In Front of the Rock Face, Self Portrait], Erwin stands atop his fake boulder from the Netherlands. With backpack and walking stick in hand, he gazes out at a mountain range shrouded in mist. The self-portrait was inspired by Caspar David Friedrich's *Der Wanderer über dem Nebelmeer* (1818) [The Wanderer above the Sea of Fog]. In both images, a solitary figure is confronted by a landscape as majestic as it is nebulous. Yet while the Wanderer stands proudly before nature, embodying the egocentric spirit of Romanticism, two hundred years later Erwin appears anything but confident as he sets out on a difficult journey that is unlikely to end well. In the Black Forest, he was also bidding farewell to his own life.

Im Wald became a series with which the German public could identify, according to Kunsthalle director Roger Diederen. What struck his colleague Anja Huber was that queer visitors told her how important Erwin's work was to them. 'But the exhibition appealed to everyone on an emotional level. The audience had the opportunity to ask Erwin questions during a number of events, and they even invited him to comment on political and moral issues, as if he were some kind of guru.'

The exhibition catapulted him to fame in Germany. It attracted 75,000 visitors – an extraordinary result in the midst of a pandemic, says Diederen. The book accompanying the exhibition sold well and was also often stolen: 'always a good sign'.

Major collectors, such as Ingvild Goetz – a political scientist and heiress of Werner Otto, founder of the Otto mail order company – acquired several works, and the media responded enthusiastically. The news bulletin *Tagesschau* ran a feature on Erwin and remarked that it was 'almost absurd' that it had taken Germany so long to discover him.

'Every journalist could relate to the exhibition because it touched on all the pressing issues of the day, from racism to gender,' says Diederen. 'The tenor in the German press was indeed: How surprising! Why haven't we heard of this photographer before? Ninety-five per cent of the comments in the visitor's book were positive; the others simply couldn't connect with his work because they found it too cool or distant.' Hardly anyone reacted to Erwin's more explicit early works, Huber notes. 'We were advised to set a minimum age for the exhibition, so we added a small warning sign.'

After his return Erwin needed time to recover. The whole undertaking had turned out to be exactly the kind of high-intensiy workload his doctors had told him to avoid, and his health had deteriorated considerably. 'I was completely exhausted; I was dizzy for three weeks with a kind of hyperventilation, which was quite frightening.'

But the effort had been worth it, Erwin realised as he walked through the rooms of the Kunsthalle in Munich on 13 May 2021 during the opening of the exhibition *Erwin Olaf. Strange Beauty*. He was ecstatic and considered the exhibition 'even more thorough and substantive' than the one in The Hague, 'if such a thing is possible'. It felt like a triumph: 'A space in that world suddenly opened up for me. I thought: I've done it; we've made it. We've conquered the world, from Korea to Germany, on our own terms and without compromise.'

'I walked around with Marline, Frans and the others and became quite emotional. Room after room after room, it went on and on, and I thought: did I make all this? Did I really make all this, starting when I was eighteen? In the first three rooms, you can see that I was searching, full of aggression and anger. And then suddenly you come to *Rain*, *Hope*, and *Grief*. And then it's clear – you're older, wiser. And then, *Im Wald*, the final chapter, far deeper than all the preceding work. In terms of posterity, if only *Im Wald* survives after my death – and perhaps *Rain* and *Grief* – that would be enough. But of course, the decision won't be mine.'

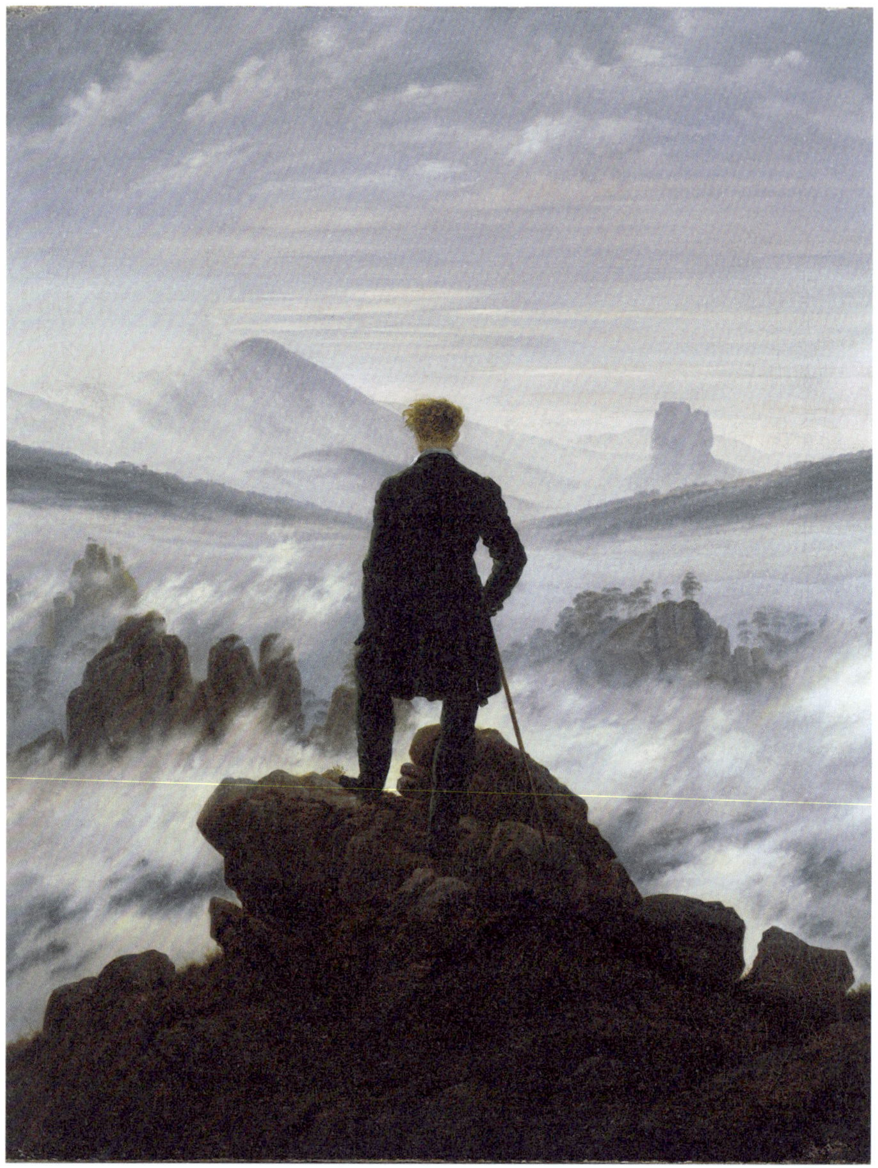

Caspar David Friedrich, *Der Wanderer über dem Nebelmeer* [Wanderer above the Sea of Fog], 1818.

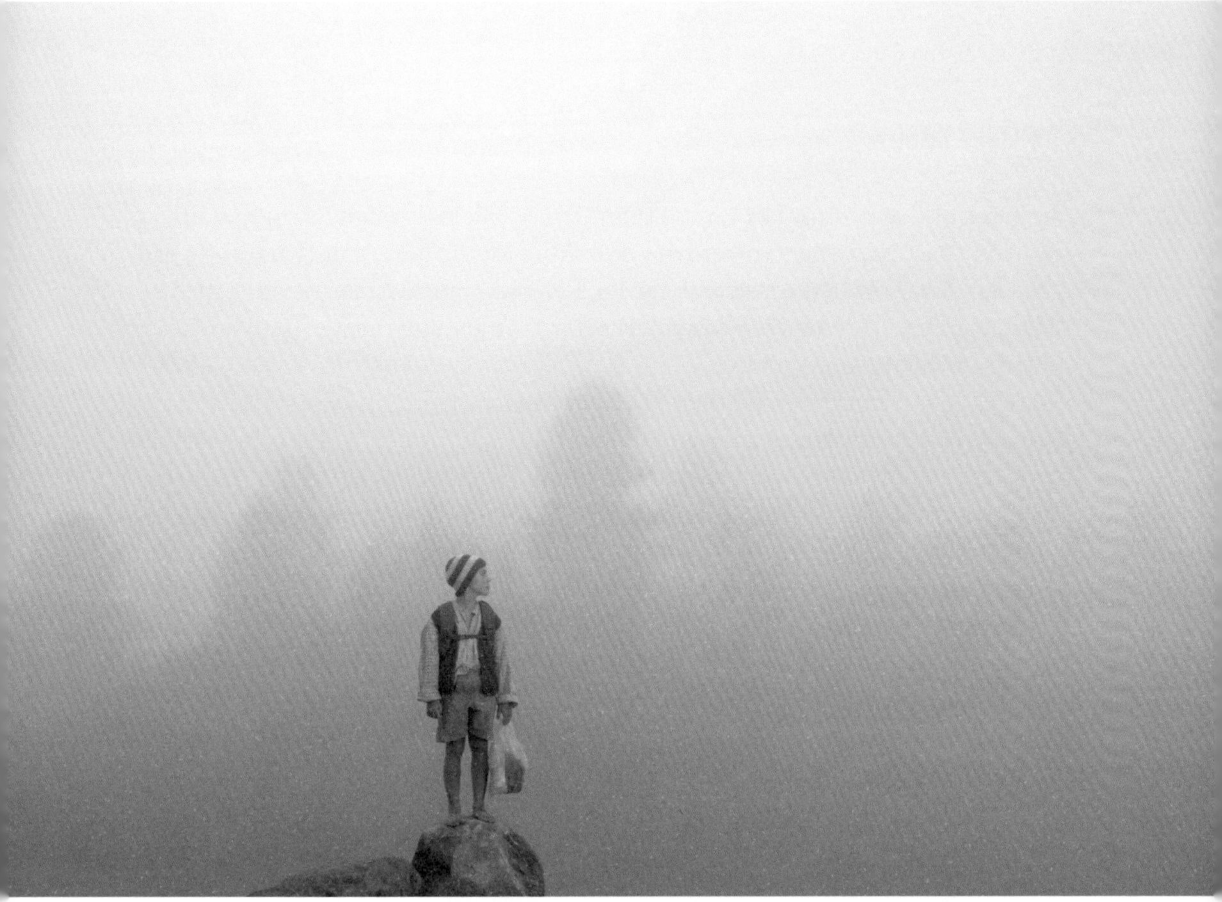

Top: *Vor der Felswand, Kevin* [In Front of the Rock Face, Kevin], *2020*.
Bottom: Erwin's sketch.

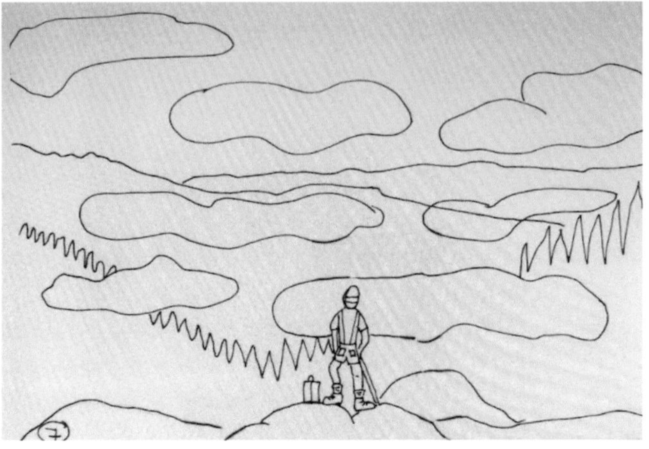

'Having "Substance X" in my safe... makes me feel very secure'

FAIRLIGHT HALL

The sun is still low in the sky when Erwin Olaf wanders through Fairlight Hall's sprawling gardens in September 2021, searching for the best camera angle. He had arrived in East Sussex the previous day for a private commission and, unsettled by the time difference, had risen extremely early, even though the morning session was not scheduled until 6:45 a.m.

The Kowitz family, owners of the estate, had flown him in by private jet to avoid the risk of coronavirus infection and the strict British pandemic measures. The rest of the team would follow on a commercial flight. Along with the British video crew, due to arrive from London a day later, there would soon be a team of seventeen people on hand to capture the Kowitz children, Douglas and Madeleine, in both still and moving images.

A foggy morning is forecast, and Erwin wants to take advantage of the weather when he photographs the twenty-somethings with the mansion in the background. He creates sketches for the family and also provides notes: 'In the middle panel of the triptych, you see Madeleine and Douglas after a ball, at daybreak, looking beautiful but slightly dishevelled, shoes in their hands, one holding a balloon, the other a suitcase – a clue that he is about to depart – some confetti, perhaps some empty glasses and a bottle of their favourite tipple.'

In addition to the mid-nineteenth-century mock-Tudor country house, the estate encompasses some 50 hectares of gardens, greenhouses, outbuildings, ponds, meadows and woodland. Fairlight Hall, complete with crenelated towers, commands views over farmland, forests and the English Channel. Owners David and Sarah Kowitz manage the estate with the support of their staff: housekeepers, butlers and gardeners.

Sarah is a former journalist; David is the founder of a hedge fund and a former employee of billionaire philanthropist George Soros. He likes to recount how he was hired. Soros asked him about his roots, and Kowitz replied that he came from a family of Eastern European Jews. Soros, who shares the same background, jokingly responded: 'I won't hold that against you.' And then he hired him.

Sarah and David lived together in New York and Hong Kong after meeting as students in Amsterdam. They run an art foundation at Fairlight Hall, where they host cultural events.

Erwin occasionally accepts assignments from wealthy clients who wish to immortalise themselves or their families. It is not primarily for financial gain; two thirds of his fee is donated to Human Rights Watch or another NGO.

He also likes to leave his own imprint on these commissions. He typically stages a *tableau vivant* in the unmistakable Erwin Olaf style, with the image then extensively edited. As an exception, he once captured the billionaire Dreesmann family – heirs to a renowned Dutch department store chain – smiling. 'In the visual arts, you rarely see a smile, whereas in the worlds of Instagram and advertising, everything is happy-go-lucky. I can't stand that strange contrast, nor the way the body, genitals and sexuality have been hijacked by bad porn, which makes everything sleazy. All the laughter has been stolen by advertising, and I want to reclaim it – like a contemporary Honthorst or Frans Hals.'

Wealthy patrons have always shaped art history, and Erwin consciously follows in that tradition. For the portraits he would create at Fairlight Hall, he drew inspiration from the work of American painter John Singer Sargent, the pre-eminent portraitist of his generation, who immortalised the European elite on canvas. 'That's exactly how it was back then – a commissioned portrait – only now there's no painter at work but a photographer, and taking it a step further, a video director.'

The combined photo and video works he is creating on the estate will never be seen beyond the walls of the country house, but they will be in distinguished company. Paintings from the Renaissance to the present day adorn the hall's staircases, hallways and rooms. A silkscreen print of Mao by Andy Warhol hangs beside a hyper-realistic work by Duane Hanson and a painting by Julian Schnabel, who was likewise commissioned to paint a portrait of Madeleine and Douglas.

During an earlier stay at Fairlight Hall, when Erwin was getting to know the family, he stepped out of the lift to the bedrooms and suddenly found himself face to face with an early sixteenth-century Flemish triptych – probably a later copy. Opening the panels revealed a scene of Saint Jerome in a landscape, while closing them showed Sodom and Gomorrah engulfed in flames, destroyed by God for the 'unprecedented sins' of their inhabitants –including homosexuality, of course.

The encounter inspired him to create the triptych he would produce there a few days later. 'Two short videos with the mansion in the middle. And when closed, you will see the portrait photos of the two children – or at least, that's my current thinking. The triptych will hang in the hallway of their parents, the clients, who will see the work every day. I asked the children for a short phrase they'd like to say. They came up with "I am you" and "you and me". The idea is that they will speak those words while slowly turning towards the camera.'

At first glance, it might seem like a far-fetched idea. Yet Erwin has never considered himself a conventional portrait photographer, so he feels he might as well tackle it in his own way. When the Kowitz family first approached him for a portrait after admiring his work at his London gallery, Hamiltons, his immediate reaction was: I'm really not good at family portraits; you'd better ask someone else. 'It's a matter of managing expectations,' he explains. The result will undoubtedly surprise them – hopefully in a good way, although there's no guarantee.

Admittedly, his enthusiasm for a commission grows if the client has a generous budget – which allows for greater photographic possibilities – and, ideally, a home that can serve as a backdrop for his imagination. Take, for instance, Schloss Nymphenburg in Munich, the former summer residence of the Bavarian court, where he photographed Franz Bonaventura Adalbert Maria Herzog von Bayern.

The duke, a patron and art collector, was approaching ninety and lived in a wing of the vast castle complex. Had the Bavarian monarchy not been abolished in 1918, Duke Franz would now be sitting on the throne. 'I was introduced to him by Roger Diederen. The duke is an extraordinarily charming man who served on the board of MoMA in New York for many years – he knows the entire American art scene. He loved to recount stories from the old days, about Andy Warhol or Bianca Jagger.

Erwin had hoped to photograph the Duke of Bavaria in full regalia, adorned with all his medals and decorations. It was also intended to be the first image in a new series, *Blue Blood*, exploring the decline of the European aristocracy. Yet the regalia proved a sensitive issue: We no longer have any power, so why should I be photographed like that? the duke reasoned. 'That's a hot potato in Germany,' explains Erwin. 'Partly because many aristocrats behaved abominably during the Nazi era. There are still far-right movements that would like to see Duke Franz back on the Bavarian throne. He wants nothing to do with that; as a boy, he and his family were imprisoned by the Nazis in Dachau and Sachsenhausen.'

In addition to the portrait with all the aristocratic regalia, it was agreed that a 'counter-photo' would be taken in which the duke would pose informally, but still in costume. In passing, Erwin broke a second taboo. Franz Herzog von Bayern's friend and confidant since 1980, Thomas Greinwald, was actually his lover. At the end of the session, Greinwald asked Erwin if he could also appear in a second photograph. 'They were both in traditional costume, the duke in long trousers, his friend in lederhosen. Greinwald stood beside the duke, I pressed the shutter, and when I looked at the photos that evening, I thought: *this is the one*. Those two elderly lovers, with the little dog – it was very moving.'

The duke initially rejected the photograph, saying he had no wish to provoke. Erwin replied that publishing it could mean a great deal to queer young people in traditional settings who are afraid to come out. 'We discussed it at length at the palace, and the duke eventually realised that the world has changed – that showing this photograph of two elderly lovers could hardly be considered provocative anymore.'

It marked the beginning of the coming out of the nearly ninety-year-old duke and his partner, twenty years his junior. Although their relationship had long been something of an open secret, Greinwald said he had 'lived in the shadows' for forty years. Now, he said, the mask could finally come off; thanks in part to Erwin's double portrait, he 'no longer had to play a role'.

After wandering through Fairlight Hall's tropical garden for a long time – sawing off branches here and there, hoisting them up on ropes, only to decide against using them as a frame – the predicted morning mist fails to appear. Instead, a beautiful, clear autumn day is dawning, much to Erwin's irritation. 'You have a preconceived idea in your head, but the weather conditions alone force you to think again. That's why I love working indoors. But you haven't heard me swear yet.'

For Erwin, adapting reality to match the image in his mind goes far beyond the weather. The Union Jack flying from one of the mansion's turrets must be lowered slightly; it is flapping just outside the frame of his Hasselblad. And those 'stupid sculptures' in the garden have to be removed.

Every position for the models is marked with duct tape, then shifted again and again. The lights behind the Hall's myriad windows must all be switched on. 'That way, I can edit the illuminated windows into my photo later.' Stress begins to mount when he cannot find the right composition. Props and people are moved endlessly for a scene that may, in the end, be discarded altogether.

Right up until the moment the shoot is due to begin, he remains 'totally unsure' about his work. 'I'm blank. I know it will be fine, but the path to the result is still completely unclear. The more people involved, the heavier the burden, because there's so much more that can go wrong.'

'I've flown so many people in for this; if it doesn't work out, I'll make a fool of myself. In that respect, you're really better off taking a passport photo in the studio.'

Later that day, the son and daughter perform in the ultra-short videos, which are more like moving photographs. Erwin shyly asks the English sound engineer whether he really has to shout 'action' before each take, as though he were directing a feature film. Laughing, he admits, 'I'm a little embarrassed about that.'

Afterwards, he wanders once more through Fairlight Hall's vast grounds. 'That wall with all the plants and flowers, that botanical garden, was a little duller than the wild garden.' He films a brief video of Madeleine in a theatrical dress, framed by silver daisies and wilted artichokes, blackened and covered with snails. His instructions are precise: 'Don't look straight into the lens. Turn slightly away from me and look as if you're lost in thought. A little arrogant.'

Madeleine has worked as a model, yet she still finds it intimidating to be watched by seventeen men and women. Erwin reassures her: 'You're great. That outfit, that light – totally Singer Sargent. Pure nineteenth century.' And to his assistants, he

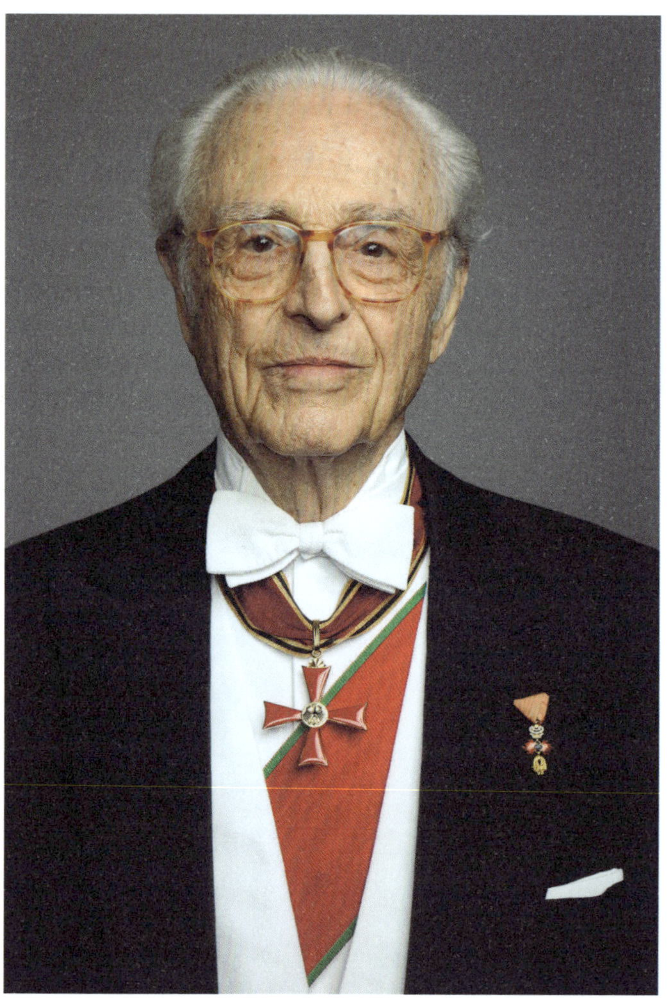

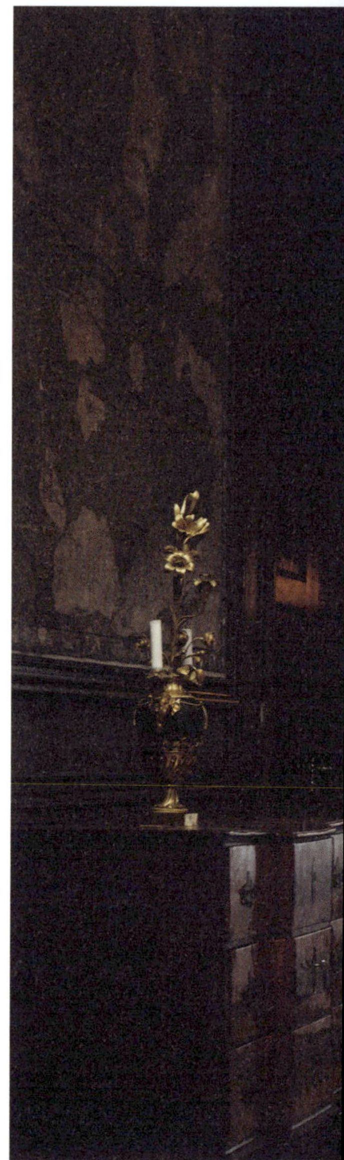

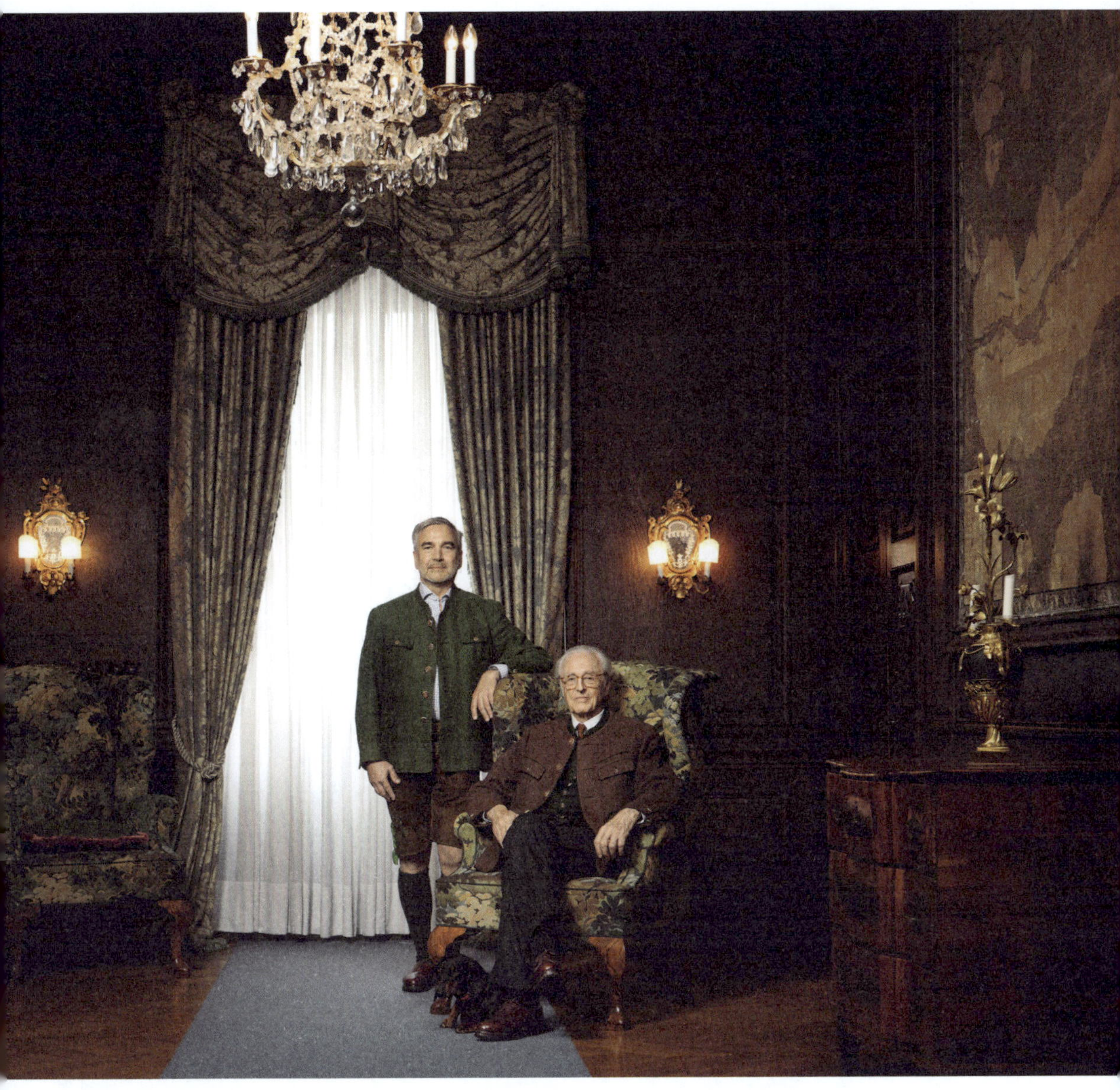

Left: The Duke of Bavaria in ceremonial attire. Right: With his partner Thomas Greinwald, both in traditional dress.

remarks: 'Photographing women is much easier than men; it was true in the beginning and it's still true today. Women like to act a little, perhaps because they've been brought up to be looked at. Men, on the other hand, often apologise when I photograph them: okay, I may be standing before the camera, but I'd rather be somewhere else. My wife signed me up for this, so to speak.'

It was Hamiltons Gallery in London that connected David and Sarah Kowitz with Erwin. Hamiltons also represents luminaries such as Mario Testino, Nobuyoshi Araki and Roger Ballen. Founder Tim Jefferies has described Erwin as 'obviously extremely talented' as well as 'compassionate and witty'. In the late 1980s, when still in his twenties, Jefferies had sought out Robert Mapplethorpe in New York and brought the already ailing photographer to London for an exhibition. Decades later, he encountered Erwin's 'crazy' *Paradise* series and immediately wanted to know its creator.

'I'd never heard of Erwin. And he's still obscure here in the UK, an outsider. Whereas he's a fucking superstar in the Netherlands. ... Erwin has been consistent for decades; he delivers. And his photographs appeal not only to Europeans, but also to people with a completely different aesthetic and mindset, such as in Korea and Japan.'

Over the years, Jefferies has consistently showcased Erwin's latest work at Hamiltons, but at a retrospective in 2019 he also exhibited vintage prints from *Chessmen* and *Blacks*, among others. 'I wanted to emphasise that Erwin is not only a talented manipulator in digital post-production, but also a craftsman – someone who understands the entire process. A genuine photographer's photographer.'

Jefferies considers himself privileged to have worked with Helmut Newton, Richard Avedon and Irving Penn. '*The* Helmut Newton. *The* Richard Avedon. *The* Irving Penn. And Erwin definitely belongs in that list. *The* Erwin Olaf. I told him: I just happen to like working with dead photographers. Erwin laughed and replied: don't worry, I have a serious lung disease, I'll soon be in my grave. Funny and maudlin at the same time – and so very Erwin.'

This jovial attitude towards illness and death has become second nature over the years, Erwin confirms in the taxi on the way from Fairlight Hall to Lydd Airport. A private jet – 'very unethical these days in light of the climate crisis, but right now, during the pandemic, it's very practical' – will pick him up there and fly him to Munich, where the exhibition at the Kunsthalle will come to a festive close in a few days' time.

'When *Grief* was released, Hans van Manen summed it up perfectly. He said, "your illness is a media blessing". And I must admit, since then, it's always the first thing I'm asked in interviews: "How are you now? How ill are you?" Nowadays, I unfortunately have to answer, "not good, things are very bad". As if they can't see that for themselves.'

To retain some control, he has been a member of the Dutch Association for Voluntary Euthanasia for the past decade. His euthanasia declaration is in order. 'Even though it hadn't fully sunk in yet, deep down I knew early on how my illness would play out.' In the summer of 2020, he signed up for informal information sessions at the Coöperatie Laatste Wil [Last Will Cooperative] about the suicide powder called 'Substance X'. 'All these interesting, highly educated white people in their seventies were sitting in a group. As the youngest, I introduced myself and said: I have terminal AATD. And I want to prepare myself.'

He threw himself into the organisation, offering his studio as a venue for information sessions and carefully noting down his own questions as well as those of others. Concerns ranged from potential side effects and the 'dignity' of dying by means of 'Substance X' – 'is it true that once ingested, you invariably die in your own faeces?' – to the possible criminal liability of the person who acquires the drug on behalf of everyone and distributes it to the group.

After five round-table discussions, the participants felt sufficiently prepared, and the question of who should collect the substance was cautiously raised. 'No one wanted to, partly because of the uncertainty about criminal liability, so I said: I'll do it,' Erwin recalls. 'I made an appointment and had to go to Haarlem. It was in the first months of the pandemic, and I felt like a courier of death. When I rang the doorbell, the person inside barked: "Go away! I'm sick! Come back tomorrow!" The next day, an elderly man opened the door and handed me the substance – more than enough for the whole group.' Since then, he has kept 'Substance X' in his safe, complete with instructions for use. 'It makes me feel very secure.'

'Thanks to Black Lives Matter, the positive aspects of woke culture, and the queer movement's own self awareness, we've made astonishing progress'

THE VALVE

On this bright summer's day on Amsterdam's Egelantiersgracht, the bells of the Westertoren chime in the distance. Erwin – wearing stylish gold-rimmed glasses and no longer reliant on an oxygen tube – is in high spirits. After a difficult period, he feels braver and is even making plans again. 'As Hans van Manen used to say in the face of the relentlessly negative reviews, "Critics and competitors all fall eventually. And if they don't die, they'll retire. So, you know what you have to do? Just keep going and grow old." And that's what I intend to do now.'

He's become more affable and optimistic about the LGBTQI+ community's social status. Whereas he once believed that the previous century's achievements were slowly being eroded and longed for the days when Amsterdam dared to call itself the Gay Capital of the World, he now feels compelled to recant. 'Aren't all your memories inevitably nostalgic? Thanks to Black Lives Matter, the positive aspects of woke culture, and the queer movement's own self-awareness, we've made astonishing progress.'

At Milkshake, the festival that has been close to his heart for a decade – where he once introduced irreverent competitions such as cock-ring and dildo throwing, with the proceeds going to projects combating discrimination and the bullying of gay young people – he saw that attitudes had visibly improved. 'Body shaming is no longer acceptable; trans people are more accepted. In the RoXY days, trans people such as Jacques Wolters and Zu Browka were seen as anomalies, who at best had a place on the fringes of society. The Netherlands may no longer be a guiding light, but the emancipation movement is now a global one: gay sex has been legalised in Singapore, and all the way from Switzerland to Chile, we can get married.'

Yet he finds himself more agitated than he would like. 'It's irritating; I feel like a broken record. But I can't help it. I find it incredibly sad that I've felt like a second-class citizen all my life, and that discrimination against me and my community ranks so low on the ladder of outrage. Homosexuals are beaten up, bullied out of their neighbourhoods, rainbow flags are set alight, but apparently that's par for the course, so it barely registers on people's radars.'

Now sixty years old, he has mellowed a great deal, yet he admits there is still something of the angry white man in him. 'My anger stems from the fact that, even within my own circle, there's no safe place, no opportunity to stare the monster in the eye and say: this is happening and this is our response. It's taboo, it's swept under the carpet. I'd rather not ask the question, especially not in this era of racism and right-wing radicalism, but still: why does that North African voice sound so loud when it comes to discrimination against homosexuals? Is it religion, is it cultural, or is it because that group is not heard? Now that's something the academics ought to research. Knowledge is power.'

His energy has returned, and things are looking up, but the past six months have been incredibly tough. 'My oxygen intake was sometimes around 80 per cent. Fortunately, that has improved now.' He clips the oximeter onto his index finger. 'Look, 97 per cent.'

First, there was the COVID-19 infection, which he contracted in March 2022 while travelling to London by train. The infection worsened his condition. Owing to his poor health, he was temporarily removed from the transplant list, and his life ground to a halt, gasping and wheezing. He even considered consulting a psychologist again. 'When you're sick, you momentarily think you're the centre of the world. But you soon realise that's not true. No matter how sorry you feel for yourself, everything and everyone carries on as normal.'

The pulmonary bulla, caused by air being trapped in the lung with every breath, was expanding at the expense of the healthy tissue. This led to extreme shortness of breath and panic attacks at the slightest exertion. 'And not just a little bit, but a real fear of death. It pushes me close to the brink.'

It has already led to some embarrassing situations. He is not shy about it; this, too, is a taboo that needs to be broken. 'My doctors said: people with emphysema tend to be mortified – we see it a lot. Because the lungs expand, they get bigger and bigger and press down on your diaphragm, your stomach and bladder, which leads to incontinence.' That was true for him as well. As a result, he almost didn't dare leave the house.

Trips to the shops, which he forced himself to make, rarely ended well. Once, in a supermarket, he accidentally knocked over a stack of cans and immediately panicked. 'At that moment, I felt a rush of anxiety and, in the middle of the shop, I peed my pants – luckily, I was wearing dark ones. It took me twenty minutes to reach the checkout, exhausted. ... The shame! Not because I was afraid of being recognised as incontinent Erwin Olaf; I was simply thinking of Erwin Springveld.'

He had gone from being someone with a minor problem to a man in need of serious help, yet he hoped for a swift recovery because 'luckily, I'm getting a valve now'. Owing to his poor condition, the bullectomy – an operation to remove the dilated air space from his lungs – had to be postponed for several months. But by the time his exhibition *Dance in Close-Up* opened at Galerie Ron Mandos in June 2022, he had recovered enough to attend and even take part in a public conversation with Hans van Manen.

To celebrate Van Manen's ninetieth birthday, Erwin had come up with an idea: to capture key scenes from his oeuvre. After all, every choreography contained a few moments that were 'typically Hans', instantly recognisable as his signature. 'It was an idea born of admiration, and it felt urgent, something I had to do before it was too late: one of us ancient, the other terminally ill.'

Working together again and returning to the kind of photography they'd explored some forty years earlier held tremendous appeal – but it was also risky. Had they not become too set in their ways in the meantime? Van Manen embraced the idea, however, and they set to work. 'I didn't expect it, but what's happening is quite magical. Absolutely fascinating – an ode to Mapplethorpe and to our early photography.' Erwin felt like the apprentice once more, while the master directed.

Paul Blanca's death just a week earlier reinforced the sense that these sessions were a tribute to a shared past. 'Not entirely unexpected, as he'd enthusiastically

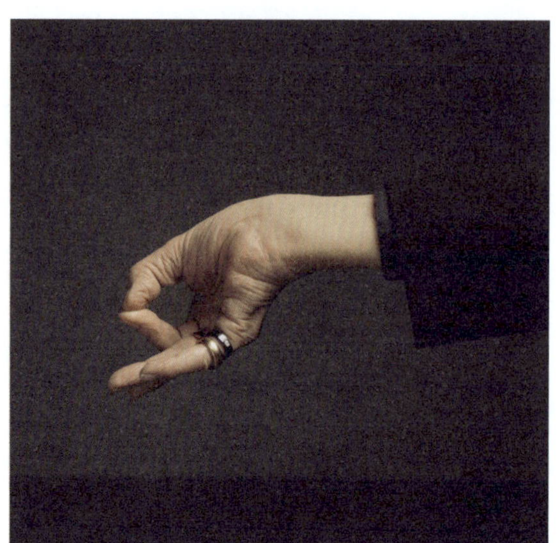

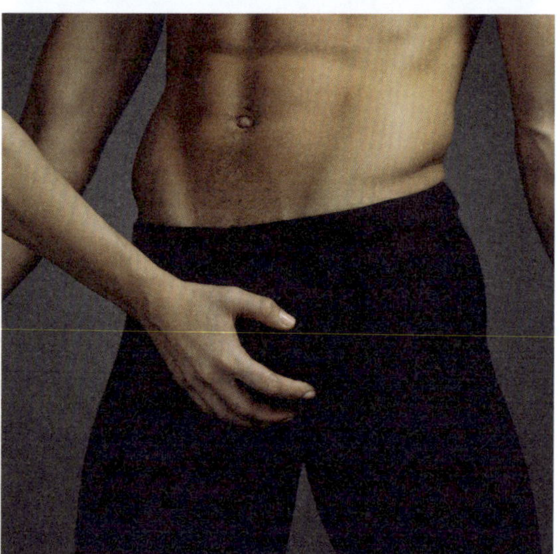

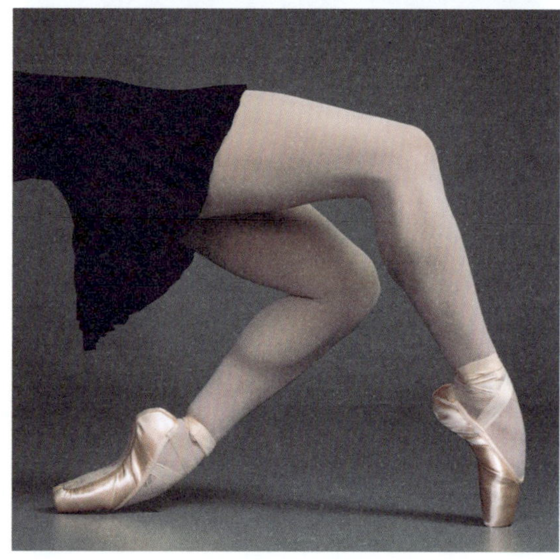

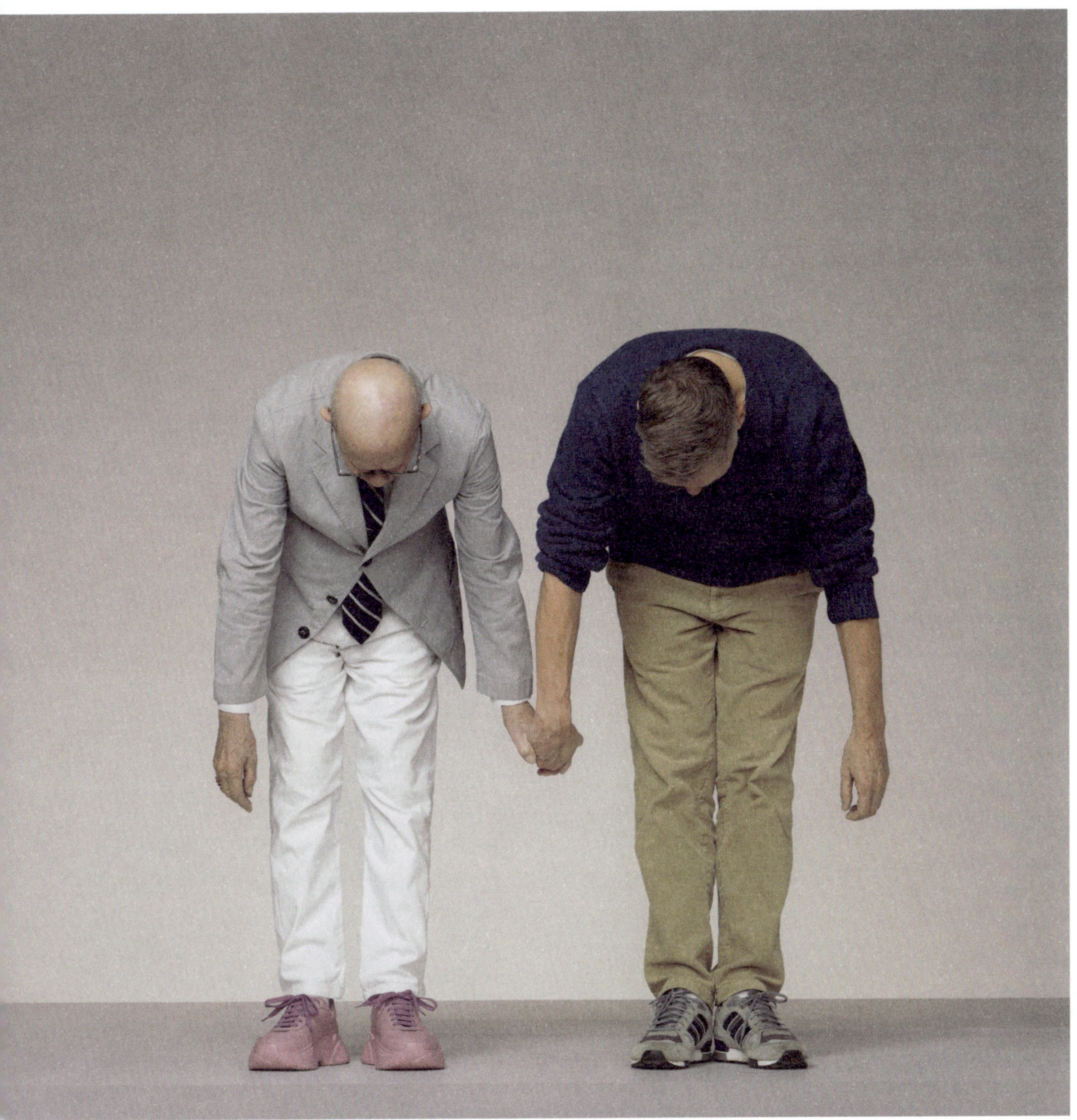

Left, from top to bottom: *Hans van Manen's Hand-Live III, Sarcasmen I* and *Sarcasmen II* from the *Dance in Close-Up* series. Right: Hans van Manen and Erwin Olaf in *Dance in Close-Up: Hans van Manen seen by Erwin Olaf, 2022.*

destroyed himself,' was Erwin's comment. 'But it's still hard to come to terms with the fact that death steals a march on us all, that it draws ever closer, and more and more people fall by the wayside. Paul was a great photographic talent who managed to self-destruct in spectacular fashion.'

Before they began, Erwin and Van Manen watched all the ballets on video, with Erwin taking screenshots of key moments that revealed the master's signature style. In his eyes, Hans was more of a visual artist than a choreographer. 'Masterful, stripped of all the excesses of which I myself am guilty.' Take the photo in *Sarcasmen* of a woman's hand grabbing a man's crotch. 'Had I designed such a scene, it would have been far more sexual. With Hans, that crotch grab carries a certain sarcasm, and you can even sense it in my photograph. That's entirely his direction. The angle and the lighting are more my contribution.'

Erwin had initially wanted to have a few scenes performed by naked dancers, both as an experiment and as a tribute to the nude photography that made both Mapplethorpe and Van Manen famous. When he asked the dancers if they felt comfortable enough to proceed, they replied that costumes are integral to Van Manen's choreography; you cannot simply omit them.

He abandoned the experiment, as well as his idea of printing the entire series in black and white. 'Colour really adds something here; it also helps bridge the gap from the 1980s to the 2020s.' Even so, he printed some of the images in black and white, using silver bromide or carbon printing. 'Call it the nostalgia of youth. I thought that last technique in particular – very old, very precise – suited Hans perfectly as a choreographer who's as sharp as he is advanced in years.'

Van Manen, Erwin and the dancers worked in the studio for six days. For Van Manen, smoking was an essential need, but for Erwin, the smoke was too great a strain on his health. As a workaround, a huge extractor hood was rented – 'a beast of a thing' that had to be brought in, mounted, and taken down again after each session. It made for an unusual sight: Van Manen, approaching ninety, sitting beneath the extractor hood, smoking his joints. In front of him a monitor showing Erwin's photographs in real time; beside him, a large ashtray and a never-ending glass of white wine.

The scenes were directed both by Erwin, from behind his camera, and by Van Manen, from a little further back. At times, it was unclear to whom the dancers should listen.

Erwin: 'And now sharp, guys.'

Van Manen: 'And very aggressive. Yes, she looks wonderful. Yes, nice. Yes. And her head a little straighter. Lower, a little lower. Lower! Lower!'

Erwin: 'But how much lower, Hans?'

Van Manen: 'Yes, like that!'

Erwin: 'Think something dirty. That's it! Beautiful! One, two. Click.'

As a symbolic finale – and also a kind of *déjà vu* in honour of their forty-year friendship – Erwin portrayed Van Manen, at his behest, with a cigarette in the corner of his mouth, a nod to Robert Mapplethorpe's famous self-portrait.

Adrenaline had carried him through the opening of the *Dance in Close-Up* exhibition, but in the aftermath, Erwin felt increasingly depressed and incapacitated. 'I really couldn't do anything anymore. Just putting the filter in the coffee machine made me gasp for breath. I was rapidly sliding into depression.'

Sex, insofar as it was possible with a nasal catheter, had become a thing of the past. 'You can throw Viagra at it, but it doesn't mean you'll actually perform.' This at a time when he had recently met a promising friend-with-benefits, process manager Erik Brink, through a dating app. What was meant to be a casual encounter quickly began to feel like the start of a serious relationship.

He had told Kevin 'from the very first second' that he wanted to stay with him forever, but that monogamy was never an option. He was open to other relationships and didn't want to hold Kevin back. 'Everyone has to define a relationship for themselves. If you say, I've explored open relationships and I want to be monogamous, then go for it. You just have to be honest. Don't deceive your partner – that's a prerequisite. I am in favour of delayed truth. You can come clean a day or two later; you don't have to confess straightaway. Be gentle with your partner. And never create the impression that you're seeking a replacement.'

Kevin, however, did not agree. 'One-night stands, fine, if necessary. But not giving someone a real place in your life. To me, that feels like a kind of rejection.'

Erwin was with his new friend in The Hague when he received a life-changing phone call – at the most inconvenient moment. 'I was tempted not to pick up: we were busy, I'd just taken the Viagra, let it ring. But when the phone kept buzzing and I finally answered, it was the transplant doctor from Groningen saying: "You need to get here immediately. I've got a new pair of lungs for you."'

While they waited for the ambulance, Erwin was emotional; he hadn't expected to move up the transplant list so quickly. There was also a practical complication: according to protocol, Kevin, as his partner, had to travel with him to Groningen with a suitcase full of clothes and toiletries. But the car was in The Hague – with Erik.

They decided that Erik would drive the car to Amsterdam and drop it off at Kevin's place, which meant that Erwin's husband and his new lover would meet for the first time. 'It was an unusual situation, but Kevin was very open and warm-hearted from the start,' Erik Brink recalls. Erwin had warned them not to argue, and to his relief, they didn't. 'The peace pipe was graciously smoked – I thought it was great.'

While Erwin was awaiting his operation in hospital, a sobering message arrived at a quarter to two in the morning: when his future lungs were removed from the donor, they were found to be too badly damaged, and the transplant was cancelled. Unable to achieve his goal and still struggling to breathe, he returned to the Egelantiersgracht, where isolation and boredom awaited him. With visitors now to be avoided, there was nothing left to do but watch the newly released series about his old hero on Netflix, *The Andy Warhol Diaries*.

The fact that he is doing better on this sunny summer day on the Egelantiersgracht is due to another operation, a bullectomy. The procedure did not cure his emphysema, but it removed a large part of the more than two litres of trapped air.

An endobronchial valve, an American invention, was inserted into the most damaged airways. 'The valve opens when I exhale, and then the balloon deflates a little. And when I inhale, the same valve ensures that no air enters the lung. They promise that it will remain in situ. It's made of silicone and titanium, so you can take it with you when you die – if you don't get new lungs, that is.'

The valve brought almost immediate relief: he could climb the stairs to his house in one go and, more importantly, he felt like taking photographs again. For a while, he had thought the series with Hans van Manen would be the epilogue to his life.

He decided to use this extra time to fulfil an old plan and rent a house in Mallorca. There, he hoped to rest, far from the publicity, and entertain friends. And occasionally – 'because there's always that homesickness' – fly back and forth to the Netherlands. 'Also in the knowledge that I don't have much time left.' Kevin will visit, but will not stay with him permanently in Mallorca. 'I want to avoid him becoming a kind of carer.'

Erwin was looking forward to a year of doing nothing, completely under the radar. He felt empty, drained, and for the first time for years, had no grand plans. Even so, he wanted to go to Mallorca, where Shirley had found a house with two large guest rooms, and set up a temporary studio for a new, small-scale project. During his absence, his canal-side home would be renovated. 'Everything needs to be in order, because in 2023 I will begin the final chapter of my life.'

'The worst thing is to create insincere work'

NO ART IN SUFFERING

It was a harsh transition from a sunny stay with friends in Mallorca to a cool auditorium filled with the art-world glitterati at the Stedelijk Museum in Amsterdam. Yet that is where Erwin found himself on 14 June 2023. His retreat, which was meant to last a year, had turned out to be a disappointment – even solitude and sunshine had failed to improve his condition.

Moreover, the valve was not the miracle it had first appeared to be – it quickly wore out. 'My lungs are like a flat tyre that you're pumping up, but in reverse. My lung function is back down to 17 per cent.'

He terminated the lease on the house in Mallorca and prepared to vacate the property by 1 July, as there was a good chance he might receive a transplant in the summer. If that happened, he would need to be able to reach Groningen within five hours.

He was briefly admitted to the Leiden University Medical Center and sent a text afterwards: 'Just got back and unfortunately feeling chronically short of breath. ... It's terrible. I feel awful. I think I'm going to die. My throat is constricted and there's a heavy weight on my chest. I can't do anything.' Yet with treatment he rallied, and more than that, he felt as though he were on speed. 'For a week, ideas kept flowing: I started making plans, calling everyone.'

During that period, he photographed singer Anouk – 'Erwin is great, I adore hyper-talented, idiosyncratic people' – with her partner Dominique for the cover of her album *Deena & Jim*. And he portrayed his old friend Arjan Ederveen in his country cottage in the Frisian countryside. They talked about 'things in the world that float around you', as Ederveen put it, somewhat cryptically. 'We made harsh jokes and gossiped a lot, but we also spoke about beautiful things. It's nice to have a friend like Erwin – not everyone sees the wonders of the world the way he does.'

His medication has since been adjusted, and the hyperactivity has subsided. Today, Erwin walked into the Stedelijk Museum for the debate accompanying the presentation of *Scherpstellen* [Focus], a collection of essays commissioned by the Mondriaan Fund on the development of photography in the visual arts. The room is filled with dozens of curators, policymakers and 'art-world bigwigs'. Feeling anxious and tense, Erwin has taken a seat in a corner so that he can easily slip away if necessary. 'I wasn't sure whether to come, but I thought: I should, otherwise I'll become a recluse.'

He still does not feel entirely at home in the Stedelijk Museum, the institution that so often rejected him, but his old antipathy has diminished along with his anger. When he walked through the galleries recently with his friend, painter Frans Franciscus, he was his usual critical self. 'Because when it comes to the Stedelijk, I'm a spoilt brat who doesn't get his own way and rants on and on about it – just like my father who, after his strokes, used to continually grumble about his football team. We don't like being told no, so we stamp our feet.'

It feels good to look around again without resentment. By now, Erwin knows exactly what he thinks about photography's place in the visual arts, and it is perfectly clear to him why his work has never been shown in the museum. 'Contemporary art has to be tormented and ragged.' His own work has never been rough around the edges; on the contrary, it is close to flawless and the product of a perfectionist. 'No matter how often I tell myself, don't get too bogged down in form, people would still accuse me of being too slick. So be it. The worst thing is to create insincere work, and no one can accuse me of that.'

As for the supposed lack of torment in his work, he likes to quote his friend Arjan Ederveen: 'There's no art in suffering. Try making a good work of art that makes you laugh.'

The world of contemporary art remained difficult for him to fathom. 'That's also due to my lack of art historical knowledge. When I'm in Venice at the Biennale and see pieces of wood strewn around in one of the national pavilions in the Giardini, I think: put them outside that pavilion and they'll go straight to the rubbish dump. To my untrained eye, contemporary art often looks like scrap; I rarely see anything in contemporary art museums that truly moves me.'

The photo debate at the Stedelijk Museum, the participants agree, is taking place at a turning point in the history of Dutch photography. *Scherpstellen* describes the growing pains of a young art form that has developed at remarkable speed. Erwin rode that wave; his career as a photographer coincided with the rapid rise of photography criticism, the founding of photography museums and archives, and the end of photography's stepmotherly treatment.

Photography is now taken seriously. It even became a craze for a time, with photographs hung in museums and galleries, and runaway auction prices. Erwin's generation benefited from this catch-up era. He had an additional advantage: the enormous advertising budgets of the 1990s and 2000s, which allowed him to survive with little or no government support. But battles are lost as quickly as they are won, and photography remains in a vulnerable position.

Erwin believes that photography's rise may have temporarily sidelined more traditional art forms, but that the pendulum is now swinging back towards classical painting and sculpture. He is not alone in experimenting with related media such as 3D printing and video. A conversation about the future of photography is therefore long overdue – though he is uncertain whether he will live to see the next chapter.

The Stedelijk debate provided no immediate answers. What Erwin did notice, however, was that certain participants clung stubbornly to outdated assumptions. Was it really still a given that documentary photography should remain at the heart of the medium within the visual arts? Erwin was bold enough to question that assumption. 'It was the first time that I, as an old white man myself, thought: just look at them – a clique of old white blokes – a demographic that everyone is sick to the back teeth of.'

Feeling uncomfortable, he stayed out of the discussion – 'I kept saying to myself: this time I'm going to keep my mouth shut' – and so did not voice his conviction that photography, especially today, should be about the imagination. Nor did he articulate that fact and fiction are not mutually exclusive. Nevertheless, he was noticed in the corner, and when the moderator mentioned his name, there was loud applause. It felt like belated recognition from the assembled photography world. 'It was an emotional moment – applause in the lion's den. I was handed the first copy of the book and then I received another ovation. Afterwards, I realised: Gosh, all that pent-up frustration has dissipated.'

It was the calm before the storm. Two weeks later, he was readmitted to hospital, where the doctors wished him to remain until he received the new lungs. On condition of extreme caution, however, he was allowed to return home.

Back in Amsterdam, he used his time to work with fellow photographer and studio assistant Feriet Tunc on printing the *Muzen* [Muses] series, which he had conceived as a contribution to this biography. Eighteen portraits which, when combined with his early work featuring the same models, form a photographic autobiography. The longer he worked on the series – capturing his peers in all their wrinkled and sagging glory, bearing the marks of time that he so disliked seeing in himself – the more it became a mirror in which he saw the reflections of his own free-spirited generation.

'Of course, I can't help but wonder why I embarked on this project. As a form of self therapy? Or perhaps, as you age, you can't resist the desire to look back? It's an incredibly simple yet fascinating concept. When the contemporary works are combined with the 1980s shots, it shifts your perspective by three decades. Every one of those faces and bodies has a story to tell of a life well and truly lived.'

He was delighted by the photographs of his female muses, such as his old friends Marline, Desiree and Suzanne. To the latter he suggested: 'For the overall picture, I'd like to create a decent nude – no visible genitalia, but an elegant pose, a semi-classical nude. Nowadays, nudity is so sexualised. In the early days, a body was just a body. And skin was just skin. Full stop. Done. Beautiful! You were never prudish. I was the most prudish of the lot.'

Ria Franken, whom he had met while photographing S&M enthusiasts in their playrooms for *Vrij Nederland*, had died. Sabien, of 'pearl earrings' fame, posed again, as did Louise, who had once performed in S&M acts with Olav. Tineke, the petite woman who starred in *Chessmen*, among other works, also modelled, as did his self-proclaimed first muse, Duck Jetten. And last but not least, Zu Browka, star of the RoXY.

'My mood dipped while shooting the series, principally because of the lack of women. Now they're here, I suddenly feel like I can breathe again. I just communicate better through women.' Erwin had planned to present all eighteen muses with

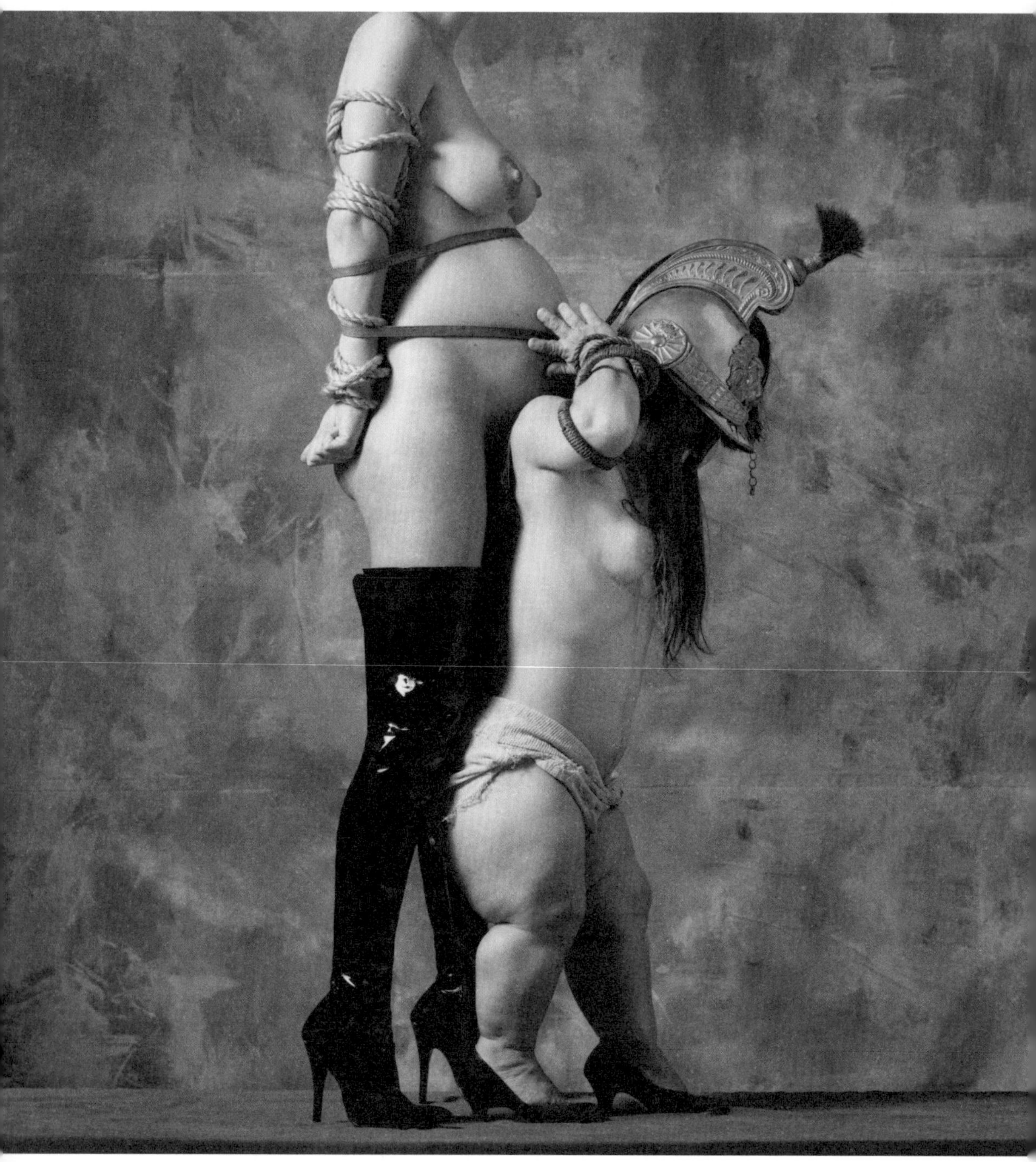

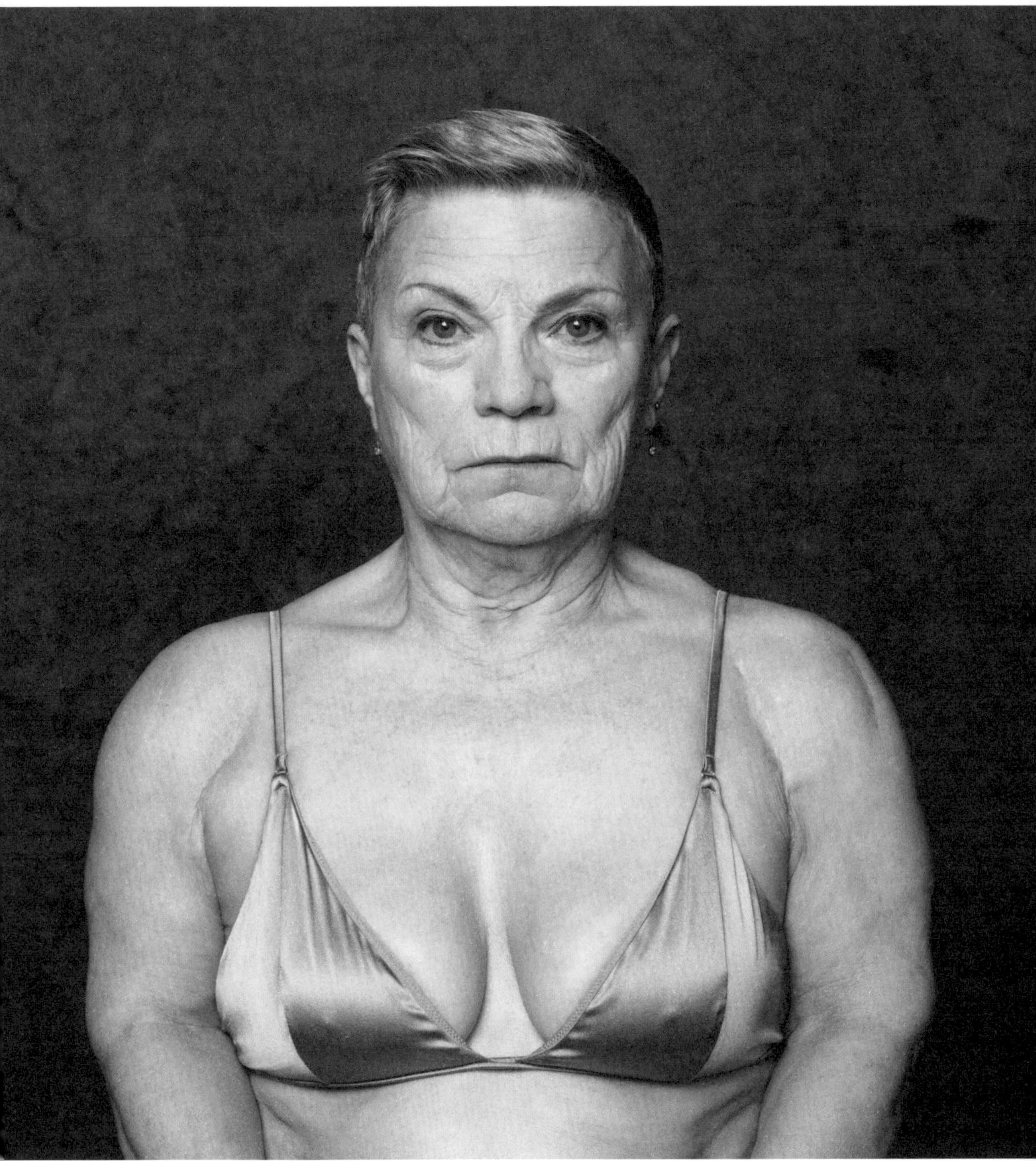

Tineke Anin in the *Muses* series, 2023. Left: In *Chessmen V, 1988*. 'That *Chessmen* photo was displayed throughout Amsterdam. I never imagined that Erwin would become renowned for it, even abroad.'

their portraits at a grand dinner in the autumn – a celebration of their shared history. It was not to be. After a respiratory crisis at his home in the Jordaan, he was admitted once more to Leiden, to an isolation room while awaiting news from Groningen that donor lungs were available. The pulmonologist in Groningen would have preferred him there, but Leiden was closer, and he was grateful that Kevin, Shirley, Frans, Marline and other old friends could visit him daily.

Take the lift to the eleventh floor. Face masks on, step into the airlock. When the red light turns green, they can enter his room. Erwin puts a brave face on the situation: 'I'm lying here with a view of The Hague. It means I can keep an eagle eye on the Binnenhof, the political centre of the Netherlands.'

'You've lost none of your cheerfulness,' said Arthur Japin when he called Erwin on his birthday, 2 July 2023. 'That's my strength,' Erwin replied. 'I don't know anything else. I'm very good at thinking about other things. I've done it all my life. About something more beautiful. Looking ahead and holding on to hope are my greatest skills.'

The titles of Erwin's series *Grief*, *Waiting*, *Separation* and *Hope* acquired a fresh resonance in his own life as he lay hovering between hope and fear in precisely the kind of small, isolated space he had built not so long ago for *April Fool*. Yet the irony of life imitating art was no match for his anxiety. 'I'm following doctor's orders but feel increasingly unhappy. Several times a day, I have to convince myself that, if I want to, I can leave and walk out of the door. That my carers are not my enemies and that my room is not a prison cell. What I do like, though, is that it's a kind of no-nonsense rehab clinic. Quitting the white wine is working wonders.'

During the crisis, he'd coughed up a large amount of blood. The initial diagnosis was thrombosis, which would have made a lung transplant impossible, leaving him powerless to alter the course of his illness. He had long since decided that he never wanted to become dependent on others. 'This hospital is one big life-sustaining factory, and it's fantastic that something like this exists. But I can't get my head around it. I wasn't brought up that way. I hate the idea of deterioration. This place is driving me crazy. Home too. Because then I miss my red button and my nurses.'

After some practice, he began using a device to help him get enough oxygen at night. 'The next step is a ventilator, which takes over completely. After that, you can't get out of your mobility scooter, you're bedridden, you go to a nursing home, and they hoist you up and wash your bum. … You become invisible; you're no longer part of things. I can't see that happening: I'm not going there.'

The sense of security that 'Substance X' had once given him faded after conversations with his ex, Teun, who also felt his own end approaching. Teun emailed him a 'rather realistic description of suicide with such a powder' and added: 'Erwin, it's not a pleasant way to die. You have to be absolutely sure that it's over, no doubts or panic, because it's irreversible. It's not always quick and there's no antidote.'

'What is the benefit of suffering? What's the point of it?'

When he had been anaesthetised for the valve insertion, he went under in just a few seconds. When he came round, his first thought was: *this is how I want to die*. Searching for an alternative to 'Substance X', he came across helium. 'It seemed like the best solution, although it's harder to acquire now because it's used as a recreational drug and has recently been added to the list of banned substances.'

Erwin didn't mind being 'phased out', as he put it, but he wanted to decide on the method himself. 'Fuck everyone, fuck morality. What is the benefit of suffering? What's the point of it? No one has ever been able to explain that to me. I've never been religious, not for a nanosecond, and I'm too stupid to imagine how bad it is to no longer be here.'

He had recently drawn up a 'withdrawal of life-sustaining treatment plan' for the point at which his quality of life would deteriorate, and he renewed his euthanasia declaration. 'I've had a wonderful life and a marvellous career, often helped by a fantastic guardian angel,' he wrote as his motivation. 'Unfortunately, this angel is becoming heavier and heavier, hanging around my neck like a dead weight, squeezing my throat tighter and tighter.'

He feared becoming even more immobile and thus ever more dependent on his loving friends. 'The idea that other people will be the arbiters of what I can and can't do is intolerable. Life has been incredibly beautiful, and I long to find eternal peace. ... And I look forward to ending my life, fearlessly, through euthanasia.'

He shared his feelings with Kevin and his closest friends. 'Why do we make such a big deal about a good death for one person? There are already 8.5 billion of us on this planet, so my presence is not strictly necessary. If my quality of life is shot to pieces, the fairy tale is over. Then I would rather be dead – long and intensely happy.'

When he was told that a transplant would be impossible, he called Shirley, who immediately realised what that meant: 'Erwin said that new lungs were no longer an option because of thrombosis. His breathing difficulties were permanent and his situation would only get worse. I went cold and it flashed through my mind: this is the moment we have to start the euthanasia process. So that protocol kicks in now.

'A moment of love, lasting no more than a few seconds'

LAST BREATH

On a sunny Monday morning, 21 August, Erwin cycles along Amsterdam's Van Baerlestraat. A nasal catheter in place, he greets me cheerfully as he rides his electric bike onto the pavement and dismounts. He's taken a wrong turn – 'what an incredible coincidence that we should bump into each other here!' – and tells me that he has not been taken off the transplant list after all and can wait for the operation at home.

Five weeks of solitary confinement had been far too long. 'I was climbing the walls.' The psychiatric nurse in Leiden reassured him that it was nothing out of the ordinary. 'It's perfectly normal; isolation does that to everyone.'

He is now waiting at home in the Jordaan, preferably on his leafy, sunny roof terrace, for a pair of donor lungs to become available. There are conditions: he and Kevin must sleep apart, and no visitors are allowed – a small sacrifice in anticipation of a new life. 'I wonder where I am on the list; it's like the Eurovision Song Contest,' he emails his doctor in Groningen.

At his request, his colleagues have built a tent in the studio and placed a vase of peonies in front of it with a camera. Just as he did during his mother's final days, he wants to capture the flowers in stop motion, this time until the moment of his lung transplant. It gives him a reason to leave his home on the Egelantiersgracht every day and, as in healthier times, make the thirty-minute bike ride to IJselstraat.

Although it is not strictly necessary, he insists on checking daily to see whether the flowers are looking good or on their way out, and whether the camera is functioning properly. After his operation, he plans to edit the images into a video so that after blooming and wilting, a new flower will always follow – and then die, and so on – in an endless cycle of life. Just as he himself hopes to climb out of his own valley thanks to his new lungs, to begin again, free of breathlessness and full of renewed spirit.

Erwin accomplished even more in the studio during that waiting period. Shirley den Hartog would later discover that he had meticulously removed every plan for his funeral and his estate. 'It was all gone: the folder in the safe, the folder on his desk, the folder on his desktop. The emails on the subject. Erwin was never very organised on the admin front, but he'd meticulously deleted everything.'

He had streamlined the structure and management of the company. The implicit message to Shirley was clear: *do whatever you think is best*. He had also drawn up a new budget, which made it clear that the funeral would have to be done on a shoestring. 'I think he wanted to cause as little trouble as possible for us and not cost us a cent,' says Shirley. 'But I also thought, that's never going to happen.'

He also gathered photographs for this biography, sketched out plans for new series and revisited some of his earlier ideas. At home, he watched a great deal of 'easy-going TV programmes', which inspired him enormously: 'Certainly formally, because that's always a sort of entertainment for me. I get the substance from the newspapers. Always.' He worried about the state of Dutch journalism and international politics, and would engage in discussions with anyone nearby – usually Kevin or the studio team.

He would then grab the newspaper to make his point or to highlight the important role of journalistic photography, his first love. 'Have you seen this? That Ukrainian soldier? Arm off, face off.' However gruesome, he thought it was vital that the newspapers printed such images. 'That's the face of war. You read about cluster bombs, but it doesn't truly affect you until you see a critically injured young man, no more than twenty-one, being comforted by his girlfriend. What kind of life is left for him? It's exactly how Otto Dix painted the casualties of the First World War and their difficult return to life. And we know how things unfolded in the 1930s – I wonder how it will turn out this time around. Putin and his clique are undermining humanity and humaneness. For what? We barely realise what's at stake – for all of us.'

This only strengthened his resolve to show – post transplant – a different, more positive side of humanity. 'Power, as pursued by dictators like Putin, is devoid of love. Oppressing people and destroying their lives is no way to live. You live to be in love, to love another person. That's what I want to show when I'm back on my feet. A moment of love, lasting no more than a few seconds, which is difficult to convey in an image. Because how am I going to capture that in videos and photos without it becoming kitsch?'

He plans to create short loops of people gazing adoringly at each other. Just that emotion, captured from a single camera angle, he explains. 'A form of video that is very close to photography, with photographs as no more than a by-product. Real actors, preferably British, and then: the fleeting glimpse of a happiness that makes life worth living. Being delighted to see someone again, being head over heels in love, laughing until it hurts. It's hard to watch; there's only so long you can gaze at other people's affection.'

Looking back, he was grateful to have experienced those feelings, which is why the film *Call Me by Your Name* had left such a lasting impression. Beyond the infatuation of the protagonist, played by Timothée Chalamet, he was deeply moved by the film's depiction of maternal love, which reminded him of his own mother. 'In the final scene, you see the boy lying on the sofa and, out of focus, his mother laying the table, like a protective mother hen. I know why it makes me want to cry: it's that mother behind the window who loves you but also pushes you out into the big bad world. ... There's no difference at all between that child, who was kicked onto the street by his mother, and the later Erwin Olaf who, as a photographer, prefers to stick to his own biotope. My work of the last twenty years has been about that emotion.'

He realised more than ever before that he'd 'wanted for nothing', received 'all the professional recognition that anyone could wish for', and been blessed with great love and lasting friendships. At this stage, it was no longer the struggle and desire to prove himself – the impulses behind early series such as *Chessmen* – that preoccupied him. It was love. 'The struggle for power stems from jealousy of others who have found the happiness you yourself have sought in vain. That's not my affliction. Of course, I know all about professional jealousy, but even the few people I dislike – and there are really no more than two – I wish them no harm. It takes too much energy to hate; they leave me cold.'

He was finding it increasingly difficult to cope with negativity – not only the baseness of others but also his own – even though anger at the world had once been his greatest fuel. 'The older I get, the more I realise that I created much of my work out of anger, but it assumed a positive form: *I can do better than that*. Tell me I can't photograph outside my studio? Then I'll go and work on a construction site in Shanghai. That my lungs are failing? Then I'll pick the highest mountain in California and, just for good measure, throw in some oxygen deficiency. And even if I can hardly walk, I'll still climb the Black Forest mountains and breathe the thin air.'

Yet his optimism and the prospect of a new post-transplant life were threatened by anxious thoughts that he tried with all his might to suppress. 'I've got to get stronger for my operation and not think too much, otherwise I'll go crazy or get really depressed.' He wasn't so much afraid of death – 'because I've done everything I could, I've played my part in my little biotope' – but he shrank from the moment of dying itself. 'I dread the last breath. That shallow gasp when you pass from life to death. That's the fear that creeps up on me when I open that door in my mind. So that door has to remain firmly closed. Because what good does it do? All that rumination? I've had a wonderful life and I don't need to make sense of anything. I'm focusing my thoughts on just one thing now: the hope that the phone will ring soon – Groningen calling.'

In the meantime, he made plans to turn his lung transplant into a photo project, creating a souvenir of the old, defective organs. He saw it as a 'farewell portrait of an essential part of my life in recent decades. Also a nice way to end the book.' The project was to take the form of a diptych: the first image, a portrait of one of his doctors holding a removed lung in each hand – a distant echo of the controversial theatre poster for the Zuidelijk Toneel, for which his model Olav de Graauw had posed thirty years earlier, clutching a bleeding cow's heart in each hand. The second image was to be a nude self portrait, showing the sutured chest incision.

He sent an email with detailed instructions to the photographers he wanted to involve. Because the exact moment the photos would need to be taken was impossible to predict, he assembled a team that included several former assistants. 'Dear all, thank you very much for agreeing to help photograph my lungs once they have been removed and I'm lying there flat on my back! It may be thankless work for you, following my instructions, but I think it could be really special. And there will only be one opportunity to take these photos.'

He had meticulously prepared this 'lung self-portrait', sketching out exactly how and where everyone should pose, including the camera position – two metres away – as well as the flash and the reflector. He had pulmonologist and intensive-care physician Anna van Gemert in mind as his model, 'a top model'. It was Van Gemert who had first suggested the idea of a lung self-portrait, and Erwin immediately recognised the image's power. 'I think it would be really cool, like a kind of farewell portrait of a fundamental part of my body. It could be a great little artwork!'

The project also gave him something to work on during the long wait for the transplant. More than ever, he realised he had no choice but to keep photographing until the very end. 'I have become my photos. What I create is who I am. And that's who I'll always be, no matter what happens.'

His doctor would need to pose in three different positions, holding a lung in each hand. According to a pathologist he consulted, lungs affected by emphysema measure about 40 cm x 25 cm x 15 cm each. The doctor was to appear in scrubs with no embellishment. 'That means green, but I'd prefer it to be completely in blue, which is possible if you ask in advance.'

According to Erwin's instructions, the photographs had to be taken 'without emotion or sensationalism'. 'This is reflected in the lighting, the serene composition, the pose and the surgeon's gaze. Looking straight into the camera, unsmiling, as symmetrical as possible, with a proud look in the eyes.' The photo was to be a half-length shot, with the lungs clearly visible yet shown 'with a certain casualness'. 'So don't present them as if they're a plate of *bitterballen*.' He concluded with a resolute directive: 'After I've physically recovered, I'll select the final image myself.'

A week after their chance encounter on Van Baerlestraat, on 29 August, Erwin and Shirley sat at the long canteen table in the studio to discuss his post-operative plans. The short films about love were definitely going ahead. It was an exceptional project, especially for Erwin, who had always been attuned to existential loneliness and had explored that emotion in much of his earlier work.

Then there was the 'long self-portrait', the peony stop-motion film, and *Muses*, the black-and-white series he had yet to complete. He had taken the stills in Gouda during the filming of *A Beautiful Imperfection*, now being directed by Michiel van Erp. He was also considering a future opera in collaboration with Arthur Japin and Van Erp. Shirley had already arranged exhibitions in Warsaw, Italy and Arles, and a major

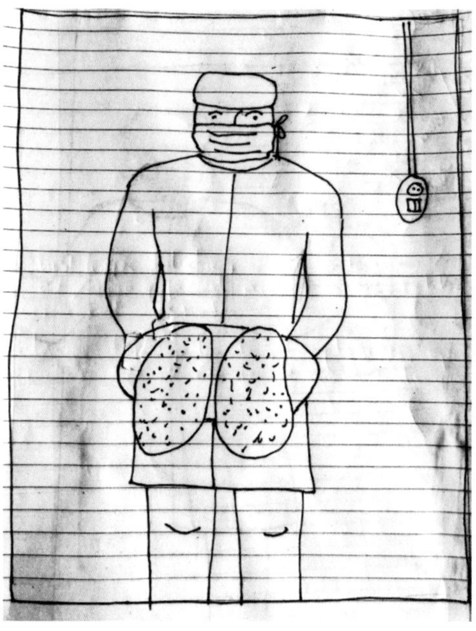

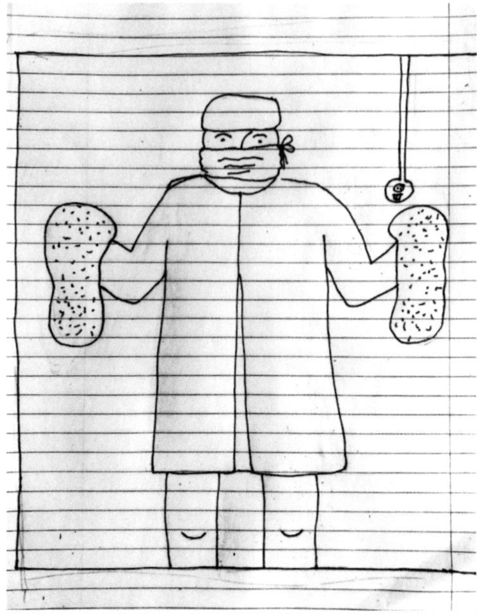

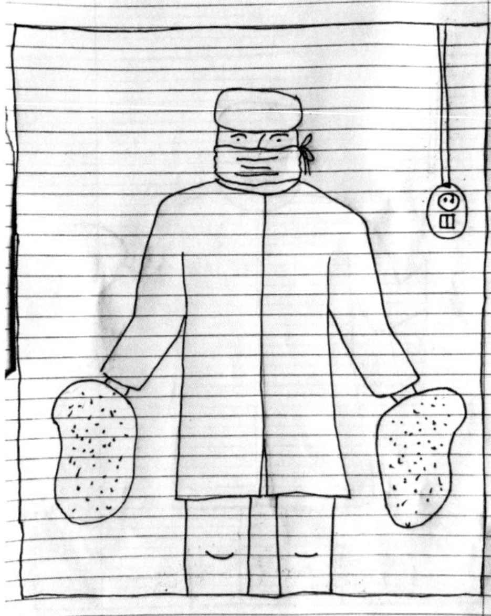

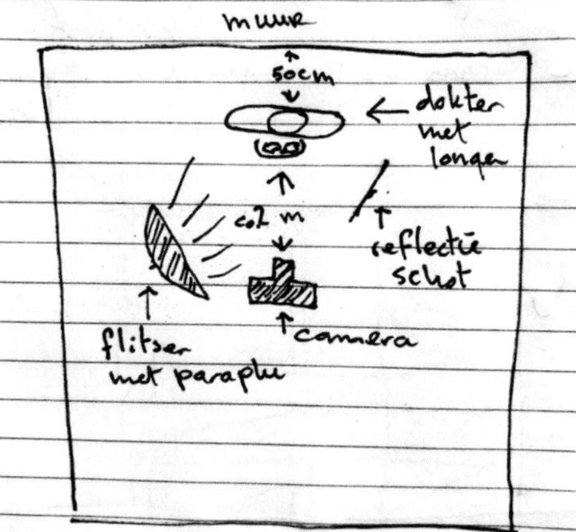

Erwin Olaf wanted to create a diptych. The first panel would be a 'farewell portrait of an essential part of my life over the last few decades'. The sketches and final work, photographed by Piotr Owczarzak and Wouter van Gens in accordance with Erwin's instructions. The second panel was never realised.

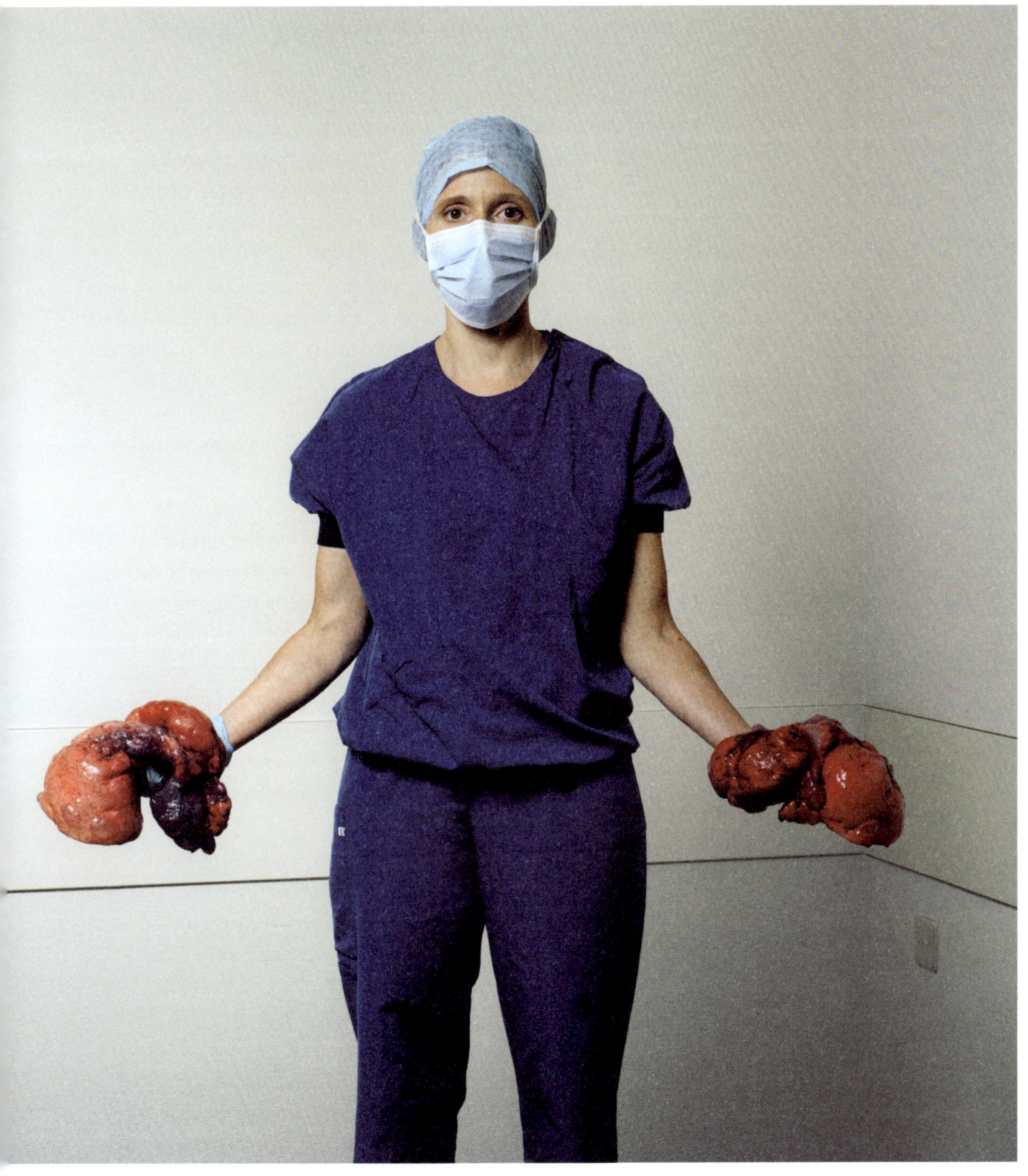

retrospective in Madrid was on the calendar. The Stedelijk Museum remained Erwin's ultimate goal; if they ever allowed his work onto their walls, he wanted the show to explore the boundaries of photography. His American publisher, Aperture, was eager to produce a new photo book. And he was determined to capitalise on his second wind by creating another series like *Im Wald* – only this time in Canada.

Quite a list, he remarked, as he said goodbye to Shirley in what would prove to be their last business meeting. But he liked the idea of making such a powerful comeback after a lung transplant at the age of sixty-five.

Two days later, his mobile phone rang: 'There's a donor, come to Groningen immediately!' The following day, on 1 September, a message arrived from Shirley den Hartog: 'Good news. The operation was a success.' The old lungs, damaged and worn out by emphysema, were removed – and then photographed exactly according to Erwin's instructions. In an operation that lasted several hours, the donor lungs were transplanted. All that remained now was to wait and see whether his body would accept them – and whether he would be able to breathe freely again.

'We're going to rock for another ten years,' were the first words he spoke to Shirley den Hartog after coming out of anaesthesia. Then he kissed her tenderly, 'even though we had never been that physical with each other'. Den Hartog and Kevin Edwards took turns at his bedside during the tense days and nights following the operation, waiting to see whether Erwin's body would accept the foreign organs or reject them.

For a few weeks, Erwin revelled in his new lungs. He was exhausted from the operation, but no longer short of breath. After all those years, he could finally breathe freely again. He threw himself into his recovery. The progress was rapid – perhaps too rapid, Kevin thought. 'Erwin was like a rocket. If he was allowed to take ten steps, he took thirty.'

On 17 September, Erwin and Kevin celebrated their seventh wedding anniversary in his hospital room. Kevin had brought in fake flowers to brighten the space, while Erwin had secretly climbed out of bed. Together they enjoyed a romantic *dîner à deux* – of the finest hospital cuisine – at a small table set up in the corner.

The loneliness that, according to Erwin, plagues everyone – 'not necessarily a negative thing, but I'm always aware of it' – seemed to vanish for a moment. 'All that suffering had made him depressed and he began to doubt everything, including love,' says Shirley. 'But after his operation, he quickly said to me: "Sorry, but the first trip I'm going to take after I recover isn't for work; it's with Kevin. I need to celebrate love again."'

The day after their wedding anniversary, Erwin sent Kevin home to rest, and Shirley came to stay instead. 'We talked about the future and laughed a lot. But I hadn't seen my children in a long time, and Erwin said, "You've got to go and see the kids."'

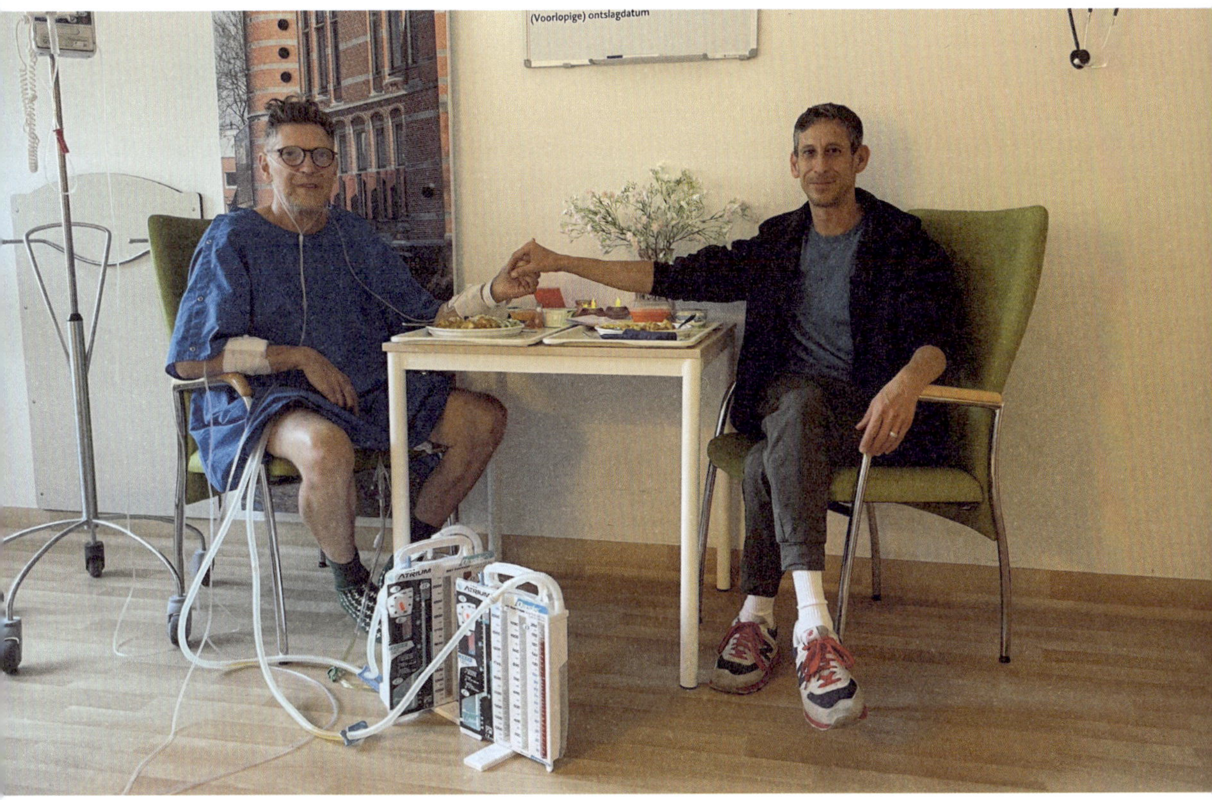

Erwin and Kevin celebrate their seventh wedding anniversary on 17 September 2023 with a dinner in Erwin's hospital room.

Neither Shirley nor Kevin stayed in Groningen that night. The following day, as planned, the second photograph for the lung self-portrait was to be taken: Erwin standing nude, marked by the still-fresh scar from the operation.

Early in the morning, Shirley left Amsterdam and set off north when she received a call from the hospital: they were resuscitating Erwin. She had to hurry. It was ten to nine, she recalls exactly. She immediately realised something was terribly wrong and rang Kevin, who was also on his way to Groningen. During the two-hour drive, he was frantic. 'All sorts of things were going through my mind, but I didn't dare think the worst.'

When Kevin arrived at the hospital, Erwin had already passed away after twenty minutes of unsuccessful resuscitation. A crisis manager had been brought onto the ward because the doctors and nurses were shaken by his sudden death, which had come as a complete shock to the care team. Kevin curled up in Erwin's arms, and they lay together in the hospital bed for another hour and a half.

They later learned that Erwin had been sitting up, ready for breakfast, with a nurse at his side. Then, without warning, he collapsed – and drew the final breath he had so long feared: his heart had given out.

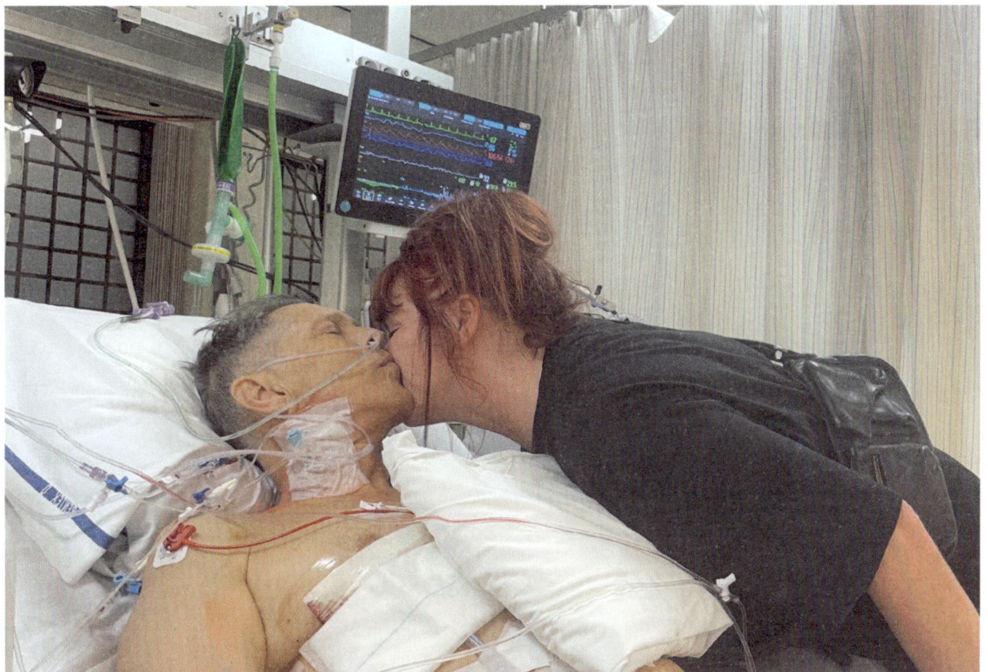

With Shirley den Hartog after his lung transplant, just after coming around from the anaesthetic. 'We're going to rock for another ten years.'

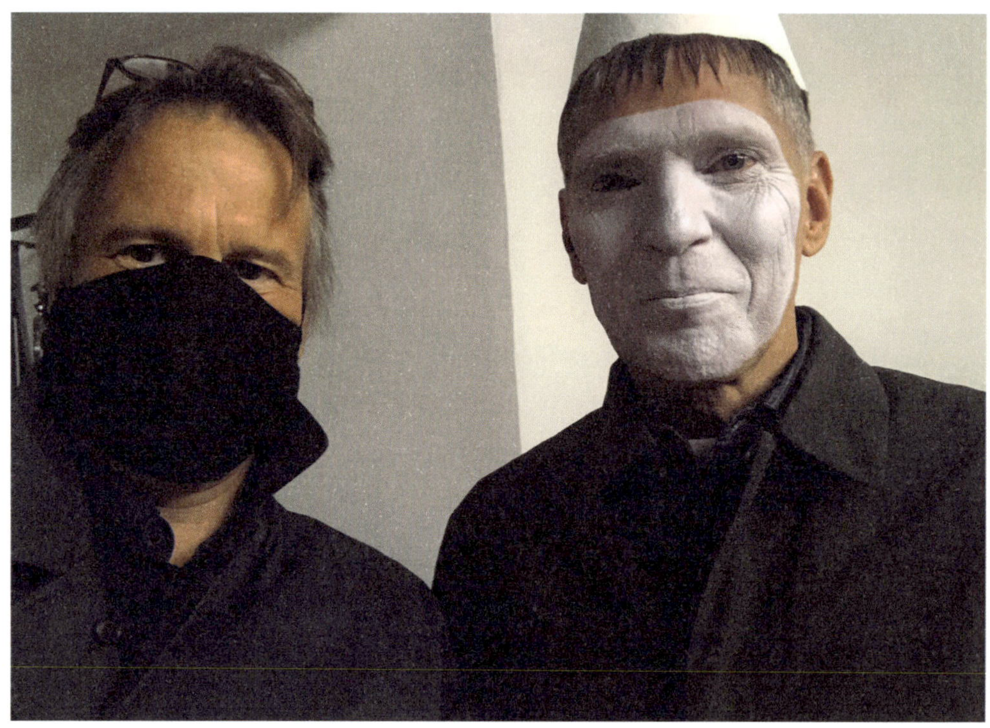

Mischa Cohen and Erwin Olaf during the video recording of *April Fool*, 6 June 2020.

AFTERWORD

The foundations for this book were laid during conversations with Erwin Olaf and publisher Robbert Ammerlaan. We discussed the idea of a biography, which Erwin was initially reluctant to pursue. 'I'm not that vain. And besides, I'm still alive!' he said. However, he did agree to collaborate on a book in which photographs, interviews, archival material and reportage would complement and reinforce one another.

At the time, I was editor of the weekly opinion magazine *Vrij Nederland*, for which I followed Erwin Olaf and his photography over the years. A book about Erwin and his work would provide an opportunity to delve deeper into his oeuvre and character, and place him in Amsterdam at the turn of the millennium, the period in which he made his name as a 'shock and baroque photographer'.

Furthermore, I was able to describe – through Erwin's eyes – the first decades of this century, a time in which he and his business partner, Shirley den Hartog, secured an increasingly prominent position in the international art world.

In addition to the photographer, I also wanted to portray Erwin Olaf the activist – the man who, often as a trailblazer, spoke out whenever he or others in the queer community were again confronted with discrimination, verbal abuse, harassment or physical violence. But also the man who, through extravagant parties – often held in the pop temple Paradiso – sought to celebrate everyone's freedom to be true to themselves in the city of Amsterdam, in the Netherlands.

It was a great pleasure to spend so much time with Erwin Olaf – and his husband, Kevin Ray Edwards – over the years. It was painful to witness Erwin grow increasingly ill, yet his energy, imagination and humour, alongside his photographs, remained the main driving forces behind this book until the very end. That Erwin decided to re-photograph friends and models from his early days for the series *Muzen* [Muses], inspired by conversations about his life, is exceptional. That series – one of the last he would create – acts as a mirror, and reflects, more poignantly than words can express, how Erwin and his contemporaries had aged since those early years. The sense of transience evoked by the series is all the more moving given Erwin's own untimely passing.

Erwin's business partner, Shirley den Hartog, was a constant presence and the font of all knowledge when it came to his plans and schedule. During his lifetime, she kept everything running smoothly in the studio. After his death, she took charge of his legacy with the same dedication. In his spirit, she established a foundation to continue his activist side. She also contributed to the posthumous fulfilment of Erwin's lifelong dream: an exhibition at the Stedelijk Museum in Amsterdam. Piotr, Feriet, Ruben, Piek, Petra, Sophie and all the other (former) members of Studio

Erwin Olaf were hospitable and kind to this outsider who, for years, appeared at the most unexpected moments – a curious witness to their world and a frequent lunch guest.

Robbert Ammerlaan was a pillar of support throughout the project. Designer Jan de Boer consistently sought – and found – the best solution to the creative challenge this book presented. And my sincere gratitude to the editors at both De Arbeiderspers and Hannibal for their patience and guidance.

Of the dozens of people I spoke to about Erwin, both at home and abroad, I would like to mention a few here. First of all, his mother, Lida Springveld, who – despite her poor health – spoke to me shortly before her death. Sadly, I can only thank Teun Frieszo posthumously. He was profoundly important to Erwin – and also to this book. Shortly before his own passing, production designer Floris Vos was able to reflect on his long-standing and close collaboration with Erwin. Hans van Manen, once Erwin's mentor and always his friend, welcomed me warmly into his home. He also kindly gave permission for several of his photographs to be included in this book, including the cover image.

Erwin's friends from secondary school and from his journalism studies in Utrecht brought those early years vividly to life through our conversations and their surviving correspondence. Henny, Anne-Marie, Frans, Rudolf, Marline, Desiree and Suzanne: thank you for your time and for sharing your memories. Erwin's muses allowed me to attend the often hours-long photo sessions, during which they bared themselves to his camera and reminisced about the days when they took the world by storm together.

And finally, my heartfelt thanks to the three dearest people in the world – Eva, Sem and Colette – who often read along and always empathised.

Mischa Cohen

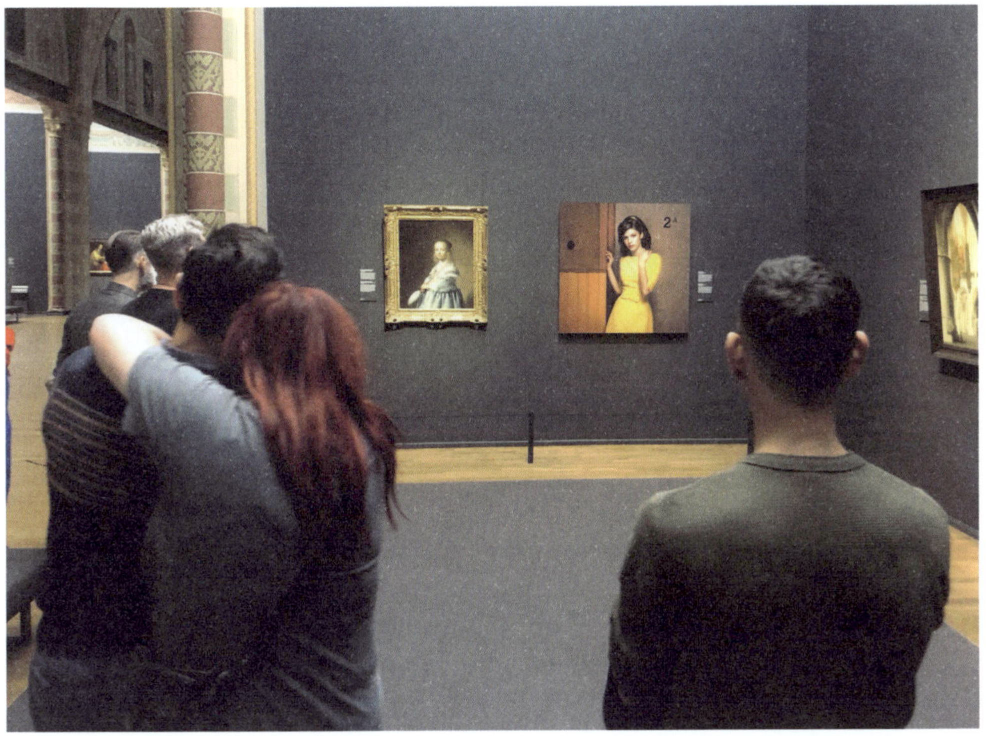

Shirley den Hartog and Kevin Ray Edwards (right) view *Portrait #5, 2005* from the *Hope* series in the Rijksmuseum's Hall of Honour on 28 September 2023. In memory of Erwin Olaf, the work was temporarily displayed next to *Portrait of a Girl Dressed in Blue*, 1641, by Johannes Cornelisz. Verspronck.

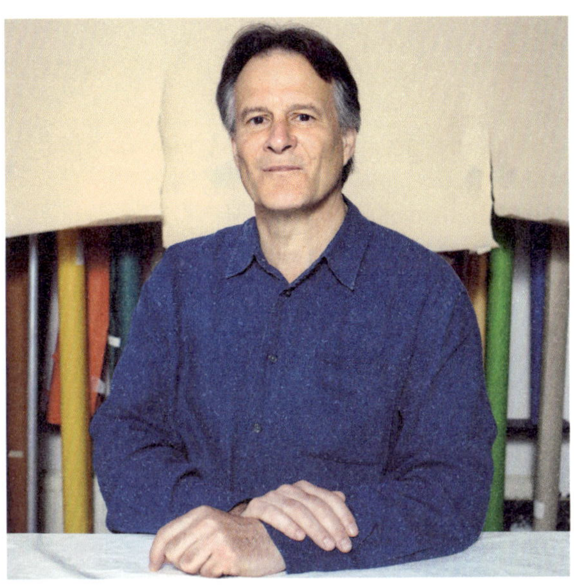

ABOUT THE AUTHOR

Mischa Cohen is a journalist and a publicist. A former editor of the weekly magazine *Vrij Nederland*, he has written extensively on the photographic work of Erwin Olaf, Bertien van Manen, Rineke Dijkstra, Dana Lixenberg, Carl De Keyzer and Ad van Denderen, among others.

He collaborated with photographer Daniel Cohen on the book and exhibition *Mijn naam is Cohen/My Name is Cohen*, and with photographer Carel van Hees on *Weerstand: Leven met aids/Resistance: Living with AIDS*.

Cohen won the Tegel journalism award for *Die fucking datum* [That Fucking Date], about the aftermath of Theo van Gogh's murder. His report on the *Charlie Hebdo* editorial team following the 2015 terrorist attack was nominated for a Mercur, the Dutch award for best magazine reportage of the year.

He is also the author of *De nazi-leerling* [The Nazi Pupil], a book about National Socialist education before and during the Second World War. Together with Harm Botje, he wrote *Mijn meningen zijn feiten* [My Opinions Are Facts], about the rise of far-right politician Thierry Baudet.

INDEX OF NAMES

PHOTO CREDITS

Unless otherwise indicated, the photographs and other images in this book are from the collection and archives of Erwin Olaf and Studio Erwin Olaf.

Archive PL / Alamy Stock Photo: p. 19 top right
Alandus Weertman collection: p. 167 top left
Alte Nationalgalerie, Berlin: p. 342 top
Daniel Cohen: p. 385
Mischa Cohen: pp. 339, 380, 383
Marc de Groot: backcover image
Kevin Ray Edwards collection: pp. 377, 379
Kunstmuseum Stuttgart collection, Sabam Belgium 2025: p. 271 top
Museum De Lakenhal collection: pp. 262–263
Piek collection: p. 113 top
Rijksmuseum collection, Amsterdam: pp. 328, 331 top
Sabam Belgium 2025: p. 271 bottom left and right
Frank van Beek: p. 283 bottom right
Hans van Manen: cover image, p. 78
Wim van Sinderen: p. 309 bottom
Hanneke Wetzer: p. 309 top

Texts: © Mischa Cohen, 2025
Editing: Mark Van Steenkiste
Translation: Helen Simpson
Copy-editing: Derek Scoins
Project management: Hadewych Van den Bossche
Image editing: Studio Erwin Olaf/Piotr Owczarzak
Design: Studio Vonk & De Boer
Printing & binding: Wilco, Amersfoort, The Netherlands
Publisher: Gautier Platteau

ISBN 978 94 6494 198 2
D/2025/11922/24
NUR 641

www.hannibalbooks.be

HANNIBAL

This publication is the revisited version of the original Dutch book entitled *Erwin Olaf Springveld – Hard werken, hard feesten*, first published in 2024 by Uitgeverij De Arbeiderspers, Amsterdam